The Burning of Moscow

The Burning of Moscow

Napoleon's Trial by Fire 1812

Alexander Mikaberidze

Pen & Sword
MILITARY

First published in Great Britain in 2014 by
Pen & Sword Military
an imprint of
Pen & Sword Books Ltd
47 Church Street
Barnsley
South Yorkshire
S70 2AS

ISBN 978-1-78159-352-3

A CIP catalogue record for this book is available from the British Library

Typeset in Ehrhardt by
Mac Style, Bridlington, East Yorkshire
Printed and bound in the UK by CPI Group (UK) Ltd, Croydon,
CRO 4YY

Pen & Sword Books Ltd incorporates the imprints of Pen & Sword
Archaeology, Atlas, Aviation, Battleground, Discovery, Family History,
History, Maritime, Military, Naval, Politics, Railways, Select, Social History,
Transport, True Crime, and Claymore Press, Frontline Books, Leo Cooper,
Praetorian Press, Remember When, Seaforth Publishing and Wharncliffe.

For a complete list of Pen & Sword titles please contact
PEN & SWORD BOOKS LIMITED
47 Church Street, Barnsley, South Yorkshire, S70 2AS, England
E-mail: enquiries@pen-and-sword.co.uk
Website: www.pen-and-sword.co.uk

Contents

Dedication

This book is dedicated to my brother Levan, whose encouragement, support and conscientious engagement have been a constant and indispensable source of strength and inspiration. I could not ask for a better, more loving brother.

Maps

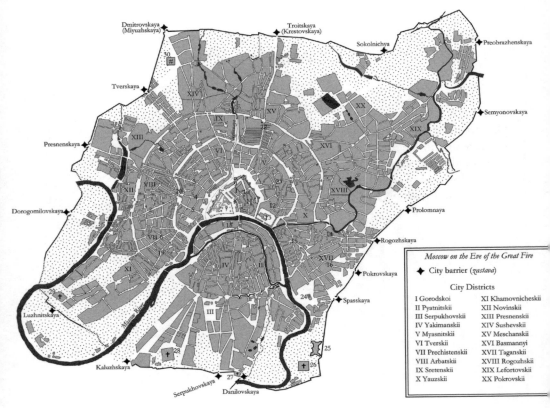

Map 1: Moscow on the eve of the Great Fire.

Key:

1. Dragomilovskaya Street
2. Arbatskaya Street
3. Nikitskaya Street
4. Vzdvizhenka Street
5. Znamenka Street
6. Prechistenka Street
7. Kremlin
8. Red Square
9. Nikolskaya Street
10. Ilyinka
11. Varvarka
12. Solyanka
13. Foundlings Home
14. Nikolaemskaya Street
15. Taganskaya
16. Semyonovskaya Street
17. Moskvoretskii Bridge
18. Zamoskvorechye
19. Ostozhenka Street
20. Tverskoi Boulevard
21. Presnenskii Ponds
22. Meschanskaya Street
23. Pokrovka
24. Novospasskii Monastery
25. Powder Magazines
26. Simonov Monastery
27. Danilov Monastery
28. Donskoi Monastery
29. Novodevichii Convent
30. Prison

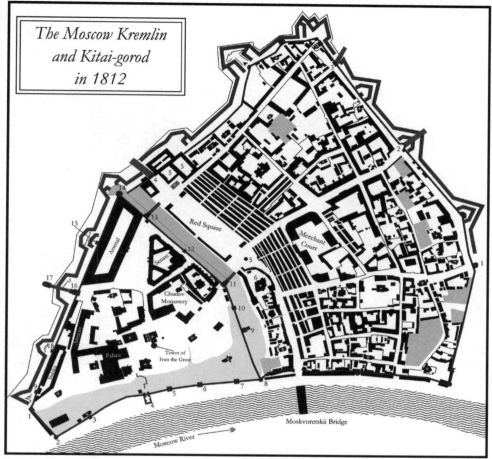

**The Moscow Kremlin
and Kitai-gorod
in 1812**

Map 2

In Kremlin:

1. Borovitskaya Tower
2. Vodovzvodnaya (Water-lifting) Tower
3. Blagoveschenskaya (Annunciation) Tower
4. Taynitskaya (Secret) Tower
5. First Unnamed (Bezymyannaya) Tower
6. Second Unnamed (Bezymyannaya) Tower
7. Petrovskaya Tower
8. Beklemishevskaya (Moskvoretskaya) Tower
9. Konstantino–Eleninskaya Tower
10. Nabatnaya Tower
11. Spasskaya (Saviour) Tower
12. Senatskaya Tower
13. Nikolskaya Tower
14. Corner Arsenalnaya (Arsenal) Tower
15. Middle Arsenalnaya (Arsenal) Tower
16. Troitskaya (Trinity)
17. Kutafya Barbican Tower
18. Komendatskaya (Commandant's) Tower
19. Oruzheinaya (Armoury) Tower

In Kitai-gorod:

1. Varvarskie Gates
2. Ilyinskie Gates
3. Nikolskie Gates
4–5. Governor's Mansion and other buildings of municipal administration
6. St Basil's Cathedral

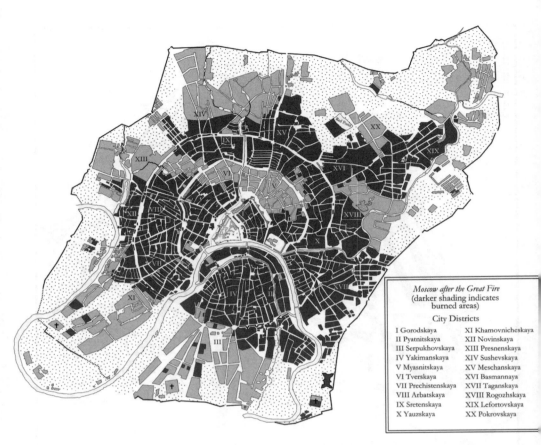

Map 3: Moscow after the Great Fire.

Map 4 Initial deployment of Allied troops in Moscow, 15–29 September 1812.

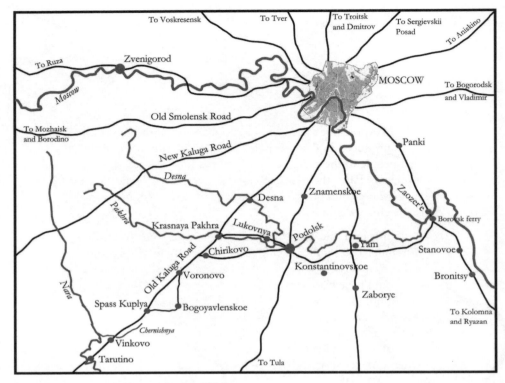

Map 5: Moscow and its environs, 1812.

Preface

'It is impossible to express the astonishment and dismay that the news of the burning of Moscow has produced in Paris. People have long forgotten about the effects of war that push people to the extremes. Despite the time elapsed since the bulletin brought this news to Paris, the impression that it has made still endures. This is one of those events whose consequences are incalculable and the more we reflect upon it, the more insights we gain.'[1]

In 1802, just slightly over one year after ascending to the throne of the Russian empire, Emperor Alexander I was informed of rather disturbing news. A certain monk Abel, who was said to have possessed a rare gift of foreseeing the future, had written a book of revelations. It would have been easy to dismiss his writing as the product of rampant imagination, were it not for the monk's correct prior predictions, including of the deaths of Empress Catherine II and Emperor Paul I. In March 1796 Catherine II, upon learning of Abel's prophecy of her death, had him confined to the Schlüsselburg Fortress but just eight months later she suddenly passed away – 'on the very day and hour predicted by Abel', as General Alexei Yermolov noted. Catherine's son Paul had him released and brought to the imperial palace. They had a long private talk, at the end of which the emperor ordered Abel to be accommodated at a privileged monastery and that all his needs be met.

A year later Abel made another 'worrisome' prediction, and history repeated itself. Arrested in May 1800 for 'various writing containing prophecies and other literary nonsense', the monk was released after Emperor Paul was assassinated by conspirators on the very night Abel had foretold. Paul's successor, Emperor Alexander, initially followed his father's example in treating the monk well until he was informed that the monk had produced yet another book of prophecies. This time the monk's predictions were even more ominous, as he spoke of a future invasion of Russia by enemy hordes and the fall of the glorious city of Moscow. Alarmed by this prediction, Alexander commanded that the prophet be thrown into prison 'and remain there until his prophecy comes true'. Ten years passed before Abel's prediction was fulfilled – Napoleon's Grande Armée crossed the Russian borders and Moscow fell and burned in September 1812. Just a month later Emperor Alexander released Abel from prison and ordered the monk to be well looked after for the rest of his life. Judging from the surviving documents, Abel lived a fairly quiet and untroubled life until his death in 1841.[2]

Historians have long agreed that the fiery destruction of Moscow was one of decisive factors in Napoleon's fiasco in 1812. Russia loomed large in Napoleon's mind. With war against Britain already entering its tenth year in 1812, the emperor was eager to find a way to subdue his stalwart enemy. The Continental Blockade, Napoleon's effort to defeat Britain by denying her access to European markets, required the involvement of all European states, most importantly Russia. In the summer of 1807 Emperor Alexander I, his army defeated by Napoleon, accepted the Treaty of Tilsit and joined the Continental

Blockade. However, Russian involvement proved to be lukewarm at best. The embargo on British trade led to a sharp decrease in Russian foreign trade, which in turned produced profound financial strains. These economic tribulations forced the Russian government gradually to relax the enforcement of the blockade, an action that incurred Napoleon's wrath. Franco-Russian relations remained tense in other areas as well, most notably over the future of Poland and the conflicting interests in Germany and the Balkan peninsula.

By 1812 it was clear that the two empires were on a collision course and both were actively preparing for war. As part of his campaign against Russia, Napoleon even revived his 'oriental' dreams. 'Imagine Moscow taken,' he had confided to his trusted aide-de-camp on the eve of the war, 'Russia overthrown, [and] the Tsar reconciled or murdered by a palace plot ... and tell me that it is impossible for a large army of Frenchmen and auxiliaries starting from Tiflis [in Georgia] to reach the Ganges, where the mere touch of a French sword would be sufficient to bring down the framework of [Britain's] mercantile grandeur throughout India.'[3] Although Napoleon never actually planned to get as far as Moscow, the prospects of overpowering Russia and then bringing the war against Britain to a conclusion clearly preoccupied him.[4]

The war, however, turned rather differently. After two months of futile pursuit of the Russian army, Napoleon found himself at the gates of Moscow, where he believed his opponent would finally sue for peace. Instead, the city went up in flames, taking with it any hopes for a triumph. 'By directing his efforts against Moscow,' wrote the famed Russian historian and war participant Dmitri Buturlin, 'Napoleon thought that he was striking at the heart of Russia. So how great his dismay must have been when he saw that the Russians looked on their ancient capital as no more than a vast accumulation of stones, with which Russia's destiny was not bound up in any way.'[5] A ruined Moscow had inflamed Russian passions, lowered the Grande Armée's morale and discipline and made retreat inevitable by destroying any prospects of peace. When in November 1816 Barry O'Meara asked the emperor to what he principally attributed his failure in the Russian expedition, Napoleon quickly named two factors – the premature cold and the burning of Moscow. 'Had it not been for the burning of Moscow,' he reminisced, 'I should have succeeded. I would have wintered there. There were in that city about forty thousand people who were practically slaves. For you must know that the Russian nobility keep their vassals in a sort of slavery. I would have proclaimed liberty to all the slaves in Russia, and abolished serfdom and nobility. This would have procured me the support of an immense and a powerful party. I would either have made peace at Moscow, or else I would have marched the next year to St Petersburg ... Had it not been for that fire, I should have succeeded in everything ...'[6] Of course, this statement, made by a man exiled to a remote island and bent on consolidating his legacy, must be treated with caution, but it does reveal Napoleon's belief that the Moscow fire was the turning point in his war against Russia.

Debate over who was responsible for the great conflagration in Moscow began even while smoke was still billowing over the ruins of the city. Young artillery officer Nikolai Mitarevskii recalled that in the evening of 14 September, as he and his comrades rested in the vicinity of Moscow, they saw dark dense clouds forming in the distance and realized that the city was burning. 'We began debating, with some arguing that the French were burning Moscow, others believing it was Count Fedor Rostopchin, the governor of Moscow, and some pointing a finger to the people themselves.'[7] Meanwhile, many

Allied soldiers and officers were simply astounded by the city's destruction and struggled to understand 'what possible advantage could this monstrous sacrifice be to Russia'.[8] Seeking answers, some pointed fingers at their greatest enemy, Britain, 'perfidious Albion', which had been at war with France for the past two decades. Soldier Marchal wrote that the fire was, in fact, caused by the 'English agents who had been detained wearing Russian clothing and holding torches'. Similarly, Guillaume Peyrusse, paymaster to Napoleon's household, cited prevailing rumours that 'it's all been a plan proposed by the English to attract us to Moscow and in the midst of the fire and the disorder of a town delivered over to pillage fall on the emperor's headquarters and the garrison'.[9] But the majority of Allied troops thought otherwise and their letters and diaries are replete with references to Russian responsibility for what they considered a 'barbaric' act.[10] Just hours after arriving at Moscow, Castellane recorded in his diary that 'many Russians had been arrested with matches in hand'.[11] Five days later Lieutenant Pierre-Laurent Paradis of the 25th Line wrote that 'the emperor of Russia forced the people to evacuate the city and then set it on fire'. Similar rumour is repeated in the letter of Pierre Besnard of the 12th Line, who wrote of the 'Emperor of Russia releasing convicts and inciting the fire'.[12] On 24 September Jean-Pierre-Michel Barriés of the 1st Division of the 1st Corps could not contain his anger at the actions of the Russian 'barbarians'. He explained that the Russians 'were hotly pursued by our legions' and, upon coming under strong fire near Moscow, they asked for a truce to save the city which 'they agreed to leave to us intact'. But alas, 'in an act of unsurpassed treachery that cannot be even compared to the actions of the worst frauds of ancient Greece', the Russians then released 'all the deranged and scoundrels from prisons' to destroy the city.[13] General Baron Louis-Joseph Grandeau d'Abeacourt, commanding the 1st Brigade of the 2nd Division (1st Corps) at least drew some consolation from the fact that even though 'the city was burned by the Russians themselves, we plundered it in the most beautiful fashion'.[14]

The bulletins Napoleon issued in Moscow, as well as his subsequent writings in exile on St Helena, played an important role in shaping the public memory of the Moscow fire. They directly accused the governor, Fedor Rostopchin, of conceiving this enterprise, collecting immense quantities of combustible materials and incendiary rockets, releasing hundreds of criminals to serve as incendiaries and removing firefighting equipment. Such claims were repeated in numerous French memoirs and studies, starting with the earliest memoirs and campaign studies, most notably by Georges Chambray.[15] The appearance of Rostopchin's brochure *La vérité sur l'incendie de Moscou*, in which the governor sought to clear his name, led to the publication of Chambray's rebuttal and Abbé Adrian Surrugues' *Lettres sur l'incendie de Moscou*, while a year later Dmitri Buturlin completed his two-volume classic *Histoire militaire de la campagne de Russie en 1812*. These works were instrumental in shaping the French historiography and, as one Russian historian justly observed, 'Surrugues' letters, Napoleon's statements, the works of Chambray created a rather well formed version of the Moscow fire that determined the course of the French historiography for the next hundred and fifty years and significantly influenced the writing of memoirs (and even publication of diaries!) of virtually every [French] participant in the Russian Campaign.'[16]

French perceptions of the Great Fire had, in turn, shaped the English-language historiography of the subject. Relying mainly on French sources, British and American scholars tend to concentrate on the military aspects of the campaign as a whole and, although one can find discussions of the Moscow fire in many books (for example those by Archibald F. Becke, Hilaire Belloc, Reginald Burton, Cate Curtis, Ronald Delderfield, Theodore Dodge, Edward Foord, H.B. George, George Nafziger, Nigel Nicolson, Alan Palmer, Richard Riehn, Achilles Rose, Digby Smith and Adam Zamoyski), the broad nature of these books meant that Napoleon's one-month stay in the Russian capital is usually described in general terms, with an emphasis on the 'French' experiences. In the last fifty years only two separate studies dealt with the burning of Moscow: Daria Olivier's *The Burning of Moscow 1812* (originally published as *L'incendie de Moscou*) and Paul Britten Austin's *Napoleon in Moscow*. Both books offer an engaging and accessible narrative to the reader but suffer from certain blemishes. Austin's book deals exclusively with the Grande Armée and has nothing to say about the experiences of the Muscovites. Olivier had consulted some Russian documents to examine the well-worn question of the origins of the Great Fire. She found her culprit in Moscow's governor, Count Fyodor Rostopchin, whom she held solely responsible for the fire. To support her argument, the author claimed that Rostopchin, given the opportunity by Emperor Alexander's failure to articulate specific orders for Moscow's defence, planned the city's destruction and carried it out through the use of incendiary bombs and willing fire-starters in the criminals he had released from Moscow's prisons. Yet some of her claims are far from conclusive and must be re-evaluated on the basis of a wider array of sources.

The Russian side of the story offers a rather different version of the event, and both public perceptions and historical assessments of what had transpired in Moscow in 1812 have varied over the past two hundred years. The news of the burning of Moscow 'struck us all like a thunderbolt,' remembered Russian noblewoman Caroline Pavlova. 'Everyone was in some sort of bewilderment and everything that had transpired seemed like a fairy tale to us; the reality seemingly turned into a daydream and the boundaries of what was feasible disappeared.'[17] The Russian public's immediate reaction to this shocking news was to point the finger at the enemy that was barbarian enough to devastate a focal point of Russian history and society, and Rostopchin's private letter reflects these attitudes when it states that, 'frustrated in his great dreams by the actions of our Sovereigns and the Russian people, [Napoleon] burned the city so he could have an excuse to plunder it'.[18] Throughout 1813 and 1814, recalled Dmitri Sverbeev, 'no one amongst us even considered [the possibility] that Moscow could have been deliberately destroyed by the Russians'.[19] Writing to his friend in March 1813, Aleksei Merzlyakov was infuriated that 'there are still half-wits who try to explain French actions and even justify them. There are even people who place responsibility for the fires on the Russians even though Napoleon publicly brags about them in Paris!'[20]

For the Russian government it was important to maintain this perception since it offered the higher moral ground in the war. The Russian struggle thus became, in the words of Emperor Alexander, the fight against 'the modern-day Attila who, furious at finding neither the treasures he thirsted for in Moscow nor the peace which he hoped to dictate there, chose to turn my beautiful capital into ashes and ruins'.[21] In October 1812, just weeks after the city was destroyed, the government's official proclamation placed the sole responsibility on the Grande Armée, describing the fire as the action of 'crazed and deprived individuals'.[22] A month later, with Napoleon's army already in full retreat and the outcome of the war all but clear, an imperial letter to Rostopchin reiterated the enemy's culpability in the devastation of Moscow but also spoke of the fire as an act of divine providence: 'As we cast our sights on the city of Moscow that has suffered so terribly at the hands of the enemy, we contemplate with extreme sadness the fate of its many victims and impoverished inhabitants. But God willed it this way! And He works in miraculous ways. Oftentimes, in the midst of violent storms, He sends us salvation, and through His rage shows us His mercy. No matter how painful it is for the Russian heart to see our ancient capital turned into ashes, and no matter how upsetting it is to gaze at the burnt churches of our Lord, we can seek solace in the fact that the enemy's misdeeds did not go unpunished and the Moscow fire was extinguished with his own blood. The ashes of Moscow have buried his pride and power ...'[23]

The purpose of this and other similar proclamations by the Russian government became evident as time passed. They served to portray the Franco–Russian conflict in apocalyptic undertones and to unite the Russian populace against the enemy. The destruction of Moscow served as just another arrow in this anti-French ideological quiver – here was an example of barbarism perpetrated by the representatives of the people considered among the most civilized in the world. In October 1812 the Russian authorities explained:

> We cannot say that we are *waging war against an enemy* [original emphasis] ... Such a statement would be too ordinary and insufficient to describe all that rabid violence that has been perpetrated [by the Grande Armée]. War, in general, causes incalculable disasters on the mortals but when it is waged by enlightened nations, its wickedness is alleviated by certain rules of honour and humanity ... Yet we are now witnessing the nation that in this enlightened era had once enjoyed a reputation for compassion but is now perpetrating abuses of such ferocity and cruelty that it would be difficult to find similar mistreatment even among the most uncultured residents of Africa and the Americas.[24]

In such a context, the Russian occupation of Paris – without plunder and destruction – in 1814 offered a rather dramatic contrast to the French entrance into Moscow and was used to augment the positive reputations of Russia and, above all, Alexander I himself. In June 1814 Semen Vorontsov, the former Russian ambassador to Britain, observed 'We are considered barbarians and the French, inexplicably, are perceived as the most civilized nation. Yet they burned Moscow while we protected Paris.'[25]

The government's desire to frame the debate of the Moscow fire was not entirely successful. Russian society and historians actively debated the causes of the fire and either acknowledged Russian involvement in it or squarely laid the blame on Napoleon's shoulders. In June 1813 Joseph de Maistre was surprised to see that 'there are still many among the commoners and [classes] above them who believe that the French burned Moscow – this only shows how powerful prejudices remain and how they suffocate any other thoughts'.[26] Over time, however, new explanations of the burning of Moscow emerged and some Russians came up with rather novel rationalizations of the event. Dmitri Runich, the infamous curator of the St Petersburg school district, rejected the accusations against Napoleon, noting that 'it would be foolish to assume that the French burnt the city where they found everything they needed to survive in abundance, and which represented a secure location from which they could conduct negotiations or military operations'. Instead, Runich claimed that 'this important undertaking [burning Moscow] could have been only conceived and carried out by the emperor [Alexander] himself',[27] who chose to sacrifice his capital but fight on! Meanwhile Sergei Glinka, editor of a prominent Russian literary journal and a close companion of Rostopchin, rejected the Moscow governor's involvement and could not make himself believe that a few 'dozen Russian peasants and foreigner craftsmen', who were executed by the Allied forces on charges of igniting fire, would have indeed 'set fires in Moscow in the presence of Napoleon's army'. For him, just as for Leo Tolstoy and others,[28] the destruction of Moscow was not premeditated but rather accidental, even a natural by-product of war. 'Moscow burnt down [because] it was supposed to burn,' proclaimed Glinka. 'Who burned Moscow? The war! It was without a doubt the result of a war the likes of which the world had never seen before …'[29] About forty years later Leo Tolstoy, whose *War and Peace* had a profound impact on popular Russian perceptions of the 1812 campaign, reiterated Glinka's assertions when he famously stated that,

> In reality, however, it was not, and could not be, possible to explain the burning of Moscow by making any individual, or any group of people, responsible for it. Moscow was burned because it found itself in a position in which any town built of wood was bound to burn, quite apart from whether it had, or had not, a hundred and thirty inferior fire engines. Deserted Moscow had to burn as inevitably as a heap of shavings has to burn on which sparks continually fall for several days. A town built of wood, where scarcely a day passes without conflagrations when the house owners are in residence and a police force is present, cannot help burning when its inhabitants have left it and it is occupied by soldiers who smoke pipes, make campfires of the Senate chairs in the Senate Square, and cook themselves meals twice a day. In peacetime it is only necessary to billet troops in the villages of any district and the number of fires in that district immediately increases.[30]

The nineteenth-century Russian imperial historians, however, followed a different path and from early on they pointed the finger towards the governor of Moscow. Dmitri Buturlin believed that, with the enemy army at the gates of Moscow, 'Rostopchin could not neglect the only means left at his disposal to remain useful to his Fatherland. No longer able to save the city entrusted to him, he set out to destroy it completely and to make the loss of Moscow beneficial to Russia's cause.' For Buturlin, Rostopchin had long prepared for this 'deed worthy of a true Roman', preparing incendiary materials and recruiting incendiaries who then scattered throughout the city under the direction of undercover police officers. But Buturlin offers no tangible evidence in support of such claims and admits that some Russians may have soberly turned to arson as a patriotic gesture.[31] More than a quarter of a century after Moscow's destruction, the Russian court historian Alexander Mikhailovskii-Danilevskii still noted that 'nowadays opinions remain divided on the Moscow fire'. His own efforts to explain what had happened produced only a contradictory account of the events: he initially rejected claims of deliberate Russian destruction of the city, focusing instead on the patriotic fervour of the Muscovites who had burned their estates, and on the plundering by Moscow's criminals and poor as well as by drunken Allied troops. Along the way he also inadvertently included sufficient information to implicate both Rostopchin and Kutuzov of contributing to the initial outbreaks of fire on 14 September. Nevertheless, in his final analysis, he blamed Napoleon and his forces for the burning of Moscow.[32] In the mid-nineteenth century Modest Bogdanovich, one of the brightest of the Russian imperial historians, published his classic three-volume history of the Patriotic War of 1812 in which he devoted one chapter to the fire of Moscow and argued that the city was destroyed not by

Napoleon or the Grande Armée (although, he argued, the latter did contribute to the fires) but through the activities of Rostopchin and zealous Muscovites.[33] Similar conclusions can be found in the works of many other late nineteenth-century Russian imperial historians,[34] although some in Russian society remained doubtful of such claims.

Following the fall of the Russian Empire in 1917, Soviet historians carried on a heated debate about the Moscow conflagration throughout the seven decades of the Soviet regime's existence; a recent study estimated that over 200 articles and books had been devoted to this issue between 1920 and the 1990s.[35] Interestingly, the first generation of Soviet historians, writing between the 1920s and the 1940s, believed that Moscow was burned by the Russians. Framing his discussion within a Communist ideological framework, Mikhail Pokrovskii spoke openly of Moscow being abandoned by the aristocracy and of '[Russian] police burning the city on the orders of Rostopchin'. These aristocratic elites could not care less about the impact the fires would have on the common people, the historian argued.[36] A more nuanced explanation was offered by the renowned Soviet historian Eugène Tarle, who spoke of several factors in the destruction of Moscow, including the carelessness of enemy soldiers. But above all, Tarle argued, Moscow was destroyed through the actions of the governor and the patriotic zeal of its residents, who preferred to have the city they loved so much destroyed rather than surrendered to the enemy.[37]

This apparent consensus on the Russian responsibility for the fire broke down after the Second World War, when the Soviet dictator Joseph Stalin sought to exploit national history to justify his own actions during the war. Stalin helped create the cult of Field Marshal Kutuzov, who was credited with developing an overarching Russian strategic plan of luring Napoleon deep into Russia and then destroying him with a masterful counterattack – ostensibly just like Stalin himself did with the invading Nazi armies in 1941–1945! After the war the Soviet historian I. Polosin sought to prove that the destruction of Moscow was just one element in Kutuzov's ingenious plan to destroy the invading enemy forces. Undaunted by the lack of concrete evidence for this plan, Polosin used circumstantial evidence to argue that the city was burned on the orders not of Rostopchin but of Commander-in-Chief Kutuzov himself. Polosin believed that Kutuzov had a plan for burning Moscow, which entailed the destruction of depots of supplies and ammunition as well as igniting fires to deceive the enemy on the direction of the Russian retreat.[38]

But this interpretation proved to be short-lived and by the early 1950s the Moscow fire was no longer thought to have been a deliberate Russian act. With the Cold War under way, it was increasingly discussed within the larger narrative of the Soviet struggle against the bourgeois and capitalist West. Any suggestions of Russian involvement in the fire were denounced as unpatriotic and were subjected to severe criticism. Scholars quickly adhered to this new official dictum. The 1950s saw the appearance of several publications by Liubomir Beskrovnyi, Nikolay Garnich and Pavel Zhilin, who claimed that the Allied forces conscientiously and deliberately destroyed Moscow. This trio of scholars (and their supporters) closely controlled Soviet publications on the subject, reviewing manuscripts for publications and ensuring they conformed to the official doctrine.[39] The sesquicentennial celebrations in the 1960s produced dozens of publications on the Patriotic War of 1812 but they were largely dominated by the Beskrovnyi–Garnich–Zhilin school of thought, while the few more balanced accounts, the most promising being the works of V. Kholodkovskii and A. Tartakovskii,[40] were tossed aside. Kholodkovskii's sensible questions on what benefit the Grande Armée could have garnered from burning the city where it hoped to spend the winter were simply ignored. The Beskrovnyi–Garnich–Zhilin 'doctrine' remained dominant throughout the 1970s and 1980s, influencing generations of Soviet youngsters. As late as 1987 the Soviet historian O. Orlik assured her readers that the 'fires were produced by pillaging, marauding and other excesses committed by the French troops'.[41] Not to be outdone, N. Ryazanov went even further, writing of special French incendiary detachments (!) 'galloping through Moscow with burning torches in hand. If a certain building failed to ignite, it was loaded with gunpowder and burnt, or ignited with incendiary shells fired from cannon.'[42]

The start of the glasnost and perestroika era allowed some Soviet scholars to defy established dogma. One of the first among them was Professor Nikolay Troitskii of Saratov State University, whose new history of the Patriotic War of 1812[43] offered a profound reassessment of the war in 1988. He rightly argued that the Beskrovnyi–Garnich–Zhilin school of thought 'simplified the debate on the Moscow fire and, most importantly, distorted its essence'. The Russian government and the church had indeed accused the French of burning the city but, Troitskii argued, one could hardly expect anything else from the authorities. He then rightly pointed to 'those great Russian historians and writers like A.S. Pushkin and N.M. Karamzin, M.Yu. Lermontov and A.I. Herzen, V.G. Belinskii and N.G. Chernyshevskii, M.I. Bogdanovich and A.I. Popov … as well as the heroes of 1812, notably A.P. Yermolov, D.V. Davydov, P.Kh. Grabbe and F.N. Glinka, not to mention M.I. Kutuzov himself, who, contrary to the official version, insisted with complete certainty that Russians themselves had burnt Moscow'.[44]

Troitskii's book played an important role in prompting both academic and public discussion of the Moscow fire, which continues to the present day. While some Russian popular history books repeat claims of the Allied involvement in the destruction of Moscow,[45] Russian scholars – notably V. Zemtsov and A. Popov – have joined their Western counterparts in holding the Russians themselves responsible for the burning of the city. Thus, V. Zemtsov's fascinating *Pozhar Moskvy* offers the most in-depth and up-to-date account of the Moscow fire based on a wide range of Russian, French, German and Polish sources. The book explores the topic thematically, looking at the fire first from the Russian perspective then 'through the eyes of the French', before concluding with three absorbing vignettes on personal experiences of the war. However, the author shies away from attributing responsibility, stating that the book does not aim to 'provide an unequivocal answer to what is often considered as the sole important question of who precisely burned Moscow: Russians or Napoleon?' Instead, he seeks to offer a 'much more multifaceted approach' on 'major issues of life and death'.[46] On the other hand, A. Popov believes that 'the question of who ignited the Moscow fire has been long resolved' and only the 'patriotic arrogance' of Russian historians 'does not allow them to accept this plain conclusion but rather compels them to reiterate propagandistic false claims that are far removed from historical truth'. In his insightful study on the Patriotic War, Popov does not loiter long on this issue but he effectively absolves the Grande Armée of the outbreak of the fires and states that 'the fire of Moscow was disadvantageous to Napoleon's army from economic, political and military points of view, and neither could it be ascribed [to the Allies] on the grounds of "plunder-marauding"'. Instead, he directly accuses Governor Rostopchin of burning the Russian capital.[47] However, it is difficult to agree with Popov's complete absolution of the Grande Armée's role in the destruction of Moscow. One cannot but wonder what part was played by the hundreds of Allied soldiers who entered the city in defiance of imperial orders and began looting the suburbs.

The purpose of this book, therefore, is to build upon the existing literature and provide an in-depth account of one of the most dramatic events of the Napoleonic Wars. It will attempt to address several important questions in this tragic story. Was the fire part of a deliberate plan conceived by Governor Rostopchin? Or was it the result of spur-of-the-moment decisions made by the governor and city officials? What was the role of common Muscovites in the event? And finally, what about the responsibility of the Grande Armée itself? In writing this book, I tried to consult the widest possible array of sources to produce a balanced account. In the process I have examined more than two hundred Russian, French, German, Polish and Dutch memoirs, diaries and private correspondences. I was fortunate to have an opportunity to peruse the archival holdings of the Russian State Military Historical Archive (RGVIA), the Service historique de la Défense at Château de Vincennes in Paris and the Central Historical Archive of Moscow (TSIAM), all of which offer unparalleled insights into the events of 1812.

This book would not have been possible without the support of many individuals. I am grateful to Rupert Harding, my editor at Pen & Sword, for his willingness to continue our collaboration after two prior volumes on the 1812 campaign. For three years he patiently waited for me to complete this book, gently reminding me of the numerous deadlines I missed and urging me forwards. In the process of researching this book, I was able to utilize materials from dozens of university libraries and am extremely grateful to Susie Davison of the Noel Library at Louisiana State University in Shreveport (LSUS) for her steadfast support. Over the last six years, as I toiled on what has now turned into the 1812 trilogy, she procured hundreds of titles from all across the United States, always attentively listening to my inquiries and quickly locating requested items. Also worthy of mention here are the staffs of the various research libraries in the United States and Europe for their generous help with materials. I would like to thank the College of Liberal Arts at LSUS for granting me the Hubert Humphreys Endowed Professorship that facilitated this research.

Beyond institutional support, I was fortunate to enjoy the friendship and support of many people. As always, I have greatly benefited from the help I received from the wonderful people at the Napoleon Series (www.napoleon-series.org) and the Russian Military Historical Forum (http://www.reenactor.ru/). Sarah Cook's careful copyediting has greatly enhanced the text, while Jonathan North and Michael Hopper looked at parts of this manuscript and shared their precious comments with me. Bart Funnekotter, who is researching the Dutch participants of the Russian campaign, turned my attention to a number of Dutch memoirs and kindly supplied translations of select passages. I was fortunate to get in contact with Tone Borren, whose ancestor Aart Kool served as a young Dutch engineer in Davout's 1st Corps and survived the campaign to write insightful memoirs. Mr Borren kindly shared his English translation of Kool's fascinating memoir. I am very grateful to my Muscovite friends Pavel and Natalya Khoretonenko, who assisted me in acquiring recent publications in Russia, while Mikhail Khoretonenko and Dmitri Ostanin helped me peruse vast maps of Moscow laid out on the floor of my living room. I am also thankful to my colleagues Gary D. Joiner, Helen Wise and Cheryl White at LSUS, Michael V. Leggiere at the University of North Texas, and John H. Gill at the National Defence University, who have cheered me on throughout these years and offered precious advice. Vladimir Zemtsov, a great scholar whose works have taught me a lot, kindly shared with me his research into the Moscow fire, while Dmitri Gorchkoff allowed me to peek into materials from his recent two-volume compilation of archival documents on Moscow during the Patriotic War of 1812. In no case, however, do any of these individuals have any share in any of the faults that may be found in these pages.

I am grateful to my family for tolerating heaps of books and papers scattered around our house for the past few years. My wife Anna endured many lonely evenings as I explored the travails of soldiers and civilians, while my sons Luka and Sergi oftentimes played underneath the desk waiting for their father to finish writing another page. This book would not have been possible without their love, patience and support.

Alexander Mikaberidze
Shreveport, Louisiana
April 2013

Chapter 1

The Road to Moscow

On a clear June day, standing on a hill overlooking the Niemen river, Emperor Napoleon watched as his Grande Armée crossed the river and invaded Russia. 'Soldiers, the Second Polish War has commenced,' he exhorted his troops in a bulletin. 'Russia is swept away by her fate; her destinies must be accomplished. She places us between dishonour and war: the choice cannot be in doubt. Let us, then, march forward! Let us cross the Niemen!'[1] Hours after the French invasion commenced, the Russian Emperor Alexander responded with his own proclamation:

> We had long observed on the part of the emperor of the French the most hostile proceedings towards Russia, but we had always hoped to avert hostilities by conciliatory and pacific measures ... We flattered ourselves that reconciliation might be effected ... alas, all these conciliatory and pacific measures could not preserve the tranquillity which we so desired [and] we are left with no other choice but to turn to arms and appeal to the Almighty, the Witness and the Defender of the truth. The ancient blood of the valiant Slavs flows in their veins. Warriors! You defend your Faith, your Country, and your Liberty! I shall be with you and the Lord will be against the aggressor![2]

The war between Russia and France was long in the making. In the summer of 1807, after suffering a major defeat at the hands of Napoleon, Russia was compelled to sign the Peace Treaty of Tilsit, which bound her in alliance with France. However, Emperor Alexander I of Russia did not forget the painful lessons of the preceding two years when his armies were repeatedly defeated by Napoleon. He was well aware of the widespread displeasure prevailing in Russia over the Franco-Russian peace. Although Napoleon and Alexander seemed to have reconciled again in 1808, the fissures became evident the following year, when Russia was reluctant actively to support France against Austria. The Continental Blockade, which Napoleon initiated in response to the British blockade of 1806, had a profound effect on Russia, leading to a sharp decrease in Russian foreign trade. Napoleon's protective tariff system sought to safeguard French manufacturers and industry, limiting Russian imports while boosting French exports. With its trade with Britain restricted, Russia looked to France for trade but the French could provide neither the volume nor the quality of products required in Russia; neither could they replace British spending power when it came to buying raw materials. The financial strains created by the Continental System soon turned into a profound economic problem, distressing merchants and nobles and affecting the imperial treasury, which struggled to deal with an increasing deficit. Such economic tribulations forced the Russian government gradually to relax the enforcement of the blockade, initially allowing neutral shipping into Russian ports. By 1810 American ships – many of them English ships with false papers – freely docked in Russian harbours. As English goods found their way from the Russian ports into Eastern and Central Europe, Napoleon realized that the new Russian policy constituted a heavy blow to his Continental Blockade, and St Petersburg's cooperation in this system could only be enforced by war. 'The sole cause [for the war]', opined a contemporary English political observer in August 1812, 'is a refusal on the part of the Czar to shut English commerce out of his dominions.'[3]

But the Continental System was not the sole bone of contention, as France and Russia also disagreed on several other political issues. Russia, which historically maintained close ties with the Germanic states, was concerned by Napoleon's aggressive foreign policy in Germany, especially after the annexation of Holland and the Duchy of Oldenburg, whose ruler was Emperor Alexander's brother-in-law. Even more important to Russia was the fate of Poland. Russia was the prime beneficiary of the eighteenth-century partitions of Poland, extending its territory deep into north-east Europe. Napoleon's establishment of the Duchy of Warsaw in 1808 naturally threatened Russian geopolitical interests in the region. Napoleon's interest in consolidating his control over the Poles was further revealed when, after the defeat of Austria in 1809, he expanded the Polish principality. Polish demands for eventual restoration of their former kingdom only increased Russia's concerns that she would be obliged to cede territory. Despite Napoleon's assurances that he had no intention of restoring Poland – 'I have no desire to become the Don Quixote of Poland,' Napoleon declared[4] – Alexander remained profoundly concerned by the existence of the Polish state and tried to convince Napoleon to give up on the Poles. Both emperors spent three years (1809–1811) wrangling over this issue and by 1812 the discussions had reached deadlock, with neither side willing to concede. Another aspect of Franco-Russian enmity lay in the Balkans, where Russia supported the local Slavic population against the Ottomans. In the eighteenth century alone Russia and the Ottoman Empire were engaged in four wars, and a fifth had been under way since 1806. At Tilsit Napoleon had agreed to give Russia a free hand in the Balkans, but Alexander gradually became convinced that France was far from willing to allow Russian expansion into the Balkans.

Thus, by late 1811 both sides were preparing for 'the Second Polish Campaign', as Napoleon described it, and the emperor's Grande Armée of some 600,000 troops (including reserves) began assembling along Russia's western frontier. Its forces were largely furnished by Napoleon's European allies, with contingents from Austria, Prussia, Saxony, Poland and Italy. By the spring of 1812 Napoleon's army was deployed in three groups – under Eugène de Beauharnais, Napoleon himself and Jérôme Bonaparte, King of Westphalia – along the Vistula river, stretching from Warsaw to Königsberg. Meanwhile, Marshal Jacques-Etienne Macdonald's X Corps (with a Prussian contingent) guarded the northern flank of the Grande Armée, close to the Baltic coastline, while Austrian troops under Karl Philip Schwarzenberg covered the southern flank.

Russia fielded about 650,000 men in 1812, but they were dispersed throughout Moldavia, the Crimea, the Caucasus, Finland and other regions, leaving some 250,000 men (organized in three major armies and a few separate corps) in the western provinces to fend off Napoleon's invasion. The 1st Western Army of Mikhail Barclay de Tolly deployed in the vicinity of Vilna, while the 2nd Western Army under Peter Bagration assembled in the area of Volkovysk and Belostock (Białystok) in the south. Alexander Tormasov commanded the 3rd Reserve Army of Observation around Lutsk, covering the route to the Ukraine. In addition to the three main armies, Lieutenant General Baron Faddei Steinheill's Finland Corps in the north and Admiral Pavel (Paul) Chichagov's

Army of the Danube in the south covered the extreme flanks of the Russian army. These forces were further supported by the three reserves corps of Peter Essen, Egor Muller-Zakomelsky and Fedor Ertel.

After a year of intensive preparations, Napoleon crossed the Niemen on 23–24 June, advancing to engage the armies of Barclay de Tolly and Bagration. The Russians retreated to Smolensk, the Grande Armée following them in the hope of forcing a decisive battle. Tormasov was more successful in the south, where he pinned down Schwarzenberg in the Volhynia region. At the same time Chichagov's Army of the Danube received orders to move from Moldavia to support Tormasov. In the north Marshal Nicolas Charles Oudinot attacked General Peter Wittgenstein's 1st Corps (tasked with protecting the route to St Petersburg) and seized Polotsk on 26 July. But in subsequent combats the Russians prevailed, forcing Napoleon to divert Gouvion St Cyr's corps to support Oudinot. In the Baltic provinces MacDonald became bogged down near Riga. Thus, by August 1812 Napoleon's initial plan to destroy the Russian armies in a decisive border battle had been frustrated. Instead, his army suffered considerable losses from strategic consumption and desertion, as well as the usual combat casualties. The hot weather was, according to Baron Lejeune, 'a veritable disaster to our troops'. There was a lack of fresh water and no forage for the horses. To cap it all, the supply system struggled to operate effectively, with the wagons laden with provisions bottlenecked near bridges or battling road conditions. These carts could not hope to keep pace with the troops that were constantly pushed forward by forced marches for a battle that forever remained on the horizon.

As the armies of Barclay de Tolly and Bagration united at Smolensk, the Russians faced a crisis of command. The constant retreat had been a subject of great consternation in the Russian army and society. In towns and at court there were angry murmurs about the Russian leadership and questions about the military strategy. What was the point of this constant retreating, and why were so many prosperous towns and villages abandoned to the enemy? The word 'treason' went from mouth to mouth and some even pointed to specific individuals. Such grievances were further exacerbated by a discord between the Russian aristocratic officers and the 'foreigners' who had gained influence at court and in army headquarters. There were two main factions that differed in their views regarding strategy. Barclay de Tolly, the Minister of War and the nominal commander-in-chief, was surrounded by a group of officers (most of them of German extraction) who supported his defensive strategy. Opposing them was the much larger 'Russian faction', led by Prince Peter Bagration (ironically a Georgian), which urged an immediate counter-offensive. Anti-Barclay sentiments were so strong among the senior officers that they openly loathed the commander-in-chief and intrigued for the appointment of Bagration to supreme command; some even suggested replacing Barclay de Tolly by force.

Bending to such pressure, Barclay de Tolly agreed to an offensive at Smolensk. But due to differences among the commanders – made worse by Barclay's vacillation – precious time was lost in futile manoeuvring, which allowed Napoleon to recognize Russian intentions and seize the initiative. He crossed the Dnieper river and rapidly advanced on Smolensk. A resolute rearguard action at Krasnyi on 14 August enabled the Russians to prepare Smolensk for defence, while Bagration and Barclay de Tolly rushed their commands back to the city. On 15–16 August the Russians repulsed the Allied assaults on Smolensk but nonetheless were forced to abandon the city. As the Russians withdrew towards Moscow, Napoleon attempted to cut their line of retreat, but Barclay's army succeeded in clearing its way to Dorogobuzh following the indecisive Battle of Valutina Gora on 19 August.

The surrender of Smolensk further stoked up the general discontent in the army and society at large. To keep up the troops' morale, they had been told over and over again that once the Russian armies linked up at Smolensk, this strategic retreat would lead to a decisive battle. But now Smolensk was left in enemy hands and vast territories were abandoned. The army and society clamoured for change and the general outcry was 'Out with Barclay! Down with foreign generals! A single command in the hands of a true Russian!' Emperor Alexander had to act. In late August he appointed General Mikhail Kutuzov as the commander-in-chief of the Russian armies. After joining the army on 29 August, Kutuzov withdrew the troops still further to the east, deploying them for battle near the village of Borodino. After receiving reinforcements, Kutuzov commanded some 155,000 troops, of whom 115,000 were regulars, supported by 636 guns. Arriving at Borodino on 5 September, Napoleon fielded some 135,000 men with 587 guns. The decisive battle took place on 7 September, with Napoleon opting for frontal attacks on fortified Russian positions instead of flanking manoeuvres that might have prompted another Russian withdrawal. In a savage and bloody fight both sides displayed great bravery and steadfastness, but suffered tremendous losses; the Grande Armée lost some 35,000 men, including forty-nine generals, while Russian losses exceeded 45,000 men, including twenty-nine generals.

Neither side was willing to concede defeat in this bloody battle. The French considered themselves victorious since the Russians eventually retreated from the battlefield. After the battle Napoleon wrote to his wife Marie Louise: 'My dear, I write to you from the battlefield of Borodino. Yesterday, I beat the Russians, their whole army [...] the battle was hot [...] and I had many killed and wounded.' His 18th Bulletin proudly proclaimed the French triumph on the field of Borodino and noted that 'the victory was never uncertain'. Yet the Russians, proud of their steadfast resistance and the fact they retained part of the battlefield under their control, had a different view on this. The battle was not even completely over when Kutuzov drafted letters with the news of the Russian victory at Borodino. His report reached the Russian capital on the night of 10/11 September, when it was presented to Emperor Alexander and his close advisers. Alexander certainly saw through Kutuzov's claims of victory, since he ordered the report to be edited and any reference to the Russian withdrawal excluded. As Joseph de Maistre described, the following day Kutuzov's courier, with the revised report in his hand, 'triumphantly arrived' at St Petersburg, which was celebrating the emperor's saint's day. The imperial family was attending a mass at the Alexander of Neva Monastery and, after the liturgy, Kutuzov's report was announced to a joyous public. The edited version was then released for publication in the newspapers.

News of the victory was rapturously celebrated throughout St Petersburg, where church bells pealed forth and trumpets blared. The American envoy to Russia, John Quincy Adams, wrote that 'St Petersburg was illuminated', while the English traveller Ker Porter described how 'with the victory being publicly declared, the *Te Deum* was chanted, every voice united in the strain which gave glory to the God who had fought, and covered her people with immortal honours'. In Moscow Governor Fedor Rostopchin, who had been publishing overly positive and patriotic proclamations for the past few weeks, issued more bulletins proclaiming that 'the accursed one [Napoleon] and his accomplices will perish through famine, fire and sword'. A *Te Deum* service was held at the Uspensky Cathedral and the air over the city reverberated with the constant pealing of church bells. The news spread to other towns and provinces and in the process became embellished. Thus Joseph de Maistre informed the Sardinian foreign minister that he had heard that 'by the end of the battle the French had completely run out of ammunition and were throwing stones'. To commemorate the Russian victory, Emperor Alexander announced that Kutuzov was to be promoted to the rank of field marshal general and every participating soldier was granted five roubles. The officer corps was not forgotten either, and dozens of generals were given promotions, various awards and golden swords for gallantry.

The Russian army spent the night after the battle at its positions, with many troops eager to resume the fight in the morning. Barclay de Tolly spent the early hours preparing defences for a new round of fighting and was enraged to receive Kutuzov's order to retreat. The officer who delivered it described the 'deep silence' reigning at the village of Gorki where he had found the peasant cottage in which Barclay de Tolly was quartered. Approaching the cottage, he 'obtained a candle with much difficulty and entered the parlour where the general [Barclay de Tolly] was asleep on the floor, side by side with his aides-de-camp and orderlies'. He gently woke him, gave him the note which he had brought with him, and explained his mission. Barclay de Tolly 'leapt to his feet, and, probably for the first time in his life, there burst from his lips, generally so mild and gentle, a torrent of the most bitter invective against Bennigsen, who, for some reason or other, he took to be the principal author of the decision to retreat'.[5] In his memoirs Barclay de Tolly lamented the 'greatest disorder' that spread through the army and believed this was 'a natural consequence of the incompetence of the people in charge'.[6] Deeply wounded by the lack of consideration shown to him, he certainly had an axe to grind against both Bennigsen and Kutuzov, and he highlighted the widespread disorders in the army and described the 'troops without guides oftentimes stopping for several hours upon encountering destroyed bridges or when passing through defiles and villages; oftentimes [engineers] tasked with repairing roads instead created obstacles with their pontoons, wagons with instruments and the *opolchenye* carts ... the troops, unaware where they should stop for the night, had to wander round until, exhausted, they threw themselves into the mud to spend the night ...'.[7] Barclay de Tolly's criticism was condemned by some Russian contemporaries and historians as unpatriotic but a few did acknowledge 'its truthfulness, even if such representation was hardly unprejudiced'. As the great nineteenth-century Russian historian Modest Bogdanovich noted, 'If the widespread disorders described by Barclay de Tolly actually existed, the Russian army, pursued by the resolute Murat, would hardly have been able to conduct an orderly retreat without leaving behind its trains and stragglers.'[8] Indeed, Carl Clausewitz, the great Prussian military thinker who served in the Russian army at the time, observed that he 'can also attest that there was no symptom of that dissolution which has been attributed to the army'.[9] On 8 September the Russian army left its positions and marched towards the village of Zhukovo, leaving a rearguard, under the Cossack Ataman Matvei Platov,[10] to cover its movement; the main army retreated in two columns, with the right wing and centre proceeding along the road leading from Borodino to Mozhaisk, while the left wing (formerly the 2nd Western Army) marched along the old Smolensk road.

The French remained bivouacked among the dead and wounded on the battlefield. Although the Imperial Guard was ready for further combat, Davout and Ney's corps were devastated by losses, while the cavalry had suffered tremendously as well; with over 90,000 artillery rounds and about a million cartridges fired, Napoleon was also anxious to replenish his ammunition supplies before waging another pitched battle. Above all, the Grande Armée was grievously depressed and a gloomy silence reigned at its bivouacs. 'Few battles won had produced such an extraordinary effect on the winners; they seemed to be stupefied,' described Georges Chambray. 'After enduring so much pain, deprivation and fatigue to compel the enemy to accept a battle, and having fought so gallantly, they now perceived the results as a terrible massacre that augmented their miseries and made it more uncertain than ever how long this war would last and how it would end.'[11] 'The soldier's former gaiety was gone, and a gloomy silence now succeeded the songs and good stories which had hitherto beguiled the tediousness of his march,' remembered Colonel Philippe-Joseph de Montesquiou-Fezensac. 'The officers themselves appeared uneasy, and were only anxious to serve from a sense of honour and duty, and this despondency, which would have created no wonder in a defeated army, was the more extraordinary after a decisive victory.'[12] Indeed, it was a Pyrrhic victory: unlike Austerlitz, Jena or Friedland, the much more sanguine slaughter at Borodino proved to be in vain – the Russians left the field of carnage and showed no desire to engage in negotiations. Napoleon had to start the pursuit all over again but in worse conditions. By now, he himself had been ill and was worn out, 'his face visibly showing burn-out, his hair dishevelled and fatigued'.[13]

Aware of the widespread fatigue in the army and personally exhausted, the emperor chose to remain idle until noon on 8 September, when Murat's advanced guard[14] moved close to Mozhaisk and fought several minor skirmishes with the Russians. The Imperial Guard, Davout's I Corps and Ney's III Corps followed in Murat's wake, while General Andoche Junot's VIII Corps was ordered to remain on the battlefield. Viceroy Eugène, reinforced by the 15th Division of General Pino, crossed the Moscow river at Uspenskoye and prepared to proceed towards Ruza in the northeast, while Poniatowski marched to Borisov to the southeast.

Throughout the afternoon of 8 September Murat's cavalry made several attacks on the Russian rearguard. Late that evening the French light infantry managed to reach the outskirts of Mozhaisk, where the Russians were stubbornly clinging on; Kutuzov sent Major General Rosen with infantry to reinforce Platov and hold on to the town. As General Count Phillippe de Ségur noted, 'Murat fancied himself already in possession of it, and sent to inform the emperor that he might sleep there.' Yet, as Napoleon and his entourage moved forward to Mozhaisk, they were warned that the town was still in Russian hands. The Emperor spent the night at Kukarino, about a mile from Mozhaisk. The very fact that Murat's advance was checked and Mozhaisk had not been seized that day showed that the Russian army was far from being routed and that Russian spirits remained unbroken. Furthermore, this advanced guard action allowed Kutuzov to claim further success for the Russians. Even so, his army still had to retreat …

On 9 September the Russian army, in two columns, proceeded to Zemlino, about 12 miles from Zhukovo. The rearguard, reinforced by the 1st Cavalry Corps, slowly retreated from Mozhaisk, which was occupied by the Allied forces in the afternoon. Napoleon moved his headquarters into the town and stayed there for the next three days. Thousands of Allied wounded were gathered and tended to in several hospitals organized on and around the battlefield, the main ones being set up at the Kolotsk Monastery and Mozhaisk. The conditions were appalling and hundreds died over the next few weeks.

Louis François Lejeune was stunned to see 'our troops using horseflesh as food' in Mozhaisk two days after the battle, while Ségur saw

> the Russians dragging themselves along to places where dead bodies were heaped together, and offered them a horrible retreat. It has been affirmed by several persons, that one of these poor fellows lived for several days in the carcase of a horse, which had been gutted by a shell, and the inside of which he gnawed. Some were seen straightening their broken legs by tying a branch of a tree tightly against it, then supporting themselves with another branch, and walking in this manner to the next village. Not one of them uttered a groan.

A yet more gruesome picture awaited Alexandre Bellot de Kergorre, a young *commissaire des guerres* at Mozhaisk, who left a vivid description of the thousands of wounded lying throughout the town and dying of deprivation:

> Our unfortunate wounded were dying of hunger and thirst. They were bandaged with hay for lack of lint and linen, and they groaned dreadfully. For the first few days they lived on the few grains they could find in the straw they lay on, and on the little flour I was able to give them … the absence of candles was a terrible privation. In the early days I had the painful misfortune to lose some men, who, hidden in the straw, were not spotted in the evening when the food was distributed by the light of a flaming pine torch. A shocking thing was the impossibility of removing the dead from among the living. I had neither medical orderlies nor stretchers. Not only was the hospital full of corpses, but so were the streets and a number of houses … Some six hundred wounded Russians had fallen in the gardens and here they lived on cauliflower stalks and human flesh. Of this there was no shortage! In the first week I could give each man no more than half a pound of meat. Many of these wretches died …[15]

At Mozhaisk Napoleon was quartered in a house near the main square. His sore throat turned to laryngitis and he could no longer speak or dictate his orders, which forced him to scribble down all his instructions. This brief respite also allowed him to regroup his troops after the bloodletting at Borodino and gather more ammunition and supplies. His advanced guard, meanwhile, pursued the Russian army and gained some success since Cossack Ataman Matvei Platov, alarmed by Murat's vigorous charges, withdrew his rearguard too soon, allowing the Allied cavalry to close on the main Russian army. Kutuzov, already dissatisfied with Platov's performance at Borodino, was furious at this latest slip-up and replaced him at once with General Mikhail Miloradovich, whom he reinforced with four infantry and two Jager regiments, and one heavy artillery company.

On 10 September Kutuzov continued his retreat, crossing the Nara river and reaching the village of Krutitsa, while Miloradovich took up positions about 3 miles away, near the village of Krymskoe. Around 5pm Murat launched an attack on the Russian rearguard, driving back its cavalry screen and reaching its main position near Krymskoe. Miloradovich had carefully selected his ground: his left wing was protected by swamps, while a narrow ravine constrained the Allied cavalry's actions in the centre, which was well protected by Russian heavy artillery. Therefore, Murat directed his efforts against the Russian right wing, where heated fighting lasted for a couple of hours. By nightfall Murat had to recall his men, who had been unable to break through; losses on both sides amounted to some 2,000 men.

The French commander's vigorous attack, however, distressed Kutuzov, who on 11 September chose to accelerate his army's movement and led it on a 16-mile march to the village of Nikolskoe (Bolshoe Vyazemy), followed by a shorter transit to Mamonovo, about 15 miles from Moscow. Miloradovich was instructed to delay the enemy advance; he slowly moved first to Kubinskoe and then to Maloya Vyazemy. On 13 September the Russian army departed from Mamonovo towards Moscow and bivouacked just a mile from the Dorogomilovskaya barrier into the capital. Special measures had been undertaken to regroup the army following the devastating losses at Borodino. Infantry regiments were reorganized into single-battalion units, since many of them now numbered just 400–500 men. Cavalry regiments were consolidated as well, with the 2nd and 3rd Cavalry Corps merged into one unit under the overall command of Adjutant General Korf. Kutuzov was glad to see some 14,000 recruits of the Moscow *opolchenye* arriving just in time to reinforce the army. These men were distributed among various regiments; bearing in mind their overall inexperience, they were placed in the third ranks and kept separate from the regular troops. 'The *Opolchenye* troops must be accepted not as soldiers, who continually maintain this status, but rather as individuals who have temporarily committed themselves to the defence of the Fatherland. Therefore, the Moscow *opolchenye* troops should not change their clothing and nor should they shave their beards.'[16] Publicly, Kutuzov was still considering fighting another battle and instructed General Baron Levin Bennigsen, the Chief of Staff of the Army, to select a new position. In fact Kutuzov was playing to popular sentiments while rationally weighing his options.

The search for a suitable battlefield finally produced a site near the Poklonnaya Gora.[17] It was selected by Bennigsen, accompanied by Colonels Karl Toll, Alexander Michaud and Jean Baptiste de Crossard, on 12 September. The position was located on the western bank of the Moscow river, straddling the heights between the villages of Vorobyevskoye and Fili, and protecting the Dorogomilovskaya suburb of Moscow. It was immediately obvious to the colonels that the position was far from suitable for battle; they voiced their concerns but Bennigsen ignored them and, making the sign of the cross, he proudly declared that 'he hoped to fight three more times before Moscow'.[18] Still, the officers questioned his rationale and debated for some time how to deploy the army in such difficult terrain. Finally, with the Russian army already approaching, the exasperated Colonel Toll, who as quartermaster general was in charge of deployment, forced Bennigsen to make the decision. As the army settled down in its new bivouacs,[19] Kutuzov instructed Barclay de Tolly and the corps commanders to acquaint themselves with the terrain, while he rested on a small bench set up on the crest of the Poklonnaya Gora and prepared for a meal. General Dokhturov, who was reluctant to spend the morning running across the ravines and 'apparently had a touch of the courtier about him', chose to stay with Kutuzov and proceeded to serve him his food. But the little picnic was quickly interrupted by Barclay de Tolly, who 'never held in high regard the small comforts of life' and, upon perceiving that Dokhturov had stayed behind, dispatched his aide-de-camp with the words, 'As usual! There they all are, dancing attendance on the Prince, and not troubling about what they [the French] may do. Fetch Dokhturov here, even if his mouth is still full.' Kutuzov apparently rather enjoyed Dokhturov's disappointment on being thus interrupted. 'You must not keep General Barclay waiting,' he remarked. 'I shall manage very well by myself,' and therewith proceeded with his meal, while poor Dokhturov was obliged to go.[20]

Barclay de Tolly, Dokhturov and their officers studied the position for about an hour and were dismayed by Bennigsen's poor choice. The western slopes, where enemy attacks would be launched, were gently rolling, while the eastern ones, over which the Russian army would have to retreat in case of need, were rather precipitous. The entire position was criss-crossed by several ravines, which complicated communications between corps. The reserves could not be deployed effectively behind the main position because of precipitous cliffs and the proximity of the Moscow river. 'It was in such a blighted area,' commented one officer, 'that the army was effectively in a hollow, where it had neither space nor communication and where the enemy could easily seize both flanks, take control of the exits and be in charge of Moscow.'[21] Barclay de Tolly, worn out by fatigue and a feverish chill, was the first to declare categorically that the position was so bad that 'in the case of a forced retreat, the entire army would have been annihilated down to the very last man'. He later wrote:

> I was surprised how disadvantageous this position was. The right wing was adjacent to the woods which extended for several miles in the direction of the enemy, who, thus, had an opportunity to send out skirmishers, seize the woods and turn our right flank. Behind the left wing there was a 20–30 metre deep ravine with such steep banks that one could only climb them single file. The reserve of the right wing was so close to the front that any enemy artillery round could target all four of our lines … The cavalry, deprived [by the deep ravines] of any opportunity to participate in this battle would have had to immediately leave the battlefield or remain idle as it was destroyed by the enemy artillery.[22]

Another general concurred: 'the position was dreadful … and unfavourable even for deploying attacking columns if circumstances allowed for launching an attack'.[23]

Returning to the Poklonnaya Gora, Barclay found Kutuzov still sitting on a campstool near the main road and surrounded by the usual crowd of officers, who were arguing loudly about the relative merits and weaknesses of the position.[24] Count Wintzingerode noted that 'by noon Kutuzov still hesitated to make a decision, so discussions continued regarding position, attacking and retreating'.[25] Barclay first conveyed his critical remarks to Bennigsen, who was so surprised (or pretended to be) to hear them that he declared that he would immediately inspect the position, starting with the left wing. Barclay then conversed with Kutuzov, pointing out the major deficiencies in the position Bennigsen had chosen. Kutuzov appeared genuinely surprised and concerned. Turning to his trusted Colonel Toll, he asked for his opinion on Barclay's comments. Toll, who was not predisposed to Bennigsen, particularly after the experiences of the previous day, replied that he himself would never have placed the army in such a dangerous position. Kutuzov then turned to General Alexei Yermolov, Barclay's Chief of Staff, who had regularly expressed hostility towards his superior but had undergone a radical change of heart since Barclay's heroic performance at Borodino. Yermolov emphatically agreed with Barclay, criticizing the position with such fervour that it prompted Kutuzov to take him by the wrist, check his pulse and inquire if he was feeling all right. But this was all part of Kutuzov's charade. As Yermolov correctly noted, many officers 'already understood that Prince Kutuzov had no need for their ideas and simply wanted to show his resolve in defending Moscow when in reality he never even considered it'. And so the farce continued. The Russian commander-in-chief next asked Colonel Jean Baptiste de Crossard, a French émigré officer who had previously served in the Spanish and Austrian armies, for his opinion. Crossard, who had earlier reconnoitred the position, bluntly declared, 'Never has a position been better suited to destroying one's own army.'[26] Kutuzov, wanting to show that he was doing everything possible to accept battle in the current position, dispatched Yermolov, Crossard and Prince Kudashev on another reconnaissance of the position.[27]

It was around 1pm already and Kutuzov still appeared to be vacillating, listening to others while keeping his genuine feelings secret. His stillness, however, was broken by the sound of gunfire as Murat's advanced guard engaged the Russian rearguard near Setun. With the enemy so close, the urgency of making a final decision became clear to everyone. Prince Eugène of Württemberg approached the aged commander-in-chief, seated on his folding stool, and whispered to him, 'You must decide, Prince, indecision is the worst thing of all.' Turning his gaze on the young general, Kutuzov responded in French, 'In this issue, my head, be it good or bad, must rely solely on itself' and departed from the crest to his headquarters set up at the village of Fili.[28] Having already decided to surrender Moscow, Kutuzov was unwilling to take sole responsibility for the decision. Yermolov recalled:

> It was late afternoon by now and yet there were still no special orders for the army. Barclay de Tolly summoned me and, with marvellous sagacity and insight, he explained the reasons for the necessity of retreat. He then went to Kutuzov, ordering me to follow him. No one knew better than Barclay the varied ways of making war and which of them were most feasible at any moment. In order to win the war, it was imperative for us to gain time, and, to that end, abandon Moscow. Listening attentively, Kutuzov could not conceal his excitement that the idea for retreat would not be attributed to him, and, to further avoid any blame, he summoned the army generals for a council of war.[29]

The council of war was supposed to meet at 4pm but it was delayed for over two hours by the late arrival of both Bennigsen, who was reconnoitring the left flank, and General Nikolai Rayevskii, who came up from the rearguard; Miloradovich could not attend because he had to remain with the rearguard. The Russian commanders gathered inside a little peasant hut in the village of Fili. Despite the specific requirements instituted by the Committee of the Ministers, the council of war inexplicably failed to maintain an official protocol, so what we know about this meeting comes from memoirs and letters written by participants. There is still disagreement on who precisely attended it; depending on sources, between seven and twelve people were present at the meeting.[30] Most sources, however, agree that under glowing candles sat Generals Kutuzov, Barclay de Tolly, Bennigsen, Matvei Platov and Dmitri Dokhturov, Lieutenant Generals Fedor Uvarov, Count Alexander Osterman-Tolstoy, Peter Konovnitsyn and Nikolai Rayevskii, Major General Yermolov and Colonel Karl Toll.[31] Some sources[32] also name *Intendant-Général* V. Lanskoi (chief supply officer) and Kutuzov's duty officer Colonel Paisii Kaissarov as participants in this council. Kutuzov's orderly Alexander Golitsyn, however, clearly indicates that Lanskoi was not invited to the council but was summoned after the meeting. As for Kaissarov, there is no direct evidence for his participation and his inclusion is usually justified in the light of his position as a duty general at the headquarters.

Bennigsen opened the meeting by asking whether it was better to give battle beneath the walls of Moscow or to abandon the city to the enemy. Kutuzov brusquely interrupted him, reprimanding him for such a 'useless and too broad question'.[33] Without preliminary discussion of the general state of affairs such a question was counterproductive, he argued, since what was at stake was not simply the army or the city but rather the preservation of the Russian realm. As Toll observes in his memoirs, this was a subtle move on Kutuzov's part since by encouraging the council of war to debate, Kutuzov in essence sought 'to shift the responsibility [for this momentous decision] from himself and to relegate it to the generals assembled here'. By letting everyone express his opinion, he could later claim not to have been the first to propose the abandonment of Moscow.[34] Thus, after making a succinct observation of the present state of affairs, Kutuzov inquired whether it was proper to await the enemy's attack in this disadvantageous position or to abandon Moscow to the enemy. Barclay de Tolly, Osterman-Tolstoy, Rayevskii and Konovnitsyn came out in support of retreating, with Osterman-Tolstoy and Rayevskii observing that 'Moscow is not the whole of Russia and our goal is not to defend Moscow but rather all of the Fatherland'. Barclay de Tolly also emphasized the need to preserve the army:

> Our current position is very unfavourable and, if we wait for the enemy in it, it will become very dangerous; considering that the French have superior forces, it is more than doubtful that we would be able to defeat them. If, after the battle, we still manage to hold our ground, we would suffer losses similar to those at Borodino and thus would be unable to defend a city as extensive as Moscow. The loss of Moscow might upset the Sovereign, but it would not be unexpected by him, certainly it would not incline him to end the war and would reinforce his resolute will to fight on. By saving Moscow, Russia will not avoid this brutal, ruinous war; but having preserved our army, the hopes of our Fatherland would persevere, and the war, our only means to salvation, would be continued on better terms ...[35]

But the 'shrewd and clever' Bennigsen was not ready 'to lose the game' yet.[36] He argued that the Russians could not give up their capital following the 'victory' at Borodino, where Napoleon had been greatly weakened; such an action would have a shattering effect on the morale of the army and the nation. Instead, he called for an attack, proposing to leave one corps on the right flank and move the rest of the army to the left for a surprise attack against the enemy's right wing. Some participants understood that Bennigsen's proposal was not serious and he was aiming at something different – he knew that the old field marshal had already made his decision and Moscow would undoubtedly be abandoned. But 'it could very well happen that Kutuzov would be removed from command for this decision – and then Bennigsen stood to benefit as one of those who refused until the last moment to consent to leaving the capital to the enemy without a fight'.[37] But the 'simple and honest' Barclay de Tolly seems to have missed the subtleties of this military intrigue and quickly voiced his opinion against Bennigsen's proposal, pointing out that it was too late for such a drastic redeployment of troops, especially over difficult terrain and in darkness. Kutuzov supported his critique, reminding Bennigsen what had happened at Friedland.

In the ensuing discussion, Barclay de Tolly expressed his preference for moving towards Vladimir to maintain communications with St Petersburg, where the imperial family resided, as well as with Kazan, Tula and Kiev, where new foundries and armament factories were established. Always an intriguer, Yermolov sensed what Kutuzov was aiming at but being 'a relatively unknown officer, I did not dare to give my consent to the surrender of Moscow'. So he spoke against a passive stance and called for an attack along the entire line. Kutuzov criticized him for proposing an attack without taking 'responsibility for such actions' and proceeded to listen to the other generals. As Yermolov observed, 'everyone based their decisions on the Minister of War's observations, without explaining their reasons or considerations'. Judging from the existing sources, Barclay de Tolly, Osterman-Tolstoy, Rayevskii and Toll recommended avoiding battle and retreating,[38] while Platov, Yermolov, Konovnitsyn, Uvarov and Dokhturov supported Bennigsen's idea of fighting another battle.[39] As the debate turned more acrimonious, Kutuzov ended the meeting by announcing, 'I am aware of the responsibility I am assuming, but I sacrifice myself for the welfare of my country. I hereby order the retreat.'[40]

It was already dark when the first orders to retreat were sent to local commanders. Kutuzov initially made the decision to retreat towards Ryazan, southeast of Moscow, and inquired from *Intendant-Général* Lanskoi about the availability of supplies. Lanskoi informed him that there were no major supply depots in this area but there were plentiful magazines at Kaluga and Tula, southwest of Moscow. But marching there would require them to make a flanking march in front of the Grande Armée and might expose the army to a dreaded flanking attack. So, while agreeing to move to Kaluga, Kutuzov decided to pretend to head for Ryazan since this would prompt Napoleon to follow him into Moscow, which would allow the Russian army a better chance of manoeuvring towards the southwest. By taking this circuitous route, the Russian army would not be exposed to a flanking attack but would be able to easily manoeuvre northwards or southwards should the occasion arise. Once on the Kaluga route, the commissariat would be well provided, since the army would have at its back the fertile provinces of the southeast and it would be in communication with the manufactories of arms at Tula and elsewhere. Consequently, Kutuzov decided to 'march to the Ryazan road but then [make a turn] and proceed to the Tula Road and further to the Kaluga Road at Podolsk'.[41]

Starting late in the evening of 13 September the Russian army proceeded in two columns through Moscow, which was hastily being evacuated. 'Goods of various kinds were piled up in all streets and it was very difficult to find one's way through them,' remembered a soldier of the Life Guard Finlyandskii Regiment. 'But this was nothing compared to the challenge of crossing the Moscow river, which all troops had to cross on a single bridge. Barclay de Tolly was there to maintain order.'[42] After slowly navigating through the city's street, the army departed via the Ryazan and Vladimir roads. 'At eleven o'clock that evening,' Bennigsen recalled, 'our artillery began to move though the city, and at three in the morning the infantry columns set off. Outside the town there was still a crowd of vehicles of all kinds, and first the guns and then the infantry prevented these from passing. Imagine the difficulties attending this march across a town about 6 miles wide, with many narrow streets and with nearly all the inhabitants departing ... The least damage to a team of horses stopped the entire column in the street!'[43] Barclay de Tolly, assisted by Jacob de Sanglen and his military police,[44] supervised the passage of the army through the city and did his best to anticipate possible disorders. His disposition of 14 September demanded the maintenance of strict discipline, prohibiting 'even a single officer or soldier from leaving the ranks, and whoever is found away from their units, should be executed [*velet' zakolot'*]'.[45] Barclay de Tolly asked Rostopchin to deploy the remaining police officials on the streets that the army would pass along in order to ensure that 'no army officials, and especially the rank-and-file, enter any houses or break their ranks under whatever reason'.[46] Baron Waldemar von Löwenstern was among those stationed 'in the various districts of Moscow to see that order was maintained. We each had a Cossack escort to turn soldiers out of the cabarets and prevent them entering houses. Anyone who in contravention of these orders was found with bottles of brandy or liqueurs was arrested on the spot and the bottles broken.'[47] Such precautions, however, did not have the desired effect and the Russian troops looted houses and taverns at the first opportunity.

The news of the abandonment of Moscow was received with a mixture of consternation and bewilderment. Governor Rostopchin, who had spent the previous weeks convincing the people of Moscow that the Russians were winning the war, expressed his distress in a letter to his wife: 'The blood is boiling in my veins. I think that I shall die of the pain.' The Russian troops, in the deepest dejection, tramped through the streets with furled standards and silent bands. Nikolai Golitsyn, who joined Kutuzov's suite at the outskirts of the city, recalled that 'we rode across Moscow in a melancholy silence, nobody expressing what was in his thoughts, and each apparently absorbed in sombre reflections. The solemnity of this silent march, of which no one except [Kutuzov] knew either the destination or the duration, had something sinister about it.'[48] Many expressed their protest publicly, some even tearing their uniforms since they felt they could not long serve in such disgrace. 'The march of the army, while being executed with admirable order considering the circumstances, resembled a funeral procession more than a military progress ...', noted Buturlin, adding that 'officers and soldiers sobbed with rage and despair.' In contrast, General Yermolov commented that the 'soldiers were not disheartened and no grumbles were uttered' although 'their commanders were astonished by the loss of our ancient capital'.[49] Indeed, senior officer were greatly affected by Moscow's abandonment. General Dokhturov wrote on 15 September:

> What a horror! We are already beyond the capital. I did my best to convince our leaders to advance against the enemy ... But this bold proposal had no effect on these cowardly people – as a result we retreated through the city. What a shame to abandon one's cradle without a single shot and without a fight! I am in a fury but what can I do? I cannot do anything but obey because it seems God's punishment is upon us. I cannot think otherwise. Without losing a battle, we kept retreating without slightest resistance to this point. What a disgrace! Now I am convinced that everything is lost and, in this case, nothing will keep me in [military] service. After all the unpleasantness, exertion, abuses and disorders committed through the weakness of our leaders – after all this, nothing would induce me to continue to serve. I am utterly dismayed by what is going on![50]

A wide range of reactions was noted by Baron von Löwenstern, who initially found it difficult to describe the reactions to the abandonment and loss of Moscow because points of view differed so sharply:

> Whereas one man grieved over the loss of his house, another regretted the loss of homes belonging to his parents or friends, while others – and they were the majority – were preoccupied with the humiliation at seeing this ancient capital occupied by foreigners. But quite spontaneously everyone forgot his personal concerns and thought only of the affront the enemy had just inflicted on us and, far from being disheartened, we felt more passionately determined than ever to continue the war

and to make every conceivable sacrifice.... After the capture of Moscow we had the Empire to save, not just a town. And from this moment everybody said, 'The war is only just beginning!'[51]

The decision to abandon Moscow was not an easy one and Kutuzov passed a sleepless night; witnesses even reported seeing more than once tears rolling down his cheeks.[52] Whether this was a calculated act or not, Kutuzov certainly understood the burden of the decision he had made; when one officer inquired whether the Russian retreat would ever end, he snapped at him, 'That is my business to know. But I am going to see to it as I did last year with the Turks that the French end up eating horseflesh!'[53] The old field marshal also hinted that the loss of Moscow might be the beginning of the end for the enemy, commenting that Napoleon's Grande Armée was akin to 'a stormy torrent' and describing Moscow as 'the sponge that will absorb it'.[54] He believed that the fall of Moscow would halt the Grande Armée's further advance as Napoleon would seek a political resolution to the war. Kutuzov needed this precious time to regroup.

And so the retreat continued and the army grudgingly obeyed its leaders. As artillery officer Ilya Radozhitskii aptly commented, 'Only Kutuzov, the genuine son of Russia who suckled on her breasts [*vskormlennyi eye sostsami*], could surrender the ancient capital of the empire without a fight. Public opinion would have condemned any other commander as an apparent traitor. So, a great sacrifice for the salvation of the whole nation was acceptable if it was offered by the chosen and foremost defender of the Fatherland.'[55] Sergei Glinka watched Kutuzov passing through Moscow, sitting in a droshki[56] and buried in deep thought. 'Colonel Toll drove up to the Russian general and reported that the French had entered Moscow. "God be praised," answered Kutuzov. "That is their last triumph."'[57]

Chapter 2

The City

On the eve of the French invasion Moscow was the largest and wealthiest of the Russian cities. Only St Petersburg, the official capital of the empire, could rival Moscow's political, economic or cultural status. 'Moscow, how much there is in this sound, that flows together for the heart of the Russian,' announced the great Russian poet Alexander Pushkin a decade after the invasion. Another poet, K. Batyushkov, who first visited Moscow in 1810, was so overjoyed by what he saw that he proudly declared that the city 'presents a sight that is worthy of the greatest capital in the world, built by the greatest nation and on a most pleasant location'.[1] Visitors to Moscow all marvelled at the spectacular views that opened to them on approaching the city, especially from the west, where the Vorobyevo Hills offered a fine vantage point to contemplate the city views at ease. 'Its immense extent, the incalculable number of steeples and churches, their domes surmounted with gilded crosses ... the neatness of the roofs of the houses which are covered with tiles of all colours, and very skilfully painted, altogether formed a charming spectacle,' observed one foreign traveller, and similar descriptions can be found in the accounts of almost all visitors to Moscow.[2] In September 1806 the Irish traveller Catherine Wilmot was charmed by the sight that was presented to her from the Vorobyevo Hills: 'The number of Churches all cover'd over in Cupolas with Metal & many with pure Dutch gold give the chief beauty to the *coup d'oeil* – 600 of these blaze like so many Suns & are contrasted to the green of the Public Gardens which everywhere abound.'[3] Looking from the bell tower of Ivan the Great, Robert Ker Porter, an Englishman who visited Moscow in April 1806, was spellbound by the 'variegated colours on the tops of innumerable buildings, the sparkling particles of snow on the earth and palaces, the fanes and crescents of the churches flashing their blazing gold, and the busy world beneath, passing and repassing in their superb dresses and decorated sledges'.[4]

Contemporary maps of Moscow[5] show that the city was a sprawling settlement in the shape of an uneven parallelogram, with most of the urban development located north of the Moscow river. The city was almost 12km wide along the southwest–northeast axis (from the Kaluzhskaya to the Preobrazhenskii barriers), and 8km wide along the northwest–southeast axis (from the Tverskaya to the Spasskaya barriers). 'Moscow is considerably larger in circumference than Paris, although the number of its inhabitants is much smaller,' opined a German visitor in 1805,[6] while an English traveller described a year later that 'on viewing it from an eminence, you see a vast plain, as far as the eye can reach, covered with houses, even to the very horizon, where the lofty towers of gorgeous palaces and the glittering steeples of churches sparkle in the sky'.[7]

Moscow was located on the rolling plains that stretched for miles along the banks of the Moscow and other rivers, which nowadays flow through tunnels beneath the Russian capital. The largest of these waterways was the Moscow river, which entered the city from the west and flowed in a southeasterly direction. The river's right (western) bank was rather low, only gradually rising towards the Vorobyevo Hills in the southwestern part of the city, where the river made a major turn towards the northeast. Here the riverbank was a largely uncluttered swathe of grassland. The left (eastern) bank, on the contrary, was both steeper and more forested (largely orchards), and intersected by numerous rivulets. Beneath the Kremlin the Moscow river was at once bucolic and commercial, though commerce and industry were clearly ascendant by 1812. On the right bank the streets were unpaved and the dirt embankment of Zamoskvorechye, across from the Kremlin, offered little protection from flooding. Contemporary prints show Muscovites strolling along the banks or, in winter time, skating and sleighing on the river. The left bank consisted of the Kremlin Embankment, which ran beneath the Kremlin citadel walls, and the Moskvoretskii Embankment, which extended further eastwards.

Of the many tributaries of the Moscow river, the Presnya (in the west), the Neglinnaya (in the centre of the town) and the Yauza (in the east) were the largest. The Neglinnaya river, which approached the city from the north, snaking along the Kitai-gorod and the Kremlin to the Moscow river, used to be an important feature in the city. At its estuary with the Moscow river, it enclosed a tall hill upon which the Russian princes built the Kremlin. However, in the eighteenth century the Neglinnaya had been re-routed to make space for the bastions surrounding the Kremlin. By 1812 the old river bed was dry and filling up with rubbish, while three bridges (see below) near the Kremlin still reminded the Muscovites of the river's earlier importance.

The various rivers and rivulets were bridged by seventeen stone and twenty-one wooden bridges connecting various parts of the city.[8] The stone-built Voskresenskii bridge on the Neglinnaya river, opposite Okhotnyi Ryad (Hunter's Row) and Moscow University and leading to Red Square, was one of the busiest intersections in the city, where one could find gentlemen and officers mingling with beggars, tradesmen, priests and craftsmen; beneath the bridge women often washed their laundry. The city's other stone bridges were the Great Stone Bridge over the Moscow river, the Kuznetskii and Troitskii bridges over the Neglinnaya, the Gorbatyi and Presnenskii bridges over the Presnya river, and the Yauzskii and Dvorstovyi bridges over the Yauza river. Among the wooden bridges the most important were the Dorogomilovskii, Krymskii and Moskvoretskii bridges over the Moscow river. The Dorogomilovskii bridge, located in the western part of the city, was maintained on a combination of rafts and pontoons, and was 185 metres long and 8.5 metres wide. At the southern end of Red Square Moskvoretskaya Street led from St Basil's Cathedral to the Moskvoretskii bridge, which connected the city's central districts with the Zamoskvorechye suburbs across the river.

The entire city was surrounded by the Kamer–Kollezhskii rampart (some 38km in length), which was built as a customs wall in 1742 but had effectively marked municipal jurisdiction since 1806; the municipal cemeteries that initially remained within the Kamer–Kollezhskii confines were moved outside the city limits following the plague epidemic of 1771. The rampart featured sixteen barriers (*zastava*) that regulated people's movements into and out of the city.

Early nineteenth-century maps of Moscow show closely packed urban development throughout the city. Its quarter of a million residents lived in 9,151 houses, including 2,367 stone and 6,584 wooden ones,[9] the majority of which were private property; only 387 buildings belonged to the state or public organizations. Under Empress Catherine II the Russian government continued the social engineering launched by Peter the Great some six decades earlier, and focused on urban renovation in an attempt to bring enlightenment to Russia. Moscow's neighbourhoods were gradually reconstructed and its old and narrow streets replaced with paved thoroughfares and street lighting: almost 7,300 street lamps illuminated its streets at night by 1812.[10] Neoclassical architecture had made an appearance, but visitors often marvelled at the mixed architectural images to be found in the city. Many were struck by the magnificence of Moscow's buildings and the vastness of some of the architectural ensembles. 'Everything appears here on a gigantic scale,' commented a Russian diplomat returning from Constantinople to St Petersburg in 1790s. 'The palaces of the men of distinction, and of the majority of the Russian nobility ... possess a colossal grandeur, and are filled with considerable numbers of domestic serfs, attached to the service of all the men of rank.'[11] 'Every object we behold in Moscow is, like the city itself, in a certain degree gigantic,' echoed the scientist and traveller Peter Simon Palas.[12] A similar observation was made by an Englishman visiting the city six years prior to the conflagration: 'It is not a city of houses in mere rank and file of streets, but rather a collection of mansions, each embosomed amidst its own lawns, gardens, pleasure grounds and the dwellings of its necessary slaves. Some of the most ancient princes of the empire have very splendid palaces in Moscow, ornamented with basso reliefs, gilding and every Asiatic decoration.'[13] One Russian contemporary, Philipp Vigel, recalled that

> every year, in December, the nobles from the neighbouring provinces considered it their responsibility to travel with their entire families from their villages to Moscow for Christmas and then return to the villages during the first week of Lent ... They were preceded by long trains of wagons loaded with frozen piglets, ducks and chickens, as well as grains, flours and butter and other necessary provisions. Each family had its own wooden house, modestly furnished, with a large yard and garden ... All of Zamoskvorechye [beyond the Zemlyanoi Val] was peppered with these houses.

Moscow had originated in the twelfth century as a small fortress at the confluence of the Moscow and Neglinnaya rivers. From this early, triangular-shaped stockade, the city grew outwards in concentric circles protected by earthworks and stone walls. By 1812 the city consisted of twenty districts[14] grouped into four historical quarters or 'cities' (gorod), the Kremlin, Kitai-gorod, Belyi Gorod and Zemlyanoi Gorod. For most of the city's history, the Kremlin was at the heart of the city, serving as a powerful symbol of the Russian rulers' authority. 'What can rival the Kremlin,' wondered the poet Mikhail Lermontov, 'which, having ringed itself with crenellated walls and adorned itself with the golden domes of the cathedrals, sits on a high hill like the crown of sovereignty on the brow of an awesome ruler?' Surrounded by its famous crenellated white-washed brick walls,[15] the Kremlin featured twenty towers (nineteen with spires and one outlying barbican tower) that were built by Italian architects (most notably Pietro Solario) in the late fifteenth and early sixteenth centuries. The most important towers, featuring gates, were those of the Saviour (Spasskaya, in the east), St Nicholas (Nikolskaya, in the northeast), Trinity (Troitskaya, in the west), and the Borovitskaya (in the southwest). Some towers have been used variously as prisons, storehouses and even as water pumping stations, as exemplified by the Vodozvodnaya (water-pumping) Tower. Perhaps the best known, and nowadays the most photographed, is the Saviour Tower on Red Square, first built in 1491; its tented roof and famous clock were installed by the Scottish clock-maker Christopher Galloway in 1625. Entering through the Saviour Gates – the main entrance to the Kremlin used by the tsars – visitors found (and still do) a remarkable ensemble of striking churches, palaces and squares inside the Kremlin confines, and were often surprised by their architectural diversity. Johann Gottfried Seume thought that there was 'a singular mixture of New Grecian half-oriental appearance, and of the more modern improved architecture of Italy'.[16] Edward Daniel Clarke found it

> difficult to say from what country [the architectural style] has been principally derived: the architects were chiefly Italians but the style is Tartarian, Indian, Chinese and Gothic. Here a pagoda, there an arcade! In some parts are richness, and even elegance; in others, barbarity and decay. Taken altogether, it is a jumble of magnificence and ruin: old buildings repaired, and modern structures not completed; half-open vaults and mouldering walls and empty caves, amidst whitewashed brick buildings; and towers and churches, with glittering, gilded or painted domes.[17]

By 1812 many of the ancient buildings in the Kremlin complex had been replaced. The decaying buildings from the sixteenth century (most of them located in the western section) were first to be pulled down and replaced by newer edifices. In 1802 repair of the crumbling walls commenced and four years later the tottering Vodozvodnaia Tower was dismantled and rebuilt, while the Nikolaskaya Tower was renovated in the neo-Gothic style. The most magnificent of the new additions was the Senate building, designed by Matvei Kazakov and built between 1776 and 1787. Designed in the classical style, the building was triangular with an inner court, its exterior corners severed and a cupola-capped rotunda (with a monumental Doric colonnade) wedged on the main entrance axis. In front of the Senate building lay three magnificent cathedrals – the Cathedral of the Assumption (Uspenskii Sobor, built in 1475–1479), the Cathedral of the Annunciation (Blagoveschenskii Sobor, 1484–1489) and the Cathedral of St Michael the Archangel (Arkhangelskii Sobor, 1505–1508) – grouped around the central square that also featured the mid seventeenth-century Cathedral of the Twelve Apostles and the adjoining Patriarchal Palace, the magnificent soaring white bell tower of Ivan the Great (1505–1508), the enormous Tsar Bell (cast in 1733–1735 but never rung) and the Tsar Cannon (cast in 1586 but never fired).

The most important of the Kremlin cathedrals was the five-domed Cathedral of the Assumption, where the tsars were crowned, patriarchs and metropolitans were buried, and important state services were held. The smaller Cathedral of the Annunciation served as the imperial family's private chapel, and Field Marshal Helmuth von Moltke, visiting Moscow in 1866 for the coronation of Alexander II, was more impressed by this 'narrower, stranger, and richer [church] than all the rest. It is a complete casket of jewels. The cross of the cupola is of wrought gold, and the floor is inlaid with jasper, agate and chalcedony from Siberia.'[18] Surrounding the cathedrals were the Palace of Facets (1487–1491) and the Terem Palace (1635–1636), which later merged into the Great Kremlin Palace complex that served as an imperial residence in the mid-nineteenth century as well as the seat of the Supreme Soviet of the USSR in the twentieth century. The grand entrance to the Palace of Facets is up the Red Staircase, which was demolished in the Soviet era but rebuilt in the 1990s. It was from this vantage point that the young Peter the Great is said to have witnessed the massacre of his relatives by the rebellious *streltsy* in 1682. Here, too, Napoleon stood and watched on the fateful day in 1812 as the fires raged through the city. Along the northwest wall of the Kremlin stood the Arsenal, which was initially laid down in 1702 but could not be completed due to lack of funds during the Great Northern War with Sweden. The building was eventually finished in 1736 under the supervision of Field Marshal Burkhard Christoph von Münnich; gutted by a fire the following year, it was fully restored only in 1796.

To the east of the Kremlin was Kitai-gorod, a bustling centre of trade since the fourteenth century. As Moscow grew, this district became a vibrant commercial hub both for the powerful merchant class and for the *boyars* (nobles) not favoured with residences within the Kremlin. The popular translation of Kitai-gorod as 'Chinatown,' which can be found in quite a few memoirs and later studies, is almost certainly erroneous since the district's name seems to have been derived from the word *kita* (woven baskets filled with dirt), the method of construction used to build the mid sixteenth-century walls that surrounded the area.[19]

Like the Kremlin, Kitai-gorod was protected by a wall and towers, although of smaller size. In addition, both the Kremlin and Kitai-gorod were surrounded by earthen bastions and a shallow moat built by Peter the Great in 1708. After a century or so of neglect, these defences were in a derelict condition; in fact, Emperor Paul had considered levelling them but never got around to accomplishing it. The houses of Kitai-gorod were principally of wooden construction, although there were a few masonry buildings. It was separated from the Kremlin Wall by Red Square, once the Russian realm's political, social and economic nerve centre, which was gradually transformed during the course of the eighteenth century. In 1812 it was smaller than it is today but it was, nonetheless, Moscow's busiest square as pedestrians and equestrians jostled for space and trade overflowed to every corner of the plaza. It was here that the infamous Tsar Ivan the Terrible had constructed the magnificent Cathedral of St Basil the Blessed in 1554–1560 to commemorate the Russian victory over the Kazan and Astrakhan Tatars. Here too Peter the Great ordered the execution of hundreds of mutinous *streltzy* in 1698. Late eighteenth-century prints show the square choked with people on foot, in carts or carriages making their way across an unpaved open space, and idlers, serfs, artisans, clergy and nobles all intermingled. In 1786 the square benefited from the construction of new commercial rows that bracketed both the east and west sides of the square and obscured from the plaza the unseemly view of hovels and shops of Kitai-gorod. A sense of how the square looked when the Grande Armée arrived there can be gleaned from the painting of Red Square by Fedor Alekseev, which shows the moat that used to run down the western side of the square, with bridges joining it to the Kremlin gates, as well as numerous trading stalls lined up along its length.

Beyond Red Square, Kitai-gorod featured narrow, crowded streets, containing numerous stores, warehouses, stalls and other commercial buildings. 'From the number of its shops and warehouses, and the Asiatic apparel of the buyers and sellers,' commented one European visitor, 'it reminded me of what I had read of Baghdad in the time of the Caliphs, when the chief merchants of the east used to assemble in its populous streets. The number of shops and warehouses which compose it are nearly six thousand.'[20] Indeed, visitors were often struck by the abundance of people, transports and goods that jammed the Ilyinka, Varvarka and Nikolskaya streets and their interconnecting alleys. The most notable building in this area was the massive *Gostinnyi dvor*, or Merchant Court, designed along classical lines by Giacomo Quarenghi and possibly Matvei Kazakov. Considering

Kitai-gorod's central role in Moscow's economy, this edifice was appropriately located in its busiest Ilyinka and Varvarka streets. Because Russian sovereigns used the nearby radial Nikolskaya street as a grand entrance into the Kremlin, triumphal arches frequently had to be erected where the street entered Red Square. The street was home to both prominent noble families (notably the Cherkasskiis and Sheremetevs) and bookshops, twenty-six of which were located there by the first quarter of the nineteenth century.

Between Varvarka Street and the embankment of the Moscow river lay Zariadye, which by the late eighteenth century was an overcrowded slum of craftsmen, tradesmen and workmen. The construction of Peter's bastions around Kitai-gorod had caused considerable traffic difficulties but, worse than that, had severed the merchant quarter's sewage connection with the river, so that the filth and waste emanating from the Varvarka shops collected in Zariadye and contributed to the outbreaks of epidemics there. In an attempt to resolve the traffic issues and improve the sanitary conditions, the Moscow river embankment was built beneath the Kitai-gorod walls in 1796–1800. A British visitor described 'the new promenade forming on its banks; immediately beneath the fortress is a superb work … it is paved with large flags [and] fenced with a light but strong iron palisade, and stone pillars executed in very good taste'.[21] On the east side of Kitai-gorod the Kitaiskii Passage, a circular boulevard skirting the district, was constructed in 1790 by filling in the moat of Peter's bastions. In 1806–1808 the houses there were demolished and rows of trees planted but the relics of the bastions remained until the 1820s.

In the first half of the eighteenth century the southeastern corner of the Kitai-gorod featured an open space known as Vasilievskii Meadow, which in 1770 became the site of the famous Foundlings Home. Designed by the architect Karl Blank, the Foundlings Home was an architectural milestone since it was the first edifice in the city to be built in the classical style. The building was designed to accommodate some 8,000 orphans and consisted of two buildings enclosing a rectangular court, where a central complex featured three structures, each of which was crowned by a cupola. Visitors often marvelled at the building's long façade (over 1,200ft) stretched along the riverbank.

While Kitai-gorod was a largely commercial district, the main residential sector lay in the city's Belyi Gorod quarter, which comprised two districts (II Tverskii and III Myasnitskii). Like the Kremlin and Kitai-gorod, this district was also once surrounded by the massive white walls built at the behest of Tsars Feodor I and Boris Godunov in 1585–1593. The wall featured over three dozen towers and gates, but was demolished during the reigns of Catherine the Great and Alexander I to create space for a series of open and long (up to 7km) boulevards that became known as the Boulevard Ring; the first boulevard, the Tverskii, was built in 1796 but the ring was not completed until after the great fire of 1812 had levelled much of the city. Today many of the traffic intersections along the Boulevard Ring still bear the names of the old gateways into Moscow. The district took its name 'Belyi Gorod' ('white city') from the tax-exempt nobility who lived there. By the late eighteenth century, however, parts of the district were also populated by commoners, and the area between the Moiseevskaya Square and Bolshaya Nikitskaya, to the west of the Kremlin, contained shops and taverns of every description jammed into narrow alleys; these were destroyed in the fire of 1790 and replaced by larger and more affluent shops. The district also featured several large open spaces, including Okhotnyi Ryad, which featured the Nobility's Meeting House, and Mokhovaya Square where, in 1793, the architect Kazakov constructed the magnificent, classical-style building of

Moscow University overlooking the Neglinnaya river. Further along the Mokhovaya, the architect Vasilli Bazhenov created one of Moscow's most famous and graceful residential estates, the Pashkov House. Built on a promontory opposite the Borovitskaya Gates of the Kremlin and surrounded by an exquisite fence, the gleaming white three-storey house was praised for its magnificence, becoming a symbol for princely living and taste in late eighteenth-century Russia. 'It comprehended within itself all conveniences and delights of life,' commented a contemporary. 'This little garden situated on a pretty high eminence presented a kind of Garden of Eden.'[22]

Outside the Belyi Gorod was the last historical quarter of Moscow, the Zemlyanoi Gorod ('earthen city'), which included six administrative districts[23] and was surrounded by the third defensive circle known as the Zemlyanoi Val ('earthen rampart'). Until the sixteenth century this territory lay outside the city proper and featured numerous settlements for palace servants, tradesmen, craftsmen, gardeners and other commoners. One area of the Zemlyanoi Gorod, adjacent to the Kremlin in the south, was called Zamoskvorechye ('beyond the Moscow river'), and was often beset by flooding. In 1593, during the Russo–Swedish War and in the wake of a Crimean Tatar raid two years earlier, the Moscow authorities decided to strengthen the city defences by building a massive earthen rampart – with a moat and more than thirty towers – encircling a wide swathe of territory around the Belyi Gorod; destroyed by the Polish invasion in 1611, it was rebuilt (and reinforced) in the mid-seventeenth century. The newly delimited territory was quickly colonized by the expanding population of Moscow and became notorious for its bustling but congested life. By the nineteenth century the earthen rampart, although repaired in its northern section, had been long ignored by the authorities and was in a decrepit state, offering no military advantages. In fact, by 1812 eleven administrative districts had spread beyond the confines of the historical Zemlyanoi Gorod quarter;[24] according to Ker Porter, these suburbs were intersected by 'numerous and antiquated streets [that] show all the varieties attached to a great capital: on one side splendid mansions, on the other dingy hovels filled with all the repressing effects of bondage. The pleasantest parts of these suburbs are inhabited by Germans, and also a band of noble Georgians,[25] who, with a large train of followers, retired hither. The districts allotted to these strangers partake of their character and are very interesting.'[26] An earlier visitor, the English clergyman William Coxe, who came to Moscow in the late 1770s, had similarly remarked on the great diversity of the city and the variety of different types of buildings that he saw:

I was all astonishment at the immensity and variety of Moscow, a city so irregular, so uncommon, so extraordinary, and so contrasted, never before claimed my attention. The streets are in general exceedingly long and broad: some are paved; others, particularly those in the suburbs, formed with trunks of trees, or boarded with planks like the floor of a room; wretched hovels are blended with large palaces; cottages of one storey stand next to the most stately mansions. Many brick structures are covered with wooden tops; some of the timber houses are painted, others have iron doors and roofs. Numerous churches present themselves in every quarter, built in the oriental style of architecture; some with domes of copper, others of tin, gilt or painted green, and many roofed with wood. In a word, some parts of this vast city have the appearance of a sequestered desert, other quarters of a populous town; some of a contemptible village, others of a great capital.[27]

Police reports reveal that Moscow's population exceeded 275,000 people in 1812.[28] The largest social group (32.5%) was the commoners, known as *dvorovye liudi*, who occupied an ambiguous status in gentry's houses. There had been two kinds of serfs, those who were tied to the soil (*krepostnye liudi*) and those who were tied to the master (*dvorovye liudi*). The latter generally comprised the entire staff of the nobleman's house, from the housekeeper to the lowest lackey. The *dvorovye liudi* were often subjected to abominable treatment from their masters, who had an almost absolute authority over them, including the right to sell them. Besides the *dvorovye*, the next largest population groups were the landlord (14.9%) and state (13.6%) peasants, who, in exchange for a tax (e.g. *obrok*) were allowed to leave their lands to find work in towns; living in teams (*artel'*) formed on a regional basis, they were engaged in commerce, manufacturing or crafts, but never fully assimilated into the urban fabric. The people who gave the city its urban character were merchants, foreigners, shop-keepers, physicians, civil servants and others who lived in the city year-round, enjoying modest material comforts and certain privileges accorded to the urban populace. Merchants (*kuptsy*), including foreign traders, represented 7 per cent of the population but were outnumbered by the combined artisans and craftsmen (*meshane* and *tsekhovye*) at 9.5 per cent, including foreigners. The rest of the population included clergy, professional groups (teachers, lawyers, writers, physicians, etc.), veterans and others.[29] Law and order was upheld by 398 senior and 3,777 minor police officials, who, according to official reports, maintained good order in the city – only 6 violent deaths (but 32 suicides) were reported in 1811.[30]

The nobles (*dvoryane*) comprised a small sliver of the population (6.3%), and a small fraction of them were aristocrats wielding enormous power and influence in the city's political, public and cultural arenas. The general perception of Russian aristocrats is derived from literary depictions by the great Russian writers. In Leo Tolstoy's *War and Peace*, the main protagonists are immensely rich Muscovites: Pierre Bezukhov has an annual income of half a million rubles, while Nikolai Rostov famously loses 43,000 rubles in a single card game.[31] Yet, in reality, very few Muscovite nobles were so rich; most of them were landless civil servants who lived on much more modest incomes. When the Russian government began assessing the damage inflicted by the great fire of 1812, some 281 noble families, who had lost their entire households, submitted their reports, which reveal that the median value of their losses was 2,500 rubles. Nobles usually spent their summers at their country estates and flocked to Moscow for the winter season, when families visited each other and attended various festivities.

Moscow held a unique status in Russian society. The city's rise to pre-eminence initially involved cultivating favour with the Mongols, who had devastated the Russian principalities in the late thirteenth century. Moscow's power was greatly enhanced when the city assumed the role of the centre of Russian Orthodoxy, and it was the Muscovite ruler who led the Russian struggle against the Mongols. In 1380, at the battle of Kulikovo Field, Moscow's Prince Dmitrii Donskoii shattered the myth of Mongol invincibility and strengthened Russia's national awakening. A century later Ivan III the Great freed Russia from the Mongol yoke and laid the foundation for the emergence of the new powerful state. Moscow thus became the centre of the grand principality of Moscow (or Muscovy), which eventually reached the shores of the Pacific Ocean. Moscow helped to develop Russian imperial and national ideology, bolstered by Russian Orthodoxy. With the fall of Constantinople, the Byzantine capital and the seat of Greek Orthodox Christianity, to the Muslim Turks in 1453, Russians increasingly perceived Moscow as the last bastion of 'genuine' Christianity. Drawing on biblical references, the Russian church embraced the doctrine of Moscow as the Third Rome and the true champion of Christianity: 'Two Romes have fallen,' Abbot Filofei wrote to Grand Duke Vasilii III in 1510. 'The Third [Moscow] stands, and there shall be no fourth.' This doctrine legitimized Russia's imperial expansion and the divine right of Russian autocracy. A visitor standing on the Vorobyevo Hills could observe the magnificent panoramic sight of Moscow with its 329 cathedrals and churches, 24 monasteries and 33 bell towers.[32]

Moscow's importance, however, diminished in the eighteenth century. Once the very incarnation of 'Holy Russia', the city was relegated to secondary status when Tsar Peter the Great, who famously disliked Moscow and what he perceived as its backwardness and obscurantism, transferred the Russian capital to St Petersburg in 1712; Catherine the Great shared Peter's aversion for Moscow, especially its unplanned and disorderly layout, which the Empress regarded as symptomatic of the city's general backwardness. Such attitudes from such august rulers naturally had a profound impact on Moscow: its population dropped considerably and it lost its dominant position in Russian political life. But while St Petersburg acquired the imperial trappings of a capital city, Moscow still retained its historic and pre-eminent role as an ecclesiastical and administrative centre. The Russian sovereigns, after all, continued to travel to Moscow for the ancient coronation rites. In addition, many governmental agencies remained in Moscow, which continued to serve as the centre for a major province. Nevertheless, there was also a sense of embitterment among the Muscovites about the decline in their city's stature, and comparisons soon began to be drawn between the old and new capitals. A certain rivalry even developed between the two cities (it continues in one form or another to this day) and Muscovites always sought to depict their hometown as the more truly Russian city, with its ancient past, onion-domed churches and narrow, winding streets, as opposed to St Petersburg with its foreign-designed architecture and European-style grid of streets and avenues. In 1834 Pushkin, remembering the Moscow of his childhood, wrote:

> At one time there really was a rivalry between Moscow and Petersburg. Then in Moscow there were rich nobles who did not work, grandees who had given up the court, and independent, carefree individuals, passionately devoted to harmless slander and inexpensive hospitality; then Moscow was the gathering place for all Russia's aristocracy, which streamed to it in winter from every province. Brilliant young guardsmen flew thither from Petersburg. Every corner of the ancient capital was loud with music, there were crowds everywhere. Five thousand people filled the hall of the Noble Assembly twice a week. There the young met; marriages were made. Moscow was as famous for its brides as Vyazma for its gingerbread; Moscow dinners became a proverb. The innocent eccentricities of the Muscovites were a sign of their independence. They lived their own lives, amusing themselves as they liked, caring little for the opinion of others ... From afar haughty Petersburg mocked, but did not interfere with old mother Moscow's escapades.[33]

Before 1812 Moscow had turned into a hotbed of political opposition that came primarily from conservative aristocratic nobles who remained resentful of the liberal reforms earlier in Alexander's reign, of the influence that the great Russian reformer Mikhail Speransky wielded before his abrupt dismissal in March 1812, and of their own failure to play a more important governmental role. This tendency persisted even two decades after Napoleon's invasion, when the English captain Charles Colville Frankland noted that 'There is a liberty of speech, and thought, and action, in Moscow, which does not exist in Petersburgh ... The fact is, Moscow is a sort of rendezvous for all the retired, discontented, and renvoye'd officers, civil and military, of the empire. It is the nucleus of the Russian opposition. Hence almost all the men whose politics do not suit those of the day, retire hither, where they may find fault with the Court, the Government, &c. as much as they please, without much fear of interruption.'[34] For many Russians the city indeed remained the heart of the empire. 'If Moscow is lost, everything will be lost,' a contemporary opined in 1812, reflecting a general belief in the city's importance for Russia. 'Bonaparte knows well of this: he never considered our capitals as equals. He knows that for Russia, only the ancient city of Moscow is genuinely important while the glittering and elegant St Petersburg is just another city in the realm. This is simply an undeniable truth.'[35] The usually sarcastic Philipp Vigel refrained from any derision when he spoke of the former capital, eulogizing it as a 'majestic and beautiful' city, 'our history, our sacred relic, the cradle of our might!' After the Russian capital was transferred to St Petersburg, Moscow became a place where aristocrats who preferred to avoid the court would spend the long winter months, entertaining with generous dinners, parties and balls. In *War and Peace*, Leo Tolstoy expressed the sentiment of many early nineteenth-century Russian noblemen when he portrayed Pierre Bezukhov viewing Moscow as a cosy and comforting place, where he could escape from the bustle and hurry of life in the capital (St Petersburg): 'he saw ... those old Moscovites who desired nothing, hurried nowhere, and were ending their days leisurely; and when he saw those old Moscow ladies, the Moscow balls, and the English Club, he felt himself at home in a quiet haven. In Moscow, he felt at peace, at home, warm and dirty as in an old dressing-gown.'[36]

Moscow was the economic and cultural centre of Russia. The last decades of the eighteenth century saw an increase in the number of manufacturers established in the city, and by January 1812 there were over 460 factories located mainly along the Yauza and Moscow rivers in the Lefortovo, Taganskii, Serpukhovo and Presnenskii suburbs.[37] The city also housed some of the earliest Russian industries, mainly textile and paper factories; according to Peter Vyazemskii, the majority of Russian books and periodicals were published in Moscow. As the commercial centre of the country, Moscow also accommodated some of the largest markets in the empire. The Merchant Court (*Gostinnyi dvor*), often referred to as the Bourse by the Allied participants, was among the oldest trade centres in Moscow; Siegmund Freiherr von Herberstein, the sixteenth-century Austrian diplomat who wrote extensively on the history and geography of the Muscovite Rus, described 'a large house, surrounded by a wall, that is called the merchant's house, where merchants live and store their goods'.[38] The Merchant Court expanded throughout the seventeenth century, especially in the 1660s when reconstruction works were led by the wealthy merchant Averkii Kirillov, and it was considered among the most gorgeous buildings in the entire city; it even featured the first apothecary in Russia. In the late eighteenth century, with the tremendous expansion of the Russian state, the decaying Merchant Court could no longer accommodate the growth of trade and had to be rebuilt. The construction works began in the late 1780s but the new building, located on the Ilyinka and Varvarka streets, was completed only in 1805. It featured over 190 trade rows with hundreds of shops.

The Merchant Court, however, was not the sole trade emporium and the city's other sixteen markets delivered every kind of provisions and supplies. Furthermore, the city featured 568 hostels, more than 40 restaurants, 166 taverns, 11 coffee houses, some 200 wine cellars, 200 pubs, 162 bread bakeries and 163 bakeries. As the leading centre of education in Russia, Moscow had a university, 3 academies, a gymnasium, 22 schools, 24 boarding schools, and 5 state and 9 private printing houses.[39] Theatre held a special place in the Muscovites' hearts and more than two dozen private and public theatres staged plays on a daily basis. Among the former were the theatres of N.P. Sheremetyev and S.S. Apraksin, famous for their lavish stage productions that occasionally even featured live animals, while at the house of P.A. Poznyakov, guests frequently attended plays performed by serfs. Among the public institutions the most famous was the Petrovskii Theatre, a large wooden building that staged both opera and ballet productions but burned down in 1805. It was replaced by a newly constructed theatre on Arbat Square, which surprised contemporaries with its opulent decorations; here people of various social backgrounds mixed together.[40] Theatre was extremely popular in Moscow and it was said that 'even lackeys often recited verses from the *Rusalka* [one of the most popular contemporary plays], while servants occasionally sang entire arias from the same play'.[41] In addition to Russian theatres, there was a French theatre that, in the years leading up to the Napoleonic invasion, was involved in a bitter rivalry with its Russian counterparts. The theatrical tastes and aesthetic standards of the Russian nobility were based on (and shaped by) French theatre, and most preferred attending the French company's productions. In 1808 the main event of the theatrical season in Russia was the debut of the famed French actress Mademoiselle Marguerite Georges in Racine's *Phaedra*, and memoirs of many contemporaries expound on her stage presence, technique and extraordinary beauty. On the eve of the war with France, and amidst a politically charged atmosphere, Russian theatres could not but become battlegrounds of ideology and aesthetics. If Russian 'gallomanes' (or Zhorzhisty) flocked to see Georges, Russian 'patriots' fervently applauded the performances of Ekaterine Semenova, a promising young actress who was praised for her ability to convey the emotional qualities of a 'Russian soul'. Passions raged violently and two factions – Zhorzhisty and Semenovisty – quickly formed around the actresses. In a stroke of marketing genius, the Directorate of the imperial theatres chose to pit the two actresses against in each other by inviting them to perform the same play on alternate days at the Arbat Theatre in Moscow. People stood in long lines to catch a glimpse of these great actresses and box office receipts exceeded expectations. The symbolism of this contest between Russian and French actresses, taking place on the eve of war between their respective countries, was, naturally, not lost on the public, which, despite earlier admiring Georges's talent, now wholeheartedly embraced Semenova's authentic Russianness.[42]

The greatest threat to Moscow's urban life came from fires – a frequent hazard since early times. In the mid-seventeenth century the German diplomat Adam Olearius observed that in this city of wooden houses 'not a month, or even a week, goes by without some homes – or if the wind is strong, whole streets – going up in smoke. Several nights while we were there we saw flames rising in three or four places at once. Shortly before our arrival, a third of the city burned down and we were told that the same thing happened four years earlier.'[43] As in many other cities of Europe, Moscow's houses were built too closely together. There was no regular street pattern and in many places houses and outbuildings were thrown together without plan. As a result, careless handling of fire could easily lead to conflagrations that, for example, destroyed much of the Kitai-gorod and Belyi Gorod in 1699. Just two years later the Kremlin and its vicinity were devastated as well. These fires were eclipsed by the conflagrations of 1712, 1730, 1736 and 1737, which all claimed the greater part of the city. Hardly had the Muscovites recovered from the last conflagration when another, in 1748, devastated a considerable part of the city. Following the plague infestation of 1771, the city suffered one more calamity in 1773.[44] These fiery incidents were naturally very difficult to contain due to the wooden construction of the city. In the first half of the eighteenth century the Muscovites often prevented the spread of fire both by using water and by pulling down houses in the fire's path and carting off the wood before it could ignite.[45] The fire of 1773, however, did compel the government to address the underlying problems that caused so much suffering among the Muscovites. The result was the general plan of 1775, one of the most important pieces of Russian urban planning of the eighteenth century, which, with modifications, influenced the subsequent growth of the city. But the plan was not carried out and the threat of fires endured; in January 1812 the Russian police reported the outbreak of sixty-eight fires in the city the year before. These fires were quickly extinguished by Moscow's firefighting brigade, consisting of about 2,100 men with some hundred fire engines. But at least one contemporary complained about the poor quality of this force:

> The firefighting brigade had poor horses, engines and other tools. There was no signal system that could have informed [firefighters] in which districts fires had broken out. As a result, fires were accompanied by great confusion, [firefighters] dragged their feet, unaware where they should go, and half of the homes had usually burned down by the time they showed up. By then, people from neighbouring houses had usually rushed to put out fires with hooks, axes and buckets of water. Water, however, had to be drawn from wells which further constrained firefighters' actions. Everywhere one could hear wailing, crying and praying for the Lord's succour. The fire, meanwhile, consumed everything... .[46]

Chapter 3

The Governor

In the spring of 1812 Ivan Gudovich, the 71-year-old governor of Moscow, who had been popular with the Muscovites because of his eccentric behaviour and limited interference in their affairs, retired from his position owing to deteriorating health.[1] The new governor of Moscow was Count Fedor Vasilievich Rostopchin, who turned 49 years old that fateful year.[2] He had been in favour under Empress Catherine the Great and enjoyed a brilliant but short career under Emperor Paul; he languished in disgrace for over a decade before making a stunning comeback as the governor of Moscow in the spring of 1812. By the end of that year his decisions concerning the defence of Moscow would earn him an everlasting notoriety. 'This Rostopchin will be looked upon as a villain or a Roman,' the famed French writer Stendhal (Marie-Henri Beyle) observed in a letter. 'We must see how he will be judged.'[3] Unfortunately for Rostopchin, history largely remembered him as a villain and 'modern-day Herostratus' who was single-handedly responsible for the burning of Moscow.

Fedor Rostopchin came from an ancient but not particularly prominent or wealthy noble family, which proudly preserved a tradition that it descended from the Crimean Tatar Prince David Rabchaka, a distant descendant of the notorious Mongol leader Chinggis Khan. As was customary at that time, the young Rostopchin was enlisted in the elite Life Guard Preobrazhenskii Regiment at a young age but did not actually serve in the regiment at that time since he was preoccupied with studies at the famous Page Corps. After graduating at the age of 19 in 1782, he began service with the LG Preobrazhenskii Regiment and it quickly became apparent that he was an intelligent and capable officer who thirsted for distinction. But his lack of patronage, so crucial in career advancement, meant that Rostopchin initially languished in the junior officer ranks, despite participating in the Russo-Swedish and Russo-Turkish Wars. In 1792, however, his chance came when he was tasked with delivering the news of the Peace of Jassy (which ended the Russo-Turkish War) to St Petersburg, for which he received the rank of *kamer-junker* (valet of the chamber). He did his best to advance at the imperial court, earning a name for his witty repartee and marrying the niece of Empress Catherine's favourite, a move which he hoped would open more doors for him at court. But his quirky and eccentric character turned many people away from him and the Empress herself teasingly called him 'Fedor the mad'. Thus, despite earnest efforts, his career had stalled, leaving the young but desperate Rostopchin pondering retirement. It was then that an auspicious incident introduced him to Grand Duke Pavel Petrovich, the son of Empress Catherine II. Mother and son were estranged, and the court largely followed the Empress's example in ignoring her son. Assigned to the Grand Duke's palace at Gatchina, Rostopchin proved to be the exception, approaching his duties in a conscientious manner while many others shirked on their responsibilities. Upset at seeing his colleagues not serving the Grand Duke in good faith, he wrote a complaint denouncing them. The letter became public and caused a scandal, effectively destroying Rostopchin's hopes for a successful career at the court of Catherine II – but it did draw the attention of Grand Duke Paul, who appreciated the young man's devotion at a time when most people stayed away from him. Thus, as Catherine II lay on her deathbed in November 1796, Rostopchin was among those few who could be confident about the future. Indeed, his career took off under Emperor Paul, who appreciated the young man's commitment and keen wit. One day Paul teasingly asked Rostopchin, in the presence of the court, why his family was not of princely rank. 'Sire, that is because my [Tatar] ancestors came to Russia in winter,' Rostopchin quickly replied. 'What does this have to do with the title?' inquired the befuddled emperor. 'When my Tatar ancestor appeared for the first time at the Russian court, the Sovereign offered him the choice between a fur coat and the title of prince. My ancestor chose the former without hesitation.'[4] Paul laughed heartily at this explanation, which further endeared the young man to him. Within three years Rostopchin was already a lieutenant general and chevalier of some of the highest imperial orders. In 1799 Paul rewarded Rostopchin's loyalty with the title of count of the Russian Empire (Rostopchin refused the princely title!), appointed him Grand Chancellor of the Order of the Maltese Knights and granted him vast estates that turned him into one of the wealthiest men in the empire. It was indeed a glorious time for Rostopchin – but all good things come to an end.[5]

In late March 1801 Rostopchin was stunned by the assassination of his benefactor. The new sovereign, Emperor Alexander I, disliked Rostopchin and many others who had been devoted to his father and who suspected him of having approved Paul's assassination. So Rostopchin was given no employment and had to settle at his estate at Voronovo near Moscow. But his inquisitive mind could not stay out of public affairs for long and over the next few years he voiced increasing criticism of the policies of the Russian government, especially in the wake of the Russian defeats at Austerlitz and Friedland – 'how can the Lord bless the armies of the wicked son?' he wrote bluntly after Austerlitz, hinting at his suspicion of Alexander's involvement in Paul's assassination.[6] He opposed the Franco-Russian rapprochement at Tilsit and openly accused some of Alexander's advisers of being stooges of France. In 1807 he published a small pamphlet denouncing the prevalence of French culture among the Russian elite, and speaking of the need to revive and maintain Russian traditions. The booklet proved to be a runaway success, selling over 7,000 copies and raising its author's public profile. Rostopchin followed up this success with a series of similar publications, effectively turning himself into an unofficial mouthpiece of the anti-French traditionalist party that gradually gained prominence in the upper circles of Russian society.[7] Among its more vocal members was Grand Duchess Catherine Pavlovna, Emperor Alexander's beloved sister, who had declined a marriage proposal from Napoleon and instead married a German princeling, George of Oldenburg. After her husband was appointed governor of Tver, Novgorod and Yaroslav, Catherine had settled in a provincial town, where she routinely invited leading personalities of Moscow society to dispel the boredom of provincial life. Rostopchin was a frequent visitor and the two quickly became friends. This rapport with the Grand Duchess, whom Alexander adored and trusted, proved to be of momentous significance for Rostopchin, for Catherine beseeched her brother to appoint her friend as the governor-general of Moscow. According to the well-informed Alexander Bulgakov, this appointment was 'almost forced out of the emperor' by Catherine, who 'admired Rostopchin's sharp wit and pleasant conversation'.[8] The Emperor, who distrusted the Russian nationalists and personally loathed Rostopchin, excused his initial evasiveness by noting that Rostopchin held the civilian position of chief chamberlain and thus could not be appointed to the position of governor of Moscow, which required its holder to wear a military uniform. 'And this is the only insurmountable obstacle?' the Grand Duchess observed cannily. 'This seems to be a simple task for a tailor.'[9] In the spring of 1812 Emperor Alexander granted his sister's wish and appointed Rostopchin military governor of Moscow, with the Senate issuing the official decree on 6 June.[10] In late July Rostopchin received even greater authority when Alexander appointed him commander-in-chief of Moscow.[11]

Governor Rostopchin took control of the city in the first days of June and threw himself wholeheartedly into his new occupation. A clever man, skilful courtier, wit and cynic, he proved an able administrator and sought to restore the order that had waned under his predecessor's lax governing. Some of his initial decisions dealt with seemingly mundane issues, such as prohibiting coffin makers from displaying coffins on their shop signs,[12] removing packs of stray dogs from the streets, forbidding the smoking of tobacco in public (ostensibly to prevent fires caused by discarded embers), introducing stricter restriction on butchers, and banning children from flying paper kites that 'frighten horses and might cause unfortunate incidents'.[13] He demanded tighter supervision of the city to put an end to 'debauchery, drunkenness, [and] outrages of various kinds', and instructed police to raid more than 390 houses that 'operate as *herbergen* [hostels], restaurants, taverns and cook shops' and get rid of 'dissolute' women who corrupted young men; all these institutions were subsequently required to close at ten o'clock in the evening.[14]

At the same time, eager to ingratiate himself with influential Muscovites, Rostopchin presided over a seemingly unending series of balls, banquets, dinners and other parties, causing some to remark that the 1812 season was the most brilliant people had known in a long time.[15] With rumours of war whirling around, Rostopchin also sought to shape and direct public opinion. At the start of the summer he assured everyone that the war would be quick and decisive in Russia's favour. 'Napoleon? We would not even let him cross the frontier,' he boasted. The news of the Grande Armée's invasion of Russia surprised him but he remained unabashed. 'War? Yes, it's war all right,' he proclaimed. 'But that does not mean that Napoleon will reach Moscow.' His benefactor Grand Duchess Catherine, who detested Napoleon and was among the first to have foreseen the impending war against France, urged the new governor of Moscow to act. 'Tell Rostopchin', Catherine wrote to her confidant Prince Obolenskii, 'that he must inflame the nobility of Moscow. All he needs to do is to show the danger the Fatherland is in and the national significance of this war.'[16] Rostopchin agreed with her, perceiving his prime duty as eradicating any signs of subversion from within and keeping up the people's morale. Therefore, he decided to 'work on the minds of the people, to arouse them and prepare them for any sacrifice for the salvation of the Fatherland'. Yet Rostopchin's form of 'patriotism' promoted a deep hatred of foreigners and incited the populace to rise up against them.

The official news from the army, published daily in the newspapers, seemed to present a depressing picture of the continually retreating Russian forces and the unremitting roll of enemy successes. Despite official propaganda, some Russians found it 'hard to believe' that Russian victories at Mir, Ostrovno and Dashkovo were of any significance.[17] So Rostopchin launched his own media blitz – his famous broadsheets (*afishy*) – that mixed nationalism and populism to inspire the people of Moscow and disparage the enemy.[18] Their content was deliberately trivial and written in what he believed to be racy but popular Russian language to allow for quick comprehension by the masses of Moscow: 'some of us found the language used in these broadsheets appropriate to our time and circumstances,' commented one resident of Moscow. 'But the majority found it vulgar and crude.'[19] Yet at least one contemporary felt that 'the broadsheets were unique – never before has a government addressed its people in such a language! The broadsheets were timely and made a forceful and indelible impact on the populace of Moscow.'[20] Another perceptive contemporary noted that the governor-general

did his best to incite the noble flames [of patriotism] among the residents of the city entrusted to him. And he succeeded in awakening the gallant spirit of our ancestors that had become dormant due to our indolence and lassitude. Like other noblemen, Rostopchin was educated abroad and was fluent in foreign languages, but he differed from other nobles in that he had also learned [the Russian] tongue and did not even disdain to speak the commoners' language. He used his knowledge of this language when, amidst the turmoil caused by the momentous events [of the summer of 1812], he addressed the people through his daily broadsheets that featured various tales designed to entertain, encourage and incite people for the greater cause.[21]

Rostopchin's broadsheets were headed by woodcuts of a drink shop and a Muscovite called Karnyushka Chigirin, 'who, having been a militiaman, and having had rather too much at the pub, heard that Napoleon wished to come to Moscow, grew angry, [and] abused the French in very bad language';[22] they were widely read and discussed among the inhabitants of Moscow. To ensure the effectiveness of his propaganda, Rostopchin recruited agents whose task was to mix with the crowds in public places and 'to spread certain rumours, maintain patriotic enthusiasm and diminish the disagreeable impression made by bad news'.

In late July throngs of Muscovites came out to greet Emperor Alexander, who had left the army after he was told, with infinite tact, that his presence in the army was onerous and it would be better if he went to Moscow and St Petersburg to cheer up people's spirits. It was already late at night when Alexander approached the former capital of his vast realm, but so many Muscovites had gone to meet him on the road that 'from their lanterns it was almost as light as in daytime'[23] and the crowds 'greeted him rapturously'.[24] Alexander, however, was uneasy, well aware of the resentment felt by many of the city's grandees towards the liberal tendencies and reforms he had championed earlier in his reign. Rostopchin assured the sovereign that he need have no fears: with a country at war, the nobility was far from being in a rebellious mood and could be counted upon, while the merchants, delighted by Russia's withdrawal from the Continental Blockade, were ready to make sizeable donations towards the national cause. But to guard against disobedience or free thinking, the governor had a couple of police carriages drawn up in front of the Sloboda Palace to prevent intemperate 'hotheads' or 'wild tongues' from attempting any excesses of speech or behaviour.[25]

On 24 July thousands of Muscovites massed in and around the Kremlin, hoping for a glimpse of their sovereign. A solemn service at the Cathedral of the Assumption, where the Russian rulers were traditionally crowned, was interrupted on a few occasions by 'thunderous shouts of "hurrah"'[26] by the vast multitudes of reverent subjects. As he was coming out of the cathedral, hundreds of hands grabbed at his uniform, hands and feet, making his entourage uneasy at the crush. 'We were like a ship without masts and rudder amidst the stormy sea,' recalled one of Alexander's adjutants.[27] The Emperor then addressed the Assembly of the Nobility and the Guild of Merchants at the Imperial Palace, where he made his plea for donations of money and recruits.[28] His speech certainly had an effect and inspired everyone to sacrifice a part of his wealth for the salvation of the Fatherland. The people thronged the emperor, crying 'We prefer to die than to surrender to the enemy!'[29] In a marvellous display of patriotism and devotion, both the nobility and merchants offered their money without stinting, while Rostopchin reassured the emperor that even though the Russian armies were currently withdrawing before the enemy, 'the Russian Empire will always remain formidable at Moscow, terrifying at Kazan and invincible at Tobolsk!' Emperor Alexander was clearly pleased with his visit to Moscow and was in brighter spirits when the time came to leave. As he bade farewell to Rostopchin during the night of 28/29 July, Alexander conferred on him full authority to act as he saw fit whatever might occur. 'Who can predict events? But I rely on you entirely,' Alexander remarked enigmatically, without specifying what those events might be.[30]

Yet not all of Moscow displayed the 'patriotic' fervour that Rostopchin wanted to see. Just as Emperor Alexander departed, 'former student Urusuv, not even drunk, publicly stated in a tavern that Napoleon's arrival in Moscow is not only possible but would be beneficial for everyone'.[31] Even more 'toxic' was the rumour that 'Napoleon was the son of the Empress Catherine, whom she ordered to be raised in foreign lands. On her death-bed she made Emperor Paul swear that he will give half of the Russian Empire to his brother Napoleon if he ever comes back'.[32] The patriotic gestures of the nobility and merchants had been largely organized in advance by Count Rostopchin, whose trusted agent 'sat next to each merchant's ear and whispered those hundreds and thousands of rubles of donations that, in his opinion, the merchant should make to the [national] altar'.[33] In addition, many merchants saw the emperor's appeal for troops as a way to turn a quick profit: realizing that 'the enemy could not be defeated with bare hands', they quickly increased the prices on weapons. Before the emperor's speech a sword and sabre cost less than 6 rubles, a pair of pistols 7–8 rubles and a musket or carbine 11–15 rubles; after the speech a sabre went for 30–40 rubles, pistols cost up to 50 rubles and muskets and carbines could not be found for less than 80 rubles. Such exploitation was not limited to arms traders: tailors, shoemakers and other craftsmen also doubled or tripled prices for their goods. 'I was greatly saddened to observe their practices,' observed one Muscovite.[34] Meanwhile, large segments of the city population remained quite indifferent to the emperor's appeal. The governor was astonished to hear that some Muscovites – 'the cowards and the malcontents', as he calls them – were, in fact, critical of the government's failure 'to avoid a third war with the enemy who has already twice defeated Russian armies'.[35] The governor was probably also aware of indifference among the lower classes. On the eve of the imperial visit to Moscow, one Russian landowner, inspired by patriotic zeal, gathered more than 200 of his serfs and gave 'a rather moving speech, appealing to each peasant to support our Orthodox Sovereign at this difficult time by contributing money or volunteering for military service against the enemy'. Despite the appeal, only one man volunteered for service, leaving the landowner 'deeply shocked by the indifference shown by [his] subjects'.[36] And the governor could hardly forget a rather embarrassing incident on the eve of the imperial visit – just as throngs of Muscovites filled all the quarters of the Kremlin for the solemn service, a rumour spread that the gates would soon be closed and all commoners found inside the complex would be forcibly enlisted into the army. 'As soon as this rumour spread,' says eyewitness Mikhail Marakuev, 'the rabble rushed to escape and the Kremlin was emptied of people in just a few moments.'[37]

Such incidents naturally caused many contemporaries to wonder if there was something or someone behind them. For Rostopchin, the answer was clear: he had long been suspicious of foreign influences in Russia and often spoke out against various secret societies and free-thinkers, be they Illuminati, Freemasons, Martinists or Jacobins. He alleged the existence of a liberal conspiracy that aimed at the destruction of traditional order in Russia, and exploited this claim to position himself as an indispensable champion of the conservative ideology, whom Emperor Alexander could trust with such an important office as the governorship of Moscow. But his struggle against freemasonry, Martinism and other radical ideologies often served as a backdrop for his settling of scores with opponents or people he disliked.[38] 'His heart is open to easy suspicions and he struggles to believe in [a person's] decency but eagerly seizes upon even the suggestion of a misdeed [the person might have committed],' one of Rostopchin's victims later bemoaned.[39] The governor was indeed keen to believe in denunciations and rumours against his perceived enemies. His hatred for anything or anyone associated with Revolutionary France was quite notorious. 'A firm supporter of serfdom and a reactionary by conviction,' one Russian historian observed, 'Rostopchin was fanatically hostile to France as the source of the revolutionary ideals and to Napoleon as the product of that same revolution.'[40] Rostopchin's acquaintances knew, for example, that 'next to his cabinet there was a small dark room, where, as the French saying goes, even the king has to go unattended. Inside this privy room there was a beautiful bronze bust of Napoleon. A slim plank nailed to the imperial head held a porcelain vessel that was so necessary for visitors seeking to relieve their natural needs.'[41] Many also amused themselves by exploiting the governor's deep antipathy for the French emperor. Just one month into the war Moscow was flooded with thousands of portraits of Napoleon, which proved to be a best-selling commodity due to their very low price of just one copper *kopeck*; rumours claimed that the governor himself had these prints made so as to make Napoleon's appearance better known to the populace and promising a handsome reward to anyone who killed him. One of Rostopchin's acquaintances thought it amusing to buy one of these prints as a gift for the governor, who was dismayed and could not stop himself defacing it (he drew a bushy moustache on Napoleon's face) and scribbled a brief but vulgar inscription:

> Indeed, it's cheap and pretty, so buy *en masse*,
> And use this mug to wipe your arse.[42]

Equally revealing was an incident that took place on the eve of the nobility's meeting with the emperor. Rostopchin's claims of Jacobin, Martinist and other conspiracies fell on fertile ground as the Russian nobles were increasingly concerned by the effect the war might have on their serfs. To them, Napoleon's name was associated with revolutionary ideals of freedom and equality, and his very presence inside Russia seemed to make the emancipation of the serfs inevitable. Such fears were certainly present among many nobles as they gathered, on 23 July, to welcome the emperor into the city. 'Common people packed the square [inside the Kremlin] and suffocated each other on staircases,' recalled one of the participants. The nobles, meanwhile, congregated inside one of the palaces, anxious to meet the emperor but also apprehensive over their own fate. One of the noblemen recalled:

> Yet the emperor had not arrived. We began to worry and loud conversations soon turned into whispers, which, in turn, soon turned into silence. Suddenly barely audible voices pronounced that 'the emperor has died'. We were all thunderstruck – everyone was ready to believe it and was afraid of everything. In the Spasskaya Tower the bells struck ten o'clock; the crowd on the square [outside the palace] began to wobble. [Upon seeing it, one of the noblemen] touched my elbow with his ice-cold hand and muttered, 'That's it, it is a revolt!' This word passed from mouth to mouth and soon turned into a dull rumble ...[43]

Yet such fears of a popular revolt and a massacre of the nobility were quickly dispelled when it became clear that the mob had quivered because of the arrival of an imperial messenger, who delivered the news that the emperor would arrive the following day. This incident is quite revealing for it shows the instinctive reaction of the Russian nobles at that tense moment: of all the possibilities, they envisioned a popular uprising.

Playing on these fears, Rostopchin was able to assert an almost autocratic authority to accomplish what he believed to be his most important mission: to rid his city of potential 'troublemakers' and to reinforce traditional order. Moscow had a sizeable enclave of French speakers,[44] consisting of émigrés, merchants, governesses, actresses and tutors. Many of them had spent most of their lives in the city and considered Russia their second homeland. The Russian elites were thoroughly immersed in French language and culture at the expense of their Russian literacy. Russian officer (and future governor of Tobolsk) Alexander Turgenev recalled that he 'knew numerous princes Troubetskoy, Dolgorukiis, Golitsyns, Obolenskis, Nesvitskis, Sherbatovs, Khovanskis, Volkonskis, Mescherskii – I cannot even name all of them now – who could not write two sentences in Russian but they all could eloquently utter improper words in Russian'. Batyushkov was startled to see this widespread emulation of foreign manners in Moscow:

> Here everyone is lisping and grimacing in a foreign manner. Upon entering a candy shop at the Kuznetskii bridge ... I encountered a great concourse of the Moscow dandies in polished leather boots and broad English frock-coats, some with glasses or without them, and all wearing a dishevelled hairstyle. These must be, of course, Englishmen ... But no, he is Russian, born and raised in Suzdal. And that one must be a Frenchman, judging how he is lisping, and trying to charm the mistress with his story of a ventriloquist acquaintance, who had entertained the Parisians last year. And yet this old beau is also a Russian, who has not travelled far and, having squandered the family estate, is now living off card games ...[45]

Similar sentiments were echoed by a British visitor, who commented:

> Russia has many other Nationalities no doubt, but my experience has not been able to distinguish any excepting amongst the lower orders of People, for with respect to the higher I am sorry to say they imitate the French in everything! ... They dress too in a bad imitation of the French & they have universally adopted their Language! ... In the midst of this adoption of manners, customs & language there is something childishly Silly in their reprobating Buonaparte when they can't eat their dinners

without a French cook to dress it, when they can't educate their Children without unprincipled adventurers from Paris to act as Tutors and Governesses, when every House of consequence (that I have seen at least) has an outcast Frenchman to instruct the Heir apparent – in a word, when every association of fashion, luxury, elegance, & fascination is drawn from France.[46]

Indeed, as one contemporary justly noted, 'Seeing our aristocracy, with its French education and French manners, berating the French in the French language, must have created a rather strange impression.'[47]

As the French emperor headed the invasion, Rostopchin – whose spoken French remained superior to his Russian – questioned the allegiance of the French residing in Moscow, seeing them as preachers of free thinking. He had long claimed that the foreigners brought nothing but harm to Russia: 'they are harmful to Russia ... and are only waiting for the arrival of Bonaparte to proclaim freedom,' Rostopchin had earlier told the emperor, beseeching him to 'Rid Russia of this disease, Sire. Order sent back beyond the frontiers these conniving wretches whose sad influence corrupts the souls and minds of your virtuous subjects.'[48] In the summer of 1812 Rostopchin still felt that his 'main concern is the foreigners who are despised by our people',[49] and were potential spies in disguise. Rostopchin's concerns were not entirely unjustified, since on the eve of the war Russian counter-intelligence had uncovered numerous French agents who, posing as merchants or travellers, had entered Russia and sought to gather intelligence on Russian preparations for war. During the war French agents were uncovered in St Petersburg and Smolensk, and even inside the headquarters of the Russian army.[50]

As far as the governor was concerned, spies could well be present in Moscow and extra diligence was required towards any foreigner. Thus, on his orders many suspected Frenchmen were arrested and some had to endure physical abuse: in late July two foreigners were exiled for 'audacious speeches'.[51] In August two more foreigners were whipped in public for their 'false prophesying that, by the 15th of this month, Napoleon would be enjoying his lunch in Moscow'.[52] The governor's own French chef, Theodore Tournay, was whipped in the public square for 'insinuations of various kinds that result in subversion of minds to the French cause'.[53] Furthermore, Rostopchin deported dozens of foreigners – mostly French, but also Germans, Italians and others – in rather deplorable conditions from Moscow to provincial towns, accusing them of spying for Napoleon[54] and warning that 'the Russian people, so great and generous, is nevertheless ready to go to extremes. Therefore I am removing you [from Moscow] to spare the people a task and to avoid soiling history with the story of a massacre ... Cease to be bad subjects and become good ones ... Remain calm and submissive or fear severe punishment.' By late August, to be taken for a free-thinking foreigner in Moscow was to risk abuse and detention. At the theatre plays were put on commemorating former Russian victories and the governor looked approvingly at the outcry against French as an aristocratic language and denounced the Russian gentry for employing French tutors.

Despite the many pressing issues he had to attend to, Rostopchin found time for a rather more absorbing task. Some months before the war David Alopeus, the Russian Minister to Stuttgart, met the young German inventor Franz Leppich, who had earlier approached King Frederick of Württemberg with the grand idea of constructing a new kind of flying machine. After Joseph and Étienne Montgolfier first flew them in 1783, hot air balloons had been used by the French military for reconnaissance. Leppich suggested improving their performance and turning them into fighting machines. The trouble with balloons, he explained, was their inability to fly against the wind, but by attaching wings they could be made to move in any direction. Although the idea seemed enticing, the King of Württemberg initially turned it down, especially after Napoleon had likewise rejected Leppich's suggestion. But King Frederick later changed his mind and provided modest funding for Leppich's experiments. The inventor was busy building his machine when, in early 1812, the Russian Minister approached him with a tempting offer to work in Russia. In his letter to Emperor Alexander, Alopeus described in detail a machine 'shaped somewhat like a whale,' capable of lifting '40 men with 12,000 pounds of explosives' to bombard enemy positions, and sailing from Stuttgart to London in an incredible thirteen hours.[55]

Leppich's project appealed to Alexander, especially as war with Napoleon was looming, and any ideas that might give Russia an edge sounded attractive.[56] On 26 April Alexander approved the project and Leppich's workshop was set up at a village near Moscow, where Rostopchin provided Leppich – now working under the alias 'Schmidt' and officially supervising the production of artillery ammunition – with all necessary resources. Maintaining secrecy around the project was of paramount importance, but difficult to maintain since suspicions were immediately aroused when guards were deployed around the estate. They were further heightened when Rostopchin placed large orders for fabric, sulphuric acid, file dust and other assets totalling a staggering 160,000 rubles.[57] By July around a hundred labourers were working 17-hour shifts at the workshop.[58] Leppich assured Rostopchin that the money was well spent and the flying machine would be completed by 15 August:[59] presumably entire squadrons would soar into the skies above Moscow by autumn!

Rostopchin believed that this invention 'could change the art of war' and in early August he made the first public acknowledgement of Russia's secret weapon, warning the residents of Moscow to expect 'a large spherical balloon' in the skies over the city. 'I am warning you about it so that when you see it you will not think it comes from the Villain [Napoleon]. On the contrary, it is devised for his misfortune and downfall.' Many Muscovites genuinely believed in the existence of this 'super-weapon' and one Senator even claimed to have seen it used in a test flight that targeted and destroyed a flock of sheep.[60] However, the deadline passed without any results. By now the invasion was under way and Napoleon was already at Smolensk. Rostopchin, beginning to doubt Leppich, demanded results. The scientist promised to deliver the machine by 27 August, but when nothing was forthcoming Rostopchin wrote a letter to Alexander denouncing Leppich as a 'charlatan and madman'. The machine was not completed by the time the battle of Borodino was fought, and the subsequent Allied advance threatened Leppich's secret workshop. So it was loaded onto 130 wagons and moved to Nizhni Novgorod, while Leppich himself was recalled to St Petersburg.[61]

Rostopchin, who had spent his life moving in the highest court and administrative circles and had no understanding of the common people he supposed himself to be guiding, genuinely believed that his was the role of director of the popular feeling of 'the heart of Russia'. Not only did it seem to him that he controlled the external actions of Moscow's inhabitants but he was convinced 'of the need to direct people's mental attitude, incite popular anger and to prepare people to any kind of sacrifices in order to save the Fatherland'.[62] He chose to accomplish this by means of newspapers and broadsheets. He closely followed the events on the front lines and corresponded with the army commanders, especially with Peter Bagration; he even dispatched a personal representative to the Russian army to receive first-hand information on the true state of affairs.[63] The official *Moskovskie vedomosti* newspaper published numerous announcements revealing a large-scale mobilization of resources and manpower in and around the city. Militiamen were called up, new regiments raised, necessary equipment solicited and monetary contributions gathered.[64] Throughout July and August Rostopchin remained convinced that the Russian armies would not allow Napoleon to approach the former capital of Russia, though his letters betray an increasing concern for such a possibility. A broadsheet on 26 August informed the Muscovites about the battle of Smolensk, though it did not convey the whole truth: the Russian retreat was described as a deliberate manoeuvre designed to weaken the enemy army. But convincing the increasingly sceptical inhabitants of the city's safety was becoming difficult. The arrival of the news of the fall of Smolensk 'astonished Moscow', recalled Sergei Glinka.[65] 'Prior to the news of the fall of Smolensk,' recalled prominent Muscovite merchant Mikhail Marakuev, 'the public still entertained some hope [that the enemy would not reach Moscow]. But once this news broke out, all our hopes expired …'[66]

As the Russian armies retreated beyond Smolensk and Vyazma and the refugees and the wounded 'arrived by the thousands each day in Moscow',[67] Rostopchin began considering evacuating key state institutions from the city. On 29 August he instructed Kriegs-Commissar A. Tatischev to 'take necessary preliminary precautions', while Major General Tolstoy, head of the military hospital, was told to make arrangements for the evacuation of the sick and wounded. The following day the Votchina Department, in charge of land management, was ordered to start removing its holdings.[68] Over the next few days Rostopchin supervised arrangements for the evacuation of the treasury and major state manufacturing, which he ordered to be carried out at night so as not to alarm the residents of Moscow. However, the movement of hundreds of transports could hardly escape the eyes of a nervous population and it served only to confirm their fears. On 30 August Rostopchin admitted that the evacuation of the state institutions had a major impact on the public so 'for the next three days I need to decide whether to evacuate the remaining items or not'.[69]

Meanwhile, to calm down the populace the governor continued publishing broadsheets and tried to contain any panic by laughing at those who fled the city and showed, in his opinion, such a premature cowardice. In a letter to Alexander Balashev, he admitted that 'women, merchants and academic swine [*tvar'*] are leaving Moscow' but also noted that 'this makes the city only more spacious'.[70] A new broadsheet declared that the report that the governor had forbidden people to leave Moscow was false; on the contrary he was glad that ladies and tradesmen's wives were leaving the city since 'there will be less panic and less gossip'. Yet he could 'not commend their husbands, brothers and other [male] relatives' who left the city together with their families. 'If there is a danger to the city, [their behaviour] is rather indecent; if there is no danger, then it is even shameful.' The governor then proudly declared that 'I will stake my life on it that the enemy will not enter Moscow.'[71] The following day Rostopchin's new broadsheet acknowledged the growing uneasiness among the city residents. As many of the inhabitants of Moscow wished to be armed, the governor declared that weapons would be available for them at the Arsenal: sabres, pistols and muskets, all could be had at a low price.[72] But the tone of the proclamation was no longer jovial and tongue-in-cheek, and its matter-of-fact delivery seemed to point to the terrible storm clouds gathering over the city. In fact, the governor's declaration that he was not forbidding anyone to leave was false. Just as he published the broadsheet, Rostopchin also issued instructions to the Moscow municipality 'not to issue passports to merchant men and urban commoners, except for their wives and little children'.[73]

By the first week of September many affluent residents, ignoring the governor's assurances about the safety of the city, had packed their belongings and left. 'There is utter confusion here,' wrote Alexander Bulgakov to his brother on 25 August. 'Hearing that the French captured Smolensk, everyone lost their heads and they are fleeing from the city.'[74] With each passing day, wrote Nikolai Karamzin, 'the city gets emptier and multitudes are fleeing'.[75] In an effort to escape from the city, employees of many state and private institutions demanded advances on their pay, while merchants refused to issue any credits or loans, which greatly affected those workers who relied on these short-term loans to procure basic essentials.[76] 'Many people began getting out of Moscow, travelling wherever and however far they could,' recalled one contemporary.[77] The French actress and singer Madam Louise Fusil, who had been living in Russia for the past six years, described 'a continuous procession of vehicles, carts, furniture, pictures, belongings of all sorts ...'.[78]

While mulling over the evacuation, Rostopchin still entertained the hope that the complete evacuation of the city would not be necessary in light of the appointment of Mikhail Kutuzov as the commander-in-chief of the Russian armies. Kutuzov made repeated requests for resources,[79] and assured Rostopchin that he would do his best to defend the former capital, noting that 'I believe that the loss of Moscow would mean the loss of Russia.' A few days later he reiterated that 'all of my movements have been hitherto directed to a single goal of saving the capital city of Moscow'.[80] In late August Rostopchin inquired about Kutuzov's intentions concerning the defence of Moscow,[81] and the Russian commander-in-chief reassured the governor that 'with our armies we are going no further than Mozhaisk and there, with the Lord's help and hope for Russian bravery, I shall give battle to the enemy'.[82] Now that 'the position near Mozhaisk has been chosen for a battle that would be crucial to saving Moscow', Kutuzov again asked Rostopchin to assist with supplies: 'Should the Almighty God bless our army, then we shall have to pursue the retreating enemy, in which case we must ensure, among other things, the procurement of victuals so that our pursuit is not stopped by supply shortages.'[83] Rostopchin was probably pleased to receive such assurances from the commander-in-chief, believing that the enemy would be soon defeated and expelled from Russia.

But as the Russian retreat continued, Rostopchin became annoyed by Kutuzov's evasive response to his questions on what would ultimately befall the city. In a letter on 31 August Rostopchin argued that there should be no discussion of whether it was better to save the army or the city: 'Our armies have been raised and deployed to defend our realm; they should have defended Smolensk and now must protect Moscow, Russia and our Sovereign.' He spoke of the political importance of Moscow to the Russian nation: 'Every Russian now assumes that our forces [are] concentrated at our [former] capital and justly considers Moscow as the nation's bastion. With its fall, the fetters that bind together popular opinion and strengthen the throne of our Sovereign would be broken ...'[84]

Rostopchin was probably surprised by the commander-in-chief's letter of 3 September suggesting the possibility that Moscow itself might be threatened: 'I shall fight a battle in the present position,' wrote Kutuzov from near Mozhaisk. 'If, however, the enemy begins flanking me, I shall have to retreat in order to block his approach to Moscow, and if I am defeated there too, I shall go close to Moscow and will defend the capital there.'[85] The governor was naturally alarmed by this prospect. 'Moscow is in a rather dangerous situation. Our army is thirteen verstas away from Mozhaisk while the French have already occupied Gzhatsk,' he wrote on 5 September, his letter revealing his misgivings about Kutuzov's claims 'that he intends to fight a battle and pursues no other goal but to defend Moscow'.[86]

Rostopchin eagerly awaited the news of the battle at Borodino. In the late afternoon of 7 September Kutuzov informed him that '[we are engaged] in the bloodiest of battles but so far all goes well. With the Lord's help the Russian army did not yield a single step, though the enemy had significant numeric superiority.' The letter made no mention of the Russian setbacks or of the commander-in-chief's intention to retreat back to Moscow, but instead requested 'as many reinforcements as possible' because 'tomorrow, I hope, placing my trust in God and in Moscow's hallowed saints, I shall fight the enemy with new forces'.[87] Rostopchin later recalled that the courier who delivered this letter also informed him of the capture of the King of Naples, Joachim Murat (in fact, it was the French General Bonnamy). The governor immediately prepared another bulletin to share these glad tidings with the Muscovites. '[Napoleon] will be defeated again, and the accursed one and his accomplices will perish through famine, fire, and sword,' he assured the 'greatly delighted residents of Moscow'.[88] A thanksgiving Te Deum service was held in the Uspenskii Cathedral inside the Kremlin, while wild pealing of church bells could be heard throughout the city.

The bells were probably still ringing when Rostopchin began receiving Kutuzov's new missives that gradually revealed the true situation at the front. Kutuzov once again spoke about the heavy fighting of the previous day[89] but he also mentioned the Russian retreat for the first time:

> Your Illustrious Excellency will agree that after the bloodiest battle that lasted 15 hours our army as well as the enemy's could not but be in disarray, and due to the losses suffered on this day the position occupied previously became larger than needed by the army. Therefore, when we do not speak of glorious victories, but the goal is the destruction of the French army, I decided, while spending the night on the battlefield, to retreat for about six verstas from Mozhaisk [towards Moscow]. Having regrouped the troops, having reinforced my artillery and become strengthened by the Moscow Militia, with my sincere hope for the Almighty Lord's help and the proven immense bravery of our troops, I shall see what I shall be able to undertake against the enemy.[90]

In another letter Kutuzov once more sought to allay Rostopchin's increasing suspicion by claiming an outright Russian victory at Borodino: 'After the bloodiest battle that took place yesterday, in which our troops naturally suffered heavy casualties commensurate to their courage. Although the battle was <u>completely won</u> [author's emphasis] by us, my intention is to hold out against the enemy in another possibly decisive battle near Moscow to inflict serious damage on the adversary who has already sustained great losses.'[91]

Four days after the battle, Kutuzov still swore that 'in spite of the bloody battle [at Borodino], my troops have retained such respectable numbers that we have enough forces not only to withstand the enemy assault, but even to get the upper hand'.[92] Throughout these days Kutuzov continually wrote to Rostopchin requesting transports, horses, ammunitions, alcohol, tools and other provisions necessary for the army,[93] without once discussing the future of Moscow.

Kutuzov's letters perplexed Rostopchin, who years later denounced them as an 'outright deception'.[94] He felt his hands were tied in the absence of clear instructions from Kutuzov, who had become his superior once the military operations entered the Moscow province. Even with the Russian army on the outskirts of the city, Rostopchin continued to assure Muscovites that the city would be defended and as late as 13 September his officials called upon local landowners 'to remain calm and not to take any precautions to protect their properties'.[95] Unsure of what Kutuzov intended to do – fight another battle or abandon the city – Rostopchin approved requests to remove the most precious state property, documents, etc., while writing once more to Kutuzov, asking him to give straightforward instructions on what to do next. 'Kindly inform me whether you have a firm intention to halt the enemy's advance on Moscow and to defend this city?' he inquired. 'I will take measures depending on your response: either by arming everyone and fighting to the last man, or by evacuating all civilians and joining you with all military resources that I possess. Your answer will prompt me to decide …'[96]

Kutuzov, of course, was in a difficult position: he well understood that Moscow could not be defended but neither could he publicly announce his intention to abandon the former capital of the empire. So, in effect, he chose to keep Rostopchin out of the loop. The Moscow governor, known for his impulsiveness and intrigues, might jeopardize the military operations. Kutuzov could imagine the logistical nightmares that might result from the governor's offer to move 'all military resources' towards the army, which was moving in the opposite direction. So, instead of clear instructions, he sent laconic and evasive responses informing Rostopchin that his suggestions for protecting Moscow were sound and should be considered, just not at present …[97]

Rostopchin's anxious behaviour during these days is understandable, given that he had grown so used to playing the fine role of leader of popular sentiments that the necessity to relinquish that role and abandon Moscow without any heroic display took him unawares. Everything he had done in the previous months was aimed at assuring the populace that Moscow would be defended. He effectively staked his own reputation on this, and surrendering the city without a fight was too bitter a pill to swallow. In a letter to the emperor, Rostopchin explained that 'prior to 7 September I did everything I could to calm down the residents and enthuse their spirits but the army's continued retreat, the approach of the enemy and numerous wounded who had arrived [in Moscow] and filled all the streets, caused shock and disbelief'.[98] He probably felt the ground slipping away from under his feet, and uncertainty about the commander-in-chief's actions and the future of Moscow clearly exasperated him. 'My heart bleeds to see now the unfortunate possibility of the enemy entering the capital,' he lamented on 10 September. The fall of Moscow 'would bring dishonour upon Russia, which would be worse than death'.[99] Deep inside his heart, he should have known that the dreadful moment was coming but he seems to have refused, till the last moment, to believe that Moscow would indeed be abandoned. If major government offices were removed in late August, this was done at the demand of officials, to whom the count yielded only reluctantly. After weeks of steadily mounting pressure, Rostopchin was clearly beginning to feel the strain.[100] Searching for scapegoats, he concentrated on the foreigners: 'The foreigners here cannot be damped down,' he reported on 10 September. 'Just yesterday one of them openly called for an uprising, describing various things that Bonaparte would do here, and berating His Majesty the emperor. Because of the extraordinary circumstances, the people are angry and are not satisfied with my leniency towards the foreigners, thus the day after tomorrow I shall have that foreigner hanged with the help of a horse cart for the disturbance.'[101]

Bestuzhev-Riumin testified that the news of the Russian army's retreat produced a 'terrible tumult' among the people. 'Thoughts, souls and the very existence of Moscow were all in disarray,' recalled Glinka.[102] Wounded officers and soldiers, streaming into Moscow, were accompanied by hundreds of fearful peasants, who declared that the French were advancing everywhere, ruthlessly plundering and burning villages. Rostopchin felt compelled to calm this popular tumult and his new proclamation resorted to even greater embellishments. He claimed that the Russian army passed though Mozhaisk only because it intended to join up with the reinforcements moving toward it: 'It has now taken up a strong position where the enemy will not attack it.' The governor assured Muscovites that

> [Kutuzov] says he will defend Moscow to the last drop of blood and is even ready to fight in the streets. Do not be upset, brothers, that the government offices are closed; things have to be put in order, and we will deal with villains in our own way! When the time comes I shall want both town and peasant lads and will raise the cry a day or two beforehand, but they are not wanted yet so I hold my peace. An axe will be useful, a hunting spear not bad, but a three-pronged fork will be best of all: a Frenchman is no heavier than a sheaf of rye.[103]

Rostopchin's suggestion that fighting might occur in the streets of Moscow further inflamed passions in the city. Some Muscovites seemed to have lost hope upon hearing this and in the ensuing 'murderous disorder' people began ransacking taverns and fights broke out in streets. By noon 'an enormous crowd had gathered near the Spasskaya Gates of the Kremlin, largely comprised of drunken men who were ready for any rowdiness.'[104] Others became animated by patriotic fervour, so that theatre actors volunteered for military service and one noblewoman offered to raise a 'squadron of amazons'![105] On 12 September the crowds were actively discussing the governor's latest proclamation that 'Moscow is our mother. She has nursed, fed and raised us. In the name of Holy Mother, I call upon all of you to rise in defence of our Lord's temples, the city of Moscow and all of Russia.' Rostopchin called upon the people 'to arm yourselves, each man as he can, come on foot or on horseback; take three days' supplies with you and assemble beneath the holy cross and banners at the Three Hills'. He promised to join this host there so 'together we shall extirpate the wretches. Glory shall be the reward of those who fight in the contest! Eternal memory awaits those who fall! And those who evade their duty shall receive retribution on the Day of Judgement!'[106]

The following day (13 September) a large crowd of factory hands, house serfs and peasants, with some officials, seminarians and gentry mingled in amongst them, had indeed gathered in the early morning at the Three Hills, brandishing pikes, scythes, pitchforks, axes and clubs. 'There were tens of thousands of people so that the distance of [2–3 miles] was so densely packed that even an apple could not fall to the ground.'[107] Waiting for Rostopchin's appearance, the crowd worked itself up to a feverish pitch of patriotic excitement and chanted 'Long live our father. [Emperor] Alexander!' Having waited for the governor for most of the day, the multitudes gradually became convinced that they had been forsaken and that Moscow would be abandoned. They dispersed all about the city, spreading ominous news and disorder. Meanwhile, this day being a Sunday, Archbishop Augustin held a mass at the Cathedral of the Assumption in the Kremlin. 'The church was packed with people,' a witness described. 'I can truthfully say that I have never attended a divine service at which every heart seemed to be so universally disposed to pray or where a more religious spirit prevailed ... The pontiff himself officiated with the most touching sincerity, and at the moment when, raising his eyes to Heaven, he pronounced in a voice filled with emotion the words, "Lift up our hearts and given thanks unto the Lord", the eyes of all present filled with tears and turned spontaneously towards the only consolation of the afflicted.'[108]

But where was the governor on 12–13 September? His daughter Natalya Narychkina later wrote that he 'busied himself with different important matters' – but going to the Three Hills was apparently not among them. Indeed, Rostopchin had never intended to go either to the Three Hills or to the mass. Speaking to Sergei Glinka, the editor of the nationalistic *Russkii vestnik*, who had to walk for miles to the governor's palace because he had been unable to hire a carriage, Rostopchin noted that 'nothing will come of this business on the Three Hills', and remarked that the broadsheet's main purpose was to 'make our peasants understand what they are to do when the enemy comes to Moscow'.[109] The governor clearly wanted to stoke up the bellicose ardour among the remaining Muscovites, hoping that the people would undertake what the army refused to do.

At 6am[110] on 13 September the governor set out 'to confer with [Kutuzov] in order to adopt, in conjunction with him, such means as will lead to the extermination of our enemies. We shall rip the living breath out of them and send them all to the devil.'[111] Upon reaching the Russian army, then deployed near the Poklonnaya Gora, the governor saw soldiers digging entrenchments on top of the heights, while officers argued ill-temperedly among themselves; everywhere was an atmosphere of 'great disorderliness'.[112] Seeing the Moscow governor, 'the accursed Kutuzov', as Rostopchin privately described him,[113] politely greeted him and took off to one side for a long, private conversation, which, Rostopchin claimed with hindsight, 'showed the baseness, timidity and the indecision of [Kutuzov] who was named the Saviour of Russia even though he did nothing to deserve it'. But at the time Rostopchin was glad to see that Kutuzov agreed with his suggestion to defend the city and declared that 'it had been decided to give battle to Napoleon at the very spot where we now stood'. He even assured the governor that 'if necessary, he would fight on even in the streets of Moscow'[114] and asked him to 'come back with the Archbishop and the two miraculous images of the Holy Virgin ... to pass in front of the army, with the clergy at the head, reciting prayers and sprinkling soldiers with holy water'.[115]

Kutuzov's orderly Prince Golitsyn was present at this conversation; he recalled that 'after the usual mutual compliments, [Kutuzov and Rostopchin] spoke about the defence of Moscow and agreed to fight and die at the walls of the city'. This was a charade. By then Kutuzov knew very well what was in store for the city. He believed that the fall of Moscow would halt the Grande Armée's further advance as Napoleon would seek a political resolution to the war. The Russian army needed this precious time to receive reinforcements and regroup to enable it to fight on. Rostopchin's arguments to the contrary would have made no difference for Kutuzov. In fact, the governor's talk of Moscow's possible destruction only alarmed the general, who regarded the city as a pawn on his strategic board. The Grande Armée 'is akin to a stormy torrent,' he observed, and Moscow 'is the sponge that will absorb it'.[116] Kutuzov would naturally have rejected any suggestions that might jeopardize his own designs and Rostopchin's idea of destroying the city *before* the enemy captured it, as he told Eugène of Württemberg, would have particularly caused him alarm. So he did his best to 'confuse and mislead Rostopchin over his actual intentions',[117] assuring the governor that the city would be defended. Golitsyn recalled that 'Rostopchin departed thrilled and delighted, but he failed to notice the surreptitious implications of Kutuzov's assurances and arrangements. Kutuzov could not reveal before time that he intended to abandon Moscow, even though he hinted at this during his conversation with Rostopchin.'

But Golitsyn seems to be mistaken here – Rostopchin's own writings suggest that he left highly disappointed, while General Yermolov believed that the governor was not deceived by Kutuzov's statements, noting that 'although he pretended to be calm and secure, in reality Rostopchin was the last to believe [Kutuzov's] statements'. Moreover, the sight of the weary army could not have been encouraging, while conversations with officers would have sown many seeds of suspicion in Rostopchin's heart. Upon encountering General Yermolov, Rostopchin took him aside for a private conversation. The governor did not hide his suspicions that Kutuzov was reluctant to defend Moscow, and his parting words particularly struck the general: 'If you abandon Moscow without a battle, you would soon see it burning in flames behind you!'[118] Similarly, upon seeing Prince Eugène of Württemberg, who was on terms of close familiarity with Kutuzov, Rostopchin told him, 'If I were asked what to do, I would say, "Destroy the city before you surrender it to the enemy." This is my opinion as a private individual but as the governor responsible for the well-being of the capital, I cannot give such advice.'[119]

Around 8pm, after returning to Moscow, Rostopchin received a brief letter from Kutuzov, finally admitting what the governor had long suspected. '[Difficult circumstances] compel me, in great grief, to abandon Moscow,' Kutuzov stated, requesting Rostopchin to dispatch 'as many police officers as possible who could guide the army by different byroads [through Moscow] to the Ryazan road'.[120] Even though Rostopchin should have realized by then that Moscow was doomed, he was incensed (or at least pretended to be) by Kutuzov's letter. 'Was not [Kutuzov] swearing just yesterday that Moscow would not be surrendered without a fight?,' he angrily asked the courier, who calmly responded, 'The war is filled with unexpected and unpleasant necessities to which we all must yield.'[121] Furthermore, coming in the form of a short note just hours before the army moved through the city, the letter was rather humiliating for the governor, who had visited, on his way back, Archbishop Augustine to convey Kutuzov's request that he come out the next day with Moscow's miracle-working icons to bless the army before the battle.[122] 'My blood boils in my veins,' he wrote to his wife that night. 'I think I shall die of grief.'[123]

Late that night Eugène of Württemberg and August of Oldenburg visited Rostopchin, urging him to come with them in a last-ditch attempt to compel Kutuzov to reverse his decision and fight at the gates of Moscow. Rostopchin declined, knowing that the die was already cast.[124] Rostopchin never forgave Kutuzov for keeping him in ignorance for so long and his immediate response was to dash off a letter to Emperor Alexander: 'Your Majesty! [Kutuzov's] resolution decides the fate of Your Empire which will foam with rage when it learns that the city which contains the grandeur of Russia and in which rest the ashes of your ancestors is to be handed over to the enemy.'[125] Writing to his wife, the governor frankly stated that 'Kutuzov deceived me when he promised he would fight.'[126] A month later he was still seething with frustration and anger, writing 'Prince Kutuzov not only lied to me but also deceived the entire Fatherland and the emperor himself, abandoning the capital to the villains.'[127]

The Day of Mourning: 14 September

In his letter to Alexander, Rostopchin mentioned in passing that he had 'put away in safety everything that was in the city, and all that is left for me to do is to weep over my country's lot'. The governor was clearly being disingenuous. Although by 14 September he had evacuated more than thirty-five state institutions,[128] including the Moscow Treasury[129] and some 300 transports laden with church treasures, numerous resources still remained in the city. Three miracle-working icons – the Vladimirskaya and Iverskaya Madonnas, as well as the Black Madonna of Smolensk – were still in the city and had to be evacuated at once. Many government institutions had not even started packing their holdings. The Votchina Department, which managed land ownership, maintained a massive archive of 'documents bound into enormous ledger books that totalled 42,160' and would have required up to a thousand horses to be evacuated.[130] Similar challenges faced officials of the Mining Department, who had to leave their vast archives with 'ledger books, journals and protocols' under the protection of just three soldiers.[131] Aside from archives, provisions and supplies, there were enormous amounts of weapons and ammunition, estimated to have required some 8,000 transports to be fully evacuated. Napoleon later acknowledged finding 150 cannon, 60,000 new muskets, 1.6 million cartridges, 400 tonnes of gunpowder and 300 tonnes of saltpetre;[132] at the Moscow Arsenal alone the Russians left 66,418 weapons and, even though most were in disrepair, there were still 27,595 functioning arms.[133] Even more weapons were available at depots at the Nikolskie Gate, Sukharev's Tower, Krasnenskii (Red) Pond, Simonov's Monastery and in the Prechistenskaya and Basmanskaya districts, where thousands of small arms, cold steel weapons and thousands of pounds of gunpowder and lead still remained, forcing Rostopchin to order it all to be dumped into the Moscow river and nearby ponds.

The night and morning of 14 September proved to be rather hectic for Rostopchin, who was besieged by a horde of last-minute supplicants as he feverishly supervised the evacuation process and organized the army's passage through the city.[134] He wrote two letters to Emperor Alexander, and arranged for all the municipal officials and garrison units to depart on the Ryazan road, while the firefighting brigade was sent to Vladimir. The remaining municipal officials and policemen were instructed to destroy those barges laden with state and private property that could no longer be evacuated. The governor then ordered the commandant of the Moscow garrison to evacuate his troops and relevant equipment from the city, and made arrangements for the evacuation of holy relics, as well as the secret workshop where Leppich had been building his 'flying machine'. He went through his copious stacks of correspondence, official papers and other documents, selecting important ones and discarding others. All the while, he was holding meetings with various officials and petitioners. Sometime after 8am, as Rostopchin was getting ready to leave the town – his coach and horses awaited him outside – a large crowd, returning from the Three Hills, gathered near his residence. 'The furious populace rushed towards the governor's palace, shouting that they had been deceived,' an eyewitness tells us. The mob scorned the governor for his abandonment of Moscow and demanded that he lead them to the Three Hills, where they wanted to fight the enemy and save the city. It was then that Rostopchin, seeking to deflect the disparagement aimed at him and place the responsibility for all that happened on someone else's shoulders, committed the heinous crime of sacrificing an innocent life. He ordered two prisoners to be brought before him: Mikhail Vereshchagin, the son of a well-to-do merchant, and a certain Mouton, 'a French deserter from the previous war',[135] who had been arrested for disseminating dangerous ideas. They stood accused of the particularly 'grave' crime of circulating translations of two apocryphal proclamations by Napoleon that had appeared in the foreign press. With an angry mob seething in front of him, Rostopchin delivered Vereshchagin – 'this traitor and state criminal' as he later described him – to the people, declaring that here was 'the only man in the whole population of Moscow to want to betray his Fatherland'. He ordered his military escorts to sabre him in front of the crowd; perhaps reluctant to kill in cold blood, they struck the poor young man a few feeble blows. This, however, did not assuage the crowd, which rushed on him and tore him to pieces. The body was fastened to the tail of a horse and dragged through the streets, while Rostopchin escaped by the back door and fled the city.[136]

By now Moscow was all bustle and commotion. 'Some were preparing to fight, others sought to escape,' observed Professor I. Snegirev.[137] But getting out of the city was a challenge in itself.[138] Even those who wanted to escape in many cases could not do so because of financial or logistical problems. Grigorii Kolchugin, a rather successful merchant, noted that evacuating his goods would have required him to spend up to 20,000 rubles, which he simply could not afford.[139] Others could not leave because of sick or old relatives (usually parents) or official responsibilities. Thus the conscientious Bestuzhev-Riumin, who worked at the Votchina Department and had a seven-week-old baby at home, chose to stay in the city to protect his department's vast archive of documents related to land ownership in and around Moscow. Even those who could leave the city found their departure complicated by the presence of the Russian army, still moving slowly through the city. 'Junctions, narrow streets, large wagon trains (which had been moved closer in anticipation of a battle) trailing the army, reserve artillery and parks, and the fleeing residents of Moscow – all these factors so complicated our movement that the army was unable to leave the city before noon.'[140] Thousands of men wounded at Borodino were brought in by the Dorogomilovskaya barrier and taken to various parts of Moscow, and thousands of carts conveyed the inhabitants and their possessions out of the city; prices for transports and horses rocketed and the streets were jammed with numerous wagons, carriages and other transports. 'The scenes on the outskirts of Moscow could have inspired an artist to paint the Exodus from Egypt,' wrote Maria Volkova in a letter. 'Every day thousands of coaches depart through all the gates, some travelling to Ryazan, others to Nizhni Novgorod and Yaroslavl.'[141]

'How different this great and imposing capital city already was from what it had been earlier!' lamented Prince Nikolai Golitsyn, upon returning to Moscow on 12

September. The people in the streets looked more like 'souls in torment who appeared to have a presentiment of some great catastrophe'. One had only to appear in military uniform to be accosted on all sides, questioned about events, the battle of Borodino or the likelihood of a battle at the gates of Moscow.[142] Desperate state officials begged their superiors to let them leave the city and save their families. Bestuzhev-Riumin recalled that one of his colleagues at the Votchina Department 'appeared to be approaching an untimely death' as he begged for a furlough to leave Moscow. 'He was deadly pale and spoke with such a weak and trembling voice that it was impossible to understand what he was saying.'[143] 'At every step we encountered poignant scenes,' reminisced another Russian officer. 'Women, elders and children crying and wailing, and not knowing where to go. Pale and frantic people ran by houses, bustling about without understanding what they should do. Everything they knew was about to be destroyed and it seemed the Antichrist himself was approaching and the Doomsday was about to start ...'[144] In some churches priests called their parishioners to mass: 'My Christian brethren, pray fervently and recant for Judgement Day has come.'[145]

By the evening of 13 September 'the popular tumult in the city reached such intensity that I cannot even describe it,' commented one contemporary.[146] The last two days before the city's abandonment were 'genuinely horrifying', recalled Fedor Lubyanovskii, who even years after the event could not speak of them without 'horror and trepidation'.[147] Similarly, Snegirev found it 'difficult to find words to describe the confusion and apprehension that reigned in Moscow ... Everyone was in commotion, fussing about, burying property in the ground or hiding their precious belongings in water wells; others were preparing to leave Moscow but still did not know to where it would be safe to flee, or were preoccupied with the search for horses and coachmen. A few intended to stay in town and were arming themselves with weapons from the arsenal or simply prayed, hoping for the Lord's intercession.'[148]

Nikolai Muravyev found the city in a woeful state, with weeping and clamour everywhere. 'Almost all the nobility had left. Carriages appearing on the streets were now stoned by the populace.'[149] In fact, there are many eyewitness accounts testifying to the hostility that the lower classes demonstrated towards the affluent and noble. Many blamed Rostopchin's jingoistic broadsheets for contributing to this popular anger. By repeatedly claiming that Moscow would be defended and the enemy would be soon vanquished, these broadsheets instilled confidence in the lower classes, and they were naturally infuriated by what they perceived as the cowardly exodus of the nobility and merchants on the eve of so decisive a moment in Moscow's history. Once the chaotic rush to evacuate began, the wealthy, who had horses, carriages and other means to move their households out of the city, were resented by poorer people, whose only options were to leave on foot with whatever they could or stay behind. Thus, while the rich escaped, 'the poor were forced to stay and breathe the same air with the [French] fiends'.[150] Sergei Glinka noted that the long line of 'coaches, carriages, carts, wagons and other transports' leaving the city 'extremely annoyed and angered the common people'.[151] The people naturally believed that 'the nobles were saving their own skins while surrendering the people and the metropolis itself to Napoleon'.[152] Thus, while taking his mother out of Moscow, Dmitri Mertvago was startled to see the common people 'impudently grumbling against the nobles who were departing from the city'.[153] Decades after the war Dmitri Sverbeyev still remembered the 'fear and anger' that he experienced as his family's carriage was harassed by the rabble. These commoners 'looked at us askance while a young lad glanced sternly at our carriages and bluntly called us cowardly runaways. Others quickly joined him and we had to travel for a long distance amidst threats and shouts that branded us as traitors and truants ... My father just sat in the carriage, without uttering a word and with his head lowered.'[154] One Muscovite townsman wrote that the fleeing noblemen were cowards and, to reinforce his point, he claimed that some of them escaped by dressing up as women or bandaged their sideburns to simulate illness.[155] Bestuzhev-Riumin observed that

> the greatest danger to [the affluent Muscovites] came from peasants residing in villages near Moscow. These peasants called them cowards, traitors and audaciously shouted in their wake, 'Boyars, why are you running away with your servants? Has hardship come upon you by chance as well? Or the threatened Moscow is no longer to your liking?' Those who were forced out of necessity to stop at these villages had to pay thrice the price for oats and hay; instead of the usual rate of five kopecks per person, they now had to pay one ruble or more, and had to do it unquestioningly if they did not want to become victims of the rage that these infuriated people felt at the sight of the fleeing [rich Muscovites]. Many of those who had fled in carriages from Moscow [soon] returned back on foot, having lost horses, carriages and property ... and told, with tears in their eyes, stories of their woeful experiences.[156]

A similar story is recounted by one Lebedev, grandson of a Moscow priest, who in his memoirs cited family stories of peasants coming at his [grandfather's family] with bear-spears and threatening to slaughter them all for having 'frittered Moscow away'. The family had to buy its way to safety with money.[157]

By noon more than two-thirds of the inhabitants of Moscow had already gone or were in the process of leaving. The precise number of people who had stayed in the city remains unknown. Participants on both sides agree that Moscow was virtually empty, and its formerly bustling streets were eerily deserted in the afternoon of 14 September. Rostopchin claimed that as few as 10,000 people – clergymen, foreigners, civil servants, servants and the poor – remained in the city by the end of that day, and at least one Russian historian argues that as few as 6,300 people had ultimately stayed behind. However, some contemporaries believed that about 20–25,000 people (and a few, less creditably, as many as 50,000) had remained in Moscow.[158]

The exodus of so many people in such a short period meant that the streets closest to the city barriers were jammed with 'carriages, *droshkis*, carts, horse-drawn vehicles of all kinds, and people on foot carrying their loads'.[159] Just in front of one of the city barriers a Russian officer saw 'a wide street jammed with several rows of carts. Carriages and wagons moved with artillery along both sides of the street. One could observe a bizarre mixture of people of all ranks and transports of all types. Wagons were filled with trunks, bundles and feather pillows on which servants sat while footmen walked behind them, leading horses and hounds.'[160] Ysarn was surprised to see 'poor women of the people crushed with the weight of burdens far beyond their strengths, carrying off even the smallest pieces of furniture in their homes, and followed by their crying children who wailed in despair'.[161] It was probably among one of these crowds that Lieutenant M. Evreinov of the Demidovskii Regiment saw the city's entire firefighting squad of some 2,100 men leaving with their equipment.[162]

At about the same time Philipp Vigel's brother also decided to leave the city, and 'his heart filled with horror' at the sights of abandoned houses and empty streets. Yet as he approached the Pokrovskaya barrier the scene changed dramatically:

[He could] barely move because of the dense crowds of fleeing residents. The utter disorder, in which these remaining residents of Moscow now rushed from the city, presented a most singularly horrifying and yet somewhat caricatural sight. One could see a priest who had put on all of his vestments, one atop another, and holding a bundle with church ornaments, vessels and other items. A heavy four-seat carriage was slowly dragged by two horses, while nearby smaller two-seat carriages had five and six horses harnessed. One could see a wagon with a commoner or merchant's wife, dressed in brocade dress and wearing pearls and numerous items of jewellery that she did not have time to pack. Men on horses and on foot thronged all around, herding cows and sheep. A remarkable multitude of dogs followed this great exodus and their miserable howling mixed with mooing, bleating, neighing and other animal sounds.[163]

By late afternoon, recalled Glinka, 'the passage of the soldiers, the crowded masses of the populace, and the serried carriages and carts had caused the dust to rise in pillars and hide the dying rays of the setting sun over Moscow'.[164]

Despite efforts to maintain strict discipline, the army's passage through the city was accompanied by numerous incidents of unruliness and plundering. As early as 12 September the Cossacks, anticipating the fall of the city, busied themselves with ransacking stockyards where they 'took away incalculable amounts of oats and hay'.[165] On 14 September, as the army passed through the city, many 'officers began to gather in groups to discuss what would happen next since none of us knew what to expect. Meanwhile, the rank-and-file, under the pretext of fetching some water, often slipped into nearby shops, houses and cellars that were left open as if to treat the passersby – and while there they bid good-bye [in their own manner] to Mother Moscow ...'[166] The clergymen of the Novodevichii Monastery soon saw the results of such leave-taking as they encountered a 'drunken Cossack with bags full of alcohol hanging on both sides of his saddle'.[167] Indeed, despite Rostopchin's orders prohibiting the sale of wine,[168] the much-reduced police force was unable to 'prevent the invasion of the wounded rank-and-file'[169] into wine cellars and taverns; all were ransacked. Andrei Karfachevskii saw 'wounded soldiers who had been in the fighting at Borodino walking about, smashing up taverns and shops in the market',[170] while General Bennigsen described 'the doors of the cellars, especially those of taverns, had been left open or were broken into by soldiers, servants, carters, hauliers and by the lowest classes of the population'.[171] To prevent the rabble and soldiers from getting drunk, the police were ordered to start smashing barrels of wine and beer but for a variety of reasons such instructions were not carried out everywhere. In some districts 'no orders prohibiting the sale of alcohol had been received and the police therefore took no action', reported one of the constables two years later.[172]

Squabbling and shouting among the drunken men further disquieted the already nervous Muscovites; one of them kept hearing loud drunken brawls and shouts of 'the French [are coming]' throughout the night.[173] In the evening the remaining residents were horrified to see 'the Bacchus devotees' running around in the streets 'armed with knives, axes, knob-sticks, clubs and other weapons' and shouting 'beat, stab, cut and murder the damned Frenchmen and show no mercy to accursed foreigners!' Such commotion continued throughout the night, one eyewitness testified, greatly frightening the remaining townsfolk.[174] These petty criminals and drunkards were joined by the soldiers as well. 'Our soldiers go pillaging under the very noses of their generals,' Rostopchin complained in a letter to his wife. 'I saw them break down the door of a house and remove all the contents ... I believe the inhabitants are less afraid of the enemy than of their own protectors.'[175] Large groups of 'men, wounded soldiers, convicts, workmen and others' wandered the empty streets ransacking taverns and shops.[176] In the morning of 14 September a retired Guard captain witnessed 'brawls and murders' taking places in the once quiet streets of the city.[177] Many merchants chose to give away their goods to soldiers and workmen, telling them 'we prefer to see you have them instead of the French'.[178] At Polyanka Square a coffin maker was giving away his stock, saying that 'there will be great demand for them soon'.[179] But in many places the soldiers took what they wanted by force. Alexander Bulgakov, who arrived in Moscow at around 5pm on 14 September, was stunned to see 'the scenes of fugitives, on foot and horse and carriage. I could not believe my eyes and continued on my way ... I soon came across a ransacked tavern and saw convicts running away from the prison. It was unclear whether they were released or simply escaped ... [As he travelled further into the city] I saw our soldiers murdering a shopkeeper. Proceeding on the Basmannaya street, I saw appalling scenes ... the wounded [Russian] soldiers and marauders are plundering everything.'[180] The city was left without any police supervision during the army's passage through Moscow, derided another contemporary. 'What a horror! This caused riots in the streets and houses ... shouts, cursing, threats and all kinds of violence that exceeded all boundaries. Anyone who attempted to transport his possessions to a safer place was abused and robbed in the most impudent manner.'[181]

Meanwhile, everywhere she looked Elena Pokhorskaya, the 17-year-old wife of the deacon at the Church of St Peter and Paul, saw 'carriages stopped at the gates of houses or stretched along in the streets'. Approaching the Kaluzhskaya barrier, in the southern part of Moscow, she 'was stunned to see an inestimable number of carriages and carts. The entire street was jammed with them. Those who travelled on government missions were let through but others waited for two and three hours before their turn came. Everyone was hurrying, fussing about, and jostling, horses frequently got frightened and trampled people on foot. Clamour, shouts and ruckus all around ...'[182] Another eyewitness remembered 'wagons queued one after another, carriages moving on the road and crowds of people walking with bundles and bags in hand: they were saving whatever they could. Women held children by the hand and everyone was bitterly crying.'[183] According to Nastasya Danilovna, the daughter of Baron Alexei Korf's estate manager, 'the streets were filled with noise, ruckus and bustle. Merchants were closing their stores and packing away their goods. A crowd stopped soldiers as they marched in the streets and asked them about the battle of Borodino; some cried bitterly, others cursed Napoleon ... One officer teasingly told me that young and beautiful girls like me would have a fun time in Moscow when the French came. I simply turned my back to him and left ...'[184] A similar tone was directed towards Anna Kruglova, the wife of a wealthy merchant, when she came out of her house to inquire about the enemy: 'Start setting the table with bread and salt for the dear guests,' one of the Russian soldiers told her sarcastically.[185]

The story of Prince Lobanov's servant Dunyasha offers a good insight into the chaotic experiences of those days. On 13 September Prince Lobanov, having earlier dispatched his entire family to Vladimir, gave orders to harness the carriage for himself, 'took out his last money and ordered [his servants] to buy a horse and ride out by the Tverskaya barrier to our country house near Moscow; if anybody was not afraid of staying at our Moscow house, then he was free to stay ... We, the servants, began to consider where we should all go. Six or so remained at the house, the others left for the country estate.' Her mother-in-law would not let the young and pretty Dunyasha go with them so far, nor would she allow her to stay in Moscow. Instead, Dunyasha was sent to her aunt, who lived about 17 miles from Moscow, travelling with a noble family heading for a village in the Orel province. 'Somehow we dragged ourselves there safely. Had there not been such distress on the way, it would have been a pleasure and real joy. Some people were riding in carriages, some on horseback, some pulling their children in little carts. Here a cow was being led, there a goat was trying to escape. Hen-coops were attached to carts ... Some people were making their way alone, others with their whole family, children clinging to their mothers, howling because they could not keep up or had grown hungry and were looking for something to eat.'[186]

The city was full of contradictory information. 'The Muscovites were confused by the gossip and numerous rumours, which often contradicted one another, as well as by Rostopchin's broadsheets. They vacillated between fear and hope, unaware where to seek shelter from the impending danger.[187] There were some who feared their fellow troops more than the enemy. Ivan Yakovlev, a retired Guard officer residing in Moscow, struggled to convince his brother Paul to leave the city; when he finally did, on 14 September, his brother received news that Cossacks had appeared on the road to his village estate. For him, the Cossacks' appearance was not a good sign and meant the prospect of being mistreated and robbed. So the fearful Paul Yakovlev 'stubbornly refused to leave Moscow and declared that he preferred to endure abuse from the French in the comforts of his home rather than from the Cossacks and [Russian] stragglers on the road'.[188] Many people believed that the governor's orders prohibited anyone from leaving Moscow, while others on the contrary said that everybody had to leave; in some cases police actually went from house to house telling the residents to leave and, in fact, warned residents that the city might be destroyed.[189] To the city's utter consternation, some rumours claimed that there had been another battle after Borodino at which the Grand Armée had been routed, while others reported that the Russian army had been destroyed. Some claimed that Sweden had joined the war and a Swedish army was marching to defend Moscow,[190] while a few thought it was, in fact, British troops.[191] Upon encountering an enemy soldier, one Muscovite's initial reaction was to inquire whether he was 'an Englishman or a Frenchman'.[192]

This confusion was made worse by Rostopchin's broadsheets and public assurances that convinced many people that Moscow would not be abandoned. Believing the governor's pronouncements, retired Major General Sergei Mosolov abandoned his village estate and returned to Moscow only 'to discover the lies that the broadsheets perpetuated'.[193] In naming his reasons for staying in Moscow, merchant Grigorii Kolchugin, who was later persecuted by Rostopchin for living under the French occupation, listed 'the assurances by our authorities that the enemy would never be allowed into Moscow' at the very top of the list.[194] His conviction was shared by Peter Kicheyev's grandfather, who, despite having three small grandchildren under his care, rejected his family's and friends' entreaties to leave the city, 'believing wholeheartedly in Count Rostopchin's broadsheets and not tolerating even the thought of Moscow being surrendered to the French'.[195] The young Alexandra Nazarova also remembered that at the Rozhdestvenskii Monastery 'no one thought that the French would capture Moscow because Rostopchin's broadsheets calmed everyone down. Our monastery had many members of the aristocracy ... and through them we usually learned what was happening outside, and everyone was saying that there was nothing to be afraid of.'[196] 'There were many who stayed because of their stubbornness and foolhardiness. They simply refused to believe that Moscow could be captured by the enemy,' recalled Alexander Ryazanov, a student at the Slavic-Greek-Latin Academy; his own father belonged to this group, which was why the entire family stayed in Moscow.[197]

One of those reluctant to believe that Napoleon had arrived in Moscow was the husband of Elena Pokhorskaya, a taciturn man who had complete faith in his God, his tsar and the governor. He ignored his wife's urging to leave the city while they could, proudly proclaiming that 'if there were a danger, our government would have known about it before us and would have certainly told us about it. The governor's broadsheets state that everyone should stay in Moscow, so Bonaparte would not be allowed to get here.' On 14 September the deacon and his wife were still at their home when the sacristan's wife appeared with the stunning news that 'the street boys are saying that Bonaparte has reached the Dorogomilovskaya and Kaluzhskaya barriers'. With his wife wailing, the deacon burst out laughing, commenting 'What a fool of a woman you are! You believe the sacristan's wife and you will not believe the governor. Here is the count's broadsheet. I have read it to you, haven't I? Well then. You would do better to prepare the *samovar*[198] and leave me in peace, I am writing my sermon.' Shortly afterwards shouts were heard in the streets. The deacon, sipping his tea, went to the window and looked outside. Then he slowly put his cup down on the table and turned to his wife, with his face 'pale as if coated with flour' and his hands shaking. 'His tongue seemed to be stuck to his palate. He could only mutter, "The French!" and then sat down. I gave him some water to drink and began telling him that one must never despair and that God is merciful. He said nothing. Bit by bit he regained his composure, and colour returned to his face. Then he stood up, grabbed Rostopchin's broadsheet, tore it to shreds, went back to the window and stayed there without moving, just as if he were dead.'[199]

Chapter 4

The Conqueror

'**A**s we approached the Russian capital,' recalled Sergeant Chrétian–Henri Scheltens of the Imperial Guard's Fusiliers-Grenadiers, 'the villages seemed to be more opulent and there were more of them. The columns of flames destroying them were also more common. At night our camps were illuminated by these huge fires. The soldiers were quickening their pace, despite the heat which good weather had brought ...' On 14 September, on just such a pleasant morning, Napoleon and Berthier climbed into their carriage at the village of Malye Vyazemy and, accompanied by the rest of the staff, set out on the main road towards Moscow. 'The road is beautifully arranged,' remarked a cuirassier captain in a letter. 'Ten transports can move on it side-by-side and two rows of tall trees enclose the road on each side.'[1] Approaching the village of Yudino, Napoleon encountered a steep ravine, where the Russians had destroyed the bridge. While French engineers busily set about restoring it, the emperor chose to mount his horse l'Emir and continue his trip on horseback.[2] About 8 miles from Moscow he encountered Murat, returning from the advanced guard. The two spent over an hour in discussion near the small church at Spasskoe as Murat reported his most recent findings on the approaches to Moscow. The Russian army was still withdrawing to the Ryazan road, having marched slowly and steadily through the winding streets of Moscow throughout the previous night. By the morning of 14 September only General Mikhail Miloradovich's rearguard remained in the Dorogomilovskaya suburb, with the task of containing the enemy and gaining sufficient time for the army to withdraw through Moscow.

General Miloradovich, though not especially well known in the West, was one of the most colourful personalities of the Napoleonic Wars. Known as the 'Russian Bayard' for his courage, Miloradovich was among the very few Russian officers to have received a higher education, having studied at the universities of Höttingen, Königsberg, Strasbourg and Metz. In 1799 he had distinguished himself under the legendary Field Marshal Alexander Suvorov in Italy and Switzerland, where he became famous for his heroics; in one of the battles, as the Russian line wavered under a French attack, Miloradovich rushed forward with a flag yelling, 'Soldiers, watch how Russian generals die!' and helped repulse the attack. His fame only increased during the War of the Third Coalition in 1805, earning him Kutuzov's praise: 'You are moving faster than angels can fly.' In 1806–1811 he fought the Turks in the Danubian Principalities, and here he revealed a more sinister side to his character. Alexander Langeron described him as 'devoured by ambition, blinded by excessive self-esteem [and] intoxicated by his initial successes ... He never concealed his untamed aspiration to become the commander-in-chief.' One of Miloradovich's principal weaknesses was a gambling addiction, and Langeron claims that he had lost tens of thousands of rubles by the time he was forced to leave the army and become the governor of Kiev. Yet Miloradovich could also be an openhearted and joyful man, who was at ease with the rank-and-file and often shared his last piece of bread with a fellow officer. His vibrant character and flamboyant sense of style often led to comparisons with Marshal Murat. A fellow general described him as a 'rare military phenomenon. He was a knight in the strictest sense of the word, unsurpassed in bravery. His calm indifference to danger was immense and so astounding that one hesitated to believe one's eyes and ears. His wit remained unquenchable under the heaviest fire and even in the face of imminent death he could draw an involuntary smile from his audience.'[3]

During the night of 14 September Miloradovich, commanding the Russian rearguard, halted his men about 6 miles from Moscow, near the porcelain factories, while Murat's advanced guard passed through the village of Perkhushkovo, guardedly following in Russian footsteps. Napoleon did not expect the Russian command to abandon Moscow without a fight and he was quite perplexed by the fact that the Russians had neither attempted to begin negotiations nor undertaken preparations to defend the city.[4] Writing to Murat, Napoleon complained that he lacked intelligence on the Russians, although he had already correctly anticipated Kutuzov's moves: 'If the enemy is not in front of you, we must verify if he has moved to the right, towards the Kaluga Road. In such a case, he might threaten our rear… . His Majesty eagerly awaits news on what is happening on your right wing, that is, the road from Kaluga to Moscow.'[5] By the evening of 13 September Murat was already near Fili, where he observed Russian earthworks at the Sparrow Hills[6] and concluded that the Russian army had chosen once more to avoid the battle and retreat to Moscow. To Napoleon, this information was quite revealing since it suggested a Russian weakness following the mauling at Borodino and raised the possibility of negotiations at the gates of Moscow. Pleased at the prospect, Napoleon had a quick lunch before resuming his journey with an escort of *chasseurs à cheval* and Polish lancers.[7] He instructed Viceroy Eugène and General Jozef Poniatowski to coordinate their movements with Murat's advanced guard so that the 4th Corps could approach Moscow from the northwest and the Polish forces from the southwest just as Murat threatened the Russians from the west. Labaume, serving in the 4th Corps, described seeing nothing but deserted villages as he marched towards Moscow. 'Upon our left were to be seen on the banks of the Moskva several splendid chateaux, which the [Cossacks] had gutted, to deprive us of the supplies they contained; for the harvest, ready for the sickle, had been trodden down or eaten by the horses, and the hayricks which covered the country, having been delivered to the flames, filled the air with a dense smoke.' On arriving at the village of Cherepkovo, Viceroy Eugène ascended a hill and for a long time endeavoured by careful examination of the surrounding country to catch a glimpse of Moscow. But he could see nothing but great clouds of dust, which, moving parallel with his corps' route, indicated the march of the Grande Armée.[8]

The converging Allied movement posed a serious threat to the Russian army. Although the evacuation of Moscow was begun during the night of 13/14 September, the streets and roads outside were choked with thousands of wounded and transports, not to mention fleeing civilians. Thus not much progress had been made by the next morning. The Russian rearguard, under Miloradovich, was still caught in a bottleneck at the gates just as the French advanced guard appeared on the city outskirts. To gain precious time, Miloradovich decided to negotiate with the enemy commander. Around noon he was informed by his headquarters that the Russian command had decided to leave some wounded men in the city, and instructed him to deliver a message to the French that 'the wounded left behind in Moscow are entrusted to the compassion of the French forces'.[9] Miloradovich ordered *Staff-Rotmistr* Fedor Akinfov of the Life Guard Hussar Regiment to deliver this message directly to Murat but also instructed him to offer the French commander a truce so that the Russians could complete their withdrawal. To drive home his point, Miloradovich warned Murat, in friendly fashion, that 'if the French want to occupy Moscow intact, they should allow us to depart it peacefully with all our artillery and trains'. Otherwise, Miloradovich threatened 'to fight to the last extremity even if he had to die beneath the ruins of Moscow'. One of Miloradovich's adjutants was somewhat surprised by the tone of the offer, noting that 'it is not brave [*on ne brave pas*] to talk in such a manner to the French army'. Miloradovich snapped back, 'It is my business to be brave, yours – to die.'[10]

Accompanied by a trumpeter, Akinfov approached the enemy outposts and a signal to parley was sounded. Akinfov was greeted by a colonel of the 1st *Chasseurs à Cheval*, who first took him to General Sebastiani, commander of the 2nd Cavalry Corps. Sebastiani initially offered to deliver the message to Murat but Akinfov insisted on doing it himself. 'After passing by five cavalry regiments deployed in chess formation in front of infantry columns,' Akinfov found himself in front of the 'splendidly dressed Murat, who was surrounded by a magnificent suite'. Greeting the Russian officer, Murat raised his richly feathered hat and, after ordering his suite to leave them alone, he asked Akinfov, 'Monsieur capitaine, what do you have for me?' Akinfov handed him a note and explained the purpose of his mission. Quickly glancing at the letter, Murat replied, 'There is no point in entrusting your wounded and sick to the compassion of the French troops. The French do not consider the prisoners as their enemies.' As for Miloradovich's request for a truce, Murat told Akinfov that he could not act without Napoleon's orders, and instructed one of his aides-de-camp to escort him to Napoleon. But just as Akinfov was riding away, Murat changed his mind and called him back, declaring that he had decided to grant Miloradovich's request and would not rush his forces to Moscow on the condition that he would be able to occupy the city that same day. Akinfov agreed and Murat immediately issued orders to halt his forward outposts and cease fire. Napoleon's aide-de-camp Gaspard Gourgaud, who happened to be with Murat at this moment, rushed back to the emperor to deliver the news. He was subjected to 'a host of questions regarding the situation in Moscow. His answers were accurate but also conveyed a sense of excitement or rather intoxication that each of us felt at the time of entering the old capital of Russia ... Indeed, Moscow was a peace! It would be a glorious peace!'[11] Napoleon confirmed Murat's decision and sent Gourgaud back to tell him so.

Meanwhile, at the advanced guard Murat continued his conversation with Akinfov. He spoke highly of Miloradovich as the two had fought against each other on several previous occasions. The King of Naples was evidently unaware of the Russian abandonment of the city and his decision to accept the Russian proposal was done to spare the city unnecessary bloodshed and destruction. Had he known about the Russian efforts to evacuate the entire city, he might have acted more vigorously to disrupt the process. But instead Murat enjoyed the prospect of the French occupation of Moscow and urged the Russian officer to convince the city residents to remain calm and that no harm would be caused to them; the French authorities would ensure their safety. At one point, however, some suspicion over the Russian designs must have crossed Murat's mind as he suddenly asked whether Moscow was abandoned – but Akinfov gave an evasive response. Murat then quickly returned to his musings, wondering aloud why 'peace has not been discussed as of yet'; he then used a strong expletive, which Akinfov did not dare to repeat on paper – and expressed his hope that the war would be over soon.[12] While Murat was conversing with Akinfov, his orders reached General Sebastiani, who appeared at the Russian outposts. Carl von Clausewitz, the famous military theorist, who was with the Russian advanced guard at that moment, noted that Miloradovich had wanted to meet Murat in person and 'was not pleased by Sebastiani's appearance but nevertheless acceded to meeting [him] and a pretty long conference ensued, to which we of the suite were not admitted'. The two generals, who had briefly met in Bucharest several years earlier, rode together a good portion of the way towards Moscow. Discussing the situation, Miloradovich spoke of the need to spare the city as far as possible, to which Sebastiani 'replied with the utmost eagerness, "Monsieur, the emperor will move his Guard at the head of his army and no disorders would be possible in the city." … Sebastiani had promised that the head of his advanced guard should not enter the city sooner than two hours after our departure.'[13]

As his conversation with Murat ended, Akinfov returned to Moscow, escorted by the same colonel of the 1st *Chasseurs à Cheval*. 'To gain a bit more time,' he tells us in his memoir, 'I asked the colonel for permission to take a look at the two Polish hussar regiments that we passed by. The colonel agreed to accompany me along the front of these two regiments. But he noticed that I rode slowly and we were losing time and asked me increase my speed. I had to comply …' In the meantime, Miloradovich left the outposts to supervise the withdrawal of his forces. Approaching the Kremlin, he was startled to see the *chef* of Moscow's garrison regiment Lieutenant General Vasilii Brozin leading the two garrison battalions out of the Kremlin with their band playing. There was a violent outcry among the retreating soldiery, who indignantly shouted that he was rejoicing amidst a national tragedy. Infuriated, Miloradovich shouted at Brozin, 'What scoundrel instructed you to march with band playing?' Brozin replied, with an annoying naiveté, that the military regulations of Peter the Great stipulated that upon surrendering a fortress, its garrison, if allowed to depart freely, must come out with band playing. 'But where in the regulations does it say anything about the surrender of [the capital city of] Moscow?' yelled Miloradovich. 'Order the music to stop at once!'

Returning from the French outposts, Akinfov informed Miloradovich of Murat's acceptance of the armistice. 'It seems the French are too eager to occupy Moscow,' the general commented. He then dispatched a messenger to inform Kutuzov of the armistice.

The Russian army was still withdrawing through the streets of Moscow. Barclay de Tolly had placed his staff officers at intervals to enforce order and facilitate the movement; knowing the especial weakness of the Russian soldiers, he issued strict orders that anyone found in a beer-shop or intoxicated was to be summarily punished. He spent the entire day directing the march (he would remain on horseback for eighteen hours) and complaining bitterly about the inefficiency of his officers, who did little or nothing to facilitate the withdrawal. Knowing that the streets of Moscow were still packed with carriages, transports and thousands of people, Miloradovich realized that he would not be able to get all of his men and equipment out of the city in time. So he instructed Akinfov to go back to Murat with a revised offer of extending the ceasefire until 7am the following morning – otherwise Miloradovich again threatened to fight 'to the last extremity'.

Shortly after noon the French advanced guard climbed the Poklonnaya Gora, from where it had a magnificent view of the city. At one o'clock in the afternoon, remembered Adrien-Jean-Baptiste François Bourgogne, 'after passing through the woods, we saw a hill some way off, and half an hour afterwards part of the army reached the highest point, signalling to us who were behind, and shouting "Moscow! Moscow!"'[14] 'The weather was warm and clear that day,' recalled a Russian contemporary. 'Not a cloud could be seen in the sky, although it was a bit windy in the morning.'[15] Standing on the Poklonnaya Gora, the men of the Grande Armée could therefore fully enjoy 'a magnificent spectacle that surpassed by far everything that our imagination had been able to conjure in terms of Asiatic splendour'. The worn-out men were bewitched by 'an incredible quantity of bell towers and domes painted in bright colours, topped with gilded crosses and linked to each other with chains which were also gilded'.[16] They greeted the emperor 'with loud cheers clearly expressing their feelings of joy'.[17] Upon reaching the Poklonnaya Gora, Napoleon and the rest of the Grande Armée paused to enjoy the panoramic view of Moscow.[18] 'There, at last, is that famous city!' Napoleon exclaimed. 'It is about time!'

The sight of Moscow and the news of the armistice 'intoxicated all with the enthusiasm of glory', recalled Ségur, and Napoleon's marshals, who had shunned him after the bloodbath at Borodino, 'forgot their grievances, pressed around the emperor, paying homage to his good fortune, and already tempted to attribute to his genius the little pains he had taken on the 7th to complete his victory'. Very few travellers had ventured as far east as Moscow and no other European army, except for the Poles in the 1600s, had ever managed to penetrate so deeply into Russia. So the soldiers found everything very strange and exotic. Napoleon himself is said to have gazed long and eagerly upon Moscow, the summit of his ambitions, now lying defenceless before his eyes. 'It was two o'clock,' Phillippe Ségur commented. 'The sun caused this great city to glisten with a thousand colours. Struck with astonishment at the sight, the [Allied troops] paused, exclaiming, "Moscow! Moscow!" Everyone quickened his pace; the troops hurried on in disorder; and the whole army, clapping their hands, repeated with delight, "Moscow! Moscow!" just as sailors shout "Land! Land!" at the conclusion of a long and toilsome voyage.'

There was 'universal enthusiasm', observed Lieutenant Serraris in his journal, noting that looking at this 'gilded city' some Allied soldiers stood still in contemplation. This moment reminded Cesare de Laugier and Fantin des Odoards of the poet Tasso's famous description of the crusaders roaring at the sight of Jerusalem:[19]

But when the gliding sun was mounted high,
Jerusalem, behold, appeared in sight,
Jerusalem they view, they see, they spy,
Jerusalem with merry noise they greet,
With joyful shouts, and acclamations sweet.[20]

To the young Private Jakob Walter of General Hugfel's 25th Division 'this holy city was like the description of the city of Jerusalem, over which our Saviour wept; it even resembled the horror and wasting according to the Gospel'.[21] The sunlight shimmering on numerous domes, spires and palaces was captivating indeed. 'Many capitals I have seen – Paris, Berlin, Warsaw, Vienna and Madrid – had only produced an ordinary impression on me,' noted Bourgogne. 'But this was quite different and the effect was to me, in fact, to everyone, magical.'[22] Indeed, Colonel Griois of the 3rd Cavalry Corps found it 'in no way resembling any cities I had seen in Europe'.[23] Captain Eugène Labaume of Viceroy Eugène's 4th Corps 'perceived a thousand elegant and gilded spires, which, glittering in the rays of the sun, seemed at a distance like so many globes of fire ... Transported with delight at this beautiful spectacle ... we could not suppress our joy but, with a simultaneous movement, we all exclaimed "Moscow! Moscow!" At the sound of this long-wished-for name, the soldiers rushed up the hill in crowds ... [to see] one of those celebrated cities of Asia, which we had thought existed only in the creative imagination of the Arabian poets.'[24] For Fantin des Odoards the sight of Moscow conjured up the fantastical world of the *One Thousand and One Nights*.[25] Ségur believed that

this glorious day ... would furnish the grandest, the most brilliant recollection of our whole lives. We felt that at this moment all our actions would engage the attention of the astonished universe; and that every one of our movements, however trivial, would be recorded by history. On this immense and imposing theatre we marched, accompanied, as it were, by the acclamations of all nations: proud of exalting our grateful age above all other ages, we already beheld it great from our greatness, and completely irradiated by our glory ... At that moment, dangers, sufferings were all forgotten. Was it possible to purchase too dearly the proud felicity of being able to say, during the rest of life, 'I belonged to the army of Moscow!'

Among those who felt the magic of this moment was the Polish Count Roman Soltyk, who served on Napoleon's staff and whose ancestors had fought in Moscow some two hundred years earlier. 'Who can understand the feeling that I experienced deep in my heart at the sight of this ancient capital of the tsars?' he wondered. 'This sight had awoken so many great historical memories. It was here that in the early seventeenth century the triumphant Poles erected their banner and the Muscovites had to kneel in front it, acknowledging the son of our king as their sovereign. And now the descendant of those Poles has come once more amidst Napoleon's columns erecting their triumphant eagles over the city. All these victories of my compatriots, both ancient and present, merged into one in my imagination ...'[26] But there were also many others who savoured more practical prospects. At the sight of Moscow 'troubles, dangers, fatigues, privations were all forgotten, and the pleasure of entering Moscow absorbed all our minds. To take up good quarters for the winter, and to make conquests of another nature – such is the French soldier's character: from war to love, and from love to war!'[27] Another French officer wondered what 'pleasures and delights' awaited them in Moscow.[28]

Atop the Poklonnaya Gora, Napoleon dismounted, drew his short spyglass from its holder and quickly examined the immense city that lay in front of him. He then asked Caulaincourt to bring him a larger telescope, which he rested on the shoulder of Anatole de Montesquiou. As he studied the city, he exclaimed several times, 'Barbarians! They are leaving all of this to us! It is not possible. Caulaincourt, what do you think of it? Tell me, can you believe it?' 'Your Majesty knows better than anyone what I think of it,' tersely replied the grand equerry, who had been against this war from the very beginning and had lost his brother in battle just a week ago.[29] To better understand the city, Napoleon asked for François Lelorgne d'Ideville, the brilliant polyglot who had served for years with the French embassy in Russia, to identify principal buildings and locations.[30] He was eager to see if the city gates would at length open and emit the deputation tamely bearing the city's keys and placing the wealth of the city at his disposal. 'It is customary, at the approach of a victorious general, for the civil authorities to present themselves at the gates of the city with the keys, in the interests of safeguarding the inhabitants and their property,' a French officer explained. 'The conqueror can then make known his intentions concerning the governance of the city.'[31] But as time went on, Moscow remained silent and inanimate and the anxiety of the emperor and the impatience of the soldiers increased. Throughout the afternoon Napoleon dispatched a number of emissaries to explore the city's suburbs. One of them, Anatole de Montesquiou, was sent to investigate a large building that Lelorgne d'Ideville could not identify. Galloping to the Dorogomilovskaya barrier, he entered the suburb, which he found completely empty. Approaching the building he had been ordered to identity, he found its entrance open and the building abandoned. A quick inspection of its tall, thick walls and bare, cell-like chambers led him to believe that it had been a penal house, now emptied of its inmates. As he came out, he encountered two tall Russians, who scowled at him and, ignoring Montesquiou's attempts to address them in French, German and Polish, shouted back 'Frantsuzy kaput!' [The French are done for.][32]

By early afternoon all the officers who had ventured within the walls of the city returned with the depressing news that the city was being abandoned completely. Losing patience, Napoleon ordered Murat to proceed towards Moscow. The leading elements of Murat's advanced guard entered the Dorogomilovskaya suburbs around 3pm, with Sebastiani's cavalry leading the way. The 10th Polish Hussar Regiment was first into the city, followed by the 1st Combined Prussian Lancer Regiment, the 3rd Württemberg *Jager zu Pferd* and the remaining troops of the 2nd Light Cavalry Division with the horse artillery. Behind them came the 2nd and 4th Cuirassier Divisions and the 4th Cavalry Corps.[33]

As the Allied advanced guard quietly followed the Cossacks of the Russian rearguard into the Dorogomilovskaya suburb,[34] the two sides came closer together and eventually intermingled and seemed to become part of the same host. The Allied troops occasionally halted to let Russian transports or stragglers pass, and officers and soldiers on both sides looked with curiosity at men whom they had frequently met on the field of battle. Captain Leopold Gluchowski, a staff officer in the 5th Corps, was in a leading group of Allied soldiers who found themselves amidst the Russians, who, upon noticing a foreign officer, shouted 'Peace! Peace!'[35] Yet, amidst this impromptu fraternization, Anatole de Montesquiou noticed 'a strange thing': 'The dogs of both armies were the least amicable, suspiciously looking at and staying away from each other while continually growling, which alerted us to their continued animosity.'[36]

The larger-than-life figure of Murat was at the centre of it all. Lieutenant Albert von Muralt of the Bavarian chevau-légers, whom Viceroy Eugène dispatched to Murat for more news, found the King of Naples 'surrounded by a brilliant and numerous suite and by Cossacks and generals who were flattering him on his bravery'. As expected, Murat was dressed flamboyantly in 'a short coat of dark-red sammet with slashed arms. A short straight sword hung from a richly embroidered belt. His boots were of red morocco leather, and on his head he wore a big three-cornered hat, embroidered with gold borders and with a long plume which he had put on back to front. His long brown hair hung down in curls on to his shoulders.'[37] A Russian officer watched as Murat, with Cossacks all around him, halted his horse and asked if anyone spoke French. As a young officer rode forwards, Murat inquired who commanded these Russian troops. The officer pointed to Colonel Yefremov, a stern-looking man in Cossack uniform. 'Ask him,' Murat continued, 'if he knows who I am.' The young man carried out this request and informed Murat that the colonel 'knows Your Majesty well and has always seen you in the heat of the battle'. The King of Naples liked the Cossack's answer and approached him. He noticed the sumptuous felt coat on Yefremov's shoulders and commented that it must be quite useful on bivouacs. Without speaking, Yefremov simply took off the coat and gave it to Murat, who was surprised by the Russian's generosity and wanted to respond in kind; unable to find anything suitable on himself, he asked his aides-de-camp for their watches and presented them to the Cossack officer and his companions.[38]

Akinfov, returning with Miloradovich's new offer to the French outposts, found Murat already near the Dorogomilovskaya barrier as he 'rode in the wake of his cavalry chain that had become mixed with our Cossacks'. Murat greeted Akinfov cheerfully and accepted the new offer but on condition that 'everything that belonged to the army would be left behind'. Remarkably, Murat then inquired if Akinfov had informed the residents of Moscow to stay calm in the face of the impending occupation. 'Even though I did not even give it a thought and there was no one in Moscow I could talk to about this,' the Russian officer commented in his memoir, 'I assured Murat that I had carried out his request.'

As the day wore on the rest of the Grande Armée closed up on the advanced guard and the Guard soldiers received orders to put on their parade uniforms for the triumphal entry into Moscow.[39] But the officers who had already been in the city were reporting that the city was deserted. The Emperor flatly refused to believe these reports. Drawn on by the movement of his troops, Napoleon mounted his horse and rode towards the city. Korbeletskii, who was in the imperial entourage, described how

> after waiting half-an-hour without any challenge from Moscow, Napoleon gave orders to fire a gun as a signal; then, when five more minutes had elapsed, he and his staff mounted their horses and galloped at full speed towards the city. At the same moment the vanguard and the division which was posted in the rear of the centre advanced with indescribable impetuosity; the cavalry and artillery galloped at full speed, keeping step together, and the infantry charged along as fast as they could double. The thud of horses' hooves, the creaking of wheels and the rattling of guns, added to the noise of running men, all combined to produce a wild and terrible rumble. The daylight was dimmed by the dense cloud of dust which they raised and the ground seemingly shook and moaned from this movement! Within twelve minutes they had reached the Dorogomilovskaya barrier.[40]

There, to incessant shouts of 'Vive l'Empereur', Napoleon dismounted near the Kamer-Kollezhskii rampart and began 'calmly' pacing back and forth just as military bands began playing music. It was clear that the emperor was still clinging to the hope that the rumours of Moscow's abandonment would prove to be untrue. Returning from his sortie into the city, Soltyk found him 'standing on the left of the road, with a large-scale map of Moscow laid out on the grass in front of him. He was studying it closely and then questioning the people who were being brought to him from the city.' The Emperor still hoped that an official delegation of Muscovite notables would appear and formally surrender the city. But none came.

Shortly after noon François-Joseph Ysarn Villefort and Armand Domergues, Frenchmen residing in Moscow, described 'a Polish general'[41] arriving in Moscow in search of deputations; he met Frederick Villers, the lecturer in French at the University of Moscow, who 'took him to the municipal administration, the Duma, the police, the governor-general, in short, to any place where at least a few magistrates could be found … After a prolonged and fruitless search, the Polish general returned to report to Bonaparte that there were no officials in Moscow, and that the city was deserted, except for some foreigners who had remained.'[42] Domergues noted that several other general officers were then dispatched to Moscow …'[43] One of them seems to have brought with him a small deputation of Muscovites. Korbeletskii, who was in Napoleon's suite, described the arrival of this group, noting that they were largely merchants and professionals who lived in Moscow and were concerned for the safety of their businesses; Domergues agreed that 'the delegation consisted of foreigners, the wealthiest of the merchants who resided in Moscow', while Bausset estimated that there were 'fifty or sixty men of various nationalities who had long resided in Moscow'.[44] The delegation included a simple typesetter named Lamour, who admired Napoleon and was eager to meet him. After Napoleon asked when Moscow was abandoned, Lamour, who had spent years living in Russia and was accustomed to using the Julian calendar, stepped forwards and replied that 'the residents of Moscow were frightened by the news of Your Majesty's triumphant procession' and began to leave on '31 August'. Napoleon was startled by this date, failing to comprehend that the date was given under the Julian calendar, and naturally found it impossible to believe that the city would have been evacuated before the battle of Borodino was fought on 7 September. 'What nonsense! Who is this imbecile?!' he exclaimed. The confused Lamour was quickly removed and he never forgave himself for this slip.[45] The remaining foreign notables (including the booksellers Riess and Sessay, and the university professor Villers), meanwhile, explained what was happening in Moscow.[46] Soltyk listened as 'one of these men, a Frenchman by origin, gave the most complete elucidation of the present situation. He assured Napoleon that all the authorities had quit Moscow or at least abandoned their posts.' But the emperor still found it difficult to believe that no official delegation would be forthcoming. He was growing anxious: 'he remained plunged in deep reflections,' wrote Soltyk, while Caulaincourt had never seen Napoleon so visibly upset. Standing nearby, Korbeletskii described the emperor in

> some sort of state of distraction or pensiveness. His tranquil and measured step at once became quick and feverish. He looked all round and about him, recovered himself, stopped in his walk, shivered, fell into a stupor, scratched his nose, pulled off his glove, and pulled it on again; drew out his handkerchief from his pocket, crumpled it between his hands and put it in another pocket as though by mistake, then took it out again and put it back; then he pulled off his glove once more and pulled it on again, repeating this action many times. He continued thus for a whole hour, and during that time the generals surrounding him stood motionless, like lifeless images of men, not one of them daring to stir.[47]

'Moscow is deserted!' Napoleon grumbled to *Intendant-Général* Pierre Antoine Noël Bruno, *comte* Daru. 'What an improbable story! We must know the truth of it. Go and bring me the *boyars*.'[48] Moments later he ordered General Durosnel to proceed into the city and 'set up an administration and bring me the keys', while Denniée was to visit government buildings and report on available resources.[49]

As the Allied troops crossed the river, many of them were struck by the ominous silence of the abandoned city. Muralt was amazed to see that 'all the streets we rode through were empty, the houses barred and bolted. Not a person appeared at any window, and all shops were closed. This deathly silence and desolation struck me as rather worrying, as it certainly did many others.'[50] Heinrich Ulrich Ludwig von Roos, a cavalry surgeon serving in the 3rd Württemberg *Chasseurs à Cheval*, wrote:

> each of us was feeling more or less deeply the pride of a conqueror; and for anyone who was not, there was no lack of officers and veterans to point out, with grave words, the importance of what was happening. It was forbidden, on pain of death, to get off one's horse or leave the ranks under any pretext ... We followed the road as far as the Moskwa river without encountering a single inhabitant. The bridge had been destroyed so we forded the river. The water came up to the axles of the guns and our horses' knees. On the far side we saw a few individuals behind their doors and windows but they did not seem very curious ... There were some gentlemen and ladies on the balconies of pretty stone and wooden houses and our officers saluted them amiably, and they replied in the same fashion. However, we saw very few inhabitants, only occasionally encountering some exhausted Russian soldiers and stragglers on foot and on horseback, as well as abandoned transports, grey oxen, etc. We bypassed all of it and slowly proceeded along the streets with numerous bends.

The Allied troops admired 'the profusion of churches, whose architecture was so alien to us, with their numerous towers and elaborate external ornaments, as well as some beautiful palaces surrounded by gardens'.[51]

Sitting on the porch of his house near the Nikitskie Gates, young F. Becker was thrilled that he did not have to go to school that day and was enjoying the beautiful weather, even though 'deathly silence and emptiness' reigned in the streets.[52] Suddenly he heard the sound of music coming from the western suburbs and soon saw 'men in blue uniforms' marching in the streets. 'There were very many of them. I was not initially impressed by the infantrymen since there was nothing unusual about them. But when the cavalry appeared, I was simply awestruck. I have never seen troops like them: on tall bay–coloured horses sat enormous cavalrymen in glistering yellow metal armour and helmets with long horse-hair. They rode calmly, holding no weapons.'[53]

Between 2 and 4pm[54] the Allied advanced guard[55] entered Moscow from the west just as the last of the main body of Russian troops were leaving it in the east.[56] Ivan Tutolmin, head of the Foundlings Home, could see that the last Russian troops were still marching on the *quai* near his Home when the enemy troops entered the Kremlin.[57] Although the Allied troops entered the city from several directions,[58] the main thrust seems to have been made through the Dorogomilovskaya barrier and along Arbat Street. After navigating their way through the maze of streets, these troops soon saw the famed crenellated red-brick walls of the Kremlin, at the gates of which there was a brief skirmish with the few remaining Muscovites. While most of Moscow's population had already departed, the city was in fact anything but empty and thousands of its residents, along with stragglers and wounded soldiers, had stayed behind. The news that the enemy had entered the city caused panic and consternation among those

Muscovites who still believed that the city would be defended. The young Kicheyev could see his neighbours 'running wherever they could. Their preparations were so sudden and hasty that they did not even take all the necessary possessions but, in panic and confusion, grabbed completely useless things.'[59] But some residents chose to arm themselves with weapons from the Kremlin Arsenal in an attempt to defend the city against the arriving enemy soldiers.

The Allied advanced guard approached the Kremlin along several streets. Murat and his suite ended up near the Troitskaya tower-gates, while Sebastiani's men, preceded by the Polish hussars, appeared at the Nikolskaya and Borovitskaya Towers, where they encountered a large crowd of armed Russians. The French émigrés François-Joseph Ysarn Villefort and Armand Domergues describe some 200–300 armed men gathered near the Nikolskaya Tower, and similar crowds were probably present at the other gates as well.[60] Many of these men were motivated by patriotic sentiments, while alcohol plundered from nearby taverns further emboldened them. One eyewitness was Vasilii Yermolaevich, a serf belonging to Alexander Soimonov, who had stayed behind to protect his master's property; he commented that 'as the French approached Moscow, orders were issued to destroy the barrels of wine in the taverns. But the people rushed at them and got completely drunk. Wine flowed on the streets and some people even lay down on the pavements and licked the alcohol off the stones. One could see fistfights and brawling[everywhere]!'[61] Similarly, Ivan Tutolmin, the head of the Foundlings Home, described how the rabble ransacked numerous taverns and 'carried off alcohol in buckets, pitchers and pots, getting drunk in the process'. In the wake of Governor Rostopchin's orders to distribute the weaponry stored at the Kremlin Arsenal, people 'freely took muskets, sabres and backswords [tesak], with even women grabbing and carrying away weapons like firewood'.[62] Vasilii Polyanskii, the son of a priest, had been present at the opening of the arsenal, where he saw some people 'taking as many sabres and muskets as they could hold, but most of the muskets lacked cocks and the sabres were rusty'.[63] Similarly, Alexander Ryazanov saw that many muskets had 'wooden flints while sabres and backswords [tesak] had no sword belts'.[64]

The appearance of Murat's troops in front of the Kremlin had a powerful effect on the crowd and some Russians fled at once. 'We were thunderstruck by fear and ran immediately through the Spasskii Gates of the Kremlin towards the Moskvoretskii Bridge,' recalled one of them.[65] But there were also those who decided to resist the invaders. Many of them were already roaring drunk. Muralt described encountering a 'mob of drunken soldiers and peasants who came rushing out from [the Kremlin] entrance and from a church opposite, and some shots were fired at us'. One of these drunkards, 'holding a drawn sabre in one hand and a bottle in the other', charged at Muralt, who dealt him a powerful blow that felled him.[66] Other Russians, however, offered a more determined resistance, closing the gates and opening fire at the Allied troops. The recently promoted Lieutenant Jean-Roche Coignet of the Imperial Guard recalled that, upon approaching the Kremlin, 'we were assailed by a perfect hail of shot, fired from the windows of the arsenal'.[67] The Allied troops responded by moving their cannon forwards and opening fire at the gates. 'We were deafened by the sound of an artillery salvo which almost felled us to the ground,' remembered one of the Russians.[68] With the gates shattered,[69] the Allied troops poured inside the Kremlin. Coignet and his comrades found buildings 'filled with drunken soldiers and peasants. A carnage ensued ...'[70] According to Roos, 'men of all kinds, above all men who seemed to be peasants, were coming out of [the arsenal] with weapons. Inside, others were swarming and jostling. The street and the square were littered with various weapons, most of them new. Underneath the Arsenal Gateway some sharp words were exchanged between [Murat's] aides-de-camp and the men who were carrying off the weapons. Some even pushed their way into the arsenal on horseback and the quarrelling became very loud and venomous. Meanwhile, an impatient and noisy mob had massed in the square ...'[71] Murat again ordered his cannon forwards and Colonel Theodore-Jean-Joseph Séruzier, commanding a light artillery company, was almost killed by bullets fired from the Arsenal's windows:

> Hearing this fusillade, I moved my cannon at gallop, surrounded the Arsenal and sent forwards a trumpeter with an officer to parley with these sharpshooters, whom I took to be inhabitants of the town who were reduced to despair. My trumpet sounded a truce but received only a discharge of musketry in reply. One of my captains, who had accompanied the trumpeter, one of my adjutants and the trumpeter himself were seriously wounded. I immediately gave the order to fire, placing my two guns under each of the vaultings serving as an entrance to the arsenal, and pitilessly rained canister on these men, who came out and fell on their knees in front of my guns, begging for mercy.

It was then that the colonel realized that these were 'not the inhabitants of Moscow nor soldiers trying to defend [their city], but rather it was the dregs of society, criminals let out of prison; they had been promised a pardon and their freedom on condition they revolted against these 'dogs' [chiens] of Frenchmen. I seized part of this scum ... and handed them over to our infantry.'[72] These infantrymen probably belonged to General Antoine Baudouin Gisbert de Dedem de Gelder's 2nd Brigade of the 2nd Division, since the general later recalled that 'the local residents and some sort of national guard retreated and locked themselves inside the Arsenal, firing at us. A canister shot dispersed them and, according to the order of the King [Murat], I rounded up anyone wearing a uniform at the imperial palace and left a company of light infantry to guard the prisoners.'[73] Dedem then led the rest of his brigade in the footsteps of Murat's cavalry, moving through Moscow's eastern suburbs.

Meanwhile, Sebastiani, unwilling to spill blood unnecessarily, tried to reason with the Russians at the Nikolskaya Tower. He saw a young man standing nearby and, on inquiring if he spoke French, discovered the man was in fact a Frenchman residing in Moscow. The young man was asked to convince the Russians to give up their arms but he was answered with musket fire, which prompted Sebastiani to order his men to charge; about a dozen Russians were sabred, while the rest fell to the ground and surrendered.[74] A letter written by an anonymous Russian provides gruesome details of how the encounter turned into a massacre: 'As the [Allies] entered the Kremlin, they found Russians holding weapons at the Arsenal, and shouted at them to drop the weapons at once; many Russians, not comprehending what they were asked to do, thought that the enemy wanted to take their weapons, and reached out their hands to give them the arms. These evil men [Allies], however, slaughtered them at once, which caused a terrible commotion as residents fled in horror in all directions, shouting that the French had entered Moscow.'[75] Likewise Andrei Karfachevskii, a postal official, noted that the Allied troops 'ordered the running populace to throw away their weapons and say "pardon". Anyone who resisted or who did not understand their language was stabbed and cut down mercilessly.'[76] But the fighting was not completely one-sided and some Russians did fight back to some effect. Vasilii Perovskii later met a French officer, his face and right leg bandaged, who recounted a frenzied attack he endured at the Kremlin. 'There was a crowd of armed residents, who fired a few shots and wounded several men in [Murat's] suite. The French had barely had time to recover from this surprise when these wild men charged with shouts of "hurrah!" … A large and strong Russian man [*muzhik*] rushed towards [the French officer], stabbed him with a bayonet in the leg, dragged him by the foot from his horse, sat on top of him and began to gnaw on his face. [The Frenchman's comrades] tried to drag him away but it proved to be impossible so he was sabred instead … The furious Frenchman assured me that the man reeked of alcohol.'[77]

With the gates opened and their path cleared, the Allied forces also entered the Kremlin through the Troitskaya and Borovitskaya Towers with 'music blaring';[78] moving across the fortress, they then emerged through the Spasskaya Tower into Kitai-gorod.[79] Sebastiani made the young Frenchman, whom he had encountered in the street, lead his troops in the footsteps of the retreating Russian army to the Rogozhskaya barrier.[80] Along the way the Allied troops passed by many wooden market stalls that were already wrecked, their merchandize scattered in disorder and thrown on the ground. It seems the Russian perpetrators of this pillage had over-indulged on their alcoholic booty, and they lay drunk and unconscious in the streets. Some of the Allied troopers realized that these men had brandy in their canteens; not allowed to dismount, they 'got the ingenious idea of using the points of their sabres to cut the cords [of the canteens] and snatch them up'.[81] On the outskirts of Moscow Sebastiani's men encountered

> several regiments of Russian dragoons, some in line, others riding slowly onwards. We approached them with the friendliest intentions, which they responded to. Officers and men went up to each other, shook hands, lent each other their water-bottles filled with brandy and chatted as best they could. This, however, did not last long, for a Russian officer of high rank, accompanied by his aides, appeared and very severely put an end to these conversations. So we remained in place while the Russians slowly withdrew. But at least we had time to notice that peace would be as welcome to them as to ourselves.[82]

The appearance of the Allied advanced guard at the Rogozhskaya and Pokrovskaya barriers greatly alarmed Miloradovich, who became concerned for the safety of the main army and believed that the Allies had acted contrary to the truce that he had concluded with Murat. He was 'much surprised, having hardly taken up his position behind the city, to see two regiments of the enemy's light cavalry deploy before us,' Clausewitz wrote. Miloradovich immediately requested a meeting with the King of Naples, who, however, declined to appear; the Russian rearguard commander was obliged again to content himself with General Sebastiani, to whom he 'made the liveliest remonstrance against the too great rapidity of the pursuit'.[83] Young Ensign Alexander Sherbinin witnessed this meeting. 'The King of Naples and I have concluded a truce till 7 o'clock in the morning,' Miloradovich told Sebastiani. 'And yet, here you are, trying to block my movement.' The French general calmly replied that he had received no information on such an arrangement from Murat and, as Clausewitz observed, he could have also noted that the Russians 'had taken a much longer time to move out than the French had anticipated'.

Nevertheless, this meeting led to both parties agreeing not to fight, and Sebastiani pledged to let the Russian stragglers and transports pass through. At one moment he even pointed towards a long line of transports moving on the road and teasingly told Miloradovich, 'You should admit that we are very kind people – all of this could have been ours.' 'You are mistaken,' Miloradovich countered. 'It would have been yours only over my dead body, while one hundred thousand Russians who stand behind me would have quickly avenged my death.'[84]

After the meeting ended, the Russian rearguard slowly continued its retreat and was about 3 miles away from the city when Miloradovich received the alarming news that two Russian dragoon squadrons[85] were cut off by French cavalry. In an act of remarkable daring and valour, Miloradovich, without guards or a trumpeter to call for a flag of truce, galloped through the Allied outposts and once more greeted Sebastiani, who was doubtless startled by his appearance; then, notwithstanding the fact that he was surrounded by Allied troops, Miloradovich commanded the trapped Russian dragoons to march forward and led them through the Allied troops.[86] By nightfall the Russian rearguard had taken up positions a few miles from Moscow, from where they could see 'how the city gradually emptied itself through the gates on either side on an endless stream of light transports, without being interrupted by the French for several hours. The Cossacks seemed rather to be yet in possession of these portions of the city while the French advanced guard occupied itself solely with the Russian rearguard. We also saw wreaths of smoke rising from several places in the furthest suburb, which were the result of the confusion that prevailed there.'[87] Murat, meanwhile, deployed his forces on the eastern outskirts of the city, covering the Pokrovskaya, Rogozhskaya, Prolomnaya and Semenovskaya barriers, and establishing a chain of outposts from the Ryazan road to the St Petersburg road.

Napoleon, back at the Dorogomilovskaya barrier, remained anxious about the whole situation. The eerie abandonment of the city had certainly affected him. It was not merely that Russian army but 'the population, the whole of Russia, that retired at our approach,' Ségur commented. 'And together with that population, the emperor saw gliding from his grasp one of the most powerful means of conquest.'[88] Napoleon certainly could enter Moscow but, with no municipal delegation offering him the city's keys, it would look as though he were entering furtively under the cover of darkness instead of in a blaze of triumph. Besides, Durosnel's report spoke about the spread of disorder and the numerous Russian soldier-stragglers still present in the city, which made it unsafe for the emperor to enter it. Instead Napoleon decided to inspect his divisions and make arrangements for securing Moscow. He briefly passed the barrier and went to the other side of the Moscow river before returning. Around 6pm Antoine-Augustin-Flavien Pion des Loches, a major in the Guard foot artillery, saw him 'watching us cross the [Dorogomilovskaya] bridge. He was surrounded by generals but nowhere near him did I see a single Russian.'[89] Muralt's Bavarian chevau-légers had also moved across the bridge, where they saw 'the emperor, wearing his chasseur uniform, with the usual four chasseurs posted in a square around him, strolling to and fro with hands clasped behind his back and talking to the prince of Neuchatel'.[90] Aart Kool, the Dutch engineer in Davout's 1st Corps, also recalled seeing Napoleon 'walking back and forth, restlessly, for over two hours. The Polish generals and officers, who had been sent to the city, came back empty-handed.'[91]

Dressed in their parade uniforms, the Italians, Germans and Poles were eager to enter Moscow, but had to wait till the morrow. 'Everyone was excited by the proximity of the city and by hopes of peace but also annoyed over the slight inflicted on us by the Guard, whom we regarded as mere parade ground troops,' derisively commented Lieutenant Carl Anton Wilhelm Wedel. At least they 'were near enough to admire the city's immense extent – its domes of a thousand colours and the endless variety of its numerous edifices. We had looked forward to this day as one of our happiest for we had expected it to mark the end of our labours, and that the victory [at Borodino] and the capture of Moscow would finish the war.'[92] To their great disappointment, Napoleon ordered the 1st, 3rd, 4th and 5th Corps to stop on the outskirts of the city: '[we] were expressly forbidden to enter Moscow,' remembered a colonel of the 4th Regiment of the 3rd Corps.[93] But many disobeyed the order since they were 'too young, too foolhardy and too hungry'.[94]

At around 3pm, the Young Guard under Marshal Mortier was instructed to enter Moscow.[95] 'The order "*Garde-à-vous!*" was now given, preceded by a roll of drums from the Guard, the signal for entering the town. We made our entrance marching in close columns, the bands playing in front.'[96] Inside the city the Guardsmen were surprised not to 'see a living soul' in the streets and homes. Some were upset that there was no one to see the Imperial Guard in all its splendour and 'listen to our band playing "*La victoire est a nous*".'[97] They could not understand this total silence and imagined that the inhabitants, not daring to show themselves, were peeping at them from behind their shutters. 'I realized that the city had been abandoned,' remembered one of them, 'and I still laugh at the sententious tone of Captain Lefrançois as he proclaimed, "No one abandons a great city, these *canailles* seem to be hiding. We will find them all right, we will see them at our feet."'[98] But the early signs were not encouraging. Sergeant Scheltens saw 'huge flocks of black birds, crows and ravens, swarming around the churches and palaces, lending the whole scene a most sinister aspect'. The first thing that struck Louis Joseph Vionnet de Maringone on entering Moscow was 'the sadness that I witnessed painted on the faces of those individuals who had stayed behind. I observed many of them weeping bitterly.'[99] 'The solitude and the silence which greeted us [in the city] calmed down in a disagreeable way the frenzy of happiness which had made our blood race a few moments before, and caused it to be replaced by a vague sense of anxiety,' recalled Fantin des Odoards.[100]

This anxiety was certainly exacerbated by occasional attacks by the few remaining Muscovites. 'As we were crossing the [Dorogomilovskii] bridge leading from the suburbs to the city itself,' wrote Sergeant Bourgogne, 'a man crept out from under the bridge … He was muffled up in a sheepskin cape, long grey hair fell down on to his shoulders, and a thick white beard came down to his waist. He brandished a three-pronged pitchfork and looked like Neptune rising from the sea.' Seeing a drum major in his smart uniform and lace, the man seems to have mistaken him for a general and charged at him with his pitchfork. The drum major dodged the blow and gave the old man a hefty kick, sending him into the river. Moments later, more Russians appeared, some of whom tried opening fire at the Young Guard but, since they did not wound anyone and most had 'only wooden flintlocks to their muskets', Bourgogne and his comrades simply contented themselves with taking their weapons from them and breaking them.[101] Lieutenant Heinrich von Brandt remembered encountering a

gigantic Russian who, as we were filing by, dashed out of one house and made for another over the road. As he crossed the street he knocked into some of our soldiers and an officer, who drew his sword. The man, who seemed rather wild, opened his coat and shouted, 'Plunge your steel into this Russian bosom!' As we had been ordered to treat the inhabitants with courtesy, we let him be and he disappeared into the house, slamming the door shut behind him. 'If they are all like that,' a sergeant said, 'our troubles have only just begun.'[102]

The Young Guard[103] reached the Kremlin at around 5pm and, 'turning sharp to the left, [we] entered a larger and finer street than the one we had left, leading to the Place du Gouvernement', where Governor Rostopchin's mansion was located.[104] Mortier chose his lodgings with an apothecary, who 'spoke French and seemed to be very learned', and whose house was on the corner of the street in front of the governor's palace.[105] Meanwhile, the Young Guard settled down in and around the Place du Gouvernement and the Kremlin, where, as Pion des Loches observed, 'the regiments that preceded [my artillery company] formed themselves as for battle in one of the public places'.[106] Vionnet de Maringone of the Fusilier-Grenadiers busied himself 'placing guards and sentries at all the public houses, stores of food, the Stock Exchange, the Bank and at the orphanage that had the appearance of a palace and contained considerable supplies'. The rest of the division was deployed inside the Kremlin and on the Kuznetskii bridge over the Neglinnaya river (north of the Kremlin), which the French called 'le Pont des Maréchaux'.[107]

As night descended on Moscow, Napoleon made preliminary arrangements for the occupation of the city. Marshal Mortier became the governor of the Moscow province, General Antoine Durosnel the military commandant, and Jean-Baptiste Barthelemy de Lesseps, formerly the French Consul General at St Petersburg, the intendant.[108] According to Ségur, when Napoleon appointed Mortier as the governor he told him, 'Above all, no pillage! For this you shall be answerable to me with your life. Defend Moscow against all, whether friend or foe.' A special proclamation was issued to the residents of Moscow requiring them to register with the French authorities and provide information on the available financial, military and supply resources.[109] At last, at around 7pm, Napoleon – 'shrugging his shoulders and exclaiming with that scornful air with which he crushed everything that opposed his wishes, "Ah! The Russians know not yet the effect the capture of their capital will produce on them!"'[110] – passed through the Dorogomilovskaya barrier and took up temporary residence in an abandoned building, which Caulaincourt described as 'a wretched tavern, built of wood, at the entrance to the suburb', although Bausset found it 'a fine wooden house'.[111] Whatever building it was, Napoleon's first valet Louis Constant Wairy found it 'so dirty and miserable that the next morning we found in [Napoleon's] bed and clothing a sort of vermin [lice] that is very common in Russia'.

'It was a gloomy night,' Ségur recalled. The building had a malodorous smell which caused Napoleon, who had a very acute sense of smell, to call out to his valet every minute to 'burn some vinegar; I cannot endure this frightful odour; it is torturing me and I cannot sleep'. So Constant spent the night burning vinegar and aloe wood, but Napoleon still could not sleep.[112] But he had more pressing concerns than the disagreeable odour of his temporary shelter. Eighty-two days had passed since the Grande Armée crossed the Niemen and in that time it had marched over 800 miles deep into Russia and lost two-thirds of its manpower without any prospect of victory or peace in the near future. At least Napoleon could now claim Moscow, and he hoped that the city's occupation would erase all the previous disappointments and provide the impetus to force Alexander to sue for peace. Alas, even this wish proved to be fleeting, for, as Caulaincourt noted, 'at about eleven o'clock in the evening news came that the city's [main] Market was on fire' and the blaze quickly spread through the city's wooden buildings. The Moscow fire had begun.

Emperor Alexander learned about the abandonment of the former Russian capital from letters written by Rostopchin and Kutuzov between 13 and 16 September. He was thunderstruck by the news. Kutuzov's first report on the outcome of Borodino had claimed a victory over Napoleon and contained many self-congratulatory lines, including one that described the Cossacks having been sent 'in pursuit of the enemy' and driving the enemy rearguard 'eleven verstas from the village of Borodino'. The news of this victory was rapturously celebrated throughout St Petersburg, where church bells pealed forth and trumpets blared. It seemed the war would be over soon and, taken in by Kutuzov's embellished dispatch, Alexander hurriedly arranged celebrations for a major victory. Just days later he learned the bitter truth. On 10 September Kutuzov wrote a short message informing the emperor that, due to heavy losses, he was compelled to withdraw the army eastwards.[113] Thereafter the shrewd commander-in-chief lapsed into a silence that he did not break until after the fall of Moscow. It was Rostopchin's aggrieved letter that made the situation clear. Complaining that Kutuzov's silence 'aggravates my astonishment', Alexander immediately dispatched one of his aides-de-camp to the main Russian army to ascertain 'the reasons that impelled [Kutuzov] to such an unfortunate resolution'.[114] Learning a lesson from the Borodino celebration fiasco, the emperor chose to keep the Petersburgers in the dark as to the full extent of the disaster unfolding in Moscow. Yet, the government's decision to evacuate some imperial institutions, including the Hermitage Palace and the voluminous state archives, only contributed to the growing anxiety in the capital.[115] Joseph de Maistre, the Sardinian envoy in Russia, was convinced that Russia's official capital would soon fall, proclaiming 'There is no more Russia! Behind us there is nothing left but Spitsbergen [island in the Arctic Ocean].' Many members of the court and nobility chose to pack their prize belongings into trunks and transport them to remote eastern regions for safekeeping. Their actions further increased the public nervousness in the capital. 'Everyone lived, as the saying has it, on axle-grease,' recalled Vasily Marchenko, a senior official in His Majesty's Personal Chancellery. 'Whoever could do so kept at least two horses in reserve, while others had hidden boats ready to leave via the canals, which were especially dyked up for their use.'[116]

Chapter 5

'And Moscow, Mighty City, Blaze!'[1]

The Grande Armée longed for rest after a prolonged campaign and hoped to enjoy some comforts, and obtain peace by means of its possession of Moscow – failing that, good winter billets in case the war should be prolonged. Those troops that entered the city occupied quarters at their own discretion. Colonel Hubert-François Biot, aide-de-camp to General Claude Pierre Pajol of the 2nd Reserve Cavalry Corps, remembered General Durosnel informing him that 'in the absence of the municipal authorities that have left the city, we have to act without consulting the hosts. We can no longer think of regular cantonment and everyone should find lodgings as he sees fit.'[2] The Imperial Guard took up quarters inside the Kremlin, with major outposts deployed at squares around it. *Intendant-Général* Daru, accompanied by Mathieu Dumas, lodged at the Mukhanovs' house located on the corner of the Place du Gouvernement. 'It was a large house built of hewn stone, of a rather bad architecture but conveniently arranged and well decorated,' Dumas recalled. 'I found two servants in the kitchen on the ground floor and they led me to the apartment. Everything was in good order as if the master of the house was expected to arrive any time now.'[3] An artillery company commander recalled that after his men had settled in near the Kremlin, he was accosted by a man who said he was French and offered the hospitality of his house. The stranger's wife also proved to be French and she treated Pion des Loches and his comrades to vermicelli soup, a large rib-piece of beef, some macaroni and a few bottles of excellent Bordeau wine. 'In my life, perhaps, I have never had a better meal,' Pion des Loches later reminisced. The hostess 'entertained us with the riches and luxury of Moscow, and the pleasures which awaited us in winter. "There are so many palaces here," she said, "that you can have one each."'[4] Indeed, both officers and the rank-and-file were only too eager to enjoy the palatial homes of wealthy Muscovites. Senior officers were often greeted at the gates of palaces by servants in livery, offering hospitality in the hopes of sparing themselves and their master's property a worse fate.

In the northwest Viceroy Eugène's corps initially took up positions near the village of Chernaya Gryaz' but some of Eugène's troops did enter the city on 14 September and established outposts near the Armenian Church of the Dormition of the Theotokos in Presnya, protecting the routes to Tver and Zvenigorod.[5] But most of the corps entered Moscow on the 15th. Labaume wrote

> At daybreak our corps marched upon Moscow. On approaching the city we noticed that it was not surrounded by walls, and that a simple parapet of earth alone marked its boundary. So far there had been nothing to show that the capital was inhabited, and the suburb by which we arrived was so deserted that not only was there no Muscovite to be seen, but not even a French soldier. Not a sound was heard in the midst of this awful solitude. A vague apprehension oppressed every mind ...[6]

Albrecht Adam, an artist who had been assigned to the staff of the 4th Corps, also commented on the 'deserted and desolate streets, and an eerie silence that hung heavily over the city, broken only by the thud of horses' hooves while the drums and trumpets echoed in the deserted streets. Officers and soldiers looked at each other in bewilderment, shaking their heads. What a stark contrast to the pompous reception accorded to the same army in the capitals of Germany, Italy and Spain!'[7] Viceroy Eugène himself was appalled by the fires that he believed the Russians intentionally set in 'twenty places' – 'one cannot act more barbarian', he confided to his wife.[8]

Eugène's troops occupied the Presnenskaya, Sushevskaya and Meschanskaya districts in the north of Moscow,[9] and the Viceroy himself took up his quarters in the palace of Prince Mamonov.[10] 'This quarter', recalled one of his staff officers, 'was one of the finest in the city, formed entirely of splendid edifices and of houses which, although built of wood, appeared to us to be of an astonishing wealth and grandeur. The magistrates having abandoned their post, everyone was at liberty to establish himself in one of their palaces, so that the obscurest officer found himself lodged in the midst of vast and richly decorated apartments, of which he might look upon himself as the owner, seeing that the only person to be found in the place was an obsequious porter, who, with trembling hand, delivered to him all the keys of the house.'[11] Cesare de Laugier, serving in Viceroy Eugène's Italian Corps, recalled that he and his comrades had been 'lodged in military fashion. The Viceroy gave the regiments the order and the officers who were to implement it indicated the lodgings in charcoal, in capital letters, on each dwelling's front door. Thus, new names for each street and square were designated, each being known as 'such or such company's street,' or 'such and such a battalion's quarter ...''[12] Next to the 4th Corps was Marshal Davout's 1st Corps, which took control of the western suburbs of Moscow, including the Khamovnicheskaya, Arbatskaya, Novinskaya and Presnenskaya districts. Michel Ney's 3rd Corps crossed the city to take up positions in the eastern Taganskaya district. While Sebastiani remained in the eastern part of Moscow, Grouchy's 3rd Cavalry Corps moved up to the Sushevskaya district in the northwest. The retired Russian Major General Molosov was returning home along Malaya Dmitrievka street when he was accosted by two dragoons (probably from La Houssaye's 6th Heavy Cavalry Division), who tried to rob him of his horse. Later in the day, looking out of the windows of his house, he could see 'enemy squadrons marching by platoons in good order. None of them had sabres unsheathed and some were even singing songs.'[13]

Meanwhile, Poniatowski's 5th Corps made a triumphant entry into the city. The Poles initially held the Yakimanskaya district in the south but were then redeployed to the northeastern districts; General Claparede's Polish division was moved to the Pokrovskaya barrier and occupied the nearby Pokrovskii (Intercession) Monastery. One wonders what these Poles felt as they entered the former capital of the empire that had destroyed their homeland just seventeen years earlier. They certainly understood the significance of this occasion and at least one of them thought of their ancestors who had captured and held Moscow in 1610–1612. 'As I came to the [Moskvoretskii] bridge near the Kremlin,' recalled Josef Zalusky of the 1st Guard Lancers, 'I stopped there, thinking about the executions of my compatriots, companions of [False] Dmitri, about the anniversary of 1612 and the massacres of Praga [in 1794].'[14] Returning to his quarters, Zalusky discovered that Dominique Radziwill, the scion of the fabulously rich and influential Polish noble family, and soon to be a major in his regiment, had recovered his ancestor's sword from the Kremlin. The Polish officers examined it 'with emotion', but the sight of the 'rows of Polish culverins and cannon, stamped with the coats of arms of the Polish kingdom and of various Polish families' lined up inside the Kremlin left a far greater impression on them.[15]

Leading the advanced guard to the Pokrovskaya and Spasskaya barriers, Marshal Murat – wearing a typically extravagant uniform of 'crimson pantaloons, sky-blue stockings and green short tunic'[16] – noticed the magnificent estate of manufacturer Ivan Batashov on the Vshivaya Gora; entering the house, he informed its manager, Maxim Sakov, that he had decided to lodge at the estate. After deploying his forces, Murat returned 'around 7 o'clock in the evening accompanied by some thirty generals and numerous officials'. Sakov had the servants prepare dinner but could not get 'any white bread or bread rolls since the bakeries throughout Moscow had been destroyed and abandoned'. So Sakov had to serve dark rye bread, though he managed to get a quarter of polar cod (*saika*) for Murat. 'The generals were initially furious at this scant offering and grumbled that only swine would eat such bread, but as they were very hungry, they still devoured it.' After dinner Murat toured the estate, which he found to his liking; he inquired about the estate and its owner, and then settled down for the night. Sakov recalled that 'Every general demanded a soft bed and separate accommodation. Although there were sufficient bedrooms, we did not have enough beds since no one wanted to sleep on a peasant's bedding and so they all used threats to get what they wanted. They dragged us back and forth like a cat by its tail throughout the night. Candles in chandeliers and lanterns were kept burning through the night – it was dangerous to leave them alight but we did not dare to extinguish them.'[17]

A few fires were already burning as the Russians evacuated the city. Shortly after midday Bestuzhev-Riumin, venturing outside the Senate Building, complained about the 'appalling stench' caused by a fire that had been ignited by some unidentified 'prince' in the chandlers' row in Kitai-gorod, which had consumed a few paint and wax shops.[18] Napoleon's secretary Agathon-Jean-François Fain noted that 'a few fires broke out from the very first moments of our entry into the city'[19] – Muralt and his comrades could indeed see 'several billowing columns of smoke' rising above the buildings in the northern parts of Moscow.[20] It was 8pm when Bestuzhev-Riumin, still in the Senate building inside the Kremlin, saw flames rising in Kitai-gorod.[21] At the same time Peter Chudimov, the archivist of the Mining Department, also saw a 'building across the Moscow river' on fire.[22]

Eyewitnesses suggest that the fires began in the trade rows of Kitai-gorod, in or around the Merchant Court (often referred to in French memoirs as the Bourse or Grand Bazaar) and in the *Solyanka* (or salted-fish market). But the precise timing of the outbreaks varies from early afternoon to late evening. Maxim Sakov recalled seeing fires in the Skobyanye and Moskatelnye trade rows and the *Novyi* Merchant Court (located across from the Nikolskii and Spasskii gates of the Kremlin) at around 9pm, while an hour later Maxim Nevzorov, director of typography at the University of Moscow, saw fires burning 'in the *Solyanka*, near the Church of the Nativity, but fires then appeared in various places as well'.[23] At about the same time Pion des Loches and his officers, still 'in an ecstasy of joy' after hearing stories of Moscow's wealth, saw their French host, 'who had left us for an instant, returning completely terrified. He cried as he trembled, "Ah gentlemen, what a misfortune! The Bourse is burning!" – "What is the Bourse?" – "A building larger than the Palais Royal [in Paris], full of goldsmiths; work and jewellery, the richest productions of the world. The loss this night will be incalculable.'"[24] Meanwhile, back at the Kremlin, Major Vionnet de Maringone of the Young Guard's Fusiliers-Grenadiers visited the posts that he had placed in the neighbouring streets. It was around midnight when, arriving at one near the Merchant Court, he saw 'thick smoke but no fire' coming out of the building. His men told him that they had seen smoke earlier as well but thought nothing of it, assuming a few remaining Russians were warming themselves by the fire; all the entrances were firmly shut and there was no evidence that the Allied troops had got into the building to cause a fire. Just as he was conversing with his men, however, Vionnet de Maringone saw flames over the building; rushing back to his camp, he rallied about a hundred men. By the time they returnmed the building was ablaze. Though there was no wind, his men struggled to contain the fire because they could not break down the doors and they lacked equipment and pumps, all of which had been removed by the retreating Russians. Marshal Mortier, finding it hard to believe that the Russians had deliberately set the building on fire, came in person to inspect it and to confirm that no Allied troops had broken into it. It took Vionnet de Maringone and his men some four hours of back-breaking labour to contain the fire but the Merchant Court was saved. Doubtless pleased with his accomplishment but 'extremely tired and barely standing on my feet', Vionnet de Maringone returned to his campsite hoping for some rest. At dawn, however, he was woken up by the news that fire had broken out in another part of the Merchant Court. 'I went in haste to the scene,' he recalled. 'My men made extraordinary efforts to contain the fire, which they did at around noon [on 15 September]. Everyone hoped that this would be the end of our troubles since we were dead tired. Alas, we soon became witnesses to a spectacle more horrible than anything we could imagine.'[25]

It was shortly after 6pm when Bourgogne, who was bivouacked with his comrades near the governor's mansion, saw 'on our right, a thick smoke, then a whirl of flames, not knowing whence it came. We were told the fire was in the Bazaar [Merchant Court], the merchants' quarter. "They are probably freebooters," we were told, "who have carelessly set fire to the shops in searching for provisions."' By 7pm, however, the fire had spread to the Place du Gouvernement, prompting a Guard officer to order that a small patrol of men should leave at once. Bourgogne was among those who 'went in the direction of the fire, but we had hardly gone three hundred steps before we heard some firing on our right'. The shots came from a blind alley and claimed a few wounded among the Allies, who advanced to the house where the firing came from, beat in the door, and came face to face with nine Russians armed with lances and muskets. The two groups plunged into a fierce hand-to-hand combat but it was an unequal struggle, with the nineteen Allies against nine Russians, who 'were drunk with the brandy they had found in quantities, so that they were like madmen'. Attempting to return to the Place du Gouvernement, Bourgogne was surprised 'to find this impossible, the fire having spread to such an enormous extent! To right and left was one wreath of flames, the wind was blowing hard, and the roofs were falling in.' Taking another course, this small group found shelter at a 'magnificent palace', where they wandered about in vast and beautiful rooms for more than an hour before hearing a terrible explosion. 'The shock was so great that we felt certain of being crushed under the ruins of the palace,' Bourgogne recalled. After a quick search they discovered that 'a bomb had been concealed in an earthenware stove', which caused significant damage to the palace and set it on fire. 'The smoke was bursting out in several places thick and black, then it became red, and finally the whole building was in flames. At the end of a quarter of an hour the roof, made of coloured and varnished iron, fell in with a frightful noise, bringing with it three-quarters of the entire building.'

At the *Solyanka* the fires threatened the nearby Foundlings Home that was established in 1763 on the initiative of I. Betskii 'to receive and take care of foundlings and homeless children'. The Home, operating under the exalted patronage of the Dowager Empress Maria Fedorovna, occupied a massive building on the bank of the Moscow river. The director of this institution, State Councillor Ivan Tutolmin, had appealed several times to Governor Rostopchin to make arrangements for the evacuation of the remaining orphans but his requests had been effectively ignored; on the eve of the Allied occupation it housed 586 children, including 275 toddlers, and had a staff of over 500 people.[26] Tutolmin, tasked with protecting hundreds of children, many of whom had not turned 11 years old yet, struggled valiantly to protect his institution amidst the disorder and pillaging. In the evening the fires erupting in the neighbouring districts threatened the Foundlings Home, prompting Tutolmin to seek help from the Allied forces, whom he saw busy mastering the blazes. He managed to get to the Kremlin and contacted General Durosnel, who immediately ordered a safeguarding picket of twelve gendarmes and an officer to be posted at the Home.[27] Throughout the night Tutolmin and the gendarmes, assisted by the Foundlings Home's remaining officials and even children, fought to protect the building from fire. Their efforts were considerably facilitated by the presence of the institution's fire equipment, which had not been removed despite Rostopchin's orders.[28]

Sometime after 7pm a colossal explosion rocked the Yauza river area, east of the Kremlin. Climbing on to the roof of her house, Madame Fusil, an actress attached to the French company in Moscow, saw 'a strange object resembling a flaming sword', while *Abbé* Adrien Surugue, who had been in charge of the Church of St-Louis des Français since 1808, recorded in his diary that, just as the Russian evacuation of the city was completed, 'a fiery ball appeared near the Yauza river, serving as an ominous sign to those remaining ... Near the Petrovskii bridge, a large house filled with alcohol, which belonged to the Wine Merchants' Court [*Vinnyi dvor*], was also consumed by fire, which spread to the neighbouring storehouse, completely destroying it.'[29] Ségur also recalled that 'the very first night, a fireball had settled on the palace of Trubetskoi and consumed it', while General Dedem der Gelder described hearing 'a violent detonation' from the direction of the Kaluzhskaya barrier and thought 'it was a powder magazine the enemy was blowing up. It seems to have been an agreed signal, for a moment afterwards I saw several rockets going up, and half an hour later fire broke out in various quarters of the town, notably in the Vladimirskii suburb.'[30] It was probably these 'rockets' that Charles de Quaij, the Dutch captain of the grenadiers in the Imperial Guard, described in his letter to his parents, noting, 'as we reached the city barrier, we saw fireworks in the city. We thought that the French inhabitants were welcoming His Majesty [Napoleon], but we were mistaken.'[31] The explosion was so powerful that Sergei Glinka, miles away from the city, heard a 'crash like thunder and [saw] a flame shooting up into the sky'. Heinrich von Roos and his Württemberg comrades, who had bivouacked in the eastern suburbs of Moscow, beside the road leading to Vladimir and Kazan, also heard 'a sudden and terrible explosion' and thought it was either 'an ammunition magazine or the so-called infernal machine of a large size'. It seemed to them that the explosion occurred in the centre of the town, 'though it is hard to be sure of one's sense of direction at night'. It was an explosion of veritable strength, causing 'an enormous jet of flames' from which balls of fire were coming out in various trajectories as if a mass of bombs and shells had been simultaneously thrown up.

> The explosion lasted three or four minutes and spread fear and terror among us. It seemed that this was a signal for starting fires to destroy the city. At first, the fire was restricted to the area where [the explosion] had occurred but a few minutes later we saw flames rising in various parts of the city. Soon we could count eighteen seats of fire, then more. We were all stricken dumb with amazement, looking at each other and seemingly sharing the same thought. Staff Captain V. Reinhardt finally gave voice to this general feeling, 'This is an ominous sign, one that puts an end to our hope of peace, the peace we all need so much!'[32]

These explosions resulted from Russian efforts to destroy any remaining military ammunition and other resources, a process that both Kutuzov and Rostopchin encouraged. A month after the conflagration Kutuzov told Napoleon's envoy that he had 'ordered the destruction of some magazines', while the subsequent investigation into the loss of state property noted that 'the remaining barges that were to sail in the wake of artillery barges but had been delayed by them and therefore could not be saved from the enemy, had been burnt and sunk on the orders of the late Prince Kutuzov'.[33] Rostopchin's orders required police officials, led by Constable P. Voronenko, to destroy any remaining artillery and commissariat supplies that had been loaded on to barges but not removed in time. Voronenko's report reveals that 'at 5am on 14 September Rostopchin ordered me to go to the Wine Merchants' Court [*Vinnyi dvor*] and Customs Office [*Mytnyi dvor*] and evacuate the state and private barges located near the Krasnyi hill and the Simonov Monastery; in the event of the enemy's prompt entry into the city, I was instructed to destroy everything with fire, which I did in various places until 10 o'clock in the evening.' Voronenko's reference to the instructions 'to destroy everything with fire' is often cited out of context, creating the impression that he was directly ordered to destroy the city as a whole. But in fact the report refers to Rostopchin's instructions to destroy military equipment and supplies so as to prevent their falling into enemy hands. Similarly, P. Kaptsevich, who commanded the 7th Infantry Division, reported that 'two ammunition magazines were blown up on the orders of General Miloradovich, causing a horrendous explosion'.[34] Sergei Glinka concurs that the explosions, at least those near the Simonov Monastery, were caused by Russian efforts to destroy barges loaded with commissariat supplies. This monastery alone contained over 8,500 *puds* of lead and almost 6,000 *puds* of gunpowder, which could not be simply abandoned to the enemy.[35]

Late at night the wind rose, carrying burning wreckage across the city and scattering it through the wood-built suburbs, where the conflagration began and rapidly spread. The young F. Becker, whose family resided near the Nikitskie Gates, was awoken late at night by his father, who ordered the family members to get dressed and leave the house at once. As he came out into the street, Becker was stunned by the 'hellish vision of the entire right side of the Arbat consumed by flames ... Trees on the boulevard were swaying from the powerful wind and it was impossible to see where the fire ended.' The family chose to move northwards, away from the flames, and walked for most of the night before resting near the Red Gates. 'We beheld a stunning view – the entire horizon, as far as the eye could see, had turned into a bright and fiery sea! The cupolas of the nearby churches appeared like some shadowy giants rising against this blazing background.'[36]

Earlier that evening (14 September) Baron de Bausset and General Count Phillippe de Ségur had been sent to inspect the Kremlin.[37] They reached the Kremlin at around 10pm, accompanied by employees of all the services so as to settle them in and prepare everything for Napoleon's reception. 'As on all these missions we had been unable to fetch our servants and carriages,' Bausset recalled. 'Ségur and I were obliged to spend the night fully clothed and stretched out on chairs or armchairs ... Between midnight and one o'clock I noticed fairly bright glows, though they were some distance away. I went to the windows and saw flames leaping up in whichever direction I looked from the eminence of the Kremlin.'[38] By then Paymaster B.-T. Duverger of the 1st Corps, resting in the western part of the city, had been abruptly awakened by 'some lamentable cries'; running out of his quarters, he was stunned to see 'the horizon entirely crimson, and the fire, moving in all directions, sounding like distant torrents'.[39] Nearby Boulart's artillery crew was surprised to see

a fire, then a second one, then a third, closer and closer, followed by a new one. These diverse fires, whose propagation nothing arrested, spread so rapidly and prodigiously that even though they began in the part of the city furthest away from us, it was easy to read by their light. Before daybreak, the fire seemed to have consumed at least half a league from right to left ... and burned in different shades of colour, from red to blue, depending on the materials it consumed. Black clouds of smoke rose above them, creating a horrific picture [and] reminding us of the fires of Troy and Rome. I was deeply affected by this sight, as was everyone else around me.[40]

Anatole de Montesquiou-Fezensac was awakened late at night by the French painter with whom he had found lodgings, who informed him about the fires. 'Just what I feared,' the painter told him, pointing at the illuminated windowpanes. Looking out of the window, Montesquiou saw flames rising some distance away but tried to downplay their significance. 'It is a misfortune common to warfare,' he calmly commented, 'Our soldiers are often careless.'[41] Similarly, Fain recalled that, despite receiving reports of the initial fires, 'we had attributed them to the carelessness of our soldiers'.[42]

Despite Napoleon's efforts, the Allied occupation of Moscow was almost immediately marred by plundering and abuses. Peter Chudimov, the archivist of the Mining Department, reported that almost as soon as the 'French' arrived at the Kremlin, they 'came to my apartments with swords unsheathed and began breaking cabinets, drawer chests and coffers, taking clothing and money ... depriving us of everything except for undershirts'. The soldiers broke down the doors of the archive rooms and tore through the leather-bound folios, scattering them all across the building; in the Proofing Section, which was responsible for the quality of items made of precious metals, all 'state and factory coffers were broken into and their contents completely looted'.[43]

The pillaging seems to have been an inevitable consequence: the municipal authorities were gone, a proper military administration had not yet been set up and the exasperated troops thirsted for loot. As one participant rightly noted, in these early hours 'no precautions of any kind had been taken to curb the disorders' unfolding in the city.[44] Durosnel, whose 'gendarmes were quite insufficient to cope' with the disorder that began to break out, 'asked the emperor for more troops, informing him that all the houses were full of stragglers and deserters'. Napoleon instructed him to direct his requests to

Mortier, who was already concerned about losses and the fatigue of his troops, and saw no need to send them out so soon into a still unsecured town. By nightfall he had sent only 'a meagre and insufficient number of troops to Durosnel'.[45]

Despite orders to the contrary, the Allied soldiers began scouring nearby buildings for food and drink almost as soon as they reached the city. 'We were told that no one, on any pretence whatever, was to absent himself,' remembered Bourgogne. 'An hour afterwards, however, the whole place was filled with everything we could want – wines of all kinds, liqueurs, preserved fruits and an enormous quantity of sweet cakes and flour, but no bread. We went into the houses on the Place asking for food and drink, but as we found no one in them we helped ourselves.'[46] Similarly, Baron de Bourgoing, whose division was halted on the outskirts of the city, saw how 'soldiers penetrated into every building in the neighbourhood and brought back boards, furniture, carpets, creating a makeshift camp'. Among the items the soldiers brought were large wooden crates from a soap factory, which they arranged to create small shelters for the night.[47] Sergeant Scheltens, who had been billeted with twelve Guard Fusiliers-Grenadiers and two corporals under his command 'at a Frenchman's house in the Kaluga suburb', had no qualms about letting his men 'go out marauding and bringing back all kinds of foodstuffs, lots of wine and Champagne, a great deal of flour and sugar, and, above all, excellent beer. They wanted for nothing, they even had mattresses to sleep on, true luxury for men who over the years had come to appreciate the value of a good bed.'[48] A mile away from them, Pion des Loches, in charge of an artillery company that was unable to find any lodgings near the Kremlin, decided to occupy an open place on 'the road from the Kremlin to the Petrovskii palace', probably on Tverskaya street near the Strastnoi Monastery. He formed up his unit in a square, with guns at the corners and men and horses in the centre. 'I forbade the troops to separate and, having dismounted, I dispatched my lieutenants with some cannoneers into the neighbouring streets in search of provisions ...' However, they found 'doors shut and barricaded everywhere. It was necessary to break them down. In an instant the pillage began, and it was doubtless the same throughout the rest of the city.'[49]

In the late afternoon of 14 September Kicheyev's family, hoping to escape from the city, encountered two Allied soldiers, who were probably among the first men from Eugène's 4th Corps to enter the city from the northwest. The soldiers – one of them a 'young man of dashing appearance, holding no weapons but a sabre and looking like a cavalry officer' – stopped the family and searched both the dray and the people to see if they had any useful items. Compelled to return home, Kicheyev's family was disturbed at midnight by a group of German soldiers demanding to be fed; they carried with them silverware plundered from nearby churches.

And the disorder only intensified as night shrouded the city.[50] With so many buildings left empty, there was nobody to guard them against plunder and fire, whether set deliberately or accidental. As the fires broke out, many Allied officers and soldiers encamped outside the city became convinced that Moscow was lost and it was vitally necessary to replenish their nearly empty supplies while they could. Thus officers often permitted, or simply ignored, the entry of their own men into the city. 'All entry into the city had been forbidden,' recalled Colonel Montesquiou-Fezensac of the 4th Line, 'but as the pillage of the city had commenced, and with [our own resources running out] it was clear that those who came last would die of hunger. I agreed then, with the Colonel [Pelleport] of the 18th Line, that we would tacitly allow our men to take their part in the plunder. After all, it was only with great difficulty that they succeeded in procuring anything.'[51] Similarly, General Bruyères, who encountered a couple of soldiers inside the city in defiance of the imperial order, simply ignored their transgression and told them 'to go and have some fun in Moscow, if you can'.[52]

The night saw such widespread pillaging that some Allied participants thought the city was being sacked, and rumours of what was transpiring in the city prompted many of the troops deployed outside the city to enter Moscow in search of prizes. Some heard about it from 'Polish lancers who had just come through the city and informed us that it was being put to the sack. This news was confirmed by some of our men who had been sent in to collect food and had come back well stocked with tea, rum, sugar, wines and precious objects of all kinds. From then on there was no restraining the soldiers. All who were not actually on duty, disappeared ... Men sent to collect wood or straw, and even men sent out on patrol, never came back.'[53] Artillery Colonel Michel Combe was among those who chose to defy the imperial orders, and, accompanied by a friend, he ventured into the city. After wandering in the desolate streets, he finally approached 'a beautiful house where loud voices and laughter could be heard'. The door into the house was broken down and the cellar windows were brightly lit. Entering the cellar, Combe found himself inside a vaulted edifice, brightly lit by torches, where French 'artillerymen, who had already consumed copious libations, were singing loudly'. They had cause to cheer since they had hit upon a veritable treasure: a vast cellar with wines from the 'best French vineyards that thrilled us and vividly reminded us of our homeland'.[54] Less cheerful were the men of the 4th Line, who had been bivouacked outside Moscow and had to sneak into the city to procure victuals. 'In returning, they had to cross the camp of the 1st Corps, which was pitched immediately in front of our own, and could only keep their booty by a fight with these, or with the Imperial Guard, who wanted to carry off everything.'[55]

Even around the Kremlin, one Allied officer saw how 'the soldiers had been allowed to remove whatever they could from burning homes and I saw them carrying booty taken from the unfortunate [residents] because under the guise of looting the burning houses, they plundered everything else'.[56]

As they sought out places to live and things to eat and drink, the Allied soldiers broke into a great number of closed and deserted houses and shops. Once the fires broke out, Pion des Loches became concerned for the safety of his men, whom he had 'rallied as best as I could and charged them to produce the essentials, that is to say, flour, liquor and warm clothes. I myself broke in the doors of a store, and, not without trouble, had a good number of sacks of flour carried off by my cannoneers, who preferred to ransack further and search for gold.'[57] The pillaging initially targeted food shops and those selling wine and spirits, but it rapidly spread to engulf private dwellings, public buildings and churches. Physician Kozma Shirovskii of the Moscow Hospital for the Poor and Elizabeth Schroeder, the widow of another physician, both complained that just hours after entering the city the French soldiers robbed them clean, taking silverware, clocks, shirts and cash.[58] The famed Russian writer Alexander Herzen's nurse later told him stories about her experiences during the Allied occupation of Moscow, noting that at first 'two or three soldiers came and went by our house, and indicated by signs that they wanted a drink. If we gave one of them a little glass of alcohol, he would go away and say "Thank you", raising his hand to his shako. But when the fires broke out, there was terrible confusion and men began to steal and rob, and one horror followed another.'[59]

Vasilii Polyanskii recalled that soon after the Allied advanced guard reached the Kremlin, '[Allied] soldiers scattered throughout the city, many of them turning to plundering at once. Passing by the deacon's house, ten men saw a cart packed with belongings and rushed to claim them. Father Mikhail tried to defend his family possessions but the soldier struck him on the head with his sabre and he fell bleeding to the ground; while his wailing family rushed to him, the plunderers took away the horses.'[60] According to merchant Andrei Alekseyev, 'Just as they occupied the Kremlin, [the Allied troops] began to wander throughout Moscow, frequently stopping by our places. On the first occasion they looked around the room and took the icon of the Holy Mother, ripping off its silver frame and trimming …'[61] During the night of 15 September the family of Anna Kruglova made a desperate attempt to escape from the city but they were 'surrounded by a crowd of enemy soldiers who proceeded to rob us. My father was searched: he had a purse with silver coins and a wallet with a considerable sum in paper money; the soldiers took the purse but they fortunately threw away the wallet, which we immediately picked up. My father's coat was snatched, as were our bags and my mantle.'[62] With the fires spreading, the family of Alexander Herzen, who was just six months old, decided to accept an offer of refuge from Pavel Golokhvastov, who was married to Herzen's aunt, and sought shelter at his stone-built house surrounded by thick walls. So the family and servants moved 'all together without any distinction', only to discover, to their horror, that the house was already on fire and 'flames were licking out of its every window'. Terrified, they took refuge in the large garden behind the house, but 'had scarcely sat down on a seat, feeling very depressed, when a party of drunken soldiers came up. One of them accosted [Golokhvastov] and tried to take his travelling coat, but the old man resisted, so the soldier drew a large knife [*tesak*] and caught him a blow right across the face: he carried the scar for the rest of his days.' Meanwhile, other soldiers mistreated the rest of the family – one soldier snatching the baby Herzen from his nurse's arms and unfastened his nappy to see whether any money or jewels had been hidden there. 'Finding none,' the nurse recalled, 'he deliberately tore the nappy and threw it away.'[63]

'A monastery close by the city walls had largely been spared due to the fact that our general was quartered there,' recalled Brandt. 'Even so, large inroads were made on the good monks' larders and cellars. One of the monks was roughly handled when he attempted to prevent this abuse and he told me that such sacrilege could only bring us bad luck …'[64] At the Rozhdestvenskii Monastery the fall of darkness also brought unexpected visitors to the frightened priests and nuns: 'There was knocking on the gates and several voices shouted something, though we could not understand them. So the nuns went to the gates and asked what they wanted. I do not know if the [enemy had] learned a few words or if some Poles were among them, but they managed to say in broken Russian that they needed bread, butter and wine.' The priest refused to open the gates but had bread thrown over the monastery wall, explaining that 'there was "no wine and no butter here since you are at the monastery"'. But the [enemy soldiers] understood this themselves, saying "monastery" as they departed.' Less fortunate was the nearby Yegorievskii Monastery, where the Allied soldiers, following the nuns' refusal to admit them, broke down the gateway and plundered the church.[65] With many Muscovites remaining in the city, it was just a matter of time before they became willing or forced guides for the invaders; there were some who readily assisted the Allies in the hope of sharing in their spoils but others were compelled to participate in the looting. The young merchant Andrei Alekseyev recalled that 'if you encountered the enemy, they forced you to go with them to help carry the loot. I twice had to carry loot for the French, who demanded that I show them where they could find supplies. There was hardly any option but to do it – my life is more precious than anything else.'[66]

The degree of disorder and insubordination that seems to have taken over the army can be seen from the experiences of Napoleon's orderly, Count Roman Soltyk, who was quartered at the house of Countess Musina-Pushkina. Late in the evening of 14 September he had barely gone to bed when he was woken up by a commotion downstairs. As the Russian servants in the house begged him for protection, Soltyk, sabre in hand, went down to see what was happening and was surprised to see grenadiers of the Old Guard plundering the wine cellar. He tried to drive them out by declaring that a general of the imperial suite was quartered at the house but this had no effect on the grenadiers; in fact, one of them raised his fist and threatened the count. Infuriated by such insubordination among the elite soldiers, Soltyk struck the grenadier with the flat of his sabre, felling him to the ground. But it proved to be a mistake. The grenadier's comrades rushed at Soltyk with their bayonets and he barely managed to escape behind the doors, threatening to shoot the first one who entered the room.[67] One may wonder, if the elite grenadiers acted in such a disreputable fashion, what could be expected of the rest of the army?

15 September

Early in the morning of 15 September,[68] amidst the smouldering fires and continuing disorder, Napoleon, riding his favourite horse l'Emir, made a solemn but hardly triumphant entrance into Moscow, followed by the Old Guard infantry. 'His entry was not accompanied by that tumult which marks the taking possession of a great city,' recalled Napoleon's secretary Claude-François Méneval. 'No noise disturbed the solitude of the city streets, save only the rumbling of the cannon and the artillery caissons.'[69] As they moved from the Dorogomilovskaya bridge along the Arbat boulevard to Znamenka and Nikitskaya streets, and on through to the Kremlin, Napoleon and his entourage admired the city's beautiful streets and buildings. 'The city is as large as Paris,' Napoleon wrote to Empress Marie-Louise, adding a few flourishes along the way: 'There are 1600 church towers here, and over a thousand beautiful palaces; the city is provided with everything.'[70] Writing to his wife later that day, Dominique Larrey also seemed struck by the sights of the city: 'I have just arrived at the most remote city in the world and can say that this is the largest and most beautiful of the cities I have ever seen, although it is deserted and all of its inhabitants, except for a few unfortunates, have fled.'[71] Napoleon's secretary echoed these sentiments when he observed, 'Moscow seemed asleep in a deep sleep, like one of those enchanted cities of which we read in Arabian tales. The streets through which we passed were lined with houses of fine appearance for the most part, with closed windows and doors. Palaces with colonnades, churches and beautiful buildings glittering with the luxury of Europe and of Asia raised themselves side by side with very modest habitations. All bespoke the ease and wealth of a great city enriched by trade and inhabited by a wealthy and numerous aristocracy.'[72] 'Each of us was stunned by the splendour of the buildings,' noted a Dutch officer of the Imperial Guard.[73]

The French were dismayed by the sight of empty streets, closed windows and smoke billowing over some suburbs. Caulaincourt was struck by the 'gloomy silence reigning throughout the deserted city. During the whole of our long route, we did not meet a single soul.' What a dramatic difference from the triumphal entries that Napoleon had made into virtually all the capitals of Europe. 'Not a single being! What people! It is incredible!' Napoleon bemoaned. At the sight of the Kremlin, Ségur tells us, 'this half-Gothic, half-modern palace of the Rurics and the Romanovs, of their throne still standing, of the cross of the great Ivan, and of the finest part of the city, which is overlooked by the Kremlin, and which the flames, as yet confined to the bazaar, seemed disposed to spare, Napoleon's former hopes revived. His ambition was flattered by this great conquest. "At last, then," he exclaimed, "I am in Moscow, in the ancient palace of the tsars, in the Kremlin!"'

On entering the Kremlin, the emperor took up residence in the tsar's private apartments in the Kremlin palace, which had been designed and built by the famed Italian architect Francesco Bartolomeo Rastrelli in the mid-eighteenth century. The baroque-style palace was famous for its bright wall paintings and interior decorations. Inside there were three drawing-rooms and a great hall used by the Russian rulers for arranging receptions and other ceremonies. The lesser rooms were sparsely furnished and the state bedroom lacked even curtains or shutters, prompting Ségur to complain that it was 'a miserable dwelling for so powerful a sovereign'. Still, the room was well ornamented and its windows opened towards a vista of houses, domes and palaces that stretched southwards over the Moscow river. Napoleon's mamluk Ali (St-Denis) recalled that

> the emperor had a very large 'salon' at the palace of the Kremlin. This room was divided into two parts by a beam or cornice supported by two columns between which one passed from one part to the other. There was a tripod between the wall and the column on either side. The salon was ornamented with gilding, but this had become blackened by time. It was the finest room in the palace in point of richness ... The windows of the bedroom opened on the Moscow river. It was a large room, ... in the left-hand corner, made by the partition and the side opposite the windows, there was a little cylindrical desk placed diagonally across the corner ... the emperor would sit at this desk either to read or to write.[74]

Napoleon explored the palace, finding its accommodations pleasing. He had a portrait of the King of Rome hung up on a wall and at around 3pm he ventured out into the city, inspecting the vicinity of the Kremlin, including nearby bridges and the Foundlings Home. Eyewitnesses report that there were no fires in the vicinity of the Kremlin at that time and Napoleon could see only a few places in Zamoskvorechye (south of the Kremlin) where smoke was billowing upwards. Consequently the emperor considered the nocturnal fires to have been inconsequential.

There is surprisingly little specific information on what Napoleon did between 14 and 17 September.[75] We may presume that he was kept occupied as a myriad urgent tasks called for his attention. He would certainly have dealt with logistics, army organization and deployment, as well as governance in France and political affairs in Europe, and so on. He made arrangements to prepare quarters for the troops and asked for a statement of the resources available in the city. *Intendant-Général* Dumas wrote that his first care upon arriving at the Kremlin was 'to ascertain what provisions for the subsistence of the army might be found in the public stores and in private houses. I caused the magazines lining the quay between the Kremlin and the Foundlings Home to be opened in my presence.

The barrels and sacks of flour and groats in these magazines were estimated at about forty thousand *quintals*, a valuable resource which might have sufficed for a short stay.'[76] Napoleon instructed Marshal Lefebvre to deploy the Old Guard in the Kremlin, where 'it will be solely responsible for maintaining order'. General Durosnel was appointed as the governor of the city, while Murat and Poniatowski were instructed to secure the Kolomna–Ryazan (in the southeast) and Troitsk–Dimitrov, SegievPosad and Aniskino roads (in the north and northeast). Eugène had headquarters assigned to him in the northwestern suburbs of Moscow and was ordered to guard the road to Tver, while Davout was tasked with guarding the remaining routes.[77] That same day the emperor also instructed Bessieres to increase patrolling in the city; the thirty-strong patrols (ten grenadiers and twenty dragoons) were to search various districts and round up all the Russians, who should be delivered to Davout.[78] Napoleon believed the moment was ripe to start negotiating with Emperor Alexander and, according to Ségur, he even began drafting peace proposals of. It was around 8pm when Napoleon decided to go to bed, confessing for once that he was exhausted. He was informed about the outbreak of new fires in the suburbs but blamed them on the imprudence of his troops and calmly retired to his chambers.[79]

The night-time disorder left a grave imprint on the city. As the news that the city had been abandoned spread through the Grand Armée, many probably shared Michel Combe's lament: 'Any illusions we still harboured had disappeared. We bade farewell to our hopes for rest, for a peaceful return home, which was so far away from us. The future held nothing but continued fighting and misery for us. Such were the cruel thoughts that beset our minds at once and manifested themselves in a single distressing exclamation that expressed them best, "The city has been abandoned!" We were stunned by this unexpected blow as if struck by lightning ...'[80] The fires raging through the night further dampened the mood. Constant reported that, before arriving at the Kremlin, Napoleon 'sent for Marshal Mortier and threatened both him and the Young Guard [for any continued fires and disorders]. Mortier, in response, showed him some houses covered with iron whose roofing was still perfectly intact. But the emperor pointed out the black smoke that was issuing from them, clenched his hands, and kicked the wretched floor in his bedroom.'[81] To Mortier's credit, his troops did their best to contain the early outbreaks. By the early morning of 15 September the Young Guard had emptied many shops of their merchandise, which was then piled up along the streets and arcades. Mortier drafted a proclamation to the residents of Moscow requiring them to make a report of all the Russians who might be in their homes (whether wounded or in good health), to declare within 24 hours any objects belonging to the state that might have been misappropriated, to reveal any supplies (wheat, flour, spirits, etc.) that were in their homes or storehouses, and to surrender any arms they possessed. In conclusion Mortier noted that 'the peaceful inhabitants of Moscow need have no fear about the maintenance of their properties and the safety of their persons, if they conform to the provisions of the present proclamation'.[82] The Allied authorities also endeavoured to control the fires and began rounding up persons suspected of arson. Thus at around 10am Bourgogne saw General Joseph-Marie Pernetty, commanding the artillery in the 1st Corps, on horseback leading a young man dressed in a sheepskin cape fastened by a red woollen belt. The general ordered Bourgogne to execute the man, who had been caught with a torch setting fire to the palace where Pernetty's men had been lodged. Bourgogne's men hesitated to carry out the order: 'French soldiers are not made for this kind of work, in cold blood. Our blows did not pierce through his sheepskin, and we should have spared his life on account of his youth; moreover, he had not the appearance of a criminal.' But Pernetty stayed around until his order was carried out, and the poor Russian was shot dead.[83]

At about the same time the men of IV Corps finally entered the city from the northwest, but by now their expectations had already been dashed. 'Moscow seemed to be a vast cadaver,' similar to the devastated ruins of Pompeii and Herculaneum, 'though here the impression was even more sepulchral.'[84] As they moved deeper into the city, the Italians encountered 'a mob of soldiers publicly selling and bartering a large quantity of movables they had looted … The number of soldiers increased as we proceeded, carrying on their backs pieces of cloth, loaves of sugar, and whole cases of merchandise …'[85] The further the men advanced, the more they found the streets leading to the Merchant Court obstructed by soldiers and beggars carrying with them all kinds of effects, while the streets were littered with discarded merchandise that the pillagers had found least valuable. Around the Merchant Court 'there were still a number of shops and there soldiers were breaking open cases, and dividing the booty which exceeded their utmost expectations. No shouts, no tumults were heard amidst this horrible scene, so intent was each upon satisfying his rapacity …' Labaume described the ruins of the Merchant Court where 'nothing was heard but the crackling of the flames, the din of the smashing in of doors, and then suddenly the appalling crash of a collapsing arch. Cottons, muslins, silks – in fact all kinds of the richest stuffs of Europe and Asia – were being rapidly consumed. Sugar had been piled up in the cellars, with oils, resin, and vitriol, and all these, burning together in the subterranean magazines, vomited torrents of flame through the thick iron gratings. It was a terrifying sight, as such a fearful catastrophe forced upon the most callous mind the conviction that divine justice would one day exact a terrible retribution from those who were the cause of this frightful devastation.'[86] Fantin des Odoards, serving in the 1st Battalion of the 2nd Grenadier Regiment of the Old Guard, recalled that his men entered the city 'less cheerful than before and we all lamented that the huge population with which we had intended to lead a happy life, had largely disappeared … Although since Smolensk, we largely advanced through hot ashes [of villages and towns burnt by the Russians], no one among us imagined that Moscow, the Holy City of Moscow itself, could be set on fire as if it were an ignoble village, but we were clearly misinformed about Russian civilization. At the first news of the fires, the emperor, who apparently shared our concerns, was convinced they were the work of our marauders, and, infuriated, he gave orders to put an end to such practices.'[87] Captain B.T. Duverger, the paymaster in Davout's 1st Corps, entered the town from the Dorogomilovskaya barrier and found the city 'peaceful and quiet, with no appearance of disorder'. But as he slowly made his way to the Kremlin and the Merchant Court, he witnessed Moscow's poor ransacking shops in the half-burnt shops and 'joined with some soldiers of the Guard to expel them. The shops were closed … Far and wide there reigned a lugubrious calm, broken only by the neighing of horses and the tramp of troops down the streets.'[88] Similarly, Roos, whose unit was deployed in the eastern suburbs, visited 'the nearby estate that resembled a monastery', hoping to refresh himself, and was surprised to find 'people preoccupied with their daily chores as if the events of yesterday had no effect on them or were not even noticed'.[89]

But such calm was misleading, as other parts of the city were far from quiet. Many Allied officers allowed their men to secure necessary provisions, effectively sanctioning looting. Pion des Loches spent most of the night ransacking stores to secure supplies for his men. After taking a short nap 'in a chair, in my clothes, with weapons handy', he woke up at dawn on 15 September, by which time the fires had damaged several quarters around the Merchant Court. 'Being without orders, and not knowing where to seek any,' he later recalled, 'I thought I would establish myself solidly with my command.' He recruited a young Frenchman, the son of the French family who had served as his hosts the night before, to explore the houses in the neighbourhood, some of which had been pillaged already. 'I lodged my cannoneers in a very large palace, the apartments of which were brilliant but unfurnished. It was moreover provided with ovens in which I proposed to bake a quantity of bread without loss of time.' Pion des Loches himself continued to explore the street and found 'another palace of a less pretentious appearance' belonging to Prince Baryatinskii. The few remaining servants told him that 'the palace was still intact, furnished, but with no other provisions than some poultry, a large quantity of oats, and a very rich cellar. A cellar! I lodged there at once.' Hoping to be safely provided for by exchanging wine for other commodities procured by the soldiers, Pion des Loches banished the servants to another part of the palace, forbidding them to approach the French quarters. He then broke down the doors into the cellar, where, to his utter amazement, he found a vast collection of wines: 'Except for an enormous cask of over 400 bottles, all the wine was in bottles buried in sand. We recognized, with glass in hand, the most exquisite brands: Bordeaux, Fontignan, Malaga, Madeira-sec, and elsewhere were liquors and syrups.' Concerned that his men would soon be subjected to great privations, he immediately had a cask with 250 Madeira bottles placed in a wagon, along with some sacks of flour and salted fish, which we found in large supply. His artillery crews likewise were busy plundering nearby buildings, but, as Pion des Loches commented, they did it 'without intelligence. From a candy store they brought me baskets full of sugar-plums, macaroons and roasted almonds. I had much trouble in getting these away from them so as to make them take casks of excellent porter and an ox recently butchered and still hung in a butcher's shop.'[90]

Across the town Kicheyev saw 'three enemy soldiers, in long blue coats and wearing blue-coloured [forage] caps that looked like sleep caps. Like almost all other marauders they had no muskets but only rods, which they began to throw to break our chickens' legs ...' They left after killing several birds but were soon followed by another group of men, who took away the family's horses and cart. Similar visits occurred throughout the next few days.[91] As some Muscovites discovered, the presence of senior Allied officers did not guarantee order. Maxim Sakov, who managed Ivan Batashov's estate, where Marshal Murat and his suite had lodged for the night, recalled that

we spent Tuesday, 3 September [the 15th] in utmost commotion since upon waking up each [Allied] official demanded whatever they wished from us: some desired tea, others coffee, while a few requested white wine, Champagne, Burgundy, vodka, Rhein-wein and white bread. In short, using harsh threats, they demanded that we satisfy all their whims. They worked us so hard that we could barely stand on our feet and many of us simply fled ... All the while, we heard women yelling that soldiers had taken away their biscuits and bread; in other rooms soldiers were breaking chests and plundering everything they could lay hands on. Although guard sentries were assigned to all plundered buildings, the pillaging went on at other locations where guards were not present. We thus spent the entire day in commotion and turmoil.[92]

Although the determined efforts of the Guardsmen had halted the initial progression of the blaze in Kitai-gorod, fires continued to break out in other parts of the city. At dawn on 15 September the Cossacks raided the Pyatnitskii, Yakimanskii and Serpukhovskii districts in Zamoskvorechye (part of Moscow that lay south of the Kremlin, across the Moscow river) and set buildings on fire near the Moskvoretskii bridge.[93] Along the Moscow river the barges laden with provisions and ammunition that the Russians had set on fire the previous day were still burning and it was the billowing smoke from these that Napoleon observed during his tour of the city. The relatively fire-free first half of 15 September proved to be illusory since the fires returned with a vengeance in the evening. Bourgogne's memoirs reveal that his company had been repeatedly deployed to fight new fires throughout the evening of the 15th and the night of 15/16 September, when they were 'busy trying to extinguish the fires round the Kremlin and were successful for a time, but the fires broke out again afterwards more fiercely than ever ... At midnight fire broke out again near the Kremlin and fresh efforts were made to extinguish it. But on the 16th, at three o'clock in the morning, it recommenced more violently than ever ...'[94]

Indeed, throughout the evening of 15 September new outbreaks were reported in the Merchant Court, which spread to Zaryadye (between Varvarka street and the river), Balchug island and further around. These fires, fanned by a strong wind, carried burning embers to other parts of the city, spawning a score of new fires in the eastern suburbs, and along the Arbat and the long avenue leading to the Dorogomilovskaya barrier. That day (the 15th) 'fierce fires had raged at the Pokrovka and devastated the *Nemetskaya sloboda* [in northeast Moscow] ... The night was equally dreadful because of the fires and the [pillaging of the] French troops,' lamented Maxim Sakov. Surrugues saw fires in the Pokrovskaya suburb but also refers to outbreaks on the Tverskoi and Nikitskii boulevards. Charles de Quaij related: 'I was put on watch with the battalion and we had just taken our post when fire broke out on three sides (the Merchant Court being the fourth side); this increased so much that [as] all of the Guard, which was in the palace, took their weapons, the city too caught fire everywhere.'[95] Castellane's journal entry for 15 September shows the gradual change in his circumstances, as it opens with the author's delight at finally having an opportunity to rest and enjoy good food, and ends with his horror at seeing 'fires near our house' and 'numerous detained Russians who held burning torches in their hands'. By the end of the day Vionnet de Maringone described conditions as 'dreadful', with the noise of houses crashing down and the sight of the unfortunates who could hardly escape from the flames creating 'a spectacle that defies human imagination'.[96] Pion des Loches believed that '15th September marked the start of the conflagration and general pillage of Moscow ... The army was completely disbanded. Everywhere officers and soldiers were seen drunk and loaded with booty and provisions taken from the burning houses. The streets were strewn with books, crockery, furniture and clothing of all kinds. The numerous female army followers furnished themselves with an incredible avidity, so as to make us pay dear during the retreat for the results of their pillage. They were seen loaded with barrels of wine and liquor, with sugar and coffee, and with expensive furs.'[97] As he crossed the river to escape the fires, Paymaster Duverger saw one of these ruthless sutlers in action: 'On the main street we saw some poor women and children with hardly any clothes on running from all directions. The fire was already threatening to cut off their retreat on all sides. At that moment, an old sutler placed herself athwart the road. I saw her repulsing with her fist a grenadier who tried to stop her coming into the town. There she stood, her savage green eyes on the hurrying fugitives, stopping and searching them.' Duverger's attention was drawn to 'an old man, two or three children, a girl, beautiful despite her pallor, and a woman who was carried on a stretcher by two men. All were weeping so piteously it broke your heart. The old sutler flung herself at the sick woman, with a sacrilegious hand searching her clothes to see if they concealed anything of value ...'[98]

Concerned about her safety on the eve of the enemy occupation, Madame Fusil, who had stayed in Moscow against her will, left the house she was living in and joined a family of artists who had occupied a large palace belonging to Prince Golitsyn in the Basmanskaya suburb, a rather isolated place at the opposite end of the city from where the Allied army entered it. On 15 September she decided to return to her apartment and was surprised to find 'all buildings occupied by the military. Two captains of the Gendarmerie were lodged at my apartment. All my belongings were ransacked and my papers were scattered around on the floor. I found these men shamelessly reading my personal papers. My appearance confused them and they assured me that they had found the apartment already ransacked.' Unable to stay there any longer, Fusil chose to return to the Golitsyn estate. However, 'the swiftly spreading fires threatened this house. As I turned back, my path was illuminated by the flames that consumed homes all around me. The fires made for a remarkably bright illumination, while the wind howled ominously. It seemed that everything conspired to destroy this ill-fated city.' Climbing to the top of one of the princely estates, Madame Fusil beheld 'the magnificent yet terrifying sight' of Moscow burning. 'For the next four nights we did not light candles since it was just as bright in the evening as at noon.'[99]

As if the situation were not bad enough, a strong wind from the east drove the flames to previously untouched areas of the city in the west. A couple of hours later the wind turned and strengthened to gale force, spreading the fires with frightful rapidity. 'Three times did the wind change from north to west, and three times did these hostile fires, as if obstinately bent on the destruction of the imperial quarters, appear eager to follow new directions,' lamented Ségur. 'Black clouds of smoke rose high into the sky,' recalled Napoleon's secretary Fain. 'In the eastern neighbourhoods the fires spread throughout the suburbs, carrying the awful smell of sulphur and bitumen. The flames spread swiftly, moving from house to house and consuming everything in their path.'[100] As one eyewitness described, 'the soldiers evacuated one shelter after another as fast as the fire reached them and sought asylum in the next house, which was soon in its turn attacked by the flames'.[101] Furthermore, some Allied participants describe rockets being fired into the air and 'wretches and rogues' seized in the act of spreading the conflagration. Interrogated under threat of instant death, the 'criminals' claimed to have been acting on the orders of Count Rostopchin, who had instructed them to burn down the city. Napoleon ordered military commissions to be formed in each quarter of the city for the purpose of judging (and executing) incendiaries taken in the act, and commanded that all available troops should be employed in extinguishing the flames. Their first action was to find the city's fire pumps, but found they had been removed – which gave the first clear indication that the fires might not be accidental. The fires that began at the *Solyanka* spread to the neighbouring wooden houses along the Yauza river towards the Shvivyi hill and soon threatened Batashev's house, where Marshal Murat was quartered. Like many of his compatriots, Murat initially dismissed the fires as insignificant, only to realize that he was dealing with a much more menacing threat. As the flames devoured the buildings around his quarters, Murat diverted troops, assisted by Batashev's servants, to contain the fire and save the house. By evening, however, the fire had become so fierce that 'every building on the [Shvivyi hill], be it wooden or stone-built, was burning ... Sparks rained down on the main building and other structures [at the Batashev's estate]. Murat, realizing there was nothing he could do to save the house, gave the order to evacuate but not before his royal kitchen and several carts were destroyed by flames. Forced to seek new shelter, the King of Naples soon found refuge at the estate of Count Razumovskii on the Gorokhovo Pole in the Basmannaya district.[102]

During the night of 15/16 September Bourgogne and two of his comrades set out to explore the city and the Kremlin. '[Despite it being night-time] there was no need of a torch to light our way,' he remembered, 'but, as we intended to pay visits to the houses and cellars of the Muscovite gentlemen, we each took a man with us armed with candles.' They quickly got lost in the winding streets of the unknown city; after walking aimlessly for some time, they encountered a Jewish rabbi 'tearing his beard and hair' at seeing his synagogue ablaze. The rabbi guided them through several districts of the town, the greater part of them already on fire, before leading them to the Kremlin, 'as clearly visible as in daylight by the light of the fires'. After ransacking a nearby cellar, Bourgogne's comrades took some wine, sugar and preserved fruits, and entered the Kremlin, where they encountered some friends from the 1st Chasseurs Regiment and, with the sun already rising, joined them for breakfast. Bourgogne was surprised to see that the Chasseurs had some silver bullion taken from the Mint, in brick-shaped ingots. But the Chasseurs were not the only ones having fun that night. When a member of Napoleon's household ventured out of the palace at dawn, he discovered that 'the greatest disorder reigned everywhere. There were some detachments bivouacking in the vast empty space before the palace, but there were very few men in each of them. Some soldiers were lying down and others were smoking, crouching or sitting beside a few embers. Some were walking about, others, again, were coming with unsteady steps to join their comrades. Empty bottles or flasks scattered about the fires showed clearly enough how the men had passed the night.'[103]

16 September

Almost all the witnesses comment on the rapid spread of the fires during the evening of 15 September. 'Just as the night began to darken the horizon,' recalled Bourgoing, 'we saw the ominous light of a couple of fires, then five fires, which soon turned into twenty and in no time it seemed that a thousand jets of flame were erupting all over the place. After two hours the horizon was a glowing circle.'[104] Vionnet could see how 'a violent wind was now fuelling the flames and causing them to advance at astonishing speed', while Boniface de Castellane believed that one contributory reason for the fires spreading so swiftly was the presence of extensive stables, mews and coach houses next to each noble house and palace. All made of wood, they acted as kindling for the flames, igniting the adjoining buildings. At 10.30pm Caulaincourt was awakened by his valet with the news that for three-quarters of an hour the city had been engulfed in flames. 'I had only to open my eyes to realize that this was so,' he recalled, 'for the fire was giving off so much light that it was bright enough to read in the middle of my room.' Caulaincourt sprang from his bed and sent his valet to wake up Napoleon's Grand Marshal, Michel

Duroc. The two men observed the burning city from their palace windows. Since the fire was spreading in the quarters furthest away from the Kremlin, they decided to send word to Mortier to mobilize the Guard but to let Napoleon sleep a little longer, especially due to his cold and bladder troubles. However, other participants offer a different version of events: Constant recalled that it was at around midnight, just as Napoleon was dictating a letter, that 'he saw from his windows an immense glow at some distance from the palace'. The fires had broken out again with greater force than ever, and the north wind was driving the flames in the direction of the Kremlin.

Shortly after midnight, in the early hours of 16 September, additional fires could be seen starting in the western suburbs and out on the Pokrovka.[105] Dutch officer Frederic Carel List recalled that 'during the night of 15/16 September fires broke out in numerous places across the city and proved to be impossible to put out because the Russians had taken all the firefighting equipment with them and the inhabitants of the burning buildings had fled. By the 16th of September, the fire grew frightfully in size and intensity.'[106] Kicheyev, whose family lived near the Presnenskii Lakes, watched as the fire spread 'from the east to the south and then to the west, burning through Nikitskaya, Povarskaya, Arbat, Kudrino and Novinskoe. The wind blew directly at us [in a northwesterly direction].'[107] In the Kremlin Napoleon's *mamluk* Ali (St-Denis) woke up because of the bright light coming in through the windows of his room, which looked westwards. 'I rose and went to one of the windows to see what caused the brightness. I was not a little astonished to see the city on fire ... It was horrible! Imagine a city as large as Paris swept by flames, and that one was on the towers of Notre Dame, watching such a spectacle at night.'[108] Alarmed by the size of the conflagration, Caulaincourt judged it necessary to inform the emperor, who at once sent more officers to find out how things stood and how these fires could be starting.' Yet Napoleon seems to have underestimated the importance of these fires since he then went back to bed.[109] St-Denis states that the emperor 'gave us no order and everybody lay down again, having nothing better to do than to wait for day'.[110] By the morning 'Moscow had turned into a sea of fire stirred up by the winds',[111] and Baron Fain was stunned by the ferocity of the fire as 'it moaned, and boiled like the waves of a tempest.'[112] Ségur saw 'sparks and burning fragments already flying over the roofs of the Kremlin, when the wind, shifting from north to west, blew them in another direction ... [yet] it was not long before fresh and vivid lights [appeared and] other flames rising precisely in the new direction which the wind had taken towards the Kremlin'.

Napoleon was still in bed at 7am on 16 September when Doctor Mestivier called to treat the cold that had plagued the emperor since the battle of Borodino. 'He greeted me with his customary question, "What is new?",' Mestivier later recalled. 'His bed was placed so that he could not see the city. I told him about the wide circle of fire that had spread around the Kremlin. 'Ah, bah,' Napoleon replied, 'it is probably a result of the carelessness of some soldiers, who have wanted to make bread, or who have established their campfire too close to wooden houses!' The Emperor still seems to have been suffering from the dysuria that had pained him from the early days of the campaign – showing an almost full flask of urine, he told the doctor that he was almost clear of the business after he had urinated so abundantly and freely but was concerned by the sediment that filled a third of the vessel. The doctor assured him that 'it was the result of a crisis' and would only help him recover his health. Then, fixing his eyes on the ceiling, Napoleon remained silent for several minutes before 'his face, full of kindness, took on a terrible expression'.

He called his valets, Constant and Roustam, and, hastily throwing himself off his bed, shaved and dressed quickly, without uttering a word, and 'kicking the Mamluk, who had tried to put the right boot on his left foot, so strongly that he landed on his back'.[113]

'On Wednesday morning [16 September],' described Ysarn, 'a hurricane of terrifying strength broke out in the city. This was the start of the great fire.'[114] Maxim Nevzorov, the head of the Moscow University's typography service, confirms that 'by five o'clock in the afternoon a powerful conflagration had erupted beyond the Moscow river and in numerous other places, prompting the tocsin to be rung in numerous churches. But this was clearly an act of desperation since one could not hope for rescue and help from ringing bells.'[115] Muscovites could see the fires taking over the entire Preschistenskaya and Tverskaya districts, then spreading into the Arbatskaya, Yauzskaya and Khamovnicheskaya districts. By then, Dominique Larrey was already troubled that 'the fires are surrounding the city from all directions and I am very concerned that the city will fall victim to the flames and pillaging'.[116] The Russian officer Perovskii, who had been in French captivity for the past few days and was inside the Kremlin during the morning of the 16th, recalled that 'a powerful wind, strengthened or maybe even caused by the raging fires, made it difficult to remain on one's feet. While there were no fires inside the Kremlin as of yet, one could see nothing but flames and terrifying black clouds of smoke from across the river. Looking at the city, you would struggle to find roofs of buildings and bell towers that were not on fire. On the right, beyond the Kremlin wall, one could see a thick cloud of black smoke rising high into the sky, and hear the reverberation of crashing walls and roofs.' The Allied officers were clearly bewildered by this sight and 'they were far from being kind in their conversations with me. Deceived in their expectations or intentions, they could no longer look indifferently at the Russian.'[117]

Napoleon now seemed to be mesmerized by the fires surrounding the Kremlin and it was a moment that he never forgot, for it seemed that 'this conquest, for which he had sacrificed everything, became a phantom which he had pursued, and which at the moment when he imagined he had grasped it, vanished in a mingled mass of smoke and flame,' as Ségur aptly put it. In agitation, he rose every moment and paced to and fro, making sudden and vigorous gestures that betrayed his painful uneasiness. He often hastened to the windows where, like his valet Constant, he watched as 'wooden houses painted in different colours, devoured in a few moments, had already fallen in, some warehouses of oil, brandy and other combustible materials darted forth flames of a livid blue, which communicated themselves to other buildings in the vicinity with lightning-like rapidity. Sparks, a rain of enormous embers, fell on the roofs of the Kremlin.' Napoleon, facing a situation far beyond his control, walked restlessly about the room, incoherent expressions occasionally bursting from his lips: 'What a dreadful spectacle! It is their own work! What extraordinary resolution! What men! These are Scythians indeed!'[118] Years later, at St Helena, Napoleon himself reminisced about

the dreadful image which will never be effaced from my memory, the whole of the city was on fire. Large columns of flames of various colours shot up from every quarter, entirely covered the horizon, and diffused a glaring light and a scorching heat to a considerable distance. These masses of fire, driven by the violence of the winds in all directions, were accompanied in their rise and rapid movement by a dreadful whizzing and by thundering explosions, the result of the combustion of gunpowder, saltpetre, oil, resin and brandy, with which the greater part of the houses and shops had been filled. The varnished iron plates with which the buildings were covered were speedily loosened by the heat and whirled far away; large pieces of burning beams and rafters of fir were carried to a great distance, and helped to extend the conflagration to houses that were considered in no danger, on account of their remoteness. Everyone was struck with terror and consternation.[119]

At around 9.30am Napoleon left the palace to make a personal evaluation of the situation in the city.[120] Just as he left the courtyard of the Kremlin on foot, two supposed incendiaries, wearing police uniforms, were brought in. Interrogated in the presence of Napoleon, they claimed that their commanding officer had ordered them to burn everything, and buildings had been designated to this end. As more detainees were brought in, their depositions seemed to confirm what the others had said: the fires were not accidental but part of a deliberate effort by the Russians to destroy the city rather than see it fall into enemy hands. Alarmed by the presence of wounded Russian soldiers and stragglers, suspecting them of incendiary activities, Napoleon instructed Berthier to issue the draconian declaration that 'starting from this day on, any Russian soldier discovered in the streets of the city must be shot'.[121] He then informed Mortier that he was henceforth granted 'supreme command in the city of Moscow' with sufficient troops and staff to control the city's twenty districts. Mortier was assisted by General Milhaud, Adjutants Commandants Puthon and Thiry and twenty *commandants d'armes*, each of whom received a city district.[122]

Colonel Jean-François Boulart's artillery company was still deployed near the Dorogomilovskaya bridge, where the fire had not yet reached the great loop formed by the Moscow river. He had billeted his men in 'a great town house to the right of and not very far from the [Dorogomilovskaya] barrier', where 'all was quiet around us, and even this silence had something frightening about it'. The fire was still gaining ground. 'As a strong north wind had got up, its progress became faster, so that during the night it approached the district I was in. I was extremely worried and never remember spending a more harassed night. No orders reached me, yet it seemed clear that I should eventually be engulfed in the flames.' So he decided to go in person to the Kremlin and seek instructions from Philibert-Jean-Baptiste Curial, commander of the 3rd Division of the Imperial Guard. While waiting for daybreak, he had 'hay and straw carried well away from my ammunition wagons. I posted gunners to watch for the fall of sparks, although there was little to fear with wagons as well enclosed as ours were and covered with sheet metal.' In the morning of 16 September he rode to the Kremlin, not knowing the precise route but simply guiding himself in the general direction of the golden domes of the towers of Ivan [the Great] that dominated that part of the town. Along the way, he experienced 'the whistling of the wind, the roar of the fire … [that] had devoured everything, flames rising above my head on both sides, the timber and metal sheets that formed the roof of many buildings crumbling down with a loud noise …' He was soon enveloped in thick smoke, forcing him to close his eyes, while his horse baulked and refused to move. 'No, I have never experienced anything as horrible,' Boulart later declared. 'And I have never again found myself in such distressing circumstances.'[123] Clearly less distressed were the French soldiers whom Christian von Martens found 'carousing cheerfully' in a large tavern not far from the Kremlin. Meanwhile, the Guard soldiers were desperately trying to save their quarters by means of wet towels.[124]

Across the city, near the Presnenskii Ponds, the residents were alarmed by the fire's swift progress and fled their houses for the safety of 'a large field near the ponds, where lilac bushes grew on the slopes of the hill that gently rolled towards the lakes'. Dozens of Muscovites, 'driven out by the fires or fear', sat near these bushes, watching as their city burned and silently enduring the pillaging by the Allied soldiers.[125] In another part of the town François-Joseph d'Ysarn de Villefort, who had been watching the progress of the fires from the window of his home, saw the flames reach the surrounding wall of his house. He left a remarkable testimony of his experiences during the conflagration that is worth citing here as an example of what it was like to live through the inferno that engulfed the city that day. A few of Ysarn's neighbours tried to run from their houses but the fire forced them to turn back and seek refuge in his courtyard, where they helped Ysarn knock down the wooden fence that separated his house from the nearby church. 'The wooden house over the ice cellars caught fire,' Ysarn recalled, 'but I did not care very much because in my defence plan I had prepared to sacrifice all the outbuildings made of wood in order to save the main part of the building.' Yet, as these outbuildings ignited, his tenants took fright and fled, abandoning Ysarn, who was 'so little aware of it that for a long time I remained in the courtyard lending a hand wherever it was most urgently required'. Eventually he returned indoors to see what his tenants were doing and was shocked to discover just the old man Monsieur de Trassène, 'infirm and deaf', who told him 'everyone has gone but I stayed here so as to live or die with you'. To reach safety, Ysarn led Trassène through 'smoke-filled rooms towards a little staircase near the well, where I reckoned on being able to shelter in the cellars on that side. I led the way down at the risk of being crushed by sheets of iron which were falling from the roofs on all sides. Imagine my horror when I found the door to the cellar burning! I only had time to climb quickly up again and to take my companion in misfortune back through the same rooms, where the smoke left us little air to breathe.' They soon realized that it would be impossible to stay inside the house any longer but the blazing buildings in the courtyard seemed to have cut off all possible escape routes. With smoke filling the room and fires heating the air, the two men faced death. But Trassène suddenly 'had a good idea and made me remove the cover of the stove in order to find some air to breathe in the mouth of this stove'. The fresh air gave them some relief but they now had to deal with the flames that reached their room and were about to scorch them. 'I sprang to the window,' Ysarn recalled, 'broke it down, and threw a mattress onto the sheets of red-hot iron which had fallen from the roof.' He and Trassène then jumped out of window and landed on the mattress; picking themselves up, they ran towards the thermolamp, the French engineer Philippe Lebon's invention designed to produce gas for heating and lighting rooms. 'We soon reached it, built between the garden and the wooden wing in which I was living. We spent nearly an hour there, between the embrasure of two walls, continually moving about to find air to breathe in one direction or another. Our resources diminished every minute.' Late in the evening Ysarn finally charged through a blazing hedge to seek another shelter. He and Trassène found refuge beyond the hedge on the grass near the pound, where they lay for a while surrounded by burning houses and fences.[126]

Many eyewitnesses were astounded by the ferocity of the fire on the 16th. Abbé Surrugues thought that the city had turned into 'an immense volcano whose crater vomited torrents of flames and smoke'. Napoleon's secretary Agathon-Jean-François

Fain also compared the conflagration to a volcanic eruption spewing out torrents of lava: 'It felt as if the earth itself had split open and ignited all the fires. While the first furrows of fire continued burning on their dreadful course, new fires appeared and these new torrents, driven by the wind, spread into the suburbs that had not been affected by the earlier fires. The fire spread furiously, and knew no bounds … engulfing that unfortunate town in a sea of flames!'[127] Throughout the day, the wind, increasing in violence every moment, spread the fires to the Kremlin as well, so that by noon Gourgaud recalled seeing 'flames in the stables of the palace, and a tower adjoining the arsenal'. Bourgogne, having breakfast with his friends from the 1st Chasseurs that morning, recalled that 'it was getting on to mid-day while we sat at breakfast with our friends, our backs against the enormous guns which guard each side of the arsenal, when we heard the cry "To arms!"'[128] The alarm was caused by the fire spreading to the Kremlin: the clock face of the Troitskii Gate tower caught fire and firebrands began to fall into the courtyard where the Artillery of the Guard – hundreds of guns with some 400 caissons and about 100,000 pounds of gunpowder – was stationed. There was also a great quantity of tow, left by the Russians, part of which was already in flames. The fear of an explosion threw everyone into confusion, and Napoleon's valet Constant recalled that 'we trembled at the thought that a single spark, happening to fall on an ammunition wagon, might produce an explosion that would blow up the Kremlin. By some inconceivable negligence, a whole park of artillery had been established underneath the emperor's windows.' Colonel Boulart, who now arrived at the Kremlin in search of General Curial, found everyone 'dejected and in a remarkable state of consternation. Fear and anxiety stood painted on all faces. Without a word said, everyone seemed to understand everyone else.'[129]

According to Caulaincourt, the wind, which had veered slightly to the west, fanned the flames to a terrifying extent and carried large and numerous sparks to a distance, where they fell like a fiery deluge, setting fire to more houses and preventing even the most intrepid from remaining in the neighbourhood in safety. 'The Kremlin became the epicentre of an immense fiery circle,' recalled Montesquiou-Fezensac.[130] The air was so hot, and the pine-wood sparks so numerous, that the beams supporting the iron plates which formed the roof of the arsenal all caught fire, while some of the windows cracked.[131] The roof of the Kremlin kitchens was saved by soldiers deployed there with brooms and buckets to gather up the glowing fragments and moisten the beams. Yet the Kremlin was still in extreme peril. In the afternoon, despite everyone's efforts, the flames reached the imperial stables located in the western part of the Kremlin, where 'some of [Napoleon's] horses were stabled and the coronation coaches of the Tsar were kept'.[132] Meanwhile, sparks falling into the courtyard of the arsenal ignited several heaps of wadding (which was used to prime Russian cannon), threatening some 400 of the Grande Armée's caissons that had been deployed there; in addition, thousands of pounds of gunpowder was stored inside the arsenal building itself. With brooms in hand, some Allied artillerymen on the roof frantically swept off any embers that might cause an explosion. Other soldiers, meanwhile, struggled around the arsenal itself, doing their best to extinguish the burning wadding and remove the caissons to less exposed areas. Using two fire pumps that had been 'completely dismantled'[133] but repaired during the night, the imperial grooms and ostlers did their best to save the Kremlin stables. The conditions, however, were brutal, since the air was seemingly charged with fire. Caulaincourt recalled:

We breathed nothing but smoke, and the stoutest lungs felt the strain after a time. The bridge to the south of the Kremlin was so heated by the fire and by sparks falling on it that it kept bursting into flames, although the Guard, and the sappers in particular, made it a point of honour to preserve it. I stayed with some generals of the Guard and the aides-de-camp of the emperor, and we were forced to lend a hand and remain in the midst of this fiery deluge in order to motivate these half-roasted men. It was impossible to stand more than a moment in one spot – even the fur on the grenadiers' caps was singed.[134]

Informed of the danger, Napoleon insisted on coming to see it for himself; according to Constant, as he came down from his apartment, 'the fire had already made such enormous headway on this side that the external doors were half-consumed. The horses would not pass them; they reared, and it was with great difficulty that they could be made to cross the thresholds. The Emperor's grey greatcoat was burned in several places, and so was his hair. A minute later we were marching on hot firebrands.' Concerned for his safety, some offered to cover the emperor from head to foot with their cloaks and carry him on their arms through this terrible passage. But Napoleon refused and instead proceeded to the arsenal, where he arrived at the moment when General Baston de La Riboisière, inspector general of the Grande Armée's artillery, was giving orders to have the caissons removed. The gunners and soldiers of the guard were surprised to find Napoleon exposing himself to so great a danger, and many members of the imperial suite were horrified by the threat the fire posed. La Riboisière pleaded with Napoleon to withdraw for his own safety, entreating that the troops, who 'stood bewildered by his presence', in the words of Gourgaud, might be permitted to save themselves without having their embarrassment increased by the presence of their Emperor. La Riboisière was joined by Berthier, Bessieres and Lefebvre, who all advised the emperor to leave at once, since there was the imminent danger that the arsenal and the neighbouring buildings might be blown up at any moment. Napoleon, however, refused to leave. He no doubt found it very difficult to reconcile himself to the prospect of abandoning the symbol of Russian imperial authority – Napoleon was the first foreigner to conquer Moscow in 200 years – in the heart of which he had hoped to negotiate a peace with the Russian sovereign. 'Moscow is gone, and with it I lose the reward that I have promised my brave army,' he was heard lamenting.[135]

Napoleon initially rebuffed his officers' pleas for him to leave. As the violent wind blew sparks and blazing fragments all around the arsenal and the artillery caissons, the threat of a potential explosion 'did not shake the emperor's resolution, for his soul never knew the feeling of fear', noted one of his secretaries. 'He did not think it necessary as yet to leave the Kremlin, the danger which he ran there, deciding him, on the contrary, to remain.'[136] Amidst the shouts and commotion, he instead insisted on climbing the tower of Ivan the Great – which reminded some of his companions of a minaret[137] – to gain a better view of the situation. Accompanied by senior officers and generals, he climbed up the spiral staircase to the top of the tower, where 'the impetuosity and violence of the wind, and the rarefaction of the air, brought on by the heat of the flames, caused a dreadful hurricane,' recalled Gourgaud, noting that he and Berthier were on the point of being blown away. The rest of the group 'remained standing slightly below on the staircase and peering through the small windows in the walls of the tower'.[138] Gazing in astonishment through a slit in the stone wall at the hellish panorama of the city engulfed by fire, Napoleon exclaimed, 'The barbarians, the savages, to burn their city like this! What could their enemies do that was worse than this? They will earn the curses of posterity.'[139]

As he descended to the ground, the emperor's vacillation on what to do next was brought to an end by shouts from the most northerly wing of the palace, announcing that part of the walls had just fallen in. 'About four o'clock in the afternoon,' noted Denniée, 'it was announced that the fire was about to break into the arsenal and that only one safe route out of the Kremlin remained.'[140] There were even rumours that the Kremlin had been mined and the fuse set, so that an explosion was expected at any moment. In fact, several suspected arsonists had been apprehended within the Kremlin. Ségur claimed that a Russian policeman was found inside the Kremlin and Napoleon caused him to be interrogated in his presence. Upon hearing the Russian's testimony that he and others had been ordered to burn the city, Napoleon realized that 'everything was devoted to destruction, the ancient and sacred Kremlin itself not excepted ... The gestures of the emperor betokened disdain and vexation: the wretch was hurried into the first court, where the enraged grenadiers dispatched him with their bayonets.'[141] Yet Perovskii, who witnessed the incident, left a rather different account. 'I saw several soldiers leading a police officer ... He was taken up to the palace and one of the staff-officers began interrogating him through an interpreter. "Why is Moscow burning? Who gave the order to burn the city? Why were the fire engines removed? Why had he stayed in Moscow?" And many other similar questions, to which the police officer responded in a trembling voice that he knew nothing and that he had stayed in Moscow because he could not depart in time.' Perovskii tried to intervene, arguing that this man was a minor police official and could not have known about the plans or intentions of the governor of Moscow. '"He serves in the police and therefore is certainly aware of everything" was the response I received. The unfortunate man was taken away and imprisoned underneath the court where I stood. "What is going to happen to him?" I inquired of the officer who interrogated him. "He will be punished as he deserves: either hanged or shot with others, who have been already detained for the same crime."'[142] Meanwhile, Peyrusse's letter, written on 21 September, speaks of at least three suspicious individuals arrested in the Kremlin: one seemed to have tried igniting a timber yard near the palace, another was caught 'sneaking into the attic with a sausage and a lighter', and the third was apprehended as he was setting fire to the bridge south of the Kremlin.[143]

Despite the raging fires, Caulaincourt informs us, military considerations weighed heavily on Napoleon's mind. He became concerned that the Russians might exploit the confusion reigning among the Allied troops inside Moscow and strike a blow at them. Gourgaud and Meneval agree with this assessment, noting that Berthier persuaded Napoleon to leave the palace by observing that 'if the enemy should attack the army corps that are stationed outside Moscow, Your Majesty has no means of communicating with them'.[144] But if the emperor could no longer stay at the Kremlin, where else could he go? Afterwards no one could say exactly who had suggested the Petrovskii Palace, located about 2 miles northwest of Moscow and sufficiently removed from the burning city. Once the decision was made, Napoleon dispatched his orderly officers to discover a passage through the burning city. The first of these officers (Mortemart) soon returned to report that the flames had not allowed him to make his way through. Shortly afterwards, another officer, however, brought the happier news that another route was passable. The Emperor then mounted his horse Tauris and, at around 5pm,[145] quitted the Kremlin, leaving for its protection only the 1st Battalion of the 2nd Grenadier Regiment. With the Borovitskaya, Troitskaya and Spasskaya gates blocked by the flames, the imperial suite was forced to escape through the Tainitskaya (Secret) Tower located in the southern wall of the Kremlin. Fantin des Odoards and Constant described a 'postern' opening towards the river, while Ségur noted that Napoleon left through 'a postern gate leading between the rocks to the Moscow river'.[146] 'Leaning on the arm of the Duke of Vicenza [Caulaincourt], [Napoleon] crossed a little wooden bridge [over the Kremlin moat] which led to the riverbank, where he found his horses.'[147]

Once they were clear of the Tainitskaya Tower, the immediate question was how to proceed to the Petrovskii Palace. The direct route would have taken them through the northern quarters of the city, which were already engulfed in flames. So it was decided to move along the river westwards, where the fire had largely burned itself out. Napoleon mounted Tauris, another of his Arab greys, and set off, followed by his entourage. The Emperor 'was preceded by one of the agents of the police of Moscow, who acted as his guide'.[148] From the Vsekhsvyatskii bridge[149] the imperial entourage turned west to the Prechistenski Gates, whence they moved north (probably along the Nikitskii boulevard) towards the Arbat. But they 'had all the trouble in the world in getting out. The streets were encumbered with debris, with burning beams and trusses. We were being grilled alive in our carriages. [At times] the horses would not move forwards. I was extremely worried on account of the treasure.'[150] Fantin des Odoards, whose unit accompanied the emperor, recalled that 'everywhere the air we were breathing seemed about to asphyxiate us by its very heat ... Many an old moustache was singed during this infernal journey.'[151] The landscape reminded some of the Frenchmen of depictions of the entrance into Hell. The imperial suite moved along 'narrow streets, where the fire, shut up as in a furnace, redoubled in intensity, and where the nearness of the roofs brought the flames together above our heads in heated domes which shut out from us the sight of heaven'.[152] The men of Bourgogne's company, struggling to keep up with the imperial suite, soon found the way blocked by the collapsed houses and decided to retrace their steps back to the Place du Gouvernement. To protect themselves from the flames, 'the idea struck us of each taking a sheet of iron to cover our heads, holding it to the windy and dusty side. After bending the iron into the shape of shields, we set out, one of the men in front; then I came leading the half-blinded man by the hand, the others following. We succeeded after an infinite deal of trouble, stumbling time after time.'[153]

The rest of the imperial entourage, meanwhile, pushed onwards. 'We issued from Moscow under a perfect hail of fire,' described Mathieu Dumas. 'The wind was so strong that it tore the red-hot iron from the roofs and hurled it down into the streets. All our horses had their legs burnt. It is impossible to describe the confusion of our headlong flight. The roar of the flames can be likened to nothing but the noise of the waves of the ocean – it was indeed a storm raging over a sea of fire. The whole length of the road to the Petrovskii Palace was littered with odds and ends of all kinds, especially with broken bottles thrown away by the soldiers.'[154] Napoleon's mamluk Ali (St-Denis) also spoke of 'great difficulty in extricating ourselves from the city whose streets were obstructed by burning beams, the ruins of fallen houses, and by flames which barred our way'. The imperial entourage was 'continually obliged to change direction, and even to retrace our steps in order to not get caught. The wind blew violently and whirled about, so that it raised a great amount of dust, which blinded men and horses.'[155] Montesquiou-Fezensac also commented on the infernal conditions in which Napoleon and his companions had to retreat from the Kremlin, noting that 'we were obliged to protect our cheeks, hands, and eyes with our handkerchiefs, hats and the tailcoats of our uniform. The extreme heat stirred up the horses so much that we had trouble keeping them at a walking pace.'[156] A much more famous description of Napoleon's departure from the Kremlin comes from Ségur, who described how the Frenchmen had encountered a Russian man amidst the fires and promised him his life if he would act as their guide; acquiescing, he led the imperial entourage through the burning streets:

> We were encircled by an ocean of flames, which blocked up all the gates of the citadel, and frustrated the first attempts that were made to depart. After some search, we discovered a postern gate, leading through rocks to the Moscow river ... The roaring of the flames around us became every moment more violent. A single narrow winding street presented itself completely on fire, and appeared rather as the entrance than as the outlet of this Hell; the emperor rushed on foot, and without hesitation, into this dangerous passage. We walked on a ground of fire, beneath a fiery sky, and between two walls of fire. The intense heat burned our eyes, which we were nevertheless obliged to keep open and fixed on the danger. A consuming atmosphere, glowing ashes, detached flames, parched our throats, and rendered our respiration short and dry; and we were already almost suffocated by the smoke. Our hands were burned, either in endeavouring to protect our faces from the insupportable heat, or in brushing off the sparks which every moment covered and penetrated our garments.

Yet this dramatic description is countered by the more grounded account of Gaspard Gourgaud, who famously accused Ségur of exaggerations and lies contained in his history of the Russian campaign. Discussing the departure from the Kremlin, Gourgaud observed that 'although we accompanied Napoleon during the entirety of this march, we did not witness the splendid horrors described by Mr de Segur. In traversing Moscow, we stepped upon ashes, it is true; but not under fiery vaults. Perhaps we had not taken the most direct road but it is untrue that the emperor ran any danger in the course of the march.' Gourgaud rejected Ségur's claim that at this moment of distress Napoleon's Russian 'guide stopped in uncertainty and agitation', or that the emperor was saved by 'some pillagers of the 1st Corps' who recognized the emperor amidst the whirling flames and led him towards the safety of a quarter that had burnt out earlier that day. It was there, Ségur claimed, and many subsequent writers repeated, that a rather warm meeting between Napoleon and Davout occurred: upon hearing about the emperor's distress, the Iron Marshal, despite being wounded, 'had desired to be carried into the flames to rescue Napoleon or to perish with him'.[157] But Gourgaud flatly denied any of this happening: 'it is untrue that our guide stopped in a state of uncertainty and agitation, or that the emperor was indebted for his life to some marauders of the 1st Corps. There is as little truth in the report of that affecting meeting with Marshal Davout ...'[158] Indeed, it is difficult to envision Davout, who was a notoriously reserved and taciturn man, being transported with joy and rushing to embrace the emperor.

Nevertheless, Napoleon and his companions managed to get safely through the burning streets. At one point they were accosted by a woman with 'dishevelled hair and torn and blackened clothes', holding her infant son in her hands. This was the wife of

Armand Domergues, the stage-manager of the imperial theatre at Moscow, who had been exiled by Governor Rostopchin and thus separated from his family. Seeking to save her infant child, the woman rushed towards Napoleon, exclaiming 'Sire, sire, have pity on me, save my son!' and grabbing the heel of the emperor with her trembling hand. At the sight of this child, who probably reminded him of his own son, Napoleon was visibly moved; he soothed the woman and assured her that 'we will take care of you and your son'.[159] The procession then made its way towards the Dorogomilovskii bridge, where its path was blocked by a slow-moving column of Guard artillery, commanded by Colonel Boulart, which was being evacuated to the safety of suburbs. During these few moments everyone remained tense, hoping that the powder-laden caissons would not explode.[160] Once safely across the bridge the imperial suite turned northwards and followed the river towards the village of Khoroshevo, where it crossed to the opposite bank on a pontoon bridge.[161]

It was early in the evening (around 7.30pm according to Caulaincourt)[162] when the imperial suite finally reached the Petrovskii Palace, from where Napoleon beheld Moscow swallowed up in a sea of flames. If anything could further deepen the grave impression that this spectacle had on the emperor's feelings, it was the increasing certainty that the conflagration was not the result of chance, but that the Russians themselves had sacrificed their city to wipe away the stain of foreign occupation and to make it impossible for the enemy to stay there. That night Napoleon lay in bed without sleeping and often came out to look at Moscow smouldering in the distance. Some of his companions seemed to have developed a macabre fascination for the conflagration. Despite being exhausted by his trip to the Petrovskii Palace, Henri Beyle (Stendhal) still managed to enjoy 'the most beautiful fire in the world that formed an immense pyramid, which, like the prayers of the faithful, had its base on the ground and its summit in heaven'.[163] Mathieu Dumas beheld 'the image of Hell – an immense city that was nothing but a plain of fire; the heavens and the entire horizon appeared to be in flames'.[164] 'The glow of the fire was so bright even at this distance,' recalled La Riboisière's aide-de-camp, 'that standing next to the window I was able to read two letters from the emperor by the light of the distant fire as easily as I would have in daylight.'[165] After resting and consuming a quick supper, Anatole de Montesquieu-Fezensac and his friends decided 'to have another look at this fiery spectacle that was doing us so much harm and to which, in spite of this, we kept returning'. Standing on the immediate outskirts of Moscow, he and his companions watched as

> the fire seemed to devour both earth and sky. Great whirlwinds of the densest black smoke arose after the collapse of the largest buildings, making long, broad transverse gashes in and above the flames. One saw volcanoes whose immeasurable eruptions had no limits but the skies ... Often the flames were drawn aside like curtains and displayed to us not only palaces, but also the amphitheatres of palaces, which, at the moment of being devoured, appeared to us thus in a fairytale splendour to bid the world a last goodbye.[166]

Chapter 6

The Great Conflagration

'It was the most grand, the most sublime, and the most terrific sight the world ever beheld!' Napoleon declared ostentatiously on St Helena.[1] For three successive days – 17, 18 and 19 September – the conflagration continued with unabated intensity. Eyewitnesses report that the sky was scarcely visible through the thick clouds of smoke that hung heavily over the city, while the sun appeared as a blood-red orb atop the city. 'During the night of 17 September,' wrote Peyrusse to his brother, 'new disasters broke out and nothing could escape them. The flames spread for more than four *lieues* [12km] and it seems the sky itself was on fire.'[2] As thousands of homes, taverns and shops burned, frightful crashes were heard at every moment, as roofs crashed down and the stately façades of princely palaces crumbled headlong into the streets. The ground was so hot that in places it was impossible to touch it, and some witnesses even assert that molten lead and copper could be seen on some streets. Claude François Madeleine Le Roy of the 85th Line recalled that as he rummaged through the streets he found 'the fires so strong that their force was lifting the metal roofing of copper plates which covered most of the houses. Soon they fell back with a crash and, thrust sideways by the wind, were as dangerous to passers-by as the fire itself.'[3] Although a light rain began on 17 September and continued throughout the 18th, it failed to damp down the flames; in fact, several new fires broke out during these days. Vionnet de Maringone recalled that 'on the 17th, the wind changed suddenly and carried the fire towards the Kremlin. We made extraordinary efforts to save at least part of the city ... On the 18th the fiery storm redoubled in violence so that it was difficult to stand in the streets and squares.'[4]

'A sea of flames flooded all areas of the city,' described Abbé Surrugues, a Catholic priest residing in the northeastern part of Moscow. 'The undulations of the flames agitated by the force of the wind were an exact imitation of the waves raised by a tempest.' The conflagration was so enormous and ferocious that many felt it was 'supernatural' as well.[5] Standing near the Kremlin, Dominique Larrey thought 'it would be difficult, under any imaginable circumstances, to find a more horrible sight than that which pained our eyes',[6] while Sergeant Scheltens of the Guard Fusiliers-Grenadiers explained that 'it is impossible to conceive what this fire was like. You had to have seen it to understand the consternation that then gripped the army.' The weather remained dry for the first few days after the Grande Armée's arrival and the wind, always violent, continued to blow and change incessantly. The men of the Grande Armée watched in utter amazement as 'the whole city burned, thick sheaves of flame of various colours rising up on all sides to the heavens, blotting out the horizon, sending in all directions a blinding light and a burning heat. These sheaves of fire, swirling in every direction through the violence of the wind, were accompanied in their upward rise and onward progress by a terrible hissing and combustion of powders, saltpetre, resinous oils and alcohol contained in the houses and shops.'[7] On 17 September Viceroy Eugène confided to his wife, 'My dear Auguste, you cannot imagine the horrifying scenes that we witnessed in the past three days and they still continue today.'[8]

Both soldiers and the unfortunate civilians who had stayed behind desperately sought shelter amidst this ocean of flames. The fires forced Napoleon's aide-de-camp Jean Rapp, who was seriously wounded at Borodino, to change residences almost half a dozen times before he managed to find a secure place to rest.[9] Many Muscovites, however, were less fortunate and their lamentable cries could be heard in the streets. Forced to flee their burning houses, they wandered through the middle of their city, carrying bundles with their most precious possessions and seeking refuge.

> Chased by the fires, the men of the lower classes went howling from house to house. Eager to save what they valued most, they loaded themselves with large bales that they struggled to carry and we often saw them abandon their possessions to escape the flames. Women, driven by their natural feeling of humanity, carried one or two children on their shoulders, dragging others by the hand and, to escape the death that threatened on all sides, ran with their skirts rolled up to seek refuge in the corners of streets and squares, but the intense fires soon forced them to abandon these shelters as well, and they fled precipitately in all directions, sometimes without being able to find their way through the maze of streets, where many of them found an unhappy ending. I saw old men, their long beards caught by the flames, laying on small carts dragged by their own children who hastened to escape from this veritable Hell.[10]

Many headed towards the stone-built churches and cathedrals, but even these centuries-old and seemingly unyielding structures were no match for the fires. In one church the residents sheltering inside it 'became increasingly frantic as they observed the approaching fires: loud sobbing, wailing and moaning could be heard all around. Frightened senseless, everyone began to run and scurry around, grabbing various items and unconsciously dropping them moments later; everyone spoke but no one listened; everyone sought advice and gave instructions. In short, complete chaos and misunderstanding reigned everywhere.'[11]

In this already deplorable situation, the civilians were exposed to the violence of soldiers who 'seeing [their] hopes dashed, thought only of enjoying the present, knew no brake, and gave themselves up to the greatest excesses'.[12] Eugène Labaume blamed the lack of proper oversight from the Allied commanders for the plundering escalating into 'the frenzy of madness'. The troops, no longer restrained by the presence of their leaders, committed the wildest excesses. 'No retreat was safe, no place sufficiently sacred to ensure protection from their bestial passions.'[13] Many Muscovites had been killed for the slightest transgressions against the soldiers: one Allied soldier murdered a young Russian maid after she washed his trousers, in the process destroying the paper banknotes that he had previously sewn inside them; he had evidently forgotten about them when he asked the unfortunate woman to wash his clothes. An eyewitness also described how a Russian man, walking near the Presnenskii Lakes, opened a silver snuffbox without noticing that a mounted lancer was passing by. The lancer demanded the snuffbox and, when the man refused, he simply ran his lance through the Russian's breast and calmly picked up the item dropped by the dying man. 'From the lancer's thrust, the poor man's body fell onto a bench, with the head suspended over it and the feet touching the ground. It remained in this position for over a week.'[14]

For days the soldiers pillaged the city, breaking in doors and windows, forcing entry to cellars and storehouses. 'Soldiers, *vivandiers*, convicts, prostitutes thronged the streets, entered the deserted palaces, and dragged out everything that excited their cupidity. Some covered themselves with cloth of gold or rich silks; others threw over their shoulders priceless furs; many decked themselves with women's and children's pelisses, and even the escaped convicts hid their rags under court robes! The remainder, rushing in a mob to the cellars, forced the doors, and, after getting drunk on the most costly wines, staggered off with their immense booty.'[15] Despite the Russians' efforts to hide their possessions, the soldiers demonstrated remarkable ingenuity and skill in finding the hiding-places, both insides homes and outdoors. Planat de la Faye was pleased when his artillerymen demonstrated 'the instinct and intelligence of veteran soldiers' in finding a hiding-place behind a wall that contained much of Prince Baratinskii's furniture.[16] 'As for our soldiers,' noted Dominique Larrey, 'tormented by hunger and thirst, they braved any danger to partake in the delights of the burning cellars and shops that contained various provisions, wines, liqueurs, and other more or less useful objects. They could be seen running through the streets pell-mell with the desperate inhabitants, taking all they could save from the ravages of this terrible fire.'[17]

Having plundered to their fill, the soldiers often forced the Muscovites themselves to carry the goods to their camps. 'Our main torment was carrying the plunder,' complained one Russian. 'The enemy sometimes forced us to carry burdens that were beyond human capacity and they beat mercilessly those who refused to carry them.'[18] After delivering the loot during the day, some Russians were kept under guard throughout the night so they could continue assisting the marauders the following morning.[19] In many of the houses, which the fire had damaged sufficiently to make their pillage excusable but without actually destroying them, the Allied troops found exquisite articles of luxury – furs, jewellery, porcelain, silverware and numerous other items – that they, in their improvidence, initially preferred to either food or clothing. It was a grotesque spectacle as the crowd of troops and the inhabitants of the city thronged the smoking embers of the once-splendid city. 'The looting and burning were walking abreast. All looted or bought cheaply the products of looting, and the interest brought together more than once in the same place the embroidered coat of a general and the humble garb of a soldier.'[20] Césare de Laugier could see the numerous Italian soldiers, who had initially followed their superior's orders in trying to 'master the fire and save pieces of cloth, jewellery, cottons, fine materials and Europe's and Asia's most precious items', were now excited by the 'example of the local populace pillaging under their eyes, and let themselves be carried away, putting everything to the sack. First and foremost the stores of flour, brandy and wine were ravaged.' What else they were supposed to do when the city was being destroyed by fires – stay outside and watch?, he wondered years later in his memoirs.[21]

And so pillage they did. Some felt ashamed to be involved in this process and wondered whether it was worth 'compromising the dignity of the uniform'. But like Michel Combe, many faced the dilemma of 'on the one hand, returning empty-handed to the camp and being taunted by your comrades; on the other hand, we were driven by the anger that arose upon seeing our hopes broken by the abandonment of the city; and finally, there was hunger that was devouring us. So all these factors led us to commit actions that we not only would have resisted if the inhabitants had remained, but would have even repressed with all our might.'[22] More practically, many found it wrong to allow precious supplies (and objects) to be destroyed by fire or claimed by others. Thus Albrecht Adam initially refused an invitation to partake in the plunder of an art collection in one of the princely estates but later could not resist claiming a portrait of the Madonna, which would otherwise have been destroyed by fire.[23] At one of the city barriers Pion des Loches found the officer in charge of patrolling, who was 'unable to partake in the pillaging and instead was levying a tax on all soldiers coming out with booty. He thought he was doing himself an honour in showing me his guardhouse filled with bottles of wine and baskets of eggs. All his men were dead drunk and he himself, thinking it his duty to set an example, could not stand upright.'[24] At the Kremlin a 'much more revolting brigandage' was committed as the Imperial Guard robbed not just the civilians but also fellow soldiers returning with booty. 'Each soldier, on coming out of the interior courtyard, was obliged to pay over five franks to the Guard Grenadiers or to abandon his booty; then, when he presented himself at the interior gate, he was called a brigand and a scoundrel, despoiled and chased off.'[25]

Alcohol was among the most sought-after items in the city and, fortunately for the soldiers, there was plenty of it. Most Russian estates possessed large wine cellars with a wide selection of wines, ports and other liquors. Even though the fires destroyed the buildings above ground, most cellars survived intact and were ransacked by Allied soldiers, Russian stragglers and local residents alike. Colonel Griois saw a large number of soldiers lying drunk and nearly dead amid the debris of bottles that covered the streets. In one place he saw a crowd of soldiers fighting bitterly in a deep cellar amidst the shells of burned-out buildings. A ladder that had been lowered into the cellar was the only way out and one could hear the 'terrible racket of dispute or rather fist-fights between the looters. They were slaughtering each other in the dark!' One dragoon managed to climb up to the surface, clutching several bottles in his hand, but he collapsed after taking just a few steps and Griois could see that in the fight a sabre had run through his body. Unexpectedly, the scene turned rather comical when Count Mathieu Dumas, the *Intendant-Général* of the Grande Armée, passed by the cellar; noticing the disorder, he rushed there with his sword drawn, striking the looters right and left. Reaching the ladder, he seized by the hair the first head to present itself – before recognizing that it was his own cook, half-drunk, his white waistcoat spattered with wine and blood, and clutching several bottles in his hand. 'It would be hard to imagine anything more comical than the general's astonishment, anger and exasperation at seeing his servant emerge among the soldiers' laughter. He did not take his sword to the unfortunate man, but kicked him and went away in despair at seeing that the disorder could not be mastered and that everyone was involved in it.'[26] Naturally Dumas made no mention of this incident in his memoirs, although he did acknowledge the widespread 'pillage of cellars that contained plenty of wines and strong liquors'.[27]

Threatened by flames, many Russian residents tried to get out to safety. Maxim Nevzorov, the head of Moscow University's typography service, who found shelter at Senator Ivan Lopukhin's house several blocks away from the walls of Kitai-gorod, remembered how he and some domestics convened a council and decided to abandon the house, which was threatened by the fires, and 'seek salvation in the fields beyond the city'. They left 'as we were, without taking any possessions, since it was said that those who carried anything were likely to be robbed and exposed to other dangers'. This decision proved to be a prudent one, since Nevzorov's group successfully navigated their way through the enemy outposts and suffered only minimal abuse. Near the Red Gates they encountered 'a small enemy patrol that let us through but, just as we passed, one of

the soldiers, a German, ran after us and robbed our companion of a flannelette bonnet'.
[28] Much less fortunate was a group of Muscovites in Zamoskvorechye, south of the
Kremlin, where about a hundred men and women had found temporary shelter inside a
church. They spent the afternoon praying for salvation but, with the fires intensifying,
they finally decided to seek another refuge. Receiving the priest's blessing, they ventured
out into the burning streets, only to be 'astonished by the darkness of whirling smoke,
and deafened by loud rumbling and the howling and hissing of the wind'. Nevertheless,
they pushed ahead against 'an almost impenetrable wall of hot ashes that was carried by
the winds, blinding eyes and burning faces'. At last they reached Polyanka, where further
misfortune befell them. As they entered a square, they were surrounded by the Allied
marauders:

> [We] fell to our knees and, raising our trembling hands to the heavens, begged for
> mercy and grace. But the concept of humanity was foreign to these barbarians
> who ignored the pleas and supplications of the vulnerable and rushed with swords
> unsheathed like wild beasts at a flock of sheep. With frenzied shouts and raging
> fury they began to pillage and beat everyone ... They tore open bundles in search
> of precious items and scattered everything else. From men they removed clothing
> and boots that they desperately needed since theirs were completely worn out. They
> snatched scarves and shawls from women's heads, angrily tore their dresses, emptied
> pockets of watches, snuff-boxes, gold and silver coins, pulled earrings straight out
> of ears and pinched rings off fingers ... I let the reader envision this scene – a square
> surrounded and illuminated by raging fires, filled with smoke, stench and hot ash
> and pierced by howling winds, and amidst such chaos, the enemy soldiers, with
> beastly expressions and unsheathed swords, ransacking through scattered items and
> among the pitiable Muscovites, crouched in various positions with faces distorted
> by fear ...[29]

Similar scenes unfolded in other parts of Moscow. 'It was impossible to tell night from
day,' recalled Andrei Karfachevskii.

> All that time the pillage continued: the [enemy] entered houses and, committing
> gross acts of violence, took from their owners not only money, gold and silver, but
> even boots, linen and, most ludicrous of all, cassocks, women's furs and cloaks,
> in which they stood on guard and rode on horseback. It was not uncommon for
> people walking in the street to be stripped to their shirt, and many were robbed of
> boots, overcoats, frock-coats. Anybody who resisted was beaten savagely, often to
> death; and in particular many priests of the churches here endured severe torture
> at the hands of the enemy seeking to extract from them information on where their
> church treasure was hidden.[30]

On 21 September Christian Christiani, an employee at the Foundlings Home, decided to
travel to the Moscow stockyard, hoping to procure a few provisions for the orphans. He
was stunned by the sight that greeted him there:

> All the fruits and vegetables were plundered, fences broken, wooden buildings
> destroyed and burned. The stone building, the yard and nearby fields and coppices
> were all full with the wounded and prisoners of all walks of life who were gathered
> together there. You could see here priests, merchants, servants and peasants and,

excluding the French guards, they must have numbered up to 6,000 men. All around lay the unburied corpses of unfortunates of both genders who had perished at the hands of the villains. There must have been as many as 400 of them, and the manure pit was topped off with a pile of corpses. In addition, the fields were strewn with numerous dead horses, cows and sheep.'[31]

Abbé Surrugues recalled that 'the wretched inhabitants of Sloboda, pursued from place to place by the flames, were obliged to take refuge in the cemeteries... . These unfortunate beings, with terror stamped on their faces, seen fitfully by the light of the burning dwellings flitting among the tombs, might have been taken for so many ghosts that had left their graves.' In the Church of St Louis, 'everything was in the greatest consternation. All the unfortunate refugees who gathered in this place, bundles in hand, were resigned to their fate.' They asked Surrugues to give them the last absolution but he begged them to wait, hoping for the best. Then, amidst the carnage and pillage, a grenadier company arrived with buckets and water; courageously entering the burning buildings, the soldiers managed to contain the fires and save the local residents.[32]

Madame Fusil has left an interesting account of these lugubrious days. On 17 September, frightened by the widespread looting, she decided to travel to the Petrovskii Palace to seek help at Napoleon's headquarters. She and her companions had to make numerous detours amidst the fires:

> We initially tried to take the usual road to the boulevards, but found it impossible to pass, the way being blocked by a wall of flame. So we turned to the Tverskoi Boulevard but the fires were even greater there. Reaching the Grand Theatre, we encountered a genuine inferno – words are simply insufficient to describe this sight ... We turned right where the fires seemed to have been subsiding but just as we stood in the middle of the street, the flames, fanned by the wind, formed an arch of fire over the thoroughfare. This may seem to be an exaggeration, but it is genuine truth. We could neither advance nor make a detour. Putting our horses to the gallop, we managed to regain the boulevard ...

Returning to their house, Fusil and her companion saw, to their horror, that it was already burning. They rushed to save their personal belongings, assisted by a group of Allied officers. Unable to stay there any longer, Fusil and her friends decided to follow a group of soldiers that happened to pass by. 'We went from street to street, from house to house. All bore the marks of devastation. This city, so rich and resplendent only a short time ago, was now nothing but a pile of ashes and ruins, where we wandered like ghosts ...' Desperate and exhausted, Fusil finally found refuge in her former apartment, which had been ransacked but not burned. 'We had scarcely eaten anything since the previous day. A table and some chairs were still intact. These were carried down into the street, and a sort of dinner was prepared and dished up in the middle of the road. Imagine a table in the middle of the street, houses in flames or smoking ruins on all sides, the wind driving dust and smoke into our faces, incendiaries shot down near us, drunken soldiers carrying away the booty which they had just pillaged.'[33]

More fortunate was the merchant Grigorii Kolchugin, who lived with his large family near the Pokrovskaya Gates in the southeastern district of Moscow. Realizing that the safety of his family, house and goods would depend on the enemy's benevolence, he made sure that the Allied troops billeted at his house were always well fed and well treated. The soldiers could always find 'a table with food, vodka, wine and beer' in exchange for promises of protection. Such an approach seems to have worked well for Kolchugin's family in the first five days of the occupation. The soldiers were pleased with their treatment and protected the family from looters. However, the fires soon reached Kolchugin's neighbourhood and destroyed nearby houses, forcing the family to seek shelter elsewhere. In the process, they were 'robbed of not only clothing, but shoes and even undergarments as well.' Returning home the following day, Kolchugin was thrilled to find his house partially pillaged but still standing, after being protected by firewalls and changing winds. To prevent any further looting, Kolchugin took on 'a wounded French captain with a medal of distinction', who protected the family for the next two weeks.[34]

Faith sustained many Muscovites through this calamity and allowed some to accept their fate calmly. Anna Grigorievna Kruglova, the wife of a wealthy merchant, lived near the Sukarevskaya Tower (in Zemlyanoi Gorod). Determined to leave Moscow with her friends, she called upon one of her acquaintances, an old woman married to another merchant, to urge her to flee with them. Kruglova later recalled:

> I found her near the icons, lighting her lamp. She was dressed as if for a holiday, all in white, with a white kerchief about her head. 'What is the matter?' I asked. 'Do you not know that your house is already on fire? Let us pack up your clothes as quickly as possible, and with God's help we may escape; we came to take you with us.' But she only replied, 'Thank you, my dear, for remembering me. For my part, I have spent all my life in this house, and I will not leave it alive. As the house caught on fire, I put on my wedding chemise and my burial garment. I shall begin to pray. And it is thus that death will find me.' We tried to reason with her; why should she become a martyr when the good God pointed out a way of escape? 'I shall not burn,' she rejoined, 'I shall be suffocated before the flames can reach me. So go, there is still time. The smoke is already filling the room, and I have my prayers to make. Let us say good-bye, and then go. God bless you.'

Weeping, Kruglova embraced her old friend and left. 'The room was already full of smoke.'[35]

Moscow was home to two dozen monasteries and over three hundred cathedrals and churches; despite the fiery devastation and pillaging, at least fourteen churches continued to perform services and provide spiritual guidance to their communities throughout the occupation.[36] However, the richly adorned monasteries and churches also naturally attracted numerous marauders. Metropolitan Platon and Archbishop Augustin tried their best to evacuate church property in good time, and Governor Rostopchin assisted them by granting some 300 transports to remove the most important church treasures. However, the sheer number of churches and convents made this task impossible to complete. Most importantly, the evacuation could not be launched too soon since the removal of icons and other holy symbols would have had a profound effect on the population and might have caused disturbances. Therefore most of the church property was evacuated in the last two days before the surrender of the city, but the process could not be completed in the time available. By 14 September there were still considerable quantities of valuables remaining in most churches and in all five women's monasteries and one male. 'I received permission to depart from the city,' wrote the priest of the Church of the Icon of the Holy Mother of Georgia, 'but our army confiscated our rented transports for the wounded soldiers and we could not find any other transports, and were thus compelled to stay in Moscow to protect our church property.'[37] Similar challenges prevented many other Russian churchmen from leaving the city or evacuating their precious possessions. To protect church property, the priests and almoners resorted to a variety of methods of concealment, including hiding property behind fake walls and burying it in the ground. But concealment often proved ineffective – the Allied soldiers broke down walls and tore apart hearths and ovens in the search for treasure. They dug into any ground that bore signs of disturbed topsoil, and even ransacked cemeteries, violating the resting-places of the dead and opening recent graves. Even goods that had been placed in 'store-rooms and basements and cleverly walled up with bricks so that it was quite impossible to perceive that there was a hole were nevertheless discovered by the French. Not even property buried in the ground escaped discovery: under vegetable gardens and courtyards they prodded the ground and pulled out chests.'[38] The small valuables of the Convent of St Alexis were hidden in a store-room; they were plundered, despite the best efforts of the priests. Some Allied soldiers here dressed themselves in the long habits of the nuns, and a few took up their quarters in the cell of the Lady Superior. They stayed at the convent for two whole days, often inviting the young nuns to join them.

'After the fire, the enemy broke into the church and, having smashed the doors, began to ransack with great fury us and all the other people who had sought shelter from the fires. This pillaging continued unremittingly for the next three weeks,' lamented one Muscovite priest.[39] Soldiers resorted to threats and violence to force priests and nuns to reveal the secret places where their treasures were hidden. At the Zaikopasskii Monastery they rounded up all the monks and, having 'robbed them of all their clothing', they made the naked monks carry their loot to their camp; along the way they threw several monks into the Moscow river. At the Pokrovskii Monastery the few remaining monks were all 'tormented to force them to reveal their treasures'. At the Bogoyavlenskii Monastery they dragged the hieromonk[40] Aaron 'by hair and beard and pressed their bayonets against his chest', demanding to know where the monastery treasures had been hidden.[41] After ransacking the monastery but finding no precious items, the soldiers forced the hieromonk to carry a few textiles and bottles of wine back to their camp, where he was freed. On his way back, Aaron was stopped by another group of soldiers, who made him carry their plunder. He managed to return the following day, only to suffer another round of abuse from a new wave of soldiers, who beat him senseless with their sabres in an effort to extract information about the whereabouts of the treasures. 'My shoulders and back remained blackened for an entire month,' complained the hieromonk in a letter to the bishop.[42] Less fortunate was the priest at the Soroka-svyatskii Church, located near the Novospasskii Monastery, who was tortured to death, his mutilated body left out in the open for days. Near the Church of St George on Vspolye a Muscovite merchant was tortured by soldiers who refused to believe that he was not a priest, and were slowly making cuts with a sword in the poor man's back demanding to know where he had hidden the church treasures.[43]

Some monasteries fared better than others. At the Devichii Monastery the news of the enemy's arrival in Moscow initially spread fear and confusion. 'We saw our priest, pale as a sheet of linen, running from the gates and shouting, "They are coming! The French are coming!",' remembered Sister Antonina. The almoner ordered the monastery gates closed, hoping to save his convent from any pillaging. The first Allied troops appeared at the Devichii Monastery on Wednesday, 16 September. Early in the morning the nuns heard A 'ruckus and commotion' outside the monastery walls. 'We looked outside and were awestruck by what we saw: there were numerous enemy soldiers in front of the monastery gates and they had two cannon in front of them.' Preparing for the worst, the nuns dropped to their knees in tears and began praying. With some troops already scaling the wall, the almoner chose to open the gates to avoid unnecessary destruction.[44] The younger nuns were all crammed into one room, and through the little windows they watched as the Allied troops entered the monastery. Spotting an officer at the head of the troops, the almoner asked him in Latin if he could help them in any way. The officer was *Capitaines adjoint* Zadera of Davout's 1st Corps,[45] who inquired about the monastery, which he said had drawn attention in the headquarters of Marshal Davout as it 'resembled a fortress'.[46] The almoner assured him it was just a monastery, and took Zadera and some other officers on a tour. When they disappeared behind the corner of the church, 'the young ones among us', relates one nun, 'were dying of curiosity to find out what they were doing, so we decided to go outside and have a look. We gently opened the door to steal out one by one. An old nun – a kind-hearted but constantly grumbling woman – saw us and ran up to us. "Where are you going?" she exclaimed. "Go back at once. You wish to look at the soldiers, shameless women that you are. See how you blush. If you were modest girls you would be pale with fear." The young nuns defended themselves: "How can we avoid having red cheeks? We are squashed like herrings in a barrel. One can scarcely breathe. If we died, we could not turn pale in here."' But the old nun went on scolding and shut the young nuns in the cell again.[47]

After inspecting the monastery,[48] Zadera informed the almoner that he intended to deploy a regiment here. As the Allied troops left, the nuns began preparing for the worst. 'We were all frightened, since we knew that this might be the last chance for us to partake in the sacraments. We listened to a mass inside the church and after the service our priest told us, "There is no time for me to receive confessions from each of you. So confess your sins to the Almighty God yourselves. He will accept your penitence while I will pray for your souls ... Only the wailing nuns could be heard in the church."[49] However, Zadera proved to be a decent man. As he inspected the church and saw its rich adornment and treasures, he told the priests to hide any precious items, adding 'the French troops [are] thieves'.[50] Zadera then took an inventory of the entire monastery. All the cells were examined and catalogued, and the nuns were asked to move into five rooms while the rest of the monastery was requisitioned. At the Rozhdestvenskii Convent, which was also treated more leniently than other monasteries, the older nuns tried to protect their younger companions from the soldiery by rubbing soot over their pretty faces. In passing through the courtyard they encountered a number of soldiers, who gathered round them. The old women spat on the ground, pretending, by their gestures, that the novices were black and ugly. But one of the soldiers picked up a bucket of water and gestured to the nuns to wash their faces. When the nuns tried to escape, the soldiers caught them and commenced scrubbing their faces. All the nuns, young and old, then began to shriek, but the soldiers laughed heartily, saying 'Jolies filles!'[51]

But it was the desecration of places of worship and religious artefacts by the Allied soldiers that particularly infuriated the Muscovites. In the burning city the stone-built churches and monasteries were often the only safe shelters and so, as Labaume explained, 'all the churches except four or five were turned into stables. They had big iron doors and locks and the French felt safer there at nights.' But for the Muscovites, the sight of enemy soldiers defiling their holy places was insufferable. 'After pillaging the churches they stabled horses, slaughtered cattle and lodged wounded soldiers there,' wrote one Russian eyewitness. 'And having stripped the sacred icons from their frames they bayoneted them and poured filth on them. They also committed other abominations which the tongue cannot mention.'[52] At the Novodevichii Monastery the troops 'despoiled everything, even stones, because they were of weak constitution. [To relieve themselves] they would stand on a stone but cover two or three other stones with their filth, which could be found everywhere.'[53] Another Muscovite was enraged to see an icon used for target practice by the Allied soldiers near the Red Gates.[54] In their search for treasures the soldiers desecrated numerous tombs and scattered countless holy relics, including the ashes of Russian martyrs and saints.[55] The young Becker was astonished to see a French soldier splitting icons with an axe near the church on the Petrovka and using the wood to cook his meal.[56] 'They slept in the sanctuary and ate off the altar,' bemoaned one Russian nun. 'In the church, there was a large icon representing the appearances of the Mother of God painted on wood and without fittings.... . The French took it from the wall and used it as a table.'[57] The Peter and Paul Church in Lefortovo was turned into a sty, while the Assumption Cathedral in the Kremlin and Trinity Church at the Syromyatniki served as stables. The Church of the Saviour in the Woods and the Church of St Nicholas (also inside the Kremlin) were used as storehouses for hay, oats and other materials. At the Kozmo-demyansk Church in the Zamoskvorechye soldiers built a bonfire in the middle of the temple, with the flames fuelled by wooden icons. In the *kliros*, where choirs once praised the Lord, the eyewitness now saw bundles of oats and rye and piles of vegetables, while horses were stationed at the altar.[58] Worse, slaughter-houses were set up inside in many churches and convents. At the Petrovskii Monastery Russian passers-by were astounded to see the monastery's entrance almost entirely covered in blood, while nearby animal intestines and other by-products lay in heaps producing an unbearable stench. 'Looking inside the church,' wrote the eyewitness, 'I saw that the [Allied soldiers] had set up a meat shop there, with meat lying on wide shelves along the walls while some animal parts hung from chandeliers and iconostasis.'[59] The Danilovskii Monastery fared a little better since the troops deployed there did not defile the church, although the area around it still presented an unseemly sight. 'A slaughter-house was established here and cattle of various kinds were gathered, so that cows, sheep, pigs and other animals were slaughtered and their intestines thrown around the monastery. The soldiers acted very untidily and walking around the monastery became a rather revolting experience.'[60] Once can only imagine the stench of blood, excrement and rotting flesh that filled the air in the city. After the French retreat, the Russian authorities collected almost 25,000 dead bodies and animal carcasses that had been left rotting in the streets in the unusually warm autumn weather. The putrid smell was so bad that even '15 *verstas* [10 miles] from Moscow it was still hard to breathe'.[61] Disposing of this mass of decomposing flesh proved to be a huge operation and 'for several weeks [after the French retreat], the police were burning corpses by the banks of the river and sweeping the ashes into the water'.[62] These fires, however, produced 'a horribly suffocating, stinking smoke that spread throughout the whole city', choking its residents.[63]

Many Russian eyewitnesses remark on the perceived lack of faith among the Allied soldiers. The desecration of the Russian Orthodox churches and cathedrals clearly showed the indifference felt by the soldiers towards Russian religious beliefs. But they also seemed unconcerned about religion in general. Although Moscow boasted a sizeable Catholic Church – St Louis des Français – very few Allied soldiers visited it. Its parish priest, Abbé Surrugues, marvelled that only a handful of officers, mostly from aristocratic backgrounds, came to mass and confession. He went around the hospitals to talk to the wounded but found them completely uninterested in spiritual issues. 'Some 12,000 men died during their stay here,' Surrugues wrote, 'but I performed a religious burial service for only two of them, an officer and a servant of General Grouchy. All the others were simply buried by their comrades in nearby gardens. They do not seem to believe in an afterlife … Faith is nothing but an empty word to them.'[64] On 2 October Russian reports from Moscow claimed that in wet weather 'Frenchmen' could frequently be seen wearing 'priestly vestments to protect their uniforms. The depth of impertinence and the range of defilement that they commit inside the church is so godless that one does not even dare to put it on paper.'[65]

In popular memory the Allied soldiers are often simply identified as 'the French', who are then associated with all the abuses and excesses committed in the city. Thus no distinction is made between the French and the Württembergers, Saxons, Bavarians, Poles, Italians and others who served in the Grande Armée. To the casual observer, they were all 'French'. But more discerning eyewitnesses did distinguish between the French and the Allied troops, speaking highly of the former and disparagingly of the latter. Many contemporaries 'ascribed most of their torments and rage to the Bavarians and Poles',[66] and many Muscovites remembered the French protecting them from the marauders. For example, Anna Kruglova's family was being robbed by some Allied troops when a 'dashing' French general (she claimed his name was Caulaincourt) appeared with a few troops and drove the robbers away, leading the family to safety and giving a pretzel to a crying baby. Decades after the event Kruglova still admired this Frenchman: 'What a kind soul he was! If he is no longer alive, may his soul rest in the heavens!'[67] Ysarn witnessed how a French general (he thought it was Sebastiani) protected a Muscovite 'bourgeois' from the 'Württemberg devils' who were about to rob him.[68] Indeed, the memoirs of the Muscovites who endured the occupation tend to describe the French soldiers as more polite, and even obliging, than some of their Allies. Thus, after enduring the first wave of plundering, Andrei Alekseyev noted that the men who robbed him 'were not true Frenchmen, who are actually very compassionate. We usually recognized them by their speech and manners and were not afraid of them because we knew they had the decency to act properly. But may the Lord protect us from their Allies! We called them a "merciless host" because neither begging nor tears affected them; it was even said among the masses that they could not be killed by a bullet. Indeed, they abused people both through word and deed … The French, on the other hand, did not abuse without a reason.'[69] Kicheyev recalled a 'French hussar officer, wearing a red dolman', who came by his house and 'politely greeted' the family. After joining them for lunch, he took aside Kicheyev's uncle and 'revealed beneath his uniform a shirt that was as blackened as tinder', humbly asking if he could spare a clean one. After receiving it, 'he left us, asking us to excuse his intrusion and saying that only extreme hardship had compelled him to disturb us'.[70] A certain mounted grenadier of the Imperial Guard left an interesting note in the great visitor's book of Moscow's city council. Written in broken French, the message reads: 'There is not one Frenchman who is not desperately saddened by the

The Cathedral Square inside the Kremlin, by F. Alekseyev, 1800–1802. The square's name relates to the great cathedrals that stand here – Blagoveshchenskii Sobor (the Cathedral of the Annunciation), Uspenski Sobor (the Cathedral of the Assumption) and Arkhangelskii Sobor (the Cathedral of the Archangel) – as well as the Church of the Twelve Apostles and the Church of the Deposition of the Robe. The Ivan the Great Bell-Tower, the Assumption Belfry and the Filaret Annexe dominate the centre of the painting.

The view from the Troitskaya (Trinity) Tower and Gates of the Kremlin. Note the earthworks and the dry bed of the Neglinnaya River.

View of the Cathedral of St Basil the Blessed from Moskvoretskaya Street, by F. Alekseyev, 1800–1802. The viewer standing in the middle of the street would have the Moscow River and the Moskvoretskii Bridge behind him, the Kremlin to the left and the Merchant's Court to the right.

View of Moscow from the southeast, on the Moscow river, by F. Alekseyev, 1800–1802. The Kremlin towers can be discerned in the distance, while the imposing building on the right is the Foundlings Home.

Inside the Kremlin complex, by F. Alekseyev, 1800–1802. The Terem Palace can be seen on the left, while the Church of the Saviour in the Woods is in the centre.

The Red Square and the St Basil Cathedral in the early nineteenth century, by F. Alekseyev, 1800–1802. Note the trade stalls in front of the cathedral, the Spasskaya (Saviour) Tower and Gates on the right and the trade stalls of the Merchant's Court on the left. The large round platform in the middle of the square is Lobnoe Mesto, where state decrees were announced.

General Domenico Pino's
15th Division on the march,
16 July 1812, by Albrecht
Adam.

The Grande Armée's units
bivouacked in the vicinity
of Moscow, 20 September
1812, by Albrecht Adam.

The devastated environs of
Moscow on 20 September
1812, by Albrecht Adam.

In the suburbs of Moscow, 20 September 1812, by Albrecht Adam.

Allied troops resting in Moscow, 22 September 1812, by Albrecht Adam.

Napoleon amidst the burned ruins of Moscow, 22 September 1812, by Albrecht Adam.

Christian von Martens's drawing of the Moscow Fire, as seen from the bastions of the Kremlin, 18 September 1812. (*Courtesy of Baden-Württemberg Landesarchiv, Hauptstaatsarchiv Stuttgart J 52 Bü 4*)

'In Moscow' – drawn by Christian von Martens, 18 September 1812. (*Courtesy of Baden-Württemberg Landesarchiv, Hauptstaatsarchiv Stuttgart J 52 Bü 4*)

Moscow burning, as drawn by Christian von Martens, 19 September 1812. (*Courtesy of Baden-Württemberg Landesarchiv, Hauptstaatsarchiv Stuttgart J 52 Bü 4*)

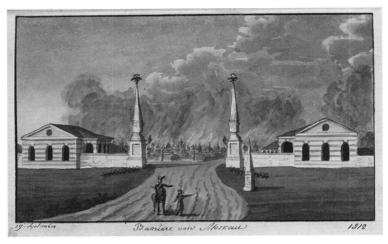

Another view of Moscow burning, as seen from one of the city barriers, drawn by Christian von Martens, 19 September 1812. (*Courtesy of Baden-Württemberg Landesarchiv, Hauptstaatsarchiv Stuttgart J 52 Bü 4*)

The Petrovskii Palace, as depicted by Christian von Martens in early October 1812. (*Courtesy of Baden-Württemberg Landesarchiv, Hauptstaatsarchiv Stuttgart J 52 Bü 4*)

'Guarding a wine cellar.' Christian von Martens, who drew this sketch on 24 September 1812, was one of the many Allied soldiers who enjoyed the vast supplies of alcohol stored in Moscow's cellars. (*Courtesy of Baden-Württemberg Landesarchiv, Hauptstaatsarchiv Stuttgart J 52 Bü 4*)

Christian von Martens's sketch of the military review held by Ney's 3rd Corps in the Kremlin on 18 October 1812. 'The review was as imposing as circumstances would admit of', commented one French officer. (*Courtesy of Baden-Württemberg Landesarchiv, Hauptstaatsarchiv Stuttgart J 52 Bü 4*)

'The Burning of Moscow' – a German engraving by Küpfer after Johan Lorenz Rugendas, early nineteenth century. (*By courtesy of Anne S.K. Brown Military Collection*)

'Napoleon's Troops entering Moscow' – German print by Friedrich Campe, early nineteenth century. (*By courtesy of Anne S.K. Brown Military Collection*)

A nineteenth-century Russian print depicting Archpriest Mikhail Gratinskii of the Chevalier Guard Regiment holding a shared service for Russian parishioners and Allied troops at the Church of St Euplius on 27 September 1812.

Panoramic view of Moscow, looking west from the Kremlin; a French print by Dubois after Henri Courvoisier-Voisin, 1812. (*By courtesy of Anne S.K. Brown Military Collection*)

French troops entering Moscow: French print by Jean, 1812. (*By courtesy of Anne S.K. Brown Military Collection*)

A nineteenth-century print depicting the Grande Armée entering Moscow on 14 September 1812.

'The French in Moscow' – D. Kardovskii, 1913.

'The Council of War at Fili' – A. Kivshenko, 1880. This is a rare version of Kivshenko's famous painting of the council at Fili. Shown (*left to right*) are: M. Kutuzov, P. Konovnitsyn, N. Rayevskii, A. Osterman–Tolstoy, M. Barclay de Tolly, F. Uvarov, D. Dokhturov, A. Yermolov, K. Toll and L. Bennigsen. The figure seated at the desk is probably P. Kaisarov.

Kutuzov and his generals on the Poklonnaya Gora before the Council of War at Fili, painted by A. Kivshenko, 1893.

An early nineteenth-century French print showing the Grande Armée occupying Moscow as the fire burns in the suburbs.

The ruins of Moscow on 24 September 1812, depicted by Faber du Faur. Note the melted copper roof in the middle and the body near the soldiers.

'Napoleon on the Poklonnaya Gora on 14 September 1812' – A. Nikolayev's illustration for Leo Tolstoy's *War and Peace*.

'An episode of 1812. French prisoners of war' – I. Pryanishkov, 1873.

'View of the Kremlin during the Moscow Fire' – Christian J. Oldendorp, coloured engraving by Schmidt, early nineteenth century.

'Russian peasant Vavila the Frost hunting hares' – Russian caricature, 1812.

'The Russian Spirit of Intrepidity' – Russian print, 1812. The caption reads: 'Exemplary spirit of resolution of twenty Russian peasants whom Napoleon had mercilessly condemned to be executed for their devotion to their Faith, Sovereign and Fatherland.'

This French print of 1816 shows the Moscow Fire as seen looking west from the Kremlin.

The meeting between Alexander Lauriston and Mikhail Kutuzov, and the Russian's rejection of Napoleon's peace offer, fancifully depicted in an early nineteenth-century print.

The Russian army abandoning Moscow on 14 September, by A. Sokolov and A. Semenov, 1958.

'Napoleon and Lauriston. Peace at any price', by V. Vereschagin, 1899.

The executions of suspected Russian incendiaries, depicted by V. Vereschagin, 1898.

A German print of 1847 showing Napoleon leaving the devastated Moscow. (*By courtesy of Anne S.K. Brown Military Collection*)

Emperor Alexander of Russia, by G. Dawe.

General Mikhail Barclay de Tolly, early nineteenth-century print.

General Levin Bennigsen, early nineteenth-century print.

Grand Equerry and General Armand de Caulaincourt, by F. Gerard, engraving by G. Kruell.

Marshal Louis Nicolas Davout, lithograph by Delpech, 1830s.

Eugene de Beauharnais, Viceroy of Italy, by H. Scheffer, engraving by C. Powell.

General Mikhail Kutuzov, by F. Vendramini, 1813.

General Jacques Alexandre Law, Marquis der Lauriston, early nineteenth-century print.

Marshal Edouard-Adolphe-Casimir-Joseph Mortier, Duke of Treviso, by Marie-Nicolas Ponce-Camus, engraving by E. Heinemann.

General Mikhail Miloradovich, by G. Dawe.

Marshal Michel Ney, Duke of Echingen and Prince de la Moskowa, by F. Gerard, engraved by E. Tietze.

Marshal Joachim Murat, King of Naples, by F. Gerard, engraved by H. Wolf.

Governor Count Fedor Rostopchin of Moscow, by O. Kiprenskii, 1809.

Cossack Ataman Matvei Platov, by G. Dawe.

misfortune which has befallen your lovely Moscow. I can assure you that as far as I am concerned, I weep for it and regret it, for it was worthy of being preserved.'[71]

The young Becker's first encounter with the French was also relatively trouble-free: three tall dragoons 'with black moustaches and sideburns' entered his house carrying four chickens, a small bag of provisions and a decanter of red wine. They asked the women to prepare the food, which they shared with the half-starved family before leaving.[72] Seeking fresh information on what was happening in the city, Madame Fusil was pleasantly surprised when 'a very polite young officer approached me and warned that it was dangerous for me to walk alone. Then he offered to accompany me ... So we went on together ... At the corner of the street, a few wailing women begged him for protection from soldiers who were looting their homes. He obliged and scattered the intruders ...' After safely delivering Fusil to her house, the young officer stayed for dinner and 'spoke to us with great delight, telling us about the latest fashion and theatre'.[73] An elderly Georgian princess living on the Presnenskaya street survived the Allied occupation of Moscow largely through the generosity of the French troops billeted in her house, who shared their food with her.[74] Madame Domergues recalled that, after the entry of the Grande Armée, she waited for some time before daring to draw aside the curtains and open the shutters. Just as she looked out of the window, however, she was frightened by a thunderous knocking on the door. She hurried to close the shutters and curtains while the knocking continued, accompanied by 'vigorous exclamations'. At last she opened the doors, and encountered some French troops led by a sous–officer of the Imperial Guard. 'Par-bleu, madame,' he exclaimed upon seeing her. 'After marching for eight hundred lieues, all by forced marches, to have the pleasure of seeing you, it would have been very nice of you to have hurried up to open the doors for us.'[75]

At the Danilov Monastery, south of Moscow, the monks first encountered the French on 15 September when 'an enemy officer and soldiers came to inspect the monastery. Two days later a larger detachment of troops occupied the monastery complex, driving the monks out of their cells but otherwise treating them leniently. '[They] walked about the church but did not touch anything, only looking and examining everything,' the monks later reported. 'One officer liked a candle that was lit in front of the icon but he did not take it and instead asked us to find a similar one for him.'[76] Later on the French officer and two of his soldiers, who were quartered in the monastery, warned the priests that artillery crews would be soon billeted there, and helped them to hide their remaining treasures. Sister Antonina of the Devichii Monastery also noted that the French (and Polish) troops deployed near her monastery acted with great courtesy, although she ascribed it to their commander's fear of committing sinful acts. 'This French commander often called our priest and assured him that he would not allow his men to rob or abuse us.' In fact, when the Russian priest lacked red wine and flour to conduct the liturgy, the commander quickly delivered them to him to ensure that the religious ceremonies continued without interruption.[77] Alexey Olenin, one of whose sons died at Borodino, while the other suffered a grievous injury, collected details on the atrocities committed by the Allied soldiers in Russia. In his 'Notebook' he recounted several examples of mistreatment of the civilian population and noted that 'among the peoples comprising Napoleon's horde the most callous torturers and barbarians were the Poles and Bavarians'.[78] Even the German resident of Moscow, who had been born during the Seven Years' War and had 'imbibed a hatred for the French with my mother's breast milk and could not stand even to see them', had to acknowledge that the French were 'the least rapacious' of the Allied troops:

> They took only what they needed to survive but did not plunder for gold, silver or other precious items, not even watches. How different from the Bavarians and the Poles, who usually left nothing behind themselves and pillaged even those items that had no value to them. The Württembergers followed in their footsteps – in fact, the idea of opening and ransacking tombs belongs to them … These soldiers committed acts of vandalism, destroying statues and Chinese bridges in the imperial garden. They were so greedy that they tore away even the upholstery of carriages and furniture, including the cloth from billiard tables. The French, on the other hand, did not commit superfluous pillaging. In fact, they acted with courtesy even in robbing people, which often presented dramatic contrasts. Thus, one French officer had a sofa cut down so he could sleep comfortably but when he departed from the apartment, he brought in a carpenter and had the sofa restored to its original condition. On another occasion some French soldiers entered the house of a professor in the middle of the night; upon learning that his pregnant wife was in labour, they approached her bed on tiptoe, covering their candles with one hand. They quietly emptied the drawers of all possessions but took nothing that belonged to the lady of the house, leaving only with her husband's possessions.[79]

In contrast, some Russians were surprised by the French soldiers' filthy boorishness, which was particularly shocking to them in light of the cultural influence that France enjoyed over much of Europe in the eighteenth century. The French were perceived as the most civilized nation, the quintessential model of European civilization. And yet, 'upon taking Moscow, the French acted themselves as a wild and uncivilized nation;' French officers, for example, were observed unashamedly relieving themselves in the libraries and ballrooms of noble estates in Moscow.[80] In his letter to the Dowager Empress, Ivan Tutolmin complained that the French soldiers billeted at the Foundlings Home had 'fouled everything: they ate and defecated where they slept'. They ruined 'the floors, doors, windows, stoves and walls' and their excrement littered the hallways and soaked into the floors.[81] One Muscovite observed, 'Maybe there was something good in the French but I personally saw nothing … One will struggle to find such know-nothing, barbarian and slovenly swine … Their officers were not averse to kneading bread in the washtubs that their soldiers used to wash their underwear, even though we warned them that the tub had been soiled.'[82]

'Of all the nations who followed Napoleon's banners,' observed one Polish officer, 'the Poles were the most hated by the Russians.'[83] And one can understand the deep-seated hostility between the two nations. In the seventeenth century the Polish–Lithuanian Commonwealth was the greatest of Russia's foes, occupying vast tracts of Russian lands, including Moscow itself. The roles were reversed a century later when the expanding Russian Empire partitioned and destroyed the Polish state. The memories of the Russian invasions of 1792 and 1794 were still fresh in the memory, and many Poles were burning with a desire for vengeance. A German officer noted that 'for the Poles, one of the attractions of joining in the pillaging was the desire to settle old scores. I saw a lancer urging on a poor Russian, laden with the lancer's booty, with a whip. When I reproached him for this brutality, he grew angry with me and hissed, "My father and mother were both massacred at Praga [in 1794].'"[84] But not all Poles were so cold-blooded, and some actively sought to lessen the hardships of Moscow's populace. At the Presnenskii Lakes Kicheyev's family and dozens of their neighbours and other refugees had their scant possessions plundered by the Allied soldiers, among whom was a tall Pole 'who appeared to be 40 years old, with long blond moustaches, dressed in military uniform and fully armed'. He did not participate in the plunder but 'seemed to be observing the other soldiers to make sure that they did not kill anyone'. At one point Kicheyev's grandfather was accosted by a tall but pale and skinny Polish soldier, who wore tattered uniform and was bare-footed. The Pole forced the old man to give up his boots but, upon seeing him crying, he offered to give them back.[85]

Of all the various disasters in Moscow, perhaps the most horrible sights were to be found in the aftermath of the fires in the Russian hospitals, which were caring for many of those grievously injured at Borodino. One of the first things that the Grande Armée's *Intendant-Général* Mathieu Dumas did upon reaching Moscow was to visit the hospitals, which he found

> already crowded with the sick and wounded of the Russian army. The most considerable of these establishments, situated at the extremity of the city near the summer-palace, appeared to me to be in a dreadful state of neglect; everything was wanting, and death made horrible ravages; the dead bodies cast into the street lay round the wall, objects of horror and compassion. Other hospitals were in a better condition; several Russian officers had been received into them, and room was reserved for ours.[86]

These hospitals, however, soon turned into deathtraps. As the flames reached each hospital, wounded soldiers were seen dragging themselves down the stairs or jumping through the windows, screaming and howling before succumbing at the end of their fall. 'When the flames took hold of the buildings in which the wounded were crammed,' wrote Chambray, 'they could be seen dragging themselves along corridors or throwing themselves out of windows, yelling with pain.'[87]

There are no precise figures for the Russian wounded who perished in the fires. On 16 September Napoleon's 19th Bulletin proclaimed that 'thirty thousand wounded or sick Russian [soldiers] are abandoned in the hospitals, without succour and nourishment'.[88] Just a day later the 20th Bulletin mentioned in passing that all of these men had perished in the conflagration,[89] and this number of some 30,000 Russian dead appeared in subsequent writings on the Russian campaign. However, writing just two days after his entry into Moscow, Napoleon could not have known the precise number of the Russian wounded, and later demanded reports detailing this information.[90] In this case, the 19th Bulletin simply twisted the truth (as bulletins usually did), and the subsequent issues further underscore this point. The 20th Bulletin claimed that all the wounded had perished in the fires, but the 23rd Bulletin noted that 'we succeeded with great difficulty in withdrawing from the hospitals and houses on fire some Russian [soldiers]. There were about 4,000 of these wretched men.'[91] So Napoleon was incorrect in his earlier claim of all Russian wounded perishing. In fact Napoleon himself does not seem to have believed the claim of 30,000 Russian wounded perishing in the fires, as in a private conversation with Ivan Tutolmin on 19 September he accused the Russians of 'callousness for abandoning 10,000 wounded soldiers without food and care'.[92] Russian documents also point to a smaller number of the wounded perishing in the flames. In the wake of the battle of Borodino between 22,000 and 26,000 wounded had been brought to Moscow: Governor Rostopchin referred to 22,000, while Jacob Wyllie spoke of 22,500.[93] On 11 September Rostopchin gave orders to evacuate all but the most seriously wounded soldiers and from the following day those soldiers who could walk were directed towards Kolomna. General Yermolov, who as the Chief of Staff of the 1st Army did his best to organize the evacuation of the wounded, spoke of some 26,000 wounded brought to Moscow, more than half of whom had been removed from the city.[94] Lightly wounded men simply followed in the wake of the army, while the more grievously injured were transported on carts.[95] Thus by 14 September more than half of the Russian wounded had been removed from the city; most Russian historians agree that some 10,000 wounded were left in the city, largely for the lack of transportation.[96] Of these, some had indeed perished in the fires, but most had got out of the burning buildings and were later seen either starving to death in the streets of Moscow or engaged in the plundering of fellow Russians. Thus, Nikolai Miritskii, the supervisor of the Widows' Home, noted that there were about 1,500 wounded at his institution. Almost half of them perished when the fires came but 'some 800, despite being weak, managed to survive the conflagration. They escaped into the yard and garden and scattered in various directions over the next few days because of lack of provisions.'[97] They could have been among those Kicheyev saw 'crawling around in garbage heaps and picking at potato peelings and other remnants'.[98]

Wounded Russian officers were a little more fortunate. Avraam Norov, who lost a leg at Borodino, was recuperating at Golitsyn's Hospital; given the nature of his injury, he was not considered for evacuation. In fact, he was largely forgotten amidst the confusion of the retreating army and the abandonment of the city, and received no medical attention for days. On 15 September, as the fires ravaged the city, Norov was lying alone in his hospital room when a marauder burst in, brusquely searched him for any loot and left without finding anything. Preparing for the worst, Norov was surprised when, a few hours later, an elderly French soldier approached his bed and shared a few biscuits and some water with him. The following day Norov was visited by Dominique Larrey himself, who gave him medical treatment for the first time since his surgery over a week earlier. Larrey's intervention probably saved Norov's life as the wound, left untreated for so long, was already showing signs of putrefaction. 'I was profoundly touched by this generous man,' Norov recalled. 'It was not for nothing that Napoleon called him "le vertueux Larrey"!'[99] Over the next few days Norov saw his room filled up with both Russian and French wounded officers, who received equal attention from the great French surgeon.

Many of the wounded were also cared for by Jean-Baptiste Turiot, an intelligent and experienced French surgeon who had long urged Napoleon to reform the French medical system and create a permanent army medical corps. However, Turiot's letters – seventeen since 1796 – remained largely ignored so that the French physicians and surgeons lacked many basic essentials in Russia, including proper field hospitals. After the bloody battle at Smolensk, Turiot wrote, 'the building of the city's archives was transformed into a hospital, the documents found there were rolled up to serve as splints, cannon plugs and gun cotton replaced bandages and linen, while government files were used as bedding for those operations'.[100] Sadly almost all the amputees died due to the unsanitary conditions. The situation was slightly better in Moscow, where the French surgeons took over existing hospital buildings but they still could not properly treat the tens of thousands of wounded and sick. Turiot appealed to Napoleon once more, arguing that the soldiers' misery and suffering was exacerbated by the lack of a proper medical system. But he also accused the 'army administrators' of not taking measures to prevent 'pillage and the waste of immense provisions that would have amply allowed us to bring much physical comfort to the troops'. These military officials, Turiot raged, 'thought only of themselves and of lining their own pockets', remarking that 'the taste for good life and blatant venality have transformed those whose job it is to devote themselves entirely to the wounded and the troops into veritable parasites'.[101] His criticism is echoed in the memoirs of Dutch officer Aart Kool, who bemoaned that 'there should have been care taken to ensure that all soldiers were well supplied with winter clothing, which would have occurred under a good administration, but the French organisation was the worst ever. The blankets stayed in storage and nothing was allocated to the officers and the soldiers.'[102]

Chapter 7

In the Ruins of the Great City

Napoleon remained at the Petrovskii Palace from the evening of 16 September to the morning of 18 September.[1] Unlike the Kremlin's oriental exotic architecture, the Petrovskii Palace divided opinions among the Allied officers. Roman Soltyk saw a 'palace of red bricks, which were not plastered with lime; the building is of Gothic architecture and resembled the palace of Hampton Court in London'. Castellane also found it 'very beautiful, surrounded by brick walls and flanked by towers of a Greek style, overall, a truly romantic place'. Less impressed was Colonel Griois, who described the palace as a 'vast building of very antique construction, surrounded by high brick walls; its heavy and stern appearance made it seem more like a state prison than a sovereign's palace'.[2] The palace, however, was large enough to accommodate the imperial and general headquarters and the Administration. Thus, General La Riboisière's entire staff – almost a dozen men – was crammed into one small room.[3]

Throughout the two days he spent at the Petrovskii Palace Napoleon remained glum and taciturn. After going to bed early on the 16th, he woke up early the next morning and came out to watch the burning Russian city in the distance. 'Absorbed by this melancholy contemplation,' observed Segur, 'he preserved a long and gloomy silence, which he broke only by the exclamation, "This forebodes great misfortunes to us!"' Returning to the palace, he dictated the 19th Bulletin, announcing both the occupation and the destruction of Moscow. 'The city of Moscow is as large as Paris, and it is an extremely rich city, full of palaces of all the nobles of the empire. Yet the Russian governor Rostopchin wished to ruin this fine city when he saw it abandoned by the Russian army … The most complete anarchy reigned in the city; some drunken madmen ran through its different quarters and everywhere set fire to them.'[4] Early in the morning of the 17th Napoleon went frequently outside to observe the city on which he had placed so many hopes smouldering in the distance. 'He beheld the fire raging with the utmost violence,' described Ségur. 'The whole city appeared like a vast spout of fire rising in whirling eddies to the sky, which it deeply coloured.' Napoleon remained 'very pensive and did not talk to anyone' for a long time.[5]

But his apathy did not last long. Pressing matters demanded his attention and the emperor was soon back to the usual routine of reviewing the continuous stream of reports and updates on troop movements, redeployments and supplies. The situation was serious, and Napoleon believed that he would need eight days to rally his remaining forces. He dictated the 20th Bulletin, informing the army (and the public back in France) of the devastating consequences of the fires, which he referred to as 'Rostopchin's crime'. To reassure the families back at home,[6] the bulletin proclaimed that the army was 'recovering from its fatigues, and has abundance of bread, potatoes, cabbages and other vegetables, meat, salted provisions, wine, brandy, sugar, coffee – in short, provisions of all sorts'. In conclusion, the emperor noted that 'the temperature is still that of autumn. The soldiers have found, and continued to find, a number of fur-trimmed coats and furs for the winter. Moscow was the depot of those articles.'[7] That same day (the 17th) Napoleon also dispatched his aide-de-camp General Narbonne to protect the beautiful Sloboda Palace (also known as the Yellow Palace) in the eastern Lefortovo suburbs of Moscow. The young Boniface Castellane, who accompanied Narbonne on this mission, remembered that they were able to reach the Lefortovo only by 'ten o'clock at night, after being forced to make long detours because flames frequently blocked our way. We saw many armed Russian soldiers walking freely in the streets, while others, being wounded, sought to escape from the flames. We encountered many people on carts carrying their most precious effects and being robbed by our soldiers. We escorted them to safety and a large number of these unfortunates settled in groups around the city.' Yet it was too late to save the Sloboda Palace, except for 'numerous paintings' that Narbonne's men removed before returning to the Petrovskii Palace.[8]

As well as his commanders and messengers, Napoleon also met with a number of the French residents of Moscow, hoping to gain a deeper insight into Russian society. Among them was Marie-Rose Aubert-Chalmé, owner of a successful milliner's shop on the famous Kuznetskii bridge, and the wife of Jean-Nicholas Aubert, who managed a hotel in Moscow. About 30 years old, a beautiful and charming woman, Aubert-Chalmé was very popular in the French community of Moscow but also maintained useful contacts among the Russian aristocracy. This, however, did not prevent Governor Rostopchin from exiling her husband, along with dozens of other Frenchmen, in August. Now, a month later, she was standing next to the emperor of the French. They held a long conversation, almost all of which remains unknown to us. It is unclear what made this young woman so important that Napoleon spent over an hour conversing with her. It certainly wasn't his desire to get away from his pressing problems in the company of a charming woman. We know that he sounded her out on a couple of important political topics, including what she thought of freeing the Russian serfs. She later claimed that her response was that one-third of the serfs would welcome his decision, while the rest would not even understand what he was attempting to do for them.[9] As it was, Napoleon did not dare to attempt such a radical reform. The rest of conversation is wrapped in secrecy. Yet this meeting proved fateful for Aubert-Chalmé: once the news of the meeting spread, the Russians branded her Napoleon's spy and accused her of having been in the service of the French government for a long time before the war. Why else, they argued, would she have met the French Emperor if not to pass on some valuable information? Even her fellow French residents of Moscow stayed well away from her, fearing retaliations for any association with her. When Napoleon left Moscow in October, Aubert-Chalmé had little choice but to join the ranks of thousands of others who followed the Grande Armée.[10] Along the way Chalmé became separated from her children and died in a typhus epidemic in Vilna in December.

After the meeting with Aubert-Chalmé, Napoleon seems to have spent some time contemplating his next moves. The troops generally expected to winter in Moscow but the emperor had grander plans. His first thought was to rally his forces, leave Moscow and either return to Smolensk or threaten St Petersburg. His so-called 'St Petersburg Plan' has long been studied by historians of the Russian campaign and most of them, based on the testimonies of Ségur and Caulaincourt, believe it was discussed in October. However, there is compelling evidence to suggest that Napoleon had considered an attack on St Petersburg as early as 17 September. His secretary noted that when the emperor arrived at the Petrovskii Palace, 'the road to St Petersburg was open, while Kutuzov's retreat had effectively exposed all of northern Russia. Viceroy [Eugène] found no forces in this direction except for a corps under the command of Wittgenstein, which retreated upon our approach and could not have stopped us. We were only fifteen marches away from Petersburg and Napoleon, therefore, contemplated launching an attack on this other capital [of Russia].'[11] Napoleon intended to regroup his forces and launch a 'simple diversion' to the north while most of the Grande Armée would remain in the environs of Moscow before marching upon Velikie Luki, about 90 miles north-east of Polotsk and some 300 miles from Moscow. This circular movement could have been accomplished by moving 'in echelons along the parallel roads' that traversed the provinces of Velikie Luki and Velikii Novgorod. Napoleon would have united the corps of St Cyr, Macdonald and Victor, and by 15 October deployed his combined forces along the new line on the Dvina river, anchored on the fortress of Riga on one side and on Smolensk on the other, with reserves at Vitebsk, Mogilev, Minsk and Vilna. 'Thus was the plan that the emperor conceived,' wrote Fain. 'He spent the night of 17 September contemplating operations on the map and already began dictating his first orders.'[12] Ségur largely concurs with Fain, although he believed that the discussion of the plan and the generals' opposition to it occurred in October, *after* Napoleon had returned to the Kremlin. According to him, 'The Emperor declared that he should march for St Petersburg. This conquest was already marked out on his maps … orders were even issued to different corps to hold themselves in readiness. But his decision was *only a feint* [author's emphasis]: it was but a better face that he strove to assume or an expedient for diverting his grief for the loss of Moscow'. The marshals convinced the emperor that he had neither time, provisions, roads nor a single requisite for so extensive an excursion. Caulaincourt also mentioned that Napoleon considered various plans at the Petrovskii Palace but he does not specify what exactly these plans entailed. But after Napoleon had returned to Moscow, Caulaincourt described a discussion of his plan for attacking St Petersburg, with Viceroy Eugène, Berthier, Dumas and Murat, who also spoke against it.[13] In the light of this evidence, the Russian historian Zemtsov rightly noted that Napoleon did indeed contemplate an attack on St Petersburg in late September but was compelled to postpone its execution since 'it was still unclear where Kutuzov was located, the [Grande Armée] itself had to be regrouped, and attempts had to be made to sound the Russians out for peace'.[14]

The prospect of a potential new campaign caused grumbling among the senior officer corps. Only Viceroy Eugène supported Napoleon's idea of marching on St Petersburg, and as of 21 September expected the launch of the offensive with his corps 'in the nearest future'.[15] The other corps commanders argued against the campaign, which would necessarily have been fought in sparsely populated and less fertile provinces in the face of the fast-approaching Russian winter. Instead, they preferred to abandon Moscow and retreat back to Poland. 'I was one of those who considered this horrible conflagration as a fortunate event, if it could decide our retreat,' recalled Mathieu Dumas. 'Whatever the difficulties might be, they seemed to me to be smaller or less dangerous than the prolongation of our stay at Moscow.'[16] Napoleon was certainly aware of the numerous challenges facing his plan to attack St Petersburg. Sending a small force northwards would have resulted only in a waste of time, manpower and resources. Yet the Grande Armée had already expended much of its resources and hardly possessed sufficient manpower to launch a major offensive in winter time. The army had to be regrouped and resupplied, which required time – the most precious resource that Napoleon lacked. Above everything else, he desired peace: the peace that he had intended to impose on Emperor Alexander in Moscow, just as he had done with the Austrian and Prussian sovereigns at their respective capitals just few years earlier. But Moscow was gone, and with it went his last hopes of forcing Russia to bend her knee to the French *imperium*. 'We have no rest!' the marshals complained openly to the emperor. 'We march constantly, and now might have to move northwards in the midst of the winter, expecting nothing but continued hardships and vicissitudes ... It is peace that we want, peace at any cost, even if we would have to beg for it on our knees.' Napoleon's initial response was brusque: 'How can you believe that the same people who burned Moscow today would accept peace just a few days later? If those responsible for this decision [to burn Moscow] continue to wield power in Alexander's cabinet, all expectations that you are flattering yourself with are in vain.' But on second thoughts, he agreed with his generals that the 'circumstances must be further examined'.[17]

Napoleon Returns to Moscow

On 18 September,[18] despite the fires still burning in the suburbs, Napoleon left the Petrovskii Palace to return to Moscow.[19] His decision was prompted by the rain that began to fall during the night and had largely damped down the fires by the morning. Around 9am, dressed in his usual great overcoat and black hat, he mounted his horse (appropriately called *le Moscou*) and slowly travelled to the southeast.[20] On his way Napoleon traversed the corps bivouacs, which presented an extraordinary sight. 'In the fields, amidst thick and cold mud, large fires were kept up with mahogany furniture, windows and gilded doors. Around these fires, on a litter of damp straw, imperfectly sheltered by a few boards, were seen the soldiers and their officers, splashed all over with mud and blackened with smoke, seated in arm–chairs or reclining on silken couches.' Luxury items were strewn all around but no one paid heed to them any longer. Some soldiers had precious cashmere shawls or rare Siberian furs wrapped around their feet, and held sumptuous silver and gold plates off which they ate black dough and half-broiled horse flesh. It was 'a singular assemblage of abundance and want, of riches and filth, of luxury and wretchedness', gloomily observed one eyewitness.[21]

The devastated city was a shocking sight. In the words of Caulaincourt, 'fortunate are those who have not witnessed this horrifying spectacle, this sight of utter destruction'.[22] Entering the city through the Tverskaya barrier, Napoleon and his entourage proceeded along the Tverskoi Boulevard towards Strastnaya Square, observing widespread destruction and misery. 'Our carriages were beset all along the route by a crowd of wretched Muscovites who came to beg for alms,' recalled Napoleon's valet. 'They followed us as far as the palace, walking in the hot cinders or on the calcined and still scorching stones. The most miserable were barefooted. It was a heartrending spectacle.'[23] Large groups of soldiers, many of them clearly intoxicated, dragged their booty behind them or forced unfortunate Muscovites to carry it for them. Some soldiers congregated at the entrances into cellars, which were nearly all intact, sharing their trophies. Desolate civilians wandered amidst the enemy troops, clinging desperately to the few possessions they had saved from the fire.

'This was a beautiful city,' Napoleon remarked in a letter later that day. 'I say it was because today more than half of it is destroyed.'[24] Indeed, there was no longer any trace of the resplendent Moscow that had greeted the Grande Armée just four days earlier. The fiery gales had left the city a blackened heap of hissing, smoking ruins. Out of more than 9,150 homes, more than 6,350 had burnt down. Over 80 per cent of the stone buildings and over 68 per cent of the wooden buildings were destroyed and, by the end of the disaster, only 521 (out of 2,367) stone and 2,078 (out of 6,584) wooden houses remained standing. Among the worst hit districts were the Pyatsnitskii, where 160 stone and 415 wooden buildings burnt down, the Yakimanskii (182 and 257 buildings respectively), the Tverskii (238 and 135), and the Arbatskii (114 and 338). In the Sretenskii district there were 630 houses before the fire; only 11 stone and 8 wooden ones survived on 20 September.[25] In addition, hundreds of taverns, shops, inns and markets had all been ransacked and destroyed; in the Yakimanskii district alone more than 100 stone and 53 wooden shopping stalls and 16 stone blacksmith shops burned down. The city also lost many state archives and important cultural centres, including Count A. Musin-Pushkin's vast collection of manuscripts on the history of Russian society and culture, Count D. Buturlin's famed private library of some 40,000 tomes, and the libraries of the University of Moscow and the Society of History and Antiquities. The total loss of property in Moscow was later evaluated at 250 million rubles, which equalled Russia's entire annual revenue for 1812.[26]

Acrid smoke billowing from the ruins and the putrid smell of rotting carcasses and corpses overwhelmed everyone's senses. 'The smell issuing from this colossus, overthrown, burned and calcined, was horrible,' recalled Ségur.[27] The city represented a landscape of collapsed houses, ruined walls and burnt trees. Blackened human corpses and animal carcasses, broken crockery, furniture and debris of various kinds obstructed movement in the streets. 'From end to end Moscow was a scene of indescribable horror and utter desolation. The houses that had survived the fire were plundered, and the churches looted. All the pavements and side-walks were littered with fragments of chandeliers, mirrors, furniture, pictures, books, church-plate and even the sacred *ikons* of the saints.'[28] Travelling across the city, Ségur could only see 'heaps of ashes, and at intervals, fragments of walls or half demolished pillars were now the only vestiges that marked the site of streets'.[29] In some places only the tall columns of chimney stacks marked the course of a street that had effectively ceased to exist. For Montesquiou-Fezensac, Moscow was at once 'a horrible and extraordinary sight'. Some of the houses appeared to have been

> razed from their foundations, others preserved their outline with walls darkened by the smoke. Debris of every kind obstructed the streets, and the smell of burning exhaled from every quarter. Here and there a cottage, a church, a palace, was standing in the midst of the widespread ruin. The churches in particular, by their many-coloured domes and the richness and variety of their construction, reminded us of the ancient opulence of Moscow. They now afforded a refuge to those of the inhabitants who had been driven by our soldiers from the houses which the flames had spared. These wretched beings, wandering like ghosts among the ruins, and clothed in rags, had recourse to the most grievous expedients for prolonging life.[30]

Entering the city after the fire, Private Walter saw 'church towers with burned roofs and half-melted bells, and copper roofs which had rolled from the buildings. Everything was uninhabited and uninhabitable.'[31]

The Emperor made a brief stop at the Kremlin, which was still standing largely intact thanks to the gallant battalion of the Imperial Guard that had preserved it. He examined the damage caused to the Kremlin buildings before changing horses and resuming his survey of the city.[32] This time he rode westwards before turning right near the Arbat Gates and proceeding along the relatively well preserved sections of the Nikitskii and Tverskoi boulevards towards the Myasnitskii district, northeast of the Kremlin. He encountered 'numerous miserable residents who had been reduced to the most frightful destitution by fire and looting', and gave orders to establish shelters and provide food rations and financial aid of some fifty thousand rubles.[33] From the Myasnitskii district Napoleon slowly moved southwards, completing his semicircular movement around the Kremlin at the Moskvoretskii bridge, where he turned west towards the Foundlings Home. The Emperor travelled along the grand *quai* of the Moscow river and amidst 'numerous heartrending scenes' he soon saw that the Foundlings Home was still standing intact. He immediately instructed one of his officers to 'go and see what happened to those unfortunate little ones' who were housed there.[34] The officer reported back that the building and children were safe under the watchful eye of Actual State Councillor Ivan Tutolmin. Napoleon then resumed his trip. Crossing the Yauza Bridge, he reached the Pokrovskaya barrier, where he examined the surrounding area, then he re-entered Moscow through the Rogozhskaya barrier and visited the military hospitals located at Lefortovo; passing by the smouldering ruins of the Sloboda Palace, he returned to the Kremlin at about 4pm.[35] Later that day he wrote a lengthy missive to his wife, sharing his impressions of the day:

> My dear, I have already written to you about Moscow. [But] I had no idea about this town. It had 500 palaces as fine as the Elysée-Napoléon, furnished in the French style with incredible luxury, several imperial palaces, barracks and magnificent hospitals. It has all disappeared. Fire has been consuming everything for four days. As all the small houses of the bourgeois are of wood, they catch fire like matches. It was the Governor and the Russians who, furious at being conquered, set fire to this beautiful town. Some 200,000 worthy inhabitants are in despair, in the streets and in misery. However, there is enough left for the army, and the troops have found no lack of riches of all kinds, for everything is exposed to looting in this upheaval. This loss is immense for Russia. Its trade will suffer a great shock from it.[36]

Napoleon was at least partially correct in stating that 'there is enough left for the army'. Despite the widespread destruction, enough buildings remained to provide shelter for the troops. Some, like Sergeant Bourgogne of the Guard, found themselves in a more than agreeable situation: 'We took possession of our quarters in a fine street hitherto preserved from fire, not far from the first enclosure of the Kremlin. Our company had a large café assigned to it; one of the rooms contained two billiard tables ... We found a great quantity of wine in the cellars and some Jamaica rum, also a large cellar filled with barrels of excellent beer, packed in ice to keep it fresh during the summer.'[37] In fact, some estates contained so much wine and alcohol that a few soldiers were drowned while pillaging in wine cellars.[38] Some soldiers found the sight of abandoned buildings with plenty of property still inside them rather suspicious and believed it was all part of an elaborate trap. 'Once inside the lodgings,' one eyewitness described, 'officers and soldiers barricaded all the entrances and slept fully dressed and with weapons within their reach.'[39]

Fortunately for the Grande Armée, the fire did not destroy all Moscow's resources. All around the city there were immense fields of various vegetables, including potatoes, beets and cabbages. Aart Kool recalled that although 'meat and bread were rationed daily, we found vegetables aplenty in the community kitchen gardens, allowing us to prepare quite good meals'.[40] Major Le Roy of the 85th Line recalled marching his men along the quay where there were still 'some boats laden with grain', and his men later found 'a grange filled with sacks of grain, made of bulrushes, sewn with string, and heaped up to the neck'. Most Russian houses had cellars and other underground stores that emerged relatively unscathed from the conflagration. 'We have found immense quantities of resources in Moscow,' Napoleon told his minister of foreign affairs.[41] That same day one French officer recorded in his diary that the city still contained vast provisions. 'Houses contain provisions for eight months and wine is plentiful. Consequently, our soldiers are getting drunk and … sit surrounded by numerous bottles of wine that they generously offer to passers-by.'[42] A Russian eyewitness observed that the Allied soldiers were at first quite finicky about food and refused to eat 'cured meats, caviar or large dried fish from the Volga river and the Caspian Sea that were in abundance in Moscow'. In addition, the French soldiers relished the French wines they found, but ignored the Ukrainian and Moldovan wines, which 'they found too flat or sour', and the Spanish and Portuguese wines that were 'too strong for them'.[43]

However, these resources were quickly consumed through carelessness and rapacious behaviour. By early October memoirs of the Grande Armée tell the same tale of plentiful luxuries but scarce essentials. While the palaces of the nobles had plenty of wine, sugar and preserved fruits, there was an acute shortage of flour and vegetables. Even though there were still considerable supplies of wheat and grain, the shortage of mills meant that both the Grande Armée and the Muscovites suffered acute shortages of both flour and groats. At the Foundlings Home Tutolmin received 10 tonnes of wheat and 2 tonnes of groats from Durosnel but his employees faced the challenge of turning the wheat into flour. After requesting gendarmes for protection, several of them wandered all across Moscow in search of mills, only to find that almost all of them had been abandoned and destroyed.[44] 'Such was the pretended abundance which the pillage of the city had procured us,' lamented one French officer. 'Liqueurs, sugar and sweetmeats there were a-plenty at the very time that we were without bread and meat. We clothed ourselves in furs, but had neither coats nor shoes, and we were on the eve of dying of hunger, with diamonds, jewels and other articles of luxury around us.'[45] Von Muraldt agreed: 'Though there was wine, sugar, coffee, etc. in superfluity, we were still suffering from a lack of bread, meat and fodder for our horses.'[46] And Césare de Laugier's diary entry for 29 September reported, 'We are swimming, so to speak, in abundance, though let me also note that this is not due to the Administration, but to our own lucky discoveries.'[47]

Lack of meat remained one of biggest challenges, as the army had mainly depended on the droves of cattle that had followed it but these supplies were now becoming exhausted. By October Russian reports from the city claimed that the 'lack of supplies is so acute that even ravens and jackdaws are being eaten'.[48] Montesquiou-Fezensac's regiment found it very difficult to procure meat and had to send out 'strong detachments' to bring in cattle from the neighbouring woods, where the peasants had sought asylum. Yet these detachments often returned empty-handed in the evening.'[49] Mathieu Dumas, the *Intendant-Général* of the Grande Armée, testified that even though the city still had considerable supplies after the fire, 'these resources were soon exhausted'.[50] Pierre Louis Valot Beauvollier of the 5th Cuirassier Division recalled that he and his comrades had found enormous amounts of supplies in Moscow. These were spared by the fire because they were stored in cellars. These provisions consisted of flour, sugar, coffee, alcohol, salted fish and mushrooms, which represent the principal fare of the local people. If this food had been distributed among different divisions of the army, it would have averted the terrible famine that contributed in so deplorable a manner to the army's destruction. But the disorganization and looting prevented any administrative action in this regard. More than once the *Intendant-Général* [Dumas] would use military force to preserve precious stores; his efforts, however, proved to be in vain ...[51]

With each passing day it became more difficult and more dangerous to forage outside the city. One officer recalled that by early October Murat's 'horses had been nearly destroyed and his men had for some time past been reduced to eating horseflesh'.[52] By early October the foragers had been compelled to move four to six hours out of the city, recalled a Dutch officer, to gather the necessary supplies for horses, which they did with great difficulty. 'This caused the steady decline of health of these poor animals, on which our very welfare depended.' One of the French generals advised his officers to 'become good walkers as we would likely lose our horses soon'.[53]

Nevertheless, the actual experience of individual soldiers varied depending on the district they were billeted in. Some troops experienced acute shortages, while others were more fortunate in procuring supplies. The Württemberg troops, billeted in the eastern suburbs, discovered 'an abundance of beets, which were as round and large as bowling balls and fiery red throughout. There were masses of cabbages three and four times bigger than cabbage heads that we would consider large.'[54] A Guard officer also recalled that his men dug up potatoes from the outlying fields, where they also managed to procure some vegetables.[55] August Thirion of the 2nd Cuirassiers was also thrilled to harvest some potatoes, 'these precious tubers' that were nothing short of 'a piece of gastronomical good luck'.[56]

Inside the city soldiers had to fight for their plunder or be repeatedly robbed of it by other troops, especially by the Imperial Guard and Davout's 1st Corps. In the words of Colonel Boulart, 'the men of Marshal Davout's 1st Corps ... flowed into the city, penetrating into every accessible place and particularly into the cellars, looting everything they could find and indulging in all the excesses of drink. One could see a continuous procession of soldiers carrying off to their camp wine, sugar, furniture, furs and so on.'[57] And who could have resisted the find of vast 'barrels that were inscribed in capital letters with the names of the most famous French vineyards'?[58] Private Walter recalled that 'everyone tried to dress as much as possible with silks and materials of all colours. Only tailors were lacking: silks, muslins and red Morocco leather were all abundant.'[59] 'On glancing at the Place du Gouvernement where the men bivouacked,' Bourgogne remarked, 'it seemed to be an assembly from all parts of the world, for our soldiers were clothed as Kalmycks, Chinese, Cossacks, Tartars, Persians and Turks, and many of them were covered with splendid furs. There were even some dressed in French court dresses, wearing swords with steel hilts shining like diamonds. Add to this that the space was covered with all kinds of dainties to eat, abundance of wines and liqueurs, a little fresh meat, a quantity of hams and fish, a little flour, but no bread.' Brandt echoes this description:

in our camp alone there was a vast quantity of silver, enamelled gold, linen, precious gems and furs for the men to sleep on, and more were being brought in on a daily basis. In addition there was a whole mass of objects such as chairs, torches and so on, which the looters were forcing Russians, as drunk as themselves, to carry. Most of the objects were quickly snatched up by dealers, who paid ridiculous prices and appeared out of nowhere. So it was that starvation quickly gave way to excess. Our camps were overflowing with fresh and preserved meats, smoked fish, wine, rum, cognac, and so on. Around each fire the men were cooking, eating, and especially, drinking. The arrival of each new consignment of pillaged items was met with loud cheers ...[60]

Senior officers were not above such practices and Albrecht Adam was surprised when he saw French officers and generals, including Viceroy Eugène, fighting over 'an immense number of new coaches and beautifully made carriages' that they had found in Moscow's market. With the fires approaching, they were all hurrying to claim the best of the carriages before the entire place went up in flames.[61] Coignet described a certain 'colonel of the staff, who had charge of the clearing of the hospitals', who went out every evening with three servants furnished with wax tapers. 'He knew that the pictures in the churches were all in relief on plaques of silver so he took them down in order to get this silver plate; he put the saints into a crucible and reduced them to ingots, which he sold to the Jews for bank-notes. He was a hard man with a face to match.' One evening the colonel showed off 'some beautiful fur robes' made of Siberian fox skins. Coignet was foolish enough to show off his own loot, including a fur coat made of sable, and was duly relieved of his treasure in return for a small fox fur. 'I feared the colonel's vengeance,' he later lamented. 'He was rascal enough to take it from me, and sell it to Prince Murat for three thousand francs. This robber of churches was a disgrace to the name of Frenchman.'[62]

The looting had a profound impact on the Grande Armée, sapping its resources and affecting its élan. 'We took possession of Moscow as if it had been built expressly for us alone,' explained an Italian officer. '[Our orders] allowed each subaltern to have a magnificent palace for himself, through whose sumptuously furnished apartments he strolled at his ease since no proprietor put in an appearance to dispute its ownership with him.'[63] Thus, as Tolstoy would later comment, 'the aim of each man was no longer, as it had been, to conquer, but merely to keep what he had acquired'.[64] Pierre Louis Valot Beauvollier of the 5th Cuirassier Division noted that 'the soldiers, exhausted and weary, thought only of satisfying their hunger for that moment, without concern for the future. They looted everything and committed all kinds of excesses, and many of them became victims of this ravenousness and haste. Over six thousand men died smothered by flames in the cellars of homes that had been preserved during the initial fires but were burned during the looting.'[65]

'The army had dissolved completely,' lamented Major Pion des Loches. 'Everywhere one could see drunken soldiers and officers loaded with booty and provisions seized from houses that had fallen prey to the flames.'[66] Brandt believed that 'the most serious consequence of the looting was that we were now to reap the full benefits of the disorder we had been sowing ever since crossing the Niemen. When order was finally re-established, there still remained bad characters in each unit who would steal away at night to continue marauding. Others, perhaps, still worse, never even rejoined the ranks. Right up to the evacuation of Moscow, there were some five or six thousand of this kind, whom we referred to as "loners". These would swell the ranks of the marauding bands, and these bands reached monstrous proportions during the misfortunes of the retreat.'[67] And there were still no signs of improvement for the thousands of civilians trapped inside the city. The courage of the people of Moscow even excited the admiration of their foes. Labaume commented, 'Although we suffered so terribly from the fire, we could not but admire the generous self-sacrifice of the inhabitants of the city, who, by their courage and steadfastness, have attained that high degree of true glory that marks a great nation ...'

Restoring Order

Settling back into the Kremlin, Napoleon found himself preoccupied with a myriad issues, leaving very little time for him to observe in personal what was happening in the city. Between 19 and 29 September he left the Kremlin only once.[68] His critics attribute this either to his 'utter apathy' or possibly to a spate of 'epileptic seizures', or suggest that he was 'paralysed by his own errors'.[69] Such claims are rather egregious. Caulaincourt's journal does show that the emperor stayed at the Kremlin throughout the first ten days after his return, but this should not be misconstrued as idleness or apathy. A quick glance at Napoleon's correspondence reveals a wide range of issues he considered and dealt with during this period.[70] As both commander-in-chief and head of state, Napoleon had to cope with a plethora of issues affecting his vast empire and one can only marvel at his ability to deliberate on such a multitude of problems at once. He had to govern the French empire, keep a close watch on the political situation throughout Europe, and conduct the war in Spain (where the French had suffered a series of setbacks in recent months), not to mention exercising command over his forces scattered in the vastness of Russia's interior, making arrangements for the Russian prisoners of war, and restoring order and discipline in Moscow. Despite the range of issues confronting him, Napoleon's legendary keen eye for detail did not falter. His letter of 24 September, for example, reprimanded officials for sending a single battalion of Swiss and Illyrian troops in the wrong direction. 'This is a mistake!' Napoleon observed and demanded the battalion be redirected to Vilna; its 900 Swiss troops were then to join Marshal St Cyr's corps while its 250 Illyrians made their way to Smolensk.[71] Just three days later Napoleon scolded his foreign minister for not delivering up-to-date reports on events in Europe. 'I receive no news from Warsaw, very little from Vienna, and none from Constantinople. Nor do I hear anything about America, and yet it is urgent to do something in that quarter.'[72] So here was a man controlling territory stretching from Spain to Russia, micromanaging a single battalion and fretting about the lack of news from America. Hardly the actions of a man 'paralysed by his own errors'!

Napoleon's most pressing concern was the need to bring some semblance of order to his weakened and fatigued Grande Armée. The Central Army Group, which he personally commanded, crossed the Niemen some 380,000 men strong; three months later its total effective force in Moscow amounted to 95,585 men.[73] Many units were mere shadows of their former selves. Montesquiou-Fezensac recalled that 'from 2,800 men, which had been the strength of the 4th Line Regiment on its crossing the Rhine, only 900 survived. Thus the four battalions equalled no more than two in the field, while each company had twice its number of officers and non-commissioned.'[74] The Württembergers crossed the Niemen on 25 June numbering some 8,200 infantry under arms, but mustered fewer than 1,000 men when they finally reached Moscow.[75] The entire 3rd Reserve Cavalry

Corps comprised just 3,000 men, while the 1st, 3rd, 4th and 5th Army Corps combined mustered just 55,000 men. There were also thousands of French wounded and sick convalescing in hospitals.[76]

Thus, one of Napoleon's immediate concerns was to maintain sufficient forces in the field. Demonstrating once again his singular talents – a remarkable memory, an eye for detail and a talent for administration – the emperor began mobilizing forces all across Europe. He called up some 140,000 men in France and 30,000 in Italy.[77] Reserves in East Prussia and Poland were placed on a war footing, while requests for new troops were conveyed to Saxony and all the courts of the Confederation of the Rhine.[78] 'The battle of Borodino and the entry into Moscow should not weaken our zeal nor send our allies to sleep,' the emperor declared.[79] Paying no heed to the fact that the Poles had already provided tens of thousands of troops, Napoleon demanded more and complained about the failure of the Polish authorities to comply. 'We need as many men as possible,' he wrote to his foreign minister, urging him to ensure that this levy was 'carried out without a delay'.[80] He instructed Poniatowski to select a sufficient number of men from his Polish corps and send them back to the Duchy of Warsaw to recruit and train additional troops. Meanwhile, the French governor of the duchy was told to 'press on with the conscription and levy of horses that are necessary to replenish our cavalry'.[81] At the same time French commandants along the lines of communication were ordered to start moving any stragglers found in their cities to Moscow immediately.[82] Napoleon also made arrangements to raise new units in those Russian provinces where the populace might be more welcoming to the French.[83] He was thus pleased to hear that 'the Tartares [probably Crimean Tatars] are impatient and eager to join and serve under my flags' and expected them to form a thousand-strong regiment.[84]

Once the fires died down, Napoleon began inspecting his armaments. He instructed General La Riboisière, the commander of the Grande Armée's artillery, to 'make a general report on my artillery, and on the means of replacing all the losses. My intention is not to lose a single piece, but to preserve my organization complete, which is not now too strong.' La Riboisière was also to take advantage of the vast quantities of ammunition and ordnance captured in Moscow and to investigate whether it would be possible to establish powder mills in the city.[85] The Emperor inspected artillery parks and workshops and was displeased to discover 'little activity and poor order' in some of them. 'I was surprised to find not a single superior officer,' he complained to General La Riboisière, urging him to pick up the pace of resupplying the artillery: 'The park produced just 10,000 artillery rounds in the fortnight that we have been here. I desire that starting the day after tomorrow you increase production rates to 6,000 per day.' Napoleon urged extra measures to be taken to replenish the artillery munitions. 'All the information we have procured leads us to believe that the enemy had a hundred thousand balls ... and they are supposed to have been thrown into the water. It being a pond, it will be easy to drain it. [La Riboisière] must, therefore, work actively at a ditch for this purpose, and recover these sunken balls.'[86] In early October La Riboisière completed a new assessment of the artillery, which revealed that more than one-third of the cannon and caissons were missing.[87] But the report was full of contradictory information and lacked sufficient detail, which infuriated Napoleon. 'The ignorance in which I remain of the state of my artillery greatly affects current operations ...', he wrote, demanding specific information on the number of cannon, caissons, ammunition without caissons and other relevant details for each corps. 'I cannot be satisfied with such a languid performance,' ended the imperial missive to the artillery commander.[88] Four days later Napoleon seems to have received a more up-to-date status report on the artillery since his letter to Berthier contains an in-depth discussion of the ammunition shortages in both artillery and infantry. The letter reveals that the Grande Armée still had a sizeable artillery arsenal – 58 12-pounder cannon, 264 6-pounders, 122 3-pounders and more than 150 other calibre guns and howitzers – but lacked sufficient ammunition.[89] To further strengthen his artillery, Napoleon ordered additional artillery units to start transferring to the control of the army. Thirteen artillery companies at Erfurt, Magdeburg, Spandau, Glogau, Custrin, Stettin, Stralsund, Thorn, Danzig, Pillau and Kovno were ordered to rejoin the army as soon as possible. [90]

One of Napoleon's greatest concerns was the weakness of his cavalry, which had been decimated during the first three months of the war. Thousands of horses perished due to poor weather, lack of forage and combat losses, and had to be replaced before hostilities resumed in earnest. 'I stand in the greatest need of 14,000 horses,' the emperor informed his Minister of Foreign Affairs. 'I have sent General Bourcier to Vilna and have placed 4 million francs at his disposal.'[91] Napoleon instructed his officials to make inquiries all across Europe to find new steeds and demanded to know 'how many men, horses and equipment' were available at cavalry depots in Prussia, Poland and the occupied Russian provinces.[92] He expected to procure some 14,000 horses from France, 7,000–8,000 from Prussia and another 2,000–3,000 from Hannover, Holstein, Mecklenburg and other German states. In addition, he sought to raise additional horses within the Russian realm. 'In the province of Mogilev', he told Maret, 'there are immensely rich Jews. Send for the chief ones and see if you cannot deal with them by paying ready money to procure 3,000 or 4,000 horses … Nothing should be spared to raise new cavalry.'[93] But gathering and delivering horses across such vast distances required considerable time, which the emperor lacked. He considered requisitioning horses from the local peasantry but this could not be easily accomplished. Irrespective of the fact that peasant horses could hardly replace well-trained war steeds, the residents of the closest villages had concealed their horses and cattle in the woods, while more distant settlements could resist the enemy detachments, requiring some commitment of military resources. Thus the Grande Armée's cavalry continued to gradually wither away.

At the same time Napoleon did his best to put an end to the disorder and pillaging. On his orders, the Old Guard was deployed inside the Kremlin, blocking all the major entrances except for the Nikolskie and Troitskie Gates and maintaining a tight perimeter around the imperial residence. 'No Russian should be allowed to enter the Kremlin under any pretext, except if accompanied by an officer … If, despite orders, any Russian attempts to get inside, you are ordered to shoot him,' stated Marshal Lefebvre's orders to the Imperial Guard.[94] General Éblé's troops received orders to 'remove all broken transports, crates, caissons and other junk of any kind' that still littered the Kremlin and its environs.[95] Pion des Loches recalled reading an order of the day which declared that 'any inhabitant who did not go to register with one of the twelve military commandants was to be killed. For individuals caught torch in hand the punishment was the same.'[96] On 18 September Napoleon instructed *Intendant-Général* Dumas to gather all the provisions and alcohol still remaining in the city and place them at specially established depots that would regulate their distribution and put an end to the disorder. The following day, however, Berthier informed Napoleon that Dumas had been unable to carry out these orders due to the continued marauding and had asked for help in reining in the imperial troops. Napoleon complied and instructed his marshals to take the necessary measures 'to put an end to plundering in Moscow, starting tomorrow', and to deploy 'sufficient number of infantry and cavalry patrols' whose task it was to detain and return soldiers to their units. They were to hold regular roster calls and ensure that soldiers did not leave their quarters. 'This is highly important,' Berthier emphasized in his letter.[97]

Their efforts produced some results. One Guard officer recalled seeing soldiers carrying pillaged items being arrested at the gates and made to hand them over. 'It was quite a sad sight to see those piles of expensive furs, fine embroidery and other precious items left there in the mud.'[98] But containing the disorder proved to be a challenging task. As Bourgogne explained, 'once they realized that the Russians themselves had torched the city, it was impossible to restrain the soldiers'. On 17 September Friedrich Wilhelm von Lossberg had recorded that 'the looting continues in the unfortunate city, and the entire army takes part in it. Even though there is an imperial command to arrest any soldier involved in pillaging, this whole thing is perpetrated so systematically that it would be impossible to carry out this order for it is done not by individuals but rather by entire units.'[99] Aart Kool, a Dutch officer in the 1st Corps, recalled that 'every day one of our officers was in charge of gathering our supplies. He would go with a small wagon, a servant, and several engineers as guards, to the centre of the city to purchase food from the very soldiers who had plundered the city.'[100]

On 20 September Berthier again informed the corps commanders that the emperor was 'displeased to see that despite his order yesterday on putting an end to plunder, acts of pillage still occurred today on the same scale as yesterday ... You must restore discipline and good order.'[101] A day later Napoleon's chief of staff again repeated the need to take immediate measures to stop looting. 'His Majesty desires not just to put an end to plundering in Moscow but to put a stop to sending out groups of soldiers for the procurement of victuals and other items. There are too many soldiers dispatched on these missions in the city. Therefore His Majesty henceforth prohibits this practice.'[102]

The Muscovites, who had spent the last few days barricaded in the cellars and warding off looters day and night, noted that the pillaging intensified after the fires subsided. Although Napoleon demanded strict measures to curb looting, he also allowed the different corps stationed in Moscow, which was now divided into twenty military districts, to dispatch detachments into neighbourhoods to secure the remaining resources.[103] Such measures, in effect, formalized the looting, as even those troops who might have earlier had qualms about looting, now joined in. Roguet, always the disciplinarian, bemoaned the fact that the 'disorders grew worse despite the efforts to contain them. The pillagers, chiefly from the Administration or foreigners, discovered the cellars and stores which had survived the fire. They laid waste to them and completed the destruction the Russians had begun.'[104] Bourgogne recalled that his captain allowed him to take ten men on a special patrol to hunt for provisions and noted that 'pillage was to be allowed but enjoining as much order as possible'.[105] In the words of one Russian eyewitness, what made this pillaging particularly unpleasant was that it was conducted in a very methodical manner as each army corps was given the right to plunder. 'The first day it was the Old Imperial Guard and the next day, the New (Young) Imperial Guard, followed by Marshal Davout's corps and so on. All the corps encamped around the city came in succession to plunder us. And you can imagine how difficult it was to satisfy these latecomers.' For eight days, almost continuously, the procession continued and it was impossible to describe 'the greed of these fellows without first experiencing it. Men without shoes, pants, with clothes in tatters – such were the soldiers of the Grande Armée, except for the Imperial Guard. So when the soldiers returned into camp in their various disguises, they could only be identified by their side-arms.' To make matters worse, many of the officers, following the example of their men, went from house to house looting. 'The less bold among them contented themselves with pillaging the houses in which they were quartered. Even the generals, under the pretence of investigation, made house to house visits, and ordered any objects that pleased them to be laid aside, or changed their apartments in order to plunder new houses.'[106] Another Muscovite described how 'as soon as one troop of marauders left the house, another took its place, so that not even a shirt or a shoe was left.... . People no longer dared to go out into the streets. Even the soldiers placed on guard began to loot, imposing silence on the wretched inhabitants by threats and blows ... Some, having lost their entire wardrobe, were obliged to wear female apparel. Men were to be seen wearing elegant bonnets trimmed with feathers or flowers ... on their shoulders were fur tippets, and their feet were squeezed into ladies' boots... .'[107]

The daily orders to the Imperial Guard provide an excellent insight into the disarray that reigned in the Grande Armée in those days. Despite its elite status, the Guard was actively involved in pillaging, which prompted its leaders to repeat their orders on a daily basis. On 20 September the Guard was informed that 'the emperor henceforth orders all pillaging in the city to cease'. Majors in each regiment were instructed to dispatch fifteen-men patrols from every battalion to restore order and detain any soldiers wandering around in the streets.[108] A day later Lefebvre reported that 'the emperor is extremely displeased that despite his express orders, detachments of marauders from the Guard still continued returning to the Kremlin'. The marshal had to remind his subordinates that 'the duty of generals and corps commanders is to enforce the orders of His Imperial Majesty'. From now on Lefebvre demanded the arrest of anyone found inside the Kremlin with 'wine, provisions or any other objects obtained through pillaging'. All cantinières had to be expelled from the Kremlin and any of their carts found within the complex had to be destroyed immediately. The Guard was again required to dispatch daily patrols 'twice a day from each battalion, while any officer who fails to contain his troops will be severely punished'.[109] Only two days later General Curial admonished the Guardsmen for ignoring the 'repeated orders' and failing to maintain proper discipline. He was particularly upset by their 'continuing to relieve all their needs in various corners of the Kremlin and even under the very windows of the emperor'.[110] That same day Napoleon was exasperated to find 'a corporal of the *chasseurs à pied* of the Guard arriving at the city gates without his knapsack and musket'.[111]

A week after returning to Moscow, Napoleon began introducing more restrictive measures to contain the disorder. He ordered small squads of troops to be deployed to keep an eye on each part of the city and ensure good order and discipline among the troops. He estimated that there were fifty barriers throughout Moscow that could be manned by ten men each. Since the city was divided into twenty districts, Napoleon decided to deploy detachments of twenty men in each district. 'There are some neighbourhoods where even ten men will be sufficient to maintain order, but there are also other places where it will require forty men.' Some 500 men were kept in reserve at various points throughout the city. In total, Napoleon believed that 'this service comprising 1,500 men will be sufficient to maintain order' in the city.[112] After learning that hundreds of troopers at a cavalry depot lacked horses – there were only 700 horses for 2,300 men – Napoleon ordered 1,600 of them moved to Moscow, where they (joined by another 400 from Mozhaisk) formed two battalions of dismounted cavalry and formed the garrison in the Kremlin.[113]

Nevertheless, the disorder persisted. Four days after the emperor's initial command Marshal Lefebvre was compelled to condemn the 'disorders and pillaging that have been committed by the Old Guard, which has acted in unworthy manner yesterday and today'. Some soldiers refused to salute the emperor properly at the reviews, while others defied officers' orders and 'even openly berated and beat them'. His order informed the Guardsmen that 'it pains the emperor to see that the elite soldiers, who are entrusted with the duty of protecting his person and should therefore be providing, in all circumstances, examples of order and subordination, have forgotten their sense of duty and commit offences, forcing their way into cellars and stores maintained by the *Intendant-Général* to service the army.' Marshal Lefebvre declared that 'it is definitely time to put an end to such abuses. A soldier of the Guard who does not appreciate the honour of being part of this corps does not deserve to be part of it.' He demanded to have special rolls drawn up listing 'men who are known to have committed excesses on daily basis ... His Excellency's intention is to make a stern example of them.' The Old Guard was warned that 'any member of the Guard who is detained in the city in violation of orders [issued by Berthier] will be judged on the spot'.[114]

If the Imperial Guard was in such a mess,[115] one can only imagine what was happening in some regular units. In fact, on 29 September the exasperated Berthier issued a new order of the day that acknowledged that 'despite previous orders' looting was still widespread in some parts of the town. Marshals and corps commanders were therefore given new and lengthy instructions to keep all their troops within the areas of their cantonments. 'Neither officers nor soldiers should be permitted, in groups or alone, to go to the city in search of flour, leather or other items.' The order condemned the continued activity of 'vivandiers and certain soldiers' who speculated on stolen items and 'perpetuated disorder'. Napoleon repeated his orders to establish depots where local provisions and 'any items that had been left behind by city residents who abandoned their properties' would be gathered together. These depots were tasked with the regular distribution of victuals. Mortier was instructed to deploy sentries and patrols throughout the city, and arrest anyone carrying provisions or items not procured at the depots. To satisfy the army's thirst for alcohol, the imperial order provided each army corps with fifteen days' rations of 'l'eau de vie' but prohibited troops from going into the city in search of alcohol; wine was restricted to medical use only. Any soldiers detained on a charge of looting were subject to court-martial by specially established military commissions. 'Ending plunder and restoring order would bring back abundance to this capital,' the order concluded.[116] Ten days later Napoleon reiterated the need to take measures to ensure that the army had at least two or three months' worth of supplies safely stored at depots.[117]

Despite their best efforts the French commanders were unable to extinguish pillaging completely throughout their thirty-five day stay in Moscow. Many regimental and divisional commanders knew all too well how much their soldiers were lacking and had no desire to impose any restrictions that would have only further increased their misery. Furthermore, Napoleon's attempt to organize the distribution of supplies through a series of depots failed once it became clear how few provisions were actually available.

While the 19th, 20th and 21st Bulletins painted a rosy picture of an army well provided with victuals, *Intendant-Général* Dumas submitted more ominous reports that showed how limited the supplies of key victuals – grain, flour and forage – actually were.[118] Mindful that the war was far from over and military operations could resume at any time, Napoleon chose to create and maintain a strategic reserve of provisions, even if that meant denying requests for supplies from individual units. Thus, when Berthier informed him that a division of the 4th Corps had no food at all and asked for permission to issue some provisions to them, the emperor simply wrote 'Refused' across the paper, effectively dooming these soldiers to feed themselves by any means necessary. The newly established general police (see below) provided incessant reports on excesses committed by Allied soldiers. On 2 October Police Commissar Georges Lalance of the 10th (Yauzskii) District described the continued pillaging by the soldiers of the 3rd Corps, who 'not only rob the destitute survivors of their meagre possessions but also furiously inflict sabre wounds on them'. Even the Allied wounded participated in this despoilment, leaving their hospital beds 'to rob the Russians carrying cabbages or potatoes'.[119] On 5 October another report from the 4th (Yakimanskii) District described a police commissioner stumbling upon four soldiers, including an Imperial Guardsman, breaking into a deacon's house with swords unsheathed and robbing a family of fourteen souls of their last two loaves of bread.[120] On 11 October the police commissioner of the 16th (Basmanskii) District complained that 'robbing and pillaging continues unabated'. There was, he wrote, 'an entire gang of robbers operating in my district and additional military forces are necessary to rein in' these criminals.[121] On 12 October it was announced that orders prohibiting pillaging were to be read aloud to military units on a daily basis. Berthier was nevertheless infuriated to find that even the troops of Marshal Davout, whose corps was previously considered exemplary, were still engaged in looting. 'Mounting my horse to accompany the emperor tonight,' he wrote to the marshal, 'I saw a number of soldiers pillaging nearby. Approaching them, I noticed that among them was one wearing captain's epaulettes. I ordered him brought to me and, after interrogating him, I discovered that he was not even an officer but rather an interpreter assigned to General Morand, who had given him permission to wear officer's epaulettes.' Berthier found this behaviour unacceptable and asked Davout to impose appropriate punishments on the guilty parties. 'You know quite well, marshal, how hard the emperor toils to restore order in this city.'[122]

Ironically, just as he was taking measures to end pillaging by his troops, Napoleon sanctioned a different type of plundering that was conducted under the pretence of collecting trophies to commemorate the glorious capture of Moscow. A special commission was set up inside the Uspenskii Cathedral to melt down precious metals from Moscow's churches, public and private houses into bullion. Peter Chudimov, the Archivist at the Mining Department, recalled seeing a 'French paymaster, two officers and a French goldsmith' arriving at the smeltery set up inside the cathedral. 'Every day gold and silver stripped from churches, vestments and objects was brought in carts and boxes and then melted during the night.' The French compelled some Russian employees of the Mining Department to participate in this operation and at least eight men were recruited to carry heavy loads of precious metals and coal into the smeltery.[123] Many were struck by the sight of the removal of the trophies from various parts of the city. *Intendant-Général* Dumas was one day alone with Berthier on the balcony of the imperial palace, from where he observed 'the fruitless efforts of the workmen, under the direction of the engineers, to loosen from the dome of the principal church the immense cross called Ivan's Cross, which was an object of veneration and admiration among the Russians'. Some believed it to be made of solid gold but the cross was in reality made of copper overlaid with several plates of gold. As this cross could not be pulled down without damaging the cupola itself, it was resolved to simply saw it off. The cross fell to the ground with a great noise and was afterwards taken to pieces and carefully packed up to be conveyed to Paris, where Napoleon intended to have it put together again and placed on top of the church that he was building near the Louvre, opposite the Museum. Upset and indignant at this spoliation, Berthier asked Dumas, 'How is it possible to do such a thing with one hand while offering peace with the other?'[124]

The Moscow Municipality

One of the problems Napoleon was grappling with was the establishment of a new municipal government in Moscow. When it became clear that the city had been abandoned, Napoleon fully intended to restore municipal authority once his army had settled down. Marquis A. Pastoret, the well-informed intendant of Vitebsk province, noted that upon entering the city one of first questions Napoleon addressed to General Dumas was whether municipal government had already been organized. Learning that the city government was non-existent, Napoleon urged Dumas to make appropriate arrangements, and then interrogated a German apothecary to learn whether there were any notables still remaining the city. That same evening Dumas submitted to the emperor a draft decree on establishing the Moscow municipality, but also informed him that he was unable to find any suitable Muscovites for this job. The outbreak of fire that same night naturally pushed the whole plan to the back and Napoleon returned to it only after the fires subsided.[125]

Throughout this time Jean-Baptiste Barthelemy de Lesseps, the former French consul-general to St Petersburg and now the civil governor of Moscow, did his best to restore normality in the city.[126] He 'has not forgotten the thirty years of hospitality he had enjoyed in Russia,' observed Caulaincourt. 'This excellent man did all he could do to put a stop to many evils ... He collected, sheltered, nourished and in fact saved quite a number of unfortunate men, women and children whose houses had burned down and who were straying about like ghosts amidst the ruins.' In late September de Lesseps received imperial permission to proceed with the establishment of the new municipal authority. He instructed Jacob Dulon, a prominent Muscovite merchant of French descent whom he had known for many years and whose house he occupied,[127] and François Xavier Villiers, reader in French at the University of Moscow, to gather together any remaining Muscovite notables. Over the next couple of days more than a dozen of them, including the officials Bestuzhev-Riumin, P. Zagryazhskii and G. Vishnevskii, and the merchants Peter Korobov, Ivan Kozlov, Ivan Isaev, Konyaev and Peter Nakhodkin, were contacted by 'strangers' who instructed them to meet at Dulon's house on 24 September.[128] Some of these affluent men could have fled from the city but they chose to stay for a variety of reasons. Merchant Gregorii Kolchugin, for example, stayed because of Rostopchin's assertion that the city would not voluntarily be evacuated, and on account of family and business matters.[129] Other notables certainly shared similar circumstances and some paid dearly for heir beliefs. Another merchant, Ivan Kulman, was robbed repeatedly during the first three days of the Allied occupation of the city and his house burned down in the fires. Previously a wealthy man, he lost everything in those days and survived on handouts he begged from Allied soldiers in the streets. He later recalled, 'when everything burned down and I had nothing left, I decided to seek any kind of employment in the French service ...'[130]

As the notables arrived,[131] Dulon led them to de Lesseps's office, where the French general informed them of the emperor's decision to set up a municipal government and offered them positions in the future municipality. Approaching Peter Nakhodkin, de Lesseps showered him with praise before revealing that 'the emperor has heard that you are a good man and therefore he appoints you as the head of the municipal government'.[132] Astonished by this news, Nakhodkin demurred and asked to be replaced. When the others joined his protest, de Lesseps informed them that he could not rescind arrangements made by the emperor, and threatened that those who resisted could face dire consequences. De Lesseps then dismissed them, instructing to come the following day to start working.[133] Kolchugin, who arrived the following day, remembered how he 'was introduced to de Lesseps, who told me that I was chosen to serve in the municipality and asked me to take my place ... I asked him to remove me from this position but de Lesseps told me that he could not do it since he did not choose me but rather my compatriots chose me to act on behalf of my fellow Russians ...' When Kolchugin continued to insist on his dismissal, de Lesseps bluntly told him: 'You are becoming rather verbose. Do you want me to inform the emperor that you are a bullhead, who could order you to be shot as an example to the others?' De Lesseps then led Kolchugin into a room where he 'found the municipal head [Nakhodkin] already holding a meeting with other members. [De Lesseps] ordered them to show me my seat and instructed me to take it.'[134] Another potential officer for the municipality was Phillip Xavier d'Horrer, a French émigré who had retired from the Russian army. He was pressured by General Dedem to collaborate with the French authorities. 'Have you visited Lauriston, Lesseps or Marshal Mortier?' the general inquired, and when D'Horrer gave a negative response, he observed that such behaviour could cause problems for his family. 'I accepted Russian citizenship and pledged an oath to the Russian Emperor. Therefore I no longer consider myself a Frenchman,' argued d'Horrer. 'This will only raise even more suspicion about you,' replied Dedem. The following day he arranged a meeting between d'Horrer and Napoleon's Secretary of State Count Pierre Daru, who tried to coerce d'Horrer into supporting the French authorities. Reminding d'Horrer that he and his entire family were émigrés, Daru noted, 'I assume you are aware of the French laws against émigrés. So go and think about it.'[135] Similarly intimidated was Professor Christian Steltzer of the University of Moscow, whose efforts to protect the university brought him into direct contact with senior officials of the Grande Armée. General Dumas offered Steltzer a position in the municipal government, noting that if he refused 'His Majesty would take certain measures that would be very unfortunate' for him. Later Steltzer also had a meeting with de Lesseps – 'that callous and miserable wretch', as he called him – who 'told me the same thing but in much coarser language'.[136] Merchant Kozlov did not require any 'coarse language' to coerce him into joining the municipality since he had already 'heard from various people that the French were shooting people for even the slightest disobedience'.[137] Bestuzhev-Riumin was offered a seat in the municipality by Marshal Mortier. He initially declined it but the marshal assured him that the primary goal of this body was to help his compatriots, and so his refusal to participate in its working seemed to be unwarranted. Mortier then showed Bestuzhev-Riumin some of the documents outlining the municipality's authority and purpose. Finding nothing 'contrary to his conscience or requiring the breaking of an oath', Bestuzhev-Riumin then agreed to participate.[138]

Thus most of the men chosen for the municipality had no choice but to submit to de Lesseps' demands, although they did try to safeguard themselves by declaring that they refused to do anything either against their faith or against the emperor Alexander. To this de Lesseps replied that the differences between the two Emperors were outside their province, and their only duty was to watch over the security and prosperity of the city.[139] But there were also some members of the municipal government who had few misgivings about collaborating with the enemy. Some, in fact, welcomed this opportunity and actively tried to shore up French authority in the city. Among these men was Paul Lacrois, a police officer who defied orders to leave the city and stayed behind.[140] He quickly rallied to the French side and delivered important intelligence, including details on the secret construction of Leppich's air balloon. François Villiers was among the first to greet the Grande Armée on the Dorogomilovskaya bridge, and later actively assisted the French military authorities in the city. It was he who helped identify candidates for municipal positions and notified selected individuals to attend the meeting with de Lesseps.[141] Villiers occasionally went beyond simple collaboration and seems to have relished his newly acquired authority. Professor Steltzer claims that on one occasion Villiers had eight Russians harnessed to pull his carriage and drove around prodding them with a stick.[142]

De Lesseps announced the establishment of the new municipal government through a proclamation issued on 1 October:[143] 'Residents of Moscow! Your miseries are great but His Majesty the emperor and the King wants to end them … [A new] administration, chosen from among you, will comprise your municipality or city government. It will take care of you, your needs, your benefits.' The new municipality,[144] divided into six bureaux, was situated in the house of Count N.P. Rumyantsev on the Pokrovka. Its members were required to wear a badge of red ribbon,[145] and enjoyed a wide range of responsibilities, including quartering troops, administering hospitals, maintaining order in the city, finding employment for the remaining workforce, ensuring regular church services and revitalizing the spirits of the city residents. In addition, the proclamation announced the formation of a general police force (lodged at Prince Dolgorukov's house not far from the municipal headquarters), comprising twenty police commissariats that were tasked with restoring and maintaining order in the city (with the help of military authorities). Most of the police officials were foreigners who 'had no other means of surviving'.[146]

The Moscow municipality proved to be ineffective.[147] Tasked with governing a city in ruins, it could hardly cope with the needs of its desperate citizens and the demands of the occupying force. Many of its members were uninterested in performing their responsibilities and tried to do as little as possible. Kolchugin and his colleagues were, for example, tasked with restoring church services in the city but, as he later recalled, it was virtually impossible to do so because 'the churches were plundered and defiled'. In fact, Kolchugin and his colleagues had no interest in even attempting it, and instead agreed 'to avoid holding meetings or signing any written proceedings'. The municipality did, however, reopen a number of taverns and bakeries in an effort to bring some sense of normality back to the city. In many districts the newly established police force was preoccupied with the removal of debris – 'the streets are now clean,' one police commissioner happily reported[148] – and human and animal corpses that presented a serious threat to the human population. Police Commissar Charles Lassan of the 8th (Arbatskii) District noted on 30 September that 'the presence of enormous numbers of corpses, only slightly covered with soil', could have a 'pernicious effect' on the army.[149] The police, however, found it difficult to put an end to the disorder, and reports from police commissioners reveal that pillaging, robbing, theft and other crimes remained widespread in the city.

The municipal government's greatest challenge was procuring supplies. During the first week of its existence the municipality could do little but ask the French military authorities for help. As a result, Mortier found himself writing incessantly to the imperial headquarters with requests for assistance, which eventually annoyed the emperor. '[Mortier] demands provisions for the police department, also for the foundlings and the Russians who are in the hospitals, for the inhabitants who are sick, &c. All these demands are proper, but it is impossible to comply with them.' Napoleon instead argued that it was the municipality's responsibility to provide for such needs: '[It] must form a Russian company, which will go by detachments to the villages and take provisions, but will pay for them.' The French authorities would provide sufficient funds to cover these expenses and furnish a storehouse, which could be appropriated for the city and stocked. 'This is the only way to supply them all,' the emperor concluded.[150] On 6 October de Lesseps issued a new proclamation addressed to the residents of the city and its environs,[151] calling upon the 'peaceful inhabitants, artisans and labourers of Moscow' to return to their dwellings, assuring them that 'peace and order have been restored in the capital. Your countrymen are safely leaving their shelters and are respected and any violence against them or their property is immediately punished.' The Emperor 'wants to put an end to your misery and return you to your homes and families.' De Lesseps assured peasants and inhabitants from nearby towns that they would be able to bring their produce safely to markets in the city and would be paid at mutually agreed rates. Sundays and Wednesdays were designated for major market fairs, on which days 'sufficient forces will be deployed on all major roads and at predetermined distances from the city, to protect transports delivering supplies to Moscow and returning back home'. One of the proclamations concluded: 'Inhabitants of towns and countryside, and you, labourers and craftsmen ... you are called on to respond to the paternal plans of His Majesty the emperor and King and to contribute with him to the well-being of all.'[152] Beauvollier recalled that 'Napoleon sent commissioners to engage the Russian peasants to bring their goods to Moscow twice a week as before, and assured them that they would be well paid. He also ordered all the church bells that had survived the fire to be rung so as to show to these villages that worship continued interrupted.'[153]

But Napoleon's hopes for peasants delivering supplies came to nothing. They had already removed or destroyed most of their foodstuffs, preferring to die of starvation than profit from supplying the occupying forces. The few who dared to trade with the enemy paid dearly for it. In October the Moscow municipal officials P. Korobov and I. Perepletchikov learned at first-hand how dangerous it was to procure provisions outside Moscow. They were each given cash and proclamations and sent to nearby villages with a military escort (ten French soldiers led by an NCO). Korobov was captured by the Cossacks, while Perepletchikov was beaten and robbed by his own escort.[154] Korbeletskii also noted in his journal that, persuaded by de Lesseps' promises of handsome rewards, some Muscovites travelled to a 'distant village to buy bread ... but one of them never returned, while the other barely escaped from the peasants'.[155] Another municipal official, Kolchugin, was not optimistic about the prospect of venturing outside the city: 'If a foraging convoy encountered Russian forces,' he mused, 'there would be a battle and neither bullets nor canisters would distinguish whether the Russian is there by choice or coercion.'[156] Indeed, the Russian peasants themselves particularly targeted those suspected of collaborating with the enemy. When Russian merchants appeared at the village of Guslitsy to procure supplies for the Grand Army, they were all slaughtered. Alexey Olenin noted in his memoirs that Russian peasants captured a Russian collaborator and buried him alive.[157]

There were also instances when peasants from nearby villages came to sell their wares in Moscow and deeply regretted it. Thus the peasants of Ostankino came to Moscow with thirty cart-loads of oats and flour, which were duly bought and paid for. Having received their money they left, with instructions to come again as soon as possible. But scarcely had they left Moscow than they were assaulted by Allied soldiers, who first robbed them and then compelled them to return to the city, where they were put to forced labour.[158] Beauvollier saw how many peasants went to Moscow with carts loaded with hay, straw and provisions, only to have their horses and carts seized. 'These good people, indignant at such unfair conduct, returned to their villages and came no more. Instead, they turned other inhabitants against the French by spreading stories of the mistreatment they had experienced and, especially, by portraying the French as wicked men who had no fear of desecrating churches.'[159] The famous engraver François Vendramini, who stayed in Moscow and befriended some French officers, was visiting a French colonel when a group of French soldiers brought in a Russian peasant. Pale and in tears, the peasant held in his hand a printed paper stained with blood. He told the French colonel that he had read the proclamation encouraging peasants to bring their produce to sell in Moscow; believing in the promise of safety, and hoping to turn a quick profit, he and his brother loaded three carts with food. Just as they approached the city, however, they were attacked by soldiers who robbed them of everything and killed his brother when he tried to defend his property. The peasant then held out the proclamation stained with his brother's blood and demanded justice. 'The French colonel was infuriated by this crime and assured the peasant that he would investigate and severely punish the perpetrators if they belonged to his regiment. He also promised to compensate him fully for his losses, but admitted that he could not bring back his brother.'[160] As the reports of such mistreatment spread, hardly anyone had any desire to deal with the French authorities and, in spite of all their efforts, de Lesseps and the municipal government of Moscow could not succeed in establishing an open and well-supplied market; the members of the municipal government themselves were horrified at 'the thought of participating in provisioning the enemy, which was against the oath to the emperor and against our Fatherland and conscience'.[161]

As the days passed, foraging expeditions had to range ever further afield and required ever heavier escorts. On 30 September Laugier recorded in his diary that 'yesterday about 1,000 soldiers, 200 cavalrymen and two cannon' were dispatched on a foraging expedition along the road to Tver. 'The greater part of the villages we passed through were totally deserted and had been searched from top to bottom by earlier reconnaissances.'[162] These foraging parties travelled as far as 20–30 miles from Moscow before encountering any still intact settlements. By mid–October 'our purveyors were no longer able to bring back anything either for the men or for the horses,' lamented Louis François Lejeune, a staff officer in Davout's headquarters. 'The accounts they gave of the dangers they had faced were appalling, and, according to them, we were hemmed in by a perfect network of Cossacks and armed peasants, who would kill any isolated parties of French, and from whom we ourselves might find it difficult to escape.'[163]

Life in the Devastated City

As the golden autumn days succeeded one another, life in Moscow was full of misery and hardship. 'Although the city has become a bit more peaceful,' wrote Tutolmin to the Dowager Empress, 'one cannot fully convey how destitute the city residents are: they are suffering the utmost deprivation in food, clothing and shelter.'[164] Priest Bozhanov recalled that everyone was 'deprived of the very staff of life – bread – which was the very last resort of prolonging one's life. Desperate to find any kind of food, we tried everything. We gathered, ground up and boiled the few burned kernels of grain but even the healthiest among us found it difficult to consume it.'[165] The Russian seminarian was astonished to see the Allied soldiers' slaughter-house at the Petrovskii Monastery. Animal intestines, bones and other by-products lay in heaps and produced an unbearable stench. Noticing him 'holding his nose and staring wildly', one of the men in the crowd told me sarcastically, 'You, brother, seem to be well fed and judging from your reaction, you might be of noble pedigree. But we are already used to this stench and come here every day with the hope of laying hands on some of these entrails to feed our orphan souls.'[166]

As well as trying to persuade the country people to bring their goods to market, Napoleon sought to induce the inhabitants to return to the city. While some residents did return, the majority were naturally out of reach of his proclamations and, even if they could read them, what incentive would they have had to return to a devastated city that was occupied by enemy forces? Some inhabitants of Moscow who had fled the city on the eve of the occupation did return because they 'wanted to visit their churches and kneel down before the altars,' observed one German officer:

> But they found to their horror that the [churches] had been desecrated and turned into stables. Others searched for their homes and found ashes instead. The public walks in the city presented a terrible spectacle. Every step trod on dead and charred bodies, and the corpses of incendiaries hung from many half-burnt trees. Amid these horrors one could see the wretched inhabitants, who had come back and had no roof over their heads, collecting the iron or lead that had once covered the roofs of palaces. They did this so as to build huts in the numerous gardens, and they stilled their pangs of hunger with raw vegetables which our soldiers had overlooked.[167]

Among the poorest class of Moscow's inhabitants there were a large number of women, who, as one German officer put it, 'believed they could derive benefit from the downfall and plundering of the city. Many of us took up these creatures who then became housekeepers in houses which had been spared by the flames. Among them were girls who deserved respect and sympathy on account of their upbringing and, in particular, their misfortune. Hunger and want drove them to offer themselves.'[168] Vionnet de Maringone adds that among the fallen women there were

some honest women who were nearly dying of hunger and were obliged to surrender themselves at their discretion to the first comers. As a result, one saw nobody except these creatures in every house that was still standing. They had installed themselves as if they owned the houses; they took possession of the ladies' adornments and they accepted as presents, in payment for their favours, often very bitter ones, rich dresses which the army had pillaged and silver bullion. This contrasted sharply with their figures, their manners and their clothes. On my walks I often came across old men who were in tears at seeing this appalling disorder.[169]

For the Muscovites, the best guarantee of safety against marauders was to have a high-ranking officer in residence. Neighbours sent messengers to alert these senior officers whenever soldiers or a gang tried to loot their houses, and more often than not an armed patrol was dispatched to put an end to any such criminal enterprise. There are also numerous accounts of Allied troops coming to the rescue of families in hardship or individuals in distress.[170] But not all crimes involved the soldiers of the Grande Armée and there are plenty of examples of Russian commoners and stragglers robbing and stealing from their own brethren. Even before the fall of Moscow Rostopchin complained in a letter to his wife: 'Our soldiers go pillaging under the very noses of their generals. I saw them break down the door of a house and remove all the contents … I believe the inhabitants are less afraid of the enemy than of their own protectors.'[171] In fact, so many Russian stragglers roamed about the streets in the days after the abandonment of Moscow that, according to Montesquiou-Fezensac, he alone had detained about fifty of them and sent them to headquarters. 'The general to whom I reported this expressed his regret that I had not shot them all,' Montesquiou-Fezensac observed, 'and instructed me to dispose of them in this way in future.'[172] Another eyewitness described Allied troops encountering 'straggler Russian soldiers for whom the lure of plunder and liquor proved to be greater than the fear of the enemy. As the result the two sides would exchange fire but their fighting quickly ended as neither was there to fight.'[173] In some instances French and Russian troops could be seen drunk or passed out next to each other in wine cellars.[174] Maxim Sakov was 'horrified' when he discovered that a group of Russian stragglers and wounded soldiers lived clandestinely near the Khovanskii Hill on the bank of the Yauza river. 'They were marauders,' he specified, 'and lived by robbing the passers-by.'[175] Sakov witnessed how these 'wounded and run-away Russian soldiers robbed an unfortunate [Russian] passer-by, broke his hands and legs and then tried to beat him to death'. Outraged by such brutality, Sakov and his comrades decided to intervene. With clubs in hand, they went in search of the soldiers and found 'twelve men lying in the grass and bushes with hands and heads bandaged [to look injured]. My men were so enraged that they charged at them … and punished them without mercy. Afterwards we found numerous articles of clothing and other items that these wounded soldiers had plundered; in fact there were two wagons full of loot …'[176]

Much of the plundering was perpetrated by commoners, who exploited the chaos and disorder to enrich themselves. As families desperately struggled to hide their remaining property behind fake walls or in the ground, their neighbours, acquaintances and, in the case of affluent families, servants naturally observed everything and later raided these locations. Anisya Poluyaroslavtseva complained that her family fretted about leaving their house because 'our renters were not trustworthy people – they had seen where we had hidden our property and my parents feared that they would take advantage of this'.[177] A serf woman of the wealthy Soimonov family recounted how, on the eve of the enemy occupation of Moscow, she and the other servants concealed the family's possessions behind a specially built fake wall in the cellar. Just as they were finishing the wall, an 'acquaintance from the neighbouring estate' came in and begged them to store his possessions in this safe place. After the Grande Armée departed, the family returned home only to discover that their safe place had been discovered and plundered, not by the enemy but rather by that very 'acquaintance' who had begged them for help.[178] One French guard officer, billeted in a nobleman's house, was pleased to find a steward who spoke a little French, but was disappointed to hear that 'his masters had had everything taken away'. Yet the officer could not but feel that 'the steward had helped himself to whatever was left and would tell his masters, upon their return, that the French had taken it'. His suspicions only increased as the days went by. 'One day I asked him for a glass of wine,' the officer recalled, 'but he told me there were only twenty-eight bottles remaining in the cellar. The very next morning my sentry told me that during the night he had seen the servant loading some wine and other items on to a cart and making off.'[179]

Contemporary Russian reports indicate that among those ransacking the Orthodox churches were the Old Believers, a dissenting Orthodox sect formed in the wake of the church reforms initiated by the Russian Patriarch Nikon in 1652–1666. Their history from the Nikonian revolution to the reign of Catherine the Great is one of persecution, flight, dispersal and factionalism. They considered Nikon's reforms a heresy and a sign that the Devil had taken control of the Russian church and state. Clinging to the old liturgy and traditions, the Old Believers suffered from government persecution that involved extremes of torture and incarceration. They felt alienated from the Russian community and hundreds of thousands of them had fled to the far-flung provinces of the empire, where they had set up self-sufficient communities. Through perseverance and hard work, they prospered in trade, commerce and industry, causing the Russian government, so rigorous in matters of political submission and ideological conformity, to soften its stance towards the sect, which was successfully expanding a Russian presence into the hinterland of the empire. The Old Believers became exempt from many of the commercial, military and labour obligations levied on Orthodox peasants and merchants, while Empress Catherine the Great invited them to return from the wild frontier lands to the heartland of Russia. In the early 1770s the first Old Believer community was set up at the Preobrazhenskoe Cemetery; true to her 'enlightened despotism', the Empress legalized this community, which was soon followed by another Old Believer settlement in the suburban village of Rogozhsk. Both communities grew and prospered over the next three decades. Early in his reign Emperor Alexander continued his grandmother's policies and extended the Old Believers' privileges, permitting the expansion of their commercial activities. By 1812 many of Moscow's manufacturing enterprises had been founded and were managed by the Old Believers.

Despite this toleration and the economic concessions they were granted, suspicion of the state remained deeply rooted in the Old Believers' philosophy. They retained vivid memories of past persecution and were well aware that the state could always reverse its policy and launch a new wave of harassment, not least because the Russian authorities still perceived the sect's social and political teachings – which included beliefs in the democratic role of the people, spiritual equality and self-government – as a real threat. In 1809–1810 Alexander became convinced that tolerating the Preobrazhenskoe community only led to 'heretical discussions'. The Old Believers, for example, rejected the government's attempts to portray Napoleon as the Antichrist – in fact, they believed that Emperor Alexander himself was the Antichrist, and a police search of the Preobrazhenskoe community produced a portrait of the Russian Emperor with horns and a tail. Consequently, the Old Believers found it hard to believe in the Russian Orthodox Church's efforts to convince the populace that Napoleon was the Antichrist. Despite the official propaganda, some Old Believers viewed Napoleon as 'the lion in the valley of Jehosaphat who was destined to overthrow the false emperor'. It was no surprise, then, that at least some Old Believers welcomed the arrival of the French army. Soon after the fall of Moscow Rostopchin was already receiving reports that 'the [Old Believers'] church and community are intact because they welcomed the French with traditional bread and salt and appealed to them for protection'.[180] In later years an Old Believer tradition claimed that Napoleon personally visited the Preobrazhenskoe Cemetery and promised to take care of their community.[181]

The Old Believers seem to have exploited the occupation of Moscow to settle old scores with their Orthodox opponents. Many of them raided nearby Russian Orthodox churches and stole icons and other relics. At the same time some leaders of the Old Believers community collaborated with the enemy and joined the Administration that Napoleon established upon his return to Moscow. 'The Raskolniki are playing a major role in all affairs,' grumbled Alexander Bulgakov, while Rostopchin informed Emperor Alexander that the sect enjoyed Napoleon's protection and eagerly supported him in return.[182]

The members of Moscow's French community, who had hoped to experience some leniency at the hands of their compatriots, were to be bitterly disappointed as they were robbed as mercilessly as the rest of the city populace. 'No distinction was made between the French and the Russians, foreigners and compatriots,' wailed one French resident of Moscow. 'Everyone was looted equally in the most despicable manner.'[183] Ysarn had been riding in his carriage when some French cavalry troopers forced him to climb out. Already robbed once before, Ysarn tried to avoid a repeat by telling the troopers that he was a Frenchman like them. But they laughed in his face: 'Why should we care that you are a Frenchman? What are you doing here? Only some [expletive] Frenchmen who are against us would be here. You are probably an émigré!'[184] Lacointe de Laveau recounted the story of a French soldier who robbed a French family of everything; noticing a pretty ring on the young woman's hand, he threatened to cut off her finger if she refused to give it up immediately.[185] During the first few days after the fires subsided, Surrugues reported, people hoped that peace and order would finally return to the city but they were to be sadly disappointed. 'In the first week [of the French occupation] no one could leave the house without being publicly abused and robbed. The unfortunate survivors had learned this quite well. The second week did not inspire any confidence either. Anything that survived the fires now became the target of a new wave of plundering ... Soldiers respected neither the decency of women nor the innocence of children in the cradle, nor the grey hairs of old age.'[186] Similar sentiments are echoed by Labaume, who witnessed how 'excesses of avarice were joined by the worst depravations of debauchery. Neither the nobility of rank nor the candour of youth nor the tears of beauty were respected in the rush of cruel licentiousness.'[187] Encountering some French Muscovites on his tour of the city, Napoleon did his best to alleviate their suffering. He instructed Berthier 'to provide all French residents of Moscow – men, women and children – with housing near the Kremlin'. Three trustees were selected to represent and direct the French community.[188]

But we should not imagine Moscow's civilian populace as peaceful men and women who tacitly bore the brunt of the violence. Far from it: many Muscovites chose to fight back against abuse and mistreatment. In some instances this took the form of passive resistance, such as concealing information or refusing to reveal the whereabouts of food and water. Roman Soltyk tried using his knowledge of the Russian language to gain a better understanding of what was happening in town. But as soon as 'our Polish uniform revealed us as enemies', the Russians would respond 'laconically or else evasively'. He was particularly impressed by the women at the college for young ladies, where the Poles came in search of provisions. The college principal pretended that she could not understand any foreign languages, even though, as Soltyk noted, 'teaching her aristocratic charges French, the second language of the elite, must have been one of her primary duties'. As the Poles complained about the lack of food, 'a 12–year-old girl who had been looking out of the window but following our conversation, turned around quickly and said vehemently, "Food for the French! The putty of these windows is good enough to nourish them!"' Soltyk was impressed by the girl's fortitude: 'One could hardly hope to subdue a population when children of twelve were so agitated,' he observed later.[189]

But Russian opposition went beyond moral resistance. Many Allied soldiers who went foraging or pillaging on their own were attacked and killed by the embittered townsfolk. Curious to see what was happening outside, Anisya Poluyaroslavtseva frequently left her shelter to peek at the street. On one occasion she watched as a Frenchman walking in the street was suddenly approached by a Russian, who struck him with a large stone. As the Frenchman fell to the ground, blood gushing from his head, his attacker jumped on him and strangled him.[190] Anna Grigorievna, a shopkeeper, described how her family was hiding in the cellar in those dreadful days when, as ill luck would have it, an enemy soldier found the cellar and forced the door. 'Over his shoulder he carried a huge cudgel,' Anna later recalled. 'He brandished it in his left hand and with his right seized my father by the throat. I rushed at the brigand, snatched his cudgel and struck him on the nape of the neck. He dropped, whereupon everyone fell on him, killing him in an instant and dragging his body off to the pond.' Over the next few days her family dispatched quite a few 'uninvited guests' into this pond and two wells, sometimes as many as four or five at once.[191] One day an acquaintance of her father's came for help: he had enemy soldiers billeted in his house and they were inquiring whether there was any means of procuring some fresh fish. 'The merchant knew that our pond, which belonged to General Kiselev's wife, had some carp in it. He asked my father, "Is there any way of casting my net into your pond?" "No need to ask permission," my father replied. "The pond does not belong to us. But the question is, what are you going to catch in your net, Gregor Nikitich? A carp – or a trooper?"'[192]

Years later Apollon Sysoev remembered vividly how his family fled from the fires into a large garden, where they found many people sitting with their possessions piled up. The garden was a large one and the people were seated in small groups of fifteen to twenty, close to one another. From time to time a group of Allied soldiers would appear, go round everybody and take anything they came across. 'They had muskets and swords and we had our bare hands,' Sysoev lamented. However, things changed when isolated Allied soldiers attempted to rob them. 'We received them in our own way,' Sysoev described:

> I recall seeing one dashing young lad going along in search of gain. He did not touch us, but went on and started to take someone else's things. All at once several men set on him and then the fun began: our people shouted [demanding to kill him] and he shouted begging for mercy. But how could he expect mercy when the people themselves were homeless and starving, and were now, on top of everything else, being robbed. I saw them drag the wretched man off somewhere, and afterwards return without him. 'We finished him off,' they said, 'We strangled him and put him down a well.'[193]

While searching for provisions amidst the burned-out ruins, Andrei Alekseyev saw a Russian man dressed in commoner's clothing approaching the gates to a wealthy merchant's estate, and calling to a French soldier, who was walking nearby, to follow him inside. Alekseyev decided to take a look at what they were doing and was startled to see how the Russian gesticulated to the Frenchman that there was some treasure hidden inside a well; when the latter tried to peer inside the well, the Russian pushed him into the deep shaft. Alekseyev 'confronted the man. "Why did you kill him? He did not even threaten you?" He looked at me: "It seems you have not lost your wife and none of your family members suffered from their bullets. And nor have you seen their horses inside our temples."'[194] G. Kozlovskii described groups of peasants, 'each carrying an iron [bar] over his shoulder', walking around the city and attacking anyone who looked foreign or behaved in a foreign manner. As he encountered one such group, he overheard 'one peasant say to the other, "Hey, look, isn't that a Frenchman?" At that moment I came up to a church and started to pray, so the other answered him, "No, he is from here, one of ours." And so the prayer saved me.' Less fortunate was the 'sick Frenchman', who was walking along a street when a couple of peasants came towards him. Approaching them, the Frenchman 'asked "Where is the hospital?" One of the peasants glanced at him, muttered "How long do we have to put up with this!" and hit him over the head with an iron bar. And that was the end of him.'[195]

Across town, a young boy searching for some sustenance for a starving girl was surprised to see a 'half-shaved red head' popping up out of a hole in the ground. The weird-looking man asked what the boy was looking for and, upon hearing his predicament, invited him to join him underground. The youngster was surprised to find 'a large cellar illuminated by thick church candles. Along one wall there was a long line of vats with numerous provisions, while several jars with jams and numerous bottles of wine were arranged on the other side of the room. In the middle there was a large pile of clothing, both male and female, various rags, and pieces of velvet, satin and brocade; carpets were covered with gold and silver tableware and church utensils, decorated with gems.' The youngster was greeted by six men 'casually sprawled around the room' and armed with muskets, sabres, daggers and other weapons; judging from the appearance of one of the men, who had torn nostrils and had been branded, these were escaped or former convicts. Upon hearing about the boy's search for food, one of the men seems to have felt a twinge of conscience as he responded, 'It is about time to think about our own souls. We cannot continue slaughtering our own Orthodox brethren like sheep – it is time for us to deal with our foreign guests as well.' In the subsequent conversation the convicts spoke of their gangs of pickpockets targeting the Allied soldiers, whom they 'at first thought to be cunning and nimble, in short, flawless thieves', but were disappointed to find them 'dim–wits and fools'.[196]

But Russian resistance extended even beyond the occasional murder. Some Russian officers had managed to infiltrate Moscow, where they deliberately targeted Allied troops. Alexander Figner, a young and ambitious artillery officer, was obsessed by the idea of ending the war by assassinating Napoleon. When the Russian army abandoned Moscow, Figner proposed the idea of ridding the world of this 'enemy of the human race'. His fellow officers found his outrageous plan difficult to swallow. 'Stunned' by Figner's proposal, General Yermolov 'scrutinized this self-sacrificing man and asked various questions to see if he was of sound mind.' Despite the poor weather, Yermolov then went personally to Kutuzov, who, upon hearing about Figner's idea, also inquired if he was 'insane'. With the glow of the Moscow fires clearly visible through the window, Kutuzov paced around the room conversing with Yermolov. 'How can we justify it?' he inquired. 'In [ancient] Rome, during the war between Fabricius and Pyrrhus, the former was once offered the chance to end the war by poisoning the latter. But Fabricius responded instead by handing over to his enemy the physician who had suggested it.'[197] 'Yes, but that was in Rome and a long time ago,' observed Yermolov. Kutuzov ignored this comment and, staring at the fiery glow illuminating the horizon, continued to reason aloud. 'How can I allow this?! If you or I were to personally fight Napoleon, the decision would be obvious ... But in this case, we talk about allowing a surreptitious act, in essence, shooting Napoleon from behind the corner. If Figner succeeds, people would say that it was not him but rather you or I who committed this murderous act.' Kutuzov vacillated for some time until Yermolov insisted on having a direct answer. 'Let him take a few Cossacks, and may Christ be with him.'[198]

Growing a short beard and cropping his hair into a circle like that of a Russian peasant, Figner sneaked back into Moscow. One of his closest friends later recounted that Figner 'rallied people of various backgrounds who still remained in Moscow and organized armed detachments to kill enemy soldiers; he ambushed them amidst the flames in the streets and inside homes and commanded his men so efficiently that the French were killed everywhere, especially at night'. Fluent in several languages, including French and Italian, Figner was well suited for this clandestine war. In daylight, wearing plain peasant clothes, he walked around the city, mixed with the Allied soldiers and served them however he could in order to listen to their conversations. At night, he attacked them with his squads, leaving the streets littered with enemy corpses. He told a friend,

> I wanted to get inside the Kremlin to assassinate Napoleon. But despite my peasant appearance, the damn sentry who stood on guard at the Spasskii Gate became suspicious and struck me in the chest violently with the butt of his musket. I was seized and interrogated on what my reason was for going inside the Kremlin. Though I did my best to pretend to be a fool and a simpleton, they kept interrogating and threatening me before releasing me with the warning that I should never ever dare to appear there again because peasants were forbidden to approach the sacred place of the imperial residence ...[199]

Figner was not the only person who tried (or at least claimed to have tried) to assassinate Napoleon in Moscow. Another was a Russian postal official, who had fought the French during General Alexander Suvorov's famous campaign in Italy in 1799, and was now eager to settle scores with his old enemies. Upon learning that Napoleon intended to visit the post office, the Russian decided to take advantage of this opportunity to assassinate the emperor. Unable to procure any firearms, he decided to hide in the attic and try to kill Napoleon by throwing a wooden log at him. For three days this 'starving and trembling' would-be assassin waited for the moment. Finally he heard a commotion in the yard and saw a group of mounted men arriving at the post office's entrance. The Russian carefully observed the crowd gathered in front of the building and, upon seeing a person whom he took to be Napoleon, he threw his log just as the man was ascending the stairs. The 'deadly' projectile, however, missed its target and only aroused suspicion among the French, who searched the building but could not find the perpetrator. The Russian spent another two days hiding in the building before he managed to escape unnoticed but starving. After the war the poor man found himself teased and ridiculed for his exploit, with many assuring him that Napoleon never visited the post office. But he angrily rejected these assertions and continued to insist that he came very close to assassinating the French emperor, repeating that it was a 'miracle' that the log did not hit its intended target.[200]

'I spent the evening with the emperor yesterday,' wrote Prince Eugène to his wife. 'We played *vingt-et-un* to pass the time but I foresee that we will find the evenings very long as there is not the slightest distraction, not even a billiard table.'[201] The three weeks Napoleon passed in Moscow were among the busiest but also the dreariest days of his career. He had once again taken up residence in the imperial apartments of the Kremlin palace, where a large bedroom and several spacious salons provided him with sufficient space to work and rest. As usual, he slept on the iron camp-bed that he always used on campaign and had the portrait of the King of Rome hung on the wall so he could admire the sweet face of his toddler son. Napoleon instructed his valet to place two lit candles near the window every night so that the soldiers in the Kremlin yard could see that he was still working on their behalf. With the communication system already established, he eagerly awaited the arrival of couriers, who covered the vast distance between Paris and Moscow in just 14–15 days. 'He was always impatient for his couriers' arrival,' noted Caulaincourt. 'He noticed the delay of a few hours, and even grew anxious, though this service did not ever break down. The Paris portfolio, the packets from Warsaw and Vilna, were the barometer of the emperor's good or bad humour.' These communications were vital for the maintenance of the empire since the emperor dealt with a myriad issues, ranging from overseeing tens of thousands of troops in the Russian theatre of war and ordering new levies of men and horses across France and Germany, to discussing the extent of censorship in France,[202] perpetuating a cattle and food fair at Donzac in rural western France, and granting the right to exploit the La Voulte mine in southern France. He also regularly wrote to his wife inquiring about her health and asking about his infant son, who turned a year and a half in late September.[203] It was probably this longing to see his son that made Napoleon take notice of the misery of two Russian orphans who were delivered to the Foundlings Home and given the last name 'Napoleonov'.[204]

'So here we are,' Césare de Laugier wrote in his diary on 25 September, 'amidst smoking ruins, walls that threaten to collapse at any moment, and half-burnt trees. The numerous sign-posts marking the limits of the various districts produce the effect of isolated columns or cenotaphs in a vast cemetery. The mass of ashes gives off a foetid stench that impregnates our clothes.'[205] Although a large part of the city had been destroyed, there were still enough buildings remaining to allow the troops of the Grande Armée stationed in Moscow to make themselves quite comfortable. 'In spite of the disasters, the fire and the flight of the inhabitants, the army is quite comfortable here,' General Charles Morand wrote to his wife. 'My division is quartered in a very large building, and I have a very fine and very comfortable house nearby on a large square.'[206] Similarly, Paul de Bourgoing was billeted in Rostopchin's house, where he loved browsing through the governor's magnificent library.[207] Dezydery Chlapowski and his comrades from the *chevau-légers* of the Guard found quarters in the palace of Prince Lobanov, while General Krasinski lived in the house of the merchant Barishnikov. 'Both houses were very well appointed, everything was in order, both upstairs and down there were very comfortable wide beds with morocco-covered mattresses.'[208] Across the city Duverger, the paymaster in General Compans' division, and eleven of his comrades were lodged in the German Sloboda in eastern Moscow, where they lived quite happily 'rich in furs and paintings, cases of figs, in coffee and liqueurs, macaroons, smoked fish and meats. Alas, [we] had no white bread, fresh meat and ordinary wine.'[209]

What Duverger fails to mention is that after weeks of campaigning, and surrounded by dirt, soot and ashes, the men of the Grande Armée bemoaned the filth of their own clothing and sought out baths[210] and washerwomen. 'Of all the hardships of this campaign,' wrote one officer, 'having to do our own laundry was one of the most humiliating.'[211] So upon settling in Moscow, many Allied soldiers and officers sought to recruit local women as laundresses. But there were not many of them remaining in the city. Bourgogne remembered how he stumbled across two Muscovite women willing to do laundry. Returning to his quarters, he found there a non-commissioned officer of his company, who had been waiting for him a long time. 'When I related my adventures, he seemed delighted as he could find no one to wash his clothes.' Wishing to keep it a secret, the two men waited till everyone fell asleep before going to meet the washerwomen. 'We found a small room at liberty, which we made over to them, furnishing it with whatever we could find – all kinds of pretty things which the noble Muscovite ladies had not been able to carry away. Although our friends had had the appearance of common servants, they were thus transformed into elegant ladies – ladies, however, who had to wash and mend for us.'[212]

Despite the devastation that the conflagration had wrought on the city, many Allied troops sought to enjoy the pleasures of Moscow. They indulged in sightseeing, visiting the Kremlin's palaces and churches, and strolling along the city's newly built boulevards. Some, like Boulart, admired the architecture, while others, especially the Poles, visited historic locations that they had read about in books.[213] To restore some normality to the city, and to soothe in some degree the anxieties of his troops, Napoleon reopened the theatre and took a personal interest in its activities. The famous Italian tenor Tarquinio and the son of Jean-Paul-Égide Martini (composer of the popular romance *Plaisir d'Amour*) were twice summoned to the Kremlin to perform for Napoleon, who was an admirer of Italian music. Bausset then took the opportunity to mention the existence of a French *troupe* in the city. The *troupe*'s director[214] had been forcibly removed by Rostopchin, but most of the *troupe* had stayed behind and now led a wretched existence. Having distributed some immediate relief to the actors, the emperor appointed Bausset to superintend them and ordered him to find out whether, given their present composition, it would be possible to stage a few performances and some light entertainment for the army. The *troupe* agreed and put on a number of short plays and vaudeville pieces.[215] Napoleon's valet Constant recalled that 'these actors had a series of performances of light comedies staged in the private court of General Pozniakov's townhouse, where in the intervals between the acts the grenadiers of the Imperial Guard served refreshments'.[216]

It is often stated that during the second week of October 1812 Napoleon spent several evenings reviewing and modifying the statute intended for the Comédie Française.[217] This matter is quite well known and is usually cited as an example of Napoleon's ability to handle diverse issues in difficult circumstances. 'Culture remained on the mind of the emperor,' observed his valet, who nevertheless found it difficult to comprehend this attention to such administrative trifles when the future was so burdened. He argued that 'it was generally believed, and probably not without reason, that the emperor was acting with a political end in view, and that these regulations concerning the Comédie Française, at a time when no bulletin had yet given a complete notion of the disastrous position of the army, were intended to impress the Parisians, who would not fail to say: "Things cannot be going so very badly if the emperor has time to occupy himself with theatres."' Yet the so-called 'decree of Moscow', which reorganized the *troupe* and the theatre and established the guidelines on structure, administration and accounting that still largely underpin the Comédie Française,[218] was, most probably, not approved in Moscow. The decree was initially adopted by the Council of State in Paris back in early August and Napoleon did not receive the portfolio of documents from the Council of State's session until late September. He reviewed them over the course of three days after returning to the Kremlin, and the documents carry his signatures dated 20, 21 and 22 September. Remarkably the original document of the 'decree of Moscow' is not in this portfolio but is instead in a separate dossier of documents labelled 'documents of October 15, 1812'. Unusually, it features two signatures of Napoleon, one stating 'Approved. Napoleon' and the second affirming 'Approved in Moscow, October 15, 1812. Napoleon.' Most interestingly, however, the document is accompanied by a note stating that 'the intention of the emperor is that the decree be dated in Moscow'. The French historian Tony Sauvel, whose study on this topic appeared almost forty years ago but has been largely ignored, justly argued that the decree reorganizing the Comédie Française 'was neither signed before Moscow, nor in the city, and could not have been so until after the [Allied] departure; either during the retreat, or in Paris once the emperor had returned. Even so, the idea of him signing the decree during the retreat is rather difficult to accept, not only because of all the circumstances of the retreat, but also because it would have been the only administrative measure made during the retreat.' Thus the only option remaining is that the decree, which was published in the official *Bulletin of Laws* on 26 January 1813, was most probably signed by Napoleon *after* his return to Paris in December 1812 and then backdated – possibly to shape public opinion – to his stay in Moscow.[219]

Many soldiers and officers preferred to spend their evenings drinking and gambling, and a few organized impromptu celebrations filled with dancing and music. In late September the fusiliers-grenadiers of the Young Guard held a 'real carnival', where everyone wore masks and costumes. 'First of all we dressed up the Russian women as French Marquises,' recalled Bourgogne. 'Our two Russian tailors were dressed as Chinese, I as a Russian boyar, Flament as a Marquis – each of us in different costume, even our cantiniere, Mother Dubois, who wore a beautiful Russian national dress. As we had no wigs for our Marquises, the regimental perruquier dressed their hair. For grease he used suet, and flour for powder. They looked splendid, and when everyone was ready we began to dance.' For music, they had a flute played by a sergeant-major, accompanied by the drum to keep time. 'We went on drinking and dancing until four o'clock in the morning.'[220] But not everyone was so cheerful. The hearts of many soldiers and officers were filled with sadness at being away from their loved ones, and they were despondent over what lay ahead. 'Enough said about the war,' wrote General Andoche Junot to his mistress. 'I now want to tell you that I love you more every day, that I am bored to death, that I desire nothing in the whole world as much as to see you again [and] that I am stuck in the most unworthy country in the world ...'[221] Soldiers felt much the same. 'I am very tired of this campaign and I do not know when God will give us peace,' grumbled Marchal, while Captain Frederic List wrote his wife, 'Another winter will go by without the happiness of being able to press you in my arms, for it is said that we are going to take winter quarters here.'[222]

Many of the letters, which were intercepted by the Russians, speak of the increasing hardship and the lack of provisions. 'Sicknesses, particularly dysentery, appeared ever more violently,' recalled one German officer. 'Few of our men were spared, and even among the officers only the youngest and strongest escaped this torment.'[223] By October Napoleon had tried to procure the necessities by deploying his advanced posts up to 30 miles from Moscow, and thus covering an area sufficiently vast to provide provisions and forage in the requisite quantities. He thanked his minister of war for sending hundreds of small portable mills that left France in mid-September and were expected to arrive in Moscow during the first two weeks of October. 'They will be of great utility to us,' Napoleon observed. 'I intend to give one such mill to each company in the army.'[224] He also tried to encourage the remaining local peasants to supply his forces in exchange for good pay. On the eve of the invasion Napoleon had secretly manufactured millions of counterfeit rubles and the army chest still contained a large quantity of them.[225] In late September he instructed the intendancy to use this counterfeit money to pay the army and cover all the expenses incurred by the authorities in Moscow and Smolensk.[226] The French authorities assured peasants in the environs of Moscow that all provisions, but especially forage, delivered to the city would be paid for and that the peasants' security during transportation would be guaranteed. The counterfeit paper money, however, was not of high quality and the Muscovites recognized it at once, especially since the banknotes were in high denominations. The Allied troops were paid both in paper banknotes and in copper money that was found in large quantities at the Moscow Mint. Neither option was particularly appealing for the soldiers. The paper money 'had one-quarter of its nominal value as one Russian ruble was being exchanged at 20 sous,' recalled one officer. 'Although pay was set at twice the usual rate, it still meant that the unfortunate officer would find himself paid at half of his usual salary ... Napoleon broadcast loudly that he was paying the army double when, in fact, he had reduced its earning by half.'[227] As for the copper money, large bags containing 25 rubles' worth of coins were used to pay all arrears due to the soldiers, who naturally found them rather unmanageable on account of their weight. Domergues noted that these bags weighed about 100lb! Thus, many Allied soldiers chose to sell this copper money to the locals, who gathered at the specially established exchanges at Nikolskaya street, the Kamennyi bridge and other locations. Russian contemporaries noted that the Muscovites could buy 25 rubles' worth of bags of copper coins for as little as one silver ruble, which naturally enticed many to barter and trade with the French.

This resulted in many 'outlandish and deplorable scenes', recalled Ysarn, who had visited the money exchange at Nikolskaya street, where for silver money one could 'have as many bags of copper coins as he wanted. The challenge was carrying the money away, first, because of its heavy weight and second, due to the crowd that gathered there.' Great was the competition to obtain a sack. There was shoving and shouting, blows from the flat end of the sword, and outright robbing. 'I saw, for example, women desperately trying to carry away bags on each shoulder but just as they were about to leave looters attacked and robbed them,' recalled Ysarn. 'Shouts, insults, blows, confusion all around; soldiers, swords in hand, came to put an end to the disorder and delivered blows right and left to disperse the crowd … Imagine this spectacle in the crowded Nikolskaya street, where numerous sellers and buyers congregated. Having gone to see this crowd, I was obliged to inch along the wall out of fear of becoming more than a spectator.' The next morning the French, having learnt their lesson the previous day, kept the crowd outside the walls and forbade entry to the lowly people. Some soldiers took a stand at the windows of the courts of justice, and set up an office for the exchange of money. After receiving the payment for a sack of 25 rubles, they would throw the bag out of the window. The crowd would then surround the buyers and make a rush for the sacks, facing even musket-shots in their delirium of greed.[228] The buyers, excited by their acquisitions, however, were 'frequently stopped and robbed by passing enemy soldiers'.[229]

Once the fires had subsided, markets began to spring up all across the city. Despite the measures taken to end the pillaging, soldiers had already accumulated plenty of booty that they were now keen to trade and exchange. 'The streets looked like a veritable fair, all of whose participants, both sellers and buyers, were military men … Driven by the lust for plunder as well as shortages of necessities, soldiers of all ranks and from all corps left their camps and flocked to Moscow … They had all turned merchant and it was to them that officers of every rank came to provision themselves.'[230] The Imperial Guard seems to have been particularly active in this regard, and Thirion accused the Guardsmen of particularly obnoxious behaviour. They set up numerous 'shops' and sold everything at high profit to the rest of the army. Because of this, the army thereafter called them 'the merchants or Jews of Moscow'.[231] The Guard paid little heed to its commanders' orders and even senior officers of the Guard were keen on procuring and trading their *emplettes* or 'little purchases'.[232] But the trade in plunder went even further up the chain of command. Many generals were busy buying silver ingots or silverware, jewels and precious stones. With winter expected to set in soon, furs were particularly popular among both officers and the rank-and-file soldiers. Upset that he could not find a 'really pretty or rare' fur coat, Peyrusse was finally able to get a pretty one from Roustam, Napoleon's mamluk, for 250 francs.[233] Lieutenant J.L. Henckens of the 6th *Chasseurs à Cheval* remembered many of his men returning to their lodgings at the 'Grand Theatre' with numerous items, including 'a sack full of gold watches' and numerous 'long shawls of very striking colours'. He was particularly pleased when one of his patrols stumbled on a store of furs, since cold weather was expected at any time and these furs would come in very handy then. In what soon proved to be a prudent move, Henckens and his comrades, including one man who had trained as a tailor, sat down to sew waistcoats.[234] Less practical was Paul de Bourgoing who, 'with youthful light-headedness and lack of foresight', ignored 'the amplest and warmest fur coats' and instead went for the 'most elegant in shape and colour'. He bought a 'very pretty Polish-style coat in dark blue cloth, richly adorned with silken fringes and lined with black astrakhan. At that moment I thought much more of my own pleasure, walking about in my general's suite with an elegant garment in the presence of [pretty actresses], than of arming myself against the icy winds.'[235]

Chapter 8

'By Accident or Malice?' Who Burned Moscow?

Count Rostopchin is widely believed to have caused the destruction of Moscow. Both his contemporaries and later generations almost universally accepted that the governor's plan of action was to burn the city and that he carried it out with the help of numerous 'gaunt and bearded prisoners and madmen'[1] whom he had set free on the eve of the occupation. 'The Russian army retreated through Moscow, which Rostopchin burned,' noted Heinrich Friedrich Karl Reichsfreiherr vom und zum Stein, the famed Prussian statesman living in exile in Russia, in his diary on 23 September.[2] 'Responsibility for the fire, which destroyed three-quarters of the wooden town, lay with its governor, Rostopchin,' proclaims one modern historian,[3] while another refers to the fire as the 'act of a man driven insane', who 'had ordered that Moscow should burn to the ground rather than be possessed by the French'.[4] Writing in 1985, the British historian Nigel Nicolson assured his readers that 'today when we can sift all the evidence, there can remain little doubt that the conflagration was started deliberately by Rostopchin's order'. In his new history of Moscow, American historian Alexander M. Martin also directly points the finger at Rostopchin, who 'ordered the city to be burned' to deny Napoleon winter quarters.[5]

To support their accusations, historians usually point to the governor's orders to remove the fire-engines and to his repeated proclamations indicating his willingness to destroy the city rather than see it in enemy hands. Yet they fail to elucidate any of the contradictions surrounding many aspects of the Moscow fire. Thus there is no written evidence confirming direct orders to prepare or distribute fuses or any other incendiary materials, or instructing saboteurs to destroy the city. Rostopchin himself had made numerous conflicting statements that both support and exclude his involvement in the burning of Moscow. Interestingly, many historians claim that Rostopchin had embraced the infamy that the destruction of Moscow bestowed on him initially, ignoring both his letters written between 1812 and 1815 that reflect his frustration with the public perception and his memoirs, which were produced with the sole purpose of rejecting responsibility for the fire. His later denials are usually branded as an attempt to evade notoriety. Yet, in doing so these critics conveniently ignore the possibility that his earlier acceptance of responsibility for the fire may have been driven by his desire for fame and/ or social advancement. One could argue that Rostopchin had initially claimed the credit in the belief that the burning of Moscow would be regarded as an heroic action, and subsequently disowned complicity when he found that posterity generally considered it shameful.

Rostopchin's letters are often cited as evidence for claims that the governor had a clear plan to destroy Moscow. But as the German historian Hans Schmidt correctly observed, the governor's letters 'amounted to nothing more than a warning to military leaders not to abandon Moscow, otherwise they would have had to bear responsibility for the destruction of the holy city in front of the tsar'.[6] An intelligent, silver-tongued and well mannered man, Rostopchin was also a man of passionate character who often allowed his emotions free rein. As early as late August, just days after the fall of Smolensk, he was already warning of the potential destruction of Moscow. He clearly exaggerated the public sentiment when he wrote to Prince Bagration that 'the local residents, out of their loyalty to the Tsar and the love of the Motherland, have all decided to perish by the walls of Moscow and, if the Lord turns away from them, to turn the city into ashes so that instead of bountiful spoils Napoleon finds only smoke and ashes'. A day later Rostopchin repeated the same warning (almost verbatim) in a letter to Balashev: 'The local populace's attitude is to follow the rule "Do not leave it to the enemy!" So if Providence decides, to the eternal shame of Russia, to let the enemy enter Moscow, I am almost certain that the people themselves will set the city on fire and deprive Napoleon of his rich prize and means of rewarding his thugs through pillage.' On 2 September another of Rostopchin's missives claimed that he was ready to lead 100,000 armed local residents to support the Russian army. At the end of the letter the governor did note, however, that in case of a setback, he could ensure 'that the villains find only ashes in Moscow'. On 8 September, just as the news of the battle of Borodino was trickling in, Rostopchin was busy writing another letter to Balashev, assuring him that 'if, due to unfortunate circumstance, it would not be possible to save the capital, I will set it on fire'.[7] Bagration seems to have become the most ardent supporter of Rostopchin's pronouncements. After reading the governor's letter, he replied, 'I must admit, as I read your letter, I cried at seeing the nobility of your spirit and honour. Indeed, we must act this way: it is better to burn than to surrender to the enemy.'[8] Bagration also discussed Rostopchin's claims with other officers; thus he confided to a small circle of senior officers in Vyazma that he did not think that 'the French would ever reach Moscow, but if they do, they will find nothing but ruins and ashes'.[9] Some of these officers later repeated this same claim, with Colonel Zakrevskii telling a fellow officer on the eve of Borodino that 'Even if we do not win the battle, another Pozharskii[10] will help us.'[11]

The governor had carefully chosen his addressees – Bagration and Balashev – knowing full well that they would either agree with his sentiments or share and discuss the content of his letters with the army. He certainly wanted to convey to these leaders that the fall of Moscow was unthinkable and that both the army and the Muscovites should be ready to make their best effort to prevail over the enemy. None of his letters to Barclay de Tolly, Kutuzov or other senior army and government officials mentions anything about the deliberate destruction of the empire's greatest city. Partially this was due to the fact that the governor did not know them well enough to confide such audacious claims. He disliked Barclay de Tolly and was apprehensive of Kutuzov, whose intentions he had already begun to suspect by early September. Rostopchin's letters do betray the governor's 'long-thought-out intention' to bring devastation upon the city rather than see it in enemy hands. Andrei Tartakovskii believes that 'it is not important whether there were indeed any "fiery" popular sentiments in Moscow in the summer of 1812 or whether Rostopchin simply invented them. More important is the very fact that he was greatly preoccupied by the idea of the possibility of burning Moscow and had clearly formulated it …' Tartakovskii argues that Rostopchin's silence on this matter in his correspondence with Emperor Alexander further underscores his cunning calculation. 'If Alexander I expressed his disapproval, Rostopchin's hands would have been tied and the very possibility of attempting such an enterprise would have been impossible.'[12]

It is difficult to agree with Tartakovskii's claim that Rostopchin was planning Moscow's destruction by late August, and 'was careful enough to present it not as his own enterprise but rather as a manifestation of spontaneous resoluteness among the local populace', or that by keeping silent on this matter in his correspondence with Emperor Alexander and other senior military and political figures, Rostopchin was able to make progress on his plan while nurturing the claim of popular reaction as a possible 'alibi' in case of 'negative reaction from the army command or the governing elites'. Rostopchin's excessive rhetoric, however, should not be misconstrued as actual preparations to destroy the city. As one historian commented, 'there was a big difference between what he desired and what he could do'.[13]

It is quite clear that Rostopchin could have taken no measures to set fire to the town before 14 September. Kutuzov assured him throughout late August and early September that he would not allow Moscow to fall. After Borodino, the old field marshal became aware of the governor's comments about burning the city and found them contrary to his own intention to turn Moscow into a 'sponge' that would absorb the 'stormy torrent'. This is perhaps why he effectively ignored the governor's inquiries and kept his plans secret until the very last minute. Somewhat dubiously, Rostopchin believed Kutuzov's reassurances and urged people to stay in the city, proudly declaring that 'I will stake my life on it that the enemy will not enter Moscow.'[14] Even while sending his letters threatening to set fire to Moscow, the governor continued publishing broadsheets ridiculing those who fled the city and appealing to the patriotism of those who remained. These publications surely cast doubt on the claims that Rostopchin had a *long-conceived plan* to destroy Moscow, unless he intended to burn the city down with the residents still inside it. Nor could Rostopchin foresee the decision of the Council of War at Fili – if he ignited the city and the council decided in favour of fighting, the Russian army might have fought the battle with the city already on fire and the reward of their victory would have been its ashes; worse, in the case of defeat, a burning city behind the lines could only have produced catastrophic results. No man in his right mind would have run such a risk and Rostopchin, perculiar as he was, was no madman. In fact, he clearly expected the Russian army to fight on the outskirts of Moscow and on 13 September he mobilized tens of thousands of Muscovites on the Three Hills to support the army. Had Rostopchin indeed had any fixed plan for the city's destruction, it seems odd that he made no actual preparations for it in the weeks preceding the fall of Moscow. He must surely have had to make an attempt to mine the vast ammunition and supply magazines that dotted the city, or to sabotage major buildings that might become useful to the enemy? Yet we lack any direct evidence that such preparations were carried out. Undertaking such a vast enterprise would certainly have produced a considerable paper trail, if not in official communications, at least in the private correspondence of the persons involved. Yet aside from Rostopchin's fervent missives, there are no other letters, instructions or reports mentioning the planning or preparations for the destruction of Moscow, either before or after 14 September. If it was indeed a carefully planned event, one would expect at the very least to find a 'mission accomplished' letter written by one of the municipal or police officials, or even Rostopchin himself, but none was written either after the Grande Armée's expulsion from Russia or after Napoleon's downfall. Prince A. Shakovskoi was among the first to greet Rostopchin upon his return to Moscow, and they spoke at length about the events that had befallen the city. Yet throughout the conversation Rostopchin made no remarks indicative of deliberate preparations or intentions to burn the city, though he was clearly content with what had happened.[15] Finally, the lack of deliberate planning and preparations for burning the city can be seen in the fact that the Allied troops actually contained many early fires – the Imperial Guardsmen were, for example, able to extinguish fires in the Kitai-gorod by the morning of 15 September, and the French theatre director Armand Domergues observed that 'through swift and energetic measures [the French] were able to completely quench the fires near the Kuznetskii bridge'.[16] The great conflagration did not start until the evening of 15 September, when the Allied troops were already inside the city, many of them industriously pillaging homes.

This is not to say that Rostopchin bore no responsibility for the fire. There is no denying the fact that he *thought* about the possible destruction of Moscow. Rostopchin, a man of fiercely nationalist temperament, believed that the fall of Moscow, the heart of the Russian Empire, the symbol of Russian imperial might, could have unforeseen political, social and cultural ramifications for the entire realm.[17] He believed that the French presence would facilitate the spread of free-thinking and radical ideas into Russia and undermine the very foundations of Russian society. 'With [Moscow's] fall, the fetter that binds together popular opinion and strengthens the throne of our Sovereign, would be broken … What obedience and commitment can we expect in the provinces when the villain [Napoleon] begins publishing his manifestoes from Moscow? What dangers would this pose to the emperor himself?'[18] Therefore Rostopchin refused to accept the possibility that the enemy would take 'his' city and was clearly willing to see it destroyed but not conquered, as he had mentioned in some of his letters and conversations. On the eve of his departure from Moscow he told his wife, 'If we do not burn the city, we will at least ransack it. Napoleon would do it later anyway, and this is a triumph that I am not willing to grant him.'[19] Writing to Emperor Alexander in late October, he admitted that 'if Kutuzov had told me about his decision [to abandon Moscow] two days earlier, I would have evacuated all the inhabitants and burned it myself'.[20] This (and other similar) pronouncements, however, must be treated cautiously since Rostopchin made them after the event when it became clear how decisive the Moscow Fire proved in defeating the enemy invasion and Rostopchin could argue that burning the city denied the enemy a political and military victory and rallied the people to the national cause.[21]

When he visited Kutuzov at Fili on 13 September, the governor was already a man on the edge. He was extremely frustrated by Kutuzov's hollow promises to defend the city and the sight of the Russian army, battered as it was in the wake of Borodino, could not have made a good impression on him. Even physically Rostopchin was not well: he later acknowledged that since the fall of Smolensk on 18 August he had not slept in bed and instead napped 'fully clothed on a couch, repeatedly awakened by dispatches that continuously reached me from all directions';[22] he had not changed his clothing in days. The sense of responsibility for what was going to happen to the city would have lain heavily on his shoulders. Yet the meeting with Kutuzov and other Russian generals only further inflamed him. Kutuzov continued to mislead him, while Barclay de Tolly bluntly informed him that defending Moscow was nothing but 'madness'.[23] Writing to his wife ten days after the fall of Moscow, Rostopchin lamented that 'my idea of burning the city before the villain entered it was a useful one but Kutuzov deceived me and by the time he readied [the troops] on the eve of his retreat through Moscow, it was already too late to do it'.[24]

Rostopchin may not have had a long-standing plan to burn Moscow but in the hours before the city fell he was determined to do everything possible to deny Napoleon his triumph. One of his numerous decisions – the removal of firefighting equipment – has been discussed by numerous memoirists and historians. In *La vérité sur l'incendie de Moscou*, Rostopchin acknowledged evacuating 'two thousand, one hundred firefighters and ninety-six pumps (for there were three for each ward) the day before the enemy's entry into Moscow. There was a body of officers attached to the service pumps, and I did not see fit to leave their services to Napoleon; instead, I had all civil and military authorities withdrawn from the city.'[25] His supporters later argued that the governor was justified in evacuating this equipment since the fire brigade was part of Moscow's *Uprava Blagochiniya* (municipal administrative police organ) and could not be left behind amidst the general evacuation of the capital city. The problem is that Rostopchin was less conscientious about other state property, which was left behind in large quantities. The vast holdings of the provincial archives were forsaken,[26] and some 300,000 rubles' worth of copper coins and stamped papers valued at almost 1.5 million paper rubles were abandoned at the municipal treasury. When it came to the firefighting equipment, Rostopchin's order is quite peculiar: he instructed the fire brigade 'to depart only with fire engines and leave other firefighting equipment behind'. The governor's decision to remove only part of the equipment may sound puzzling but the spontaneity of his resolution to doom Moscow to destruction does explain it. He could not remove everything in the few remaining hours (which once again points to the lack of long-term planning) and so chose to take the most important gear: without the pumps, the other equipment would have been less useful. Observing a group of soldiers accompanying transports out of the city, Ludwig Wolzogen approached them and discovered that they were removing the fire pumps, which, he wrote, 'greatly perturbed me'. Finding Rostopchin, he asked the purpose of the removal of this equipment and was told that the governor had 'a good reason for it'.[27] Wolzogen could not have known that just moments earlier Rostopchin had penned a letter to his wife: 'By the time you receive this letter, Moscow will have turned to ashes. I hope I will be forgiven for acting as the Roman.'[28]

Available evidence suggests that Rostopchin did not issue a direct order to set the city on fire. Such an act would have involved considerable personal liability. Instead, he simply created conditions in which the city could burn out of control. This way he avoided direct responsibility and could portray the fire as the manifestation of popular will. He was well aware of the inherent fire hazard that any largely wooden city faced – in June–July he had become so concerned about the risk of fire in the city that he prohibited smoking in the streets – and doubtless anticipated that, amidst the turmoil of evacuation and enemy occupation, the city would inevitably catch fire. Somebody was bound to leave a burning hearth or accidentally drop a candle, which was all that might be needed to ignite the initial fires. Writing to his wife on 21 September, he admitted, 'I knew that fire would be inevitable [when] 30,000 French brigands and a few thousand Russian marauders plundered the city.'[29] Removing the fire pumps guaranteed that, even in the case of accidental outbreaks of fires, the enemy would find it difficult to contain the flames and the city would suffer greater damage, denying Napoleon the benefits he hoped for.

Most studies point to Rostopchin's removal of the firefighting equipment as the prime evidence for his deliberate effort to burn the city. Yet we cannot but wonder how useful the firefighting equipment would have been if it had been left behind. The

Soviet historian V. Kholodkovskii believed that Rostopchin's decision revealed his real intentions, for 'to deprive the city of the means of protection from fire meant preparing it for fiery destruction'.[30] This is true, but we must also bear in mind that the presence of fire engines does not equate to total fire safety. The risk of fire was a common hazard in all early modern European cities that had been built predominantly of wood, and they were vulnerable to fires even during peacetime. Moscow suffered several devastating fires (in 1712, 1730, 1736, 1737, 1748, 1752 and 1773) even in peacetime when it had manpower and equipment to fight the flames. The Great Fire of London of 1666 was sparked off by a minor accident but it rapidly turned into a fiery inferno that consumed much of the city – over 13,000 houses and 87 churches – despite the best efforts of the inhabitants. The presence of municipal authorities and firefighting equipment did not prevent the Copenhagen Fire of 1795, which raged for two days and destroyed 941 houses and made homeless some 6,000 residents; it came in the wake of the 1728 fire that had already destroyed much of historic Copenhagen. Across the Atlantic the city of New Orleans fell victim to fires in 1788 and 1794 that destroyed more than a thousand buildings. Taking these global examples into account, one cannot but wonder if the presence of fire engines in Moscow would have made any difference in a city that was largely abandoned by its citizens, lacked the municipal authorities to coordinate a response and was being pillaged both by its own citizens and by the occupying force?

Over the years Rostopchin adopted a dubious position over his involvement in the burning of Moscow. On one hand, he firmly rejected claims that he had burned the city and insisted that the fire was caused by the French, who had 'pillaged and burned this poor city for five days'.[31] As early as November 1812 he argued that the French were trying to turn him into a scapegoat, and later complained that 'in his effort to blame this shameful misdeed on someone else, Bonaparte rewarded me with the title of arsonist and many people actually believe him'.[32] Yet, while denying his involvement in the fire, Rostopchin also basked in the glory that it bestowed on him. Starting in 1814, he had been warmly welcomed in conservative circles throughout Europe, hailed as a hero who had contributed to the downfall of the Corsican ogre. 'In German lands, they show me all the marks of esteem and consideration,' he boasted in a letter to a manager of his estates. 'They all acknowledge me as the main weapon in the destruction of Napoleon, which the latter himself had acknowledged, for if there were a popular uprising in Moscow what would the nobility have done and what consequences would this have produced?' He lamented that instead of similar acclaim, Muscovite society in fact poured scorn on him. 'Back home everyone talks about their burned houses and property but no one thinks beyond that. Yet, here [in Germany] my portraits are everywhere and even many monuments [can be seen]. So while my own compatriots cannot be gratified, foreigners are thanking me.'[33]

Rostopchin's acceptance of such homage reinforced the public's perception that he was the architect of the great conflagration. But such an assessment weighed heavily on his mind, and in 1823 he published a pamphlet entitled *La Vérité sur l'incendie de Moscou* (The Truth about the Fire of Moscow), in which he surprised his contemporaries by denying any involvement in the fire. 'Ten years have elapsed since the burning of Moscow,' he wrote, 'and I am still being pointed out to history and posterity as the author of an event, which, according to accepted opinion, was the principal cause of the destruction of the army of Napoleon, his downfall, the salvation of Russia and the delivery of Europe.' But now Rostopchin stood ready to 'renounce the finest role of the epoch' and to 'personally bring down the edifice of my celebrity'.

In just forty-seven pages Rostopchin sought to refute the charge that he had deliberately destroyed Moscow. His main argument was the same as that he had used in letters written immediately after the liberation of Moscow in 1812:[34] the fire was caused by the actions of the Grande Armée, and Napoleon had subsequently sought to shift the responsibility for it. He analysed Napoleon's bulletins, pointing out inconsistencies and mistakes. He rejected Napoleon's claim that he had planned to use a flying machine designed by 'Schmidt'. How can one believe, he argued, that 'Schmidt could destroy the French army with a balloon similar to the one which the French themselves used at the Battle of Fleurus'?[35] Rostopchin denied both the existence of any special incendiary devices and the use of police and convicts to ignite the city. Instead, he blamed the fire on the actions of the Muscovites, who had 'preferred to destroy rather than surrender'.[36] He justified his decision to launch a general evacuation of Moscow because he 'wanted to deny Napoleon any means to establish local contacts, to communicate with the interior of the empire, and to take advantage of the influence that the French have gained in Europe through their literature, fashion, cuisine and language'. Instead, the abandonment of Moscow rallied Russians to the national cause. It incited an 'ardent patriotism, the sense of sacrifice, military ardour and desire for vengeance against the enemy who had the audacity to penetrate so far into the Motherland'.[37]

Many contemporaries refused to accept the governor's belated denial and wondered what persuaded him, 'after a silence of more than ten years, to open his mouth to deny what has become a universal opinion'.[38] We will never know what impelled him to do it, although one of his descendants mentioned some factors. Rostopchin seems to have been exasperated at seeing his countrymen ignoring 'the glorious side of this great deed' and instead 'contemplating the disastrous consequences of the fire in terms of their material losses'. He must have wanted to punish them: 'the Muscovites complain about the glorious halo that I have placed around their heads. Well then, I will deprive them of it.' Or Rostopchin could have written the book out of 'sublime sentiment and wounded patriotism', after he realized that he personally had been largely credited with 'the deed that saved the nation' and wanted to 'attribute it to all of his countrymen'.[39]

The memoir of Rostopchin's daughter Natalya Naryshkina, written some fifty years after the event, offers a few more tantalizing insights. She described how, during the night of 14 September, 'Police Constable [Adam] Brokker brought several people, some of whom were civilians and others police officials. They held a secret discussion in my father's cabinet in the presence of Brokker and my brother.' Naryshkina, who was not present at the meeting, claimed that 'these people received precise instructions on which buildings and districts had to be burned immediately after the passing of our troops through the city'. Naryshkina argued that she wanted to reveal these detail to challenge the belief that 'criminals and convicts' burnt the city. Instead, it was the handiwork of 'men devoted to their Fatherland and to their duty'. Among these men Naryshkina named Ivan Prokhorov (who was later shot by the French), Anton Gerasimov (who disappeared, and probably perished in Moscow) and District Supervisor and Police Constable P. Voronenko. The latter is particularly noteworthy, for it was he, wrote Naryshkina, who

was among the first to begin implementing this plan. Around ten o'clock in the evening he courageously undertook this enterprise when part of the enemy army occupied the city's suburbs. In one instant, stores with provisions, barges with grain on the river and stalls with various goods ... – everything became prey to the flames. The wind spread the flames and since fire pumps and firefighters were absent and could not stop the fire, the sacrifice inspired by that moment was accomplished, as was my father's desire.

Naryshkina's testimony is usually cited as evidence in support of Rostopchin's direct order to destroy the city, especially since it seems to be supported by Voronenko's own report submitted not long after Moscow burned to the ground. Voronenko enjoyed a close relationship with Rostopchin, who in August had entrusted him with a mission to the Russian army headquarters to report on military operations. Voronenko remained with the army for a couple of weeks before returning to Moscow on the eve of its abandonment. 'At 5am on 14 September,' he later described, '[Rostopchin] ordered me to go to the Wine Merchants' Court [*Vinnyi dvor*] and Customs Office [*Mytnyi dvor*] and evacuate the state and private barges located near the Krasnyi hill and the Simonov Monastery; in the event of the enemy's prompt entry into the city, I was instructed to destroy everything with fire, which I carried out in various places until 10 o'clock in the evening.'[40] Voronenko's reference to instructions 'to destroy everything with fire' is often cited out of context, creating the impression that he was directly instructed by Rostopchin to destroy the city as a whole. Yet a closer reading of the report shows that it actually refers to Rostopchin's instructions to remove supplies and ammunition and destroy any that remained so as to prevent it falling into the enemy hands. Less well known is the report of Adam Brokker, another 'conspirator' named by Naryshkina, who was asked in 1817 to submit a report on his action. Brokker explained that 'during the night of [14] September I was left behind by Police Chief Ivashkin to destroy barrels of wine stored in the Wine Merchants' Court and the shops [around it]. I executed this mission until 7am, when I received an order to appear with my squad before my superiors on the occasion of the departure of the police from the capital.'[41] Thus Brokker, who attended the same meeting as Voronenko, was also tasked with the destruction of state property to prevent its falling into the enemy hands.

Even if we assume that Rostopchin was the mastermind of the Moscow fire, we must also note that he must share, at least partially, this notoriety with others, since he was not the only one igniting storehouses. General P. Kaptsevich, who commanded the 7th Infantry Division, reported that as the Russian army passed through the city, 'two ammunition magazines were blown up on the orders of General Miloradovich, causing a horrendous explosion'.[42] A month after the conflagration, Kutuzov acknowledged that he had 'ordered the destruction of some magazines', while the subsequent investigation into the loss of state property noted that 'the remaining barges that were to sail in the wake of the artillery barges but had been delayed by them and therefore could not be saved from the enemy, had been burnt and sunk on the orders of the late Prince Kutuzov'.[43] Looking out of the windows of his apartment in the Foundlings Home, Christian Christiani watched the result of these orders as 'barges, some empty and some carrying wheat and other grains, anchored on the Moscow river right next to our building, were all in flames, as were flours and grains unloaded on the riverbank'.[44] Did Miloradovich and Kutuzov realize the consequences that igniting these storehouses and barges might have on the wooden city that surrounded them? They certainly should have. Yet neither is accused of burning Moscow. These explosions, carried out in the chaotic atmosphere of the enemy's initial occupation of the city, could by themselves have caused the outbreak of the initial fires as the city's markets and wooden buildings were filled with combustible materials that could be easily ignited by the falling smouldering debris.

Another incident cited in favour of Rostopchin's culpability was his burning of the magnificent estate at Voronovo, which was decorated in the most superb and costly manner with precious and antique articles. 'The very stabling was of rare grandeur, surmounted over the gateways by colossal casts of the Monte Cavallo horses and figures which he had brought from Rome, with costly models of all the principal Roman and Grecian buildings and statues that filled a large gallery in the palace, the interior of which was most splendidly and tastefully furnished with every article of luxurious use and ornament that foreign countries could supply.' When the French threatened the place in late September, Rostopchin had it all burnt down, leaving a note: 'Frenchmen, I abandon to you my two houses at Moscow, with their furniture and contents worth half a million of rubles. Here you will only find ashes.'[45] Some have used this incident as further proof that Rostopchin had indeed ordered the fire in Moscow. But this seems far-fetched. The burning of the Voronovo estate seems to be more a direct response to the approach of the enemy army than part of any larger design. It took place on 29 September, almost two weeks after the Moscow conflagration, and only when threatened with French occupation. Robert Wilson, who was present at Voronovo, described how distraught Rostopchin was in the wake of Moscow's fall:

> During the night preceding the retreat from Voronovo, Rostopchin, Bennigsen, Yermolov, and various generals and officers, with the English general [Wilson] and Lord Tyrconnel, his aide-de-camp, bivouacked round a fire in front of the palace stabling. Rostopchin had prevented all sleep by his bitter complaints against Kutuzov 'for his evacuation of Moscow without giving him the "covenanted notice", and for having thus deprived the authorities and inhabitants of an occasion to display, not Roman, but more than Roman – Russian dignity by a municipal and popular ignition of their city before it had been contaminated by an invader's presence.

It was in this state of depression that he decided to set fire with his own hands to the palace that all so much admired. But there is one more factor that we cannot overlook: Rostopchin burnt his estate at Voronovo after it became clear that both his large houses in Moscow had escaped the flames. This would have placed him in a rather awkward position: the fire he helped to bring about had brought hardship and misery to some quarter of a million people, while he personally suffered no harm. He must have felt an urge to do something to remedy this.

Some Allied participants described finding incriminating evidence in the governor's palace in Moscow. Bourgoing recalled that when General Delaborde was lodged in Rostopchin's palace, the French troops found 'physical evidence' that seemed to implicate the governor in deliberate preparations for the fire. Bourgoing encountered 'some poor people' near the house whom he 'gradually reassured about our intentions, and some of them even offered us their services. We need these men to learn about local circumstances.' Their help became particularly valuable when some of them removed from inside the stove ovens and pipes 'an assortment of small wooden barrels filled with incendiary material'. Bourgoing specified that these were not the usual 'barrels', but rather cylindrically shaped, single pieces of pine wood, carved and rounded on both ends; they were 9 inches long and almost 2½ in diameter.[46] Paul Berthezène also remembered seeing these weird items that 'by their shape and size, resembled tobacco rolls [*carotte de tabac*], about 9 or 10 inches long and 2 inches in diameter; once lit, they burned even in water'.[47] Similar testimony comes from Bausset, the prefect of the imperial palace, who was informed about the discovery of 'the small infernal machines' at the governor's palace.[48]

In his *La Vérité*, Rostopchin denied the presence of any special explosives at his palace, arguing that if any were found, they could 'have been placed there after my departure to provide additional proof to the claim that there had been a plan to burn Moscow'.[49] He observed that there was no need for special combustible materials to ignite the city since straw and hay would have been within reach of any would-be incendiary. Assuming the Allied participants were telling the truth, these explosive devices were most probably intended for Leppich's flying machine, which was supposed to conduct air attacks against the Grande Armée and drop these explosives devices from the air. Throughout the late summer Rostopchin and Obreskov supervised the preparation of munitions for Leppich's machine and their letters contain numerous references to incendiary and explosive materials. These supplies were largely stored in Moscow and their presence would naturally have surprised the French, many of whom interpreted them as evidence for the deliberate Russian planning for the fire. As early as 15 September the French authorities were informed about the large volume of sulphuric acid that Muscovite merchant Auguste Prêtre was contracted to deliver. The French agent suspected that it could have been used in 'secret operations conducted by civilian and military authorities of Moscow'.[50] In reality, it was one of the many acquisitions that Rostopchin had made for Leppich's project.

Incendiary Criminals

The letters and memoirs of French, German, Polish and other soldiers and officers offer contrasting insights into the Moscow fire, but they do agree on one thing: there were hundreds, even thousands, of people running around the city and igniting buildings. 'The Russian governor Rostopchin wished to ruin this fine city when he saw it abandoned by the Russian army,' the 19th Bulletin proclaimed on 16 September. 'He had armed 3,000 malefactors, whom he had taken from the prisons. He also summoned together 6,000 men and distributed arms among them from the arsenal.' A day later the 20th Bulletin repeated: 'The Russians set fire to the money market, the bazaar and the hospital. On the 16th, a violent wind started blowing; 3,000 to 4,000 brigands set fires in the city in 500 places at once, by orders of Governor Rostopchin ... The majority of the houses are made of wood; the fire spread with prodigious rapidity, it was an ocean of flames ... This is the crime of Rostopchin, carried out by felons liberated from the prisons.'[51]

Napoleon's bulletins played an important role in shaping the public memory of the Moscow fire. The letters of French soldiers writing home from Moscow often repeated the information contained in the bulletins, although their estimates of the numbers of incendiaries involved in the fire varied wildly. One intendancy official informed his father that the conflagration was the handiwork of '2,000 convicts',[52] while on 28 September *Sous-Lieutenant* Jean Dauve of the 12th line (1st Corps) wrote to his father that the fire was spread by a 'vast number of Russian soldiers and convicts'.[53] Likewise, *Lieutenant* Pierre-Laurent Paradis of the 25th Line (1st Corps) thought as many as '10,000' convicts had set fires in various parts of the city,[54] while the wife of another intendancy official learned from her husband that it was in fact '20,000 convicts, as well as [Russian] soldiers and officers', who carried out this action.[55]

The belief in the widespread involvement of convicts in the burning of Moscow was repeated and buttressed in dozens of memoirs of French, German, Polish and other participants, who recounted their experiences years after the event. In a passage typical of other Allied memoirs, Montesquiou-Fezensac described how Rostopchin 'collected about 3,000 or 4,000 men from the dregs of the people, amongst them were several criminals who had been set at liberty for the occasion. Combustible materials were distributed to them, and the agents of police were ordered to conduct them into every part of the city.'[56] These memoirists varied in their estimates of the numbers of convicts involved in igniting the fires, with some referring to as few as 1,000 (Fantin des Odoards) and others to as many as '10,000 criminals unleashed to burn down the city' (General François Roguet).[57] Similar claims can be found in the memoirs of French residents of Moscow. Chevalier d'Ysarn, for example, recounted one of the stories he had heard after the fire:

A few days before the Grande Armée's arrival, a tramp in prison outfit and with his head half shaved appeared at the doors of a German locksmith, Gourny, who lived in the Nemetskaya Sloboda. The mistress of the house took pity on the wretch and gave him some food and money. Before leaving, the convict then told her, 'Madame, in gratitude for your kindness to me, I will give you a piece of advice – leave the city as soon as possible.' 'But why?' inquired the woman. The convict initially refused to explain but, pressed with questions, he finally declared that 'all convicts had been released without exception and compelled to swear an oath to burn the city; to reinforce their oath, they had been pledged in front of the icons of the saints.[58]

It was even said that, upon their release, Rostopchin gave a short speech instructing the convicts what to do. F. Vaudoncourt put the following words in Rostopchin's mouth: 'You have, of course, committed crimes but can now atone for them by doing a great service to the state.'[59]

Such claims, frequently cited in later studies, are almost entirely fictional and documents in the Russian archives reveal a very different reality. There could not have been 'thousands' of convicts roaming the streets of Moscow, since the total number of detainees held in the city's prisons was far short of the numbers claimed in the bulletins and memoirs. There were just 631[60] convicts (including more than 90 women and 110 military detainees) in the Prison Castle and another 173 (including 26 women)[61] in the Temporary (Debt) Prison.[62] The majority of these convicts were evacuated before the city was abandoned. Late on 13 September Rostopchin instructed the civilian governor of Moscow and the city's chief of police to make arrangements for their transportation to Ryazan and Nizhnii Novgorod.[63] The detainees of the Prison Castle were removed under escort (Major Nittelhorst and a squad of soldiers from the newly established 10th Infantry Regiment) to Nizhnii Novgorod.[64] Although the Russian historian A. Popov argues that this order was not carried out and the convicts were simply released, Alexander Mikhailovskii-Danilevskii cites good evidence to the contrary: in mid-October the governor of Nizhnii Novgorod acknowledged the arrival of 540 convicts.[65] The eighty-seven 'missing' convicts probably included the 'eighty sick men' mentioned in an official report,[66] and it is possible that they were left somewhere along the route to convalesce.

This still leaves the 170 convicts held in the Temporary Prison. The word 'convict' might conjure up visions of hardened and ruthless criminals, but the detainees at the Temporary Prison hardly fitted this stereotype. They came mostly from Moscow's servitor class and peasantry,[67] but they also included a merchant's son, six officials, one retired officer, etc. All had been convicted for minor offences, such as failing to repay a debt. Given the nature of their crimes, Rostopchin and N.V. Obreskov, the civilian governor of Moscow, chose simply to release them 'under written assurance to appear [before the authorities] upon request'.[68] In the morning of 14 September V.A. Obreskov, Rostopchin's aide-de-camp, conveyed the order to the Temporary Prison and the prisoners were released.[69] It was probably these people that Alexander Bulgakov saw 'running away from the prison' late in the afternoon, prompting him to wonder 'whether they were released or simply escaped'.[70]

Rostopchin himself was not present when the prisoners were released, and therefore could not have made any speeches, as some memoirists claimed. Many, if not all, of these convicts had undoubtedly stayed in the city and some might have participated in the pillaging. But there is no tangible evidence – aside from the French court proceedings that will be discussed shortly – that these convicts were instructed or compelled to perform any actions intended to destroy the city. Aside from the memoirs of the Allied participants, who could not in any case have witnessed such an event, there is no evidence to back up the suggestion made by one modern historian that 'some eight hundred common-law prisoners' were given 'Congreve fuses' and instructed to set fire to buildings occupied by the French invaders.[71] Confessions made by 'incendiaries', and cited in the memoirs of Allied participants, must be treated cautiously. They were made under duress, and some detainees, in an effort to secure more lenient treatment, might simply have claimed that they were following orders from above, especially since they had already been exposed to the governor's inflammatory broadsheets. Discussing this issue, Rostopchin correctly wondered how 'can one really believe that I would have given freedom to criminals and convicts provided that they burned the city, and that these malefactors would then actually execute my orders in my absence and in front of the entire enemy army?'[72] As one Russian historian astutely pointed out, 'Why would people detained at [the Temporary Prison] for debt default and other minor transgressions suddenly turn into the most disreputable criminals, eager to burn, murder and plunder?'[73]

It is difficult to agree with scholars who find it suspicious and sinister that Rostopchin, beset as he was with numerous problems, found time to consider the convicts' fate and order their release. What else was he supposed to do? In the evening of 13 September he finally received a clear indication that the city would not be defended and immediately began a flurry of preparations to evacuate the city. The issue of the convicts was just one of the myriad concerns he faced in the few hours remaining before the enemy's arrival, and the decision to release them seems to have been something of an after-thought; as Zemtsov aptly observed, 'hardly anyone [in the governor's circle] even remembered them until then'.[74] Evacuating convicts would have required additional resources – a military escort, daily allowances for food and transportation[75] – and releasing them was clearly the most convenient way of dealing with a group that did not present any threat to society but could not simply be left incarcerated in the soon-to-be-occupied city.

In the first two weeks after the Allied occupation of Moscow hundreds of Muscovites were shot or hanged in extrajudicial killings all across the city. Allied participants later claimed that all those executed were involved in incendiary activities, but Russian eyewitnesses paint a more sinister picture. 'The French sought scapegoats and kept finding them among the Russians, who were then shot without further investigation or hanged on posts ... Many innocent lives were thus lost,' lamented one Muscovite.[76] This is hardly surprising considering the chaotic nature of those days. There is a Russian proverb, 'Fear has magnifying eyes',[77] and this was particularly true for the Allied soldiers caught in the fiery inferno, where any local was perceived as a suspect. There are numerous accounts by Allied soldiers and officers describing the swift justice brought upon 'convicts', 'incendiaries' and 'criminals', but the liberal use of these terms reveals that the Allied soldiers made no distinction between actual offenders and civilians caught in the wrong place at the wrong time. The ever-curious Anisya Poluyaroslavetseva was among the Russians who witnessed public hangings at one of the city squares:

> There I stood and watched as these villainous [French] dragged our men to the gallows. They claimed these were incendiaries who had been caught. But these were no incendiaries. One of them, for example, was a half-blind old serf from the Korsakov's estate. What was there for him to burn when he already had one foot in the grave? The [French] simply grabbed the first people they encountered and denounced them as incendiaries. As the ropes were placed around their necks, our poor men began to pray and many even cried. But the villains did not even blink – they hanged some, shot others and left their bodies on the ground as a warning. I witnessed everything and was so frightened that I could not move or breathe.[78]

Among the papers of Alexander Bulgakov, who directed the Moscow Post Office, there is a report from late September claiming that the Allied authorities promised monetary compensation to any incendiary who willingly appeared before them. Coveting what seemed to be easy money, eight Muscovite 'drunkards' came to claim the reward but were quickly arrested, charged with incendiary activity and hanged.[79] The Russian officer Perovskii, who had been detained during the armistice negotiations on 14 September, was initially locked up inside a church in the Kremlin complex. In the turmoil of the first few days he was completely forgotten about by the French authorities, only to be accidentally 'rediscovered' by a patrol. Without inquiring into the details, a French captain ordered Perovskii placed with other detainees suspected of incendiary activity, effectively sentencing him to death. Fortunately for Perovskii, his fluency in French saved him and he was able to explain what had happened to him. But hundreds of Muscovites were less fortunate. Anyone suspected of incendiary activity – whatever that might constitute – or merely looking suspicious (for example, having a bushy beard, a common feature among Russian peasants) was treated mercilessly. Such violence was further buttressed by an order of 16 September that provided a legal sanction for the execution of suspects in incendiary activity. Bourgogne remembered that such orders were 'carried out at once and a little open space near the Place du Gouvernement was called by us the Place des Pendus, as here a number of incendiaries were shot and hanged on the trees'.[80] Another officer saw a dozen or so Russians hanged in the square where his unit was deployed, and noted that many more were summarily court-martialled and hanged from the gates of nearby houses.[81] In some cases simply looking like a convict was enough to bring arrest or death. Bourgogne admitted that some Russians were arrested even though 'nothing about their actions showed that they were incendiaries'. Years after the event one participant still remembered how, upon encountering a crowd of suspicious-looking Muscovites, 'our Lieutenant Serraris ... charged into the courtyard of a palace and thrust his sabre between the shoulderblades of one such wretch. The sabre broke and our Russian took a dozen more steps with the best part of a Guardsman's sword stuck in him. The others scattered in order to try to save their lives, but we brought them crashing down with our muskets.'

The hapless Muscovites found themselves caught between two extremes. To survive in the ruins of the city, they had to make fires to cook meals and stay warm at night. Yet such an act could easily see them branded as incendiaries and might cost them their lives. 'We execute anyone we find igniting fires,' wrote an officer of the 1st Tirailleurs of the Imperial Guard. 'They are then left in public squares with inscriptions indicating their crimes ... I cannot give any further details since they are horrible.'[82] Ysarn was stunned by 'a change that had taken place in Moscow' within days of the enemy army's arrival. 'Everywhere the streets and yards were strewn with corpses, mostly of bearded men. Dead horses, cows and dogs littered the streets, mingled with the corpses of hanged men: these were incendiaries who had been shot and then hanged. We walked past all this with inconceivable indifference.'[83]

In late September the French authorities organized well publicized court proceedings against the incendiaries. On 20 September Napoleon announced the arrest of hundreds of incendiaries who 'were armed with fuses 6 inches long, which they had between two pieces of wood. They also had explosives, which they threw upon the roofs of the houses.'[84] A special Military Commission[85] was organized after Napoleon's return from the Petrovskii Palace and it convened on 23–24 September in the house of Prince Dolgorukii.[86] Of the numerous individuals suspected of incendiary activity, the Military Commission tried only twenty-six suspects,[87] whose cases were presented by *Chef-d'escadron* François Weber of the *Gendarmerie d'élite*. The commission heard testimonies from eyewitnesses and examined the evidence, which included 'fuses, rockets, phosphoric pellets,[88] sulphur and other combustible materials found partly on the accused and partly already placed in numerous houses'.[89] The accused were given a chance to address the Military Commission, which conducted its proceedings in both French and Russian.[90] Afterwards, members of the commission deliberated behind closed doors before reaching verdicts on all twenty-six cases. They condemned ten individuals to death, while the remaining sixteen individuals, whose crimes were not 'sufficiently proven', were sent to prison. On 25 September the condemned men were all taken to the Novodevichii Monastery, lined up against the walls and shot by firing squad. Their corpses were then tied to posts under inscriptions reading 'Incendiares de Moscou'.[91]

The Military Commission's protocol, which was published in French and Russian, with a thousand copies distributed throughout the city, went beyond simply determining the guilt or innocence of the twenty-six men. It offered a broader look at the events in Moscow and, together with the imperial bulletins, laid the foundation for the official French version of the Moscow fire. The establishment of this commission was part of Napoleon's attempt to defend himself against charges of culpability for the conflagration. In the words of Caulaincourt, Napoleon had to exculpate both the army and himself 'of the odium of having caused the fire [which] it had in fact done its utmost to put out, and from which self-interest was enough to exonerate'. Napoleon understood that the 'public opinion of the entire world would turn against him once it learned that the entrance of his troops into the abandoned ancient capital of Russia was accompanied by a devastating fire. He understood that responsibility for the fire would be placed, first of all, on his shoulders. Therefore, he thought it of paramount importance to shift the burden to the Russians and the Russian government.'[92] The primary task of the Military Commission was not to deliver justice but rather to provide sufficient foundation for this official contention. The commission's protocol thus dealt in passing with the twenty-six defendants, but was largely focused on proving the charge that the 'Russian government' had made preparations to burn Moscow since the start of the war. The Russian authorities, it concluded, recruited a 'certain Englishman by the name of Smith who claims to be a German', who designed a special machine – 'une machine exterminatrice' – that could carry incendiary material and burn the city. The Military Commission also cited Rostopchin's broadsheets and his orders to remove the firefighting equipment as evidence for a plan to destroy Moscow, and claimed that '800 convicts' were purposely released to 'ignite the city within twenty-four hours after the entry of the French troops'.[93]

Yet many of these claims are false. It was inconceivable that the Russian government could have planned the destruction of the city three months in advance, since no one expected that Napoleon would actually advance so far into Russia. The claim of the flying machine was factual, but Leppich's device was not intended for burning the city and was nowhere near completion by the time Moscow fell. As seen above, Rostopchin's broadsheets should not be taken at face value since their primary purpose was to shape public opinion, and Rostopchin frequently adopted colourful and inflated expressions to appeal to his audience. Yet, to drive its point home, the Military Commission even resorted to forgery by inserting direct references to the burning of Moscow into translated texts of Rostopchin's broadsheets. Finally, it is rather peculiar that the Military Commission declared that hundreds of convicts had been ordered to burn the city, and yet not a single convict was arrested and present at its proceedings. Such flaws in the French court-martial caused many Russian historians to reject its findings. Modest Bogdanovich thus flatly refused to attach 'any importance to the work of the French military commission', in whose findings 'falsehoods became interwoven with truth to such a degree that no clarity was brought to the issue that the commission was tasked with investigating'.[94]

Similarly problematic are claims of police involvement in the burning of the city. Many Allied participants and historians speak of police officials being detained in the process of igniting fires, and accuse them of being incendiaries. Bogdanovich, for example, bluntly states that 'some police officials were left in the capital to ignite fires in various points',[95] but to support this claim he cites only the French Military Commission's protocol, despite the fact that just a few pages later he rejects its veracity outright. Of the twenty-six men tried by the Military Commission nine identified themselves as policemen, but only one was found guilty of incendiary activity and shot.[96] Even if he wanted to utilize the police to burn the city, Rostopchin could hardly involve large numbers of police officials since they had been committed to more pressing tasks. On the eve of Moscow's abandonment, Kutuzov had ordered Rostopchin to dispatch available police officers to guide the army through Moscow to the Ryazan road'.[97] Throughout the evening of 13 September and the next morning the majority of police officials were busy maintaining a fragile order in the city, supervising the evacuation of various state and private property, and guiding columns of troops through the city, which they then left together with the Russian army. A few did stay in the city to serve as the governor's eyes and ears, making clandestine trips to the Russian army's headquarters with information about the enemy's activities in the abandoned capital. Rostopchin later described how he asked police officers to volunteer for this mission. He wanted six 'agents' but only five volunteered, compelling Rostopchin to select the sixth one himself.[98] The report by the acting Chief of Police, K. Gelman, prepared in late October 1812, reveals that, in total, twenty-two police officials had stayed behind in Moscow and were involved in clandestine work procuring information for the Russian authorities; based on available evidence, none of these officers had been arrested by the Allied authorities but some did choose to collaborate with the enemy.[99] In contrast, there were also some policemen who stayed behind due to other circumstances and were captured by the enemy. Moscow's Police Chief Ivashkin noted that 'the order for the police to depart was received at midnight on 14 September. At 5am police squads were instructed to gather at designated spots', but the passage of large numbers of people and the army meant that some police officials became separated and were unable to get to their squads in time. As a result, 'some of the police rank-and-file, unable to get to the designated concentration points and unaware where to go next, were captured by the enemy'.[100] Also among the captured were some members of the fire brigade, who had been sent to various stores to destroy barrels containing alcohol but seem to have enjoyed doing it a little too much. Thus Ivashkin complained that some firefighters were 'senselessly drunk' and had to be left behind.

The People of Moscow

So if neither convicts nor police officials played a decisive role in the start of the fire, who did? To this author, the answer lies in the multitudes of Russian army stragglers and Muscovite poor who had stayed behind. During the previous month Rostopchin had managed to inflame the inhabitants to such a degree that emotions had reached fever pitch by 14 September. At the start of the war his broadsheets and other appeals sought to calm down sentiments in the city by reassuring the residents that the enemy posed no direct threat to them. But as the war progressed, the governor completely reversed direction and sought to incite what he considered to be a patriotic zeal in the populace. This meant embracing increasingly xenophobic rhetoric and inciting people to violence and armed struggle. He carefully cultivated the idea that Moscow was central to Russian culture and must be protected at all costs. 'Glory shall be the reward of those who take part in this struggle! Eternal memory awaits those who fall! And those who evade their duty shall receive retribution on the Day of Judgement!'[101] Such appeals naturally had a profound impact on the Muscovites, especially the lower classes, who gathered in their tens of thousands on the Three Hills on 13 September. Glinka, one of Rostopchin's keen companions, recalled that after writing his appeal to muster the Muscovites at the Three Hills, the governor instructed him to print it as a broadsheet and noted, '[As for ourselves,] we will have nothing to do at the Three Hills but this will teach our peasants what they should do if the enemy takes Moscow.'[102] Consequently, as one Russian contemporary aptly commented, 'Moscow and Rostopchin perfectly understood each other'.[103]

Two principal factors influenced the actions of the Muscovites. One was the strong patriotic sentiment, which Rostopchin did his best to nurture, and which was easily inflamed by the news from the army and the influx of refugees from the western provinces already devastated by war. A number of eyewitnesses testified that many Muscovites chose to destroy their property instead of leaving it to be plundered by the enemy. Elizaveta Yankova, for example, recalled that 'it was later discovered that many houses were set on fire by their owners, many of whom were driven by the sentiment, "Let my entire property perish and my house burn so none falls into the hands of the cursed dogs [the Grande Armée]. Let's destroy whatever I cannot take so it does not belong to the abominable French."'[104] After the city fell, those merchants who had hoped that Moscow would fare no worse than Berlin or Vienna were quickly disillusioned by the widespread looting and burned their stores themselves. General Hermann von Boyen, deployed to the vicinity of Vladimir, recalled meeting a Muscovite merchant who had a small wooden store in the trading stalls near Red Square. The merchant told him that when the Allied troops began to plunder stores, he and his companions 'became seized with the desire for revenge and burned their property with their own hands rather than let it fall into the enemy hands'. Boyen added that many other refugees from Moscow recounted similar experiences.[105] In his *La Vérité*, Rostopchin cited his conversation with the owner of the carriage shop, who decided to burn his store when French officers began to take carriages for themselves.[106] Such acts could easily have contributed to a general conflagration.

But there was also a second, more powerful, factor at play. The absence of authority encouraged many Muscovites to steal, rob and cause mayhem. As early as the beginning of June Rostopchin complained about numerous 'vagabonds who have flooded the city. They beg in the morning, steal in the evening and cause various disorders at night.'[107] He later recounted that two merchants overheard men brawling in the streets, one of whom declared that 'it was time to set fire to some suburbs, ring the tocsin and start robbing. The other man, however, counselled caution and suggested waiting, noting that it was still full moon.' The alarmed merchants managed to seize one of the men and delivered him to the governor, who offered him freedom and money in exchange for full disclosure. The man declared that there were 'twelve of them, all scoundrels', and they intended to ignite fires to cause confusion so they could plunder the richest stores in town.[108] It is probably that such sentiments are reflected in another Muscovite's recollection that 'for many months' prior to September, 'there was a [popular] rumour about the expected and, in a certain turn of military events, even very probable, burning of the city'.[109] It was probably this rumour that prompted Dmitri Volkonskii, one week before the battle of Borodino and two weeks before the enemy approached Moscow, to comment in his letter of 31 August, 'many residents are leaving Moscow fearful that all homes would be burned'.[110] The Moscow police maintained control of public order throughout July and August but as the municipal authorities withdrew on 13–14 September, so the city's riff-raff emerged onto the streets. Bourgogne was probably describing some of them when he noted in his memoirs that on the outskirts of the town 'we met several miserable creatures … they all had horrible faces, and were armed with muskets, staves and pitchforks'.[111]

The chaos that enveloped Moscow in mid-September thus served as a catalyst for mischief perpetrated by the poor, who found themselves, probably for the first time in their lives, free from any supervision by higher authority and took advantage of the moment to seek quick enrichment and settle old scores.[112] In addition, the presence of Russian soldiers hungry for some bounty – 'many of our marauders stayed behind in Moscow', admitted one Russian staff officer[113] – would only have further exacerbated the situation. Maxim Nevzorov, head of the typography service at the University of Moscow, complained about 'certain rascals who exploited these tragic circumstances and confusion among people to perpetrate their mischief'.[114] The Allied participants do acknowledge that 'there was a huge mass of people from the lower classes prepared to act as guides and assist the invaders in the hope of sharing in the spoils'.[115] Rostopchin confided to the Russian Minister of Police S. Vyazmitinov that he was convinced that among 'the 10,000 residents remaining in Moscow, probably 9,000 stayed behind because they intended to rob and plunder'.[116] This is clearly an exaggeration but it still points to his belief in the presence of a large number of people capable of criminal enterprise. Indeed, we have numerous accounts of Muscovites wandering around the city, getting drunk, ransacking taverns and shops, and attacking the houses of the affluent, whom they resented for abandoning the city. For some of them, it was all part of a purposeful assault on the authorities that had long oppressed them. But for merchant's wife Anna Kruglova, 'this was a terrifying time: our own people burned Moscow'.[117] Her sentiment was shared by Peter Chudimov, the archivist of the Mining Department who lamented the sight of government buildings ransacked and 'strewn with hay, potatoes, cabbages and wine barrels, with doors, windows and cabinets broken … The Russian people themselves plundered all of the government offices.'[118] In some cases this popular anger was manifested in the deliberate burning of noble mansions and estates. Some domestic servants might have been tempted to ransack their masters' estates and then set fires to cover up their actions. One of Soimonov's serfs recounted a rumour that 'our own people were burning Moscow to drive Bonaparte out of it. I do not know whether it was true or not but can testify that our house was set on fire [by Russians]. The fire was still far away from us when the house [suddenly] caught fire from inside.'[119] At Prince Kurakin's estate a drunken man dressed in a peasant's smock was caught attempting to set fire to the house; when the estate's steward and four footmen drove him out with blows, the man kept exclaiming, 'Look how well it burns!' The footmen finally gave the man up to the French, who promptly shot him. Upper-class Russians prided themselves on embracing French culture, language and fashion. But amidst the disorder reigning in Moscow, their appearance and manners could easily become a liability, since the peasants looked with suspicion at anyone dressed or behaving in a foreign manner. Thus some Russian nobles felt more 'threatened by Russian peasants than by the French'.[120] A priest recalled that the peasants 'were merciless in pillaging Moscow and proffered all sorts of insults against the [affluent] inhabitants of Moscow, calling them runaways and traitors and declaring resolutely that whatever stayed behind in Moscow now belonged to them'.[121] When the deacon of the Novodevichii Monastery returned to Moscow in October, he found his house still standing but already occupied by others. 'Five or so peasants came suddenly running to him. "Where are you going?" they shouted. "Back home," he answered. "I am the master of this house." "There are no longer any masters here so get lost," one of them screamed in response.' The German physician Nordhof wrote of a crowd of peasants, led by a sabre-wielding priest who declared that it was not a crime to loot the houses of the affluent and foreigners because they were all traitors.[122]

The presence of the Russian soldiers, who took what they wanted by force, further exacerbated the situation. Colonel Toll recalled that during the Russian army's procession through Moscow, General Barclay de Tolly was informed that soldiers were looting the Merchant Court. He immediately dispatched there his aide-de-camp, who soon returned with the news that 'the merchants themselves had invited the soldiers to plunder their stores because they were about to lose their riches and preferred to enrich their compatriots rather than the enemy'. Toll notes that more than six thousand soldiers were drawn in by this 'enticing invitation'.[123] 'Near the Pokrovskii Monastery,' wrote one eyewitness on 13 September, 'we encountered some 5,000 wounded, who were ransacking shops.'[124] Another Muscovite 'saw our soldiers murdering a shopkeeper. Proceeding along Basmannaya street, I saw appalling scenes ... wounded [Russian] soldiers and marauders were plundering everything.'[125] Rostopchin later described the misery of Moscow's residents, caused by 'the wounded sick and [healthy] rank-and-file who were meandering around solely to despoil their own compatriots'.[126]

Would it be far-fetched to suppose that in the chaos and turmoil of the first two days some of these newly minted pillagers accidentally caused fires in the buildings they were ransacking? The repeated references to numerous 'criminals and convicts' in the memoirs of Allied participants can perhaps thus be explained in the context of actions perpetrated by the rabble, who certainly numbered in the hundreds. Seeking personal enrichment or avenging their past wrongs by society, these men were not inspired by any grand patriotic designs, nor did they follow any plans. If Rostopchin's above-mentioned testimony is to be relied on, these criminally minded men (and probably women) would have been keen to cause confusion and mayhem to prevent the enemy authorities from establishing control over the city. The greater the disorder, the easier it was for them to steal and rob. But to a French, German or Polish observer, the actions of so many individuals, seemingly acting in concert in combing the streets, and robbing and burning houses, could easily have been perceived as part of a deliberate plan to destroy the city.

The Grande Armée

No discussion of the Moscow fire would be complete without some inquiry into the role of the Grande Armée. It is indeed remarkable that the majority of existing accounts focus exclusively on Russian culpability and ignore the possibility that the Allied forces might have had anything to do with the fire. To be fair, most accounts do acknowledge the widespread pillaging that the French, Germans, Poles and others committed but it is usually portrayed as a response to the fire. In fact, the soldiers of the Grande Armée began looting the city almost as soon as they had reached it and before the city-wide conflagration became apparent. It is certain that the soldiers, finding the town largely abandoned by its inhabitants, broke into the houses to search for plunder on the night of their arrival. As one prominent contemporary, evidently with considerable expertise in this subject, commented, 'light for this purpose is generally procured by flashing off a firelock, and setting fire to the oil rag with which the musket is commonly kept clean. This oil rag is kept in the hand as long as the latter is not burnt; the rag is then thrown upon the ground or anywhere, and something is found and set fire to, to answer the same purpose. It is thus that a house abandoned by its inhabitants, if plundered by troops, is generally burnt.'[127] Indeed, the immediate reaction of many Allied officers, generals and even Napoleon himself was to discount the initial fires simply as the result of carelessness among the troops.

In the first day and a half of its occupation of Moscow the Grande Armée found itself in a position where many of its soldiers were actively looting, while others, especially the Young Guard around the Kremlin, had to deal with the consequences. But as the fires spread, Allied officers and soldiers encamped outside the city became convinced that the city was being plundered, and believed they should replenish their nearly empty supplies while they could. This sparked a new wave of looting that could have only worsened the situation in the city and doubtless contributed to the outbreak of new fires. There are a number of testimonies that directly acknowledge the Grande Armée's culpability in this respect. On 27 September Philibert Poulachard of the 21st Line told his wife, 'we burned every region we have marched through. On arriving in Moscow, we burned this ancient capital as well.'[128] Pion des Loches did not doubt that 'on the night between the 14th and 15th, as the soldiers, torch in hand, entered into the houses, they may have set them on fire unintentionally'.[129] Similarly, Castellane wrote in his diary on 15 September that 'our soldiers may well have set fires in some places, but not everywhere'.[130] Johannes von Horn witnessed how, almost immediately upon the Grande Armée's arrival in Moscow, bands of looters infiltrated into the city. 'Soldiers bundled together several wax candles, which they found in large quantities in candle stores, and used them to light their way.' As a result, some stores caught on fire and 'French officers later confessed that it was their troops who caused it because of carelessness'. Horn later saw Polish troops setting a bakery on fire because it had no bread left. The Poles then proceeded, with torches in hand, to enter nearby houses, which later caught fire.[131] Soltyk explains that some troops may have been misled by the appearance of wooden houses that were covered with white lime and appeared to be built of stone. Writing on 19 September, Friedrich Wilhelm von Lossberg complained that 'many houses fell to the flames because soldiers used ovens to bake their bread inside them, notwithstanding the strictest prohibitions'.[132]

* * *

In respect of the origin of the fire, it may be regarded as certain that it was not a deliberate action by Napoleon, who had every motive for preserving the city for his own convenience. But nor was it the outcome of long-term Russian planning. The fire had already begun while the Russian army was still withdrawing through the city, and no Russian leader would have deliberately sanctioned such a potentially catastrophic action. Had there been any settled plan of destruction, surely the major buildings and magazines would have been fired first to ignite the city. Arthur Wellesley, Duke of Wellington, was right to marvel that 'in a town abandoned by its inhabitants, doomed by its native governor to be destroyed by fire, surely the object to which [the Russians] would first have turned [their] attention, that in which [they] would most willingly have tried [their] infernal machines, would have been the magazines of arms, cannon, etc. and above all the powder magazine'.[133]

The conflagration itself seems to have been caused by a combination of factors. The general evacuation of Moscow was an unprecedented move on the part of the Russian authorities, since no major European city – not Milan, Venice, Vienna, Rome, Berlin nor Madrid – had been completely evacuated in the face of the arrival of the French army. The French had never had to deal with such a situation and this may explain their underestimation of the challenges they faced. Rostopchin did play an important role in the conflagration and, although he did not 'personally execute or order it, [the fire] was still desired and facilitated by him'.[134] That he left men to destroy supplies and ammunition is undeniable – but so did the Russian generals, including Field Marshal Kutuzov himself, and thus they too should be held responsible for the fire that their actions might have caused. Rostopchin's broadsheets had a powerful impact on the popular psyche, encouraging people to destroy their property rather than see it despoiled by the enemy. His orders to remove the police and fire brigades effectively left the city vulnerable to the fire hazard that is inherent in any city built of wood – a fact Rostopchin was well aware of. Removal of the municipal authority also encouraged the disreputable elements in the Muscovite population, who had stayed behind during the evacuation and were willing to take their chance of making a profit out of the fall of the city. And we cannot discount the actions of those patriotic citizens of Moscow who, whether under the influence of Rostopchin's broadsheets or through their own convictions, chose to set their property on fire. Plundering on the part of the invaders commenced almost immediately after their entry into Moscow; with the soldiers, and a supporting cast of camp-followers, beggars, criminals and prostitutes, all looting indiscriminately, there was every opportunity for fire to break out. And once it had started, the spell of dry weather, plus the strong winds, which were further strengthened as the conflagration intensified, helped to spread the flames, which found plenty of fuel in the thousands of wooden buildings.

On a final note, it is interesting to look at another incident from this period – the Great Fire of New York of 1776 – as it bears close resemblance to events in Moscow. After early setbacks at Lexington and Concord during the American Revolutionary War, the British managed to capture New York in mid-September 1776, when General William Howe's troops landed on Manhattan. The British were still celebrating their victory when, on 21 September 1776, fire erupted in the city. Some eyewitnesses claimed that it began in the Fighting Cocks Tavern near Whitehall Slip, and, abetted by dry weather and strong winds, it then spread rapidly north and west as the few fire engines available proved useless and there were too few buckets and not enough water at hand. Dozens of houses were torn down in advance of the flames that ultimately consumed as much as a quarter of the city before being contained both by changes in the wind and by the actions of citizens and British marines sent to help them.[135] As in Moscow, each side accused the other of deliberately starting the fire. General Howe's report claimed that the fire was deliberately set in 'a most horrid attempt ... by a number of wretches'.[136] The British Royal Governor William Tryon suspected that General George Washington was responsible for it, asserting 'many circumstances lead to conjecture that Mr Washington was privy to this villainous act'. Washington was accused of sending 'all the bells of the churches out of town, under pretence of casting them into cannon, whereas it is much more probable to prevent the alarm being given by ringing of the Bells before the fire should get ahead beyond the reach of Engines and Buckets'. In addition, 'some officers of his army were found concealed in the city'.[137] Even some colonists believed that the fire was the work of Patriot arsonists. John Joseph Henry recorded accounts of marines returning to HMS *Pearl* after fighting the fire, in which men were 'caught in the act of firing the houses'. On the other hand, many American colonists held the British responsible for setting the fire so that the city might be plundered. One Hessian officer noted that some who fought the blaze managed to 'pay themselves well by plundering other houses nearby that were not on fire'. George Washington denied any knowledge of the fire's cause and claimed that 'Providence – or some good honest Fellow – has done more for us than we were disposed to do for ourselves'.[138] It was never determined, then or later, that the fire was anything other than accidental. But unlike New York, the Moscow fire was the result of both Providence and some fellows, though few of them could be described as 'good and honest'.

Chapter 9

In Search of Peace

Napoleon spent thirty-five days in Moscow and, as one Russian historian aptly commented, his sojourn here represented 'the complete opposite to his stay at Dresden [in May 1812], where he felt at the height of his powers, the conqueror of Europe, surrounded by servile rulers and high court officials'.[1] There he was at the centre of a carefully choreographed display of power. One eyewitness observed that anyone who wished to give themselves a true idea of the commanding power that Napoleon exercised in Europe 'should transport themselves in imagination to Dresden so as to behold him at the period of his greatest glory ... His levée was, as usual, at nine o'clock, and only by being there could one possibly imagine the cringing submission with which a crowd of princes, confounded with the courtiers, who for the most part paid them but the slightest heed, awaited the moment of his appearance ... In effect, Napoleon was the God of Dresden, the ruler of all those rulers who appeared before him, the king of kings ... It was, without doubt, the highest point of his glory.'[2] Now, just four months later, this 'ruler of rulers' found himself stuck amidst the ruins of Moscow, presiding over an increasingly chaotic force and anxiously trying to find a way to end the war and get out of Russia. 'It is impossible to explain Napoleon's pertinacity in prolonging the stay of the army in the centre of Russia, amidst the smoking ruins of the ancient capital, except by supposing that he was nearly certain of the speedy conclusion of peace,' recalled a French general.[3] Simply abandoning Moscow and retreating was not an option since, in Napoleon's opinion, this would be tantamount to acknowledging defeat. Yet staying in the burnt-out city offered only bleak prospects for ending the war. Signing a peace treaty, on the other hand, offered a way out of this complicated situation. Napoleon was convinced that, in the wake of the battle of Borodino and the burning of Moscow, Emperor Alexander would not hesitate to accept if he received a letter offering peace.

On his return to Moscow, Napoleon persuaded Ivan Tutolmin, the director of the Foundlings House, to carry a letter to Alexander. Tutolmin had first encountered the French authorities in Moscow on 14 September when, amidst the spreading disorder, he personally went to the Kremlin and asked General Durosnel to provide protection for the orphans at the Foundlings Home. Durosnel immediately ordered a safeguarding picket of twelve gendarmes and an officer to be posted at the Home.[4] When the fires broke out, Tutolmin and the gendarmes, assisted by the Foundlings Home's remaining officials and even some of the children, fought to protect the building from the flames throughout the night of 15 September and the subsequent days. Upon returning from the Petrovskii Palace on 18 September, Napoleon passed by the Foundlings Home; seeing the massive building towering over the nearby ruins, he inquired about it. Informed about the institution, he dispatched *Intendant-Général* Mathieu Dumas[5] to see what had become of all those unfortunate children. It was early afternoon when Dumas knocked on the doors of the Foundlings Home and was greeted by its director Ivan Tutolmin; the two men had already met three days earlier when Dumas inspected the 'magazines which line the quay between the Kremlin and the Foundlings Home' and had 'ovens set up to bake biscuits'.[6] Dumas declared that he was sent to convey Napoleon's gratitude for Tutolmin's efforts in saving his institution from the flames, and his desire to meet him in person.

The following day, at noon, Napoleon sent his interpreter Lelorgne to bring the Russian to the palace.[7] Tutolmin found the emperor a thoughtful and considerate person, and thanked him 'on behalf of all the unfortunates who had been saved at the Foundlings Home'.[8] Napoleon responded that he had desired to do the same for the entire city, which he had 'intended on treating in the same way as I did Vienna and Berlin that are still standing unharmed', and lamented that the Russians had chosen to abandon and 'burn their capital and, in trying to cause me harm, they in fact destroyed what has been created over centuries'. He complained that 'I have never adopted this method of warfare; my troops can fight, but not burn. All the way from Smolensk I have seen nothing but ashes.' Napoleon then quizzed Tutolmin about the Russian arrangements on the eve of the Grande Armée's entry into Moscow and repeated his accusations that Rostopchin had intentionally set fire to the city. 'Maybe the Russians initially set fire to it and the French then contributed to it,' Tutolmin countered. 'That's untrue,' replied Napoleon. He then inquired about the children housed at the Foundlings Home and, after reviewing a roster,[9] teasingly told Tutolmin, 'I see that you have evacuated all the young women.' After further quizzing Tutolmin, Napoleon ended their meeting and advised the Russian to write a letter to Emperor Alexander describing what had transpired in the city.[10] Although it was casually mentioned, this was in fact Napoleon's first attempt to open direct communications with the Russian sovereign and he certainly hoped that it would lead eventually to peace. He did not want to make an open appeal for peace and thus sought a more indirect approach.

As promised, Tutolmin wrote a short letter in the evening of 19 September, describing his meeting with Napoleon and mentioning his request to contact the Russian sovereign.[11] The following day he instructed College Secretary Phillip Rukhin to carry the letter to St Petersburg for him; he was to go first to Marshal Murat's chancellery, where he would receive a passport and the necessary paperwork.[12] Rukhin was guided by French dragoons as far as the village of Chernaya Gryaz', where he was detained by a Cossack outpost from Count Wintzingerode's flying detachment. Despite his explanations, the unfortunate Rukhin was accused of being a French spy and was arrested; happily for his mission, he was then dispatched under escort to the Russian capital, where he was finally able to explain his mission and deliver Tutolmin's letter to Emperor Alexander.[13]

Just hours after meeting Tutolmin, Napoleon made a second attempt to establish communications with the Russian sovereign. This time it was through Ivan Yakovlev, a retired Guard captain and former dashing courtier during the reign of Empress Catherine II.[14] Yakovlev had failed to convince some of his family of the need to leave Moscow before Napoleon's army arrived,[15] and it was only on 14 September that they finally departed. But it was too late and Yakovlev's family was caught by French troops who robbed it clean, taking away even their clothing and shoes.[16] Thus, Yakovlev, who had rubbed shoulders with members of the imperial family, was reduced to begging as he roamed the streets of Moscow in search of provisions. It was during one such outing that he accidentally encountered a colonel who served in the headquarters of the Young Guard. Yakovlev asked him for help in getting his family out of the city but was advised to appeal to Marshal Morthier. Yakovlev actually knew Mortier from his earlier visit to Paris and pleaded with him for a *laissez-passer* to leave the city. Mortier agreed to help and sought permission from Napoleon, who quickly realized that here was another opportunity to contact the Russian court. Napoleon was already aware of the Yakovlev family since Ivan's brother, Lev Yakovlev, had served as a Russian plenipotentiary envoy to Cassel (Westphalia). On 21 September he sent Lelorgne to bring Yakovlev to the palace.

Unlike Tutolmin, who was received in the emperor's study, Napoleon greeted Yakovlev in the throne hall at the Kremlin palace. After the usual pleasantries, Napoleon subjected Yakovev to a tirade of self-justification and complaints. He accused the Russians of acting like barbarians in despoiling their own country and deplored the conflagration that had claimed the larger part of Moscow. 'We, of course, are not responsible for this since I have occupied almost all the capitals of Europe but not a single one of them has been burned.'[17] There had never been any reason for war between Russia and France, he claimed, and if there had been one, the war should have been fought in Lithuania, not in the heartland of Russia. 'I have no reason to be in Russia,' Napoleon stated. 'I do not want anything from her, as long as the Treaty of Tilsit is respected. I want to leave here, as my only quarrel is with England. Ah, if only I could take London! I would not leave that. Yes, I wish to go home. If the emperor Alexander wants peace, he only has to let me know.'[18] Yet Napoleon's tone kept veering from the cajoling to the bullying.[19] 'If Alexander wants to continue the war, I will keep on fighting as well. My soldiers impatiently demand to march on St Petersburg. So if the war continues, we will indeed march northwards and St Petersburg will share Moscow's fate!'[20] After a few more complaints and reproaches, Napoleon, adopting a much gentler tone, asked if Yakovlev would agree to deliver a message to Emperor Alexander. Yakovlev initially declined, explaining that he had 'neither the right nor the appropriate status' to be introduced to the Russian sovereign and so could not guarantee the success of such an undertaking. But Napoleon persisted in his demands until Yakovlev agreed.

Later that night Napoleon dictated his letter to Alexander. He began by informing the tsar that 'the beautiful and superb city of Moscow no longer exists. Rostopchin had it burnt.' Napoleon described this conduct as 'atrocious and pointless', a genuine act of barbarism. 'Is it intended to deprive me of a few supplies? But these supplies were in the cellars that the fire could not reach. Besides, why destroy one of the most beautiful cities in the world – the work of centuries – to achieve such a feeble end?' He reminded Alexander that no other European capital or city had suffered such a fate. 'Humanity, the interests of Your Majesty and this great city required that it be put into my hands on trust, since the Russian army left it exposed. Administrators, magistrates and civil guards should have been left there. That was what was done at Vienna, twice at Berlin and at Madrid. That was how we ourselves acted in Milan at the time of [Alexander] Suvorov's entry [in 1799].' He expressed his conviction that Rostopchin had acted on his own, in contravention to Alexander's wishes or orders. In conclusion, Napoleon assured Alexander: 'I have waged war on Your Majesty without animosity: a letter from you before or after the last battle would have halted my advance and I would have liked to be in a position to sacrifice the advantage of entering Moscow in return for it. If Your Majesty still retains some remnant of your former feelings for me, you will take this letter in good part. In any case, you cannot but be grateful for my having informed you about what is happening in Moscow.'[21] In the morning of 20 September[22] Lelorgne delivered this letter to Yakovlev, who used his *laissez-passer*[23] to lead many other people out of the city. By evening he was already at Chernaya Gryaz', where, like Rukhin before him, he encountered the Cossacks. Unlike his predecessor, who was a minor official, Yakovlev was treated well by Wintzingerode, who immediately made arrangements to transport him to St Petersburg.[24]

Napoleon's conversations with Tutolmin and Yakovlev and his letters to Emperor Alexander reveal that he had profoundly misunderstood both his circumstances and the Russian attitudes towards war. He dismissed the burning of Moscow as the irrational, barbaric act of a lunatic governor but failed to comprehend that Russian society perceived it in a different light. For the Russians, the destruction of Moscow was the work of French 'monsters', who could no longer be shown any quarter. The city's smouldering ruins served as a powerful symbol that united Russian society and turned the war into a popular conflict that sought, in the words of one contemporary, to have Napoleon 'drowned in the tears he has caused to be shed'.[25] Negotiating peace with the French 'barbarians' had effectively become impossible. Meanwhile, Napoleon clung to Moscow as his trump card, waiting for his foe to deal. He hinted that he was willing to embark on a long war and spoke of new Polish levies and reinforcements. Yet, the reality was that the army could not remain a fighting force for much longer. Although the army had some supplies, many essentials were lacking and, most importantly, there was only a limited supply of fodder for the horses, whose well-being was crucial to the French war effort. The Russian army, on the other hand, continued mobilizing reinforcements and its flying detachments, together with peasant partisans, had already begun to threaten the Grande Armée's lines of communication. On 24 September Napoleon informed General Raymond-Gaspard de Bonardi de Saint Sulpice, commanding the Guard dragoons, that he attached 'great importance' to ensuring that the routes to Mozhaisk remained open and urged him to dispatch strong patrols to guard against any Russian threat to French communications.[26]

The situation in the rear was not encouraging. While Polish troops remained steadfast in their support of Napoleon, contingents from other parts of Europe were less inclined to do so. General van Hogendorp, the Governor General of Lithuania, complained that 'the Bavarian soldiers left the colours in their hundreds and came to Vilna, pretending to be ill, in order to get into the hospitals'.[27] The Austrians continued to drag their feet in the southwest, while the Prussians stalled in the north.[28] Worst of all, the condition of the troops along the Grande Armée's lines of communication left much to be desired. As early as August Jean Rapp was appalled to see unmotivated and exhausted troops slowly trudging along the roads.[29] A month later Prince Wilhelm of Baden lamented that 'from the moment of our leaving Vilna, in every village, in every farm, we found isolated soldiers who were abandoning the army under various pretexts'.[30] Writing to the emperor in late September, Lieutenant J. de Merville complained that his convoy of over 100 transports found it difficult to keep its military escort. 'After three days all our escorts disappeared, with men dispersing on both sides of the road. I demanded and received a new escort, which stayed with me for a longer time but soldiers disappeared with each passing day despite the best efforts of their officers.'[31] The countryside was awash with thousands of stragglers and deserters, who ransacked nearby villages and alienated the peasantry, and thereby contributed to the intensifying 'little war'. Napoleon might well have known, as Rapp asserts, 'to the last man how many men he had stationed between the Rhine and Moscow', and he might have believed that he was still in a position to dictate to the Russians. But the reality was dramatically different. His forces were slowly disintegrating and with each passing week it was becoming a more difficult task to turn the war in his favour.

And yet Napoleon persevered in Moscow, still believing that the Russian leaders 'do not know the effect that the fall of the capital will have on them'.[32] He expected Alexander to cave in and was willing to make the first move to nudge the Russian sovereign towards peace. 'Like everyone else, the emperor realized that his repeated messages would, by showing up the difficulty of his position, only confirm the enemy in his hostile dispositions,' Caulaincourt pondered. 'Yet he kept sending him new ones! For a man who was so politic, such a good calculator, this reveals an extraordinary blind faith in his own star, and one might almost say in the blindness or the weakness of his adversaries! How, with his eagle's eye and his superior judgement could he delude himself to such a degree?'[33] Maybe he still entertained thoughts of the grand campaign that he had confided to his trusted aide-de-camp a month before the war began. 'Imagine Moscow taken, Russia overthrown, [and] the tsar reconciled or murdered by a palace plot ... and tell me that it is impossible for a large army of Frenchmen and auxiliaries starting from Tiflis to reach the Ganges, where the mere touch of a French sword would be sufficient to bring down the framework of [Britain's] mercantile grandeur throughout India.'[34] Indeed, there were even rumours that he took the insignia of imperial dignity – robe, sceptre and crown – with him on the journey to Russia, in order that after he had dictated peace he might be proclaimed in the Kremlin 'the emperor of the West, Supreme Head of the European Confederation, Defender of the Christian Religion'. There was just too much at stake for Napoleon to admit defeat, turn round and leave Moscow. He seems to have forgotten his own earlier premonition: 'How can you believe that the same people who had burned Moscow today would accept peace just a few days later? If those responsible for this decision [to burn Moscow] continue to wield power in Alexander's cabinet, all expectations that you are flattering yourself with are in vain.'

Like many of his contemporaries, Napoleon also misread Alexander's character. The British historian Dominic Lieven has justly pointed out that 'most European statesmen and much of the Russian elite shared some of the doubts on Alexander's strength of will'.[35] Napoleon believed that Alexander would not hesitate to make peace if he had but received a letter offering it. He 'nourished his hopes [for peace] with the recollections of Tilsit and Erfurt',[36] and hoped that the Francophiles in the Russian court would push Alexander in that direction. Napoleon thus failed both to understand Alexander's character and to perceive how profoundly his relationship with Alexander, as well as the sentiments of Russian society, had changed since 1807. The Russian emperor was well aware of the widespread displeasure prevailing in Russia over the Franco-Russian peace. 'The spirit of patriotism burst out forcefully without any particular efforts on the part of the government,' remarked one contemporary. 'Hatred of the French and foreigners spread vehemently among the Russians and left deep seeds inside the hearts of contemporaries; many of those, who have survived to the present day, still feel loathing towards foreigners and especially the French ... Everyone wanted to avenge Austerlitz, Friedland and other setbacks from previous wars that had humiliated us so much.'[37] Prince Sergei Volkonskii remembered how on the eve of the war 'the peace of Tilsit [and] the meekness of Emperor Alexander to the policies of Napoleon left deep wounds in the heart of every Russian. Vengeance – and vengeance once more – was the unshakeable feeling with which all hearts were burning.'[38] Such sentiments only further intensified in the wake of the continued withdrawal by the Russian armies and the loss of Russian provinces. Just days after the fall of Moscow, the Grand Duchess Catherine confronted her august brother:

> The taking of Moscow has put the finishing touches to people's exasperation. Discontent is at its highest and your person is far from being spared. If such news reaches me, you can imagine the rest. You are openly accused of having brought disaster upon your empire, of having caused general ruin and the ruin of private individuals, lastly, of having lost the honour of the country and your own personal honour. I leave it to you to judge the state of affairs in a country whose leader is despised.[39]

Even if he had wanted to, against this backdrop Alexander could not afford to come to terms with the man who had invaded and despoiled his realm. Public opinion was against it and any sign of weakness on Alexander's part might have led to tragic consequences. A second Tilsit would have sealed the condemnation of his reign and Alexander knew only too well what happened to unpopular monarchs in Russia: the preceding eighty years had witnessed a number of palace *coup*s and murders of reigning sovereigns, including Alexander's own father.

Alexander consistently demonstrated his refusal to compromise with Napoleon. During their final audience, he warned Caulaincourt that in case of war he was ready to retreat as far as Kamchatka in Siberia's frigid borderland before he would give up any provinces or sign any treaties. Napoleon brushed this statement off as mere posturing but Alexander meant every word of it. Now, in late September, the Tsar remained resolute in his determination to resist the invader. 'Once war begins,' he had said to Caulaincourt, 'one of us – either he, Napoleon, or I, Alexander – must lose his crown.' In mid-September the Grand Duchess urged Alexander to remain steadfast in his struggle: 'Do not abandon your resolution: no peace and you still have the hope of recovering your honour … My dear friend, no peace, even if you were at Kazan, no peace!' Responding to his sister's appeals, he assured her that 'my resolve to struggle is more unshakeable than ever. I should rather cease to be what I am than compromise with the monster who is the curse of the world.'[40] On 20 September Colonel Michaud, one of his aides-de-camp, visited him in the Winter Palace at St Petersburg to deliver a verbal report of the abandonment of Moscow and the fire. Alexander was visibly shaken but once again he reassured Michaud that under no conditions would he make peace with Napoleon. He instructed the colonel to transmit a special statement to the army:

> Tell all my good subjects, wherever you go, that when I have not one soldier left, placing myself at the head of my dear nobles, of my good peasants, I shall use up the last resources of my empire. But if ever it is written in the decrees of Divine Providence that my dynasty is to cease to reign on the throne of my ancestors, after having exhausted all the means at my disposal, I shall let my beard grow down to here and go and eat potatoes with the least of my peasants in the furthest confines of Siberia, rather than sign away my beloved country, whose sacrifices I fully appreciate. Colonel Michaud, do not forget what I say to you here: Napoleon or I, he or I; now we can no longer reign together. I have learned to know him, he will not deceive me again.[41]

This speech, even if Michaud embellished it as he recounted it years later, reveals that Alexander was profoundly affected by the events in Moscow. He later confided to Baroness von Krüdener that 'the burning of Moscow has illuminated my soul!' The great fire did not weaken his resolve; on the contrary, it made him more determined to pursue the war to the end. Admittedly, there were few, if any, viable alternatives. He was well aware of the disgruntlement in Russian society over the Treaty of Tilsit, and knew that another compromise with Napoleon could lead to dire consequences. The annual commemoration of his imperial coronation on 27 September only further underscored how gloomy the public mood was. Countess Edling, lady-in-waiting to Empress Elisabeth, described how, on its way to the Holy Mother of Kazan Cathedral, the emperor's glassed-in carriage slowly travelled through 'a huge crowd, whose ominous silence and irritated faces contrasted with the festival that was being celebrated. Never in my life will I forget the instant when we walked up the steps of the cathedral, between two hedgerows of people who did not utter a sound of acclamation. One could have distinguished the sound of our footsteps, and I have never doubted that a spark at this moment could have set off a general conflagration. A glance at the emperor told me what was going on in his soul, and I felt my own knees sagging beneath me.'[42]

Alexander had to fight on. It was becoming perfectly clear to him that Napoleon had overplayed his hand and feared the prospect of wintering in Moscow's ruins, where the climate, the lack of resources and the relaxation of discipline might succeed where the Russian armies had failed. As one modern scholar aptly put it, Alexander understood that 'Napoleon could stay in Moscow all he liked, but Russia still had more armies, more beasts of burden to haul the ordnance through the inhospitable terrain, more carts on which to load the stores, and indeed a ready store of arms in the arms factory to the south of Moscow'.[43] On 29 September Alexander acted to calm public opinion and shore up support from any allies who might question the Russian determination to continue the war now that their great city had fallen. He had Kutuzov's lengthy report of 16 September published in the official *Sankt-Peterburgskie vedomosti*, along with a proclamation informing Russian society that Moscow had been abandoned. 'But the great Russian people should not feel dejected,' the emperor appealed to his subjects. 'To the contrary, let us swear to be guided by a new spirit of valour and determination and hope that by fighting for a just cause we shall hurl back on the enemy all the misfortunes he wants to heap on us.' Alexander spoke of the resilience of the Russian nation and the valour of Russian troops, while also describing the difficult conditions the enemy experienced in Moscow. He beseeched the Almighty to 'preserve the courage and constancy of the [Russian] people! May it triumph over its and Thy adversary! May it be in Thy hands the instrument of his destruction and, by delivering itself, redeem the liberty and independence of nations and kings!'[44]

This proclamation was the response to Napoleon's peace overtures. It made it abundantly clear that Alexander not only refused to negotiate peace terms but would from now on fight to reclaim Russian soil and 'redeem the liberty and independence' of the rest of Europe. Napoleon failed to grasp this and waited for an answer that never came. 'At the Kremlin,' recalled Constant, 'the days were long and tedious.' Napoleon rode almost daily through the city,[45] mounted on one of his Arab stallions and accompanied by a few generals and aides-de-camp. He rarely spoke to anybody in the street. Among other things his spirits were depressed by the flocks of crows and jackdaws that appeared in the city. 'Mon Dieu!' he cried. 'Do they mean to follow us everywhere?' It was at this period that his valets noticed that Napoleon usually had on his night table Voltaire's history of Charles XII's disastrous campaign in Russia in 1709.[46] The Emperor probably endured some very painful reflections every time he turned the pages of that book.

Lauriston's Mission

By early October, two weeks after Yakovlev had taken Napoleon's letter, it was becoming plain that Alexander would not condescend even to reply. Napoleon was naturally disappointed. On 3 October, 'after a night of restlessness and anger', he summoned his marshals. As soon as they appeared, he had Eugène read out his new plan.[47] Over the next few minutes the marshals listened as the proposals that Napoleon had first elaborated at the Petrovskii Palace surfaced once more. Napoleon envisioned burning the remains of Moscow, marching via Tver to St Petersburg, where he would be joined by Macdonald. Murat and Davout would form the rear-guard. 'The Emperor, all animation, fixed his sparkling eyes on his generals, whose frigid and silent countenances expressed nothing but astonishment. Then, exalting himself in order to rouse them, "What!" said he. "Are you not inspired by this idea? Was there ever so great a military achievement? Henceforth this conquest is the only one that is worthy of us! With what glory we shall be covered, and what will the whole world say, when it learns that in three months we have conquered the two great capitals of the North!"'[48] But the marshals thought otherwise. Davout and Daru tried to dampen Napoleon's enthusiasm by pointing out the lateness of the season, the scarcity of provisions, the bare and exposed nature of the road from Tver to St Petersburg. Why, they urged, go north, when winter was already at their very doors? And what about the thousands of wounded and sick in Moscow? Most importantly, what about the Russian army? It would certainly pursue them and the Grande Armée would then have to fight on two fronts. The time, they added, had come to end the campaign, not to prolong it. The question was not that of securing another superfluous victory, but of getting as quickly as possible into winter quarters. The marshals clearly saw not just the dangers of advancing in to the north through the fast-approaching winter, but also the precarious condition of the army. Irate at their lack of enthusiasm, Napoleon did not ask any further questions and ended the meeting abruptly.

The marshals' obstinacy prompted Napoleon to pursue peace once more: Emperor Alexander must be persuaded to take the hand which Napoleon had proffered so late in the game. It is possible, as Popov argues, that Napoleon believed Alexander's silence was the result of Yakovlev's failure to deliver the letter – it was not impossible that Yakovlev, who had been very reluctant to undertake this mission, simply accepted it to get his family out of the city and never intended to deliver the letter to the addressee.[49] Therefore Napoleon decided to make a third attempt to contact Alexander, and this time he chose a trusted man to accomplish the mission. Napoleon initially considered sending one of his most capable diplomats, Caulaincourt, who had served as the French ambassador to Russia and established good relations with Emperor Alexander. Well informed and honest, Caulaincourt was a vigorous and outspoken critic of the war against Russia, and on at least one occasion Napoleon had accused him of Russian partisanship; in fact, for the past few weeks he had kept him at arm's length. On 3 October Napoleon summoned Caulaincourt to discuss his decision to send him to negotiate peace with Russia. Caulaincourt, however, could not see the point in this and smartly observed that 'the man does not burn his capital to sign a peace treaty on its ashes'.[50] This was not what the emperor wanted to hear and he tried a change of tactics. Ségur tells us that Napoleon suddenly informed Caulaincourt that he planned to attack St Petersburg, knowing full well that 'the destruction of that city would no doubt give pain to his grand-equerry'. With its capital sacked, Russia would then turn against the emperor Alexander, Napoleon argued. There would be a conspiracy against that monarch and he would be assassinated, which would be 'a most unfortunate circumstance for us'. Alexander's character, Napoleon added, was suitable to French interests and 'no prince could replace him with such advantage to us'. He thought therefore of sending Caulaincourt to him, to prevent such a catastrophe. 'Will you go to St Petersburg? You will see Emperor Alexander. I shall entrust you with a letter and you will make a peace.' But Caulaincourt was unfazed and assured Napoleon that no one would receive him in St Petersburg. Napoleon countered that 'Alexander will be all the more eager to seize this opportunity because his nobility, ruined by this war and the fire, desires peace.' But Caulaincourt reminded him of Alexander's earlier pledge not to listen to any proposals as long as a single French soldier remained in Russia. He warned that making a peaceful overture might actually be detrimental to the Allies, inasmuch as it would demonstrate Napoleon's need for peace, and betray all the difficulties of his current situation. Thinking that he detected a personal motive behind Caulaincourt's refusal to go to St Petersburg, where he had been popular and welcomed just a year and half ago, Napoleon suggested a compromise: he could travel instead to the headquarters of Field Marshal Kutuzov. But Caulaincourt refused again; he saw no point in meeting the Russian commander-in-chief, who would be unable to make any decisions without imperial consent. Irritated by Caulaincourt's remarks, the emperor abruptly ended the conversation. 'Very well, then, I will send Lauriston. He shall have the honour of having made peace and saving the crown of your friend Alexander.'[51]

General Jacques Alexandre Bernard Law, Marquis de Lauriston, aged 44, was descended from a Scottish family that had settled in France in the early eighteenth century. After a successful career in the army during the Revolutionary Wars, he became aide-de-camp to Napoleon, whom he first encountered as a student at the famed École Militaire in Paris before the revolution. In 1805–1811 he earned a reputation as a capable officer and diplomat and in February 1811 was rewarded with the position of French ambassador to Russia, where he served until the start of the war. Now, in early October 1812, the emperor resolved to send him to Kutuzov's headquarters, and this choice only underscored the 'sense of importance' that he attached to the mission.[52] Lauriston was probably pleased to supplant Caulaincourt, whom he loathed, but he shared the grand equerry's assessment. He ventured to argue that at this season of the year it was time not to be negotiating from Moscow, but to be retiring to Kaluga. Napoleon answered that he liked 'simple plans, and the least tortuous roads', but he would not leave Moscow until peace had been concluded. He then showed Lauriston, as he had showed Caulaincourt, his letter to Alexander, then bade him approach Kutuzov and request a pass to St Petersburg. The desperation of Napoleon's position was expressed in his last words to Lauriston: 'I want peace, I must have peace, I absolutely will have peace. Save my honour by any means you can!'[53]

At dawn on 4 October Berthier informed Murat that 'the emperor has decided to send one of his aides-de-camp to Commander-in-Chief Kutuzov' and instructed him to contact the enemy advanced guard commander to convey the emperor's message: 'His Majesty wishes to know the day and hour when and where Kutuzov can meet [Lauriston].'[54] It was already evening when Lauriston reached Murat's headquarters, but the following morning Murat, Lauriston and a number of senior officers rode up to the Russian lines and made contact with the Russian outposts, which conveyed their message back to their headquarters. Kutuzov received the news around 10am[55] while he was conferring with Emperor Alexander's trusted aide-de-camp Prince Peter Volkonskii, who had recently arrived to ascertain the situation at the Russian army's camp at Tarutino. Kutuzov was naturally intrigued by the French overture, especially because it was entrusted to a former ambassador to Russia. He instructed Volkonskii to meet Lauriston and drag out the negotiations to gain time. Reaching the Russian outposts, Lauriston was greeted by Prince Volkonskii, who inquired into the purpose of his mission and offered to deliver any letters to the Russian headquarters. But Lauriston, offended at being fobbed off, refused to confer with Volkonskii, declaring that he would speak only with Kutuzov himself. Volkonskii responded by saying that the Russian commander-in-chief might be willing to meet Lauriston that same night at a station several miles from the Russian outposts, but he needed to confirm this. He ordered his aide-de-camp to return to headquarters for further instructions, but then added a few words in Russian, telling him to gallop off for the first hundred yards or so, until he was out of sight, and then to slow down to a walk.[56]

The news of the French request for a truce and Kutuzov's willingness to consider it had provoked strong opposition from the Russian generals and more than a dozen of them – including the British Commissioner Robert Wilson – anxiously gathered at the headquarters.[57] They erroneously believed that Kutuzov had agreed to discuss the terms of a peace convention that would allow the Grande Armée to leave Russia unmolested. Considering such an act tantamount to treason, they were resolved to take drastic measures, including 'not allowing Kutuzov to return and resume the command once he quitted it for this midnight interview in the enemy's camp'.[58] Robert Wilson, who enjoyed Emperor Alexander's confidence, agreed to voice these concerns to Kutuzov himself. It was late in morning of 5 October when Wilson entered Kutuzov's room. They spoke at length and the conversation frequently became heated. Kutuzov defended his decision to meet the French envoy, while Wilson reminded him of Emperor Alexander's refusal to conduct any negotiations while an armed Frenchman was in the country. Wilson argued that Kutuzov's intention of 'meeting an enemy's general and envoy beyond his own advanced posts at midnight was unheard of in the annals of war, except when illicit communications had been intended, so illicit as not to admit of a third person being employed'. He charged that the 'army would believe, and would be authorized to believe, that [Kutuzov] on quitting the Russian lines was about to make a treaty, or enter into some transaction with the enemy, in defiance and contravention of their Emperor's promises and orders; that the interests of Russia and the honour of the imperial army would be compromised by any treaty, however speciously framed; and that the destruction or capitulation of the enemy was the only "point de mire" which should be entertained by the Marshal'.[59] One can only imagine Kutuzov's reaction upon hearing this brash British meddler's threat that 'under such circumstances the Russian generals and army might and would feel themselves under the terrible necessity of withdrawing his authority until the emperor's decision could be known'.

Kutuzov knew that although he was popular with the rank and file, he had many critics (and enemies) in the officer corps. Bennigsen openly tried to have him removed so he could replace him at the helm of the armies. Prince Bagration (who passed away on 24 September) described Kutuzov as 'a fine piece of work' and similar criticism was voiced by other officers: General Nikolay Rayevskii considered Kutuzov a 'mediocrity', Miloradovich derisively called him 'a petite courtier' and Dokhturov regarded him as a 'coward'. Upon his appointment to lead the Russian armies in August, Kutuzov had promised to end the retreating that had made Barclay de Tolly so unpopular. Yet in the wake of Borodino and the abandonment of Moscow, Kutuzov's reputation was dented. 'There was a general suspicion', wrote Wilson, 'that Kutuzov did not wish to push the enemy to extremity and a corresponding vigilance was exercised over his transactions.'[60] Kutuzov might have heard of this discontent but on 4 October he actually faced it at first hand. To drive home his point, Wilson brought in 'reinforcements': Duke Alexander of Württemberg (Emperor Alexander's uncle), the Duke of Oldenburg (the emperor's brother-in-law) and Prince Peter Volkonskii. Considering their connections to the emperor and their knowledge 'of his most intimate feelings', these men were 'less liable to objection on the ground of subordination than any of the other generals under [Kutuzov's] orders'.[61] The four of them then proceeded to pressure Kutuzov into revising his decision. 'After much controversy and an expression of dissent', Kutuzov complied and dispatched a note to Lauriston advising him that he was unable to keep the appointment made and inviting him instead to his headquarters.[62]

Around 11pm Lauriston was taken to the Russian camp at Tarutino. Although Wilson claims the French envoy was 'blindfolded' to prevent him from observing the Russian deployment, other Russian eyewitnesses disagree. Kutuzov wanted to make the most of this opportunity to impress the French envoy and had ordered the men to 'ignite numerous bonfires so that it appeared that more than 200,000 men were in the camp'. Soldiers were told to cook porridge, sing songs and create the impression of a joyous atmosphere.[63] 'Travelling in an open carriage, Lauriston arrived as darkness descended,' recalled Alexander Sherbinin, who served on Kutuzov's staff. 'He was accompanied by Lieutenant Mikhail Orlov of the Chevalier Guard Regiment. It was then that we saw, for the first time, Kutuzov in full uniform, [even] wearing a feathered half-moon hat. Not pleased with the tarnished appearance of his epaulettes, Kutuzov asked [General] Konovnitsyn to lend him his, although Konovnitsyn was no dandy and Miloradovich [who was famous for his sense of style] would have been a much better choice.'[64]

Lauriston was ushered into Kutuzov's hut, where he found a small group of high-ranking officers. After some general conversation, everyone withdrew, leaving Kutuzov and the envoy together. Lauriston at first complained of the 'barbarity' of Russian behaviour towards the French, and cited examples of peasants attacking isolated French troops, and burning their own homes and harvests to deny the French any resources. Kutuzov replied that 'he could not civilize in three months a nation who regarded the enemy as worse than a marauding force of the Mongols of Genghis Khan'. Lauriston tried to interject: 'But there is at least some difference.' 'There may be,' retorted the field marshal, 'but none in the eyes of the people; besides, I can only be responsible for the conduct of my troops.' Lauriston then briefly spoke about the fire of Moscow, noting that it was not the French who burnt the city. At last he came to the real point of his mission. 'Is this strange war, this unique war, to go on eternally?' he inquired. 'The emperor, my master, has a sincere desire to end this dispute between two great and generous nations and to end it for ever.' Kutuzov replied that he had no instructions on that subject. 'When I left for the armies, the word peace was not mentioned a single time ... I should be cursed by posterity if I were regarded as the prime mover behind any kind of accommodation, for such is the present mood of my nation ...' Returning to the subject of the armistice, Lauriston continued, 'You must not think we wish it because our affairs are desperate. Our two armies are nearly equal in force. You are, it is true, nearer your supplies and reinforcements than we are, but we also receive reinforcements.' He tried to play down the effects of the French defeat at Salamanca in July. 'Perhaps you have heard that our affairs are disastrous in Spain?' he inquired. 'I have,' said Kutuzov, 'from Sir Robert Wilson, whom you just saw leave me, and with whom I have daily interviews.' Lauriston argued that things were not as bad as Wilson might have described them. The British 'have reasons to exaggerate our reverses'. He acknowledged setbacks in Spain, including the British occupation of Madrid, but expected to see the situation reversed soon. 'Everything will be retrieved in that country by the immense force marching thither.' At the end of the conversation Lauriston asked for a safe-conduct to get to St Petersburg with a view to possible negotiations. Kutuzov, however, refused to let him through and instead promised to submit the matter to Emperor Alexander. After half an hour's talk, Lauriston departed.[65]

The following morning Kutuzov dispatched Peter Volkonskii with a report to St Petersburg, recommending that Napoleon's offer be ignored. On receiving the letter, Alexander was enraged by the field marshal's decision to meet the French envoy at all and sent him a sharp reproof:

> In the interview I had with you at the very moment of your departure, and when I confided my armies to your command, I informed you of my firm desire to avoid all negotiations with the enemy, and all relations with him that tended to peace. Now, after what has passed, I must repeat with the same resolution that I desire this principle adopted by me to be observed by you to its fullest extent, and in the most rigorous and inflexible manner ... All the opinions and suggestions you have received from me – all the resolutions which I have expressed in the orders addressed to you, should convince you that my determination was unalterable, and that at this moment no proposition of the enemy can induce me to terminate the war, and by that to weaken the sacred duty that I have to perform in avenging my injured country.[66]

However, in defying the imperial order not to negotiate with the enemy, it must be said that Kutuzov was guided by military considerations. Just one and half months later, while conversing with a captured French official, he admitted that he had done everything he could to draw out and prolong the negotiations because 'in politics you do not miss an opportunity that presents itself to you spontaneously'. He had agreed to meet Lauriston and send letters to St Petersburg only because 'the distance between St Petersburg and Moscow required time, and it was precisely that time which the marshal needed to mobilize all the armies of Russia'.[67] As before, Kutuzov was convinced that 'winter is our greatest ally' and he was willing to bend, and if necessary defy, imperial instructions to gain precious time.

Upon returning to the Kremlin, Lauriston briefed Napoleon on his meeting and stressed that the letter would be delivered by the Russian emperor's own aide-de-camp and a response should be forthcoming within a fortnight. This seemingly minor detail had important implications. 'Had Lauriston returned to say that Kutuzov had simply refused to receive him,' reasoned one historian, 'Napoleon would have been stung to the quick, and he would have lost no time in hastening his departure.'[68] As it was, the news that his request was being transmitted directly to Alexander revived Napoleon's hopes for peace and resulted in his insistence on staying in Moscow, ignoring all advice to retreat; evidently, he remained convinced that the food supplies were adequate for the army's needs. He also seemed unwilling to consider the threats that the arriving Russian reinforcements, including Admiral Paul Chichagov's Army of the Danube, could pose, and continued to believe in the security of his rear. General Dumas later wondered whether the emperor was 'misinformed respecting the situation of the Russian army, which he believed to be weakened and dispirited, whereas it was receiving powerful reinforcements'.[69]

Searching For a Way Out

Outsmarted by Kutuzov, Napoleon was also misled by Nature itself. Throughout the first two weeks of October the weather was beautiful, and golden autumn days succeeded one another. 'The weather is so lovely for the time of year that one is tempted to believe God is with the Emperor Napoleon,' commented one participant.[70] Napoleon had been frequently warned about the rigours of the Russian climate but so far the autumn of 1812 was so mild that 'even the natives were amazed'.[71] Enjoying warm and sunny days on his regular outings,[72] Napoleon frequently compared the weather with that of France. On 4 October he wrote to Marie Louise, 'the weather here is beautiful, as warm as in Paris. We have just had those lovely Fontainebleau days.'[73] He brushed aside the concerns of Caulaincourt, who, based on his experiences as an ambassador to St Petersburg, warned Napoleon of the impending cold. Napoleon frequently teased him: 'So this is the terrible Russian winter that Monsieur de Caulaincourt frightens the children with.'[74] But this misplaced sense of complacency proved to be consequential, since the mild superb weather 'doubtless contributed to dispel any apprehensions that [Napoleon] might have entertained respecting the difficulties of a retreat'.[75] He was willing to allow the lapse of the ten or twelve days necessary to receive an answer from St Petersburg, and could not suppose that by departing in late October he would be setting out too late. 'The mild temperatures that lasted much longer than usual this year all contributed in lulling him,' believed Caulaincourt. 'Even in private so strongly did the emperor express his convictions of remaining in Moscow now that those held in his closest confidence continued to believe him for quite some time.'[76]

In those days, some historians assure us, Napoleon kept 'sinking into depression, sometimes spending whole hours without saying a word'[77] or 'dwelling in the palace of the tsars, sometimes full of confidence, sometimes much depressed, at the very solstice of his power, or in other words, at that undetermined period which separates the moment of the greatest elevation of the stars from that of their decline'.[78] But this image of the downcast and gloomy emperor should not be overplayed or interpreted as representing complacency and idleness. His valet Constant Wairy, while acknowledging that the emperor 'exhibited the depressing calm of a careworn man who cannot foresee how things will result', also noted that Napoleon was 'a prey to his genius for administration, even in the midst of the ruins of this great city; and in order to divert his mind from the anxiety caused by outside affairs, occupied himself with municipal organization'. Indeed, while awaiting

Alexander's response, Napoleon remained engaged in the day-to-day administration of the army and the empire, receiving daily deliveries of reports, letters, state documents and other materials from all across Europe. Among the daily minutiae, he reviewed stacks of promotion papers rewarding troops for their performances in the preceding months of campaigning. Promotions and decorations rained down on the army[79] but captured French documents in the Russian Archives reveal that the emperor did not simply blindly approve such documents but attentively reviewed each dossier and, in some cases, expunged individuals (or even entire regiments) that he found unworthy of reward.[80] A good example of his attention to detail and his micromanagement of issues that his intendants should have taken care of can be found in his 6 October letter to Maret:

> Forty portable mills left Paris by post on 6 September. It is now 6 October. So they should have passed through Vilna. I have exhorted you to inform yourself on the progress of this convoy. It is my intention that you shall withdraw one of these mills to serve as a model. Have it operated under your eyes, and let me know how much [corn] it has ground in 24 hours and how many men successively have done this work. I want you to have fifty of these mills constructed at Vilna on the basis of the one you use as a model. As soon as you have had two or three made, you will send one by post to Warsaw and Konigsberg. In the same way you will send one more to Minsk for fifty more copies to be made. I assume there are workmen in the countryside who will do it promptly. You must also send one to [Macdonald] to have some made on this model at Mittau.[81]

As the days passed, and it became clear that Lauriston's mission had failed, Napoleon summoned Caulaincourt once more. Their conversation is quite revealing about the emperor's misconceptions. 'Emperor Alexander is stubborn,' he grumbled. 'He will regret it. Never again will he be able to obtain such good terms as I would have made now.' Napoleon spoke of inciting the Poles to rise 'en masse' to defend themselves against the Russians and look after their 'particular interests'. He claimed that Alexander was endangering himself by insisting on continued hostilities. 'I am going to attack Kutuzov. If I beat him, as is probable, Alexander runs grave risks. But he can stop it by a single word. Who can tell what will happen in the forthcoming campaign? ... I have learned much from this war; my army is getting to know the country and the troops confronting them. There are incalculable advantages.' He envisioned establishing winter quarters at Moscow and Kaluga, or withdrawing westwards to winter around Smolensk and Vitebsk. 'Russia will be lost,' he believed. 'Having offered all the concessions that I can be expected to make, I shall have no choice but to pursue the interests of my system, to pursue the great political aim which I have set for myself. If Emperor Alexander ponders this, he would realize that he could go a long way with a man of my character.' Caulaincourt, probably weary from voicing the same arguments over and over again, reminded the emperor that the Russians were hoping to 'lull' him into a false sense of security and were well aware that the French were in no bargaining position and faced insurmountable 'difficulties'. At the words 'lull' and 'difficulties' the emperor became irritated. 'What do you mean by 'difficulties?' Caulaincourt replied:

> The winter, Sire, is a major difficulty to begin with. The lack of stores, of horses for your artillery, of transport for your sick and wounded, the poor clothing for your soldiers. Every man must have a sheepskin, stout fur-lined gloves, a cap with ear-

tabs, warm boot–socks, heavy boots to keep his feet from getting frost-bitten. We lack everything. Our smiths do not even have the proper heavy horseshoes used here in winter. How can teams of horses be expected to haul our artillery across ice? And then there is the question of our lines of communications. It is still unseasonably warm now, but what will it be in two weeks' time when winter sets in?

The emperor listened with growing impatience. 'So you think I intend to leave Moscow?' he inquired. 'Yes, Sire,' Caulaincourt replied but Napoleon quickly interjected: 'I have decided nothing yet. I could hardly be better situated than where I am now, at Moscow, to sit out the winter.'[82]

But Napoleon was being disingenuous with his grand equerry. After days of waiting for a Russian response to his peace overtures, he had at last realized that it was necessary to adopt decisive measures. Further offensive operations were clearly out of the question. He explained to his trusted aide-de-camp Narbonne that until now he had been obliged to wait in Moscow to see what effect 'those two thunderbolts, the battle of Moscowa [Borodino] and the taking of Moscow, would have. I had reason to believe in a peace. But whether it comes or not, there is a limit for us.' He now faced two choices: he could take the army, 'which has largely rested up', back to Lithuania and Poland, where it would take up comfortable winter quarters. Or he could follow the advice of Secretary of State Daru – which Napoleon called 'the lion's advice' – of rallying his troops, collecting provisions and hunkering down for the winter in Moscow.[83] Daru argued that it would be easier to feed the army in Moscow and to secure its communications than to risk marching back to Smolensk. The city still offered sufficient means of subsistence, including plenty of corn, rice, vegetables, spirituous liquors and salted provisions. But remaining in Moscow entailed several major challenges. While troops could be sufficiently well fed, the army was desperate for forage for the horses that were already dying of inanition. Losses had already weakened the cavalry, artillery and transport in a season that was far from being the least favourable of the year. Furthermore, Moscow was hundreds of miles away from the heartlands of the French Empire, and maintaining communications over such vast distances was a challenging task. In the face of attacks by the hostile local populace, not to mention roaming Cossack and partisan detachments, Napoleon would have to commit considerable resources to guarding his lines of communications. By October the Allied convoys were already so threatened that the emperor had to specify that no convoy should leave Smolensk without an escort of 1,500 men of both infantry and cavalry. 'The cavalry and artillery of each convoy must march together, bivouac in square battalion round the convoy, and not separate from it under any pretext whatsoever; that the commander of the convoy must bivouac in the centre – that every commander who shall neglect these instructions will be punished as negligent and culpable of the loss of the convoy.'[84] General St Sulpice, commander of the dragoons of the Guard, was tasked with keeping open the road from Mozhaisk to Moscow, one of the most threatened sectors in the long line of communications, and was obliged to dispatch strong patrols to accompany each courier travelling along the route.[85] The thought of what would happen in Paris or the rest of Europe if, in spite of all his efforts, there should some week be no news about his whereabouts, would have certainly preoccupied Napoleon. 'One must not be away from home too long,' he told his companion. 'I feel Paris calling me even more than St Petersburg tempts me.'[86] More importantly, what advantage would he gain by being in Moscow at the commencement of the succeeding spring? Emperor Alexander had already rebuffed his repeated attempts to open negotiations and there were no signs of a Russian willingness to compromise. The situation in Moscow was becoming increasingly precarious. Throughout October the Russian army was daily strengthening its positions on the banks of the Nara river and the various flying detachments, dispersed round Moscow, became more enterprising. In the villages surrounding the city popular anger was already spilling out into a guerrilla war that targeted isolated Allied detachments as well as lines of communication. The Grande Armée's detachments and convoys on their march to and from the army were routinely attacked on the main road to Smolensk, despite the presence of the escorts. The Cossacks, reinforced by newly arriving recruits from the Don and other regions, kept the roads into Moscow under close watch, attacking Allied foragers in the vicinity of Moscow and frequently launching daring raids into the city itself. On one occasion, a young seminary student, who had survived the devastation of Moscow by cleaning stables for the French troops, was sent as servant to a squad of hussars quartered at the extreme end of the city. He noticed, one evening, an individual looking through the lighted windows, watching all that went on inside the house. 'What are you doing there?' he cried. The stranger stepped back quickly, then approached the young man; leading him into the garden, he questioned him, and showed him the Cossack uniform under his caftan of coarse cloth. He wished to find out whether the hussars were numerous, whether they all slept in the same room, and where they deposited their arms and horses, and he enjoined the most absolute secrecy. Two days afterwards the seminarian was awakened by an extraordinary commotion as a Cossack detachment raided the place, killed all the hussars and escaped with their weapons and horses.[87] There were many similar cases and the Allied troops deployed on the outskirts of the city, and especially near the barrier gates, were particularly vulnerable to Cossack raids. One Muscovite recalled seeing a group of 'seven enemy men, virtually unarmed and looking more like batmen or footmen, loading a wagon with their possessions. Suddenly a Cossack flew into the yard and, within just a few seconds, he slew all of them with his lance, jumped off his horse, searched the corpses and then galloped away.'[88] At the Novodevichii Monastery Semen Klimych recalled that the French troops billeted there held daily roster calls that revealed the unending loss of men. 'This continued for three weeks and rarely did a day pass [without loss of life], causing them to complain in broken Russian to the priests, "Russian Cossack, devil, eat French."'[89] Some Russian troops managed to infiltrate into Moscow and rallied local residents. Among them was Alexander Figner, a young man of medium height, with a round face and pale complexion, who spoke half a dozen languages and virulently hated the French. 'Contempt for any and all dangers and unmatched gallantry revealed his unwavering intrepidity and presence of mind,' recalled one of his comrades. After sneaking into Moscow in late September, Figner

> rallied people of various backgrounds who still remained in Moscow and organized armed detachments to kill enemy soldiers; he ambushed them amidst the flames in the streets and inside homes and commanded his men so efficiently that the French were killed everywhere, especially at night. And so, accompanied by just a handful of gallant lads, Figner began to kill the enemy inside the city itself, amidst the horrors of burning and plunder. In the flaming ruins of the Russian capital the French faced a methodical and clandestine war from this courageous avenger, but they searched for him in vain. Even though they had him before their eyes, they still could not find him. In daylight, wearing plain peasant clothes, he walked

between French soldiers and served them however he could so he could listen to their conversations. At night, he attacked them with his gallant lads and by morning the streets were covered with the bodies of the killed Frenchmen.[90]

Napoleon was well aware of these challenges and understood the benefits that departing from Moscow could bring. Withdrawing towards Vitebsk (if not all the way back to the Duchy of Warsaw) would bring the Grande Armée closer to its reinforcement and supply depots in Prussia and Poland, and shorten the lines of communication, making them easier to defend. It could spend the next few months in winter cantonments, regrouping and preparing for the next stage of the war in the spring. But besides the purely military aspect, the emperor also had to consider the political implications of his actions and, in this regard, he was convinced that leaving Moscow without any tangible gains, not even an armistice, would have the appearance of acknowledging defeat and thus could undermine his standing in Europe. According to Ségur, Napoleon told Daru, 'As if I do not know that from a military point of view Moscow is of no value! But Moscow is not a military position, it is a political position.' He then argued that 'in political measures we ought never to recede, never to retrograde, never to admit ourselves to be wrong, as it lessened our consideration; that, even when in error, we should persist in it, in order to have the appearance of being in the right'.[91]

So, throughout early October Napoleon insisted on staying in Moscow. For a week or more his companions listened to the emperor 'in his intimate circle conversing, acting and issuing orders all on the presumption that he was going to stay in Moscow'.[92] To this end, Napoleon continued to strengthen the city's defences, including enhancing the Kremlin[93] and fortifying some principal convents,[94] as well as the approaches to the city.[95] He raised a new (dismounted) cavalry brigade to 'guard the defences of the Kremlin and the city'.[96] He ordered that ample provisions of ammunition should be prepared for the army and that the surplus should be carefully managed so as to last the troops the five or six months that winter was expected to last in this region. The long network of posting stations connecting Paris to Moscow – so crucial for maintaining control over the vast empire – was reinforced to ensure the daily arrival of couriers.[97] Napoleon continued holding military parades in the courtyard of the Kremlin, ordered the construction of large new baking ovens[98] for the troops and mills for the preparation of flour, and sent out strong detachments to collect cattle and forage for the long winter ahead. On 6 October Napoleon instructed Eugène to push his forces towards Dmitrov and Kline, where he was supposed to issue proclamations reassuring the peasants of his intentions and collect necessary provisions. Napoleon hoped that by 'not pillaging and paying [for everything] with money', the 4th Corps would find 'plenty of resources' in this region.[99] Similarly, the 1st Corps was allowed to expand its reaches beyond Moscow,[100] while the 3rd Corps was ordered to move further westward, where it eventually advanced as far as Bogorodsk,[101] where Ney's men spent several days 'constructing barracks round this small town as if they intended to pass the winter there'.[102]

Even Napoleon's closest companions believed that staying in Moscow for the winter was the emperor's favorite idea. 'For some time even those most closely in his confidence', noted Caulaincourt, 'entertained no doubts on that score. Seeing the season so far advanced without any preparations made for our departure, I too ended by doubting whether we would evacuate Moscow voluntarily. It seemed to me impossible the emperor would even think of a retreat when the frost set in, especially as no measures had been taken to protect the men nor any steps taken to enable the horses to cross the ice.'[103] However, even though he was still in two minds about attempting a retreat, Napoleon was also keen to find a way he could accomplish it without political repercussions. In early October he devised a manoeuvre which, whilst it carried him towards Poland by an oblique march towards the north, would have made him appear to be not in retreat but rather carrying out an offensive movement. In a lengthy memorandum, Napoleon outlined his thoughts on this subject, showing how clearly he appreciated the difficulties of his situation. He first offered a broad overview of the situation across the entire theatre of war. 'The enemy is marching on the road from Kiev. His object is evident – he seeks reinforcements from the Army of Moldavia. To march against them would be to march in the direction of their succour, and to find ourselves deprived of any *points d'appui* during winter cantonments. Moscow, having been burned and deserted by its inhabitants, must not be taken into account; that city cannot contain our sick and wounded; the resources found there, once exhausted, no more will be forthcoming ...' So Napoleon urged breaking the stalemate through vigorous action. The question was, which way? Advancing further eastwards was clearly pointless: the Russian army had already manoeuvred itself to Tarutino, southwest of Moscow. Therefore, 'should the army fall back to Smolensk,' the emperor wondered, 'would it be wise to seek engagement with the enemy, and to risk losing, in a march which would resemble a retreat, several thousand men in the presence of an enemy acquainted with the country, having a large number of secret agents and a numerous light cavalry?' Napoleon expected the Russians to have established themselves at a strong position, possibly already fortified, and received continued reinforcements. 'Although the French army is victorious,' the emperor argued, a retrograde movement would place it at a disadvantage. 'We might dispute terrain and lose 3,000–4,000 wounded, but it would look like a defeat. A withdrawal of 100 leagues, with subsequent losses and events, would allow the enemy to claim it as a success and portray us as beaten.'

After considering whether it would be feasible to return by the same route that had brought him to Moscow, the emperor asked himself:

> What is the object to be fulfilled? First, to place the emperor as near France as possible, and to give the country confidence that the emperor during his winter cantonments is in the midst of his people. Second, to quarter the army in a friendly country, close to its magazines. Third, to place ourselves in a position to back up the emperor's negotiations for peace by threatening St Petersburg. Fourth, to sustain the honour of our arms at the height to which it has been raised by this glorious campaign.[104]

The Emperor then indicated a series of movements calculated to fulfill these goals. He envisioned two army corps launching an offensive northwards to St Petersburg. St Cyr's corps would secure Polotsk and threaten St Petersburg from the southwest. It would be supported by Marshal Victor's 9th Corps, which was supposed to be at Velikie Luki within nine days; Victor would coordinate his actions with St Cyr.[105] Further west, Marshal Macdonald would remain in the vicinity of Dunaburg and Riga, protecting the Grande Armée's extreme left flank. Once Victor had secured Velikie Luki, Napoleon would march his army westwards out of Moscow, moving beyond the Dvina and closer to Polish lands.[106] Such plans were probably drawn up early in October, as on the 9th the emperor confided to Maret, 'Everything leads me to believe that when the last half of November arrives, that is to say, the real season for winter quarters, I will take position between the Dvina and the Dnieper to be closer to my reinforcements, to rest the army and to attend to many other pressing issues.'[107]

Thus, even while still professing his intention to stay in Moscow, Napoleon began to take measures to prepare the territory between Moscow and Smolensk for a possible retreat of the Grande Armée. He gained a sense of urgency after the daily *estafette* from Moscow to Paris was attacked and captured near Moscow on 12 October, and more messengers were intercepted by the Russians over the next two days. These attacks underlined the gravity of the situation for Napoleon, who had already started making inquiries about the status of major supply depots in the rear and frequently complained about his subordinates' failure to follow through on his orders.[108] 'Have I not said and said again a hundred times to bring up all the clothing which is in Danzig to Kovno and Vilna?' he wrote to Maret. 'So write to Danzig that my orders must be carried out.'[109] He paid particular attention to the grand supply depot at Minsk, where vast supplies of provisions had been already amassed, and more was still expected. On 14 October the emperor instructed Maret to send rice collected from all over Europe to Minsk.[110] Heavy transports and artillery were no longer allowed to pass beyond Smolensk,[111] while thousands of wounded and sick were slowly taken westwards. Moving them represented a major challenge and in early October *Intendant-Général* Dumas informed the emperor that it would take forty-five days to evacuate all the wounded left behind at Mozhaisk, the Kolotsk Monastery and Gzhatsk. Startled by this claim, Napoleon replied, 'The accounts of the *Intendant-Général* appear to me to be wrong. I can scarcely believe that it will require forty-five days to remove the wounded, for I will only remark that if nothing is done during these forty-five days, some must die and some recover; therefore, it can only be the remainder that are to be removed, and experience has proved that three months after a battle only a sixth part of those wounded remain. Thus, reckoning six thousand wounded, there would only be, at the end of three months, one thousand to remove.' He was furious at the commissioners of war and administrative officials for failing to provide accurate reports on circumstances in their hospitals, and demanded they 'establish precisely how many patients' were convalescing between Moscow and Vyazma. 'In all circumstances, I need to be aware of sacrifices that might have to be made if [military] operations require abandoning these institutions.' Therefore, all patients had to be assessed and separated into three groups depending on the severity of their condition.[112] The emperor then requested some 200 transports from the 1st and 3rd Corps to deliver flour, alcohol, wine and medicine and evacuate the wounded, starting with the most seriously wounded.[113] The same day he instructed Minister of War Clarke to dispatch a couple of hundred additional physicians to the army 'because there is a great need for them here'.[114] On 6 October Napoleon ordered Junot to use transports at the cavalry depot in Mozhaisk to start removing the wounded to Vyazma, while General Baraguay d'Hilliers was tasked with transporting them further west to Smolensk. For this purpose, both generals were ordered to 'scour the country for ten leagues round and collect a large number of transports necessary for the said evacuations'. They were also permitted to employ military transport that carried flour supplies to French hospitals. 'My intention', declared the emperor, 'is to have not a single wounded man remaining at Ruza, the Kolotskii Monastery, Mozhaisk or Gzhatsk within the next eight days ... This is of the utmost importance.'[115]

Napoleon's efforts on behalf of the wounded are commendable indeed but they came a bit late. Had he begun this process in late September thousands of men would have left Russian unmolested and survived. Even those evacuated in the first week of October managed to reach France in relatively good condition. But now, moving thousands of wounded along the old Smolensk road became fraught with challenges. This route had been devastated by both armies during the summer campaign. 'The road from Smolensk to Mozhaisk is completely exhausted,' observed Napoleon. 'It is appropriate, therefore, to have the commandants of Dorogobuzh, Gzhatsk, Vyazma and other locations to reconnoitre two parallel roads, two or three leagues to the right [from the main road], where there would be sufficient resources [for the army].'[116] Napoleon instructed Marshal Victor to 'detain all detachments of infantry, cavalry, artillery, military crews, trains of artillery, clothing, etc ... at Smolensk'. The intention was to keep 'this road open for the evacuation of hospitals and parts of the army to Smolensk, while nothing should pass from Smolensk to Moscow'.[117] On 15–17 October thousands of wounded were moved from hospitals in the direction of Smolensk, and General Nansouty, who escorted these convoys, received instructions to turn back any transports he encountered on the road.[118] Russian prisoners of war were also moved to Smolensk; en route, they suffered numerous abuses and mistreatment from their captors. One of them recalled that the prisoners included many innocent Muscovites. 'Among us were many merchants and peasants because the French, upon seeing their beards, were convinced that they were Cossacks. There were also many servants and even footmen still wearing their liveries, whom the French accused of being disguised Russian soldiers.' Anyone showing signs of fatigue or illness was simply shot by the side of the road.[119]

To avoid any 'embarrassing incidents'[120] at the start of the retreat, Napoleon gradually concentrated his forces. Marshal Ney, who had spent several days with his corps around Bogorodsk, was ordered to return to Moscow. Napoleon ordered Murat to observe closely the Russian camp at Tarutino, affording his troops as much rest and as good subsistence as possible. He also began redeploying the troops left in the rear and gave directions as to the manner in which the stragglers who had been assembled at Vilna, Minsk, Vitebsk and Smolensk were to rejoin the army. On 13 October a slight frost occurred and first light snow shower fell on the ruins of Moscow. Although the season remained fine, this cold spell had finally shown that the weather could change abruptly and the moment had come when it was necessary to decide what to do. 'Let us make haste,' he told his secretary. 'We must be in winter quarters in twenty days' time.'[121]

And yet there was no follow up and Napoleon continued to demonstrate extraordinary indecisiveness. Finally he assembled his council of war. Viceroy Eugène, Berthier, Daru, Mortier, Davout and Ney obeyed his summons; Murat and Bessieres could not attend due to their responsibilities in the advanced guard. The council first discussed the state of the army, reviewing each corps' strengths and preparedness. One cannot but wonder how disheartening it must have been to these men to hear about the much-reduced strength of the Grande Armée. Davout's corps was reduced from 72,000 to about 30,000, while Ney saw his corps shrink from 39,000 to just 10,000. Poniatowski's 5th Corps numbered no more than 5,000 and Junot's Westphalians mustered just 2,000. At least the condition of the men was largely satisfactory. The council then considered what plan of operations it would be best to adopt. This issue produced a diversity of opinion: Daru continued to insist that the army ought to remain at Moscow, while Davout, supported by Ney, strongly argued in favour of retreating along the Kalouga route that would open up to the army previously untouched provinces. In contrast, Berthier, supported by

Mortier and Eugène, proposed that the army should proceed by a northern route through Volokolamsk and Zubkov to Vitebsk. Napoleon listened to all these opinions before deciding in favour of the plan to march on Kaluga. On 14 October Berthier informed Murat that Napoleon was taking the first steps to leave Moscow. 'His Majesty desires you to reconnoitre routes so if you have to retreat before the enemy, you know these roads well. The emperor suggests making arrangements so your transports, parks and most of your infantry could depart without the enemy noticing.'[122] The first trains with trophies – the regalia used in the tsarist coronations, the Ottoman standards that the Russians had captured in previous wars, the imperial eagles from the tops of the Kremlin towers, the cross of the Ivan the Great Tower and other treasures – departed from Moscow under the protection of General Claparede's troops on 15 October.[123] The following day Napoleon informed his Minister of Foreign Relations that he had made the decision to depart from Moscow and withdraw his forces to Smolensk and Vitebsk. 'I intend on leaving on the 19th[124] towards Kaluga,' he wrote, 'and beating the enemy army if it decides to oppose me ... I will then proceed to Tula and Bryansk, or return immediately to Smolensk if the weather turns bad.' As for the reasons for his departure, Napoleon explained that Moscow 'no longer exists ... therefore, it cannot serve as a military position for my future operations; it no longer has any significance'.[125]

Unaware of the emperor's decision, many officers in Ney's 3rd Corps, arriving in Moscow on 15 October, hoped that their return would be the precursor to a general withdrawal. 'Two days passed over and we heard nothing of our departure,' grumbled Montesquiou-Fezensac.[126] Napoleon instead kept rallying troops and holding reviews in the court of the Kremlin. On 6 October it was the Old Guard infantry, followed by a review of the Young Guard, while a general parade was held on 8 October, only to be followed by a review of the divisions of the 1st Corps on 10–12 October. 'We were almost constantly on duty or on parade. These tasks took up much of the day ... [Reviews] exhausted the soldiers,' recalled a Guard officer.[127]

On the 18th it was the turn of Ney's 3rd Corps, and 'the review was as imposing as circumstances would admit of,' commented one officer. 'The colonels rivalled each other in their efforts to display their regiments to the best advantage. No one would have imagined from their appearance how much their men had suffered and were still suffering. I am persuaded that this good outward show confirmed the emperor in his obstinacy, by inducing him to believe that, with such men, nothing was impossible.'[128] But Napoleon's experienced eye could not have ignored the meagre state of the once-imposing corps that once counted almost 40,000 men and now barely listed 10,000. As he contemplated the sight of his war-weary troops, reports circulated that gunfire had been heard in the direction of Vinkovo.[129] It was some time before anyone dared to apprise Napoleon of the circumstances: 'some from incredulity or uncertainty, and dreading the first movement of his impatience; others from love of ease, hesitating to provoke a terrible signal, or apprehensive of being sent to verify this assertion, and of exposing themselves to a fatiguing excursion.'[130] But suddenly M. de Berenger, Murat's aide-de-camp, turned up, 'crestfallen and with a worried air'.[131] He hardly took time to shake hands with Biot and simply muttered, 'Thing are going badly!' Berenger was rushed to the emperor who listened anxiously to his account of the surprise enemy attack at Vinkovo, where Murat barely escaped destruction.[132]

Chapter 10

The Die is Cast

In the evening of 14 September the disheartened officers and soldiers of the Russian army streamed through Moscow in an easterly direction. On leaving the city, the army made two unhurried marches on the Ryazan road to cross the Moskva river, about 20 miles from the capital. Despite claims by certain Russian/Soviet historians, Kutuzov had no premeditated plan of what was to become the famous flanking manoeuvre to Tarutino. Instead, it was the result of circumstances and a gradually formed consensus. At the council of war at Fili the Russian generals considered two possible directions: Barclay de Tolly suggested proceeding eastwards to Vladimir, which would secure direct communications with St Petersburg and protect the provinces east and north of Moscow. Bennigsen and Toll, on the other hand, favoured turning southwards and moving to Kaluga, which would allow the Russians to protect the resources-rich provinces and threaten the enemy lines of communications.[1] The latter offered many advantages but also represented a considerable threat, as Kutuzov feared that Napoleon would continue pursuing the Russian army and a flanking manoeuvre might expose it to devastating attacks by the Grande Armée.

Kutuzov's orders on 13–14 September reveal that he initially considered accepting Barclay de Tolly's suggestion and even made preparations to move his forces to the Vladimir road. In a letter to the commander of the 9th Reserve Regiment, for example, he noted that this unit should 'proceed to Vladimir, where the main army is currently turning from the Ryazan road'.[2] However, as it became clear that the Grande Armée had no intention of pursuing the Russians beyond Moscow, Kutuzov felt confident enough to adjust his plan. On 15 September he decided against moving to Vladimir and instead chose the opposite, southwesterly, direction. He explained to Wintzingerode that he intended to 'make a march to the Ryazan road tomorrow and then reach the Tula road with a second march. From there I will proceed to Podolsk on the Kaluga road. With this movement I intend to turn the enemy's attention to this army and threaten his rear. Podolsk is such a place where I hope to find [an advantageous] position and receive reinforcements, and from where I can dispatch detachments to the Mozhaisk road [to harass Napoleon's line of communications].'[3] Further details can be gleaned from Kutuzov's letter to Emperor Alexander, the first he had written since the fall of Moscow. After explaining the factors that caused him to abandon Russia's ancient capital, Kutuzov laid out his plan of launching a flanking manoeuvre that would take the Russian army to the Kaluga and Tula roads, which 'will allow me to safeguard the city of Tula, where our most important munitions factory is located,[4] and Bryansk, where we have an equally important casting factory'. Furthermore, the army would have not only the rich plains of the Ukraine at its rear but the whole of southern and southeastern Russia, with its abundant resources and vast pool of recruits. The flanking manoeuvre would also allow the main Russian army to maintain communications with the armies of Tormasov and Chichagov that had began to move up northwards from Volhynia to threaten the enemy's right flank.[5]

On the 17th, leaving a small Cossack force under Colonel I. Efremov[6] on the Ryazan road to divert the Allied advanced guard,[7] Kutuzov turned westward at the Borovsk ferry on the Pakhra river and proceeded by forced marches along the river's southern bank.[8] 'The crossing of the Moscow river [at the Borovsk ferry]', recalled General Yermolov, 'was accomplished with great difficulty and in incredible confusion because of the vehicles belonging to the fleeing residents of Moscow. Gunfire could be heard but the enemy did not attack.'[9] Instead, General Sebastiani, who had replaced Murat at the head of the Grande Armée's advanced guard, proceeded, seeing always before him parties of Cossacks, to the Moskva river, where the Russians burned the bridge on the 18th. By the time Sebastiani managed to move his forces across on 21 September, the Cossacks had simply 'disappeared' – in reality, they turned westward and proceeded by rural paths to join the main army. Realizing the potential consequences of this mistake, Sebastiani frankly sent word to Napoleon that he knew not where to find the Russian army.

Meanwhile, as it became clear that the Cossack feint was a success and the enemy had failed to detect the Russian manoeuvre, Kutuzov decided to revise his earlier plan and advance further westwards (and deeper into Napoleon's rear) to take a position on the old Kaluga road.[10] By late on 18 September, 'despite the most appalling weather and dreadful country roads',[11] as well as alarming rates of looting carried out by soldiers,[12] the Russian army was already at Podolsk,[13] where it spent two days before making another forced march to reach the old Kaluga road and complete its flanking manoeuvre. On the 21st Kutuzov took up a position at the village of Krasnaya Pakhra behind the Pakhra river, with two strong advanced guards deployed around it. Miloradovich, with the 8th Corps and the 1st Cavalry Corps, halted at Desna, only some 10 miles from Moscow, while Rayevskii, with the 7th Corps and the 4th Cavalry Corps, camped at the village of Lukovnya, protecting the Russian right flank and guarding the road from Podolsk to Krasnaya Pakhra.[14] At the same time Dorokhov, with the flying detachment of hussars, dragoons and Cossacks, was sent towards Mozhaisk both to reconnoitre and to harass the enemy lines of communications.[15]

Not everyone was pleased with Kutuzov's flanking manoeuvre and some generals thought halting on the old Kaluga road was premature. Barclay de Tolly argued that the army should move further westwards and take a stand on the new Kaluga road, which would in effect interdict Napoleon's lines of communication, forcing him to leave Moscow and fight.[16] However, this was exactly what Kutuzov wanted to avoid for now. He was well aware that the Russian army needed time to regroup and recuperate, as well as to train and equip the newly raised units. Kutuzov argued that his position on the old Kaluga road gave him a central base that allowed him to control all the routes leading southwards from Moscow. He could therefore access the vast supplies in the southern provinces, while harassing the enemy around Moscow. 'Currently our main concern is to replenish the troops,' he informed the emperor on 23 September.[17] By then he had already begun making arrangements to have supplies and recruits delivered to Ryazan, Tula and Kaluga, from where they could be easily absorbed into the army.[18]

On receiving Sebastiani's initial report on the 'disappearance' of the Russian army, Napoleon was furious at the general's failure to conduct a proper pursuit. He was particularly upset about the news of the tacit cease-fire that developed between the French and Russian outposts. 'The advanced guard of our army was wrong in concluding a kind of suspension of hostilities with the Cossack advance posts,' he privately complained.[19] Napoleon showed Caulaincourt several letters he had received from Murat in which he quoted the Cossacks expressing both war-weariness and a readiness to desert the Russian command and serve under his (Murat's) leadership. To Napoleon, it was clear that the Cossacks sought to flatter Murat's ego and pull the wool over his eyes. 'Murat, king of the Cossacks! What folly!' the emperor scoffed. On 22 September Napoleon sent a terse letter to his brother-in-law informing him that detailed intelligence about the Russian army was needed immediately. He declared that the cease-fire was nothing but a ruse with which the Cossacks had diverted Murat's attention. While some Cossacks had been 'befriending' the French on the Ryazan road, others were preoccupied attacking the Grande Armée's lines of communication and destroying munitions convoys in the vicinity of Moscow.[20] These attacks, especially a Cossack raid that inflicted heavy losses on the dragoons of the Imperial Guard at Malo-Vyazma,[21] came as a surprise to Napoleon and, in the words of Caulaincourt, 'this slight reverse irritated the emperor as much as the loss of a battle'.[22] Consequently Napoleon decreed 'the penalty of death to every officer who shall parley with the enemy's advanced posts, without authority. His Majesty wishes that they should not correspond with the enemy, except by their cannon and muskets.'[23] The emperor ordered Murat to proceed immediately to the head of the advanced guard, taking with him Poniatowski's Polish corps in order that, being accompanied by troops who could communicate in Slavic language, he might the more easily discover the whereabouts of the Russian army.[24] The reports of Cossacks raids south of Moscow led Napoleon to surmise that Kutuzov was executing a flanking movement towards the Kaluga route. 'Particular information leads us to believe that the enemy is no longer at Podolsk,' he wrote to Murat on 23 September.[25] Therefore Murat was directed to proceed from the Ryazan road to the Toula road (in other words, from south-east to south), and to continue his march until he procured information on the Russian army's location. At the same time, unwilling to leave the search for the Russian army in the hands of Murat alone, Napoleon dispatched Marshal Bessieres with some 11,000 men[26] in the direction of Kaluga.[27] He correctly anticipated that the double object of threatening the Allies' rear and protecting the richest provinces of the empire would compel the Russians to move beyond Podolsk towards the Kaluga road, but he rejected suggestions that the Russians might intercept the old Smolensk road, the Grande Armée's main line of communication. 'The idea of marching to Mojaisk appears to his majesty as mere boasting,' Berthier informed Mortier. 'A victorious army, says he, would not consider itself in a proper condition to attempt such an undertaking; how then believe that a conquered one, that has abandoned its fine city, would think of such a movement.'[28] Nevertheless, Napoleon still wanted detailed information on the enemy's whereabouts: he was resolved to prevent Kutuzov from taking up a threatening position in his rear. Marshal Davout had entreated the emperor to leave Moscow at once and engage the enemy. Napoleon was disposed to follow this advice, provided it could be executed without too many protracted marches. He therefore eagerly awaited the arrival of intelligence with respect to the new positions taken up by the Russian army.[29]

On 22 September Murat, with his advanced guard strengthened by Claparede's division, advanced along the Ryazan road; he was supported by Poniatowski, whose Polish troops moved on the Tula road. Since the Russians had burned the bridge at the Borovsk ferry, Murat forded the river and proceeded towards Bronitsy.[30] Finding no Russian forces in this direction, he then turned westward and dispatched scouts towards Podolsk. By the 23rd he had ascertained the true direction of Kutuzov's march and reported it back to Moscow. Napoleon initially instructed Murat to press the Russians' right flank, while Bessieres marched from Moscow against their front.[31] The troops marched in miserable weather and one of them complained that 'never in my life have I seen a muddier place nor wetter mud. We were in it up to the middle of our legs, in the middle of the road; [it was] impossible to walk along the roadsides.'[32]

On 21–23 September Miloradovich informed the main headquarters about the enemy troops moving from Moscow and engaging his outposts. Without precise intelligence on the size of this force, and already in receipt of Rayevskii's reports about Murat's movements from the east, Kutuzov chose to avoid direct confrontation and pull Miloradovich back from Desna, which was occupied by the Allied troops. Meanwhile, Murat was already approaching Podolsk, where Poniatowski's Polish troops awaited him.[33] The news of the enemy advances from both north and east caused many in the Russian headquarters to assume that 'Napoleon was attacking with all his forces our flank and rear'.[34] Another council of war was held at the Russian headquarters, where some senior commanders urged attacking to seize the initiative and surprise the enemy. Bennigsen in fact instructed Miloradovich to launch an attack on Bessieres' forces at dawn on 25 September, while Rayevskii was asked to 'undertake a feint attack on the enemy facing him in order to distract his forces'.[35] But the cautious Kutuzov demurred, arguing that if the Russians attacked so close to Moscow, they would have the whole Grande Armée, still a potent force, upon them at once and the army's current condition could scarcely be relied upon to deliver more than a doubtful success. On the other hand, if the Russian army avoided combat, time was on their side as every day would ensure the steady increase of Russian numbers. Therefore Kutuzov forbade Miloradovich from engaging in a major battle and instead limited him to forceful reconnaissance. 'Even if you find it convenient to attack the enemy, you must not pursue him too far and only limit yourself to reclaiming Desna.'[36] Just an hour later Bennigsen, upset by Kutuzov's reluctance to fight, jotted down a brief message cancelling the offensives altogether.[37] Instead, General Alexander Osterman-Tolstoy was instructed to take command of a new *corps de bataille* (consisting of the 4th Corps and 2nd Cavalry Corps), which moved forwards to support Miloradovich's advanced guard.[38]

By 26 September Napoleon had learned with certainty that Kutuzov's main forces were on the old Kaluga road. The appearance of Russian flying detachments on the old Smolensk road prompted him to move up strong cavalry reinforcements to guard the lines of communications.[39] Then, as soon as he was informed of the position occupied by the Russian army, he ordered Murat, supported by Bessieres if necessary, to engage the Russian army and drive it away from Moscow. Napoleon was convinced that Kutuzov would choose to retreat as soon as he heard about the Allied advance. If, however, he chose to stand his ground, Napoleon was ready to lead the rest of the Grande Armée out of Moscow to attack the Russians.[40]

Napoleon was largely correct in his reckoning. Had the commander of the Russian army at this time been Bennigsen rather than Kutuzov, it is likely that the Russians would have accepted battle; considering the difficulties the Russian army was experiencing, this might well have resulted in a French victory, profoundly affecting the outcome of the campaign. But unlike Bennigsen, Kutuzov understood that this was not the time for provoking Napoleon into a decisive battle. The wounds of Borodino had barely healed. Every day Kutuzov had to face the grim reality of ill-discipline and marauding in the Russian ranks, while thousands of soldiers were still unaccounted for after the march through and from Moscow. Like Barclay de Tolly, Kutuzov understood early on that time was on Russia's side and each day gained without a battle in fact brought him closer to a triumph over the enemy. He was therefore unwilling to fight a major battle, and his reaction to the news of the French offensive was to order a withdrawal southwards at dawn on 27 September. The new round of retreating caused a lot of grumbling among both officers and the rank and file. The British commissioner Wilson was among the more vocal critics of Kutuzov,[41] while Governor Rostopchin, impressed by what the Cossacks and Russian flying detachments were already accomplishing, could not hide his disdain for the commander-in-chief. 'What is maddening', he wrote to his wife, 'is that our troops have everywhere the upper hand, but the general to lead them is missing … Kutuzov never shows himself, he eats and sleeps alone, he drags around with him a young girl dressed as a Cossack and he lets two scoundrels carry out his functions for him. At times the soldiers even call him a traitor …'

That day there were several brisk encounters between the Russians and the Allied troops in the environs of Desna and Podolsk.[42] Brandt, whose Vistula Legion had been attached to Murat's advanced guard, recalled that 'we were on the move at an early hour on the 27th and soon closed with the enemy, who unmasked a considerable body of cavalry. There followed a series of skirmishes in which artillery played the dominant part. The Russians retreated when they saw we were about to launch a general assault.'[43] Nevertheless, the Russian rearguard actions revealed the relative weakness of the enemy forces and Kutuzov, who was closely following the events, at one point even pondered counterattacking Murat.[44] However, this idea was quickly abandoned when Russian reconnaissance reports indicated a strong position near the town of Tarutino. 'This simple message caused Kutuzov to order the withdrawal to resume, which greatly upset Bennigsen,' observed one of Kutuzov's orderlies.[45]

Over the next few days the Russian army slowly retreated to Tarutino, where it arrived on 2–3 October and took up a new position; entrenchments were immediately put in hand to protect it. Meanwhile, Miloradovich fought a series of rearguard actions at Chirikovo and Voronovo,[46] where Rostopchin had already set on fire his magnificent estate, and retreated to Spas Kuplya, 10 miles north of Tarutino. The 4th and 7th Corps were drawn back towards the main army, covered by the 8th and most of the cavalry. Early on 3 October Murat and Poniatowski marched on two separate roads from Voronovo and sought to flank Miloradovich near Spas Kuplya.[47] Brandt recalled that 'throughout the whole of 3 October we continued our march hard on the heels of the Russian rearguard'.[48] Despite Miloradovich's resistance,[49] Murat was able to capture Spas Kuplya on 4 October but the Russian 4th (Osterman-Tolstoy) and 7th (Rayevskii) Corps successfully crossed the Chernishnya river, half-way to Tarutino, and Miloradovich, protected by Korff's cavalry, held firm upon the river until night.[50] The 2nd, 3rd and 4th Cavalry Corps (the first two now amalgamated) and some Cossacks remained to observe the French north of the Nara. By then, Murat's offensive power had exhausted itself, and he halted, disposing the bulk of his force along the Chernishnya, with his outposts at the village of Vinkovo.[51]

The Tarutino Camp

Over the next two weeks the reorganization of the Russian army proceeded energetically at Tarutino. In the preceding three months of campaigning, especially the bloody battles at Ostrovno, Smolensk and Borodino, all the regiments had been grievously weakened, and some were practically destroyed. Kutuzov's immediate task, therefore, was to rebuild his army. Shattered units were either dissolved or sent back into the interior to reform. The veterans of the combined grenadier battalions were split up and distributed into new units, and recruits were then drafted in to bring the new units up to strength. To maintain each unit's cohesion and battle readiness, only recruits who had received some training were brought in. Since horsemen could not be trained as readily as infantry, the Russian cavalry received far fewer reinforcements and many of its regiments remained in a greatly reduced condition. The Russian artillery remained in admirable order, while the irregular cavalry, especially the Don Cossacks, saw the influx of dozens of new regiments. The Russian army at Tarutino experienced little or no privation as supplies of food were plentiful. Forage after a time grew scarce in the immediate neighbourhood but the horses remained in excellent condition. The only item in short supply was dry fuel, and to obtain it the villages within the Russian lines were almost entirely demolished.

The three weeks spent at Tarutino had naturally had a profound effect on the army. By late October the strength of the Russian army, which counted just 75,000 men upon its arrival at Tarutino,[52] had risen to 105,000 regulars, including 12,000 cavalry and nearly 20,000 Cossacks, with an artillery train of some 650 guns excellently appointed and horsed. The regular cavalry remained organized in four corps: Lieutenant General Prince Golitsyn I received the command of the Cuirassier Corps, while the 1st and 3rd Cavalry Corps were given to Major Generals Baron Muller Zakomelski and Vassilchikov respectively. Baron Korff continued to command the 2nd, which was increased to eight regiments of dragoons, and one or two of light cavalry. The various army corps still retained their old leaders, except the 3rd, which was now commanded by General Stroganov. At the same time some changes were made in the higher command. On 24 September Prince Peter Bagration, grievously injured at Borodino, had passed away. Four days later Kutuzov announced the merger of the 1st and 2nd Western Armies into a single army that was placed under the command of Barclay de Tolly.[53] However, after reaching Tarutino Barclay de Tolly, who had been deeply offended by the insulting attacks made upon him throughout July and August, and whose relations with some senior commanders were rather strained, departed from the army. Miloradovich practically took the place of Bagration, while General Tormasov, who had commanded the 3rd Army of Observation, was brought in to succeed Barclay. The Russian army was divided into an advanced guard led by Miloradovich, the *Corps de Bataille* under Tormasov, six flying columns and six irregular detachments.[54]

Throughout the first two weeks of October the two sides maintained an unofficial armistice. Senior officers from both sides frequently visited the outposts and each occasion became 'a battle of politeness between the French and Russian generals', as Tascher described it in his diary. The encounters between Murat and Miloradovich were particularly fascinating, for there never was a man better qualified to treat with the famously flamboyant Gascon than Miloradovich, whose manners, tone of voice and gestures branded him the 'Russian Murat'. The two met on more than one occasion and always sought to outdo the other. General Yermolov recalled, 'If it were possible to forget we were enemies, the meetings would have seemed like an entertainment at a local fair,' recalled one Russian general. 'Murat appeared either dressed in the Spanish fashion or in unbelievably ridiculous costumes, with a velvet hat and flashy pantaloons; Miloradovich – on a Cossack horse, with a whip in his hand, and three bright scarves, which did not match, wrapped around his neck and flapping in the winds. There was no third man like them in either army.'[55] On one occasion Murat asked Miloradovich 'to let his cavalry forage to the right and left of his camp without being disturbed'. 'Nay, would you wish,' replied Miloradovich, 'to deprive us of the pleasure of taking your finest cavaliers of France, comme des poules?' 'Oh then, I shall order due measures of precaution,' said Murat, 'and march foraging columns with infantry and artillery on their flanks.' 'That is what we desire,' replied Miloradovich. 'We are impatient for an encounter.' The following night and morning (8/9 October) the Russian outposts captured almost a hundred cuirassiers and carabiniers, prompting a gleeful Miloradovich to send a special notice of the capture to Murat.[56]

During these impromptu meetings the Russian officers were often pleasantly surprised by their opponents, and by their prognoses for the war and calls for peace. The Allied officers believed that it was only a matter of time before peace was signed, and some even thought that Franco-Russian forces would then embark on a joint expedition to India. 'We are expecting to leave soon,' noted Boniface de Castellane on 5 October. 'There is talk of going to India. We have such confidence that we do not reason as to the possibility of success of such an enterprise … We are accustomed to the infallibility of the emperor and of the success of his projects.'[57] To escape the harsh reality, young Sergeant-Major Thirion of the 2nd Cuirassiers and his comrades dreamt of

> taking up winter quarters in the Ukraine … In the spring the Russian and French armies would march together to conquer Turkey. Each of us already saw himself a *pasha*. We made it a duty in advance to restore their liberty to numerous victims shut up in harems. Instead of being herded together waiting for their despotic shepherd to select a favourite, it would be they who would toss a handkerchief amid our squadrons. Each of us wanted to bring a beautiful slave back to France. One fancied a Greek, another a Circassian, still others a Georgian, and some pined for a daughter of the Caucasus. Our discussions of the beauty of our future slaves and the chateaus in Turkey helped us to pass a very dreary, very painful time in this camp we had named the 'Camp of Famine', a title it merited all too well since we lacked for everything. No tents, no shelter, simply sleeping under the open sky on a little straw, eating horseflesh, drinking river water from the infected stream.[58]

On at least one occasion Marshal Murat himself expressed the desire to see the war ended, and similar sentiments were expressed by other French generals as well. During one meeting General Armande La Houssaye (of the 3rd Reserve Cavalry Corps) told General Korf, 'We are really tired of this war: give us passports and we will depart.' Korf answered, 'General, you came without being invited; when you go away you must take French leave.' La Houssaye smiled but replied gravely, 'Is it not a pity that two nations who esteem each other should be carrying on a war of extermination? We will make our excuses, our apologies if you insist, for having been intruders, and shake hands upon our respective frontiers.' 'Yes,' said Korf, 'we believe you have lately learned to think us more worthy of your esteem than you did; but would you, General, continue to do so if we let you withdraw with arms in your hands?' 'Parbleu!' sighed the French general. 'I see that there is no talking to you about peace now, and that we shall not be able to make it.'[59]

Such conversations only motivated the Russians to fight on. 'That the enemy is in dire circumstances is revealed by the fact that the French are begging for peace, undoubtedly offering us every potential advantage,' wrote one Russian officer. 'During our various negotiations at the advance outposts the French generals and Murat, the King of Naples, tell us directly that they do not wish anything as much as peace to end the war. One of them even told us, "Just give us a pass and we will get out of here at once, leaving everything as it was before and accepting peace." He would not have dared to speak about this if this were not what Napoleon desired as well.'[60] Johann Friedrich von Uxküll noted in his diary that 'an armistice is being discussed; that would be bitter. Our motto must be either exterminate them or perish, for the enemy is a Hydra that sooner or later will be reborn if a single head is left.'[61]

The relative tranquillity of the front line could be deceptive. Russian flying detachments and Cossacks constantly prowled the countryside in search of isolated Allied troops or patrols. The official Journal of Military Operations reveals that dozens of Allied soldiers were captured and delivered to the Russian camp on a daily basis.[62] 'We hold a position that is, by nature, advantageous and has been reinforced so much that the enemy will not dare to attack us and disrupt the peaceful stay which is necessary to prepare the newly arrived troops,' wrote one officer in mid-October. 'Meanwhile, our detachments constantly harass the enemy, targeting all roads connecting Moscow to the provinces … and delivering hundreds of prisoners every day. If one counts losses inflicted by our detachments and peasants, the enemy's daily casualties can be estimated at more than 500 men per day.'[63]

The Battle of Tarutino (Vinkovo), 18 October

The Russians would have had to be blind not to see the growing weakness of the enemy force in front of them. Murat's position was so poor as to tempt even the most cautious enemy commander to attack and, after some vacillation, Kutuzov finally gave in to the energetic representations of his senior officers, in particular Colonel Karl Toll, who had spent several days carefully examining the enemy positions, which he found weak and exposed. The Allied left flank was anchored on a wood that was not sufficiently well protected or patrolled. The Allies seem to have been convinced that peace would soon be declared and security was thus lax. The front line stretched from the confluence of the Chernishnya river with the Nara to the hamlet of Teterinka, some 5 miles to the west, and about 4 miles south of Spas-Kuplya. Vinkovo, which lay south of the Chernishnya, was occupied by Claparede's Poles, supported by the 3rd Cavalry Corps (under General St Germain) and a division of the 1st Corps. To the left rear of Vinkovo lay Dufour's division, with the rest of Nansouty's cavalry corps on its left. Even further to the south of the Chernishnya stood Poniatowski's 5th Corps, with Sebastiani's cavalry on the extreme left. Latour-Maubourg was observing the Nara on the right rear.

Murat's forces amounted to some 26,000 men, encumbered rather than supported by 187 horsed guns. The troops were in a wretched state. They were mostly camped out in the open fields, with no shelter to protect them from the wind, rain and cold. The autumn days were becoming colder and there were frosts at night. The shortage of forage and food had a ruinous effect on the troops, who could neither travel regularly to Moscow for provisions nor forage freely in the vicinity. The once resplendent cavalry thus comprised between 7,000 and 8,000 fatigued and malnourished horsemen. Visiting the 11th Hussars, Captain Biot, aide-de-camp to the wounded General Pajol, was stunned to see 'men and horses dying of hunger. Literally. They never received any distributions.'[64] Some squadrons were down to two dozen troopers, while some regiments had fewer than a hundred men. Lieutenant Mailly-Nesle, who had just joined his 2nd Carabiniers Regiment, was shocked to find that it had lost so many men that 'we were no more than 100 men in the two carabinier regiments all told. We had left France 1,400 strong and several detachments had joined us later.' Many units lacked basic essentials and had been eating only unground rye and horseflesh: Kutuzov's sullen promise to make 'the French eat horseflesh' was now being fulfilled.[65] Almost every day Colonel Griois and his companion Jumilhac had to fend off desperate soldiers who wanted to dismantle their timber cottage for firewood.[66] The condition of the horses was even more dreadful. According to Lieutenant Henryk Dembinski, the horses were so malnourished that 'even though we had folded blankets to the thickness of sixteen, their backs had rotted through completely, so much so that the rot had eaten through the saddlecloth, with the result that when a trooper dismounted, you could see the horse's entrails'.[67] Murat was aware of these difficulties and tried to inform Napoleon of the critical condition of the cavalry. 'My position is atrocious. I have the whole enemy army in front of me. Our advanced guard is reduced to nothing. It is starving, and it is no longer possible to go foraging without the virtual certainty of capture. Not a day passes without me losing two hundred men in this way.'[68] But the emperor, probably influenced by the splendid parades at the Kremlin, dismissed such warnings.[69] 'My army is finer than ever,' he told Murat's aide-de-camp. 'A few days of rest have done it the greatest good.'[70]

After examining the terrain, Toll proposed a way for the Russian army to score a decisive victory at Vinkovo: part of the army would make an attack against Murat's extended front, while Bennigsen, with a force composed of the bulk of the army, turned his left flank. There was a bottleneck just 6 miles behind the Allied front line at Vinkovo, where the old Kaluga road ran through a narrow defile between two forests. The two-pronged attack would overwhelm the enemy, cut the only road along which Murat's men could withdraw, and result in encirclement and a decisive victory. Most of the Russian generals agreed with Toll and emphatically supported his plan of attack, forcing Kutuzov to yield.

The attack was planned for 17 October but staff mismanagement forced a day's postponement. At dawn on 18 October the Russians advanced in multiple columns, surprising the enemy and scoring a quick success.[71] The Russian cavalry on the right swept away Sebastiani's horsemen, captured most of the baggage and artillery, and pushed on towards Spas-Kuplya, where they cut Murat's line of retreat. This development would have been critical had the Russian cavalry been supported by infantry. But poor staff work once again intervened. Only one Russian column advanced on time and, as the rest got delayed, the attack soon became disjointed. The second column, consisting of General Baggovut's 2nd Corps, arrived late and suffered the misfortune of losing its commander in the very first minutes of the fight. Murat's bold charge contained its advance, while the third and fourth Russian columns failed to advance with the necessary speed and acted indecisively. The result was that the entire Allied advanced guard, though in great disorder and suffering considerably from Russian artillery fire, succeeded in evading the Russian envelopment and effected a retreat through Spas-Kuplya, which the Russian cavalry was obliged to abandon. Murat retreated to Voronovo, where he rallied his shaken troops, while the Russian forces returned to Tarutino. The Allies lost some 2,800 men, of whom 1,150 were prisoners or missing; two generals were killed and two more wounded. The Russian losses amounted to 1,500 killed and wounded but they captured thirty-eight cannon, a standard and the bulk of the enemy baggage.[72]

The Russian success at Vinkovo, incomplete as it was, none the less dealt a heavy blow to Murat's advanced guard, further damaging the already shaken morale of the Grande Armée; it also had a significant effect on the strategic situation. This action was the last straw that forced Napoleon to finalize his plans. It was now clear that, niceties aside, there would be no peace with Russia and it was time to think of the future.

The Departure From Moscow

The news of the battle of Tarutino/Vinkovo startled Napoleon, who 'without being frightened, was none the less very agitated'; he finished his review of the 3rd Corps, distributed promotions and awards and then returned to his rooms where he instantly began to issue a series of orders to prepare the Grande Armée for the resumption of hostilities. 'He kept opening the door to the room where those on duty waited, calling now for one person, now for another, and he put so much urgency into all his ideas and plans that I believe that the fatal consequences of his long stay in Moscow were suddenly revealed to him on that day,' wrote Bausset.[73]

Napoleon needed this jolt – it made him rediscover 'the fire of his earliest years', as Ségur aptly observed. 'A thousand general and detailed orders, all different, all concording, all necessary, gushed all of a sudden from his impetuous genius!' Among the first to receive his orders were Marshals Davout, Ney and Lefebvre, who were instructed to start redeploying their forces to the Kaluga road at once and to be prepared to leave tomorrow at daybreak for 'a hard day's marching'.[74] The insult to French arms had to be avenged[75] and Napoleon decided to set out with the army in pursuit of the Russians, leaving Mortier with about 10,000 men[76] to take up his quarters at the Kremlin and 'remain in the city, and defend the Kremlin under all circumstances'.[77] Mortier was to fortify and mine the Kremlin and 'keep a strong force at the nearby monastery' that had previously been occupied by Davout. Once the army departed, Napoleon wanted Mortier to 'issue a proclamation, through the municipality, warning the inhabitants that the rumours of evacuation are false, that the army is advancing on Kaluga, Tula and Bryansk to take possession of these important places, and the arms factories they contain; and to engage the inhabitants to maintain public order and prevent anyone from trying to complete the destruction of the town'. Mortier was told 'to keep up tight policing' and to 'shoot every Russian soldier found in the streets, and give orders to all those who are in the hospitals not to leave them'.[78] Napoleon urged the marshal to evacuate and save as many wounded and sick soldiers as possible.[79]

That Napoleon did not intend to abandon Moscow completely is made plain by his instructions to Mortier, and in a letter to La Riboisière he acknowledged that 'it is possible I may return to Moscow: therefore, nothing of value – such as gunpowder, musket and cannon cartridges, lead to make balls – must be destroyed'.[80] However, just in case circumstances turned differently, Napoleon wanted a number of artillery officers to stay behind at the Kremlin and be 'responsible for blowing up the Kremlin, when it will be time'.[81] Deep in his heart, Napoleon must have known that returning to Moscow would be pointless. Now that the army was on the move, he needed to press on. He planned to move his forces to the western provinces of Russia, where supplies and magazines had already been prepared. 'We are going to withdraw to the frontiers of Poland by the Kaluga road,' he told his trusted aide Jean Rapp. 'I shall take good winter quarters and hope that [Emperor] Alexander will make peace.' For him, it was a strategic withdrawal, not a retreat – a point he tried to reinforce in his memoirs dictated at St Helena.[82] The route from Moscow to Smolensk, via Gzhatsk, was still devastated after the Allied forces had fought their way along it to the Russian capital between July and September. Therefore Napoleon decided to advance by the Kaluga route, towards the intact southwestern regions, before veering north.

The news of the impending departure caused an indescribable commotion in the city. As soldiers and officers began making last-minute preparations, many Muscovites were confronted with the dilemma of whether to leave or to stay. Some had compromised themselves 'by their trust in Napoleon's fortune', in the words of Chevalier d'Ysarn, but many more, especially foreigners, were simply seized with panic and feared retribution once the Russians reclaimed the city. In these chaotic few hours they had little time for reflection and most simply rushed to grab as much as they could before departing. The city's streets turned into bustling markets as small traders sought to profit from the confusion and snapped up anything the Allied troops could not carry off with them.

After spending just over a month in Moscow, Napoleon finally departed from the city on 19 October 1812.[83] The vanguard, commanded by Eugène, Ney's 3rd Corps and Davout's 1st Corps left at dawn and were followed by the Old and Young Guard and the remnants of the cavalry. Late in the day Napoleon himself left the city that he had entered in all its splendour – and now left a mass of smoking ruins. His forces amounted to about 115,000 men,[84] who were overall in relatively good condition and many 'marched along gaily, singing at the tops of their voices'.[85] Observing the troops marching out of Moscow, Captain François Dumonceau was particularly impressed by the Italians, who had 'a fine martial look. It was evident that they had recovered well from their previous exertions. The soldiers appeared to be joyous and ready for anything.'[86] In contrast, the Allied cavalry had suffered great losses in horses and was just a shadow of its former self. Several thousand troopers, formed into a dismounted unit, were issued carbines and ordered to fight as infantry, a role they greatly disliked. 'The worst infantry regiment is more effective than four regiments of dismounted cavalry,' lamented Castellane. 'They bleat like donkeys that they were not made for this work.'[87] Unfortunately, neither Napoleon nor any of his marshals, not even the meticulous Davout, took measures to prepare the troops fully for the rigours of the Russian winter.[88] They probably assumed that there was still enough time to reach their winter quarters before the onset of freezing temperatures. Smolensk, with its supply magazine, was only ten or twelve days' march from Moscow, and the great depots at Vilna and Minsk were only another two weeks of marching from there. Bausset noted that on Napoleon's orders 'Russian almanacs for the past forty years had been reviewed' to see temperature averages and 'it was agreed that the coldest weather appeared around the first day of December'.[89] This information probably led many into complacency, believing that the Grande Armée, departing on 19 October, had more than thirty days before the winter arrived. A few individual officers were clever enough to prepare themselves for the winter by buying winter clothing and obtaining sufficient supplies and horses, but the army remained woefully unprepared for the cold. This was especially true of the remaining cavalry and horse artillery. Accustomed to a northern climate, the Polish troops prepared for the march by setting up their forges and shoeing their horses. They urged their Allied comrades-in-arms to do likewise but few listened to them. 'The stubbornness and arrogance of the French, who felt that having been through so many wars they knew better than everyone else and did not need their advice, did not allow them to sharp-shoe their horses,' grumbled Jozef Grabowski.[90]

The Allied army was, however, burdened with an enormous transport train, which, depending on sources, is estimated to have included between 15,000 and 40,000 wagons.'The first big mistake [of the retreat] was made as early as the gates of Moscow,' lamented one Dutch officer. 'It had been generally accepted that people could bring along all that had been plundered.'[91] Yet during their month's sojourn in Moscow soldiers and officers had accumulated booty, which they hoped would make their fortune back home. Philippe de Ségur likened the departing Grande Armée to 'a Tartar horde after a felicitous invasion', while Dominique Larrey suggested that the treasures carried off from Moscow by the Allied troops outdid all that the Persians seized in ancient Babylon. 'Many generals who until then had contented themselves with only one carriage,' explained Chambray, 'now left with several, while a large number of officers who had not had any on reaching Moscow had procured some for themselves.'[92] These were transports of all shapes and forms: 'Charabancs, drozhkies wurts, calèches, kibitkas, contending with each other in elegance and speed, covered the road, overflowed everywhere and inundated the plain,' described an eyewitness.[93] In every battalion and regiment soldiers and officers sought to protect themselves against the rigours of a winter campaign by procuring furs or woollen clothing and amassing as much wine and strong liquor as possible. The officers, having helped themselves to any carriages they could find, naturally had more space to transport provisions and loot. The newly promoted Major Pion des Loches explained, 'As a captain I had had one wagon for myself and my lieutenant, half filled with my troops' effects. Now that I was a major I had a wagon to myself, smaller it is true, but sufficient for my victuals for a retreat of three to four months: a hundred cakes of biscuit a foot in diameter, a sack holding a quintal of flour, more than 300 bottles of wine, 20–30 bottles of rum and brandy, more than 10 pounds of tea, and as much again of coffee, 50–60 pounds of sugar, 3–4 pounds of chocolate, some pounds of candles.' In addition, Pion des Loches also had a stack of books and a few furs.[94] Even the less well-off Captain Louis Bro of the Guard *Chasseurs à Cheval* was able to procure two horses to carry his possessions. 'I bought two little Cossack horses used to surviving off straw and the branches of pine trees,' Bro wrote. 'They carried my personal effects and 100 kilograms of reserve victuals, principally chocolate and eau-de-vie … I also furnished myself with a fur-lined cloak, a fox fur, a fur-lined cap, felt boots and resin bricks that would allow me to light a fire at any moment.'[95] The Imperial Guard was no better than the rest of the army, and many followed the example of Sergeant Bourgogne of the Young Guard, whose knapsack contained several pounds of sugar, rice and dry biscuits, as well as half a bottle of liquor, a Chinese silk embroidered dress, two silver-framed paintings, several medallions, a diamond-studded decoration, a lady's riding coat and his dress uniform. He carried additional silver and porcelain items in a large bag slung over his shoulder.[96] Soldiers groaned under their heavy knapsacks but refused to part with their precious possessions, preferring rather to throw out parts of their uniform, cartridges and musket-cleaning equipment instead. In some cases, soldiers even impressed unfortunate Russian peasants to carry their loot for them or to push barrows piled with booty. 'Anyone who did not see the French army leave Moscow,' observed Pierre-Armand Barrau, lamenting the state of the army, 'can only have a very weak impression of what the armies of Greece and Rome must have looked like when they marched back from Troy and Carthage.'[97]

Aside from the personal possessions of officers and soldiers, there were also hundreds of wagons belonging to non-combatants and hundreds of cannon and caissons. Napoleon, fearful that the Russians would treat any abandoned ordnance (even spiked guns) as trophies, insisted on withdrawing all artillery pieces (over 600 in total) with hundreds of caissons.[98] In addition, the emperor did his best to evacuate the remaining wounded and sick soldiers from Moscow. He told Mortier that he could not stress enough how important it was 'to place the men who remain in the hospitals, on the wagons of the Young Guard, on those of the dismounted cavalry, and upon all he can find. For as the Romans gave civic crowns to those who saved their fellow citizens, [Mortier] will merit one if he shall save soldiers.' Mortier was instructed to mount the wounded and sick upon his own horses, and those of all his officers – 'It was thus the emperor acted at St Jean d'Acre [in 1799] and [Mortier] ought to adopt this measure as well.'[99]

Traffic on this scale not only slowed the army's movements but also distracted the troops, many of whom were more concerned about securing their portion of booty than maintaining discipline and battle readiness. As Colonel Griois summed up: 'This mass of men, of horses and of vehicles resembled rather the migration of a people on the move than an organized army.'[100] This 'was no longer the Grande Armée of Napoleon', thought one cavalry officer, but rather that of Darius returning from a far-flung expedition, more lucrative than glorious'.[101] Sergeant Bourgogne has left us a vivid description of this chaotic departure from Moscow:

> We found ourselves amongst a great number of carts and wagons, driven by men of every nationality, three or four in a line, and stretching for the length of a league. We heard all round us French, German, Spanish, Italian, Portuguese and other languages also, for there were Muscovite peasants among them, and a great number of Jews. This crowd of people, with their varied costumes and languages, the canteen masters with their wives and crying children, hurried forward in the most unheard-of noise, tumult and disorder. Some had got their carts all smashed, and in consequence yelled and swore enough to drive one mad.[102]

'It was ridiculous to see what was being taken,' recalled one participant. 'Couches, armchairs, mirrors, etc. In a word, everything was being hauled along ... This slowed the army's march and during that first day we only made four hours of progress.'[103] The army, burdened with its vast train and stragglers, struggled along roads cluttered with carriages, people and animals, with gridlock setting in whenever streams and gorges were encountered. Many carriages struggled to advance over the sandy terrain, frequently either getting stuck, losing a wheel or breaking an axle. And to make matters worse, heavy rains on 22 October turned the roads into rivers of mud. More and more vehicles were abandoned by the side of the road while the army's line of march grew longer and longer as stragglers failed to keep up.

A detailed study of the Grande Armée's retreat through the snowy expanse of Russia is beyond the remit of this book, but suffice it to say that Napoleon's attempt to break through to Kaluga and the still intact southern provinces was thwarted by the Russian army at Maloyaroslavets on 23–24 October. As a result, the Grande Armée was compelled to return to the old route to Smolensk, pursued by the Russian army that now had a unique chance of trapping it on the Berezina river. As Kutuzov pursued Napoleon from the east, Wittgenstein's 1st Corps converged from the northeast and Chichagov's Army of the Danube from the southwest. However, due to Russian indecision and mismanagement, as well as the skill and heroism of the Allied troops, Napoleon managed to extricate most of his army from the trap and get them across the Berezina. Nevertheless, by December the Grande Armée, suffering vast casualties from the weather, exhaustion and constant attacks, had in effect ceased to exist as an organized military force. On 5 December Napoleon put Murat in charge of the army and left for Paris. By the end of the month the last remnants of the Grande Armée crossed the Niemen river. The Russian campaign was over.

The Second Fire of Moscow

The day the enemy departed from Moscow was 'one of the most horrible' for the Muscovites, recalled one eyewitness. 'We took every possible precaution and no one even thought of sleep that night.' [104]

The term 'Moscow fire' is usually associated with the initial Allied occupation of the city on 14–18 September. But there was also another major conflagration in the city, this time deliberately caused by the retreating Grande Armée. These fires broke out for two main reasons. On the one hand, the Allies' departure from Moscow was not well coordinated or organized. Napoleon made his decision hurriedly and this accelerated departure compounded the work of quartermasters, who for weeks had been gathering supplies in accordance with imperial directives, only to be told to abandon them. Many units chose to destroy whatever victuals and possessions they could not take. Montesquiou-Fezensac, whose regiment lacked many basic provisions, was infuriated at the sight of another regiment setting fire to a store of flour and fodder because it had no means to transport them. By the evening of 18 October some monasteries in the suburbs were already burning. [105] The conflagration further intensified as the Allied troops began destroying the remaining ammunition and supplies in the city. Christian Christiani recalled that the departing enemy troops set fire to a large warehouse with spirits and then began burning other buildings as well. [106]

But there was also a more deliberate effort under way to destroy what was left of Moscow. On the 19th, before leaving Moscow, the emperor wrote to Maret that 'it has been decided to blow up the Kremlin'. Just one day after leaving Moscow Napoleon sent a remarkable set of instructions to his chief of staff. 'On the 22nd or 23rd,' he wrote, 'Marshal Mortier will arrange for setting fire to the warehouses containing spirits, the barracks, and to the public establishments, with the exception of the Foundlings Hospital. He must set fire to the palace of the Kremlin. He must take care to have the muskets broken in pieces, and powder placed under the towers of the Kremlin … Having accomplished these things, and when fire has been set to the Kremlin in several places, Marshal Mortier must leave it and take the road to Mojaisk… .' At the end of the letter

Napoleon again stressed that Mortier 'must take care to remain in Moscow until he has personally seen the Kremlin blow up'.[107]

Mortier remained in Moscow for the next four days, concentrating his troops in the Kremlin for protection against the encroaching Cossacks and the revitalizing animosity of the people. To mine the Kremlin his troops impressed many Muscovites to dig trenches and mine towers. 'The French took me there,' recalled a Russian eyewitness, 'and there were many other Russians forced to work there. The French made us dig under the walls of the Kremlin, under the cathedral and the palace, and they dug trenches themselves as well. We tried to resist – if everything was destined to perish, we would at least have no role in it. But, alas, it was not up to us to decide and, no matter how bitter it was, we had to dig. Those accursed [French] stood nearby and mercilessly beat with the butts of their muskets anyone whom they saw not working properly.'

Ordered to retreat in the evening of 22 October, Mortier complied with the imperial wish to see the Kremlin destroyed. Shortly after midnight on 23 October he gave the order to light the fuses.[108] 'Around half past one we saw fire in the Kremlin and ... part of the Kremlin blew up with a terrifying roar,' recalled an eyewitness. 'Four more explosions took place over the next hour.'[109] The powerful blasts shook the ground, causing frightened Muscovites to flee in all directions. Among them was Apollon Sysoev's family: 'beside themselves with fear', they stood in panic in the middle of the yard when another blast completely terrified them. 'We thought this was indeed the last moment of our lives and began to bid farewell to each other.'[110] Half-naked, injured by fragments of glass, stone and metal, many other Muscovites fled in terror into streets still shrouded in darkness as cold autumn rain drizzled down on them. 'Everyone one could hear screams, shrieks, groans ... Many called for help but there was no one to assist them. The Kremlin was ominously illuminated by flames. One explosion followed another and the earth itself was trembling. It looked like Judgement Day had come at last.'[111]

These explosions were powerful enough to inflict serious damage on the Kremlin complex and neighbouring buildings. They destroyed part of the arsenal, both belfries of the Ivan the Great Bell Tower, and the Nikolskaya, Borovitskaya, 1st Bezymyannaya and Petrovskaya Towers, while a stretch of the Kremlin wall completely collapsed; the corner Arsenalnaya Tower suffered extensive damage but remained standing. Fortunately for the Russians, the drizzling rain had dampened some of the fuses, while the actions of some quick-thinking Muscovites and the arrival of Russian troops prevented the majority of the planned explosions.[112] Thus the Spasskaya and Troitskaya Towers escaped unscathed, while the Kremlin Palace, the Facet Palace, the Senate and the Commandant's Quarters suffered limited damage.[113] It is indeed incredible that Napoleon, who just one month before had condemned the Russians for being 'vandals' and uncivilized 'Scythians', had now turned into one himself. Georges Chambray was correct when he observed that this act was 'not justified by any military consideration, and was nothing but an act of senseless revenge on the part of Napoleon, who was furious that he could not subdue Alexander to his will. Such an act could benefit only his enemies, fanning their hatred and further embittering the Russian people against the French, while prompting Alexander to conduct a war of extermination against the French army.'[114]

With the departure of the Grande Armée, Moscow was plunged into anarchy as once again the city's riff-raff sought enrichment. 'Instead of being excited by the departure of the enemy,' recalled one Muscovite, 'we were terrified by the explosions in the Kremlin and expected the worst.' At dawn numerous Muscovite poor and peasants came out into the streets to plunder and seek vengeance against the remaining enemy troops. 'We heard the shouts of peasants, armed with weapons that they had plundered in Moscow or captured from the French. These brigands immediately rushed to the [municipal] treasury building and plundered the remaining copper coins left there. They were joined by the city's rabble. But a different scene caused even greater indignation. At Petrovka a priest, with a sword in his hand, called upon the mob to loot the homes of foreigners.'[115] There are many eyewitness accounts describing the Russian rabble despoiling the city before Russian troops restored order. The foreigners, who had already endured the hardships of the past month, now became the targets of another wave of violence.[116] Major Gelman, who was among the first to reach the city, was astonished by the 'most terrible sight' of 'thousands of pillagers roaming the streets'.[117] Fedor Toll admitted that 'Moscow was devastated not just by the French but also by peasants from nearby villages, servants and other rabble; getting drunk, they all plundered the houses that survived the fires. All around Moscow villages are filled with stolen items and furniture.'[118] A. Shakhovskii described how the Moscow peasants, who 'are among the shrewdest and most perceptive but also the most depraved and ravenous peasants in all of Russia', sought to exploit the moment to enrich themselves and 'once they ascertained that the enemy had departed, they rushed on carts to the city to seize what had been left behind'.[119] The pillaging only further intensified with the appearance of the Cossacks, who were the first to enter the city and used the opportunity to pillage it. They made no distinction between fellow Russians or foreigners, robbing both mercilessly; at the Foundlings Home, which had been converted into a hospital, these marauders robbed both the French wounded and the Russian officials living in the building.[120] At other hospitals the Allied and Russian wounded and service personnel joined the efforts to protect their institutions from marauders.[121]

The first regular Russian troops, from Ferdinand Wintzingerode's detachment,[122] entered the city at noon on 23 October. 'This ancient capital was still smouldering,' recalled Alexander Benckendorf, who led these men. 'We could barely find our way through the bodies of men and beasts, the debris and the ashes that obstructed all the streets. The churches, pillaged and blackened by smoke, served as gloomy markers for finding one's bearings amidst the immense devastation.'[123] Benckendorf first led his troops to the Kremlin, where 'an enormous crowd was trying to get inside'. The appearance of the Guard Cossack Regiment forced the mob back and the troops formed a perimeter around the Kremlin. Entering the great Uspenskii Cathedral, officers were 'seized with horror at seeing this revered church, which even the flames had spared, desecrated by the unrestrained soldiery … The relics of the saints were defaced, their tombs filled up with filth, the ornaments of the tombs were pulled off, the images which decorated the cathedral were defiled, torn up … the altar was thrown down, casks of wine had flooded these sacred floors and the bodies of men and horses tainted these vaults.' Benckendorf and his officers agreed that, because of the state it was in, the cathedral must be hidden from the eyes of the people. So the cathedral doors were sealed and a large patrol deployed to guard the place.

Noticing the vast building of the Foundlings Home, Benckendorf hastened to see the fate of its orphans, only to discover that several hundred children and a quantity of women and Russian wounded had shared their meagre residences with hundreds of Allied sick and wounded who had been abandoned by the Grande Armée.[124] 'All asked for bread, but the devastation in and around Moscow did not allow me to provide immediately for a need so pressing. The hallways and the courtyard of this enormous building were filled with dead, the victims of destitution, sickness and terror.'[125]

Despite securing the Kremlin, the Russian detachment was not large enough to safeguard the rest of the city and mobs of peasants and urban riff-raff continued their rampaging for the next few days. 'Lost in the vastness of Moscow, my detachment could barely contain the rabble armed with weapons it had seized from the enemy,' Benckendorf later recalled. In the first two days his men arrested more than 200 people who had been robbing, looting and igniting fires throughout the city. Benckendorf responded with harsh measures, shooting criminals if they resisted and holding the general public responsible for any damage done to their property. 'He ordered the inhabitants of houses to protect them day and night, and warned them that if their houses caught fire or were robbed, they would be held accountable as criminals.'[126] Such measures seem to have had some effect in restoring a semblance of order in the city and the process only accelerated with the arrival of further reinforcements, including the Moscow Police, led by Ivashkin, on 28 October.[127]

Rostopchin was still in Vladimir when he received the good news of the liberation of Moscow. He returned to the city on 5 November and was stunned by the 'horrifying sight' it presented. 'I fear, Your Majesty,' he wrote gloomily to Emperor Alexander, 'that Moscow will never rise up again. Nobles may not return because they no longer have their social order, while merchants may not find sufficient profit here. Besides, they would be concerned that Bonaparte might return the following year, especially if he is allowed to winter in Vilna.'[128] Settling in his governor's palace, which had survived intact despite Napoleon's orders to blow it up, Rostopchin began feverishly working on reviving the city. It was an enormous task: the brigandage had to be ended, order fully restored and criminals as well as those who had collaborated with the enemy detained and punished. The city was in ruins and littered with numerous corpses that had to be disposed of as soon as possible to prevent the spread of pestilence. Thousands of Muscovites were homeless and required sustenance, as did the numerous Russian and Allied wounded and sick, who cluttered up the few surviving hospitals. The winter of 1813 proved to be rather cold for people huddled amidst the ruins of the burned city. Broken street lights and long winter nights kept many in the literal darkness and Dmitri Zavalishin recalled that in much of Moscow 'there was no glimmer from even the smallest flame'. Life in the ruined city was quite dangerous, recalled Anna Khomutova: 'we did not hear the rumble of carriages or for that matter, any noise at all. It was the silence of a burial vault. In the evenings, all of a sudden, a pistol shot would ring out, but no one knew if it was an accident or a crime.'[129]

Over the next months, as Russia continued to fight Napoleon on the battlefields of Germany and France, the Muscovites slowly cleared the ruins, repaired and replastered their surviving buildings, reopened markets and rebuilt shops and taverns. The Kremlin and its environs were carefully inspected and cleared of any remaining mines.[130] The wounded were moved from their shelters to a handful of military hospitals and provided with care and sustenance.[131] Soon there was a general return of Muscovite refugees, who flooded the governor's office with countless claims for lost property.[132]

'There is no end to the complaints on stolen items,' the governor wrote in mid-November. 'Those who are in possession of these items claim right of possession because they argue that the city was under the control of the French, who had the authority to give whatever they wanted to whoever they liked.'[133] Already overwhelmed by numerous urgent problems, Rostopchin now faced growing criticism of his leadership. Instead of hailing him as a hero, as Rostopchin had expected, Muscovite landowners and proprietors held him responsible for the destruction of their property. In 1815, while travelling in Germany, Rostopchin lamented the fact that 'in German lands, they show me all the marks of esteem and consideration', while the Muscovite society poured scorn on him. 'Back home everyone talks about their burned houses and property but no one thinks beyond that.'[134] The most pressing issue was clearing the city of the thousands of decomposing carcasses that might cause outbreaks of disease. Thus, Ivan Tutolmin described how at the Foundlings Home between twenty and fifty men died every day and had to be buried in shallow graves next to the building. He estimated that some 1,500 men were buried around the Foundlings Home, but other witnesses claimed the figure was as high as 2,500.[135] Thousands of putrid horse carcasses lay throughout the city.[136] Over the next five months the Muscovites, supported by three battalions of the Moscow garrison and the militiamen of the Vladimir and Tver *opolchenyes*,[137] scoured every building, street and garden looking for corpses. 'We burn 200 to 300 human bodies and 100 horse carcasses every day,' reported Rostopchin in December.[138] By April city officials could report that 11,955 human bodies and 12,360 animal carcasses had been removed and burned.[139] An eyewitness recalled how 'rotting horse and human corpses lay everywhere. The police were trying to get rid of them long after the enemy was gone. These corpses were piled in enormous heaps and burnt on the banks of the [Moscow] river or in the fields beyond the city barriers. I once saw a pile of human corpses near the Lefortovo barrier and decided to approach it to get a better view. The sight terrified me so much that I could not eat meat for almost a month.'[140]

At the same time Rostopchin faced another urgent issue. Thousands of commoners had acquired weapons as the result of the events in Moscow and it was paramount to have them disarmed. This proved to be a long and arduous process that lasted for over two years.[141] All Muscovites who remained in the city during the occupation were placed on special rosters and supervised by the police. Those who collaborated with the enemy began to be arrested almost immediately after the city was liberated and dozens of them were detained by 30 October.[142] These individuals were then investigated by a special commission of inquiry that was established on 21 November. This commission, whose task was to 'look into the affairs of employees and persons of all classes having held employment under the enemy', investigated numerous suspected cases for the next three months. It ultimately charged 103 individuals (six of them members of the Smolensk municipality) with collaborating with the enemy and, dividing them into five categories depending on the severity of the charges, transferred their cases to the imperial Senate for final judgment. The Senate finished its work by the summer of 1814. Foreigners accused of collaborating with the enemy were expelled from the realm. Naturalized foreigners and Russian subjects received punishments of varying severity, ranging from whipping and denial of state employment to loss of property and hard labour in Siberia. However, in nearly all cases these sentences were not carried out: on 11 September 1814 Alexander pardoned all except two of the condemned[143] to celebrate the re-establishment of peace in Europe.

That same day the emperor also signed a decree dismissing Rostopchin from his post as governor of Moscow. By then, Russian public opinion, especially in Moscow, had begun to look for explanations for what had transpired in Moscow and soon found its scapegoat in the governor. After all, it was Rostopchin who had assured everyone that Moscow would not be abandoned, and ridiculed those who chose to leave the city; many now held him solely responsible for the fire. In the face of public anger and mistrust, Rostopchin tried to find support in St Petersburg, but society turned away from him. 'It is difficult to get used to the fact that you are well treated when you are needed and cast aside and called a wild beast when the danger has passed,' he lamented in November 1812.[144] After his dismissal from the governorship, Rostopchin became a member of the State Council, a largely honorary function that gave him plenty of free time to tend to his family and pursue other interests.[145] 'I wash my hands of Moscow and everything else,' he told his wife in the wake of his discharge.[146] In the autumn of 1814 Rostopchin decided to travel abroad to improve his health and was surprised by his enthusiastic reception in the salons of Berlin, Paris and London, where he was hailed as a hero and as a man who had contributed to the fall of the despised Corsican ogre. He stayed abroad for almost a decade, returning home only in 1823. Settling back in his estate in Moscow, he watched cheerfully as the city rose from the ashes. The death of his beloved daughter Elizabeth in March 1825 had a profound impact on him, and his already weakened health never recovered from this blow. He died on 30 January 1826 and was buried at the Pyatnitskoe cemetery.

Rising From the Ashes

The Russian campaign had disastrous consequences for Napoleon. The loss of up to half a million men in Russia shattered his military might. The French cavalry was virtually wiped out and never fully recovered during the subsequent campaigns in 1813–1814. More importantly, Austria and Prussia exploited the moment to break their alliance with France and turned their efforts to destroying the French empire, which was accomplished in 1815. The war, of course, had important effects on Russia. The Russian army became the main force in the subsequent struggle for Germany, adding tremendous clout to Russia in European affairs so that by 1815 Emperor Alexander had become one of the arbiters of European affairs. The war also deeply influenced cultural and social life in Russia. It launched a period of national self-definition when the century-long identity crisis since Peter the Great began to resolve into a sense of Russia's place and purpose in the world.

For Moscow, the war meant a disaster of unparalleled severity, as no European city of comparable size had suffered such devastation in generations before or after the event. Yet, the calamitous conflagration in 1812 precipitated a momentous urban rebuilding programme that turned Moscow into one of Europe's foremost classical cities. During the half-century before 1812 Russia had been actively adopting the new classical architectural style as the newly emancipated nobility embarked on extensive constructions of estate houses in town and country. These new constructions reflected the growing sense of the 'golden age of the nobility,' and the government's own planning enterprises only further underscored this appreciation of the new style. The rebuilding of St Petersburg with its grandiose ensembles is quite well known but Catherine II, the mastermind behind many of these efforts, also sought to rebuilt Moscow, which by the time of her accession still retained its medieval character. Catherine had a distaste for the city[147] and was keen on changing it. By 1775 the Commission for Building of St Petersburg and Moscow had developed a plan of rebuilding for Moscow which Catherine supported and sought to carry out. As discussed in chapter 2, this Project Plan of 1775[148] was the most important of numerous plans for Moscow developed in the late eighteenth century. It intended to revitalize the city by razing numerous buildings to make way for the construction of vast squares and public buildings. In the Belyi Gorod alone, the plan called for the demolition of ancient fortifications and densely packed housing and their replacement with a semicircular chain of squares embracing the Kremlin and Kitai-gorod. New canals would revitalize smaller rivers, such the Neglinnaya, which served largely as rubbish dumps, by pumping more water through them, improving their appearance and enhancing the buildings and squares built along their banks. The 1775 Plan was only partly implemented in the 1780s and early 1790s but, despite its shortcomings, it still had a profound impact on the central parts of the city. The Soviet historian S. Zombe described it as 'one of the most interesting examples' of municipal planning, and remarked that it was outstanding for 'its great comprehension of realistic ideas over abstractions'. Indeed, as the result of these rebuilding efforts an ordered and classical central Moscow had emerged in the midst of the ancient, and rather dilapidated, city on the eve of 1812. The great radial thoroughfares – the Prechistenka, Great Nikitskaya and Tverskaya – cutting through the city were a good example of the dichotomy between old and new.

The Great Fire of 1812 was a turning-point in Moscow's history. The fiery destruction of almost the entire city offered a remarkable opportunity for the city to be rebuilt in a better and grander style. To the Russian authorities there were three aspects to the restoration. First, housing had to be provided for the returning residents. At the same time a long-term plan for the new city had to be developed and implemented. Finally, this rebuilding had to incorporate monumental architecture to fulfil the new aesthetic objectives that Russia had embraced in the wake of its triumph over Napoleon. In May 1813 the Moscow Building Commission (*Komissiya dlya stroeniya v Moskve*) was established to supervise this mammoth undertaking.

Emperor Alexander selected the Scottish architect and planner William Hastie, who had already earned fame for his constructions in St Petersburg and Tsarskoe Selo, to lead the drafting of a plan for the new Moscow.[149] For Hastie, the fire offered opportunities unimagined by Moscow's architects before. He adopted the 1775 Plan as the basis of his own vision of the new Moscow but made several important revisions to it. Hastie's 1813 Plan focused on the districts surrounding the Kremlin that were almost completely gutted in the fire. He envisioned eliminating the trading stalls opposite the Kremlin, removing the earthen bastions of the Kitai-gorod and widening Red Square. In the Belyi Gorod Hastie adopted the earlier idea of a series of squares around Moscow's centre but also intended to build new radial thoroughfares. In the Zemlyanoi Gorod he called for the demolition of the remaining old structures and the elimination of the ancient crooked alleys and the construction in their place of linear streets and radial highways, with eleven major squares dispersed throughout the suburbs. Although Alexander liked the boldness of Hastie's vision, the plan met with strong objections from the building commission, which complained that it took little account of the natural or man-made environment, and many of his suggestions indicated rather a decorative than utilitarian purpose. The new plan, with its vast demolitions and constructions, also would have been excessively costly. The commission's detailed critique and its own suggestions for Moscow's development were delivered to St Petersburg in early 1814 when the Russian army, together with Emperor Alexander, was still fighting abroad. So it was not until 1816 that the new plan, which the commission continuously revised, was reviewed. At last the 'Project Plan for the Capital City of Moscow' was approved on 19 December 1817 and this served as the basis for restoring and renovating the city. The new plan downscaled Hastie's earlier proposals by eliminating the most dramatic proposals and focusing more on Moscow's immediate needs, but adhering to the city's natural and historic contours. It divided the city into four construction zones, each including several city districts, with each zone directed by a carefully chosen architect and his staff. A number of brick factories were placed at the commission's disposal and military labour battalions committed to assist the construction. One of the important elements in the plan was the construction of masonry dwellings that would both provide better accommodation and embrace the aesthetics of the classical style. The so-called 'model façade' programme involved developing design standards to which all new constructions had to adhere.

The reconstruction of central Moscow brought forth a new generation of talented architects, including Joseph (Osip) Bove, Domenico (Dementii) Giliardi and Afanasii Grigoriev, whose architectural visions transformed much of the city. Their work resulted in the removal of hundreds of trading stalls and the defence bastions of Peter I in the Kitai-gorod, while a number of streets were widened and de-cluttered. Bove was particularly instrumental in transforming Red Square into Moscow's most iconic sight: he filled in the Kremlin moat, demolished shops and constructed a new set of buildings in the classical style. In 1818 a bronze statue of Prince Dmitry Pozharsky and Kuzma Minin, who had played a prominent role in rallying Russian forces against the Poles during the Time of Troubles in the seventeenth century, was erected in front of St Basil's Cathedral on Red Square, symbolising the rise of patriotic consciousness during Russia's recent struggles as well. In the rest of the city numerous masonry and wooden houses were erected, all conforming to the 'façade model' guidelines, causing one British traveller to observe that 'there is something captivating in this display of Grecian and Palladian architecture intermingled among the old national structures'.[150] Most of Moscow's smaller rivers, including the Neglinnaya, were converted into underground channels. The Moscow river embankment was further improved in an effort to both exercise flood control and impose a new classical aesthetic. Along the Kremlin's west wall Bove created the 20-acre Alexander Gardens, which some visitors described as a 'magnificent ornament and an elegant promenade'.[151] The 1820s and 1830s saw the construction of the Boulevard and Garden (sadovoe) rings – derived from Moscow's historic encompassing ramparts – which became delightful garden areas with both modest and elegant dwellings. The city's aesthetics further benefited from the appearance of spacious squares at the intersections of major boulevards and radial streets. Work on Theatre Square was completed between 1817 and 1819, resulting in the creation of another of Moscow's iconic public squares, further embellished by the monumental edifice of the renowned Bolshoi Theatre, completed in 1825.

With the enemy defeated and expelled, many Muscovites embraced the sense of greater destiny that Heaven itself had chosen for Moscow. One of them proudly shared his feelings with a friend:

We are experiencing divine miracles that, one may say, Moscow has long been destined for. How many times did it burn? How many times has it been in the hands of the most fierce enemies? And yet there exists no power that can destroy Moscow, the city most beloved by Heaven, and nothing can extinguish the love that the Muscovites feel towards their beloved and ancient mother-city. Not even a Hades with millions of Napoleons is capable of accomplishing this. Just recently destroyed and devastated, Moscow is already the best city in Russia ... Thousands of axes are at work and buildings are built; devastated alleyways are once again rebuilt and streets are once more jammed with transports full of timber and building material. Numerous people are all around and one can hardly move about ... May dim-witted Europe see who she is dealing with![152]

Notes

Preface

1. Joseph Fiévée to Napoleon, October 1812, *Correspondance et Relations de J. Fiévée avec Bonaparte* (Paris, 1836), III, 239.
2. 'Proritsatel Abel,' in *Russkii arkhiv* 7 (1878), 353–365; 'Predskazatel monakh Abel,' in Russkaya starina (1875), 414–435; N.P. Rozanov, 'Predskazatel monakh Abel,' in *Russkaya starina* (1875), 815–819; L.N. Engelhardt, *Zapiski* (Moscow, 1867), 218.
3. A. Villemain, *Souvenirs contemporains d'Histoire et de Littérature* (Paris, 1854), I, 175–180.
4. On the eve of the war, the head of the French intelligence in the Duchy of Warsaw, discussing massive preparations for the war with Russia, wondered 'what would be a worthy reward for such a vast undertaking? What goal is sufficiently grandiose to justify these preparations?' For him, the answer was clear – the impending war with Russia ultimately aimed at India, for Russia would 'have to join, willingly or on the basis of the laws of victors, the greatest undertaking that would change the history of the world'. Many Russian participants, including Denis Davydov, Peter Chuikevich, Alexander Bulgakov and Pavel Grabbe, shared such beliefs, which were seemingly confirmed when, in 1813, the Russian police arrested French spies as far as Astrakhan, carrying draft map drawings of eastern Russian provinces that lay on routes to India. For an insightful discussion, see V. Bezotosnyi, *Razvedka i plany storon v 1812 godu* (Moscow, 2005), 80–85.
5. Buturlin, I, 306.
6. Barry Edward O'Meara, *Napoleon at St Helena* (New York, 1889), I, 177–178.
7. Mitarevskii, 88.
8. Méneval, III, 67–68.
9. Marchal to curé Thugnet, 25 September 1812, in *Lettres interceptées par les Russes durant la campagne de 1812*, 34; Peyrusse, *Mémorial*, 102–103.
10. For just a few examples of letters see Joseph Ficher to Roch, 25 September 1812; Baron Jean-Louis Charrière to Tostch, 27 September 1812; Corneille-Gérard-Iman Van Boecop to his father, 27 September 1812, in *Lettres interceptées par les Russes durant la campagne de 1812*, 36–37, 49.
11. Castellane, I, 154–155.
12. Paradis to Geneviève Bonnegrace, 20 September 1812; Pierre Besnard to his wife, 23 September 1812, in *Lettres interceptées par les Russes durant la campagne de 1812*, 22, 30.
13. Barries to his wife, 24 September in Ibid., 33.
14. Grandeau d'Abeacourt to Baron Joseph-Francois Noos, 27 September 1812, in Ibid., 39. On the other hand, there were also a number of Grande Armée troops who disagreed with the majority. Brandt, thus, noted that he did not 'hear the shots supposed, by many writers, to have been signals to the incendiaries to start fires'. Regarding the explosions that occurred on 14–15 September, he believed that 'there was no question of these explosions being anything other than accidents. They were in the wrong part of the city and the smoke was white, which is certainly not the case when houses are on fire.' Brandt, 229.
15. Labaume's *Relation Circonstanciés de la Campagne de Russie,* initially published in 1814, proved very popular in Europe. Within three years, it was released in multiple editions in French, Italian, German and Spanish. Chambray's two-volume *Histoire de l'Expédition de Russie* remains one of the most important early works on the Russian Campaign and it exercised great influence on subsequent French historiography of this subject.
16. Zemtsov, 96.
17. Caroline Pavlova, Vospominaniya, in *Russkhi arkhiv* 10 (1875), 224.
18. Rostopchin to Semen Vorontsov, 10 May 1813, in *Russkii arkhiv* 6 (1908), 274.
19. Sverbeev, I, 79.
20. Alexey Merzlyakov to Fedor Velyaminov-Zernov, 26 March 1813 in *Russkii arkhiv* 1 (1865), 112–113.
21. Emperor Alexander to Crown Prince Karl Johan (Bernadotte) of Sweden, 1 October 1812, in Mikhailovskii-Danilevskii (1843), II, 395–396.

22. 'Iz pravitelstvennogo soobsheniya o prebyvanii v Moskve Napoleonovskikh voisk', 29 October 1812, in *M.I. Kutuzov: Sbornik Dokumentov*, IV, part 2, 149–152.

23. *Moskovskie vedomosti*, 23 November 1812.

24. *Iz pravitelstvennogo soobsheniya o prebyvanii v Moskve Napoleonovskikh voisk*, in *M.I. Kutuzov: Sbornik Dokumentov*, IV, part 2, 150.

25. Vorontsov to Rostopchin, 19 June 1814, *Russkii arkhiv* (1872), 2188.

26. Joseph de Maistre to King Victor Emmanuel I of Sardinia, 14 June 1813, in *Russkii arkhiv* 1 (1912), 48.

27. Runich, 604–605.

28. For example see Dmitri Sverbeev, 'O Moskovskikh pozharakh' in *Vestnik evropy* 11 (1872), 427–449.

29. Sergei Glinka, *Zapiski o Moskve* (St Petersburg, 1837), 65–66.

30. Tolstoy, *War and Peace*, 963–964.

31. Dmitri Buturlin, *Istoriya nashestviya imperatora Napoleona na Rossiyu v 1812 godu* (St Petersburg, 1837) I, 305. Nikolai Okunev's classic analysis of the Russian Campaign concurred with Buturlin in assigning responsibility to the Russians. Nikolai Okunev, *Razsuzhdenie o bolshikh voennykh deistviyakh, bitvakh i srazheniyakh proiskhodivshikh pri vtrozhenii v Rossiyu v 1812 godu* (St Petersburg, 1833), 198–200. The book was originally published in French in 1829.

32. Mikhailovskii-Danilevskii (1843), II, 363–379. For an insightful critique of Mikhailovskii–Danilevskii's account see I. Liprandi, *Russkie ili Frantsuzy zazhgli Moskvu?* (St Petersburg, 1855).

33. Modest Bogdanovich, *Istoriya voiny 1812 goda po dostovernym istochnikam* (St Petersburg, 1859), II, 314–318.

34. For example, S. Melgunov, 'Kho szheg Moskvu?' in *Otechestvennaya voina i Russkoe Obschestvo* (St Petersburg, 1911), IV, 162–171; Hans Schmidt, *Vinovniki pozhara Moskvy v 1812 godu* (Riga, 1912).

35. A. Smirnov, 'Evolutsiya vzglyadov otechestvennykh istorikov na prichiny pozhara Moskvy v 1812 g.: analiticheskii obzor,' in *Moskva v 1812 godu: Materialy nauchnoi konferentsii* (Moscow, 1997), 20.

36. Mikhail Pokrovskii, *Diplomatiya i voiny tsarskoi Rossii v XIX stoletii* (Moscow, 1923), 56.

37. Eugène Tarle, *Nashestvie Napoleona na Rossiyu. 1812 god* (Moscow, 1943, reprint 1992) 167–168. In 1951 the journal *Bolshevik*, a mouthpiece of the Communist party, accused Tarle, arguably the most renowned Soviet historian at the time, that in his classic study of the 1812 Campaign he had not been sufficiently critical of 'aristocratic-bourgeois' historians. He was accused of distorting the history of the Patriotic War and seeking to remove responsibility for the 'deliberate' destruction of Moscow from Napoleon and his soldiers. Already hardened in earlier squabbles and exile to Central Asia, Tarle avoided direct confrontation with these critics and appealed directly to Joseph Stalin for help. Two months later, the same periodical retracted its statements but noted that Tarle's study did require 'some' corrections. Understanding what he was asked to do, Tarle conformed to the 'party line' and the 1952 edition of his work contained greater emphasis on the culpability of Napoleon in the destruction of Moscow.

38. I. Polosin, 'Kutuzov i pozhar Moskvy,' in *Istoricheskie zapiski* (1950), XXXIV, 162–165. Polosin pointed out that the wooden bridge at the Dorogomilov barrier was not demolished after the withdrawal of the Russian forces, which would have delayed the enemy forces for at least few hours. For Polosin, the answer lay in Kutuzov's intention to lure the Allied forces into Moscow where he had already sprung a trap.

39. Thus, in her *Istoriya Moskvy* (1954), historian Militsa Nechkina was convinced that 'the Moscow fire was above all the result of the actions of the Napoleonic forces. Afterwards Napoleon did everything he could to shift his responsibility for it [on to the Russians].' Ignoring numerous documents to the contrary, Nechkina insisted that 'the French marauders burnt Moscow because they sought to plunder it and the French military command made no effort to curb their activities'. Interestingly, just a few years prior, Nechkina gave a public lecture 'Moscow in 1812', in which she considered three possible versions of culpability (accidental burning, French involvement or deliberate Russian act) and came to the conclusion that 'the Moscow fire was an act of heroic people's patriotism'. See Militsa Nechkina, *Moskva v 1812 gody* (Moscow, 1947), 25; Idem, *Istoriya Moskvy* (Moscow, 1954), III, 102–103.

40. V. Kholodkovskii, 'Napoleon li podzheg Moskvu?' in *Voprosy istorii* 4 (1966); A. Tartakovskii, *Voennaya publitsistika 1812 g* (Moscow, 1967).

41. O. Orlik, *Groza dvenadtsatogo goda* (Moscow, 1987).

42. N. Ryazanov, ed. *M.I. Kutuzov general-feldmarshal. Pisma, Zapiski* (Moscow, 1989), 558.

43. Nikolai Troitskii, *1812. Velikii god Rossii* (Moscow, 1988).

44. Troitskii, 189.

45. For example, N. Shakhmagonov, *Taina moskovskogo pozhara: kto szheg belokamennuyu?* (Moscow, 1999).

46. Zemtsov, 3.

47. Popov, 181–183.

Chapter 1: The Road to Moscow

1. 2nd Bulletin, 22 June 1812, *Imperial Glory: The Bulletins of Napoleon's Grande Armée, 1805–1814*, ed. J. David Markham (London, 2003), 246.
2. Order to the Armies, 25 June 1812, in *Vneshnaya politika Rossii XIX i nachala XX veka* (Moscow, 1962), VI, 442–443.
3. *Cobbett's Political Register*, 8 August 1812, XXII, 173.
4. Napoleon to King Frederick of Württemberg, 2 April 1811, *Correspondance de Napoléon*, XXII, No. 17553, 17.
5. Grabbe, 467–468.
6. Barclay de Tolly, *Izobrazhenye*, 24.
7. Barclay de Tolly, *Izobrazhenye*, 24–25.
8. Bogdanovich, II, 236.
9. Clausewitz, 131.
10. In addition to the Cossacks, Platov also received four *jager* regiments from the 2nd Corps, one hussar regiment and twelve horse artillery guns.
11. Chambray, II, 82.
12. Montesquiou-Fezensac, *Journal de la Campagne de Russie en 1812*, 51–52.
13. Bausset, II, 110.
14. It comprised four reserve cavalry corps and Dufour's 2nd Division (from I Corps).
15. Bellot de Kergorre, 60–61.
16. Order to the Armies, No. 14, 11 September 1812.
17. 'Mount of Salutation'. It lies a few miles from the capital and is so called because travellers, upon seeing the great city, saluted it by prostrating themselves.
18. Jean Baptiste de Crossard, *Mémoires militaires et historiques* (Paris, 1829), IV, 361.
19. As the Russian army occupied its positions, its right wing was protected by the Moscow river near the village of Fili, its centre was located between the villages Volynskoe and Troitskoe and the left flank was anchored on the Vorobyevo ('Sparrow') Heights; Miloradovich's rearguard bivouacked at the village of Setun'.
20. Löwernstern, I, 280.
21. Mayevskii, 141.
22. Barclay de Tolly, *Izobrazhenye*, 25–26.
23. Wintzingerode to Emperor Alexander I, 25 September 1812, in Dubrovin, *Otechestvennaia voina v pis'makh sovremennikov*, 138.
24. Toll, II, 139–142.
25. Wintzingerode to Emperor Alexander I, 25 September 1812, in Dubrovin, *Otechestvennaia voina v pis'makh sovremennikov*, 138.
26. Crossard, IV, 363–365.
27. Yermolov, 168–169; Grabbe, 469.
28. J.M. von Helldorff, ed. *Aus dem Leben des kaiserlich-russischen Generals der Infanterie Prinzen Eugen von Württemberg* (Berlin, 1862), II, 58–59; Toll, II, 143.
29. Yermolov, 169–170.
30. Buturlin, I, 306; Rostopchin (1889), 717; Rayevskii, 71; Mikhnevich, 'Fili' in *Otechestvennaya voina i Russko obshchestvo* (Moscow, 1911), IV, 32; *Sovetskaya Istoricheskaya Entsiklopedia* (Moscow, 1974), XV, 80; *Bolshaya Sovetskaya Entsiklopediya* (Moscow, 1977), XXVII, 392; Mikhailovskii-Danilevskii (1839), II, 323; Bogdanovich, II, 248; Kharkevich, 34; Beskrovnyi, 415; Zhilin, 176–177; Tarle, *Nashestvie Napoleona na Rossiu*, Chapter 6 (on-line edition); Garin, 275; Troitskii, 183.
31. In his memoir, Konovnitsyn mentions that General Karl Baggovut had also attended the council but no other source confirms this information. Konovnitsyn, 128.
32. Cate, 268; Garin, 275; Troitskii, 183.
33. Barclay de Tolly, *Izobrazhenie*, 26–27; Toll, II, 143–144.
34. Toll, II, 143–144.
35. Yermolov, 170. Barclay de Tolly's *Izobrazhenye* differs in some details of this speech.
36. Toll, II, 145.
37. Ibid.
38. Barclay de Tolly, *Izobrazhenie*, 26–27; Rayevskii, 72–73; Bennigsen 9 (1909), 503; Yermolov, 170–171; Löwernstern 1 (1901), 105.
39. Bennigsen 9 (1909), 503. Bennigsen states that he left the meeting after it became clear that his opinion was discounted and the debate was not recorded as required by regulations. Kaissarov's opinion (if he

indeed took part in the council) remains unknown. Challenges inherent to memoir literature become apparent when one considers Dokhturov's position. Writing to his wife just two days after the council, Dokhturov noted that he wanted to fight and 'did everything I could to convince [the council] to advance against the enemy. Bennigsen was of the same opinion … But this gallant idea had no effect on these pusillanimous men so we retreated through the city.' Yet Yermolov, in his memoirs, states, 'General Dokhturov said that it would be good to march against the enemy, however, because of the loss of so many commanders at Borodino, who had been replaced by less familiar officers, success in the ensuing battle could not be guaranteed; therefore, he proposed to retreat.' Dokhturov to his wife, 15 September 1812, in *Russkii arkhiv* 1 (1874), 1098; Yermolov, 171.

40. Rayevskii, 74.
41. Kutuzov to Wintzingerode, 15 September 1812, in *M.I. Kutuzov: Sbornik Dokumentov*, IV, part 1, 231.
42. Rastkovskii, 31.
43. Bennigsen (1908), III, 94–95.
44. Sanglen, 553.
45. Disposition for the 1st and 2nd Western Armies, 14 September 1812, in *M.I. Kutuzov: Sbornik Dokumentov*, IV, part 1, 225. A similar order was issued on 12 September and specified that any official or officer who left the ranks without permission should be hanged or shot while rank-and-file 'should be bayoneted [*zakolot'*] on the spot'. *Journal of Incoming Correspondence*, in General Staff Archives, XVII, 192.
46. Barclay de Tolly to Rostopchin, 13 September 1812, in Dubrovin, *Otechestvennaia voina v pis'makh sovremennikov*, 118–119.
47. Lowenstern, I, 283.
48. Golitsyn, *Ofitserskie zapiski*, 21.
49. Yermolov, 172.
50. Dokhturov to his wife, 15 September 1812, in *Russkii arkhiv* 1 (1874), 1098–1099.
51. Lowenstern, I, 284.
52. Toll, II, 148–149.
53. In late 1811 Kutuzov routed the Ottoman army near Rousse (in present-day Bulgaria) and starved its remnants into submission.
54. A.B. Golitzyn, 'Zapiski o voine 1812 goda,' in *Voennyi sbornik* 12 (1910), 24.
55. Radozhitskii, 87–88.
56. A four-wheeled open carriage, popular in Russia.
57. Sergei Glinka, 'Iz zapisok o 1812 gode,' <http://www.museum.ru/1812/library/glinka1/glinka. html#p40>

Chapter 2: The City

1. K. Batyushkov, 'Progulka po Moskve,' in K.N. Batyushkov, *Sochineniya* (Moscow, 1934), 299.
2. *Travels in the Crimea: A History of the Embassy from Petersburg to Constantinople in 1793* (London, 1802), 51.
3. Catherine Wilmot to Anna Chetwood, 24 September 1806, in *The Russian Journals of Martha and Catherine Wilmot*, edited by Harford M. Hyde (London, 1934), 192.
4. Porter, 161.
5. While researching this book I consulted more than two dozen maps of Moscow spanning the period between 1770 and 1852. A vast collection of digitized city maps can be accessed at www.retromap.ru.
6. Johann Gottfried Seume, *A Tour through Part of Germany, Poland, Russia, Sweden, Denmark, etc.* (London, 1807), 35–36.
7. Robert Ker Porter, *Travelling sketches in Russia and Sweden* (Philadelphia, 1809), 160.
8. 'Statisticheskaya tablitsa o sostoyanii g. Moskvy v 1811 g.,' in Gorshkov, *Moskva i Otechesvennaya voina*, I, 16.
9. 'Statisticheskaya tablitsa o sostoyanii g. Moskvy v 1811 g.,' in Gorshkov, *Moskva i Otechesvennaya voina*, I, 15.
10. 'Vedomost'' o sushestvuyushikh v Moskovskoi stolitse tserkvakh, kazennykh i obyvatelskikh domakh, 1812 goda,' in *Russkii arkhiv* (1864), 1207–1208; 'Statisticheskaya tablitsa o sostoyanii g. Moskvy v 1811 g.,' in Gorshkov, *Moskva i Otechesvennaya voina*, I, 16.
11. *A History of the Embassy from Petersburg to Constantinople in 1793*, 53.
12. *Travels through the Southern Provinces of the Russian Empire in the years 1793–1794* (London, 1812), I, 7.
13. Porter, 166–167.

14. The city was also divided into ninety police districts. 'Statisticheskaya tablitsa o sostoyanii g. Moskvy v 1811 g.', in Gorshkov, *Moskva i Otechesvennaya voina*, I, 15.
15. Originally the Kremlin of the fifteenth century was red but later it was whitewashed all over; the first reliable evidence of this practice goes back to the late seventeenth century. The Kremlin remained white-coloured until the early twentieth century (a fact often missed by artists), when the Soviet authorities removed the whitewash and coated the Kremlin with a special red paint to make it look like brick.
16. Seume, 36.
17. Edward Daniel Clarke, *Travels in Various Countries of Europe, Asia and Africa* (London, 1813), I, 128–129.
18. Graf Helmuth von Moltke, *Field-marshal Count Moltke's letters from Russia* (New York, 1878), 122.
19. Some scholars do suggest, however, that the term may have been developed from the Tartar word *kitay* ('fortress' or 'centre').
20. Porter, 162.
21. Clarke, 130.
22. Pavel Svinin, *Sketches of Russia* (London, 1814), 30–31.
23. These districts were: IV Pyatnitskii, V Yakimanskii, VI Prechistenskii, VII Arbatskii, VIII Sretenskii and IX Yauzskii.
24. These districts were: X Basmannii, XI Rogozhskii, XII Taganskii, XIII Serpukhovskii, XIV Khamovnicheskii, XV Novinskii, XVI Presnenskii, XVII Suschevskii, XVIII Meschanskii, XIX Pokrovskii and XX Lefortovskii.
25. The Georgian community grew in Moscow in the early eighteenth century when King Vakhtang of Kartli (eastern Georgia), unable to resist joint invasions of Iran and the Ottoman Empire, fled with a large retinue to Russia in 1724.
26. Porter, 164.
27. William Coxe, *Travels in Poland, Russia, Sweden, and Denmark* (London, 1802), 282.
28. *Istoriya Moskvy* (Moscow, 1948), III, 168; Sytin, *Pozhar Moskvy v 1812*, 13–15. The official *Statistical Report on the Number of Residents of the City of Moscow*, completed in February 1811, shows the population of Moscow at 263,423 people. Gorshkov, *Moskva i Otechesvennaya voina*, I, 12–13. However, the report seems to be incomplete. For example, the ethnic breakdown of the city shows 260,472 Russians but only 703 French, even though most Russian studies suggest that the French community in Moscow was much larger. The German population, shown at 1,029 'Germans', 34 'Saxons', 129 'Prussians' and 18 'Liflandians', also seems to be under-reported. Another official 'Statistical Report on the Well-Being of Moscow in 1811,' completed in February 1812, showed the city population at 270,184 people. Gorshkov, *Moskva i Otechesvennaya voina*, I, 12–17.
29. 'Statisticheskaya vedomost' o kolichestve zhitelei g. Moskvy,' February 1811, in Gorshkov, *Moskva i Otechesvennaya voina*, I, 12–13.
30. 'Statisticheskaya tablitsa o sostoyanii g. Moskvy v 1811 g.,' 1 February 1812, Gorshkov, *Moskva i Otechesvennaya voina*, I, 13–14.
31. For comparison, a colonel's salary was about 1000 rubles per year.
32. 'Statisticheskaya tablitsa o sostoyanii g. Moskvy v 1811 g.,' in Gorshkov, *Moskva i Otechesvennaya voina*, I, 15; 'Vedomost' o sushestvuyushikh v Moskovskoi stolitse tserkvakh, kazennykh i obyvatelskikh domakh, 1812 goda,' in *Russkii arkhiv* (1864), 1207–1208.
33. T.J. Binyon, *Pushkin: A Biography* (New York, 2004), 9.
34. Charles Colville Frankland, *Narrative of a visit to the courts of Russia and Sweden* (London, 1832), II, 269.
35. Maria Volkova to Varvara Lanskoi, 15 September 1812, in *Pis'ma 1812 goda M.A. Volkovoi k V.A. Lanskoi* (Moscow, 1990) <http://az.lib.ru/w/wolkowa_m_a/text_0010. shtml> (accessed on 4 April 2012).
36. Leo Tolstoy, *War and Peace*, translated and edited by Louise Maude and Aylmer Maude (Oxford, 2010), 574.
37. 'Statisticheskaya tablitsa o sostoyanii g. Moskvy v 1811 g.,' in Gorshkov, *Moskva i Otechesvennaya voina*, I, 16; 'Vedomost' o sushestvuyushikh v Moskovskoi stolitse tserkvakh, kazennykh i obyvatelskikh domakh, 1812 goda,' in *Russkii arkhiv* (1864), 1207–1208.
38. Siegmund Freiherr von Herberstein, *Rerum Moscoviticarum Commentarii* (Russian edition) (Moscow, 1988), Part 4, 128.
39. 'Statisticheskaya tablitsa o sostoyanii g. Moskvy v 1811 g.,' in Gorshkov, *Moskva i Otechesvennaya voina*, I, 16.
40. For details see Robert Leach and Victor Borovsky, *A History of Russian Theatre* (Cambridge, 1999), 57–85.

41. *Russkii Arkhiv* 8 (1891), 173.
42. For details see Catherine A. Schuler, *Theatre and Identity in Imperial Russia* (Iowa City, 2009).
43. Samuel H. Baron, ed. *The Travels of Olearius in Seventeenth-Century Russia* (Stanford, 1967), 112.
44. For an insightful discussion of the impact these calamities had on Moscow's development see John. T. Alexander, *Bubonic Plague in Early Modern Russia: Public Health and Urban Disaster* (Oxford, 2003).
45. John Perry, *The State of Russia under the Present Tsar* (London, 1716, reprint 1968), 264–265.
46. Glushkovskii, 122.

Chapter 3: The Governor

1. Emperor Alexander to Ivan Gudovich, 25 May 1812, in Gorshkov, *Moskva i Otechesvennaya voina*, I, 81.
2. Some sources suggest he may have been born in 1765. A. Meshcheryakova, *F.V. Rostopchin: U osnovaniya konservatisma i natsionalisma v Rossii* (Voronezh, 2007); Lydie Rostoptchine, *Les Rostoptchine* (n.p., 1984); Alexander M. Martin, *Romantics, Reformers, Reactionaries: Russian Conservative Thought and Politics in the Reign of Alexander I* (DeKalb, Ill.: Northern Illinois University Press, 1997).
3. Stendhal to Felix Faure, 4 October 1812, in *Correspondance de Stendhal*, I, 391.
4. Pierre de Ségur, 'Rostopchin en 1812,' in *La Revue de Paris* (1908), IV, 88.
5. Rostopchin fell victim to a court intrigue and was dismissed by Paul I in mid-March, less than ten days before his assassination. See Ségur, 'Rostopchin en 1812,' in *La Revue de Paris* (1908), IV, 89–90; Gornostaev, General-gubernator Moskvy F.V. Rostopchin <http://www.museum.ru/museum/1812/Library/Gornostaev/part1.html>
6. Ségur, 'Rostopchin en 1812,' in *La Revue de Paris* (1908), IV, 93.
7. Fedor Rostopchin, *Sochineniya* (St Petersburg, 1853), 1–19; Anatole Henri de Ségur, *Vie du Comte Rostopchine, Gouverneur de Moscou en 1812* (Paris, 1893), 117–120; Ségur, 'Rostopchin en 1812,' in *La Revue de Paris* (1908), IV, 91–92; Gornostaev, General-gubernator Moskvy F.V. Rostopchin <http://www.museum.ru/museum/1812/Library/Gornostaev/part1.html>
8. Many contemporaries remarked on the governor's wit and intelligence. Thus, the perceptive Prussian general August Wilhelm Antonius Graf Neidhardt von Gneisenau, who briefly encountered Rostopchin in 1816, found him a 'capable and well informed' man. Gneisenau to Madame Clausewitz, 15 August 1816, in Georg H. Pertz and Hans Delbrück, eds. *Das Leben des Feldmarschalls Grafen Neithardt von Gneisenau* (Berlin, 1880), V, 140.
9. Bulgakov, *Vospominaniya*, 99–100.
10. The Senate's decree of 5 June granted Rostopchin the rank of general of infantry and appointed him the military governor of Moscow. Minister of Police Alexander Balashov congratulated Rostopchin on 6 June. Alexander Balashov to Rostopchin, 6 June 1812, in Dubrovin, 5. Also see Gudovich to Provincial Administration of Moscow, 13 June 1812, in Gorshkov, *Moskva i Otechesvennaya voina*, I, 96.
11. Decree of the Senate, *c.*29 July 1812, in Gorshkov, *Moskva i Otechesvennaya voina*, I, 194–195. Alexander signed the decree during his stay in Moscow in late July. Also see Rostopchin to Emperor Alexander, 19 June 1812, in *Russkii arkhiv* 8 (1892), 422.
12. Rostopchin to Major General Ivashkin; Major General Ivashkin to City Constable Putyatin, 25–26 June 1812, in Gorshkov, *Moskva i Otechesvennaya voina*, I, 100.
13. Rostopchin to Major General Ivashkin, 16 June 1812, in Gorshkov, *Moskva i Otechesvennaya voina*, I, 97.
14. Rostopchin to Major General Ivashkin, 22 June 1812, in Ibid., 99.
15. M. Evreinov, 'Pamyat' 1812 g,' in *Russkii arkhiv* 1 (1874), 95; Bulgakov, *Vospominaniya*, 98–135.
16. A. Popov, 'Moskva v 1812 g.,' in *Russkii arkhiv* 7 (1875), 313.
17. Vigel, IV, 35.
18. See Afishy 1812 goda ili druzheskie poslaniya ot glavnokomanduushego v Moskve k zhitelyam eye, <http://www.museum.ru/museum/1812/Library/rostopchin/>. Rostopchin was not the sole 'rabid patriot' willing to use the press for propaganda purposes. Sergei Glinka played a central role in this undertaking and his memoirs are very enlightening on this topic. See S.N. Glinka, *Zapiski o 1812 gode* (St Petersburg, 1836).
19. Bestuzhev-Riumin (1859), 77.
20. Dmitriev (1854), 166–167.
21. Vigel, IV, 34.
22. No. 1 Broadsheet, in Afishy 1812 goda <http://www.museum.ru/museum/1812/Library/rostopchin/>
23. Komarovskii, 775.
24. Runich, 598. Another eyewitness, however, writes that the crowds waited for the emperor until late at night and, with the emperor not coming, returned back home. Ryazanov, 25.

25. Rostopchin (1889), 673–674.
26. Ryazanov, 26.
27. Komarovskii, 775.
28. Bestuzhev-Riumin (1859), 74.
29. Komarovskii, 776. Rostopchin was bemused by this ethos, noting, 'It was, in its own way, a unique spectacle for the Russian expressed his feelings freely, and forgetting that he was a slave, he rose in anger at being threatened with chains that a foreigner was preparing.' Rostopchin (1889), 674.
30. Rostopchin (1889), 683.
31. Rostopchin to Balashov, 4 August 1812, in Dubrovin, *Otechestvennaia voina v pis'makh sovremennikov*, 59.
32. Fedor Rostopchin, *Okh, frantsuzy!* (Moscow, 1992), electronic version <http://az.lib.ru/r/rostopchin_f_w/text_0190.shtml>
33. Sverbeyev, 65.
34. Bestuzhev-Riumin (1859), 74–75.
35. Rostopchin (1889), 655.
36. Sverbeyev, I, 62–63.
37. Marakuev, 112. Although this rumour was untrue, there was a grain of truth in it. In early July Rostopchin was given the authority to raise militia forces in Moscow and he used forcible recruitment to satisfy the quotas. Men captured for crimes, drunkenness and debauchery were forced to enlist in the army. The governor also requested (and received) authority to impress for any petty crimes 'men lacking any craft skills, residence or property as well as retired officers and lower classes of officials who remain indolent'. Alexander Balashev to Fedor Rostopchin, 10 July 1812, in Dubrovin, *Otechestvennaia voina v pis'makh sovremennikov*, 32.
38. For details see Runich, 599–600; Rostopchin to Balachev, 22 August 1812, in Dubrovin, *Otechestvennaia voina v pis'makh sovremennikov*, 90–91. 'Zapiska o Martinistakh predstavlennaya v 1811 godu grafom Rostopchinym velikoi knyagine Ekaterine Pavlovne', *Russkii arkhiv* 13/3 (1875), 75–81. Rostopchin occasionally sent rumour-mongers to lunatic asylums, where they were treated to 'daily cold showers and, on Saturdays, they were made to swallow medications'. Rostopchin (1889), 689.
39. Kolchugin, 46.
40. S. Melgunov, 'Rostopchin – Moskovskii glavnokomanduyushii,' in *Otechestvennaya voina i Russkoe obschestvo* (Moscow, 1911), IV, 36.
41. Bulgakov, *Vospominaniya*, 103. Rostopchin's wife, who had converted to Catholicism, tried her best to save Napoleon, a fellow Catholic, from this unsavoury fate. But her argument that Napoleon was a crowned head blessed by the Pope himself had no impact on Rostopchin, who continued to use the bust for the above-mentioned purpose.
42. Bulgakov, *Vospominaniya*, 102–103.
43. Anna Khomutova, 'Vospominaniya A.G. Khomutovoi o Moskve v 1812 godu,' in *Russkii arkhiv* 3 (1891), 315.
44. Bogdanovich estimates at least 3,000 Frenchmen living in Moscow in 1812. Bogdanovich, II, 258.
45. K. Batyshkov, 'Progulka po Moskve,' in I. Semenko, ed. *Batyshkov K.N. Opyty v stikhak i proze* (Moscow, 1977), 382–383.
46. Catherine Wilmot to Anna Chetwood, 24 September 1806, in *The Russian Journals of Martha and Catherine Wilmot*, edited by Harford M. Hyde (London, 1934), 194.
47. Caroline Pavlova, Vospominaniya, in *Russkii arkhiv* 10 (1875), 224.
48. Rostopchin to Emperor Alexander, 29 December 1806, in *Russkii arkhiv* 8 (1892), 420.
49. Rostopchin to Emperor Alexander, 4 August 1812, in *Russkii arkhiv* 8 (1892), 435.
50. For details see V. Bezotosnyi, *Razvedka i plany storon v 1812 godu* (Moscow, 2005).
51. 'Ob inostrantsakh vyslannykh iz Moskvy v raznye goroda v 1812 gody', in Shukin, I, 156.
52. Rostopchin to Major General P. Ivashkin, 31 August 1812, in Gorshkov, *Moskva i Otechesvennaya voina*, I, 299.
53. Rostopchin to Major General P. Ivashkin, 8 August 1812; Police Constable I. Mikhailov to Major General Ivashkin, 10 August 1812; Journal of Deliberations of Police Officials, 10 August 1812; Major General Ivashkin to Rostopchin, 22 August 1812, in Gorshkov, *Moskva i Otechesvennaya voina*, I, 226–229.
54. For details see 'Ob inostrantsakh vyslannykh iz Moskvy v raznye goroda v 1812 gody' in Shukin, I, 151–162.
55. *Sbornik istoricheskikh materialov* (1876), 92–100.
56. Rumyantsev to Alopeus, 26 April 1812, in *Russkii arkhiv* 9 (1875), 44; Emperor Alexander to Rostopchin, 24 May 1812, in *Russkaya starina* 1 (1902), 217–218.

57. Rostopchin to Emperor Alexander, 25 August 1812, in *Russkii arkhiv* 9 (1892), 520.
58. For details on Leppich's work see a series of letters Rostopchin wrote to Emperor Alexander between May and early September 1812 in *Russkii arkhiv* 8 (1892), 419–446; 9 (1892), 519–536.
59. Rostopchin to Emperor Alexander, 16 July 1812, in *Russkii arkhiv* 8 (1892), 432.
60. Bestuzhev-Riumin (1859), 77.
61. Leppich continued his experiments at the famous Oranienbaum observatory. In November 1812 his first prototype balloon collapsed as it was wheeled out of the hanger. By September 1813 he finally built a flying machine that could ascend 12–13m above the ground – a far cry from his earlier promises of soaring squadrons in the skies above Russia. In October 1813 General Alexei Arakcheyev launched an investigation into Leppich's experiments and branded him 'a complete charlatan, who knows nothing whatever of even the elementary rules of mechanics or the principles of levers'. Deprived of funding and in disgrace, Leppich left Russia in February 1814. By that time the Russian government had spent a staggering 250,000 roubles on Leppich's project. For details see A.A. Rodnykh, *Tainaya podgotovka k unichtozheniyu armii Napoleona v dvenadtsatom godu pri pomoshi vozdukhoplavaniya* (St Petersburg, 1912); A. Popov, 'Leppich i ego shar,' in *Russkii arkhiv* 9 (1875), 30–47; S. Iskul, *Rokovye gody Rossii. 1812 god. Dokumentalnaya khronika* (Moscow, 2008), 145–153.
62. Rostopchin (1889), 669.
63. Rostopchin to Voronenko, 6 August 1812, in *Russkii arkhiv* 1 (1909), 38; *Russkii arkhiv* (1866), 689–691; Rostopchin to Emperor Alexander, 6 August 1812, in *Russkii arkhiv* 8 (1892), 437.
64. For example see *Moskovskie vedomosti* Nos. 62–69 (15 August-9 September). The last issue (No. 70) came out on 12 September.
65. Glinka, *Zapiski o 1812 gode* <http://www.museum.ru/1812/library/glinka1/glinka.html#p16>
66. Marakuev, 115.
67. Rostopchin (1889), 706.
68. Bestuzhev-Riumin (1859), 77.
69. Rostopchin to Balashev, 30 August 1812, in Dubrovin, *Otechestvennaia voina v pis'makh sovremennikov*, 102.
70. Rostopchin to Balashev, 30 August 1812, in Dubrovin, *Otechestvennaia voina v pis'makh sovremennikov*, 102.
71. No. 7 Broadsheet, 29 August 1812, in *Afishy 1812 goda* <http://www.museum.ru/museum/1812/Library/rostopchin/>
72. No. 8 Broadsheet, 30 August 1812, in *Afishy 1812 goda* <http://www.museum.ru/museum/1812/Library/rostopchin/>. The memoir of Vasilii Polyanskii offers fascinating details on the distribution of arms at the arsenal. Tolycheva, 38–40.
73. Bestuzhev-Riumin (1859), 79.
74. Alexander Bulgakov to Constantine Bulgakov, 25 August 1812, in *Russkii arkhiv* 5 (1900), 32.
75. Nikolai Karamzin to I. Dmitriev, 1 September 1812 in Garin, 6.
76. M. Nevzorov to P. Golenischev-Kutuzov, 3 December 1812, in Gorshskov, *Moskva i Otechestvennaya voina 1812 g.*, II, 19.
77. Blagovo, 161.
78. Fusil, 228.
79. For example, Kutuzov asked Rostopchin to provide 1,000 axes, 1,000 iron spades and 250 drills, and instructed him to deliver muskets from the depots and arsenals in Moscow. He was particularly interested to learn if it would be possible to use the air balloon, which Leppich was secretly building near Moscow, in the impending battle. On 4 September Kutuzov instructed Rostopchin to 'take all possible measures to ensure quick procurement of 1,000 carts at each station from Moscow to Mozhaisk'. The governor did his best to fulfill Kutuzov's requests and on 6 September he reported that 'The required horses, 1,000 per station, from Moscow to Mozhaisk will be ready, the work-sheet has already been prepared ... I have already quite successfully carried out a monthly procurement of more than 1,000 horses for the army. Tomorrow I am signing a contract which I shall send you with horses and carts filled with biscuits. Tools for the workers, that is spades and drills, have been purchased according to your prescript and already dispatched today.' Kutuzov to Rostopchin, 31 August-4 September 1812, in *M.I. Kutuzov: Sbornik Dokumentov*, IV, part 1, 99–100, 125–126, 133–134.
80. Kutuzov to Rostopchin, *c.*1–2 September 1812, in *Feldmarshal Kutuzov: Sbornik dokumentov i materialov* (Moscow, 1947), 156–157; Nikolai Dubrovin, 'Moskva i Graf Rastopchin v 1812 godu,' in *Voennyi sbornik* 7 (1863), 148.
81. Rostopchin to Kutuzov, 31 August 1812, in *Russkii arkhiv* 2 (1875), 457.
82. Kutuzov to Rostopchin, 2 September 1812, in *Borodino: dokumenty, pis'ma, vospominaniya*, 54.

83. Kutuzov to Rostopchin, 2 September 1812, in *M.I. Kutuzov: Sbornik Dokumentov*, IV, part 1, 119–120.

84. Rostopchin to Kutuzov, 31 August 1812, in *Russkaya starina*, 1870, II, 305.

85. Kutuzov to Rostopchin, 3 September 1812, in Dubrovin, *Otechestvennaia voina v pis'makh sovremennikov*, 108.

86. Rostopchin to Peter Tolstoy, 5 September 1812, *Zarya* 8 (1871), 186.

87. Kutuzov to Rostopchin, 7 September 1812, in *Borodino: dokumenty, pis'ma, vospominaniya*, 93–95; *M.I. Kutuzov: Sbornik Dokumentov*, IV, part 1, 151.

88. Rostopchin (1889), 706.

89. 'The battle that started yesterday in the morning and continued to the very night was the bloodiest. Casualties on both sides are heavy: the losses the enemies suffered judging by their stubborn attacks on our fortified position must be much greater than ours. Our troops fought with incredible bravery. Batteries kept changing hands, and it ended with a situation that the enemies, with their superior numbers, did not gain a single pace.'

90. Kutuzov to Rostopchin, 8 September 1812, in *M.I. Kutuzov: Sbornik Dokumentov*, IV, 155–156. The governor later wrote that he would have remained unaware of the Russian retreat if not for 'the courier's slip of the tongue when he accidentally mentioned that our troops were at Mozhaisk, that is, already ten verstas from the battlefield'. However, Kutuzov's letter (No. 71) clearly informed him of the army redeployment to Mozhaisk. Rostopchin (1889), 706.

91. Kutuzov to Rostopchin, 8 September 1812, in *M.I. Kutuzov: Sbornik Dokumentov*, IV, 158–159.

92. Kutuzov to Rostopchin, 11 September 1812, in *M.I. Kutuzov: Sbornik Dokumentov*, IV, 183–184.

93. See Kutuzov to Rostopchin, 7–12 September 1812, in *Borodino: dokumenty, pis'ma, vospominaniya*, 95f, 124–126, 129. Two days after the battle Rostopchin replied that 'tomorrow at dawn two regiments, consisting of 4,600 men ready for service, will start moving in accelerated march to Mozhaisk. In two days one more regiment of 2,300 men will come from Podolsk. From here the day after tomorrow a battery with a pontoon company and 100 men from militia fully trained in firing cannon. Arapetov's three companies with cannon and shells have already begun marching. All the caissons belonging to the artillery division moving to Kolomna and found by my courier between Podolsk and Borovsk have been turned to Mozhaisk. Moreover, tomorrow 26,000 artillery rounds will be carried to the army in carts. Tomorrow I hope I shall send 500 horses with horse-collars.'

94. Rostopchin (1889), 707.

95. Sverbeyev, I, 438–439.

96. *Russkii vestnik* 2 (1842).

97. Kutuzov to Rostopchin, 1 September 1812, in *M.I. Kutuzov: Sbornik Dokumentov*, IV, 115. Just days later Rostopchin received another letter from Kutuzov that spoke of his determination to protect Moscow and asked for more reinforcements to 'fight a decisive battle near Moscow'. Kutuzov to Rostopchin, 9 September 1812, in *Feldmarshal Kutuzov: Sbornik dokumentov i materialov*, 173–174.

98. Bogdanovich, II, 268.

99. Rostopchin to Balashov, 10 September 1812, in *Borodino: dokumenty, pis'ma, vospominaniya*, 85.

100. On 11 September alone Rostopchin received half a dozen letters from Kutuzov and other commanders that must have left him befuddled. One letter informed him that a French corps (Eugène's 4th Corps) was outflanking the Russian army and approaching Moscow from the northwest. Remarkably, Kutuzov wondered if Rostopchin could not prepare a hot reception for the enemy by calling out the Moscow militia. One wonders why such a suggestion was made, considering Kutuzov's own low opinion of the militia. In another letter Kutuzov assured Rostopchin that 'we are approaching a general battle near Moscow' and asked him to 'provide as rapid aid as possible'. Further missives sounded even more frantic, requesting as many battery guns from the Moscow arsenal as possible, along with supplies of munitions, transports, axes, spades and mulled wine. Kutuzov to Rostopchin, Barclay de Tolly to Rostopchin, 11 September 1812, in *M.I. Kutuzov: Sbornik Dokumentov*, IV, Part 1, 183–188. For Rostopchin's responses see Rostopchin (1889), 712–714.

101. Rostopchin to Balashov, 10 September 1812, in *Borodino: dokumenty, pis'ma, vospominaniya*, 85.

102. Glinka, *Iz zapisok o 1812 gode*, <http://www.museum.ru/1812/library/glinka1/glinka.html#p40>

103. No. 14 Broadsheet, 11 September 1812, in Afishy 1812 goda <http://www.museum.ru/museum/1812/Library/rostopchin/>

104. Bestuzhev-Riumin (1859), 82.

105. Rostopchin (1889), 710–711.

106. No. 15 Broadsheet, 11 August 1812, in Afishy 1812 goda <http://www.museum.ru/museum/1812/Library/rostopchin/>

107. Bestuzhev-Riumin (1859), 83.

108. Golitsyn, *Ofitserskie zapiski*, 19–20.
109. Glinka, 'Iz zapisok o 1812 gode,' <http://www.museum.ru/1812/library/glinka1/glinka.html>. Around ten o'clock in the morning Sergei Glinka visited Rostopchin and the two had a brief chat. The governor looked fatigued and upset. 'Let us speak like sons of the Fatherland,' he told Glinka. 'What do you think will happen? Will Moscow be surrendered?' Glinka argued that such a prospect had to be considered. The more important question was how would the city be given up – with or without bloodshed? Rostopchin tersely replied, 'Without bloodshed.'
110. Rostopchin (1889), 714.
111. No. 16 Broadsheet, 12 September 1812, in Afishy 1812 goda <http://www.museum.ru/museum/1812/Library/rostopchin/>
112. Rostopchin (1894), 214–215.
113. Rostopchin to his wife, 13 September 1812, in *Russkii arkhiv* 8 (1901), 461.
114. Rostopchin (1889), 715; Narichkine, 161–162; Rostopchin to Peter Tolstoy, 13 September 1812, in *Russkii arkhiv* 3 (1885), 441; Rostopchin to his wife, 13 September 1812, in *Russkii arkhiv* 8 (1901), 461; Rostopchin to the Senate, 9 August 1814, in *Russkii arkhiv* 6 (1868), 884.
115. Pierre de Ségur, 'Rostopchin en 1812,' in *La Revue de Paris* 7 (1902), 104; Rostopchin (1889), 715.
116. A.B. Golitzyn, 'Zapiski o voine 1812 goda,' in *Voennyi sbornik* 12 (1910), 24.
117. Tartakovskii, 93.
118. 'Razgovor s A.P. Yermolovym,' in *Russkii arkhiv* (1863), 856–857; Grabbe, 470.
119. Württemberg, 98–100; J.M. von Helldorff, *Aus dem Leben des kaiserlich-russischen Generals der Infanterie Prinzen Eugen von Württemberg* (Berlin, 1862), II, 58–59.
120. Kutuzov to Rostopchin, 13 September 1812, in *Borodino: dokumenty, pis'ma, vospominaniya*, 143–144; Rostopchin (1889), 717; Rostopchin to his wife, 13 September 1812, in *Russkii arkhiv* 8 (1901), 461; Rostopchin to the Senate, 9 August 1814, in *Russkii arkhiv* 6 (1868), 884.
121. *Russkii invalid*, 3 December 1846, No. 279, 1077. 'At 1 pm on [13] September [Kutuzov] assured me that the city would be defended,' Rostopchin later complained to the Imperial Senate. 'And yet, by midnight, he informed me that it would be abandoned.' Rostopchin to the Senate, 9 August 1814, in *Russkii arkhiv* 6 (1868), 884.
122. Rostopchin (1889), 716–717.
123. Rostopchin to his wife, (11pm) 13 September 1812, in Narichkine, 164–165.
124. Rostopchin (1889), 719–720; 'Zametki o 1812 gode,' in *Russkii arkhiv* 8 (1901), 503.
125. Rostopchin to Alexander, 13 September 1812, in *Russkii arkhiv* 8 (1892), 530–531.
126. Rostopchin to his wife, 15 September 1812, in Narichkine, 175; Rostopchin to his wife, 25 September 1812, in *Russkii arkhiv* 8 (1901), 474.
127. Rostopchin to Mikhail Vorontsov, 30 October 1812, in *Russkii arkhiv* 6 (1908), 270–271.
128. Dubrovin, *Moskva i graf Rostopchin*, VIII, 437. For various orders and instructions on evacuating government institutions see Gorshkov, *Moskva i Otechestvennaya voina 1812 g.*, I, 405–429.
129. For details see S. Tsvetkov, *Vyvoz iz Moskvy gosudarstvennykh sokrovisch v 1812 godu* (Moscow, 1912).
130. Bestuzhev-Riumin (1859), 80.
131. P. Chudimov to V. Soimonov, 17 November 1812, in Gorshkov, *Moskva i Otechestvennaya voina 1812 g.*, II, 16.
132. Napoleon to Alexander I, 20 September 1812, in *Correspondance de Napoléon*, XIV, No. 19213, 222.
133. For details see S. Shvedov, 'Sud'ba zapasa ognestrelnogo oruzhiya Moskovskogo arsenal v 1812 g,' in *Sovetskie arkhivy* (1985), No. 5; Idem, 'O zapasakh voennogo imushestva v Moskve v 1812 g,' in *Sovetskie arkhivy* (1987), No. 6.
134. Rostopchin (1889), 721.
135. Rostopchin to Balashov, 11 August 1812, in Dubrovin, *Otechestvennaia voina v pis'makh sovremennikov*, 70.
136. Dmitriev (1869), 237–238; Vyazemskii, 209–213. Vereshchagin's body, after being dragged through the market-place, was dropped in front of a small church, and was buried at the very spot on which it fell. For an insightful discussion of this case see 'F.V. Rostopchin i 'delo Vereshchagina," in Zemtsov, *1812 god. Pozhar Moskvy*, 26–40.
137. Snegirev, 540.
138. The main routes out of Moscow were: 1. Along the Nikolaemskaya Street towards the Rogozhskaya barrier in order to reach the Vladimirskaya road that led to Vladimir and Nizhnii Novgorod in the east. 2. Along the Taganskaya street towards the Pokrovaskaya and Spasskaya barriers that connected to the Bronitskaya/Ryazanskaya road that led to Ryazan in southeast. 3. Crossing the Moscow river to the Yakimanskaya district, then along the Bolshaya o Malaya Kaluzhskaya streets towards Kaluzhskaya

barrier that was on the Old Kaluga Road leading to Kaluga in the southwest. 4. Along the Meschanskaya street towards Krestovskaya (Troitskaya) barrier that led to the north.

139. Kolchugin, 46.
140. Yermolov, 172.
141. *Pis'ma 1812 goda M.A. Volkovoi k V.A. Lanskoi* (Moscow, 1990) <http://az.lib.ru/w/wolkowa_m_a/text_0010. shtml> (accessed on 4 April 2012).
142. Golitsyn, *Ofitserskie zapiski*, 18–19.
143. Bestuzhev-Riumin (1859), 81, 84.
144. Radozhitskii, 88–89.
145. Semen Klimych, 417.
146. Bestuzhev-Riumin (1859), 84.
147. Fedor Lubyanovskii, *Vospominaniya* (Moscow, 1872), 281.
148. Snegirev, 541.
149. Muravyev, 346.
150. Peter Zhdanov, *Pamyatnik Frantsuzam, ili priklyucheniya Moskovskogo zhitelya P … Zh …* (St Petersburg, 1813), 4.
151. Glinka, *Iz zapisok o 1812 gode* <http://www.museum.ru/1812/library/glinka1/glinka.html#p22>
152. 'Rasskazy ochevidtsev o dvenadtsatom gode: Na Mokhovoi,' *Moskovskie vedomosti*, March 1, 1872.
153. Mertvago, 316.
154. Sverbeyev, I, 72.
155. 'Rasskaz meshchanina Petra Kondratieva,' in *Russkii vestnik* 102 (1872), 275–276.
156. Bestuzhev-Riumin (1859), 79–80. Also see T. Tolycheva, *Rasskaz starushki o dvenadtsatom gode* (Moscow, 1878), 40–41.
157. Lebedev, 257.
158. Rostopchin to Vorontsov, 10 May 1813, in *Russkii arkhiv* 2 (1887), 181; Andrei Tartakovskii, 'Naselenie Moskvy v period frantsuzskoi okupatsii,' in *Istoricheskie zapiski* 93 (1973), 356–379; Bestuzhev-Riumin (1896), 376.
159. Ysarn, 2–3.
160. Radozhitskii, 89.
161. Ysarn, 2–3.
162. Evreinov, 104.
163. Vigel, IV, 54.
164. Sergei Glinka, 'Iz zapisok o 1812 gode,' <http://www.museum.ru/1812/library/glinka1/glinka.html#p41>
165. Christiani, 47.
166. Radozhitskii, 89.
167. Semen Klimych, 418.
168. Rostopchin to Major General Ivashkin, 12 September 1812, in Gorshkov, *Moskva i Otechesvennaya voina*, I, 430.
169. Police Constable A. Danilov's report, 27 December 1814, in Gorshkov, *Moskva i Otechesvennaya voina*, I, 430–431.
170. Karfachevskii, 165.
171. Bennigsen (1908), III, 94–95.
172. Police Constable Perkov's report, 10 November 1814, in Gorshkov, *Moskva i Otechesvennaya voina*, I, 431.
173. Fusil, 5–6.
174. Ryazanov, 46.
175. Rostopchin to his wife, 15 September 1812, in Narichkine, 175–176.
176. Kozlovskii, 106.
177. Ivan Yakovlev to E. Golokhvastova, 13 November 1812, in *Russkii arkhiv* (1874), 1057.
178. Rastkovskii, 31.
179. Pokhorskaya, 47–48.
180. Alexander Bulgakov, 'Zametka na pamyat,' in *Russkii arkhiv* (1866), 701–702.
181. 'Zapiski moskovskogo zhitelya …' in *1812 god v vospominaniyakh sovremennikov* (Moscow, 1995), 51.
182. Pokhorskaya, 48.
183. Nazarova, 79.
184. Nastasya Danilovna, 31.
185. Kruglova, 60.

186. 'Rasskaz dvorovoi zhenshiny o dvenadtsatom gode,' in Garin, 26.
187. Snegirev, 540.
188. Ivan Yakovlev to E. Golokhvastova, 13 November 1812, in *Russkii arkhiv* (1874), 1057.
189. Fusil, 5.
190. Alekseyev, 25.
191. Sub Lieutenant Vasilii Kalashnikov to State Councillor Grigorii Spiridov, 14 November 1812, in Gorshkov, *Moskva i Otechestvennaya voina 1812 g.*, II, 28; Kicheyev, 12.
192. Semen Klimych, 418–419. He later had to convince the manager of Count Golovkin's estate that it was French, not British, troops entering the city.
193. Mosolov, 336. Also see Fedor Golitsyn, 'Zapiski ...' in *Russkii arkhiv* 5 (1874), 1331.
194. Kolchugin, 46.
195. Kicheyev, 3.
196. Nazarova, 77.
197. Ryazanov, 45.
198. A samovar is a heated metal container traditionally used to boil water for tea in Russia.
199. Pokhorskaya, 48–49.

Chapter 4: The Conqueror

1. Bréaut des Marlot, 21–22.
2. Itinéraire des Archives de Caulaincourt, in Caulaincourt, *Mémoires*, 7.
3. Theodor Rehtwisch, *1812–1815. Geschichte der Freiheitskriege* (Berlin, 1908), I, 308.
4. Caulaincourt, *Mémoires*, 440.
5. Berthier to Murat, 13 September 1812, Chambray 1839, III, 404.
6. Berthier to Eugène, (9pm) 13 September 1812, in *Mémoires et correspondence politique et militaire du Prince Eugène*, VIII, 44.
7. Korbeletskii, 22–23.
8. Labaume, 181.
9. Un billet de Kaissarov, 14 September in Chuquet, *Lettres de 1812*, 31.
10. Akinfov, 206; Miloradovich, 59–60.
11. Denniée, 85–86.
12. Akinfov, 206; Miloradovich, 59–60.
13. Clausewitz, 136–137.
14. Bourgogne, 13.
15. Kicheyev, 7.
16. Combe, 96.
17. Dedem de Gelder, 248–249.
18. The precise time when Napoleon saw Moscow varies depending on source but most agree that it happened around 2pm.
19. Laugier, 71; Fantin des Odoards, 331–332.
20. Torquato Tasso, *Gerusalemme Liberata* (Florence, 1895), 102. English translation at 'Jerusalem Delivered' <http://omacl.org/Tasso/>
21. Walter, 43.
22. Bourgogne, 13.
23. Griois, II, 49.
24. Labaume, 183–184.
25. Fantin des Odoards, 331–332.
26. Soltyk, 259–260.
27. Bourgogne, 13.
28. Fantin des Odoards, 332.
29. Montesquiou-Fezensac, *Souvenirs*, 226–227.
30. Fain described this scene as taking place at the Dorogomilovskaya barrier. Fain, II, 53.
31. Damas, I, 118.
32. Montesquiou-Fezensac, 227.
33. Roos, 115; Seruzier, 215; Cerrini di Monte Varchi, 389.
34. Murat acknowledged entering Moscow at 2pm on 14 September. Murat to Eugène, [n.d.] in *Mémoires et Correspondance de Prince Eugène*, VIII, 47. Brandt's memoirs also refer to 2pm.
35. Kukiel, 213; Soltyk, 265.
36. Montesquiou-Fezensac, *Souvenirs*, 226.

37. Muralt, 69.
38. Combe, 102; Dedem de Gelder, 249–250; Bausset, II, 87–88; Fain, II, 52; Denniée, 85–87; Ségur, II, 31. Caulaincourt certainly repeats hearsay when he writes, 'The Russian officer in command could not speak highly enough of [Murat's] courage ... "Such is our admiration of you," he said, "that our Cossacks have passed word round that no one is to fire a shot at so brave a Prince. However, one of these days," he added, 'you will meet with misfortune.'" Armand de Caulaincourt, *With Napoleon in Russia: The Memoirs of General de Caulaincourt, Duke of Vicenza* (New York, 1935), 111.
39. Bourgogne, 13. Most were preoccupied with more mundane tasks, including securing provisions. Thus, Dedem de Gelder was thrilled to seize 'a herd of magnificent bulls', even though he had to give twenty-two of them to the Cossacks, who demanded a fair shair of the spoils. Dedem de Gelder, 250.
40. Korbeletskii, 24–25.
41. Ysarn, 7; Domergues, II, 42. Zemtsov suggests it was M. Sokolnicki (Zemtsov, 23) but it might have been Roman Soltyk.
42. Ysarn, 7–8.
43. Domergues, II, 42.
44. Chambray, 117; Soltyk, 270; Domergues, II, 42–43; Bausset, II, 89.
45. Vsevolozhskii, 22.
46. Bookseller Riess later recounted his conversation: 'Who are you ?' asked Napoleon. 'A French bookseller.' 'Ah! then you are one of my subjects.' 'Yes; but I have lived for a long time in Moscow.' 'Where is Rostopchin?' 'He has gone.' 'Where are the magistrates/municipal council?' 'Gone also.' 'Who is left in Moscow?' 'None of the Russians.' 'C'est impossible!' Riess swore that what he said was true. Napoleon frowned and remained for some time buried in thought.
47. Korbeletskii, 27.
48. Ségur, II, 32; Dumas, III, 443.
49. Denniée, 88–89; Korbeletskii, 25–26.
50. Muralt, 69.
51. Roos, 116–117.
52. Becker, 510.
53. Becker, 511.
54. Most Allied and Russian eyewitnesses testify to Murat's entry around 4pm. But some advance elements of Murat's force may have entered the city as early as 2pm. See Murat to Eugène [15 September 1812] in *Mémoires et correspondence politique et militaire du Prince Eugène*, VIII, 47; Brandt, 226.
55. Its composition remains unclear. Murat's cavalry was naturally present. Lagneau claims that only two regiments of the Old Guard were sent in to maintain order in the city but Dedem de Gelder's memoirs indicate that his division was present as well. Guyot, 142; Lagneau, 135; Dedem de Gelder, 249.
56. Major General Ivashkin to Titular Councillor Domontovich, 11 January 1813, in Gorshkov, *Moskva i Otechestvennaya voina 1812 g.,* II, 12; Tutolmin to Empress Maria Feodorovna, 17 December 1812, in *Chteniya v Imperatorskom Moskovskom obshestve istorii i drevnosti* 2 (1860), 164; Anonymous, 28.
57. Tutolmin to Empress Maria Feodorovna, 17 December 1812, in *Chteniya v Imperatorskom Moskovskom obshestve istorii i drevnosti* 2 (1860), 164. See also *1812 god v vospominaniyakh sovremennuikov,* 28.
58. According to Bestuzhev-Riumin, the Allied forced entered through the Dorogomilovskaya, Presnenskaya, Tverskaya and Miusskaya barriers. He also notes that the Allied entrance was preceded by an eighteen gun salvo. But another eyewitness, F. Becker, who lived at the Nikitskie Gates, makes no mention of the gun salvo. Bestuzhev-Riumin (1859), 87; Becker, 510–511.
59. Kicheyev, 8–9.
60. Domergues, II, 39; Ysarn, 4–5. According to one eyewitness, 'the square in front of the Spasskaya tower-gates was so full with people it was difficult to move'. Bestuzhev-Riumin (1859), 86. General Guyot recorded in his journal that some 'six or seven hundred criminals' attacked the Allied troops. Guyot, 142.
61. Vasilii Yermolaevich, 66.
62. Ryazanov, 50.
63. Vasilii Polyanskii's recollections, in Tolycheva, 40. Anna Kruglova recalled that her father, a wealthy merchant, had visited the arsenal on the eve of the Allied entry into the city and brought back a musket without a cock, saying 'though it is in disrepair, it might still be useful, maybe we will scare off the French'. Ibid, 59.
64. Ryazanov, 50.
65. Ryazanov, 51.
66. Muralt, 70. Philippe-Paul Ségur, who could not have witnessed the scenes in Moscow, offers a rather vivid image of 'the gates of the citadel appearing to be closed [and] ferocious cries issuing from within it:

men and women, of ferocious and disgusting appearance, appeared fully armed on the walls. In a state of filthy inebriety, they uttered the most horrible imprecations.' Ségur, II, 36.
67. Coignet, 322.
68. Ryazanov, 51.
69. Depending on the source, the Allies fired between two and five shots before shattering the gates and dispersing the crowd.
70. Coignet, 322.
71. Roos, 118.
72. Seruzier, 216–217.
73. Dedem de Gelder, 249.
74. Bestuzhev-Riumin, 363–364. Bestuzhev-Riumin was an official at the Votchinskii Department and witnessed this scene from the windows of the Senate building.
75. 'Otryvok iz chernovago pisma neizvestnogo litsa', in Schukin, III, 262.
76. Karfachevskii, 165.
77. Perovskii, 261–262. Ségur mentions a similar (possibly the same?) incident: 'We penetrated partly without opposition, partly by force, among these wretches. One of them rushed close to the king [Murat], and endeavoured to kill one of his officers. It was thought sufficient to disarm him, but he again fell upon his victim, rolled him on the ground, and attempted to suffocate him; and even after his arms were seized and held, he still strove to tear him with his teeth.' Ségur, II, 36.
78. Bestuzhev-Riumin (1859), 88.
79. Bestuzhev-Riumin, 364; *Histoire de la destruction de Moscou en 1812*, 77–78.
80. Ysarn, 4–5.
81. Roos, 117.
82. Roos, 120–121.
83. Clausewitz, 137–138.
84. Sherbinin, 26–27.
85. Mikhailovskii-Danilevskii and Bogdanovich refer to two squadrons; Miloradovich himself claimed these were two regiments, but it seems improbable.
86. Miloradovich, 60. Vasilii Perovskii, an eyewitness, however, speaks of General Panchulidzev negotiating with Sebastiani. Perovskii, 258–259.
87. Clausewitz, 138.
88. Ségur (1826), I, 245.
89. Pion des Loches, 295.
90. Muralt, 70.
91. Kool, 51.
92. Montesquiou-Fezensac, *Journal de la Campagne de Russie*, 52–53.
93. Montesquiou-Fezensac, *Journal de la Campagne de Russie*, 52.
94. Combe, 100.
95. The 4th Corps approached Moscow from the northwest and bivouacked near the village of Khoroshevo. The 1st RCC moved around the northern suburbs of Moscow, halting near the road to St Petersburg. The 5th Corps marched south of the Grande Armée and appeared near Moscow's Kaluga barrier. The 1st and 3rd Corps deployed on both sides of the main road leading to Moscow. The Old Guard bivouacked at the Dorogomilovo suburb. For details see Pelleport, II, 31–32; Fain, 53–54; Bonnet, 660–661; Montesquiou-Fezensac, 52; Fantin des Odoards, 332; Thirion de Metz, 199–201; Bourgoing, 111–112.
96. Bourgogne, 14–15.
97. Bourgogne, 15–16.
98. Pion des Loches, 295.
99. Vionnet de Maringone, 24–25.
100. Fantin des Odoards, 332
101. Bourgogne, 15.
102. Brandt, 226–227.
103. Mortier sent Roguet's division and the Vistula Legion, while keeping Delaborde's division outside the city. Paul-Charles Amable de Bourgoing recalled that 'Delaborde's division advanced to the suburbs that spread widely around the city. We had to spend the night in the open air because it was forbidden, at first, to take lodgings inside houses: it was feared that our scattered soldiers might commit disorders and cause fire – that is the usual consequence.' Bourgoing, 111.
104. Bourgogne, 16.
105. Vionnet de Maringone, 24–25.

106. Pion des Loches, 295–296.
107. Vionnet de Maringone, 24; Surrugues, 15.
108. Napoleon to Berthier, 15 September 1812, in Chambray, III, 405.
109. Chambray, I, 348–349; Mikhailovskii-Danilevskii, II, 287; Dubrovin, *Otechestvennaia voina v pis'makh sovremennikov*, 118–119.
110. Ségur, II, 33.
111. Ysarn refers to a 'tavern' – *la maison d'un traiteur* – near the Dorogomilovskii barrier. Ysarn, 8.
112. Constant, III, Chapter XXIV, <http://napoleonic-literature.com/Book_11/V3C24.html>
113. Kutuzov to Emperor Alexander, 10 September 1812, in *M.I. Kutuzov: Sbornik Dokumentov, IV, Part 1*, 175–176.
114. In his report of 16 September Kutuzov explained the difficult decision he had to make at the council of war at Fili. He noted that after 'the so bloody but victorious battle' his forces, particularly the Second Western Army, were in disarray and he could not have continued to make war without first receiving sufficient reinforcements. Otherwise, with both his flanks threatened by the enemy's enveloping manoeuvres, another battle would have resulted not just in 'the destruction of the remains of the army but in the bloodiest destruction and reduction to ashes of Moscow itself'. So to save the army, he decided, after 'consulting our most prominent generals', to abandon Moscow, from which, he hastened to note, 'all the treasures, the arsenal, and practically all belongings, both state and private, had been removed, and in which not a single gentleman remained'. To drive home this positive point, Kutuzov underscored that 'the enemy's entry into Moscow does not mean the conquest of Russia'. As long as the army remained in the field, Russia could still hope to prevail in this struggle. Alexander was quite impressed with this deftly couched dispatch and had it printed, with slight revisions, in the official newspaper *St Petersburgskie vedomosti* on 29 September. Kutuzov to Emperor Alexander, 16 September 1812, RGVIA, f. VUA, d. 3572, l. 47–50.
115. On 24 September John Quincy Adams noted in his diary that the Russian government was still silent regarding the recent events in Moscow. 'It was said there was a formal capitulation, but nothing has yet been officially published by the government respecting it.' The following day he wrote that 'the English are all preparing to leave the country; their fears are greater than I believe there is occasion for. My landlord, Strogovshikov, also came to me much alarmed and mortified at the present condition of his country – hinting, but afraid expressly to say, that Moscow is in the hands of the French, and still reposing confidence in the cunning of General Kutuzov. Nothing official has yet been published by the government concerning the occupation of Moscow, and the rumours are innumerable. Several persons, it is said, have been made to sweep the streets for having said that Moscow was taken; so that the people are afraid of talking.' It was only on 29 September that 'the occupation of Moscow by the French is at length officially announced by a report from Prince Kutuzov, and by a proclamation of the government. It is attenuated into a circumstance of trifling importance as to the ultimate issue of the war.' Adams, II, 404–408.
116. Marchenko, 500–501.

Chapter 5: 'And Moscow, Mighty City, Blaze!'

1. Alexander Pushkin, *Sochineniya* (St Petersburg, 1859), 254. 'Fight on, embattled Russia mine, / Recall the rights of ancient days! / The sun of Austerlitz, decline! / And Moscow, mighty city, blaze!'
2. Biot, 41–42.
3. Dumas, III, 445.
4. Pion des Loches, 296–297.
5. Berthier to Eugène, 15 September 1812, in *Mémoires et correspondence politique et militaire du Prince Eugène*, VIII, 46.
6. Labaume, 194.
7. Adam, 203–204
8. Eugène to his wife, 15 September 1812, in *Mémoires et correspondence politique et militaire du Prince Eugène*, VIII, 46. See also his letters of 17–18 September in Ibid, 47–48.
9. According to Labaume, in the morning of 15 September, 'While the 13th and 15th Divisions encamped around the Petrovskii Palace, the 14th established itself in the village situated between Moscow and the palace, and the Bavarian light horse, under the orders of Count Ornano, were a league in advance of that village.'
10. Adam, 204. Also see Biot, 42.
11. Labaume, 195.
12. Laugier, 73.

13. Molosov, 337.
14. Zalusky, 527. Zalusky was referring to the infamous massacre of the Polish residents of Praga, a suburb of Warsaw, by the Russian troops led by General Alexander Suvorov in 1794.
15. Zalusky, 528.
16. Maxim Sakov to Ivan Batashov, [n.d.] September 1812, in *Russkii Arkhiv* (1871), 0218.
17. Maxim Sakov to Ivan Batashov, [n.d.] September 1812, in *Russkii Arkhiv* (1871), 0218–0219.
18. Bestuzhev-Riumin, 362.
19. Fain, II, 86–87.
20. Muralt, 74–75.
21. Bestuzhev-Riumin, 370.
22. Chudimov to Soimonov, 17 November 1812, in Gorshkov, *Moskva i Otechestvennaya voina 1812 g.*, II, 16.
23. Maxim Sakov to Ivan Batashov, [n.d.] September 1812, in *Russkii Arkhiv* (1871), 0218–0219; Nevzorov to Golenischev-Kutuzov, 3 December 1812, in Gorshkov, *Moskva i Otechestvennaya voina 1812 g.*, II, 20. Ysarn agrees with them, noting that the first fire broke out in the *Solyanka*, near the Foundlings Home, and subsequent break-outs took place in the Merchant Court. Ysarn, 8–9. Interestingly, F. Becker recalled seeing the first fires starting in the Merchant Court on 'Sunday', that is 13 September, while the Russians were still abandoning the city. Becker, 509.
24. Pion des Loches, 297.
25. Vionnet de Maringone, 27–30.
26. *Materialy dlya istorii Imperatorskogo Moskovskogo Vospitatelnogo doma* (Moscow, 1863), 100.
27. Tutolmin to Emperor Alexander, 19 September 1812, in Gorshkov, *Moskva i Otechestvennaya voina 1812 g.*, II, 64; Tutolmin to Dowager Empress Maria Fedorovna, 23 November 1812, in *Russkii arkhiv* 11 (1900), 462–473; Christiani, 47. For the costs of maintaining these gendarmes at the Foundlings Home see the Register of Expenses in Provisions and Forage, 23 November 1812, in Gorshkov, *Moskva i Otechestvennaya voina 1812 g.*, II, 44–47.
28. Christiani, 47–48.
29. Surrugues, 27–28.
30. Dedem, 250–251. When Madame Fusil's companion went to check the nature of these rockets, he reported that it was 'a small balloon with the Congrève rockets [*fusée à la Congrève*] that exploded at the house of Prince Trubetskoi in the Pokrovka district'. Fusil, 7.
31. Quaij, 103.
32. Roos 122–123.
33. *M.I. Kutuzov: Sbornik Dokumentov*, IV, part 1, 473.
34. Kaptsevich to Arakcheyev, 16 September 1812, in Dubrovin, 122.
35. Rostopchin to Golitsyn, 28 December 1812, *Journal of Outgoing Correspondence of Governor Rostopchin*, 234.
36. Becker, 512.
37. Bausset, II, 89, 91.
38. Bausset, II, 91–92.
39. Duverger, 142.
40. Boulart, 258–259.
41. Montesquiou-Fezensac, 233.
42. Fain, II, 86–87.
43. Chudimov to Soimonov, 17 November 1812, in Gorshkov, *Moskva i Otechestvennaya voina 1812 g.*, II, 16.
44. Brandt, 227–228.
45. Caulaincourt, *Mémoires*, II, 4–5.
46. Bourgogne, 16.
47. Bourgoing, 111–112.
48. Scheltens, 154.
49. Pion des Loches, 296.
50. Kicheyev, 12–16.
51. Montesquiou-Fezensac, *Journal de la Campagne de Russie*, 55–56.
52. Combe, 102–103.
53. Brandt, 227.
54. Combe, 106.
55. Montesquiou-Fezensac, *Journal de la Campagne de Russie*, 56.

56. Vionnet de Maringone, 30.
57. Pion des Loches, 298.
58. Letters of Shirovskii and Schroeder to the Moscow Trustee Council, January 1814, in Gorshkov, *Moskva i Otechestvennaya voina 1812 g.*, II, 51–52.
59. Herzen, 32.
60. Polyanskii, 40–41.
61. Alekseyev, 25–26.
62. Kruglova, 60–61.
63. Herzen, 32–33.
64. Brandt, 228.
65. Nazarova, 81.
66. Alekseyev, 26.
67. Soltyk, 273–278.
68. The precise moment of Napoleon's entry varies depending on source. Ségur states that it took place at dawn, Gourgaud and Constant refer to 6am, Denniée to 8am, Korbeletskii and René Bourgeois to 11am, Caulaincourt to noon and Ysarn to around 2pm.
69. Meneval, III, 63–64.
70. Napoleon to Marie-Louise, 16 September 1812, in *Correspondance générale*, XII, 1099; *Lettres inédites de Napoléon 1er à Marie-Louise écrites de 1810 à 1814* (Paris, 1935), 78.
71. Dominique Larrey to his wife, 15 September 1812, in *L'Intermédiaire des chercheurs et curieux: Notes and queries français* (Paris, 1912), vol. 66, 278.
72. Meneval, III, 63–64.
73. Quaij, 103.
74. St Denis, 28.
75. None of the existing biographies or campaign histories deals in detail with Napoleon's activities during the first week in Moscow. Neither the famous *Correspondance de Napoléon*, nor the *Correspondance militaire de Napoléon*, *Correspondance inedite de Napoléon* or other compilations of Napoleon's papers contain much information on Napoleon's activities between 14 and 20 September. Thus, Picard and Tuetey's *Correspondance inedite de Napoléon* contains only the 19th and 20th Bulletins, while the *Correspondance de Napoléon* includes just two orders that Napoleon had issued on the 15th. The *Correspondance militaire de Napoléon* skips from 6 September directly to 23 September. Fortunately the newly published *Correspondance générale* contains over a dozen documents from this period. In addition, some insights can be gleaned from correspondences of Eugene, Davout and other marshals and generals who received orders and instructions from Napoleon.
76. Dumas, III, 446.
77. Napoleon to Berthier, 15 September 1812, *Correspondance de Napoléon*, XIV, Nos. No. 19,207, 218.
78. Napoleon to Bessieres, 15 September 1812, S.H.D., département de l'Armée de Terre, 17 C 113; *Correspondance de Napoléon*, XXIV, No. 19,206, 218.
79. Caulaincourt, II, 11.
80. Combe, 104.
81. Constant, Chapter XXIV, <http://www.napoleonic-literature.com/Book_11/V3C24.html>
82. Proclamation aux habitants de Moscou in Chuquet, *La guerre de Russie*, I, 78.
83. Bourgogne, 23.
84. Laugier, 73.
85. Labaume, 197–198.
86. Ibid, 199–200.
87. Fantin des Odoards, 333.
88. Duverger, 141–142.
89. Roos, 125.
90. Pion des Loches, 298–300.
91. Kicheyev, 20.
92. Maxim Sakov to Ivan Batashov, [n.d.] September 1812, in *Russkii Arkhiv* (1871), 0218–0219.
93. Zemtsov questions the veracity of this attack, which has been mentioned by most Russian historians. Zemtsov, 98.
94. Bourgogne, 24.
95. Quaij, 104.
96. Maxim Sakov to Ivan Batashov, [n.d.] September 1812, in *Russkii Arkhiv* (1871), 0218; Surrugues, 28–31; Castellane, 154–155; Vionnet de Maringone, 29.

97. Pion des Loches, 300.
98. Duverger, 143.
99. Fusil, 8–9.
100. Fain, II, 87.
101. Pion des Loches, 300.
102. Maxim Sakov to Ivan Batashov, [n.d.] September 1812, in *Russkii Arkhiv* (1871), 0218; Ysarn, 8–9.
103. St Denis, 24.
104. Bourgoing, 112–113.
105. Ysarn, 9.
106. List, 89.
107. Kicheyev, 20.
108. St-Denis, 23.
109. Napoleon's letter to Marie Louise, written in the morning of 16 September, betrays no hint of the disaster unfolding in Moscow and instead describes the wealth of the city, briefly mentioning that Napoleon was recovering from a cold. Napoleon to Marie Louise, 16 September 1812, in *Lettres inédites de Napoléon Ier à Marie-Louise, écrites de 1810 à 1814*, 78.
110. St-Denis, 23.
111. Chambray, I, 355.
112. Fain, II, 86–87.
113. Mestivier's attestation in Ségur, *Histoire et mémoires*, VI, 17–18.
114. Ysarn, 10.
115. Nevzorov to Golenischev-Kutuzov, 3 December 1812, in Gorshkov, *Moskva i Otechestvennaya voina 1812 g.*, II, 21–22.
116. Dominique Larrey to his wife, 15 September 1812, in *L'Intermédiaire des chercheurs et curieux: Notes and queries français* (Paris, 1912), vol. 66, 278; Larrey, *Mémoires*, IV, 64.
117. Perovskii, 264–265.
118. Ségur, 292–293.
119. Las Cases, III, 172.
120. Caulaincourt, II, 12–13.
121. *Ordre du Jour*, 16 September 1812, RGVIA, f. 846, op. 16. d. 3588, l. 1.
122. Berthier to Mortier, 16 September 1812, in Chuquet, *La guerre de Russie* (1er Sér), 79.
123. Boulart, 259–261.
124. Martens, 133.
125. Kicheyev, 21.
126. Ysarn, 15–20.
127. Fain, II, 88.
128. Bourgogne, 26–27.
129. Boulart, 260–261.
130. Montesquiou-Fezensac, 234.
131. Caulaincourt, II, 13; Fain, II, 90.
132. Caulaincourt, II, 14; Gourgaud, 276.
133. Caulaincourt, II, 14.
134. Caulaincourt, II, 14.
135. Chambray, I, 355–356.
136. Meneval, III, 68–69.
137. Montesquiou-Fezensac, *Souvenirs*, 235; Larrey, IV, 65.
138. Montesquiou-Fezensac, *Souvenirs*, 235.
139. Gourgaud, 283–284; Montesquiou-Fezensac, *Souvenirs*, 234–235; Caulaincourt, II, 14–16.
140. Denniée, 95.
141. Ségur, *Histoire de Napoléon et de la Grande-Armée*, II, livre VIII, 50–51.
142. Perovskii, 265–266.
143. Peyrusse to Andre, 21 September 1812, in Peyrusse, *Memorial*, 96.
144. Gourgaud, 278; Meneval, III, 69; Caulaincourt, II, 15.
145. *Itinéraire des Archives de Caulaincourt*, in Caulaincourt, II, 15. Mathieu Dumas says 3pm. Dumas, III, 448.
146. Interestingly, Fantin des Odoards describes the passage as rather narrow and difficult, with the Imperial Guard troops marching through in single file. Yet, Peyrusse also speaks of the imperial treasury, moved

in carriages, accompanying Napoleon. It is unclear if the treasury wagon used a different gate to leave the Kremlin. Fantin des Odoards, 334; Peyrusse to Andre, 21 September 1812, in Peyrusse, *Memorial*, 96.
147. Denniée, 95.
148. Gourgaud, 280.
149. The Vsekhsvyatskii bridge was the first permanent stone bridge in Moscow and was completed in 1693. It was located some distance away from the Kremlin's southeastern tower (Vodovzvodnaya or Sviblov's Tower) and connected the city centre to the Zamoskvorechye. It was demolished in the 1850s.
150. Peyrusse to Andre, 21 September 1812, in Peyrusse, *Memorial*, 96.
151. Fantin des Odoards, 334.
152. Constant, Chapter XXIV, http://napoleonic-literature.com/Book_11/V3C24.html
153. Bourgogne, 30.
154. Dumas, III, 449–450.
155. St-Denis, 26.
156. Montesquiou-Fezensac, 235.
157. Ségur, *Histoire de Napoléon et de la Grande-Armée*, II, livre VIII, 53–54.
158. Gourgaud, 280.
159. Domergues, II, 68–70.
160. Boulart, 261.
161. Korbeletskii, 33.
162. Caulaincourt, II, 16.
163. Stendhal to Felix Faure, 4 October 1812, in *Correspondance de Stendhal*, I, 390.
164. Dumas, III, 450.
165. Planat de la Faye, 90.
166. Montesquiou-Fezensac, *Souvenirs*, 237. Similar description in Prosper to his stepfather, 15 October 1812, in *Lettres interceptées pendant la Campagne de 1812*, 149.

Chapter 6: The Great Conflagration
1. O'Meara, I, 196.
2. Peyrusse to Andre, 21 September 1812, in *Lettres inédites*, 93.
3. Le Roy, 169. See similar descriptions in Rigau, 60–61.
4. Vionnet de Maringone, 30–32.
5. Surrugues, 23.
6. Larrey, IV, 73.
7. Larrey, IV, 73–74.
8. Eugène to his wife, 17 September 1812, *Mémoires et correspondence politique et militaire du Prince Eugène*, VIII, 47.
9. Rapp, 209–211.
10. Larrey, IV, 75.
11. Ryazanov, 72.
12. Chambray, 355–356.
13. Labaume, 213.
14. Kicheyev, 31, 39.
15. Labaume, 211–212.
16. Planat de la Faye, 90.
17. Larrey, IV, 76.
18. Kicheyev, 39–40.
19. Norov, 208.
20. Chambray, 355–356.
21. Laugier, 75.
22. Combe, 105.
23. Adam, 208f.
24. Pion des Loches, 302.
25. Pion des Loches, 302.
26. Griois, II, 56–57.
27. Dumas, III, 453.
28. Nevzorov to Golenischev-Kutuzov, 3 December 1812, in Gorshkov, *Moskva i Otechestvennaya voina 1812 g.*, II, 22.

29. Ryazanov, 76–77.
30. Karfachevskii, 166.
31. Christiani, 48.
32. Surrugues, 24–25. Their actions, noted the abbé, 'saved the entire district, including [the Kuznetskii bridge], the Rozhdestvenka and Lubyanka streets, the post office, the bank, the Clean Ponds [Chistye prudy] and part of the Pokrovka between the boulevards and the Maroseika street.' Built in the mid-eighteenth century, the Kuznetskii bridge was a stone three-arched bridge across the Neglinnaya river. It was 16 metres wide and some 30 metres long. In 1818–1819, after the Neglinnaya river was placed in an underground masonry canal, the bridge was buried as well. The Clean Ponds is a large pond located in the Basmanny district.
33. Fusil, 11, 15–17.
34. Kolchugin, 47–48.
35. Kruglova, 60.
36. Priest Legonin to Bishop Augustin of Moscow, 11 March 1813; Priest Vasilii Gavrilov to Bishop Augustin of Moscow, 17 December 1813; Archpriest Romodanovskii to Bishop Augustin of Moscow, 25 March 1813, in Gorshkov, Moskva i Otechestvennaya voina 1812 g., II, 88–90, 100. Also see Popov, Frantsuzy v Moskve, 144–147; L. Melnikova, Armiya i Pravoslavnaya tserkov' Rossiiskoi imperii v epokhu napoleonovskikh voin (Moscow, 2007), 113.
37. Priest Vasilii Gavrilov to Bishop Augustin of Moscow, 17 December 1813, in Gorshkov, Moskva i Otechestvennaya voina 1812 g., II, 90.
38. Karfachevskii, 166.
39. Priest Vasilii Gavrilov to Bishop Augustin of Moscow, 17 December 1813, in Gorshkov, Moskva i Otechestvennaya voina 1812 g., II, 90.
40. In Orthodox Christianity, a hieromonk can be either a monk who has been ordained to the priesthood or a priest who has received monastic tonsure.
41. Hieromonk Aaron to Bishop Augustin, January 1813, in Gorshkov, Moskva i Otechestvennaya voina 1812 g., II, 30.
42. Hieromonk Aaron to Bishop Augustin, January 1813, in Gorshkov, Moskva i Otechestvennaya voina 1812 g., II, 30.
43. Ryazanov, 81, 135–137.
44. Semen Klimych, 420.
45. Sister Antonina, 9; 'Tableau synoptique de la Grande Armée' in Emile Marco de Saint-Hilaire, Histoire de la Campagne de Russie, 1812 (Paris, 1846) II, 374.
46. Semen Klimych, 420.
47. Sister Antonina, 9.
48. For details see Semen Klimych, 420–421.
49. Ibid., 9–10.
50. Semen Klimych, 421–422.
51. Nazarova, 84–85.
52. Karfachevskii, 166.
53. Semen Klimych, 427.
54. Histoire de la destruction de Moscou en 1812, 149.
55. See letters of A. Nikiforov, Priest V. Veniaminov, Priest T. Tankovskii, Privy Councillor N. Obreskov to Bishop Augustin of Moscow, November 1812–February 1813, in Gorshkov, Moskva i Otechestvennaya voina 1812 g., II, 136–137, 139–140.
56. Becker, 519.
57. Sister Antonina, 14.
58. Ryazanov, 143–144.
59. Ryazanov, 191–192.
60. 'Opisanie proischestvii v Moskovskom Danilove monastyre vo vremya nashestviya nepriyatelya v Moskvu v 1812 godu,' in Chteniya v Imperatorskom Moskovskom obshestve istorii i drevnosti 1 (1861), 195.
61. 'Griboedosvkaya Moskva v pismakh M.A. Volkovoi k V.I. Lanskoi, 1812–1818gg.' in Vestnik Evropy 8 (1874), 613.
62. 'Rasskazy ochevidtsev o dvenadtsatom gode: Na Mokhovoi,' Moskovskie vedomosti, March 1, 1872.
63. Lebedev, 259.
64. Surrugues, 10–11.
65. Russkii arkhiv (1864), 1195.

66. Kicheyev, 40.
67. Kruglova, 61–62.
68. Ysarn, 23. Also see Kool, 56.
69. Alekseyev, 26.
70. Kicheyev, 19.
71. Schukin, VII, 214.
72. Becker, 513.
73. Fusil, 10–11.
74. Kicheyev, 39.
75. Domergues, I, 46.
76. 'Opisanie proischestvii v Moskovskom Danilove monastyre vo vremya nashestviya nepriyatelya v Moskvu v 1812 godu,' in *Chteniya v Imperatorskom Moskovskom obshestve istorii i drevnosti* 1 (1861), 195.
77. Sister Antonina, 13–14.
78. Alexey Olenin, 'Rasskazy iz istorii 1812 g.' in *Russkii arkhiv* 12 (1868), Entry No. 14, <http://www.museum.ru/1812/library/Ra1/index.html>
79. *Histoire de la destruction de Moscou en 1812*, 111–112.
80. 'Griboedosvkaya Moskva v pismakh M.A. Volkovoi k V.I. Lanskoi, 1812–1818gg.' in *Vestnik Evropy* 8 (1874), 615–616.
81. Tutolmin to Dowager Empress Maria Fedorovna, 23 November 1812, in *Russkii arkhiv* 11 (1900), 472; *Chteniya v Imperatorskom obshestve istorii i drevnostei rossiiskikh* 2 (1860), 179.
82. Sokolskii's letter in Garin, 48.
83. Soltyk, 253f.
84. Brandt, 227.
85. Kicheyev, 23–24.
86. Dumas, III, 446–447.
87. Chambray, II, 124.
88. 19th Bulletin, 16 September 1812, *Les Bulletins de la Grande Armée*, V, 298.
89. 20th Bulletin, 17 September 1812, *Les Bulletins de la Grande Armée*, V, 302–303.
90. See Arthur Chuquet, ed. *Ordres et apostilles de Napoléon, 1799–1815* (Paris, 1911), II, 453.
91. 23rd Bulletin, 9 October 1812, *Les Bulletins de la Grande Armée*, V, 308.
92. Tutolmin to Dowager Empress Maria Fedorovna, 23 November 1812, *Chteniya v Imperatorskom obshestve istorii i drevnostei rossiiskikh* 2 (1860), 168–169.
93. Rostopchin to his wife, 13 September 1812, in *Russkii arkhiv* 8 (1901), 461–462; Wyllie to Arakcheyev, 24 September 1812 in Dubrovin 1882, 133–136. According to Wyllie, 8,000 wounded were at the Golovinskie Kazarmy and another 5,000 at the Spasskie Kazarmy. Some 4,000 were lodged at the Alexandrov and Ekarinenskii Institutes, 3,000 at the Kudrinskii Institute, about 2,000 at the Western Palace and some 500 were billeted at private apartments.
94. Yermolov (1863), 190.
95. For example see Nikolai Raspopov, 'Iz vospominanii Nikolaya Maksimovicha Raspopova,' in *Russkii arkhiv* 9 (1879), 39–41.
96. For details see Mikhailovskii–Danilevskii, II, 331; S. Melgunov, 'Rostopchin – Moskovskii glavnokomanduyushii,' in *Otechestvennaya voina i Russkoe obschestvo* (Moscow, 1911), IV, 79–80; A. Smirnov, 'Tak skolko ze ikh bylo. Ob ostavlennykh v Moskve ranenykh,' in *Proceedings of the III All-Russian Scientific Conference*, 2000, <http://www.chasseurs.ru/Biblio/ssmirnov.html>
97. Miritskii to Tutolmin, 9 December 1812, in Gorshkov, *Moskva i Otechestvennaya voina 1812 g.*, II, 50; Tutolmin to Emperor Alexander, 17 December 1812, in *Chteniya v Imperatorskom Moskovskom obshestve istorii i drevnosti* 2 (1860), 170.
98. Kicheyev, 41.
99. Norov, 206–207.
100. Turiot's letter of 27 September 1812, cited in Soubiran, 257. Similar description in Larrey, IV, 31.
101. Turiot's letter of 27 September 1812, cited in Soubiran, 263–264.
102. Kool, 53.

Chapter 7: In the Ruins of the Great City

1. Chambray, Labaume and others claim that Napoleon returned to the Kremlin on 20 September. However, Caulaincourt's journal, together with Castellane's diary and the memoirs of Peyrusse, Denniée, Pion des Loches and others clearly refer to his return on 18 September.
2. Soltyk, 263–265; Castellane, I, 155; Griois, II, 54.

3. Planat de la Faye, 90.
4. 19th Bulletin, 16 September 1812, *Les Bulletins de la Grande Armée*, V, 294, 297.
5. Caulaincourt, II, 16.
6. For reactions in Paris, see *Correspondance et Relations de J. Fiévée avec Bonaparte*, III, 239–240.
7. 20th Bulletin, 17 September 1812, *Les Bulletins de la Grande Armée*, V, 302–304.
8. Castellane, 155–156; Méneval, III, 66. Bourgogne, however, describes being dispatched with some 200 men to the Yellow Palace on 19 September, when Napoleon was already in the Kremlin. His account also confirms the burning of the palace 'a quarter of an hour' after his arrival there. Bourgogne, 38.
9. Much of what we know about her meeting with Napoleon comes from Aubert-Chalmé's conversation with Chevalier d'Ysarn. Ysarn, 13–15. A slightly different version is reported in Popov, *Frantsuzy v Moskve*, 83–84.
10. Alexander Bulgakov to Natalya Bulgakova, 31 October 1812, in *Russkii arkhiv* (1866), 704–705.
11. Fain, II, 93–94.
12. Fain, II, 94–95.
13. Caulaincourt, II, 18.
14. Zemtsov, 84.
15. Eugène to his wife, 21 September 1812, in *Mémoires et correspondence politique et militaire du Prince Eugène*, VIII, 50.
16. Dumas, III, 450.
17. Fain, II, 95–97.
18. A number of historians date Napoleon's return to 19 September but a closer examination of sources shows that he returned the day before.
19. Dumas notes that 'I was much astonished when I heard that the emperor had ordered [Berthier] and the Count de Narbonne to go themselves to the east part of [Moscow], where the ravages of the fire had been less extensive, and examine the fine summer-palace which had been preserved. This order clearly indicated the fatal resolution which the emperor had taken to return to Moscow, instead of falling back to the frontier of Lithuania, and going to meet his reinforcements and supplies, before the Russians should be able to harass his retreat. Dumas, III, 450–451.
20. Itinéraire des Archives de Caulaincourt, in Caulaincourt, *Mémoires*, II, 19f.
21. Ségur, *Histoire de Napoleon*, II, 63–64.
22. Caulaincourt, *Mémoires*, II, 21. 'The city is almost completely reduced to ashes,' confided Viceroy Eugène to his wife later that day. Eugène to his wife, 18 September 1812, *Mémoires et correspondence politique et militaire du Prince Eugène*, VIII, 48. See also Fantin des Odoards, 335; Castellane, I, 157.
23. Constant, III, Chapter XXV, <http://www.napoleonic-literature.com/Book_11/V3C25.html>
24. Napoleon to Cambacéres, 18 September 1812, in *Correspondance générale*, XII, 1100. Also see Napoleon to Marie Louise, 18 September 1812, Ibid., 1101.
25. Report on Destroyed Buildings, July 1817, in Gorshkov, *Moskva i Otechestvennaya voina 1812 g.*, II, 218–219; 'Kratkaya zapiska ostavshimsya v tselosti zdaniyam v Moskve,' in *Russkii arkhiv* (1864), 1203–1204.
26. Gorshkov, *Moskva i Otechestvennaya voina 1812 g.*, II, 218f; *Ministerstvo finansov 1802–1902* (St Petersburg, 1902) I, 616–617. 'Even two hundred years from now,' Napoleon lamented, 'Russia will not recover what has been lost here. It will not be an exaggeration to state that the losses will exceed one billion [francs].' Napoleon to Maret, 18 September 1812, in *Correspondance générale*, XII, 1101.
27. Ségur, *Histoire de Napoleon*, II, 64–65.
28. Korbeletskii, 38.
29. Ségur, *Histoire de Napoleon*, II, 64–65.
30. Montesquiou-Fezensac, *Journal de la Campagne de Russie*, 57.
31. Walter, 43.
32. Itinéraire des Archives de Caulaincourt, in Caulaincourt, *Mémoires*, II, 19f.
33. Napoleon to Berthier, 18 September 1812, S.H.D., département de l'Armée de Terre, 17 C 113; Fain, II, 99. Fain notes that 'this charitable mission was entrusted to an auditor of the State Council, *Busch*, who was known for his religious zeal'. Also see Napoleon to Berthier, 18 September 1812, in *Correspondance de Napoléon*, XXIV, No. 19209, 219; Korbeletskii, 36–39.
34. According to Fain, it was Napoleon's secretary and interpreter Lelorgne. Fain, II, 99. Tutolmin's letter of 19 September also notes that it was Lelorgne. However, his more detailed report, submitted on 17 December, notes that Napoleon also passed by the Foundlings Home on 17 September and dispatched General Dumas to pay his respects to Tutolmin. Zemtsov correctly points out that Napoleon could not have been near the Foundlings Home on the 17th since he was still at the Petrovskii Palace, and argues that Tutolmin simply made a mistake in dating the incident. It probably occurred on the 18th. Tutolmin

to Emperor Alexander, 19 September 1812, in Gorshkov, *Moskva i Otechestvennaya voina 1812 g.*, II, 64; Tutolmin to Empress Maria Feodorovna, 17 December 1812, in *Chteniya v Imperatorskom Moskovskom obshestve istorii i drevnosti* 2 (1860), 164; Zemtsov, *Pozhar Moskvy*, 106–107.

35. Itinéraire des Archives de Caulaincourt, in Caulaincourt, *Mémoires*, II, 19f.
36. Napoleon to Marie Louise, 18 September 1812, in *Lettres inédites de Napoléon Ier à Marie-Louise*, 78–80.
37. Bourgogne, 37.
38. Surrugues, 19.
39. Domergues, I, 47–48.
40. Kool, 53.
41. Napoleon to Maret, 18 September 1812, in *Correspondance de Napoléon*, XXIV, No. 19208, 219.
42. Castellane, I, 156–157.
43. *Histoire de la destruction de Moscou en 1812*, 103–104.
44. Christiani, 48.
45. Montesquiou-Fezensac, *Journal de la Campagne de Russie*, 59.
46. Muralt, 76.
47. Laugier, 83.
48. *Russkii arkhiv* (1864), 1201.
49. Montesquiou-Fezensac, *Journal de la Campagne de Russie*, 59.
50. Dumas, III, 453.
51. Beauvollier, 37.
52. Montesquiou-Fezensac, *Journal de la Campagne de Russie*, 64.
53. Kool, 53, 57.
54. Walter, 45.
55. Vionnet de Maringone, 42. Also see Kool, 53.
56. Thirion, 204.
57. Boulart, 262.
58. Combe, 106.
59. Walter, 45.
60. Brandt, 228.
61. Adam, 208.
62. Coignet did not mention the colonel's name but observed that he 'saw him afterwards at Vilna, frozen to death. God punished him. His servants robbed his body.'
63. Laugier, 73–74.
64. Tolstoy, *War and Peace*, 227.
65. Beauvollier, 37–38
66. Pion des Loches, 300.
67. Brandt, 228.
68. Itinéraire des Archives de Caulaincourt in Caulaincourt, II, 37f-38.
69. Schom, 634–635.
70. Caulaincourt's journal also shows that Napoleon made extended daily trips to visit various parts of Moscow between September 30 and October 11, staying at the Kremlin only on four days when he was reviewing troops.
71. Napoleon to Maret, 24 September 1812, in *Correspondance générale*, XII, 1110. In another incident Napoleon advised his Chief of Staff, 'I noticed in the status reports that the 6th Battalion of the 19th Line has been ordered to proceed to Smolensk. This is an error. Convey orders to Vilna and to Minsk to direct this battalion to Polotsk, where its corps is located.' Napoleon to Berthier, 4 October 1812, in Ibid., 1131.
72. Napoleon to Maret, 28 September 1812, in *Correspondance générale*, XII, 1119.
73. Napoleon mobilized over 650,000 men for the campaign and about 500,000 of these actually entered Russia. Of these, the Central Army Group – the Imperial Guard, the 1st, 2nd, 3rd, 4th, 5th, 6th, 7th and 8th Army Corps, and the 1st, 2nd, 3rd and 4th Reserve Cavalry Corps – amounted to some 380,000 men. Strategic and operational considerations, battle losses, illness and desertion in the first two months of the war reduced this force to some 180,000 men at Smolensk and 134,000 at Borodino. The Grande Armée lost some 35,000 men in the subsequent battle at Borodino. Berthier to Napoleon, 28 September 1812, in General Derrécagaix, *Le Maréchal Berthier, Prince de Wagram & de Neuchatel* (Paris, 1905), II, 437–438. This total excludes Andoche Junot's 8th Corps at Mozhaisk.
74. Montesquiou-Fezensac, *Journal de la Campagne de Russie*, 51.

75. John H. Gill, 'The Rheinbund in Russia 1812: The Württemberg Experience,' paper presented at the Consortium on the Revolutionary Era (Dallas TX, 2013). I am grateful to the author for allowing me to consult it.

76. In late September Davout's corps continued to hold the western suburbs of Moscow, while Ney's 3rd Corps held positions in the southeastern suburbs, controlling the roads to Tula and Ryazan. The troops from the 8th Corps were initially west of the Dorogomilovskii barrier but were then moved back to Mozhaisk. The 5th Corps initially took up positions near the village of Petrovskoe on the Vladimir road, but then moved to the Tula road around 21 September. Murat's advanced guard, consisting of the 2nd and 4th Cavalry Corps, with additional light cavalry brigades and infantry divisions of the 1st and 3rd Corps, held positions in the eastern suburbs of Moscow in the first two days of the occupation. On 16–17 September Sebastiani led part of the advanced guard (the 4th Cavalry Corps and part of the 2nd Cavalry Corps) in the wake of the Russian army as far as Bronitz, before realizing he had lost the enemy force. Defrance's carabiniers, meanwhile, remained on the Kaluga road until 23 September. Claparade's Vistula Legion, supported by Subervie's 16th Light Brigade, initially observed the Vladimir road but the Poles were then moved to the Ryazan road, where they took quarters in the village of Panki. Subervie's men, meanwhile, remained on the Vladimir road, advancing beyond Bogorodsk before veering to the southeast and arriving at Podolsk. When Napoleon moved to the Petrovskii Palace, he was followed by the Old Imperial Guard, which took up positions around the palace; the Young Guard remained deployed around the Kremlin, which was in turn held by a sole battalion of the Old Guard. The Guard Cavalry Division was still southwest of Moscow and approached the city only after 19 September. The 4th Corps, which approached Moscow from the northwest, also retained considerable forces in that area. It was soon joined by the 1st and 3rd Reserve Cavalry Corps, which took up positions on both sides of the roads leading to Tver and Dmitrov. According to one eyewitness, the officers of the Grande Armée demonstrated a thorough knowledge of Moscow's streets as they deployed the units throughout the city. 'Our consul Dorfland had supplied the best information and topographical details before the start of the war. He was present with the army and his directions were conveyed to everyone, from officers to the last soldier. It was remarkable to observe the French amidst this enormous city, some eight hundreds lieues from the motherland, orienting and moving their units in the Kremlin, Kitai-gorod or Belyi Gorod as if it was all taking place in their garrison hometown.' Domergues, I, 50.

77. Napoleon to Maret, 23 September 1812, in *Correspondance générale*, XII, 1110. For conscription issues see Napoleon to Clarke, 8 October 1812, Ibid., 1169–1170.

78. Napoleon to Maret, 23 September 1812; Napoleon to Berthier, 5–6 October 1812, in *Correspondance générale*, XII, 1110, 1135–1137, 1154. Napoleon told Clarke, his Minister of War, to raise reinforcements for the Guard voltigeurs and tirailleurs and dispatch four foreign regiments, deployed in Italy and Holland, to Poland. Napoleon to Clarke, 21 September–5 October 1812, in Ibid., 1106, 1137–1138.

79. Napoleon to Maret, 23 September 1812, in *Correspondance générale*, XII, 1110.

80. Napoleon to Maret, 23 September 1812, in *Correspondance générale*, XII, 1110. A week later, in a letter to his foreign minister, Napoleon voiced his harshest criticisms of the Poles: 'It seems my ambassador is an imbecile who does nothing and that the ministers of the grand duchy do not do anything either … Inform them of my strongest dissatisfaction at this exceedingly ill will … It is ridiculous that while I am suffering huge expenses for their cause, they do not want to cover even the simplest expenditures related to the maintenance of their corps.' Napoleon to Maret, 30 September 1812, in Ibid., 1123.

81. Napoleon to Berthier, 27 September–5 October 1812, S.H.D., département de l'Armée de Terre, 17 C 113.

82. Napoleon to Berthier, 19 September 1812, S.H.D., département de l'Armée de Terre, 17 C 113; Napoleon to Berthier, 21–23 September 1812 in *Correspondance de Napoléon*, XXIV, Nos. 19216–19217, 19220. He also made arrangements to have Russian prisoners of war transported from Poland and east Prussia to France. Napoleon to Berthier, 19 September 1812, in *Correspondance générale*, XII, 1101.

83. Napoleon to La Riboisière; Napoleon to Maret, 23 September 1812, in *Correspondance générale*, XII, 1109–1110.

84. Napoleon to Maret, 29 September 1812, in *Correspondance générale*, XII, 1121.

85. Napoleon to General La Riboisière, 18 September 1812, *Correspondance de Napoléon*, XXIV, No. 19210.

86. Napoleon to General La Riboisière, 3 October 1812, *Correspondance générale*, XII, No. 31793, 1127.

87. According to the report, the 1st, 3rd and 4th Corps, the reserve cavalry and the Guard were supposed to have 524 pieces, but only 381 were actually present in Moscow (with another 83 en route). Equally alarming was the situation with the artillery caissons. The 1st Corps was supposed to have 200 caissons but mustered 139, the 4th Corps had 310 instead of 390 and the reserve cavalry had 266 out of 310. This meant that only 715 caissons were available, instead of the supposed 900.

88. Napoleon to General La Riboisière, 3 October 1812, *Correspondance générale*, XII, No. 31794, 1127.
89. Napoleon to Berthier, 7 October 1812, S.H.D., département de l'Armée de Terre, 17 C 114.
90. Napoleon to La Riboisière, 8 October 1812, *Correspondance générale*, XII, 1173; Napoleon to Clarke, 11 October 1812 S.H.D., département de l'Armée de Terre, 17 C 326; Napoleon to Berthier, 12 October 1812, in Chuquet, *Ordres et apostilles de Napoléon*, 461.
91. Napoleon to Maret, 29 September 1812, in *Correspondance générale*, XII, 1121. Similar sentiment – 'I have the greatest need for horses' – in Napoleon to Maret, 6 October 1812, Ibid., 1158–1159.
92. Napoleon listed 'Hannover, Berlin, Glogau, Elbing, Thorn, Modlin, Koenigsberg, Gumbinen, Kovno, Vilna, Minsk, Merech, Lepel, Glubokoe, Smolensk, Mozyr, etc.' Napoleon to General Durosnel, 19 September 1812, *Correspondance générale*, XII, 1102.
93. Napoleon to Maret, 29 September 1812, in *Correspondance générale*, XII, 1121.
94. *Ordre du jour*, 18 September 1812, 'Extraits du Livre d'Ordres du 2e Régiment de Grenadiers a pied de la Garde imperiale,' in *Carnet de la Sabretache* 8 (1900), 575.
95. *Ordre du jour*, 18 September 1812, 'Extraits du Livre d'Ordres du 2e Régiment de Grenadiers a pied de la Garde imperiale,' in *Carnet de la Sabretache* 8 (1900), 576.
96. Pion des Loches, 303.
97. Berthier to Davout, 19 September 1812, RGVIA f. 846, op. 16, d. 3587, 1.1; Berthier to Eugène, 19 September 1812, in *Mémoires et Correspondance … du Prince Eugène*, VIII, 49.
98. Vionnet de Maringone, 33.
99. Lossberg, 190.
100. Kool, 52–53.
101. Berthier to Davout, 20 September 1812, RGVIA f. 846, op. 16, d. 3587, 1.2; Berthier to Eugène, 20 September 1812, in *Mémoires et Correspondance … du Prince Eugène*, VIII, 49–50.
102. Berthier to Davout, 21 September 1812, RGVIA, f. 846, op. 16, d. 3587, 1.3.
103. Chambray, I, 366; Napoleon to Berthier, 21 September 1812, in *Correspondance générale*, XII, 1105.
104. Roguet, IV, 492.
105. Bourgogne, 30–31.
106. Ysarn, 26–27. Also see G. Lecointe de Laveau, *Mosca avanti e doro l'incendio* (Milan, 1818), 111–112.
107. *Histoire de la destruction de Moscou en 1812*, 105–107.
108. *Ordre du jour*, 20 September 1812, 'Extraits du Livre d'Ordres du 2e Régiment de Grenadiers a pied de la Garde imperiale,' in *Carnet de la Sabretache* 8 (1900), 683.
109. *Ordre du jour*, 21 September 1812, 'Extraits du Livre d'Ordres du 2e Régiment de Grenadiers a pied de la Garde imperiale,' in *Carnet de la Sabretache* 8 (1900), 684–685.
110. *Ordre du jour*, 23 September 1812, 'Extraits du Livre d'Ordres du 2e Régiment de Grenadiers a pied de la Garde imperiale,' in *Carnet de la Sabretache* 8 (1900), 685–686.
111. Napoleon to Lefebvre, 23 September 1812, in *Correspondance générale*, XII, 1109.
112. These troops were drawn from the Young Guard, Roguet's division and the 1st, 3rd and 4th Corps. Napoleon to Berthier, 25 September 1812, in *Correspondance générale*, XII, 1111.
113. Napoleon to Berthier, 28 September 1812, S.H.D., département de l'Armée de Terre, 17 C 113. One battalion comprised carabiniers and cuirassiers, while the other included chasseurs, hussars and chevau-légers. See also Napoleon to Berthier, 30 September 1812, in *Correspondance générale*, XII, 1122.
114. *Ordre du jour*, 29 September 1812, 'Extraits du Livre d'Ordres du 2e Régiment de Grenadiers a pied de la Garde imperiale,' in *Carnet de la Sabretache* 8 (1900), 690–691.
115. To keep the Guard occupied, Napoleon required it to parade every day, at noon, in front of the imperial palace inside the Kremlin. 'The troops must be in full military uniform, with music, and all officers and staff of the Guard must be present as well.' *Ordre du jour*, 21 September 1812, 'Extraits du Livre d'Ordres du 2e Régiment de Grenadiers a pied de la Garde imperiale,' in *Carnet de la Sabretache* 8 (1900), 684. Nevertheless, some Guardsmen continued to rob and pillage. For example, Michel Marc, Police Commissar of the 13th District, reported that a *fourrier* of the 10th Guard Cavalry Company had robbed a Russian straggler. Marc's Report of 9 October 1812, RGVIA, f. 846, op. 16, d. 3587, 1. 12.
116. *Ordre du jour*, 29 September 1812, 'Extraits du Livre d'Ordres du 2e Régiment de Grenadiers a pied de la Garde imperiale,' in *Carnet de la Sabretache* 8 (1900), 692–693; *Russkii arkhiv* (1864), 408–410; *Ordre du jour*, 30 September 1812, RGVIA, f. 846, op. 16, d. 3587, 1. 4.
117. Napoleon to Berthier, 8 October 1812, in *Correspondance de Napoléon*, XXIV, No. 19264.
118. See 'Tableau par apercus des ressourses existantes après l'incendie dans la place de Moscou, 27 September 1812', in Popov, *Frantsuzy v Moskve*, 122f.
119. Commissar George Lalance's Report of 2 October 1812, RGVIA, f. 846, op. 16, d. 3587, 1. 7.
120. Joseph de Roch's Report of 5 October 1812, RGVIA, f. 846, op. 16, d. 3587, 1. 9.

121. Humbert Droz's Report of 11 October 1812, RGVIA, f. 846, op. 16, d. 3587, l. 14.
122. Berthier to Davout, 12 October 1812, in Popov, *Frantsuzy v Moskve*, 120.
123. Chudimov to Soimonov, 17 November 1812, in Gorshkov, *Moskva i Otechestvennaya voina 1812 g.*, II, 16.
124. Dumas, III, 455–456. A Russian report claims that once the cross was removed, Napoleon had an optical telegraph built on top of the Ivan the Great's tower. Perechen' izvestii iz Moskvy po 3–e oktyabrya, in *Ruskii arkhiv* (1864), 1202.
125. Pastoret, 530.
126. For example, he recruited foreigners residing in Moscow to provide intelligence. Major General Ivashkin to Emperor Alexander I, 11 November 1812, RGVIA., f. 846, op. 16, d. 3586, ll. 9–9b.
127. Interrogation Protocol of Jacob Dulon, July 1814, in Gorshkov, *Moskva i Otechestvennaya voina 1812 g.*, II, 114. Dulon lived in merchant Clementz's house at Maroseika.
128. Major General Ivashkin to Rostopchin, 7 August 1814; Interrogation Protocols of Paul Lacrois, F. Kotov, I. Kozlov, P. Nakhodkin, J. Dulon and V. Konyaev, July 1814, in Gorshkov, *Moskva i Otechestvennaya voina 1812 g.*, II, 107, 111–115. For biographical details of leading members of the municipality, see Zemtsov, 52–60.
129. Kolchugin, 46.
130. Cited in Zemtsov, 52; S. Bakhrushin, *Moskva v 1812 godu* (Moscow, 1913), 30–31.
131. There are several lists of notables who served in the municipal government and the total number of people differs depending on the document. See 'Raspisanie osobam, sostavlyavshim frantsuzskoe pravlenie ili munitsipalitet v Moskve 1812 goda,' in *Russki arkhiv* 4 (1864), 839–842; Schukin, Bumagi, I, 58–61; Gorshkov, *Moskva i Otechestvennaya voina 1812 g.*, II, 102–103.
132. Interrogation Protocol of Ivan Kozlov, July 1814, in Gorshkov, *Moskva i Otechestvennaya voina 1812 g.*, II, 113.
133. Interrogation Protocols of P. Nakhodkin and P. Korobov, July 1814, in Gorshkov, *Moskva i Otechestvennaya voina 1812 g.*, II, 112, 114.
134. Kolchugin, 49–50.
135. Cited in Popov, *Frantsuzy v Moskve*, 119. Popov consulted d'Horrer's handwritten manuscript which has not been located since.
136. A. Andreyev, '"Ya sluzhil gorodu, a ne vragu." Pismo professora Kh. Steltzera rektory Moskovskogo universiteta I.A. Heimu, 1812 g.' in *Istoricheskii arkhiv* 3 (1997), 44–45.
137. Interrogation Protocol of I. Kozlov, July 1814, in Gorshkov, *Moskva i Otechestvennaya voina 1812 g.*, II, 113.
138. Bestuzhev-Riumin (1859), 172–173.
139. Ysarn, 28.
140. Major General Ivashkin to Rostopchin, 7 August 1814; Interrogation Protocols, July 1814, in Gorshkov, *Moskva i Otechestvennaya voina 1812 g.*, II, 106–107, 110–111.
141. Interrogation Protocol of P. Nakhodkin; Interrogation Protocols of P. Nakhodkin and J. Dulon, July 1814, in Gorshkov, *Moskva i Otechestvennaya voina 1812 g.*, II, 112, 115.
142. Andreyev, 52.
143. *Proclamation*, 1 October 1812, in Schukin, I, 163; Gorshkov, *Moskva i Otechestvennaya voina 1812 g.*, II, 100–101; Popov, *Frantsuzy v Moskve*, 116–117. For an interesting discussion of the Russian historiography of this issue, see Zemtsov, 48–50.
144. For a concise overview see V. Zemtsov, 'Moskovskii munitsipalitet' in *Otechestvennaya voina 1812 goda i Osvoboditelnyi pokhod russkoi armii 1813–181 godov. Entsiklopediya* (Moscow, 2012), II, 527. Overall, the municipality employed over a hundred men in various capacities. V. Ulanov, who analysed eighty-seven high- and mid-ranking individuals of this municipality, concluded that more than twenty of them were foreigner subjects while thirty came from the Russian bureaucratic and merchant class. In addition, there were four retired officers and four scholars, including one professor. For details see V. Ulanov, 'Organizatsiya upravleniya v zanyatykh frantsuzami russkikh oblastyakh,' in *Otechestvennaya voina i Russkoe obschestvo*, IV, 121–140, <http://www.museum.ru/museum/1812/Library/sitin/book4_09.html>; E. Boldina, 'O deyatelnosti Vysochaishe uchrezhdennoi komissii dlya issledovaniya povedeniya i postupkov nekotorykh zhitelei vo vremya zanyatiya stolits nepriyatelem,' in *Otechestvennaia voina 1812 goda. Istochniki. Pamyatniki. Problemy* (Moscow, 2001), 30–63. Upon liberating Moscow, Major General Ilovaiskii IV prepared a list of individuals suspected of collaboration and submitted it to Rostopchin. The initial list consisted of just twenty-eight names. Ilovaiskii to Rostopchin, 28 October 1812, in *Russkii arkhiv* (1866), 697–699. To see forty-three top officials of the municipal government see Gorshkov, *Moskva i Otechestvennaya voina 1812 g.*, II, 102–103. A longer list of sixty-five names, ostensibly found in the municipal headquarters after the French retreat and preserved in Alexander Bulgakov's personal

papers, can be seen in 'Rospisanie osobam sostavlyavshim frantsuzskoe pravlenie ili municipalitet v Moskve, 1812 goda,' *Russkii arkhiv* (1864), 412–416.

145. Proclamation of 1 October 1812, in Gorshkov, *Moskva i Otechestvennaya voina 1812 g.*, II, 100–101. Members of the municipality wore two bands of red ribbon – a larger one across the right shoulder when acting in their official capacity, and a small one round their left arm when off duty. The head of the municipality also wore a white sash. Constables and minor officials wore bands of white ribbon round their left arms. Bestuzhev-Riumin, who served in the sixth department (dealing with the poor and sick), recalled that he did not wear a band on his arm but instead wore a red band across his chest. This band was made from the ribbon of the prestigious Order of St Alexander of Neva, which he inherited from his grandfather. Bestuzhev-Riumin also informs us that the houses of members of the municipality were marked with a special sign to protect them against any attacks. The gate to his house featured an inscription, 'logement d'adjoint au maitre de la ville'.

146. Ysarn, 28. For details on police officials see Zemtsov, 51; Gorshkov, *Moskva i Otechestvennaya voina 1812 g.*, II, 101f.

147. For the subsequent prosecution of the members of the municipal government see 'The Governing Senate's Decree of 31 October 1814', in Gorshkov, *Moskva i Otechestvennaya voina 1812 g.*, II, 116–125.

148. 2nd (Pyatnitskii) District's Commissioner Daniel Fabre's Report of 4–5 October 1812, RGVIA, f. 846, op. 16, d. 3587, l. 8.

149. Lassan's Report of 30 September 1812, RGVIA, f. 846, op. 16, d. 3587, ll. 5–5b.

150. Napoleon to Berthier, 6 October 1812, in *Correspondance générale*, XII, 1145.

151. *Proclamation*, 6 October 1812, in Schukin, I, 165.

152. Proclamation of 6 October, in Chambray (1825), 272–274.

153. Beauvollier, 38–39.

154. Zemtsov, 57–58. In contrast the third municipal official, Kozlov, successfully procured forty-six cows and thirty sheep.

155. Korbeletskii, 80.

156. Kolchugin, 50.

157. Alexey Olenin, 'Rasskazy iz istorii 1812 g.' in *Russkii arkhiv* 12 (1868), Entries Nos. 8 and 12, <http://www.museum.ru/1812/library/Ra1/index.html>

158. Perechen' izvestii iz Moskvy po 3–e oktyabrya, in *Ruskii arkhiv* (1864), 1201.

159. Beauvollier, 38–39.

160. Vendramini, 105.

161. Kolchugin, 50.

162. Laugier, 83–84.

163. Lejeune, II, 197.

164. Tutolmin to Dowager Empress Maria Feodorovna, September 1812, in Gorshkov, *Moskva i Otechestvennaya voina 1812 g.*, II, 93.

165. Bozhanov, 261–262.

166. Ryazanov, 191–192.

167. Kurz, 95–96.

168. Kurz, 95–96.

169. Vionnet, 42–43.

170. For just some instances see Chevalier, 208; Adam, 213; Lecointe de Laveau, 125–126.

171. Rostopchin to his wife, 15 September 1812, in Narichkine, 175–176.

172. Montesquiou-Fezensac, *Journal de la Campagne de Russie*, 59–60. Castellane bragged that he personally disarmed a dozen drunken Russian soldiers wandering around in the streets; nudging them along with a 'Cossack lance', he took them all to the headquarters. Castellane, I, 154.

173. Domergues, I, 49.

174. Combe, 106–107.

175. Maxim Sakov to Ivan Batashov, [n.d.] September 1812, in *Russkii Arkhiv* (1871), 0222.

176. Maxim Sakov to Ivan Batashov, [n.d.] September 1812, in *Russkii Arkhiv* (1871), 0223.

177. Poluyaroslavtseva, 7. Also see interrogations of peasants suspected of ransacking Count Stroganov's estate, Schukin, III, 44–56.

178. 'Razskaz o dvenadtsatom gode', in *Russkii arkhiv* 6 (1871), 0198–0199, 0206.

179. Vionnet de Maringone, 32–33.

180. 'Vypiska iz izvestii iz Moskvy, 30 September 1812,' in *Russkii arkhiv* (1864), 1193.

181. Popov, 72–73.

182. Alexander Bulgakov to Natalya Bulgakov, 31 October 1812, in *Russkii arkhiv* (1866), 705; Rostopchin to Alexander, 13 October 1812, in *Russkii arkhiv* 8 (1882), 547–548.
183. Surrugues, 20.
184. Ysarn, 21, 25.
185. Lecointe de Laveau, 112.
186. Surrugues, 28–29.
187. Labaume, 226.
188. Napoleon to Berthier, 18 September 1812, S.H.D., département de l'Armée de Terre, 17 C 113.
189. Soltyk, 255.
190. Poluyaroslavtseva, 9.
191. Years later Anna Grigorievna observed, 'All this sickened me, but the instinct for self-preservation is uppermost. If we had let them go after beating them, you can see that they would have gone away in a fury and returned with a band of their comrades to exterminate us to the last man. And so we had no pity. To the death!'
192. Kruglova, 64.
193. Sysoev, 13–14.
194. Alekseyev, 28–29.
195. Kozlovskii, 113.
196. Ryazanov, 90–94.
197. 'After this Fabricius took the consulate, a person came with a letter to the camp written by the king's principal physician, offering to take off Pyrrhus by poison, and so end the war without further hazard to the Romans, if he might have a reward proportional to his service. Fabricius, hating the villainy of the man, and disposing the other consul to the same opinion, sent despatches immediately to Pyrrhus to caution him against the treason. His letter was to this effect: "Caius Fabricius and Quintus Aemilius, consuls of the Romans, to Pyrrhus the king, good health. You seem to have made an ill-judgement both of your friends and enemies; you will understand by reading this letter sent to us, that you are at war with honest men, and trust villains and knaves. Nor do we disclose this to you out of any favour to you, but lest your ruin might bring a reproach upon us, as if we had ended the war by treachery, as not able to do it by force." When Pyrrhus had read the letter, and made inquiry into the treason, he punished the physician, and as an acknowledgement to the Romans sent to Rome the prisoners without ransom.' *Plutarch's Lives of Illustrious Men*, translated by John Dryden (New York, 1887), II, 26.
198. This conversation was retold by I.M. Kovalevskii, who heard it from Yermolov. See N. Rozanov, 'Zamysel Fignera, 1812 g.' in *Russkaya starina* (1875), XIII, 450–451.
199. Radozhitskii, 107–108.
200. 'Rasskazy iz istorii 1812 goda,' in *Russkii arkhiv* 11 (1868), 1867–1868. On a lighter note, it must noted that some Russian officers visited enemy-occupied Moscow as a dare. Prince Fedor Gagarin was well known for his gallantry as well as for recklessness and gambling. He earned his notoriety for a wild exploit he performed in the autumn of 1812. One evening, as a group of officers gathered for another round of drinking and gambling, Gagarin surprised everyone by announcing his bet that he would deliver two pounds of tea to Napoleon. Officers eagerly accepted this outlandish wager and Gagarin set out for Moscow. Precise details of what transpired next remain unclear but contemporaries were convinced that Gagarin had indeed reached the Kremlin, where he was detained and brought before Napoleon, who was amused by the prince's exploit and let him return to the Russian army. N.I. Kulikov, 'Vospominaniya', in *Russkaya starina* 12 (1880), 992.
201. Eugène de Beauharnais to his wife, 21 September 1812, in *Mémoires et Correspondance de Prince Eugène*, VIII, 50.
202. 'My intention is to allow complete freedom of the press, that it be entirely unhindered, and that only obscene works or those tending to foment political trouble be stopped.' Napoleon to Montalivet, 11 October 1812, in *Correspondance générale*, XII, 1181.
203. See Napoleon to Marie Louise, 24–27 September 1812 in *Correspondance générale*, XII, 1114, 1117.
204. Main Register Book of the Foundlings Home, September-October 1812, in Gorshkov, *Moskva i Otechestvennaya voina 1812 g.*, II, 37–42; Tutolmin to Dowager Empress Maria Feodorovna, 23 November 1812, *Russkii arkhiv* 11 (1900), 467; Tutolmin to Dowager Empress Maria Feodorovna, 17 December 1812, in *Chteniya v Imperatorskom Moskovskom obshestve istorii i drevnosti* 2 (1860), 171. Napoleon was not the only one to take care of orphans. Marshal Mortier, Duc de Treviso, made arrangements for the care of nine children (given the last name of Trevizskii) at the Foundlings Home, as did General Edouard Milhaud (given the last name Milievyi). At the Dowager Empress's request, all last names given to

children after French generals were later deleted from the records. Most of these orphans, aged between 2 weeks and 7 years, died between November 1812 and January 1813.
205. Laugier, 82.
206. Morand to his wife, 10 October 1812, in *Lettres interceptees par les Russes durant la campagne de 1812*, 66–67.
207. Bourgoing, 134.
208. Chlapowski, 127.
209. Duverger, 11–12.
210. For a fascinating discussion of the Moscow baths see Vionnet de Maringone, 51–55.
211. Britten-Austin, 84.
212. Bourgogne, 42–44.
213. Boulart, 262–264; Zaluski, 527–528.
214. Bausset claimed that Aurore Bursay directed this *troupe*, and in 1814 Bursay herself claimed that she was 'the manageress of the Imperial Theatre of Moscow'. Neither claim is true. The stage-manager of this *troupe* was Louis Antoine Domergues.
215. Bausset, 99–103; Fusil, 18–21.
216. Combe, 126; Count Dunin-Stryzewski to his wife, 12 October 1812, in *Lettres interceptees par les Russes durant la campagne de 1812*, 79.
217. For an interesting discussion between Napoleon and Narbonne see Villemain, I, 225–230.
218. For details see *Quand Napoléon inventait la France. Dictionnaire des institutions politiques, administratives et de cour du Consulat et de l'Empire* (Tallandier, 2008).
219. See Tony Sauvel, 'Le "décret de Moscou" mérite-t-il son nom?', *Revue historique de droit français et étranger*, 4e série, 53 (July 1975), 436–440.
220. Bourgogne, 50–51.
221. Andoche Junot to Baroness Elizabeth-Augusta Daniels, 13 October 1812, in *Lettres interceptees par les Russes durant la campagne de 1812*, 84.
222. Frederic-Charles List to his wife, 22 September 1812; Marchal to curé Thugnet, 25 September 1812, in *Ibid.*, 25, 34.
223. Muralt, 78.
224. Napoleon to Clarke, Napoleon to Maret, 24 September 1812, in *Correspondance générale*, XII, 1112–1113. On Napoleon's intentions to distribute these portable mills, see Napoleon to Berthier, 6 October 1812, Ibid., 1154. On 6 October the emperor complained that one month after departing from Paris these portable mills still had not reached Moscow. Napoleon to Maret, 6 October 1812, Ibid., 1159.
225. At Vilna alone the French authorities had 2 million rubles' worth of counterfeit money. Napoleon to Berthier, 27 September 1812, in Arthur Chuquet, *Ordres et Apostilles de Napoleon*, II, 431; Napoleon to Maret, 27 September 1812, in *Correspondance générale*, XII, 1117.
226. Napoleon to Berthier, 25 September 1812, S.H.D., département de l'Armée de Terre, 17 C 113; Napoleon to Berthier and Dumas, 25 September 1812, in Chuquet, *Ordres et Apostilles de Napoleon*, II, 429. Napoleon allowed troops who desired to send their pay to France to exchange these forged rubles for genuine 'franc-germinal'.
227. Vionnet de Maringone, 58.
228. Ysarn, 41–43.
229. Polyanskii, 44.
230. Griois, II, 55–56.
231. Thirion, 209.
232. Coignet, 212.
233. Peyrusse, *Mémorial*, 98.
234. Henckens, 132–139.
235. Bourgoing, 121.

Chapter 8: 'By Accident or Malice?' Who Burned Moscow?

1. Owen Connelly, *The French Revolution and the Napoleonic Era* (New York, 2000), 325.
2. 'Denkwürdigteiten des Freiherrn vom Stein aus dem Jahre 1812,' in *Nachrichten von der Königlichen gesellschaft der wissenschaften zu Göttingen* (1896), 190.
3. Tim Chapman, *Imperial Russia, 1801–1905* (London, 2001), 30.
4. Todd Fisher, *The Napoleonic Wars: The Empires Fight Back 1808–1812* (Oxford, 2001), 71.
5. Nigel Nicolson, *Napoleon 1812* (Cambridge, 1985), 94. Alexander M. Martin, *Enlightened Metropolis: Constructing Imperial Moscow, 1762–1855* (Oxford: Oxford University Press, 2013), 180, 193. Martin

cites two short articles from *Otechestvennaya voina 1812 goda: Entsiklopediya* but neither article refers to any <u>direct</u> orders by Rostopchin to burn the city.

6. Schmidt, 28.
7. *Russkaya starina* 12 (1883), 650–651; Dubrovin, 94, 114; Bogdanovich, II, 313–314.
8. Bagration to Rostopchin, 26 August 1812, in Dubrovin, 98. Alexander M. Martin, Enlightened Metropolis: Constructing Imperial Moscow, 1762–1855 (Oxford: Oxford University Press, 2013), 180, 193. Martin cites two short articles from *Otechestvennaya voina 1812 goda: Entsiklopediya* but neither article refers to any <u>direct</u> orders by Rostopchin to burn the city.
9. Nikolai Golitsyn, *Souvenir d'un officier russe pendant les campagnes 1812, 13, 14* (St Petersburg, 1848); Bertin, 123. Interestingly the Russian edition of Golitsyn's memoirs does not contain this passage.
10. Dmitrii Pozharskii was the Russian prince who led the Russian national struggle for independence against the Polish-Lithuanian invasion known as the Time of Troubles. Zakrevskii is playing on the meaning of his name, Pozharskii, derived from *pozhar*, meaning fire.
11. Wolzogen, 152.
12. Andrei Tartakovskii, 'Obmanutyi Gerostrat: Rostopchin i Pozhar Moskvy,' in *Rodina* 6/7 (1992), 89.
13. Schmidt, 46.
14. No. 7 Broadsheet, 29 August 1812, in *Afishy 1812 goda* <http://www.museum.ru/museum/1812/Library/rostopchin/>
15. Shakovskoi, 56.
16. Domergues, II, 54–55.
17. Rostopchin to Bagration, 24 August 1812, in *Zhurnal dlya chteniya vospitannikam voenno-uchebnykh zavedenii* (1842), XXXVI, 328–329.
18. Rostopchin to Kutuzov, 31 August 1812, in *Russkaya starina* (1870), II, 305.
19. Rostopchin to his wife, 14 September (8am) 1812, in Narichkine, *Le comte Rostopchine et son temps*, 171.
20. Rostopchin to Alexander, 25 October 1812, in *Russkii arkhiv* 8 (1892), 551.
21. Rostopchin's daughter pointed out that her father believed that 'the fire's effect would have been doubly terrifying to the French if it ignited before Napoleon entered the city'. Narichkine, *Le comte Rostopchine et son temps*, 170.
22. Rostopchin, *La Vérité*, 19–20.
23. Rostopchin (1889), 716.
24. Rostopchin to his wife, 23 September 1812, in *Russkii arkhiv* 8 (1901), 471.
25. Rostopchin (1889), 717–718.
26. Only the three most important archives – Archives of the College of Foreign Affairs, of the Votchina Department and of Ancient Affairs (*starykh del*) – had been removed back in August.
27. Wolzogen, 156.
28. Rostopchin to his wife, 14 September (8am) 1812, in Narichkine, *Le comte Rostopchine et son temps*, 171. Relying on family tradition, Count Anatole de Ségur (Rostopchin's grandson) cited an interesting incident involving his grandfather: upon leaving the city Rostopchin supposedly told his son Serge, who accompanied him, 'Salute Moscow for the last time. Within a half-hour it will be in flames.' However, it is doubtful that the younger Rostopchin, who served as an officer in the Akhtyrskii Hussar Regiment and aide-de-camp to Barclay de Tolly, would have been with his father at that moment. Ségur, *Vie du comte Rostopchine*, 173.
29. Rostopchin to his wife, 21 September 1812 in *Russkii arkhiv* 8 (1901), 465.
30. V. Kholodkovskii, 'Napoleon li podzheg Moskvu?' in *Vorposy istorii* 4 (1966), 35.
31. Rostopchin to Semen Vorontsov, 28 April 1813, in *Arkhiv Vorontsova*, VIII, 313.
32. Rostopchin to Vyazmitinov, 11 November 1812, in *Russkii arkhiv* 1 (1881), 225; Rostopchin to Vorontsov, 10 May 1815, in *Russkii arkhiv* 6 (1908), 279.
33. Rostopchin to a village manager in the Orlov province, 15 October 1815, in *Russkii arkhiv* (1864), 407–408.
34. For example, Rostopchin to Vyazmitinov, 11 November 1812, in *Russkii arkhiv* 1 (1881), 224.
35. Rostopchin, *La Vérité*, 5.
36. Ibid., 12.
37. Ibid., 20–22.
38. Ségur, *Vie du comte Rostopchine*, 193.
39. Ibid., 193.
40. RGVIA, f. VUA, d. 3465, part 11, ll. 203–207.
41. Brokker, 1432–1434.

42. Kaptsevich to Arakcheyev, 16 September 1812, in Dubrovin, 122.
43. *M.I. Kutuzov: Sbornik Dokumentov*, IV, part 1, 473; *Mnenie Gosudarstvennogo soveta o poteryakh artilleiiskogo i intendantskogo imushestva*, 718.
44. Christiani, 47.
45. Wilson, 178–179. Rostopchin's inscription is cited in a number of French and Polish memoirs (i.e. Brandt and Dumonceau), though they cite it as: 'I have set fire to my chateau, which cost me a million, so that no dog of a Frenchman shall lodge in it.'
46. Bourgoing, 116–117.
47. Berthezène, II, 69.
48. Bausset, II, 90.
49. Rostopchin, *La Vérité*, 6.
50. Unsigned report to the French authorities, 15 September 1812, in Gorshkov, *Moskva i Otechestvennaya voina 1812 g.*, II, 52–53.
51. Markham, *Imperial Glory*, 298–299.
52. Prosper to his step-father, 15 October 1812, in *Lettres interceptées par les Russes durant la campagne de 1812*, 148.
53. Dauve to his father, 28 September 1812, in Ibid., 54.
54. Paradis to Geneviève Bonnegrace, 20 September 1812; Paradis to his son, 26 September 1812, in Ibid., 22, 24.
55. Coudère to his wife, 27 September 1812, in Ibid., 51.
56. Montesquiou-Fezensac, *Journal de la Campagne de Russie en 1812*, 54.
57. Fantin des Odoards, 336; Roguet, IV, 488.
58. Ysarn, 54.
59. Frederic-François Vaudoncourt, *Mémoires pour server à histoire de la guerre entre la France et la Russie en 1812* (London, 1815), 192.
60. For the list of convicts see Spisok Gubernskago Tyuremnago Zamka … in Schukin, VI, 6–7.
61. Due to space constraints, seven detainees of the Temporary Prison were transferred to the Prison Castle, leaving 166 detainees. In addition, Welttman acknowledged 'more than twenty Jews' who had been under his authority but imprisoned in the Castle. Temporary Prison Warden Welttman to Moscow's *Uprava blagochiniya* (municipal administrative police organ), 10 April 1813, in Schukin, II, 212–213.
62. Prison Castle Warden Ivanov to Moscow's Chief of Police Ivashkin, 26 September 1812, Schukin, VI, 5. In his letter to the emperor, Rostopchin refers to 620 but in his memoirs he mentions 810 men, which probably refers to all convicts in general. On 13 September Civilian Governor Obreskov referred to 529 convicts in the Prison Castle and 166 detainees in the Temporary Prison but he specified that his number for the Prison Castle did not include military detainees. Obreskov to Ivashkin, 13 September 1812, in Schukin, VI, 4; Rostopchin, *La Verité*, 8. The Prison Castle (*Tyuremnyi zamok*) was Moscow's main penitentiary.
63. Rostopchin to Emperor Alexander, 29 November 1812, in *Russkii arkhiv* (1892), 555; Rostopchin to Vyazmitinov, 8 November 1812, in *Russkii arkhiv* 1 (1881), 225; Prison Castle Warden Ivanov to Moscow's Chief of Police Ivashkin, 26 September 1812, Schukin, VI, 5; Moscow's *Uprava blagochiniya* to the 1st Department of Moscow Aulic Court, 18 June 1813, in Schukin, II, 213; Major Nittelhorst to Kutuzov, 21 September 1812, in *General Staff Archives*, XVIII, 42–43.
64. Prison Castle Warden Ivanov to Moscow's Chief of Police Ivashkin, 26 September 1812, Schukin, VI, 5. It is noteworthy that to escort 627 convicts, Nittelhorst's squad consisted of just 4 NCOs, 6 veteran soldiers, 10 newly trained soldiers and 284 recruits. Major Nittelhorst to Kutuzov, 21 September 1812, in *General Staff Archives*, XVIII, 42–43.
65. Civil Governor of Nizhnii Novgorod Runovskii to Count Rostopchin, 15 October 1812, in Mikhailovskii-Danilevskii, II, 410–411. Also see Ibid., 347. Four prisoners had been freed before departure from Moscow so 627 convicts should have left the city on 14 September. Spisok Gubernskago Tyuremnago Zamka … in Schukin, VI, 7.
66. Obreskov to Ivashkin, 13 September 1812, in Schukin, VI, 4.
67. Prison Warden Welttman to Moscow's *Uprava blagochiniya*, 10 April 1813, in Schukin, II, 212–213.
68. Obreskov to Ivashkin, 13 September 1812, in Schukin, VI, 4.
69. Prison Warden Welttman to Moscow's *Uprava blagochiniya*, 10 April 1813, in Schukin, II, 212–213; Prison Castle Warden Ivanov to Moscow's Chief of Police Ivashkin, 26 September 1812, Schukin, VI, 5.
70. Alexander Bulgakov, 'Zametka na pamyat,' in *Russkii arkhiv* (1866), 701–702.
71. Cate, 273.
72. Rostopchin, *La Vérité*, 7.

73. Zemtsov, 43.
74. Zemtsov, 45.
75. Obreskov to Ivashkin, 13 September 1812, in Schukin, VI, 4–5; Ivashkin to Commandant of Moscow Lieutenant General Hesse, 13 September 1812, in Schukin, III, 195.
76. Kharuzin, 168.
77. 'U strakha glaza veliki.'
78. Poluyaroslavtseva, 9–10.
79. *Russkii arkhiv* (1864), 1201.
80. Bourgogne, 30.
81. Pion des Loches, 303.
82. Van Boecop to his father, 27 September 1812, in *Lettres interceptées par les Russes durant la campagne de 1812*, 50. See also Dauve to his father, 27 September 1812, in Ibid., 54.
83. Ysarn, 30.
84. 21st Bulletin, 20 September 1812, in Markham, *Imperial Glory*, 300.
85. The Military Commission included nine members. Its chair was General Jean Lauer, the head of the gendarmerie and chief justice (*grand-prévôt*) of the Grande Armée. Other members of the commission were: General Claude Etienne Michel, commander of the 2nd Brigade of the 3rd Guard Infantry Division; Louis Charles Saunier, head of the gendarmerie of the 1st Army Corps; Major Pierre Bodelin, commanding the Fusiliers-Grenadiers of the Young Guard; *Adjutant-Commandant* Louis Noel Théry, the Commandant of the Quarter-Impérial; *Chef-d'escadron* Jeannin of the *Gendarmerie d'élite*; General François Bailly de Monthion; *Chef-d'escadron* François Weber of the *Gendarmerie d'élite*, and *Sous-officier* Jouve de Guibert of the Gendarmerie. Monthion served as a prosecutor, and Weber as a *rapporteur* responsible for presenting cases. Protocol of Proceedings of the Military Commission, in Schukin, I, 129–130.
86. Peyrusse, *Mémorial*, 102; Protocol of Proceedings of the Military Commission, in Schukin, I, 129.
87. These men came from various walks of life, including a lieutenant of the 1st Moskovskii Infantry Regiment, three housepainters, nine policemen, a merchant, a tailor and a farrier. Their average age was 42–45 years; the oldest were 70–year-old Ivan Maksimov, a servant of Prince Simbirskii, and 67–year-old Ivan Ivanov, a sexton at the church of St Philipp, while the youngest were two 18–year-olds, the farrier Ilya Yagokomov and the upholsterer Semen Ivanov.
88. The Military Commission described these *cadenats phosphorique* as hollow spheres filled with phosphorus and wrapped in canvas covered with sulphur.
89. Protocol of Proceedings of the Military Commission, in Schukin, I, 132.
90. Protocol of Proceedings of the Military Commission, in Schukin, I, 131–132.
91. Protocol of Proceedings of the Military Commission, in Schukin, I, 134–140. Also see Rostopchin, *La Vérité*, 9–10; Georges Chambray, *Réponse de l'auteur de l'Histoire de l'expédition de Russie, a la brochure de M. le comte Rostopchin, intitulée La Vérite sur l'incendie de Moscou* (Paris, 1823), 5–10.
92. A. Yelnitskii, 'Rostopchin, F.V.' in *Russkii biograficheskii slovar* (Petrograd, 1918), 281–282.
93. Protocol of Proceedings of the Military Commission, in Schukin, I, 132–134.
94. Bogdanovich, II, 311.
95. Bogdanovich, II, 270.
96. Protocol of Proceedings of the Military Commission, in Schukin, I, 132–134.
97. Kutuzov to Rostopchin, 13 September 1812, in *Borodino: dokumenty, pis'ma, vospominaniya*, 143–144; Rostopchin to his wife, 13 September 1812, in *Russkii arkhiv* 8 (1901), 461; Rostopchin to the Senate, 9 August 1814, in *Russkii arkhiv* 6 (1868), 884.
98. Rostopchin (1889), 721.
99. '*Spisok chinovnikov moskovskoi politsii …*' [Roster of Officials of the Moscow Police …] in Gorshkov, *Moskva i Otechestvennaya voina 1812 g.*, II, 13–15. Some of these officers had been rewarded after the war: police supervisors Egor Rovinskii of the Pyatnitskii district and Fedor Pozharskii of the Tverskoi district were, for example, rewarded with gold watches for their services. It must be noted that some policemen chose to collaborate with the French authorities and served in the newly established municipal police, for which they were later prosecuted by the Russian authorities.
100. Ivashkin to Tormasov, 21 August 1816, in *Istoricheskii arkhiv* 3 (2003), 162–165.
101. No. 15 Broadsheet, 11 August 1812, in Afishy 1812 goda <http://www.museum.ru/museum/1812/Library/rostopchin/>
102. Glinka, 'Iz zapisok o 1812 gode,' <http://www.museum.ru/1812/Library/glinka1/glinka.html>
103. Liprandi, 168.
104. Blagovo, 166.

105. Boyen, II, 231. Young artillery officer Nikolai Mitarevskii recalled that 'after the fall of Smolensk the residents of the Russian heartlands eagerly offered soldiers everything that they could not hide or evacuate. It was they who destroyed the remaining furniture and other property in landowners' estates. All of this was done to prevent [property and resources] from falling into French hands.' Mitarevskii, 88.

106. Griois described how 'several generals and some of my own comrades had helped themselves to carriages to replace their own, rendered more or less unserviceable by the road'. He himself chose 'one of the lightest calèches' and decided to move it the following day. However, during the night the fire consumed the carriage yard. Griois, II, 57.

107. Pierre de Ségur, 'Rostopchin en 1812,' in *La Revue de Paris* 7 (1902), 94.

108. Rostopchin (1889), 697–698.

109. *Ueber die Verbrennung der Stadt Moskau*, 4.

110. Volkonskii, 141.

111. Bourgogne, 15.

112. In fact, even some Russian government officials could not resist the lure of quick profit and partook in the plunder. The employees of the Moscow post office were later charged with accompanying and assisting the enemy in pillaging. A. Karfachevskii to D. Runich, December 1812; Investigation File of Employees of the Moscow Post Office, January 1814, in Gorshkov, *Moskva i Otechestvennaya voina 1812 g.*, II, 142–143, 146–147.

113. Muravyev (1885), 349.

114. Nevzorov to Golenischev-Kutuzov, 3 December 1812, in Gorshkov, *Moskva i Otechestvennaya voina 1812 g.*, II, 20–21.

115. Brandt, 228.

116. Rostopchin to Vyazmitinov, 12 November 1812, in Schukin, VII, 417–418.

117. Kruglova, 62.

118. Chudimov to Soimonov, 17 November 1812, in Gorshkov, *Moskva i Otechestvennaya voina 1812 g.*, II, 16. Titular Councillor Vasilii Popov, a blind and ageing civil official, stayed in Moscow, believing the governor's assurances that the city would not fall. On 14 September he was robbed by his maid and landlady and abandoned in a park amidst the burning neighbourhood. He begged passers-by to help him but was instead beaten mercilessly and robbed threadbare by three young men. Popov barely made it to a village where a kind old woman sheltered him. Alas, the next morning the enemy soldiers savagely beat him after finding that he had no valuables to steal. 'Proshenie titulyarnogo sovetnika Vasillia Popova grafu F.V. Rastopchiny', 22 November 1812, in Schukin, I, 121–2.

119. Vasilii Ermolaevich, 69.

120. Kozlovskii, 113.

121. 'Kratkoe opisanie proizshestvii, byvshikh pri Pokhvalskoi, chto v Bashmakove, tserkvi v 1812 godu,' in *Chteniya v Obshchestve lyubitelei dukhovnogo prosveshcheniya* 36 (March 1914), 71. A house serf recalled, 'the people grumbled very much about the lords, saying they had surrendered Moscow, that they had frittered everything away'. A Moscow priest later told his grandson that 'a horde of peasants came to him with bear-spears and threatened to slaughter [the affluent] for having "frittered Moscow away".' 'Razskaz nabilkinskoi bogadelenki, Anny Andreyevny Sazonovoi,' in Tolycheva (1872), 291; A. Lebedev, 'Iz razskazov rodnykh,' in Schukin, III, 257.

122. Lavrov, 110–111; Nordhof, 234.

123. Toll, II, 152.

124. Cited in Zemtsov, 42.

125. Alexander Bulgakov, 'Zametka na pamyat,' in *Russkii arkhiv* (1866), 701–702.

126. Rostopchin to Kutuzov, 29 September 1812, in *Journal of Outgoing Correspondence of Governor Rostopchin*, 182.

127. Arthur Wellesley, Duke of Wellington, 'Memorandum on the War in Russia in 1812,' in George R. Cleig, ed. *Personal Reminiscences of the First Duke of Wellington* (London, 1904), 387–388.

128. Philibert Poulachard to his wife, 27 September 1812, in *Lettres interceptées par les Russes durant la campagne de 1812*, 51.

129. Pion des Loches, 301.

130. Castellane, I, 155.

131. Horn, 118–121.

132. Lossberg, 196.

133. Wellington, 'Memorandum on the War in Russia in 1812,' 387.

134. Ségur, *Vie du comte Rostopchine*, 192.

135. For an eyewitness account see Lieutenant Frederick Mackenzie's account in George F. Scheer and Hugh F. Rankin, *Rebels and Redcoats: The American Revolution Through the Eyes of Those Who Fought and Lived it* (New York, 1957), 188–189.
136. William Howe to Lord George Germaine, 23 September 1776, in *The Parliamentary Register* (London, 1802), X, 346–347.
137. Governor Tryon to Lord George Germain, 24 September 1776, in *Documents Relative to the Colonial History of the State of New-York,* ed. John Brodhead (Albany NY, 1857), VIII, 686.
138. For details see Barnet Schecter, *The Battle for New York* (New York, 2002); Ron Chernow, *Washington: A Life* (New York, 2010).

Chapter 9: In Search of Peace

1. Popov, *Frantsuzy v Moskve*, 149.
2. D. Dufour de Pradt, *Histoire de l'Ambassade dans le Grand Duché de Varsovie en 1812* (Paris, 1815), 52–54, 64–65.
3. Dumas, III, 454–455.
4. Tutolmin to Emperor Alexander, 19 September 1812, in Gorshkov, *Moskva i Otechestvennaya voina 1812 g.,* II, 64; Tutolmin to Dowager Empress Maria Fedorovna, 23 November 1812, in *Russkii arkhiv* 11 (1900), 462.
5. French contemporaries and Western studies refer to Napoleon's interpreter Lelorgne's visit to Tutolmin. However, Tutolmin's own letters (dated 19 September and 23 November) make it clear that Dumas's visit preceded Lelorgne's and Western accounts simply confused them. Daria Olivier's account of this meeting contains considerable deviations from Tutolmin's letters.
6. Dumas, III, 446–447; Tutolmin to Dowager Empress Maria Fedorovna, 23 November 1812, in *Chteniya v Imperatorskom obschestve istorii i drevnostei rossiiskikh* 2 (1860), 165.
7. Tutolmin to Emperor Alexander, 19 September 1812, RGVIA, f. 846, op. 16, d. 3586, ll.3b; Tutolmin to Dowager Empress Maria Fedorovna, 23 November 1812, in *Russkii arkhiv* 11 (1900), 465; *Chteniya v Imperatorskom obschestve istorii i drevnostei rossiiskikh* 2 (1860), 168–169.
8. Tutolmin to Emperor Alexander, 19 September 1812, RGVIA, f. 846, op. 16, d. 3586, ll.3b.
9. The roster showed 275 children, 207 healthy children aged 1 to 12 years, and 104 sick children aged 1 to 18 years.
10. Tutolmin to Emperor Alexander, 19 September 1812, RGVIA, f. 846, op. 16, d. 3586, ll.4; Tutolmin to Dowager Empress Maria Fedorovna, 19 September 1812, in Gorshkov, *Moskva i Otechetsvennaya voina 1812 g.,* II, 67–68; Tutolmin to Dowager Empress Maria Fedorovna, 23 November 1812, in *Russkii arkhiv* 11 (1900), 465.
11. Britten Austin cites some passages from this letter but they do not appear in Tutolmin's original document. Britten Austin, 56.
12. *Passeport,* 20 September 1812, RGVIA, f. 846, op. 16, d. 3586, l.8. The passport was signed by Alexander Berthier but Rukhin's name was misspelled as RouKine.
13. Tutolmin's certificate to Rukhin, 19 September 1812, RGVIA, f. 846, op. 16, d. 3586, l. 7; Winzegerode to Alexander Balashov, 22 September 1812, RGVIA, f. 846, op. 16, d. 3586, ll.5–6.
14. Yakovlev was also the father of Alexander Herzen, one of the founders of Russian socialism and a leading proponent of agrarian populism. Herzen was the result of an affair Yakovlev had with Henriette Wilhelmina Luisa Haag, a young German woman from Stuttgart; he gave the boy the last name Herzen because he was a 'child of his heart [*herz*]'. Young Herzen was just five months old when his father met Napoleon.
15. In Western accounts Yakovlev is sometimes accused of being 'an almost pathological procrastinator' (Britten Austin, 56), and it was said that he 'dithered and talked too much' (Olivier, 106). These claims are largely based on Alexander Herzen's memoirs but Yakovlev's letters reveal that he was in fact prepared to depart with his family but could not convince his brother to follow him and refused to leave him behind. See Yakovlev to Golokhvastova, 13 November 1812, in *Russkii arkhiv* (1874), 1060–1061.
16. Yakovlev, 1066. Yakovlev wrote his recollections after finding certain inaccuracies in the memoirs of Baron Fain. However, this document remained unpublished for many years. In 1872 Yakovlev's experience, including his meeting with Napoleon, was recounted in the memoirs of Madame Passeck, who, however, exaggerated or invented many elements in the story. This prompted Dmitri Golokhvastov, Yakovlev's relative, to publish Yakovlev's private letters and his memoir to refute Passeck's claims. Adolphe Thiers' account of Yakovlev's meeting with Napoleon is also erroneous.
17. Napoleon did note, however, that 'in all of my life, I burned only one city – it was in Italy – and only because its residents continued to resist us in the streets'.

18. Yakovlev, 1066–1067. Yakovlev's memoir, written in French, is also available in N. Stchoupak, 'L'entrevue de I. Iakovlev avec Napoléon,' in *Revue des Études Napoléoniennes* 33 (1931), 45–48.
19. Yakovlev described Napoleon's speech as filled with intermittent 'bragging' and 'dishonesty'.
20. Yakovlev, 1067; Fain, 105–106.
21. Napoleon to Alexander, 20 September 1812, *Correspondance de Napoléon*, XXIV, No. 19213, 221–222; *Correspondance générale*, XII, 1103.
22. Western accounts claim that Yakovlev met Napoleon on at least two occasions, but Yakovlev's letters and memoirs refute such claims and show that there was only one meeting.
23. Mortier's order of 19 September, published in *Correspondance de Napoléon* (XXIV, No. 19212, 221) contains no name but might have been intended for Yakovlev.
24. Wintzingerode's letter of 25 September reveals that he was suspicious of Yakovlev, whom 'I could not consider as a normal man and could not conceive how he had the audacity to take such a mission upon himself.' The general initially dispatched Yakovlev under escort to Minister of Police Balashov. However, Yakovlev is silent about Wintzingerode's suspicions and simply remarks that the general 'immediately sent me, accompanied by an officer, to St Petersburg'. Arriving there, Yakovlev received orders to go directly to Count Alexei Arakcheyev, who then delivered Napoleon's letter to Alexander. Yakovlev, 1066–1068; Wintzingerode to Emperor Alxander, 25 September 1812, in Dubrovin, 140. Fain is usually the main source for Western accounts but Fain and Yakovlev differ in a number of points. I gave preference to Yakovlev, who wrote his memoir in response to Fain's account. In her *The Burning of Moscow 1812*, Daria Olivier offers a very stylized and literary version of this meeting, including quotes that neither memoir contains. Britten Austin's version is based on Olivier's.
25. Choiseul-Gouffier, 130.
26. Napoleon to Berthier, 24 September 1812, in *Correspondance générale*, XII, 1111.
27. Hogendorp, 324.
28. Berthier argued that the Austrians were teetering on the verge of defection and begged Napoleon to give the order for the move back to winter in Poland. 'You want to get to Grosbois to see [your lover] Madame Visconti,' mocked the emperor. Caulaincourt, II, 51.
29. Rapp, 185.
30. Hochberg, 69.
31. Merville to Napoleon, 23 September 1812, in Chuquet, *La guerre de Russie* (1er Sér), 80–81.
32. Ségur (1825), 40.
33. Caulaincourt, II, 49.
34. Villemain, I, 175–180.
35. Dominic Lieven, *Russia against Napoleon* (London: Penguin, 2010), 251.
36. Ségur (1825), 77.
37. Muravyev (1955), 170–171.
38. Volkonskii, 147.
39. Grand Duchess Catherine to Emperor Alexander, 18 September 1812, in *Correspondance de l'empereur Alexandre 1er avec sa soeur*, Letter, XXXIII.
40. Grand Duchess Catherine to Emperor Alexander; Emperor Alexander to Grand Duchess Catherine, 15–18 September 1812, *Correspondance de l'empereur Alexandre 1er avec sa soeur*, Letters Nos. XXXII, XXXIII, LXXII.
41. Bogdanovich, II, 288–289.
42. Edling, 79–80.
43. Peter Hicks, *Beyond Smolensk*, <http://www.napoleon.org/en/reading_room/articles/files/481833.asp>
44. *Sankt-Peterburgskie vedomosti*, 29 September 1812.
45. See Itinéraire des Archives de Caulaincourt in Caulaincourt, II, 37–38.
46. Constant, III, Chapter XXV, <http://www.napoleonic-literature.com/Book_11/V3C25.html>
47. Ségur (1825), 79–80.
48. Ségur (1825), 79–80.
49. Popov, *Frantsuzy v Moskve*, 154.
50. Caulaincourt, II, 46.
51. Caulaincourt, II, 46–47; Ségur (1825), 81–83. Also see *Souvenirs du Duc de Vicence* (Paris, 1837), I, 92–93.
52. Fain, II, 106–107.
53. Ségur (1825), 83.

54. Napoleon to Kutuzov, 3 October 1812, *Correspondance générale*, XII, 1126; Berthier to Murat, 4 October 1812, in Fain, II, 192–193; Gourgaud, 531–532.
55. Mikhailovskii-Danilevskii, III, 82.
56. Mikhailovskii-Danilevskii, III, 83 (based on a conversation with Volkonskii).
57. Mikhailovskii-Danilevskii, III, 82–84. In the morning of 5 October Robert Wilson received a message from Bennigsen asking him 'to return instantly to headquarters, as the Field Marshal had agreed, not merely proposed, but actually agreed in a written note, to meet Lauriston at midnight beyond the Russian advanced posts'.
58. Wilson, Narrative, 182–183.
59. Wilson, *Narratives*, 185–186.
60. Wilson, *Narratives*, 182.
61. Wilson, *Narratives*, 187.
62. Mikhailovskii-Danilevskii, III, 84–85. In his classic *Histoire du Consulat et de l'Empire* (XIV, 419–420), Adolphe Thiers included a very different version of Lauriston's arrival at the Russian camp; his version can be found unchanged in the works of subsequent generations of historians. Thiers described how, upon reaching the Russian outposts, Lauriston was greeted by Prince Volkonskii, who intended to entertain the French envoy at Bennigsen's quarters. But Lauriston, offended at this reception, refused to confer with Volkonskii and returned to Murat's headquarters, declaring that he would only speak with Kutuzov himself. 'This sudden rupture of relations somewhat disturbed the Russian staff,' wrote Thiers. 'For the vehement national hatred against the French began to subside amidst the higher ranks of the army, and they were unwilling to render peace quite impossible. And even the persons opposed to peace regretted the manner in which M. de Lauriston had been treated, although for a different motive – their fear that this offensive treatment might induce the French army to advance against them full of anger and determination before the Russian army had been reinforced or reorganised.' Consequently, Thiers argued, Russians agreed to receive Lauriston at the main headquarters.
63. Mikhailovskii-Danilevskii, III, 76–77.
64. Sherbinin, 36.
65. Kutuzov to Alexander, 5 October 1812, RGVIA, f. VUA, d. 3697, l. 2; Wilson, *Narrative*, 187–190; Langeron, 31–32. Also see *Vestnik Evropy*, No. 21–22, November 1812, 155–158.
66. Alexander to Kutuzov, 16 October 1812, in Wilson, *Narrative*, 203–204.
67. Puybusque (1817), 141–48.
68. Cate, 318.
69. Dumas, III, 455.
70. Muralt, 78.
71. Caulaincourt, II, 42; Castellane, I, 166.
72. See Napoleon to Cambacérès; Napoleon to Marie-Louise, 23–24 September 1812, in *Correspondance générale*, XII, 1109–1110, 1114.
73. Napoleon to Marie-Louise, 4–6 October 1812, in *Correspondance générale*, XII, 1133, 1161.
74. When the grand equerry continued to raise his concerns about the protracted sojourn in Moscow and the onset of winter, Napoleon again ridiculed him, telling Berthier and Michel Duroc that 'Caulaincourt is already half-frozen'.
75. Dumas, III, 455.
76. Caulaincourt, II, 25–26.
77. Vincent Cronin, *Napoleon* (London, 1990), 321.
78. Thiers, XIV, 426.
79. Among those who received awards was the Dutch officer Aart Kool, who noted: 'You can well imagine the pride and joy with which we walked back home. You would need to understand the culture of the French army, the way they strove to wear the French Legion of Honour on their chest, to see what this meant. The joy was immediately diminished by the way our fellow officers, who had not been honoured, greeted us, their eyes heavy with distaste. Still, it was an honour rather than an indictment. On the day of my investiture I purchased a small cross and a ribbon for the Legion of Honour, which cost me 100 francs, although I suspect I might have paid 500 to be able to wear the cross straightaway.' Kool, 55–56.
80. Thus, on 5 October he rejected all nominations for promotions of the Portuguese officers from the 3rd Corps, drawing a large cross over their names. Dossier 3604 at the Russian State Military Historical Archive alone contains over 500 pages of promotion lists reviewed and signed by Napoleon between June and November 1812. His load varied but on 14–15 October he reviewed and approved more than thirty pages of promotional lists. All documents are in RGVIA, f. 846, op. 16, d. 3604.
81. Napoleon to Maret, 6 October 1812, in *Correspondance générale*, XII, 1159.

82. Caulaincourt, II, 62–64.
83. Villemain, 230.
84. Napoleon to Berthier, 23 September 1812, in *Correspondance générale*, XII, 1107–1108.
85. Napoleon to Berthier, 24 September 1812, in *Correspondance générale*, XII, 1111.
86. Villemain, I, 230.
87. Ryazanov, 205–220.
88. Kicheev, 43.
89. Semen Klimych, 424.
90. Radozhitskii, 107–108.
91. Ségur (1825), I, 80.
92. Caulaincourt, II, 25–26.
93. On 1–2 October twelve cannon (howitzers, 12pdr and 3 pdr guns) were deployed in the Kremlin towers, taking control of all approaches to the complex. Another eighteen cannon were kept inside the Kremlin. The emperor also undertook major repair works designed to strengthen the Kremlin's defences. He demolished some buildings adjacent to towers and strengthened defences around four gates by building palisades and earthworks. Inside the complex he had several walls demolished to allow for greater manoeuvrability. Outside the Kremlin walls French engineers were ordered to rebuild three major lunettes that were connected by a series of palisades. They also repaired covered ways and glacis and began demolishing all buildings on Red Square to clear up the approaches to the fortress. Napoleon to Berthier, 1 October 1812, in *Correspondance générale*, XII, 1123–1124.
94. Napoleon to Berthier, 8 October 1812, Ibid., 1167. Aart Kool, the Dutch engineer in the 1st Corps, was tasked with fortifying the Novodevichii Monastery in the southwestern suburb of Moscow. 'In front of the gates we built earthen walls and palisades. We installed light cannon in the stone towers. Close to the cloister, at around 30 to 40 paces, stood a large church, its highest part just taller than the 50–foot walls of the cloister. I was ordered to destroy that building and learned a lot about military destruction from this job. We created sixty points in the walls and pillars of the building in which to install mines and explosives. These points were connected by wooden ducts to carry fast fuses to each explosive. Once this was in place, we went to light the fuse from behind the stone tower. Marshal Davout came to see it with his entire entourage. The collapse was completely successful, almost like an earthquake. The tip of the church tower, with the St Andrew's cross, stood on the ruins, still upright, about 150 feet lower than before, a message that the cross of Christ lasts for ever even amidst destruction and devastation.' Kool, 54.
95. One thousand men from Marchand's 25th Division were thus committed to building a strong redoubt and fortified observation post on the bank of the Moscow river. Napoleon to Berthier, 4 October 1812, Ibid., 1130.
96. Napoleon to Berthier, 11 October 1812, Ibid., 1177–1178. The brigade, commanded by General Charrière, consisted of two regiments. The 1st Regiment included light cavalrymen while the 2nd Regiment consisted of cuirassiers, carabiniers and dragoons.
97. For details see Caulaincourt II, 23f.
98. Napoleon seems to have allowed the designing of new ovens. According to Aart Kool, 'In early October I was asked to design a transportable iron bread oven, and to build it in the engineers' workshop, so I lodged for eight days with the colonel in charge of the workshop. I made model drawings of the design and took it to the headquarters of the engineers, at General Haxo's request. These drawings received the high honour of being reviewed by the emperor. There was no time to make more of these ovens, but the oven I built was used during the eventual retreat.' Kool, 54.
99. Napoleon to Berthier, 6 October 1812, in Chuquet, *Ordres et apostilles de Napoléon*, II, 451.
100. Berthier to Davout, 7 October 1812, RGVIA f. 846, op. 16, d. 3587, l. 11.
101. Napoleon to Berthier, 6–7 October 1812, in *Correspondance générale*, XII, 1146, 1161–1162.
102. Montesquiou-Fezensac, *Journal de la Campagne de Russie*, 65.
103. Caulaincourt, II, 26.
104. Notes, [n.d] October 1812, *Correspondance de Napoléon*, XXIV, No. 19,237, 235–236.
105. To guard Smolensk and the lines of communication, Napoleon ordered the formation of a 'division of twelve thousand infantry and four thousand cavalry'. In addition, he agreed to form a strong corps – *un gros corps* – at Vyazma, Gzharsk and Dorogobuzh from stragglers passing through these towns. Napoleon to Berthier, 6 October 1812, in *Correspondance générale*, XII, 1147–1148; Napoleon to Berthier, 10 October 1812, in Chambray (1839), III, 429.
106. Notes, [n.d] October 1812, Correspondance de Napoléon, XXIV, No. 19,237, 237–238.
107. Napoleon to Maret, 9 October 1812, in *Correspondance générale*, XII, 1176, No. 31882.

108. According to Meneval, the emperor often criticized Berthier for his carelessness. "Berthier,' he used to say to him, 'I would give an arm to have you at Grosbois [the chateau that Napoleon gave to Berthier]. Not only are you no good, but you are actually in my way.' After these little quarrels Berthier would sulk, and refuse to come to dinner (he was Napoleon's habitual table-fellow). The emperor would then send for him, and would not sit down to dinner until he had come; he would put his arms round his neck, tell him that they were inseparable, etc., would chaff him about Madame Visconti, and in the end would seat him at the table opposite him.' Meneval, III, 42.

109. Napoleon to Maret, 9 October 1812, in Chuquet, *Ordres et apostilles de Napoléon*, II, 456.

110. Napoleon to Maret, 14 October 1812, in *Correspondance générale*, XII, 1184.

111. Napoleon to Berthier, 14 October 1812, in *Correspondance de Napoléon*, XXIV, No. 19273.

112. Napoleon spoke of three 'classes': the lightly wounded who were capable of leaving on their own; those in serious condition who could be evacuated on transports; and finally, men in grave condition who, in surgeons' opinion, might further worsen during transportation. Napoleon to Berthier, 5–6 October 1812, in *Correspondance générale*, XII, 1133–1134, 1146.

113. Napoleon to Berthier, 5 October 1812, in *Correspondance générale*, XII, 1133–1134.

114. Napoleon to Clarke, 5 October 1812, S.H.D., département de l'Armée de Terre, 17 C 326.

115. Napoleon to Berthier, 6 October 1812, in Chambray (1839), III, 425–426; *Correspondance générale*, XII, 1145.

116. Napoleon to Berthier, 10 October 1812, in Chambray (1839), III, 428.

117. Napoleon to Berthier, 10 October 1812, in Chambray (1839), III, 428–430. Also see Napoleon to Berthier, 16 October, Ibid., 433.

118. Fain, II, 150–153; Larrey, IV, 79–80; Napoleon to Berthier, 16 October 1812, in *Correspondance générale*, XII, 1187.

119. Perovskii, 275–277.

120. Berthier to Murat, 14 October 1812, in Chambray (1839), III, 432–433.

121. Fain, II, 152.

122. Berthier to Murat, 14 October 1812, in Chambray (1839), III, 432–433.

123. Fain, II, 150–153; Kool, 54..

124. The date of departure was later rescheduled to 20 October.

125. Napoleon to Maret, 16 October 1812, in *Correspondance générale*, XII, 1192; Maret to Otto, 26 October 1812, in *Correspondance de Napoléon*, XXIV, No.19,275, 265–266.

126. Montesquiou-Fezensac, *Journal de la Campagne de Russie*, 63–64.

127. Vionnet de Maringone, 40–41. Also see Kool, 55–56.

128. Montesquiou-Fezensac, *Journal de la Campagne de Russie*, 64.

129. Fain, II, 158.

130. Ségur (1825), 325.

131. Laugier, 89.

132. Biot, 51–52; Montesquiou-Fezensac, *Journal de la Campagne de Russie*, 64.

Chapter 10: The Die is Cast

1. Yermolov, 170–171; Bennigsen 9 (1909), 502–503; Journal of Military Operations, RGVIA, f. VUA, d. 3465, Part 5, ll. 229–230.

2. Kutuzov to Lieutenant Kalinov, 14 September 1812, in *M.I. Kutuzov: Sbornik Dokumentov*, IV, Part I, 227.

3. Kutuzov to Wintzingerode, 15 September 1812, in *M.I. Kutuzov: Sbornik Dokumentov*, IV, Part I, 231. He instructed Prince Dmitri Lobanov-Rostovskii, who was responsible for the formation of reserve forces, to direct the newly formed unit to Kolomna and Serpukhov in preparations for the main army's flanking manoeuvre. Kutuzov to Lobanov-Rostovskii, 15 September 1812, in Ibid, 230.

4. See Kutuzov's letters to Governor N. Bogdanov of the Tula Province and Major General F. Voronov, Head of the Tula Munitions Factory, 19 September 1812, in *M.I. Kutuzov: Sbornik Dokumentov*, IV, Part I, 250.

5. Kutuzov to Alexander I, 16 September 1812, in Ibid., 232–234.

6. Yefremov commanded a Cossack detachment consisting of Andrianov II's Cossack, Simferopolskii Horse Tatar and the 1st Bashkirskii Regiments. The first two regiments remained on the Ryazan road while the Bashkirs moved to the road to Serpukhov.

7. Kutuzov to Miloradovich, 16–17 September 1812, in Ibid., 236–237, 240–241.

8. For details see Journal of Military Operations, RGVIA, f. VUA, d. 3465, Part 5, ll. 229–231b; Disposition of the 1st and 2nd Western Armies, 16 September 1812; Kutuzov to Miloradovich, 17 September 1812;

Kutuzov to Emperor Alexander, 18 September 1812, in *M.I. Kutuzov: Sbornik Dokumentov*, IV, Part I, 237–238, 241, 243; Order to the Armies, 18 September 1812, RGVIA, f. VUA, d. 3524, ll. 15–16b.

9. Yermolov, 174.

10. Kutuzov to Alexander I; Kutuzov to Chichagov; Kutuzov to Tormasov, 18 September 1812, in Ibid., 243–245.

11. Yermolov, 174.

12. Kutuzov to Emperor Alexander, 18 September 1812, in *M.I. Kutuzov: Sbornik Dokumentov*, IV, Part I, 243.

13. Kutuzov to Miloradovich, 18 September 1812, in Ibid., 248.

14. Journal of Military Operations, RGVIA, f. VUA, d. 3465, Part 5, ll. 231–231b; Disposition of the 1st and 2nd Armies for 20 September 1812; Kutuzov to Miloradovich, 19 September 1812, in *M.I. Kutuzov: Sbornik Dokumentov*, IV, Part I, 252–253; Miloradovich to Konovnitsyn, 22 September 1812, in *General Staff Archives*, XVIII, 45–46.

15. Kutuzov to Dorokhov, 20 September 1812, RGVIA, f. VUA, d. 3463, l. 52.

16. Barclay de Tolly, *Izobrazhenye*, 28.

17. Kutuzov to Alexander I, 23 September 1812, in *M.I. Kutuzov: Sbornik Dokumentov*, IV, Part I, 277–278.

18. Kutuzov to Lobanov-Rostovskii, Lanskoi and Miloradovich, 18–21 September, in Ibid., 247, 254, 261–262.

19. Napoleon to Bessieres, 27 September 1812, in Gourgaud, 529.

20. Napoleon to Murat and Bessieres, 22–26 September 1812, in Gourgaud, 525–528; Reports of Dorokhov and Wintzingerode, 22–25 September 1812 in *Severnaya pochta*, Nos. 75–77, 30 September–7 October 1812.

21. Everts, 692–695; Castellane, I, 161.

22. Caulaincourt, II, 56–57.

23. Napoleon to Murat, 22 September 1812, in Gourgaud, 525.

24. Napoleon to Bessieres, 22 September 1812, in Gourgaud, 525.

25. Napoleon to Murat, 23 September 1812, in Gourgaud, 526.

26. Bessieres' force consisted of the 4th and 5th Guard Cavalry Brigades, the 3rd Cavalry Corps, the 1st Light Cavalry Brigade and the 4th Division of the 1st Corps.

27. Fain, II, 110–111; Chambray, II, 148–149.

28. Berthier to Bessieres, 27 September 1812, in Gourgaud, 528.

29. Napoleon to Bessieres and Murat, 22–23 and 27 September 1812, in Gourgaud, 525–526, 529.

30. Efremov to Miloradovich, 22 September 1812, in *General Staff Archives*, XVIII, 55.

31. Napoleon to Murat and Bessieres, 22–23 September 1812, in Gourgaud, 525–527.

32. Le Roy, *Souvenirs*, 185–189.

33. Chambray, II, 149.

34. Barclay de Tolly, *Izobrazhenye*, 29.

35. Bennigsen to Miloradovich, 24 September 1812, in *M.I. Kutuzov: Sbornik Dokumentov*, IV, Part I, 291–292.

36. Kutuzov to Miloradovich, 24 September (7 pm) 1812, in *M.I. Kutuzov: Sbornik Dokumentov*, IV, Part I, 292–293.

37. Bennigsen to Miloradovich, 24 September (8 pm) 1812; Toll to Miloradovich, 25 September (midnight), in Ibid., 293–294.

38. Disposition of the 1st and 2nd Armies for 27 September 1812, in *M.I. Kutuzov: Sbornik Dokumentov*, IV, Part I, 308–309; Bennigsen to Osterman-Tolstoy, 27 September 1812, RGVIA, f. VUA, d. 3463, l. 69.

39. Napoleon to Berthier and Bessieres, 24–26 September 1812, in Gourgaud, 527–528; Chambray, II, 150.

40. Napoleon to Bessieres and Murat, 27–28 September 1812, in Gourgaud, 529–530.

41. Wilson, *Private Diary*, 173–175; Idem., *Narrative*, 178–180.

42. Butulin, I, 312–313.

43. Brandt, 233.

44. Kutuzov to Osterman-Tolstoy and Yermolov, 27 September 1812, RGVIA, f. VUA, d. 3463, ll. 40, 70–70b.

45. Golitsyn, 72; Buturlin, I, 314.

46. In the combat at Chirikovo on 29 September the Russian rearguard lost 804 men, including an officer and 96 soldiers killed. The following day the fighting at Voronovo claimed just twenty-one Russian casualties. Roster of the Killed, Wounded and Missing in the 1st Western Army in *M.I. Kutuzov: Sbornik Dokumentov*, IV, Part I, 714; Journal of Military Operations in Ibid., 339–341.

47. Miloradovich to Konovnitsyn, 3 October 1812, in *General Staff Archives*, XVIII, 100.

48. Brandt, 236.
49. Miloradovich to Konovnitsyn, 3 October 1812, in *General Staff Archives*, XVIII, 100–101.
50. Miloradovich to Konovnitsyn, 3 October 1812, in *General Staff Archives*, XVIII, 100–101; Buturlin, I, 315–316.
51. For a critical view of Murat, see Brandt, 236–237.
52. Army Roster, 5 October 1812, in *M.I. Kutuzov: Sbornik Dokumentov*, IV, Part I, 355–358. On 23 September the 1st Western Army had fewer than 50,000 men.
53. Order to the Armies, 28 September 1812, RGVIA, f. VUA, d. 3524, ll. 26b–28.
54. The advanced guard included the 2nd and 4th Army Corps, the 2nd and 3rd Cavalry Corps and the Cossacks. The *Corps de Bataille* consisted of the 3rd, 5th, 6th, 7th and 8th Army Corps, plus Golitsyn's and Muller-Zakomelski's cavalry corps. The flying columns were:

Platov's, comprising thirteen regiments of Cossacks, one of light infantry, and a horse battery;

Wintzingerode's, of one hussar regiment, one of dragoons, seven of Cossacks, and a battery, observing Moscow in the north;

Dorokhov's, observing Mozhaisk, ultimately increased by detachments to five battalions, sixteen squadrons, a battery and some Cossacks;

Orlov-Denisov's, consisting of six regiments of Cossacks and six guns;

Karpov's, comprising seven regiments of Cossacks; and

Ozharovski's, composed of four regiments of Cossacks, one of Hussars, a regiment of light infantry and six guns.

In addition, irregular detachments infested the Moscow–Smolensk road. These were led by Colonel Kaisarov (three regiments), Colonel Prince Kudachev (two regiments), Colonel Yefremov (two regiments), Lieutenant Colonel Davidov (two regiments), Captain Seslavin (one regiment) and Captain Figner (one regiment).
55. Yermolov, 175f.
56. Wilson, *Narrative*, 200–201.
57. Castellane, I, 165.
58. Thirion de Metz, 216.
59. Wilson, *Private Diary*, I, 188; Idem., *Narrative*, 200–201.
60. Peter Kikin to his brother, 19 October 1812, in Schukin, V, 3–4.
61. Uxküll, 91–92.
62. Journal of Military Operations, October 1812, in *M.I. Kutuzov: Sbornik Dokumentov*, IV, Part I, 400–401, 408–410, 434–435.
63. Sergei Marin to an unknown addressee, 14 October 1812, in Schukin, I, 60–64. Also see A. Muravyev, 205–206.
64. Biot, 49.
65. The Polish Lancer Brigade was an exception. Stationed at the village of Voronovo, Rostopchin's former estate, it was relatively well provided for. Zaluski, 529–530.
66. Griois, II, 69–72.
67. Dembinski, I, 167.
68. Murat to Belliard, 10 October 1812, in Belliard, I, 112.
69. Denniée, 101.
70. Chambray, II, 204–205. Writing to Murat on 13 October, the emperor argued that 'the position at Voronovo is good and commanding, and can be defended by the infantry, which will easily cover the cavalry. If you are of the same opinion, you are authorized to take it up.' The following day, however, Napoleon hinted to Murat that the Grande Armée might depart Moscow and urged him to 'reconnoitre well the road which will take you to Mojaisk, that if you are obliged to retreat before the enemy, you may be perfectly conversant with the route'. Berthier to Murat, 13–14 October 1812, in Gourgaud, 537–538.
71. The memoirs of Auvray, Bréaut des Marlots, Dupuy, Griois, Mailly-Nesle and Séruzier offer fascinating insights into the Allied side of the battle.
72. For an in-depth study of the battle see V. Bessonov, *Tarutinskoe srazhenie* (Moscow, 2008), as well as a series of articles by A. Ulyanov and A. Vasiliev. A. Ulyanov, 'Tarutinskoe srazhenie: problemy izucheniya,' in *Sobytiya Otechestvennoi voiny 1812 g. na territorii Kaluzhskoi gubernii* (Maloyaroslavets, 1993); Idem., 'Boi na reke Chernishne,' in *Ot Tarutino do Maloyaroslavetsa. K 190–letiyu Maloyaroslavetskogo srazheniya. Sbornik statei* (Kaluga, 2002) <http://www.museum.ru/museum/1812/Library/Mmnk/1994_4.html>; A. Vasiliev, 'Frantsuzskie karabinery v boyu pri Vinkovo 18 oktyabrya 1812 goda,' in *Sobytiya Otechestvennoi voiny 1812 g. na territorii Kaluzhskoi gubernii* (Maloyaroslavets, 1998) <http://www.museum.ru/museum/1812/Library/Mmnk/1998_6.html>

73. Bausset, II, 126.
74. Napoleon to Berthier, 18 October 1812, in *Correspondance générale*, XII, 1198, No. 31932. Generals Éblé and Chasseloup were told to start preparing their *pontonniers* and engineers for immediate departure the following morning. Napoleon to Berthier, 18 October 1812, in *Ibid.*, 1197, No. 31930.
75. Aart Kool colourfully notes, 'On 18 October just before lunchtime I was talking to the Dutch General Matuscheurtz in the Kremlin when we heard that the King of Naples had been tricked, the Russians were scum and had broken the truce, and that on the following day we would leave to revenge their defiance.' Kool, 57.
76. Napoleon to La Riboisière, 18 October 1812, Ibid., 1201–1202.
77. Napoleon to La Riboisière, 18 October 1812, Ibid., 1201–1202. Mortier was given 'Laborde's division, General Charrier's brigade (composed of four battalions of dismounted cavalry), two companies of sappers, one company of artillery, the artillery of Laborde's division and finally one brigade of cavalry 500 strong'.
78. Napoleon to Berthier, 18 October 1812, in *Correspondance générale*, XII, 1198–1199.
79. Napoleon to Berthier, 21 October 1812, Ibid., 1211–1212.
80. Napoleon to La Riboisière, 18 October 1812, Ibid., 1201–1202.
81. Napoleon to La Riboisière, 18 October 1812, Ibid., 1201–1202.
82. Rapp, 221–222; Charles Tristan Montholon, *Mémoires pour server a l'Histoire de France sous Napoléon, écrits a Sainte-Hélène* (Paris, 1823), II, 104.
83. To distract the Russians, on 18 October Napoleon dispatched Colonel Berthémy, Murat's aide-de-camp, to Kutuzov on a mission of 'making arrangements to give the war a character in conformity with the established rules and the taking of the indispensable measures resulting from the state of war'. Kutuzov met Berthémy but refused to make any compromises. Berthier to Kutuzov, 18 October 1812, *Correspondance de Napoléon*, XXIV, 267, No. 19,277; Kutuzov to Berthier, 20 October 1812, in *M.I. Kutuzov: Sbornik Dokumentov*, IV, Part 2, 38–39.
84. Chambray, II, 314–315.
85. Mailly, 66. Also see Lieutenant Colonel K. de Baudus, Études sur Napoléon (Paris, 1841), II, 247; René Bourgeois, *Tableau de la Campagne de Moscou en 1812* (Paris, 1814), 85.
86. Dumonceau, II, 175.
87. Castellane, I, 169.
88. There were some exceptions. Caulaincourt, who had spent several winters in Russia, took no chances and had all members of the horse-and-carriage service buy warm cloaks lined with furs, wool-lined gloves and fur bonnets. He also had every one of the more than 700 saddle and draft horses under his command roughshod with crampons to be able to move over frozen ground. He also acquired sleighs. Caulaincourt, II, 26–28.
89. Bausset, II, 108.
90. Grabowski, 7.
91. Kool, 57.
92. Chambray, II, 316.
93. Montesquiou-Fezensac, *Souvenirs*, 243–244.
94. Pion des Loches, 306–307.
95. Bro, 119.
96. Bourgogne, 56–57. This was all in addition to his full equipment. After dragging these possessions for a few miles, he finally decided to lighten his load but ended up 'leaving out my white trousers [of the dress uniform], feeling pretty certain I should not want them again just yet'.
97. Barrau, 91.
98. Napoleon to La Riboisière, 18 October 1812, *Correspondance de Napoléon*, XXIV, 275; Fain, II, 162, 162f; Planat de la Faye, 92.
99. Napoleon to Berthier, 21 October 1812, in *Correspondance générale*, XII, 1211.
100. Griois, II, 82.
101. Mailly, 72.
102. Bourgogne, 56.
103. Kool, 57.
104. Christiani, 49.
105. Montesquiou-Fezensac, *Journal de la Campagne de Russie*, 68.
106. Christiani, 49.
107. Napoleon to Berthier, 20 October 1812, in *Correspondance générale*, XII, 1208. Napoleon also instructed Mortier to 'set fire to the two houses of the former governor [Rostopchin] and the house of Razumovskii'.

108. Chambray, II, 324–325.
109. Christiani, 49. According to Benckendorf, his troops heard the sound of an explosion at 2am. Benckendorf, 119–120.
110. Sysoev, 15.
111. Cited in S. Knyazkov, 'Ostavlenie frantsuzami Moskvy,' in *Otechestvennaya voina i Russkoe obschestvo*, <http://www.museum.ru/museum/1812/Library/sitin/book4_16.html>
112. Rostopchin to Emperor Alexander, 7 November 1812, in *Russkii arkhiv* 8 (1892), 553. 'The evening proved to be cold and it rained incessantly.' Christiani, 49.
113. Norov, 213–214.
114. Chambray, II, 325.
115. Christiani, 49.
116. For example, in one of his letters, Rostopchin mentioned two women, sarcastically referring to them as 'Citoyennes Heck and Armand', who had been mistreated by the Cossacks. 'Despite my hatred of this vile [French] nation, I could not but laugh upon seeing these madames, who once trotted in stylish fur coats on the Kuznetskii bridge. Now the Cossacks despoiled their bodies both internally and externally.' Rostopchin to Balashev, 1 January 1813, *Russkii arkhiv* 1 (1881), 227.
117. Helman to Ivashkin, 27 October 1812, in Schukin, I, 100.
118. Toll to unknown addressee, 11 December 1812, *Russkaya starina* 12 (1873), 992. Similar account in Rostopchin to Vyazmitinov, 8 November 1812, in *Russkii arkhiv* 1 (1881), 222. Nikodim Kazantsev, the son of a sacristan, lamented that many villagers in his village died due to an epidemic that broke out as the result of the villagers' greed. 'Some stupid peasants', he explained, went to the Borodino battlefield, which was still littered with thousands of bodies, and looted the corpses. Unable to strip the boots from the corpses because of muscle stiffness and frost, they simply hacked off the legs and took them home to thaw out. The rotting flesh consequently led to outbreaks of lethal diseases. Nikodim Kazantsev, 'Zhizn arkhimandrita Nikodima Kazantseva,' in *Bogoslovskii vestnik* 1 (1910), 77.
119. *Russkaya starina* 10 (1889), 47.
120. Tutolmin to the Dowager Empress, 23 November 1812, in Schukin, V, 160. Rostopchin to Vyazmitinov, 11 November 1812, *Russkii arkhiv* 1 (1909), 42.
121. Norov, 210–212.
122. These troops belonged to Ferdinand Wintzingerode's detachment. On 22 October, upon hearing rumours of the Allied departure and French mining of the Kremlin, Wintzingerode made a reckless decision to enter the city accompanied only by his aide-de-camp. He was stopped on the Tver Boulevard by a French patrol which refused to consider him as a truce-bearer and took him to Mortier, who held Wintzingerode as prisoner of war. The detachment thus came under the command of General Ivan Ilovaiskii IV, who then entrusted it to Alexander Benckendorf.
123. Benckendorf, 120–121.
124. Tutolmin reported 1,500 Allied wounded, including sixteen officers, who had been left behind by the French authorities 'without any food, medicine or other necessities'. Tutolmin to Rostopchin, 5 November 1812, in Gorshkov, *Moskva i Otechestvennaya voina 1812 g.*, II, 168.
125. Benckendorf, 123–124.
126. Major General Ivan Ilovaiskii IV to Fedor Rostopchin, 28 October 1812, in *Russkii arkhiv* (1866), 696.
127. Journal of Outgoing Documents of Police Chief Ivashkin, in Gorshkov, *Moskva i Otechestvennaya voina 1812 g.*, II, 158.
128. Rostopchin to Emperor Alexander, 7 November 1812, in *Russkii arkhiv* 9 (1892), 553–554.
129. Khomutova, 327.
130. Lieutenant Colonel Afanasiev II and the 2nd Company of the 1st Battalion of the 2nd Pioneer Regiment took the lead role in this process.
131. Ivashkin to Rostopchin, 20 November 1812, in Gorshkov, *Moskva i Otechestvennaya voina 1812 g.*, II, 164; Major General Ivan Ilovaiskii IV to Fedor Rostopchin, 28 October 1812 in *Russkii arkhiv* (1866), 695–696.
132. For documents of property claims see Chapter 5 in Gorshkov, *Moskva i Otechestvennaya voina 1812 g.*, volume 2. A special commission on property claims, chaired by Count N. Golovin, was set up in February 1813. Muscovites were required to submit their claims, verified by police authorities, by the end of March. Throughout the year the commission reviewed over 18,000 claims and began granting loans as compensation. It eventually gave away over 13 million rubles in ten-year interest-free loans. For details see E. Boldina, 'O deyatelnosti Komissii dlya rassmotreniya proshenii obyvatelei Moskovskoi stolitsy i gubernii, poterpevshikh razorenie ot nashestviya nepriyatel'skogo,' in E. Boldina, A. Kiselev, and L. Seliverstova, eds, *Moskva v 1812 godu: Materialy nauchnoi konferentsii posvyashchennoi 180-letiyu*

Otechestvennoi voiny 1812 goda (Moscow, 1997); Alexander M. Martin, 'Precarious Existences: Middling Households in Moscow and the Fire of 1812,' in Marsha Siefert, ed., *Extending the Borders of Russian History: Essays in Honor of Alfred J. Rieber* (Budapest, 2003); Alexander M. Martin, 'Down and Out in 1812: The Impact of the Napoleonic Invasion on Moscow's Middling Strata,' in Roger Bartlett et al., eds, *Eighteenth-Century Russia: Society, Culture, Economy* (Munster, 2007).

133. Rostopchin to Vyazmitinov, 11 November 1812, in *Russkii arkhiv* 1 (1881), 224.

134. Rostopchin to a village manager in the Orlov province, 15 October 1815, in *Russkii arkhiv* (1864), 407–408.

135. Tutolmin to Rostopchin, 5 November 1812, in Gorshkov, *Moskva i Otechestvennaya voina 1812 g.*, II, 168; Professor Schloezer's letter of 20 December 1812, in *Russkii arkhiv* (1866), 247; Rostopchin to Vyazmitinov, 11 November 1812, in *Russkii arkhiv* 1 (1881), 223.

136. Rostopchin to Vyazmitinov, 11 November 1812, in *Russkii arkhiv* 1 (1881), 224–225.

137. Mikhail Kutuzov to Lieutenant General Prince B. Golitsyn, Chief of Vladimir *Opolchenye*, 29 October 1812, RGVIA, f. VUA, d. 3510, ll. 311–311b; Alexander to Kutuzov, 2 November 1812, RGVIA, f. VUA, d. 3495, l. 6; Lieutenant General Prince B. Golitsyn to Kutuzov, 4 November 1812, RGVIA, f. VUA, d. 3510, ll. 19–19b; Kutuzov to Emperor Alexander, 31 October 1812, and 'Zapiski o Tverski voennoi sile' (1836) in Liubomir Beskrovnyi, ed. *Narodnoe opolchenye v Otechestvennoi voine 1812 goda. Sbornik dokumentov* (Moscow, 1962), 211, 220–222.

138. Rostopchin to Emperor Alexander, 14 December 1812, in *Russkii arkhiv* 8 (1892), 560.

139. Vedomost' Moskovskoi upravy blagochiniya o kolichestve sozhzhennykh trupov ... in Gorshkov, *Moskva i Otechestvennaya voina 1812 g.*, II, 225.

140. Sysoev, 16.

141. Emperor Alexander's decree of 5 December 1812; Register of Weapons delivered to Police Stations, January–June 1813, in Gorshkov, *Moskva i Otechestvennaya voina 1812 g.*, II, 234–240.

142. Arriving in Moscow on 28 October, Ivashkin was already armed with secret instructions from the governor, who ordered the arrest of anyone suspected of collaboration with the enemy, and demanded detailed accounts on conditions in the city. Rostopchin to Ivashkin, 25 October 1812, in Schukin, I, 102–103. For Ivashkin's first actions see his letter to Rostopchin on 30 October in Gorshkov, *Moskva i Otechestvennaya voina 1812 g.*, II, 163. Also see Rostopchin to Vyazmitinov, 8–19 November 1812, in *Russkii arkhiv* 1 (1881), 222–223, 225–226.

143. The two men were merchant Ivan Poznyakov, who was accused of procuring supplies for the enemy, and clerk Orlov, who was charged with treason and espionage. The former was sentenced to whipping and the latter to hard labour. For police reports and trial proceedings see Gorshkov, *Moskva i Otechestvennaya voina 1812 g.*, II, 288–294.

144. Rostopchin to his wife, 13 November 1812, in *Russkii arkhiv* 8 (1901), 482.

145. Rostopchin to his wife, 13–30 September 1814, in *Russkii arkhiv* 8 (1901), 492–498.

146. Rostopchin to his wife, 30 September 1814, in *Russkii arkhiv* 8 (1901), 498.

147. For example see, John T. Alexander, 'Catherine II, Bubonic Plague, and the Problem of Industry in Moscow,' *American Historical Review* 79 (1974), 637–671.

148. For details see P.V. Sytin, *Istoriya planirovki i zastroiki Moskvy* (Moscow, 1950–1954, 2 vols); Albert J. Schmidt, *The Architecture and Planning of Classical Moscow: A Cultural History* (Philadelphia, 1989); M. Budylina, 'Planirovka i zastroika Moskvy posle pozhara 1812 goda (1813–1818 gg.),' *Arkhitekturnoe nasledstvo* 1 (1950), 135–174.

149. For details see Albert J. Schmidt, 'William Hastie, Scottish Planner of Russian Cities,' *Proceedings of the American Philosophical Society*, 114, 3 (1970), 226–243.

150. William R. Wilson, *Travels in Russia* (London, 1828), I, 52–53.

151. Robert Lyall, *The Character of the Russians and a Detailed History of Moscow* (Moscow, 1823), 525.

152. Alexey Merzlyakov to Fedor Velyaminov-Zernov, 26 March 1813, in *Russkii arkhiv* 1 (1865), 109–110.

Select Bibliography

Archival Material

Rossiiskii Gosudarstvennii Voenno-Istoricheskii arkhiv (RGVIA)
[Russian State Military Historical Archive]
Fond 846 (Voenno-Uchebnii Arkhiv), *opis* 16, delos 3465, 3572, 3586, 3587, 3588, 3604, 3697.

Archives de la Guerre, Château de Vincennes
Expédition, S.H.D., département de l'Armée de Terre, 17 C 113; 17 C 114; 17 C 326.

Tsentralnyi istoricheskii arkhiv Moskvy (TSIAM)
[Central Historical Archive of Moscow]
Gorshkov, Dmitri. *Moskva i Otechestvennaya voina 1812 goda* (Moscow, 2011–2012), two volumes.

Published Archival Material and Private Papers
Beskrovnyi, Liubomir, ed. *Borodino: dokumenty, pis'ma, vospominaniya*. Moscow, 1962.
Beskrovnyi, Liubomir, ed. *Narodnoye opolchenye v Otechestvennoi voine 1812 goda*. Moscow, 1962
General Staff Archives: *Otechestvennaya Voina 1812 goda: Materialy Voenno-Uchenogo Arkhiva Generalnogo Shtaba*. St Petersburg, 1910–1917, volumes 15, 16, 18, 19 and 20.
Journal of Outgoing Correspondence of Governor Rostopchin – 'Zhurnal iskhodyashim bumagam kantselyarii moskovskogo general-gubernatora grafa Rostopchina, s iunya po dekabr' 1812 goda' in P. Shukin, ed., Bumagi…, X, 50–259.
Journals of Military Operations: 'Zhurnaly voyennykh deistvii' in *Sbornik istoricheskikh materialov izvlechennykh iz arkhiva sobstvennoi Ego Imperatorskago Velichestva Kantselyarii*. St Petersburg, 1906, volume 13.
Kharkevich – Kharkevich, V. *1812 god v dnevnikakh, zapiskakh i vospominaniyakh sovremennikov*. Vilna, 1900–1903, 4 volumes.
Kutuzov, Mikhail. *M.I. Kutuzov: Sbornik Dokumentov*, ed. L. Beskrovnyi. Moscow, 1954, volume 4, parts 1 and 2.
Napoleon I, Emperor of the French. *Correspondance de Napoleon Ier*. Paris, 1858–1869.
Napoleon I. Emperor of the French. *Correspondance générale. Tome XII. La Campagne de Russie, 1812*. ed. Thierry Lentz, François Houdecek and Irène Delage. Paris, 2012.
Napoleon I, Emperor of the French. *Lettres inédites de Napoléon 1er à Marie-Louise écrites de 1810 à 1814*. Paris, 1935.
Napoleon I. Emperor of the French. *Correspondance inédite de Napoléon Ier conservée aux Archives de la Guerre*. Publiée par Ernest Picard et Louis Tuetey. Paris, 1912–13.
Napoleon I. Emperor of the French. *Correspondance militaire de Napoléon Ier*. Paris, 1876–77.
Schukin, P. ed. *Bumagi otnosyaschiesya do Otechestvennoi voiny 1812 goda*. Moscow, 1897–1908. 10 volumes.
State Council Archive: *Arkhiv Gosudarstvennogo soveta*. St Petersburg, 1888, volume 2.
Tolycheva, T. *Razskazy ochevidtsev o Dvenadtsatom gode*. Moscow, 1872.
Tolycheva, T. *Razskazy ochevidtsev o Dvenadtsatom gode*. Moscow, 1912.

Periodicals
Carnet de la Sabretache
Cobbett's Political Register
Le Moniteur
Moskovskie vedomosti
Russkaya starina
Russkii arkhiv

Russkii invalid
St Petersburgskie vedomosti
Severnaya pochta

Primary Sources

Adams, John Quincy. *Memoirs of John Quincy Adams, comprising portions of his diary from 1795 to 1848.* Philadelphia, 1874.

Akinfov F. 'Iz vospominanii Akinfova,' in Kharkevich I, 205—212.

Albrecht, Adam. *Aus dem leben eines Schlachtenmalers.* Stuttgart, 1886.

Alekseyev, Andrei. [Recollections,] in Tolycheva 1912, 24–29.

Alexander I, Emperor of Russia. *Correspondance de l'Empereur Alexandre Ier avec sa soeur la Grande-Duchess Catherine.* St Petersburg, 1910.

Anonymous. 'Nekotorye zamechaniya, uchinennye so vstupleniya v Moskvu frantsuzskikh voisk (i do bvybedu ikh iz onoi),' in A. Tartakovskii, ed. *1812 god v vospominaniyakh sovremennikov* (Moscow, 1995), 25–32.

Aubry, Thomas Joseph. *Souvenirs du 12e Chasseurs.* Paris, 1889.

Bakunina, Varvara. 'Dvenadtsatyi god,' in *Russkaya starina* (1885), 392–410.

Barclay de Tolly, Mikhail. *Izobrazhenie voennykh deistvii 1-oi armii v 1812 godu.* Moscow, 1859. Also *Chteniya v Imperatorskom Moskovskom obshestve istorii i drevnosti* 2 (1858), 1–32.

Barrau, Jean-Pierre. 'Jean-Pierre Armand BArrau, Quartier-Maitre au IVe Corps de la Grande Armée, sur la Campagne de Russie,' in *Rivista Italiana di Studi Napoleonici* (1979), No. 1.

Bausset-Roquefort, Louis François Joseph. *Mémoires anecdotiques sur l'interieur de Palais de Napoléon sur celui de Marie-Louise, et sur quelques evénemens de l'Empire, de puis 1805 jusqu'en 1816.* Paris, 1827.

Beauharnais, Eugène de. *Mémoires et Correspondance politique et militaire de Prince Eugène,* ed. A. Du Casse. Paris, 1860.

Beaulieu, Drujon de. *Souvenirs d'un militaire pendant quelques années du regne de Napoléon Bonaparte.* Verpillon, 1831.

Beauvollier, Pierre Louis Valot. Mémoires secrets et inédits, pour servir à l'histoire contemporaine, Paris, 1825, volume 2.

Becker, F. 'Vospominaniya Bekkera o razorenii i pozhare Moskvy v 1812 g'. in *Russkaya starina* 6 (1883), 507–524.

Belliard, Augustin Daniel. *Mémoires* ... Paris, 1842.

Benckendorf, Alexander. 'Zapiski' in Kharkevich, II, 53–138; also *Zapiski Benkendorfa* (Moscow, 2011).

Benckendorf, Alexander. 'Opisanie voennyh deistvii otryada, nakhodivshegosya pod nachal'stvom generala Winzengerode v 1812 godu,' in Schukin VII, 249–256.

Bennigsen, Levin. *Mémoires du Général Bennigsen.* Edited by Eutrope Cazalas. Paris, 1908.

Bennigsen, Levin, 'Zapiski grafa L.L. Bennigsena o kampanii 1812 g.,' in *Russkaya starina,* 1909, Vol. 138 (Nos 4, 6); Vol. 139 (Nos 7, 9), Vol. 140 (Nos 11–12).

Berthézène, Pierre. *Souvenirs militaires de la République et de l'Empire.* Paris, 1855.

Bertin, Georges. *La Campagne de 1812 d'apres des témoins oculaires.* Paris, 1895.

Bertrand, Vincent. *Mémoires du Capitaine Bertrand.* Angers, 1909.

Bestuzhev-Riumin, A. 'O proisshestviyakh sluchivshikhsya v Moskve vo vremya prebyvaniya v onoi nepriyatelya v 1812 godu. Doneseniya...' in Chteniya v Imperatorskom Moskovskom obshestve istorii i drevnosti 2 (1859), V, 163–184.

Bestuzhev-Riumin, A. 'Proizshestviya v stolitse Moskve do vtorzheniya v onuyu nepriyatelya,' in Chteniya v Imperatorskom Moskovskom obshestve istorii i drevnosti 2 (1859), V, 69–89.

Beyle, Henri (Stendhal). *Correspondance de Stendhal (1800–1842),* ed. Ad. Paupe and P.-A. Cheramy. Paris, 1908.

Beyle, Henri (Stendhal). *Mémoires sur Napoléon.* Paris, 1929.

Beyle, Henri (Stendhal). *Journal* (Paris, 1934), volume 4.

Beyle, Henri (Stendhal). *Campagnes de Russie. Sur les traces de Henri Beyle dit Stendhal.* Paris, 1995.

Biot, Hubert Francois. *Souvenirs Anecdotiques et Militaires* ... Paris, 1901

Blagovo, Dmitrii. *Razskazy babushki: iz vospominanii pyati pokolenii.* St Petersburg, 1885.

Bonnet, Guillaume. 'Journal du capitaine Bonnet du 18e de ligne (Campagne de 1812)' in *Carnet de la Sabretache,* No. 239 (November 1912), 641–672.

Boudon, Jacques-Olivier. *Lettres de Russie, 1812.* Paris, 2012.

Boulart, Jean Francois. *Mémoires militaires* ... Paris, 1892.

Bourgogne, Adrien-Jean-Baptiste François. *Mémoires du Sergent Bourgogne, 1812–1813.* ed. Paul Cottin and Maurice Hénault. Paris, 1910.

Bourgoing, Paul-Charles de. *Souvenirs militaires* ... Paris, 1897.

Boyen, Hermann von. *Erinnerungen aus dem Leben des General-Feldmarschalls Hermann von Boyen*, ed. Friedrich Nippold. Leipzig, 1889.

Bozhanov, S. 'Rasskaz svyaschennika Uspenskogo sobora I.S. Bozhanova,' in *Russkii arkhiv* 10 (1899); 256–267.

Brandt, Heinrich von. *In the legions of Napoleon: the memoirs of a Polish officer in Spain and Russia, 1808–1813*. Ed. by Jonathan North. London, 1999.

Bréaut des Marlot, Jean. 1812. *Lettre d'une Capitaine des Cuirassiers sur la Campagne de Russie*. Poitiers, 1885.

Bro, Louis. *Mémoires* ... Paris, 1914.

Brokker, Adam. 'Ego Zapiski,' in *Russkii arkhiv* (1868), 1413–1445.

Bulgakov Alexander. 'Razgovory neapolitanskogo korolya s grafom Miloradovichem na avanpostakh armii 14 oktyabrya 1812 goda,' in *Russkii arkhiv* 7 (1900), 265—277.

Bulgakov, Alexander. 'Vospominaniya o 1812 gode i vechernikh besedakh u grafa Fedora Vasilievicha Rostopchina,' in *Starina i Novizna*, VII, 98–135.

Buturlin, Dmitri. 'Kutuzov v 1812 godu,' in *Russkaya starina* 10 (1894), 201–220; 11 (1894), 193–213; 12 (1894), 133–154.

Castellane, Boniface de. *Journal du Maréchal de Castellane, 1804–1862*. Paris, 1895.

Cathcart, George. *Commentaries on the War in Russia and Germany in 1812 and 1813*. London, 1850.

Caulaincourt, Armand Augustin Louis, Duc de Vicence. *Mémoires*. Paris, 1933.

Caulaincourt, Armand Augustin Louis, Duc de Vicence. *With Napoleon in Russia: The Memoirs of General de Caulaincourt, Duke of Vicenza*. New York, 1935.

Cerrini di Monte Varchi, Clemens Franz Xaver von. *Die Feldzüge der Sachsen, in den Jahren 1812 und 1813: aus den bewährtesten Quellen gezogen und dargestellt von einem Stabsoffiziere des königlich sächsischen Generalstabes*. Dresden, 1821.

Chicherin, Alexander. *Dnevnik*. Moscow, 1966.

Chłapowski, Dezydery. *Pamietniki*. Poznan, 1899.

Chłapowski, Dezydery. *Mémoires sur les guerres de Napoléon, 1806–1813*. Paris, 1908.

Choiseul-Gouffier, Sophie de. *Historical memoirs of the emperor Alexander I and the court of Russia*. London, 1904.

Christiani, Christian. 'Zapiska' in *1812 god v vospominaniyakh sovremennikov* (Moscow, 1995), 46–49.

Chuquet, Arthur, ed. *Lettres de 1812*. Paris, 1911.

Chuquet, Arthur, ed. *1812: La guerre de Russie. Notes et documents*. Paris, 1912.

Chuquet, Arthur, ed. *Ordres et Apostilles de Napoleon (1799–1815)*. Paris, 1912.

Clausewitz, Carl von. *Der feldzug 1812 in Russland und die befreiungskriege von 1813–15*. Berlin, 1906.

Coignet, Jean-Roch. *Les Cahiers du Capitaine Coignet*. Paris, 1907.

Combe, Julien. *Mémoires* ... Paris, 1853

Constant (Louis Constant Wairy). *Recollections of the private life of Napoleon*. Akron OH, 1915.

Crossard, Jean Baptiste de. *Mémoires militaires et historiques pour servir à l'histoire de la guerre depuis 1792 jusqu'en 1815*. Paris, 1829.

Damas, Roger de. *Mémoires* ... Paris, 1914.

Davout, Louis Nicolas. *Correspondance du Maréchal Davout Prince d'Eckmuhl*. Paris, 1885.

Davout, Louis Nicolas. *Mémoires et souvenirs*. Paris, 1898.

Dedem van der Gelder, Antoine Baudouin Gisbert de. *Mémoires du général Bon De Dedem der Gelder, 1774–1825: un général hollandais sous le premier Empire*. Paris, 1900.

Denniée, P.P. *Itinéraire de l'Empereur Napoléon pendant la campagne de 1812*. Paris, 1842.

Dmitriev, Mikhail. *Melochi iz zapasa moei pamyati*. Moscow, 1854 (first edition); 1869 (expanded second edition).

Domergues, Armand. *La Russie pendant les guerres de l'empire (1805–1815), Souvenirs historiques*. Paris, 1835.

Dubrovin, Nikolai, ed. *Otechestvennaya voina v pismakh sovremennikov, (1812–1815)*. St Petersburg, 1882.

Dumas, Mathieu. *Souvenirs* ... Paris, 1839.

Dumonceau, Francois. *Mémoires* ... Brussels, 1960.

Dupuy, Victor. *Souvenirs Militaires*. Paris, 1892.

Durdent, René Jean. *Campagne de Moscow en 1812*. Paris, 1814.

Dutheillet de la Mothe, Aubin. *Mémoires* ... Brussels, 1899.

Duverger, B.-T. *Mes Aventures dans la Campagne de Russie*, in Georges Bertin's *La Campagne de 1812 d'apres des témoins oculaires* (Paris, 1895).

Eugène von Württemberg. *Journal des Campagnes du Prince de Württemberg*. Paris, 1907.

Evreinov, M. 'Pamyat' o 1812 gode,' in *Russkii arkhiv* (1874), 95–110.

Faber du Faur, Christian Wilhelm von. *La Campagne de Russie 1812*. Paris, 1895.

Fain, Agathon Jean Francois. *Manuscrit de Mil Huit Cent Douze*. Paris, 1827.

Fain, Agathon Jean Francois. *Mémoires du Baron Fain*. Paris, 1908.

Fantin des Odoards, Louis Florimond. *Journal du Général Fantin des Odoards. Étapes d'un Officier de la Grande Armée*. Paris, 1895.

Fievée, Joseph. *Correspondance et relations de J. Fiévée avec Bonaparte*. Paris, 1836.

Fusil, Louise. *Souvenirs d'une Actrice*. Brussels, 1841.

Fusil, Louise. *Souvenirs d'une Femme sur la retraite de Russie*. Paris, 1910.

Garin, F.A. ed. *Izgnanie Napoleona iz Moskvy. Sbornik*. Moscow, 1938.

Glinka, Sergei. 'Cherty iz zhizni grafa F. V. Rostopchina: Moskva i graf Rostopchin: 1812 god,' in *Russkoe chtenie* (St Petersburg, 1845), I, 237–248.

Glinka, Sergei. *Iz zapisok o 1812 gode*. <http://www.museum.ru/1812/library/ glinka1/glinka.html>

Glushkovskii, Adam. 'Moskva v 1812 godu,' in *Krasnyi arkhiv* 4 (1937), 121–159.

Golitsyn, Nikolai. *Ofitserskie zapiski ili Vospominaniya o pokhodakg 1812, 1813 i 1814 godov*. Moscow, 1838.

Gourgaud, Gaspard. *Napoléon et la grande armée en Russie*. Paris, 1825.

Grabbe, Pavel. 'Iz pamyantnykh zapisok,' in *Russkii arkhiv* 3 (1873), 416–0418.

Griois, Charles-Pierre-Lubin. *Mémoires ...* Paris, 1909.

Grouchy, Emmanuel. *Mémoires ...* Paris, 1873.

Guyot, Claude-Etienne. *Carnets de Campagnes (1792–1815)*. Paris, 1999.

Henckens, J.L. *Mémoires se rapportant à son service militaire au 6me régiment de chasseurs à cheval française de février 1803 à août 1816*. La Haye, 1910.

Herzen, Alexander. *Byloe i dumy*. Moscow, 1958.

Holzhausen, Paul. *Les Allemands en Russie avec la Grande Armée, 1812*. Paris, 1914.

Horn, Johannes von. *Versuch einer darstellung der verbrennung und plünderung Moskwas durch die Franzosen im September 1812*. St Petersburg 1813.

Ivanov, Gavrila. *Neschastiya Gavrily Ivanova, komissara Moskovskoi Senatskoi tipografii vo vremya zlodeyanii v Moskve frantsuzov*. Moscow, 1813.

Ivanov, Gavrila. *Russkii vestnik*, 1813, No. 12, 68–79.

Ivanov, P. 'Vospominaniya o prebyvanii frantsuzov v Moskve,' in Schukin V, 161–163. Also *Russkii arkhiv* 11 (1900), 473–475.

Ivashkin, P. 'Moskovskaya politsiya v 1812 g. Raport ober-politsmeistera P.A. Ivashkina na imya glavnokomanduyushego v Moskve A.P. Tormasova,' ed. A. Shakhanov, *Istoricheskii arkhiv* 3 (2003), 162–165.

Karfachevskii, Andrei. [Recollections] in Schukin, V, 165–167.

Kharuzin, Egor. 'Melkie epizody iz vidennogo i slyshannogo mnoyu i iz moikh detskikh vospominanii, perezhitykh mnoyu v godinu dvenadtsatogo goda, pri zanyatii frantsuzami Moskvy,' in *1812 god v vospominaniyakh sovremennikov* (Moscow, 1995), 163–169.

Khomutova, Anna. 'Vospominaniya A.G. Khomutovoi o Moskve v 1812 godu,' in *Russkii arkhiv* 3 (1891), 309–28.

Kicheev, Peter. *Iz nedavnei stariny. Razskazy i vospominaniya*. Moscow, 1870.

Klimych, Semen. 'Moskovskii Novodevichii monastyr' v 1812 godu. Razskaz ochevidtsa – shtatnogo sluzhitelya Semena Klimycha,' in *Russkii arkhiv* (1864), 416–434.

Kolchugin, Gregorii. 'Zapiski..'. in *Russkii arkhiv* 9 (1879), 45–62.

Konovnitsyn, Peter. 'Vospominaniya,' in Kharkevich, I, 121–133.

Kool, Aart. *An Account of My Life, Aart Kool, 1787–1862 : A Dutch Engineering Officer in Napoleon's Campaign to Moscow*, translated and introduced by Tone Borren. Wellington, NZ, 2012.

Korbeletskii, F. *Kratkoe povestvovanie o vtorzhenii frantsuzov v Moskvu i o prebyvanii ikh v onoi*. St Petersburg, 1813.

Kozlovskii, G. 'Moskva v 1812 godu, zanyataya frantsuzami. Vospominaniya ochevidtsa,' in *Russkaya starina* 1 (1890), 105–114.

Kruglova, Anna. [Recollections,] in Tolycheva 1912, 59–67.

Kurz, Hauptmann von. *Der Feldzug von 1812. Denkwürdigkeiten eines württembergischen Offiziers*. Leipzig, 1912.

Labaume, Eugène. *Relation circonstanciée de la campagne de Russie en 1812*. Paris, 1815.

Lagneau, L. *Journal d'un Chirurgien de la Grande Armée 1803–815*. Paris, 1913.

Larrey, Dominique. *Mémoires de Chirurgie Militaire et Campagnes*. Paris, 1817.

Las Cases, Émmanuel Auguste Dieudonne. Memoirs of the Life, Exile and Conversations of the Emperor Napoleon. New York, 1894.

Laugier, Césare de. *Épopées Centenaires. La Grande Armée. 1812.* Paris, 1910. Russian edition: *Dnevnik oficera Velikoi armii v 1812 godu.* Moscow, 2005.

Lavrov, Nikolai. 'Razskaz' in Tolycheva 1912, 106–112.

Le Roy, Claude Francois Madeleine. *Souvenirs de Leroy, major d'infanterie, vétéran des armées de la République et de l'Empire.* Dijon, 1914.

Lebedev, A. 'Iz rasskazov rodnykh o 1812 gode.' in Schukin, III, 255–261.

Lecointe de Laveau, G. *Mosca avanti e doro l'incendio.* Milan, 1818. French edition: *Moscou, avant et après l'incendie, par un témoin oculaire.* Paris, 1814.

Lejeune, Louis François. *Memoirs of Baron Lejeune: aide-de-camp to marshals Berthier, Davout and Oudinot.* New York, 1897, Volume 2.

Les Bulletins de la Grande Armée, ed. by A. Pascal. Paris, 1844.

Lettres interceptées par les Russes durant la campagne de 1812. ed. S. Goriainow. Paris, 1913.

Liprandi, Ivan. *Materialy dlya Otechestvennoi Voiny 1812 goda.* St Petersburg, 1867.

List, Frederic Carel. *Herinneringen van den luitenant-generaal Frederic Carel List. Uit zijn nagelaten papieren samengesteld door zijn zoon C. L. Scheidler List.* 'SGravenhage, 1889.

Lossberg, Friedrich Wilhelm von. *Briefe in die Heimath: Geschrieben während des Feldzuges 1812 in Russland.* Kassel, 1844.

Löwernstern, Waldemar Hermann, 'Zapiski generala V. I. Lewernsterna,' in *Russkaya starina,* 1900–1901, Vol. 103 (Nos 8–9), Vol. 104 (Nos 10–12); Vol. 105 (Nos 1–2).

Löwernstern, Waldemar Hermann. *Mémoires ...* Paris, 1903.

Mailly, Adrien. *Mon journal pendant la campagne de Russie.* Paris 1841.

Maistre, Joseph de. *Correspondance Diplomatique.* Paris, 1860.

Marakuev, Mikhail. 'Zapiski rostovtsa M.I. Marakueva,' in *Russkii arkhiv* 5 (1907), 107–129.

Marchenko, Vasily. 'Autobiograficheskie vospominaniya,' *Russkaya starina* 3 (1896), 471–505.

Maret, Hugues Bernard. *Souvenirs intimes de la Révolution et de l'Empire.* Brussels, 1843.

Markham, J. David, ed. *Imperial Glory: The Bulletins of Napoleon's Grande Armée, 1805–1814.* London, 2003.

Martens, Christian Septimus von. *Vor funfzig Jahren. Tagebuch meines Feldzugs in Russland, 1812.* Stuttgart, 1862.

Martin, Alexander M. *Enlightened Metropolis: Constructing Imperial Moscow, 1762–1855* (Oxford, 2013).

Martin, Alexander M. 'The Response of the Population of Moscow to the Napoleonic Occupation in 1812,' in Eric Lohr and Marshall Poe, eds. *The Military and Society in Russia, 1450–1917* (Leidein, 2002), 469–90.

Mashkov I. '1812 god: Sozhzhenie Moskvy. Pokazanie ochevidtsa,' in *Russkii arkhiv* 12 (1909), 455–463.

Maslov, S. *Puteshestvie v Moskvu vo vremya prebyvaniya v onoi frantsuzov.* Moscow, 1813.

Maslov, S. *Russkii arkhiv* 7 (1908), 403–415.

Mayevskii, Sergei. 'Moi vek ili istoriya Sergeya Ivanovicha Mayevskogo, 1779–1848,' in *Russkaya starina* 8 (1873), 125–167.

Memoirs of the History of France during the Reign of Napoleon, dictated by the emperor at Saint Helena to the Generals who shared his Captivity. London, 1823.

Meneval, Claude-François. *Mémoires pour servir a l'histoire de Napoléon Ier depuis 1802 jusqu'a 1815.* Paris, 1894.

Mertvago, Dmitri. *Zapiski ...* Moscow, 1867.

Miloradovich, Mikhail. 'O sdache Moskvy. Rasskaz zapisannyi v 1818 g. A.I. Mikhailovskim-Danilevskim,' in *1812 god v vospominaniyakh sovremennikov* (Moscow, 1995), 59–60.

Mitarevskii, Nikolai. *Vospominaniya o voine 1812 goda.* Moscow, 1871.

Montesquiou-Fezensac, Raymond-Aymery-Philippe-Joseph de. *Journal de la Campagne de Russie en 1812.* Paris, 1850.

Montesquiou-Fezensac, Anatole de. *Souvenirs sur la révolution, l'empire, la restauration et le règne de Louis-Philippe.* Paris, 1961.

Mosolov, Sergei. 'Istoriya moei zhizni,' in Schukin, VIII, 335–344.

Muralt, Albrecht von. *Beresina: Erinnerungen aus dem Feldzug Napoleons I in Russland 1812.* Bern, 1940.

Muravyev, Alexander. 'Zapiski,' in *Dekabristy: Novye materialy* (Moscow, 1955), 57–207.

Muravyev, Nikolai. 'Zapiski,' in *Russkii arkhiv* 10/11 (1885), 225–262, 337–408.

Narichkine-Rostopchine, Natalie. *1812. Le Comte Rostopchine et son temps.* St Petersburg, 1912.

Nastasya Danilovna, [Recollections,] in Tolycheva 1912, 30–37.

Nazarov, Alexander. [Recollections,] in Tolycheva 1912, 91–97.

Nazarova, Aleksandra. [Recollections,] in Tolycheva 1912, 76–91.

Nordhof, A.W. *Die Geschichte der Zerstorung Moskaus im Jahre 1812.* Munich, 2000.

[Nordhof, A.W]. *Histoire de la destruction de Moscou en 1812, et des événemens qui ont précédé accompagné et suivi ce désastre*, Translated and edited by Jean Baptiste Joseph Breton de La Martinière. Paris, 1822.

Norov, Avraam. 'Vospominaniya,' in *Russkii arkhiv* (1881), 173–214.

O'Meara, Barry. *Napoleon in Exile or a Voice from St Helena*. London, 1822.

'Opisanie proischestvii v Moskovskom Danilove monastyre vo vremya nashestviya nepriyatelya v Moskvu v 1812 godu,' in *Chteniya v Imperatorskom Moskovskom obshestve istorii i drevnosti* 1 (1861), 193–197.

Pavlova, Caroline. Vospominaniya, in *Russkii arkhiv* 10 (1875), 222–240.

Pelleport, Pierre. *Souvenirs militaires et intimes du général vte. de Pelleport de 1793 à 1853*. Paris, 1857.

Perovskii, Vasilii. 'Iz zapisok pokoinogo Grafa Vasiliya Alekseevicha Perovskogo,' in *Russkii arkhiv* (1865), 257–286.

Peyrusse, Guillaume. *Lettres Inédites* ... Paris, 1894.

Peyrusse, Guillaume. *Mémorial et Archives du M. le Baron Peyrusse*. Carcassonne, 1869.

Pion des Loches, Antoine-Augustin-Flavien. *Mes campagnes (1792–1815)*. Paris, 1889.

'Pismo k vdovstvuyushei imperatritse Marii feodorovne, pisannoe posle nashestviya Frantsuzov aptekarem Sheremetevskago strannopriemnogo doma,' in *Russkii arkhiv* 6 (1871), 0191–0197.

Planat de la Faye, Nicolas Louis. *Vie de Planat de la Faye*. Paris, 1895.

Pokhorskaya, Elena. [Recollections,] in Tolycheva 1912, 46–58.

Poluyaroslavtseva, Anisya. [Recollections,] in Tolycheva 1872, 7–10.

Polyanskii, Vasilii. [Recollections,] in Tolycheva 1912, 38–46.

Puibusque, Louis Guillaume de. *Lettres sur la guerre en Russie en 1812*. Paris, 1816.

Quaij, Charles de. *Charles de Quaij, capitaine de grénadiers de la garde impériale sous Napoléon I: sa correspondance inédite, précédée d'un aperçu biographique*, ed. A.F. van Beurden. Ruremonde, 1900.

Radozhitskii, Ilya. *Campaign Memoirs of the Artilleryman. Part I: 1812*. Translated by Alexander Mikaberidze. Tbilisi, 2011.

Rapp, Jean. *Mémoires* ... Paris, 1823.

Raspopov, N. 'Iz vospominanii o Moskve v 1812 godu,' in *Russkii arkhiv* 9 (1879), 36–44.

Rastkovskii, F. *Ob Otechetsvennoi voine 1812 g.: Rasskaz starika finlyandtsa*. St Petersburg, 1900.

Rayevskii, Nikolai. 'Zapiski o 1812 gode,' in Denis Davydov, *Zamechaniya na nekrologiyu N.N. Rayevskogo s pribavleniem ego sobstvennykh zapisok na nekotorye sobytiya voiny 1812 goda v koikh on uchavstvoval* (Moscow, 1832), 33–89.

Raza, Roustam. *Souvenirs de Roustam, Mamelouk de Napoléon*. Paris, 1911.

'Razskaz Moskvicha o Moskve vo vremya prebyvaniya v nei Frantsuzov v pervye tri nedeli sentabrya 1812 goda,' in *Chteniya v Imperatorskom Moskovskom obshestve istorii i drevnosti* 2 (1859), V, 93–114. Also in *Russkii arkhiv* 8 (1896), 521–540.

'Razskaz o dvenadtsatom gode,' in *Russkii arkhiv* 6 (1871), 0198–0218.

Roguet, Christophe Miche. *Mémoires militaires*, Paris, 1865.

Roos, Heinrich Ulrich Ludwig von. *Ein Jahr aus meinem Leben* ... St Petersburg, 1832.

Rossetti, Marie-Joseph. *Journal d'un Compagnon de Murat*. Paris, 1998.

Rostopchin, Fedor. 'Pisma Grafa F.V. Rostopchina k Feldmarshalu Knyazyu M.I. Kutuzov Smolenskomy v 1812 godu,' in *Russkii arkhiv* 12 (1875), 456–460.

Rostopchin, Fedor. 'Tysyacha vosemsot dvenadtsatyi god v zapiskakh grafa F.V. Rostopchina,' in *Russkaya starina* 12 (1889), 643–725.

Rostopchin, Fedor. 'Pisma grafa F. V. Rostopchina k Imperatoru Aleksandru Pavlovichu v 1812 godu,' in *Russkii arkhiv* 8 (1892), 419–446; 9 (1892), 519–565.

Rostopchin, Fedor. *Oeuvres inédites*. Paris, 1894.

Rostopchin, Fedor. 'Kratkoe opisanie proisshetviyam v Moskve v 1812 godu.' in *Russkii arkhiv* 7 (1896), 341–385.

Rostopchin, Fedor. 'Pisma k svoei supruge v 1812 godu,' in *Russkii arkhiv* 8 (1901), 461–507.

Rostopchin, Fedor. 'Graf F.V. Rostopchin. Ego bumagi,' in *Russkii arkhiv* 1 (1909), 26–51.

Rostopchin, Fedor. *Okh, frantsuzy!* Moscow, 1992. Electronic version <http://az.lib.ru/r/rostopchin_f_w/text_0190.shtml>

Runich, D. 'Iz zapisok D.P. Runicha,' in *Russkaya starina* 3 (1901), 597–633.

Ryazanov, Alexander. *Vospominaniya ochevidtsa o prebyvanii Frantsuzov v Moskve v 1812 godu*. Moscow, 1862.

Ryazanov, N. ed. *Kutuzov M.I. Pis'ma, zapiski*. Moscow, 1989.

St-Denis, Louis-Etienne. *Napoleon from the Tuileries to St Helena*. New York, 1922.

Sanglen, Jacob de. 'Zapiski Yakova Ivanovicha de Sanglena, 1778–1831 gg.' in *Russkaya starina* 3 (1883).

Scheltens, Henri. *Souvenirs d'un vieux soldat belge de la garde imperiale*. Bruxelles, 1880.

Ségur, Philippe-Paul. *Histoire et mémoires*. Paris, 1873.

Ségur, Philippe-Paul. *Histoire de Napoléon et de la grande-armée pendant l'année 1812*, Paris, 1825. English translation available in numerous editions, including *History of the expedition to Russia undertaken by the Emperor Napoleon in the the year 1812*. London, 1825.

Semen Klimych. 'Moskovskii Novodevichii monastyr' v 1812 godu. Razskaz ochevidtsa – shtatnogo sluzhitelya Semena Klimycha,' in *Russkii arkhiv* (1864), 416–434.

Serraris, Jean-Théodore. 'Biographie du lieutenant-général messire Jean-Théodore Serraris,' in *Annalen van den oudheidskundigen kring van het Land van Waas* (St Niklaas, 1869), 341–374.

Séruzier, Theodore-Jean-Joseph. *Mémoires militaire*. Paris, 1823.

Shalikov, P. *Istoricheskoe izvestie o prebyvanii v Moskve frantsuzov 1812 goda*. Moscow, 1813.

Sherbinin, A. 'Moi zapiski o kampanii 1812 goda', in Kharkevich, I, 14–53.

Simeonov P. 'Iz zapisok, vedennyh v Moskve 1812 goda, pri zayatii onoi vragami,' in *Istoricheskii, statisticheskii i geograficheskii zhurnal*, 2/2 (1826), 101–107.

Sister Antonina, [Recollections,] in Tolycheva 1912, 5–19.

Snegirev, I. 'Vospominaniya,' in *Russkii arkhiv* (1866), 513–562.

Sokolskii. 'Vospominaniya o prebyvanii frantsuzov v Moskve,' in Schukin I, 1–6.

Sołtyk, Roman. *Napoleon im Jahr 1812*, trans and ed. by Ludwig Bischoff. Leipzig, 1838.

Surrugues, Adrian. *Lettres sur l'incendie de Moscou*. Paris, 1823.

Surrugues, Adrian. 'Vospominaniya o prebyvanii frantsuzov v Moskve,' in *Russkii arkhiv* (1882), 196–204.

Surrugues, Adrian. *Mil huit cent douze. Les Français à Moscou*. Lille, 1909.

Sverbeyev, Dmitri. *Zapiski* ... Moscow, 1899.

Sysoev, Apollon. 'Rasskaz,' in Tolycheva 1872, 11–16.

Tascher, Maurice de. *Journal de Campagne d'un cousin de l'Impératrice*. Paris, 1933.

Thirion, Auguste. *Souvenirs militaires*. Paris, 1892.

Toll, Carl. *Denkwurdigkeiten aus dem Leben des Kaiserl russ. Generals von der Infantrie Carl Friedrich Grafen von Toll*, ed. Theodor von Bernhardi. Leipzig, 1856–1858.

Tutolmin Ivan. 'Vospominaniya o prebyvanii frantsuzov v Moskve,' in Schukin V, 147–151. Also *Russkii arkhiv* 11 (1900), 457–462.

Über die Verbrennung der Stadt Moskau: ein Privatschreiben aus der russischen Stadt Wladimir. Leipzig, 1813.

Vasilii Yermolaevich, [Recollections,] in Tolycheva 1912, 67–76.

Vendramini, Francois. 'Souvenirs de 1812. Les Français à Moscou,' in *L'Économiste Belge* 8 (1864), 93–96; 9 (1864), 104–108.

Vigel, Philipp. *Vospominaniya* ... Moscow, 1864.

Villemain, Abel François. *Souvenirs contemporains d'Histoire et de Littérature*. Paris, 1854.

Vionnet de Maringone, Louis Joseph. *Campagnes de Russie & de Saxe (1812–1813) Souvenirs d'un ex-commandant des grenadiers de la vieille-garde*. Paris, 1899. English edition: *With Napoleon's Guard in Russia. The Memoirs of Major Vionnet, 1812*. Translated and edited by Jonathan North. Barnsley [UK], 2012.

Volkonskii, Dmitrii, 'Dnevnik, 1812–1814,' in *1812 god. Voennye dvevnniki*, ed. A. Tartakovskii (Moscow, 1990) <http://militera.lib.ru/db/1812/02.html>

Volkonskii, Peter. 'U frantsuzov v Moskovskom plenu 1812 goda,' in *Russkii arkhiv* 11 (1905), 351–359.

Volkonskii, Sergei. *Zapiski* ... St Petersburg, 1902

'Vospominaniya ob ostavlenii Moskvy,' in Kharkevich II, 185–196.

Vsevolozhskii, [Recollections,] in Tolycheva 1912, 19–24.

Vyazemskii, Peter. *Polnoe sobranie sochinenii Knyazya P.A. Vyazemskago*. St Petersburg, 1882.

Walter, Jakob. *A German Conscript with Napoleon. Jakob Walter's Recollections of the Campaigns of 1806–1807, 1809, and 1812–1813*. Edited and Translated by Otto Springer.. Lawrence KS, 1938.

Wilson, Sir Robert. *Narrative of the events during the invasion of Russia by Napoleon Bonaparte and the retreat of the French army*. London, 1860.

Wilson, Sir Robert. *Private Diary of Travels, Personal Services and Public Events During Mission and Employment in 1812, 1813 and 1814 Campaigns*, ed. by H. Randolph. London, 1861.

Wolzogen und Neuhaus, Ludwig. *Memoiren des Königlich Preussischen Generals der Infanterie Ludwig Freiherrn von Wolzogen*. Leipzig, 1851.

Yakovlev, Ivan. [Memoir] in Dmitri Golokhvastov, 'Wahrheit und Dichtung,' *Russkii arkhiv* (1874), 1061–1068.

Yermolov, Alexey. *Zapiski Alekseya Petrovicha Yermolova*. Moscow, 1863. English edition: *The Czar's General: The Memoirs of a Russian General in the Napoleonic Wars*, trans. by A. Mikaberidze, Welwyn Garden City, 2005.

Ysarn-Villefort, François Joseph. *Relation du séjour des Français à Moscou et de l'incendie de cette ville en 1812 par un habitant de Moscou suivie de divers documents relatifs à cet évènement*. Bruxelles, 1871.

Zakharov F. 'Vospominaniya o prebyvanii frantsuzov v Moskve,' in Schukin V, 163–164.
Zaluski, Jozef. 'Les Chevau-Légers Polonais de la Garde dans la Campagne de 1812,' in *Carnet de la Sabretache* 5 (1897), 521–533. Also see *Wspomnienia*. Krakow, 1976.
Zhdanov P. *Pamyatnik frantsuzam ili priklyucheniya Moskovskogo zhitelya*. St Petersburg, 1813.

Secondary Sources
Austin, Paul Britten. *1812: Napoleon's Invasion of Russia*. London, 2000 (combined edition).
Belloc, Hilaire. *Napoleon's Campaign of 1812 and the Retreat from Moscow*. New York, 1926.
Beskrovnyi, Liubomir. *Otechestvennaia voina 1812 goda*. Moscow, 1968.
Bezotosnyi, Viktor. *Donskoi generalitet i Ataman Platov v 1812 godu: Maloizvestnye i neizvestnye fakty na fone znamenitykh sobytii*. Moscow, 1999.
Bezotosnyi, V. ed. *Otechestvennaia voina 1812 goda: Entsiklopedia*. Moscow, 2004.
Blocqueville, Louise Adélaïde d'Eckmühl. *Le maréchal Davout, prince d'Eckmühl; correspondance inédite, 1790–1815. Pologne—Russie—Hambourg*. Paris, 1887.
Bogdanovich, Modest. *Istoria Otechestvennoi voiny 1812 g. po dostovernym istochnikam*. St Petersburg 1859.
Boudon, Jacques-Olivier. *Napoléon et la campagne de Russie, 1812*. Paris, 2012.
Burton, Reginald. *Napoleon's Invasion of Russia*. London, 1914.
Buturlin, Dmitri. *Istoriya nashestviya Imperatora Napoleona na Rossiyu v 1812 godu*. St Petersburg, 1823.
Buturlin, Dmitri. 'Kutuzov v 1812 g.' in *Russkaya starina*, 10 (1894).
Cappello, Girolamo. *Gli Italiani in Russia nel 1812*. Città di Castello, 1912
Cate, Curtis. *The War of the Two Emperors. The Duel between Napoleon and Alexander: Russia 1812*. New York, 1985.
Chambray, Georges. *Histoire de l'expédition de Russie*. Paris, 1823.
Chandler, David. *The Campaigns of Napoleon*. London, 1967.
Derrécagaix, Victor Bernard. *Les Etats-Majors de Napoléon: le Lieutenant-Général Comte Belliard, Chef d'Etat-Major de Murat*. Paris, 1908.
Djevegelov A. and N. Makhnevich, eds. *Otechestvennaia voina i Russkoye obshestvo*. Moscow, 1911–1912, 7 volumes.
Duffy, Christopher. *Borodino and the War of 1812*. London, 1972.
Foord, Edward. *Napoleon's Russian Campaign of 1812*. London, 1914.
Girod de l'Ain, Maurice. *Grande artilleurs: Drouot, Senarmont, Eblé*. Paris, 1895.
Grunwald, Constantine. *La Campagne de Russie, 1812*. Paris, 1963.
Hartley, Janet. *Alexander I*. London, 1994.
Hasquenoph, Sophie. *Les Français de Moscou en 1812. De l'incendie de Moscou à la Bérézina*. Paris, 2012.
Josseslson, Michael. *The Commander. A Life of Barclay de Tolly*. Oxford, 1980.
Kharkevich, V. *Voina 1812 goda. Ot Nemana do Smolenska*. Vilna, 1901.
Kharkevich, Vladimir. *Barklai de Tolly v Otechestvennuyu voinu posle soedineniya armii pod Smolenskom*. St Petersburg, 1904.
Kudryashov, K. *Moskva v 1812 godu*. Moscow, 1962.
Kukiel, Marian. *Wojna 1812 roku*. Krakow, 1936.
Lieven, Dominic. *Russia against Napoleon*. London, 2010.
Mikhailovskii-Danilevskii, Alexander. *Opisaniye Otechestvennoi voiny v 1812 godu*. St Petersburg, 1839.
Mikhailovskii-Danilevskii, Alexander. *Imperator Aleksandr I i ego spodvizhniki v 1812, 1813, 1814, 1815 godakh: Voennaia galereia Zimnego Dvortsa*. St Petersburg, 1845–1850, 6 volumes.
Moskva v 1812. Istoricheskii ocherk. Moscow, 2008
Nafziger, George. *Napoleon's Invasion of Russia*. Novato CA, 1988.
Nicolson, Harold. *Napoleon 1812*. Cambridge, 1985.
Palmer, Alan. *Napoleon in Russia*. London, 1967.
Petiteau, Natalie, Jean-Marc Olivier and Sylvie Caucanas, eds. *Les Européens dans les guerres napoléoniennes*. Toulouse, 2012.
Popov, A.N. *Frantsuzy v Moskve v 1812 godu*. Moscow, 1876.
Popov, A.I. *Velikaya armiya v Rossii: pogonya za mirazhom*. Samara, 2002.
Promyslov, Nikolai. 'La guerre et l'armée Russe à travers la correspondance des participants Français de la campagne de 1812' in *Annales Historiques de la Revolution Francaise*, n369 (2012), 95–115.
Rey, Marie-Pierre. *Alexander I: The Tsar Who Defeated Napoleon*. DeKalb, IL: NIU Press, 2012.
Rey, Marie-Pierre. *L' effroyable tragédie: une nouvelle histoire de la campagne de Russie*. Paris, 2012.
Riehn, Richard. *1812. Napoleon's Russian Campaign*. New York, 1991.
St-Hilaire, Emile Marco de. *Histoire de la Campagne de Russie, 1812*. Paris, 1846.

Schmidst, Hans. *Vinovniki pozhara Moskvy v 1812 g.* Riga, 1912.

Ségur, Anatole Henri de. *Vie du Comte Rostopchine, Gouverneur de Moscou en 1812.* Paris, 1893.

Ségur, Pierre de. 'Rostopchin en 1812,' in *La Revue de Paris* 1902, IV, 85–117.

Soubiran, André. *Napoléon et un million de morts.* Paris, 1969.

Sytin, P. *Istoriya planirovki i zastroiki Moskvy. Materialy i issledovaniya.* Moscow, 1950.

Tarle, Eugène. *Nashestvie Napoleona na Rossiyu 1812.* Moscow, 1992 (on-line text available at www.1812.ru).

Tartarovskii, Andrei. *1812 god i russkaia memuaristika.* Moscow, 1980.

Tartakovskii, Andrei. *Nerazgadannyi Barklai: legendy i byl' 1812 goda.* Moscow, 1996.

Tartakovskii, Andrei. 'Obmanutyi Gerostrat: Rostopchin i Pozhar Moskvy,' in *Rodina* 6/7 (1992).

Thiers, Adolphe. *Histoire du Consulat et de l'Empire.* Paris, 1845.

Thiry, Jean. *La Campagne de Russie.* Paris, 1969.

Tranié, Jean and C. Carmigniani. *La campagne de Russie: Napoléon, 1812.* Paris, 1981.

Troitskii, Nikolay. *1812: Velikii god Rossii.* Moscow, 1988.

Troitskii, Nikolay. *Aleksandr I i Napoleon.* Moscow, 1994.

Tzenoff, Gantscho. *Wer hat Moskau um Jahre 1812 in Brand gesteckt?* Historische Studien, Heft 17. Berlin, 1900.

Zaichenko, L. *Moskva v Otechestvennoi voine 1812 goda.* Moscow, 2006.

Zamoyski, Adam. *Moscow 1812: Napoleon's Fatal March.* New York, 2004.

Zemtsov, V. *1812 god: pozhar Moskvy.* Moscow, 2010.

Zhilin, Pavel. *Gibel Napoleonovskoi armii v Rossii.* Moscow, 1974.

Index